SHAKESPEARE SURVEY

ADVISORY BOARD

SHAKESPEARE SURVEY

AN ANNUAL SURVEY OF
SHAKESPEARE STUDIES AND PRODUCTION

60

Theatres for Shakespeare

EDITED BY

PETER HOLLAND

CAMBRIDGE
UNIVERSITY PRESS

CAMBRIDGE UNIVERSITY PRESS
Cambridge, New York, Melbourne, Madrid, Cape Town, Singapore, São Paulo

Cambridge University Press
The Edinburgh Building, Cambridge CB2 8RU, UK

Published in the United States of America by Cambridge University Press, New York

www.cambridge.org
Information on this title: www.cambridge.org/9780521878395

First published 2007

Printed in the United Kingdom at the University Press, Cambridge

A catalogue record for this publication is available from the British Library

ISBN 978-0-521-87839-5 hardback

EDITOR'S NOTE

Volume 61, on 'Shakespeare, Sound and Screen', will be at press by the time this volume appears. The theme of Volume 62 will be 'Close Encounters with Shakespeare's Text'. For volume 63, the theme will be 'Shakespeare's English Histories and their Afterlives'.

Submissions should be addressed to the Editor at The Shakespeare Institute, Church Street, Stratford-upon-Avon, Warwickshire CV37 6HP, to arrive at the latest by 1 September 2008 for volume 62 and 1 September 2009 for volume 63. Pressures on space are heavy and priority is given to articles related to the theme of a particular volume. Please send a copy you do not wish to be returned. Submissions may also be made via e-mail attachment to pholland@nd.edu. All articles submitted are read by the Editor and at least one member of the Advisory Board, whose indispensable assistance the Editor gratefully acknowledges.

Unless otherwise indicated, Shakespeare quotations and references are keyed to *The Complete Works*, ed. Stanley Wells, Gary Taylor, John Jowett and William Montgomery, 2nd edition (Oxford, 2005).

Review copies should be addressed to the Editor as above. In attempting to survey the ever-increasing bulk of Shakespeare publications our reviewers inevitably have to exercise some selection. We are pleased to receive offprints of articles which help to draw our reviewers' attention to relevant material.

As this volume was going to press, we learned of the sudden death of Tony Nuttall, a long-serving member of *Shakespeare Survey*'s Advisory Board. A superb scholar, a generous teacher and a kind friend, he is much missed. To say that I valued his advice is a cliché but, as Tony would have appreciated, the language of clichés is often also true.

P. D. H.

CONTRIBUTORS

RICHARD ABRAMS, *University of Southern Maine*
JAMES P. BEDNARZ, *University of Long Island*
MICHAEL BOGDANOV, *Theatre Director*
JULIAN M. C. BOWSHER, *Museum of London Archaeology Service*
S. P. CERASANO, *Colgate University*
ROB CONKIE, *University of Winchester*
STEPHEN DICKEY, *University of California, Los Angeles*
JANETTE DILLON, *University of Nottingham*
MICHAEL DOBSON, *Birkbeck, University of London*
JOHN DRAKAKIS, *University of Stirling*
BRIDGET ESCOLME, *Queen Mary, University of London*
JON GREENFIELD, *Architect*
BARBARA HODGDON, *University of Michigan*
ANDREAS HÖFELE, *University of Munich*
GRAHAM HOLDERNESS, *University of Hertfordshire*
J. R. MULRYNE, *University of Warwick*
SHARON O'DAIR, *University of Alabama*
ERIC RASMUSSEN, *University of Nevada, Reno*
JULIE SANDERS, *University of Nottingham*
JUNE SCHLUETER, *Lafayette College*
JAMES SHAW, *University of Oxford*
EMMA SMITH, *Hertford College, University of Oxford*
MICHAEL TAYLOR, *University of New Brunswick*
RUTH VANITA, *University of Montana*
MICHÈLE WILLEMS, *University of Rouen*
YUKARI YOSHIHARA, *University of Tsukuba*

CONTENTS

vii

CONTENTS

ILLUSTRATIONS

LIST OF ILLUSTRATIONS

LIST OF ILLUSTRATIONS

PROFESSIONAL PLAYERS IN THE GUILD HALL, STRATFORD-UPON-AVON, 1568–1597

J. R. MULRYNE

The following article summarizes professional theatre in Stratford-upon-Avon in the years from 1568 to 1597, a period when payments for more than thirty visits to the town by travelling companies are recorded in the *Minutes and Accounts of the Corporation of Stratford-Upon-Avon*.[1] Stratford was, in the years in question, a fairly average Midlands town with a population of 1500–2000. It may therefore stand for any number of towns visited by travelling companies, an aspect of England's theatre culture being progressively revealed by volumes in the *Records of Early English Drama* series. The present discussion is indebted to the generosity of Alan Somerset, editor of the forthcoming Warwickshire volume, who has allowed me to quote from his unpublished work. I am also much indebted to Sally-Beth MacLean, whose remarkable *The Queen's Men and their Plays*, written with the late Scott McMillin, has set a scholarly standard for everyone working in the field. Published studies by Andrew Gurr and Siobhan Keenan have made my own immeasurably more modest enquiries possible. Research by Edgar I. Fripp, J. O. Halliwell, Richard Savage, Levi Fox and John Tucker Murray, sometimes neglected by today's scholars, has been called on, as well as recent historical and sociological studies by Robert Bearman and others. I am grateful to Margaret Shewring for scholarly and practical help.[2]

The immediate stimulus for writing lies with archaeological and historical research on the Stratford Guild Hall by Jonathan Clark and Kate Giles of the University of York.[3] Clark and Giles's study has considerably altered our understanding of the Guild Hall's history and fabric, and several conclusions below depend on their work. The Hall, now part of King Edward VI School, is the almost certain location for performances by visiting players, when these were authorized and paid for by the Stratford Corporation.[4] Guild Halls, Moot Halls and

---

[1] *Minutes and Accounts of the Corporation of Stratford-Upon-Avon, 1553–1620 and other records*, 5 vols., vols. 1–4 transcribed by Richard Savage, with Introduction and Notes by Edgar I. Fripp (London, 1921–1929), vol. 5 edited and introduced by Levi Fox (Stratford-upon-Avon: The Dugdale Society, 1990). The manuscripts on which the volumes are based are held, mainly, in the archives of the Shakespeare Birthplace Trust. Manuscript entries referring to visits by travelling players have been checked and where necessary corrected by Professor Alan Somerset, editor of the forthcoming *REED* volume on Warwickshire, and, for the purposes of this article, by myself.

[2] See Scott McMillin and Sally-Beth MacLean, *The Queen's Men and their Plays* (Cambridge,1998); Andrew Gurr, *The Shakespearian Playing Companies* (Oxford, 1996); Siobhan Keenan, *Travelling Players in Shakespeare's England* (Basingstoke, 2002); Edgar I. Fripp, Introductions to *Minutes and Accounts* (see note 1); James O. Halliwell, *The Minute Book of Stratford Corporation* (London, 1863); John Tucker Murray, *English Dramatic Companies 1558–1642* (London, 1910). See also Park Honan, *Shakespeare: A Life* (Oxford, 1998); Stanley Wells, *Shakespeare For All Time* (London, 2002); Alan Somerset, '"How Chances it they Travel?": Provincial Touring, Playing Places and the King's Men', in Stanley Wells, ed., *Shakespeare Survey 47* (Cambridge, 1994), pp. 45–60; G. E. Bentley, *The Professions of Dramatist and Player in Shakespeare's Time, 1590–1642* (Princeton, NJ, 1986).

[3] The work, funded by the Heritage Lottery Fund, has resulted in the compiling of a detailed but unpublished report, from which I have drawn many of the details mentioned here in connection with the fabric of the Guild Hall.

[4] Gurr, *The Shakespearian Playing Companies*, p. 39, writes that 'from 1559 plays had either to be licensed directly by the

Common Halls were the usual location country-wide for such performances, and there is no reason to doubt that the same location was employed in Stratford. I have speculated below on one possible setting – the town's inns – for performances other than those presented before the Bailiff and members of the Corporation. Innkeepers did not compile permanent records, and no legal action took place in Stratford with reference to an inn-based performance, as happened, for example, at Norwich.[5] My focus remains, therefore, on the Guild Hall and the professional theatre mounted there.

It is perhaps surprising that, while the main outlines are well known, detailed work on this setting has not been published hitherto, given that the Hall provided the schoolroom in which William Shakespeare was educated and, more than likely, in which he first saw professional theatre. His presence in Stratford for part or even the whole of the period 1568–97 remains a subject for debate, and this is not the place to enter that fray. But a more exact understanding of the conditions under which the playwright saw, or may well have seen, professional companies in performance may throw light on his concept of theatre as he prepared to travel to London and join the players. At the least, the records offer a useful survey of a typical Stratford resident's opportunities to experience professional and London theatre. Only groupies, one assumes, would travel to Coventry, Leicester or Gloucester to see the professionals, and only the elite and money-eyed made business trips to London, allowing them to take in a theatre visit there.

Drawing on existing research, this study also attempts, in a necessarily limited and speculative way, to map visiting theatre on to the micro-history of Stratford during the period, so far as this can be reconstructed from surviving documents, asking whether bumper and lean years for visiting theatre can be attributed to events in the town, and whether cultural and religious change over the period can be discerned through the partial, and perhaps arbitrary, prism of travelling theatre. There has been considerable discussion, by Patrick Collinson among others, of the extent of puritan influence on the town's corporate life during the

last third of the century.[6] The interaction of this religious climate with visiting performance, and more particularly with its cessation, may tell us something, however narrowly focused, about the relationship between theatre and the confessional upheavals of the period. A glance at local events, particularly the more technicolour happenings of pestilence, storm and fire, may also lead to some partial conclusions, and may at the least remind us that theatre, including visiting theatre, takes place not in a vacuum but in the context of society.

The Stratford Corporation's *Minutes and Accounts*, so far as they relate to travelling theatre, have been newly read and checked by Alan Somerset and myself. The occasions on which travelling players visited the town are listed in Appendix 2 below, together with the companies' names and the monetary reward each was given. The old-spelling orthography of *Minutes and Accounts* has been retained, but for ease of reference the lay-out has been simplified by omission and emboldening. We cannot be sure the accounts document every professional visit but, given the fairly rigorous – and

---

mayor, or seen in performance by the whole corporation' and cites instances in Bristol and York where the Common Hall or Guild Hall is specifically named. Keenan, p. 24, indicates that while the official performance 'might be staged within the mayor's house . . . the more usual venue for civic-funded performances appears to have been the town hall or its equivalent' – in Stratford's case the Guild Hall. See also *REED Devon*, ed. John Wasson (Toronto, 1986), pp. xxv–xxvi, where a distinction is drawn between the preferred playing place of amateurs (the parish church) and that of professionals (the Guild Hall). King Edward VI School is in the process of restoring the Guild Hall with funds provided by the Heritage Lottery Fund, and is seeking support to make it possible to open the Hall to public access.

5 See *REED Norwich 1540–1642*, ed. David Galloway (Toronto, 1984), and Keenan, *Travelling Players*, esp. pp. 99–106.

6 For authoritative studies of radical Protestantism in England, see Patrick Collinson, *The Religion of Protestants: the Church and English Society 1559–1625* (Oxford, 1996) and *The Birthpangs of Protestant England* (London, 1988). For a closer focus on Stratford, see Robert Bearman, ed., *The History of an English Borough: Stratford-upon-Avon 1196–1996*, especially the essays by Robert Bearman, Christopher Dyer, Christine Carpenter, Alan Dyer and Ann Hughes.

tightening – official control of travelling theatre, it is probable that all performances taking place before the Bailiff and members of the Corporation – taking place, that is, so far as we know, in the Stratford Guild Hall – are mentioned.

To examine the chronological record of visiting companies, it may be best to start at the end – the end, that is, of civic-authorized playing in the Guild buildings. The Borough Council Minute Book for 1593–1628 records a meeting of the Council held on 17 December 1602, at which a decision was taken to permit no further play-performances in (to quote) 'the Chamber the guild hall nor in any p[ar]te of the howsse or Courte'. The full minute is reprinted in Appendix 1. I shall return to the details of the phrasing later. For the moment, we may note that the minute does not specifically ban *all* professional playing in the town, only performances taking place under the Council's auspices (though strictly speaking an outright ban should be the effect, since no playing was permitted without the authorisation of the Bailiff and civic authorities). The fine of a considerable, though not crippling, ten shillings will be levied, we are told, on 'whosoeuer of the Baylief Alderman & Burgesses' should give leave for future playing in the civic buildings – an act, it implied, of civic irresponsibility.

An altogether saltier Minute was written for a subsequent Council meeting held on 2 February 1612. This reveals that the earlier decision had not achieved the desired effect, or not without exception (see Appendix 1 for the full text). Referring to plays, it says, 'The sufferance of them is againste the orders hearetofore made', which can only mean that, despite the ban, plays have continued to be performed in the Guild buildings. No payments are recorded in the Council's accounts – presumably none was made, at any rate by town officials. Perhaps the Council is simply reaffirming, ten years after its first enunciation, a socio-moral principle: that plays are not appropriate to the decorum and dignity of the town's civic buildings. Robert Tittler shows in his *Architecture and Power: The Town Hall and the English Urban Community* (Oxford, 1991) that such a stance was becoming widely

shared across the country in the late sixteenth and early seventeenth centuries. The revised imposition in this Minute of a fine of ten *pounds* – that really is crippling – suggests that the meeting it records was characterized by something approaching righteous indignation. Use of the nice word 'inconvenience' – 'the *inconuenience* of plaies' as the Minute puts it – tends to confirm this. Among obsolete, but then current, meanings the *OED* offers 'impropriety' and 'unfitness', citing for the latter the antiquary John Hooker (1600): 'They plead against the inconvenience not the unlawfulness of popish apparel.' The present context alleges both impropriety and unlawfulness (because the earlier ruling had been defied). We can detect, perhaps, beneath the phrasing, an earnest discussion of the 'impropriety' of plays, as though local pressure was being exerted to sway Council members' minds. The matter was, in the words of the Minute, 'verie seriouslie considered of'. The whopping twenty-fold increase in the fine reads like a self-righteous gesture meant to impress. The rather limp tailing-off that follows may be equally revealing: the order will stay in effect 'vntill the nexte common councell' (only weeks or at most months away) or until it is then revoked – a less than confident forecast. The full minute reads as though there may have been moderating or opposing voices present – which would line up with inferences below about the religio-cultural climate of the early seventeenth century town.

It may be illuminating to diverge from Stratford for a moment. Other towns and cities also issued banning orders about this time. Chester, for example, issued a ban in 1596, one of the earlier prohibitions on record. The really gutsy order comes later, however, in the Chester Assembly Book for 20 October 1615 (Appendix 1). The City, it says, has incurred 'Common Brute and Scandall' through permitting 'Stage Plaiers to Acte their obscene and vnlawfull Plaies or tragedies in the Common Hall of this Citie' – standard rhetoric, this, from the lexicon of the anti-theatrical writers. A little less derived is the indignation arising from the alleged perverted use of the civic buildings. The Common Hall, we are told, has been desecrated by

being turned into 'a Stage for Plaiers and a Receptacle for idle persons', whereas it was 'ordained for
the Iudiciall hearinge and determininge of Criminall offences and for the solempne meetinge and
Concourse of this howse'. Such sentiments speak to
a relatively new sense of civic dignity and order, as
much as to sectarian prejudice. A regard for commercial profit also (unsurprisingly) rears its head:
the apprentices 'manie times wastfullie spende their
Masters goodes' by attending play performances.
What is interesting, further, is that the order concludes not in a universal ban but in a ban on playing,
in the Common Hall or elsewhere, 'in the night
time or after vje of the Clocke in the eveninge',
a restraint not unique to Chester. Admittedly, the
expression is ambiguous: a total ban on playing in
the Common Hall may be intended. But it looks as
if the wretched minute-taker is trying to summarize
a lively meeting at which various factions weighed
in with their particular stances, without the meeting reaching a coherent outcome. This reflects poor
chairmanship, perhaps, but is also characteristic, in
my reading, of the complex attitudes to playing
obtaining at the time, even in areas of the country
known for radical sectarianism.

The list of pre-ban visits to Stratford by professional companies (Appendix 2) offers the opportunity for a number of inferences about playing and its
context in the later sixteenth century. There were
more visits, first of all, than one might expect for
a small market town in the midst of Warwickshire.
The town authorities paid for thirty-one visits over
the period, twenty-five of them by named companies. In the years we are looking at, England
was a network of touring routes, as the maps in
Scott McMillin and Sally-Beth MacLean's invaluable *The Queen's Men and their Plays* graphically
illustrate (illustrations 1 and 2). Stratford lay close to
the hub of a communications network that linked
the important provincial centres of Leicester and
Coventry to the north with Banbury and Oxford to
the south and Gloucester and Bristol to the south-
west. The town-to-town itineraries described in
the *REED* volumes, and detailed also by J. Tucker
Murray, Andrew Gurr and, in a less complete form,
by E. K. Chambers, show these routes to have been

habitual for the Stratford visitors. The small devia-
tion from the main inter-urban roads necessary to
allow the companies to play Warwick and/or Stratford may have been occasioned, we might guess,
by the political importance of the former, the seat
of the powerful Earls of Warwick. Coventry, less
than twenty miles away, was a major city and a
major touring centre, the axis of a Midlands network of tour destinations that was among the busiest in the country. In an obvious sense, therefore,
Stratford was well placed to play host to professional
touring theatre.

A second glance at the list indicates that the visiting companies were in no way marginal to mainstream theatre. On the contrary, these were major
players, in every sense of the word. Leicester's Men
came early (in 1573–4 and 1576–7) and stayed late –
they were in Stratford in 1587, on the brink of
the company's dissolution (their patron Leicester
died in 1588). When they first visited the town
(1573–4) the company was the most celebrated in
the land, dominating the court seasons of 1572–3
and 1573–4, during which they gave six of the nine
royal command performances.[7] About their patron
Leicester's own eminence, there cannot, notoriously, be any argument. Favourite of Elizabeth,
'practically', in Simon Adams's recent phrase, 'a
surrogate husband',[8] protector of advanced Protestantism, absolute governor, towards the end of his
life, of the United Provinces, Leicester exercised
from court and from his seat at Kenilworth – even
closer than Coventry, a dozen miles down the
road from Stratford – an extraordinary influence.
Through Elizabeth's generosity, Leicester and his
brother Ambrose, Earl of Warwick, became 'the
leading landed interest in the west Midlands and
north Wales', ensuring a respectful reception for
their servants when they chose to visit the Midlands

---

[7] See E. K. Chambers, *The Elizabethan Stage* (Oxford, 1923, 1951), vol. II, pp. 85–91, and Gurr, *The Shakespearian Playing Companies*, pp. 185–95, esp. pp. 187–8.
[8] Simon Adams, 'Robert Dudley, Earl of Leicester', *Oxford Dictionary of National Biography* (Oxford, online edn, May 2006).

MAP 2

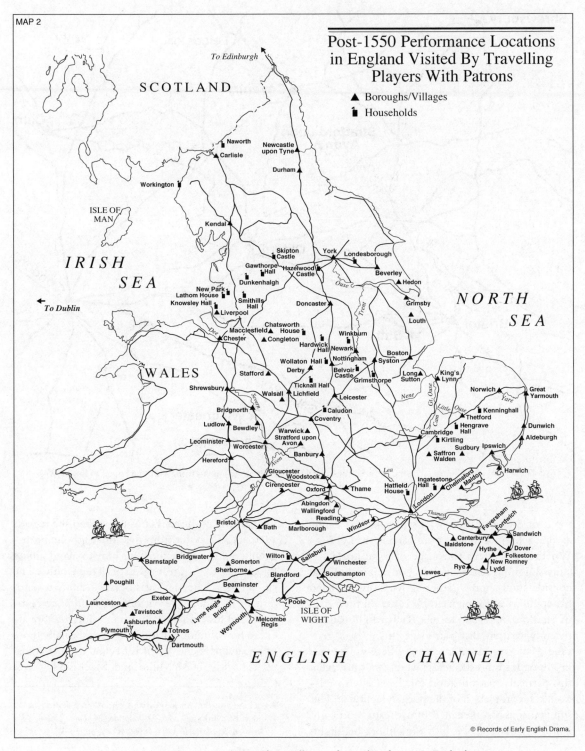

Post-1550 Performance Locations
in England Visited By Travelling
Players With Patrons

▲ Boroughs/Villages
⌂ Households

SCOTLAND

To Edinburgh

IRISH

SEA

To Dublin

ISLE OF
MAN

WALES

NORTH

SEA

Naworth
Carlisle
Newcastle
upon Tyne
Durham
Workington

Kendal

Skipton
Castle
Gawthorpe
Hall
Dunkenhalgh
New Park
Lathom House
Knowsley Hall
Smithills
Hall
Liverpool
Macclesfield
Chester
Congleton
Chatsworth
House
Hardwick
Hall
Wollaton Hall
Stafford
Derby
Walsall
Ticknall Hall
Shrewsbury
Lichfield
Bridgnorth
Caludon
Coventry
Ludlow
Bewdley
Warwick
Leominster
Worcester
Stratford upon
Avon
Hereford
Banbury
Gloucester
Woodstock
Cirencester
Oxford
Thame
Abingdon
Wallingford
Reading
Bristol
Bath
Marlborough
Windsor

York
Londesborough
Hazelwood
Castle
Beverley
Hedon
Doncaster
Grimsby
Louth
Winkburn
Newark
Nottingham
Belvoir
Castle
Grimsthorpe
Leicester
Boston
Syston
Long
Sutton

Ouse
Trent

King's
Lynn
Norwich
Great
Yarmouth
Kenninghall
Thetford
Hengrave
Hall
Cambridge
Kirtling
Sudbury
Ipswich
Dunwich
Aldeburgh
Saffron
Walden
Harwich
Ingatestone
Hall
Chelmsford
Maldon
Hatfield
House
London

Nene
Cam
Gt. Ouse
Little Ouse
Yare

Lea

Thames

Faversham
Fordwich
Sandwich
Canterbury
Maidstone
Hythe
Dover
Folkestone
New Romney
Lydd
Lewes
Rye

Bridgwater
Barnstaple
Poughill
Launceston
Exeter
Tavistock
Ashburton
Plymouth
Totnes
Dartmouth
Somerton
Sherborne
Beaminster
Lyme Regis
Bridport
Weymouth
Melcombe
Regis
Wilton
Blandford
Poole
Salisbury
Winchester
Southampton
ISLE OF
WIGHT

ENGLISH   CHANNEL

© Records of Early English Drama.

1. Post-1550 locations and routes for travelling professional performers in England.

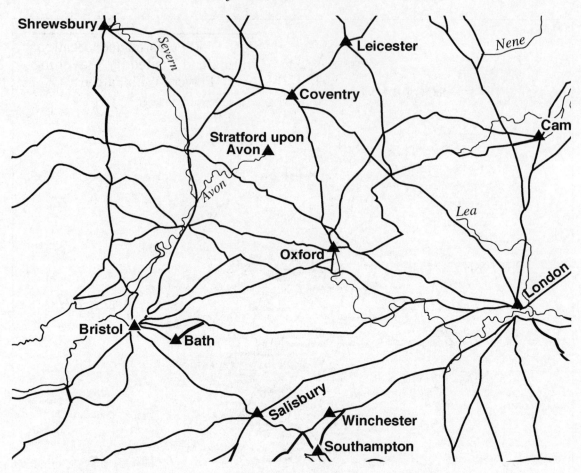

2. Detail from illustration 1, showing the area immediately around Stratford-upon-Avon, with tour routes to local towns.

town of Stratford. (Warwick's players also came, at the zenith of their court career, in 1574–5.) Whether Leicester's patronage of a theatre company was motivated by political or religio-political considerations, and whether his Men disseminated his opinions and supported his cause on their days in Stratford, it is hard to tell. Richard Dutton has recently written that patronage 'involved a genuine relationship with a patron, whose public face in important ways the actors were',[9] but just what this particular patron stood for, especially in relation to his protection of the puritan faction and his simultaneous maintenance of a theatre company, is not crystal clear. Eleanor Rosenberg highlights

the paradox of the Earl's position when she reports a letter to Leicester from the anti-Catholic propagandist John Field exhorting him to avoid aiding the players 'to the greate greif of all the Godly'. The rift between Leicester's aristocratic leaning towards display, including the patronage of a theatre company, and his espousal of puritan values was apparent to his contemporaries, it seems, especially those of a Calvinist bent. What is beyond dispute is that up to 1583, in McMillin and MacLean's words,

9 Richard Dutton, 'Shakespearian Origins', in Takashi Kozuka and J. R. Mulryne, eds., *Shakespeare, Marlowe, Jonson: New Directions in Biography* (Aldershot, 2006), pp. 69–84, p. 75.

'Leicester's Men were by far the most widely travelled, the most knowledgeable professionals on the road.'[10] And, as MacLean points out elsewhere,[11] Leicester was prepared to spend the considerable sum of £20 kitting out his players in expensive silks, satins and taffetas for court performance. They must have seemed to him worth the investment. In Stratford they may have made, in consequence, something of a splash, though we know almost nothing about players' costuming on tour.

The Queen's Men in effect took over from Leicester's. Formed in 1583 through the agency of Secretary Walsingham, with the advice of Master of the Revels Edmund Tilney – who knew the theatre scene in England better than anyone – they swept up the country's most talented actors, including three of Leicester's Men.[12] Whether their formation could be called political is arguable, though it is true that almost nothing Walsingham did was non-political. There are grounds for supposing that in the unsteady 1580s the Queen's advisers felt that theatre-touring in her livery would assist the further integration of the realm, an endeavour parallel to her assiduous distribution of her image by other means.[13] Whether it was in that spirit or not, the 'new' Queen's Men came three times to Stratford, in 1587, 1593 and 1594, the only professional players to do so in the latter two years. The Queen's company was high-profile, being repeatedly awarded coveted slots in the entertainment programme at court: three performances in 1583–4 and five commissioned (four given) in the following year – shortly before their first Stratford visit. It has been suggested by McMillin and MacLean, on evidence from Shakespeare's re-writing of Queen's Men plays, that the actor-playwright travelled to London and joined the celebrated Queen's company after seeing their performances in Stratford.[14] This is debatable territory, and only one of several hypotheses relating to Shakespeare's early career. Nevertheless, the possibility raised by McMillin and MacLean serves to underline the potential significance of professional theatre in the Stratford of Shakespeare's day.[15]

The most frequent visitors were the Earl of Worcester's players, a company somewhat different in background, and probably in esteem, from Leicester's Men or the Queen's. Worcester's Men came five times to town between 1568 and 1583–4. They were a wholly provincial company, specializing in the Midlands circuit, in contrast to the two companies just mentioned, both of which toured nation-wide and were based in London. The company patron, William Somerset, third Earl of Worcester, was an altogether less prominent nobleman than Leicester or Warwick, or than those of Privy Council status associated with the Queen's Men. His son Edward the fourth Earl, became a more notable figure, sharing responsibility under James for mounting spectacular court masques. The Stratford visitors, we may easily infer, offered entertainment a good deal less remarkable than that afforded by Leicester's or the Queen's companies. This suggests a mixed theatre economy for the town, with standards of performance varying from year to year – except that, in the increasingly regulated and restrictive theatre profession of the later sixteenth century, the standard of performance, judging from the personnel involved, and the limited number of companies, may never

---

10 McMillin and MacLean, *The Queen's Men*, p. 21; Eleanor Rosenberg, *Leicester, Patron of Letters* (New York, 1955), p. 255. Field made his views plain in the same letter, dated 25 November, 1581, referring to 'those impure enterludes and playes that were in vse. Surely the schooles of as great wickednesses as can be.'

11 'Tracking Leicester's Men: The Patronage of a Performing Troupe', in Paul Whitfield White and Suzanne R. Westfall, *Shakespeare and Theatrical Patronage in Early Modern England* (Cambridge, 2002), pp. 246–71, p. 260.

12 For information on the Queen's Men see Chambers, *The Elizabethan Stage*, II. 104–15; Gurr, *The Shakespearian Playing Companies*, pp. 196–217; McMillin and MacLean, *The Queen's Men*, *passim*.

13 See, for example, Roy Strong, *The Cult of Elizabeth: Elizabethan Portraiture and Pageantry* (London, 1977), *passim*.

14 McMillin and MacLean, *The Queen's Men*, pp. 160–6.

15 The company of 'Queenes Players' mentioned at the head of the list of visitors (1568–9) is an altogether more obscure group, a purely provincial company whose status Gurr is inclined to question, even wondering whether it was a theatre company in the accepted sense, or a group of tumblers. See Gurr, *The Shakespearian Playing Companies*, p. 196.

have dropped seriously low.[16] The repeated visits of Worcester's Men also suggests an element of habit, or even customary booking, in the structure of sixteenth-century touring.

Some conclusions may be drawn from the town's payments to the named visitors. A pattern emerges, if rather uncertainly. One unambiguous feature stands out. The highest reward – twenty shillings, consistently – is given to the 1583 Queen's Players, suggesting a correlation between the patron's political status and the level of payment offered. To some extent this is followed through, but not without exception. The Earl of Leicester's Men, to take the most obvious example, received a considerable sum, fifteen shillings, in 1576–7, echoing their patron's standing, but only three years earlier had received no more than five shillings and eight pence. In 1587, the same Company's reward falls back from its peak of fifteen to no more than ten shillings. Perhaps this lower sum is influenced by Leicester's mixed fortunes in the Netherlands (1586–7). In the case of the visit of 1576–7, the reward may have been boosted, in contrast, by the acclaim surrounding his staging of a series of spectacular royal entertainments at Kenilworth from 1566 on, climaxing in 1575. The Stratford Borough officials may have been influenced in their relative generosity by the fame of the theatricals just a few miles down the road. The town was getting reflected glory, they may have reasoned, as a result of hosting a company associated with such splendour – a company that may have brought some of the splendour with them, not only in their liveries, but also in their stage costumes and properties. On the larger platform provided by the city of Coventry, Leicester's Men received thirty shillings in 1580 and twenty shillings in 1582, rewards fit for a Queen's Company in smaller Stratford. Rank and file visitors to the town, or rather companies with rank and file patrons (though never less than noble) are good in the Stratford accounts for three, four and five shillings, as indeed such companies are at Coventry, if we transfer the Stratford earnings to a big-city scale: the parallel Coventry payments did not normally rise above ten shillings.[17] Social and political status seems, therefore, to play

a part in the calculation of rewards, even if these are sometimes affected by temporary fluctuations of esteem. A similar pattern of political privilege is replicated in other towns, where the Queen's Men are routinely given the highest sums, not infrequently well above, even double, the Stratford payment.

What looks like an anomaly in the Stratford accounts, the seventeen shillings paid, as early as 1574–5, to 'my lord of warwicke players' tends on the contrary to confirm the payment-by-patronage hypothesis, since, in Christine Carpenter's words, 'the earls [of Warwick] were territorially and politically . . . dominant around Stratford' in the fifteenth century and after. Ambrose Dudley, the current Earl, was restored to favour by 1573 (a year or so before his company's Stratford visit) despite, in 1554, a charge of treason arising from his assistance with the royal ambitions of Lady Jane Grey.[18] The local influence of a company's patron, that is to say, may have affected the level of payment. It is difficult to know, it must be conceded, whether features other than the patron's prestige played a part in calculating rewards, for example how elaborate a show was, or how large the playing company or (in the case of 1587, when the payment to Leicester's company fell) the number of visiting companies paid for by the town authorities during a busy year.

Further analysis of the visitors' list, coupled with information from other studies, will help to reveal the membership of the visiting companies. Borough officials did not think it worth recording the names of actors, a lack of interest shared by other

---

16 The regulations on patronage of companies had the effect, even if sometimes flouted or circumvented, of ensuring that a relatively restricted number of companies were in existence to be received by town officials as part of the officially-sanctioned touring network, thus broadly maintaining standards.

17 For payments in Coventry see *REED Coventry*, ed. R. W. Ingram (Toronto, 1981).

18 Christine Carpenter, 'Town and "Country": the Stratford Guild and Political Networks of Fifteenth-century Warwickshire', in Bearman, *The History of an English Borough*, pp. 62–79, p. 68; Patrick Collinson, 'Ambrose Dudley, Earl of Warwick', *Oxford Dictionary of National Biography*.

towns – except, for example, in the rare instance when a legal hearing took place. Appendix 3 gives information, from sources such as Chambers, Murray and Gurr, about the three companies discussed above. What this shows – to summarize – is that Stratford audiences had access to performances by some of the leading names in contemporary theatre. The touring companies that came to Stratford may have differed from the touring companies of the same name that visited elsewhere. We have no means of knowing. But it seems probable that Edward Alleyn, the most celebrated actor of his day, came to Stratford with Worcester's Men in 1583–4. This was, admittedly, at the age of seventeen or eighteen, before the triumphs of his later career. James Burbage, theatrical entrepreneur, actor and irascible leader of men, was one of the Earl of Leicester's company in 1572, 1574 and 1576 and probably came to Stratford with them in 1573–4 and perhaps in 1576–7. The famous comic actor Richard Tarlton, a founder-member of the Queen's Men in 1583 who remained with the company until his death in 1588, probably played Stratford in 1587. Given the complex history of the Queen's Men and the company's split in 1587–8 (Gurr says 'by 1590'),[19] we cannot, however, be sure. These are names to conjure with. There were others only a little less high-profile who visited, especially when the star-studded Queen's company became almost regulars after 1587. In brief, experience of theatre in Stratford seems likely to have measured up with the best in the land, so far as casting was concerned, even if shows of high calibre were less regularly available than in London.

Increasing evidence exists that touring theatre far exceeded in scale the four or five men, a cart and a drum of popular caricature.[20] This is apparent from documents relevant to the three visiting companies considered above. In 1577, the Earl of Worcester's Men had ten players at Southampton and the same number at Norwich and Leicester in 1583/4. They visited Stratford in 1576–7, presumably with a similarly numerous company as on the Southampton visit of the same year. The Earl of Leicester's Men comprised twelve players at Southampton in

1577, and took in Stratford on the same tour. The Queen's Men were formed with twelve players in 1583 and were in Stratford in 1587 before, so far as we can tell, the company split. These are viable numbers for the performance of even elaborate plays. Whether companies also recruited locally for minor parts and backstage assistance it is hard to say. There is, to my knowledge, no reliable information. In any case, nothing suggests that plays were scaled down from their London performances when they came to Stratford, or were under-cast. The evidence in fact tends to the contrary.[21]

One minor feature of the list of visitors suggests what is apparently the case: that Stratford had a particular talent for attracting the more robust companies at their more robust moments. The 1587 entry records payment 'for mendinge of a forme that was broken by the queenes players xvj d.', a token of the risk to civic property that hosting theatre entailed. Robert Tittler notes that records of damage are widespread, at Bath, York, Bristol, Leicester and Canterbury, and speculates that the decline in – and bans on – Guild Hall performances after 1590 may have been connected with defensive local pride in increasingly elaborate civic buildings.[22] However that may be, Stratford's visitors are connected with some of the more spectacular run-ins with authorities elsewhere, just at the time they visited the town. In 1583–4, the Earl of Worcester's Players got into hot water with the Mayors of both Norwich and Leicester, accused of defying their official authority. They were in Stratford during the same accounting year. The Queen's Men, right at the start of their illustrious career (June 1584), precipitated the most notorious theatrical incident of the period when three of their leading actors, Tarlton, Singer and

[19] Gurr, *The Shakespearian Playing Companies*, p. 71.
[20] See, for example, Gurr, *The Shakespearian Playing Companies*, pp. 42–3, and David Bradley, *From Text to Performance in the Elizabethan Theatre* (Cambridge, 1992), pp. 58–74.
[21] The figures for company numbers given in this paragraph are taken from Gurr, *The Shakespearian Playing Companies*, and Murray, *English Dramatic Companies*.
[22] Robert Tittler, *Architecture and Power: the Town Hall and the English Urban Community* (Oxford, 1991), pp. 146–7.

Bentley, stage-swords in hand, were involved in a brawl at Norwich that led to the death of an innocent local. They may have cooled off by the date of their visit to Stratford four years later, but the incident serves to suggest that at this period Stratford theatre was in all likelihood a full-blooded activity, as well as theatrically high level and relatively well-resourced.[23]

It is inviting to attempt to map the list of theatre visits on to Stratford's local history. The discussion will, however, be short and, in the absence in a majority of cases of unequivocal evidence, more gesture than substance. The overall pattern of the century from 1540 countrywide was, to quote Alan Dyer, 'marked by rising social and economic stress caused by an expanding population and price inflation, coupled with rapid economic change'.[24] In Stratford, this pattern was particularly marked, and was exacerbated by local disasters such as famine, fire and epidemic. Bubonic plague struck in 1564 (Shakespeare's birth year), just before the period of theatre visits, when 13 per cent of the population died. Mortality from disease, probably typhus and dysentry, linked with malnutrition and crop-failure, peaked from November 1596 until the spring of 1597. Does the cessation of playing after 1597 have anything to do with the town's distressed state (there are no recorded visits after that year up until the ban on playing in 1602), or were the deaths, which occurred chiefly among the poor, irrelevant to hosting players? There may be a glimpse here of the select nature of Stratford audiences, though the evidence is too slight to support a conclusion. The town burned in 1594 and 1595, when, it was claimed, 'over 200 houses were destroyed' and total damage, including goods spoiled, was estimated at the huge sum of £12,000. Collections for the relief of the Stratford poor were taken in the neighbouring counties, in Oxford and in London.[25] Yet as many as six (unnamed) companies visited in 1596 and 1597, as if nothing of fiscal significance had happened. In all probability, the Queen's Men were not among them, since the rewards do not look Queen-sized. The reward of 19s 4d in 1596–7 is, however, anomalous for a single, unnamed, company, so we cannot be sure. The likely absence of the Queen's Men may, it is true, be explained by the fact that by 1594 they were, in Gurr's words, 'ripe for reallocation'.[26] There is another possibly significant item in, or rather missing from, the visits list. Jeanne Jones's study of the Borough Chamberlain's accounts reveals that in the sixty years from 1570 to 1630 the accounts were in deficit on only twelve occasions, three of these being the years 1570, 1571 and 1572.[27] There are no records of players in the town in those years. Is there a correlation, due to the depletion of the treasury, between the deficit and the absence of visiting players? Overall, these scraps of information are intriguing, but, in the absence of more detailed documentary evidence, not easily woven into any local-history explanation for the irregular pattern of visits.

What, then, are we to make of the more obvious fact that Stratford was one of the earlier towns, a few years after Great Yarmouth in 1595 and Chester in 1596, to impose a ban on playing in the Guild or Common Hall? Historians are agreed that an accelerating trend towards Puritan attitudes made itself apparent in the town in the last years of the century. Jeanne Jones writes: 'the puritan faction within the [Stratford] Corporation became more powerful at the turn of the century. It began to

---

[23] For further information about the incidents mentioned, see Appendix 3.

[24] Alan Dyer, 'Crisis and Resolution: Government and Society in Stratford, 1540–1640', in Robert Bearman, *The History of an English Borough*, pp. 80–96, p. 80.

[25] Alan Dyer in Bearman, *The History of an English Borough*, p. 95; Levi Fox ed., *Minutes and Accounts* v, pp. xix and 133; *The Victoria History of the Counties of England: Warwick* (London, 1945) III, pp. 221–82. Lewis Bayly, vicar in 1597 of Shipston-on-Stour, a few miles from Stratford, attributed the fire in his hugely popular *The Practice of Piety* (12 edns by 1620) to 'prophaning the Lords Sabbaths, and . . . contemning his word in the mouth of his faithfull Ministers', suggesting that the godly did not hold unrestricted sway in late sixteenth-century Stratford (quoted Fox, *Minutes and Accounts* v, p. xix).

[26] Gurr, *The Shakespearian Playing Companies*, p. 71.

[27] Jeanne Jones, *Family Life in Shakespeare's England: Stratford-upon-Avon 1570–1630* (Stroud, 1996), p. 124.

show its hand in the 1590s.'[28] Patrick Collinson sees such a development as part of a national movement of opinion, led by the Protestant earls including, notably, Leicester. The trend, he suggests, may be discerned in Stratford in the issues chosen for resolution by the Borough Council. In contrast to an earlier preoccupation with commercial and social matters, 'by the early 1600s, Shakespeare's neighbours were concerned with offences against God: swearing, contempt for God's ministers and God's sabbath, drunkenness. Stratford had become a little Geneva.' This is a striking phrase, if difficult to reconcile with detailed contemporary records as an overall assessment of the town's outlook. Prominent as well as less noted townspeople varied, it becomes clear, in their moral as well as religious convictions, and in their behaviour, though the direction of trend amongst opinion formers, the clergy, the social elite and the town officials, is also evident.[29]

The inclination towards Puritan attitudes, while unmistakable, was not, in Stratford, abrupt in origin. A 1586 survey of Warwickshire ministers found that of 186 incumbents fewer than thirty were able to 'preach the Word', and many were not resident in their cures. A notable exception to this apparent tide of incompetence and neglect was Richard Barton, vicar of Stratford, presented by the Earl of Warwick at Michaelmas 1584 and instituted on 17 February 1585. Barton was found to be 'learned, zealous and godlie, and fit for the ministrie. A happie age, yf our Church were fraight [provided] with manie such.' He features in the survey as a contrast to Martin Delane, to take a single example, the incumbent of St Mary's, Warwick, who was judged to be a lover of 'the alehouse and verie much subiect to the vice of good felowshippe', a coded formula for unserious and unreliable.[30] The survey was Puritan-inspired, and biased, and cannot be taken as more than a hint of clerical opinion in Stratford – at a time, it is true, when the opinion of the clergy to a considerable extent both reflected and moulded lay attitudes. A detail from the list of theatre visits to Stratford under 1582–3 offers what may be a further, token corroboration of emerging Puritan sentiment in the town. The entry reads: 'Payed to Mr Berman . . . & to a preacher'. The preacher on this occasion is unnamed, but preachers were, it is well known, front-line troops in the Puritan–Calvinist mission, and the invitation may therefore be thought a significant one. The Corporation's favoured preacher four years later, in 1586, was the learned and unquestionably Puritan Thomas Cartwright, opponent of Archbishop Whitgift and critic of most things episcopal, whom Leicester had appointed Master of the Lord Leycester Hospital in Warwick the previous year. Cartwright was a noted controversialist and a highly popular preacher. An early biographer reported that 'grave men ran like boys in the streets to get places in the Church' when he delivered sermons in Cambridge in the 1580s. He preached in Stratford by invitation of the Corporation at least twice, in 1586 and 1587, and was entertained at the Swan, accompanied, in 1586, by Job Throckmorton of Haseley, ten or eleven miles distant from Stratford, an altogether more robust writer and controversialist, and a suspected author of some at least of the notorious Martin Marprelate tracts.[31]

---

[28] Jones, *Family Life*, pp. 110–11.

[29] See Collinson, *The Religion of Protestants*, esp. pp. 182–3 and *The Birthpangs of Protestant England*, p. 55.

[30] Fripp, ed., *Minutes and Accounts* iv, pp. xv–xvi; Ann Hughes, 'Building a Godly Town: Religious and Cultural Divisions in Stratford-upon-Avon, 1560–1640', in Bearman, *The History of an English Borough*, pp. 97–109, p. 102.

[31] For Cartwright and Throckmorton, see the articles on both men by Patrick Collinson in the *Oxford Dictionary of National Biography*, and appended bibliographies. The early biographer is S. Clarke in *A generall martyrology* (1651), quoted by Collinson. Throckmorton's authorship of some at least of the Marprelate Tracts is now widely accepted. See Leland H. Carlson, *Martin Marprelate, gentleman: Master Job Throkmorton laid open in his colors* (San Marino, CA, 1981). While Collinson, *Oxford Dictionary of National Biography*, thinks Carlson takes his case too far, he broadly agrees with him in the attribution to Throckmorton of at least a number of the Marprelate tracts. The story of Cartwright's opposing the proposition 'Monarchia est optimus status Reipublicae' when Elizabeth visited Cambridge in 1564, an undertaking that looks like an act of reckless folly, has to be understood, as Collinson points out, in the context of a formal academic exercise. It is nevertheless by no means inconsistent with Cartwright's courageous

It is impossible to recover, at this distance in time, and in the absence of written records, either the theme or the detail of Cartwright's sermons. Given the tenor of his published work, their emphasis would have been, it seems probable, on the godly life and the absolute need for 'the lampe of a preaching ministery'.[32] The surviving writings emphasize these matters repeatedly, together with Cartwright's unwavering preference for a presbyterian form of Church government. If he turned in his preaching to matters of public entertainment, it is unlikely he would have endorsed play-performance as more than an occasional diversion. His friendship with Throckmorton, reciprocated by the latter's admiration, was qualified by a difference of style and temperament, and by an earnestness and moderation of argument in contrast to Throckmorton's altogether more ebullient and sometimes outrageous views. Throckmorton was an influential resident of the Stratford area, who in 1586 secured the parliamentary seat of Warwick by some distinctly unparliamentary lobbying. If the *Theses Martinianae* (1589), attributed to him, are indeed his work, it is not difficult to infer the opinion of theatre he may have shared with any Stratford resident who cared to listen. 'The stage players', he writes,

poore seelie hunger-starued wretches, they haue not so much as an honest calling to liue in the common-wealth: And they, poore varlets, are so base minded, as at the pleasure of the veryest rogue in England, for one poore pennie, they wil be glad on open stage to play the ignominious fooles, for an houre or two together. And therefore, poore rogues, they are not so much to be blamed; if being stage-players, that is, plaine rogues (saue onely for their liueries)[33]

and so on. The concession relating to the players' liveries is interesting, since it represents Throckmorton's otherwise less than evident regard for their noble patrons. The general opinion is however unmistakable, as is the bias of Throckmorton's outlook in another treatise which, while conceding that audiences may be 'edified' by 'these plaies or Theater Spectacles' nevertheless asserts that theatres are places where God's 'holy ordinance is

prophaned'.[34] If Throckmorton's views are typical of Stratford opinion in the 1580s, or at the least of an influential strand of Stratford opinion, it is hardly surprising that playing ceased within a few years, and was banned by the town authorities shortly thereafter.

The prevailing socio-religious climate in Stratford in the years surrounding the cessation of playing looks, then, to have been of a broadly Puritan cast. When the Throckmorton faction or its fellow-travellers were in the ascendant, plays in the Guild buildings were always likely to be banned. We should not forget, however, that several prominent families, including leading members of the Corporation – there are multiple references in the *Minutes and Accounts* – were not only recusants of the clerical left or right but declared Papists.[35] The

---

facing up to hardship and persecution both before and after his appointment as Master of the Lord Leycester Hospital. Who else would have accepted the poisoned chalice offered by his Cambridge contemporaries and the university authorities?

[32] Cartwright's letter as printed in Robert Browne, *An answere to Master Cartwright* (London, 1585), p. 87.

[33] *Theses Martinianae* (1589), printed by John Hodgskin (or Hodgkins) at Wolston Priory, Warwickshire, sig. D2v. As the well-informed internet source www.oxford-shakespeare.com/drk/marprelate notes, 'all the Marprelate tracts with the exception of Martin's *Epistle* were printed within a few miles of Leicester's brother Ambrose Dudley's seat of Warwick Castle and Leicester's own Warwickshire seat of Kenilworth'.

[34] *M Some laid open in his coulers* (La Rochelle, 1589), p. 118. 'M Some' was Robert Some (1542–1609), Master of Peterhouse, Cambridge and Fellow of Queens' College. He took a middle course between high Anglicans and Puritans, and tried to damp down the Marprelate controversy.

[35] The most colourful and controversial of the Papist members of the Corporation was probably George Badger, who on 27 July 1597 'for his wylfull refusing to come to the Halle havinge lawfull warninge shalle forfeit the some of ffyve poundes' – a considerable fine (*Minutes and Accounts*, v, pp. 105–6). Evidently Badger had his supporters among members of the Corporation, for he was elected Bailiff at a meeting on 7 September 1597. He refused to serve, despite having stood for election. Local politics, within which religious politics presumably played their part, may well have been as complicated and fraught as they are now. The episode is only one of a number of similar tussles relating to the Corporation's affairs in the last years of the century, suggesting that the town was not of a uniform mind in matters of religion.

town remained, even at the end of the century, a mixed-faith community. Ann Hughes, referring to an essay by Patrick Collinson, has remarked on the comparative lateness of Stratford's elimination of its 'papist' images in the Guild Chapel, under the supervision of John Shakespeare, suggesting the town's reluctance to embrace wholeheartedly the Protestant spirit.[36] What we are seeing, I suggest, is a developing cast of mind, not so much confessional in nature – Catholic or Calvinist – but more broadly cultural, increasingly moralistic and Borough-proud. Yet a disinclination to support playing on the part of an influential section of town opinion may not, of itself, have been responsible for touring theatre's effective disappearance, even in combination with adverse local events. Several scholars[37] have noted the larger-cast plays that became characteristic of touring in the post-1583 period, making a stop at a small and comparatively low-paying town such as Stratford a less than attractive proposition. Visits may have fizzled out, that is to say, for commercial reasons. As with most historical events, the causes of the cessation of playing are likely to have been multiple.

The focus of this article has been on the Guild Hall, and we shall return to it below. We should not suppose, however, that the Guild Hall was the only performance venue in Stratford at the time. It seems likely, on the model of other towns, that after the official preview the companies played in one or other of the inns – so making their visit financially viable. There were four inns in Stratford in the later sixteenth century, if we observe Peter Clark's distinction between *inns* ('large, fashionable establishments offering wine, ale and beer, together with quite elaborate food and lodging'), *taverns* ('selling wine to the more prosperous, but without the extensive accommodation of inns') and *alehouses* ('normally smaller premises serving ale or beer').[38] The Stratford inns were all located in Bridge Street, the town's main traffic axis. The two principal were the Bear and the Swan, both situated at the foot of the street, the former on the south side, the latter on the north. The Bear survives, much altered, and is now known as the

Encore. The Swan has been demolished and its site swallowed into BHS, the department store. Both inns were extensively used by the Borough Council for entertaining, as the *Minutes and Accounts* show, with local celebrities including Sir Thomas Lucy and Sir Fulke Greville wined and dined, as well as national figures including, in 1577, John Whitgift (Cartwright's opponent), bishop of Worcester, subsequently archbishop of Canterbury, and, in 1582, Ambrose Dudley, Earl of Warwick.[39] An inventory of the Swan in 1602–3 shows it to have been a large country inn, its contents assessed at £327 19s 7d – a formidable sum. The Swan incorporated a 'hall', five chambers (Dickenson's, Lyon, Cock, Talbot and the 'lower parlour') and a 'great upper chamber', with a yard, stables and outbuildings.[40]

---

[36] Hughes, 'Building a Godly Town', p. 97.

[37] See, for example, Gurr, *The Shakespearian Playing Companies*, p. 43; McMillin and Maclean, *The Queen's Men*, p. 108.

[38] Peter Clark, *The English Alehouse: A Social History 1200–1830* (Harlow, 1983), p. 5. If Clark is right in his generalisation (p. 145) that 'a storm of criticism erupted against alehouses in the late sixteenth century . . . Puritan preachers, government ministers, magistrates and village worthies all raised their voices loud in condemnation', this further illustrates the distinctions that were drawn in Stratford, for the Bear and the Swan (inns rather than alehouses) were much favoured by the authorities, and were by no means regarded with a 'hostility [which] was also fuelled by a fear, sometimes bordering on the hysterical, that alehouses were being transformed into the strongholds of a populist world which aimed to overthrow established, respectable society'.

[39] For the two inns, see, among other references, *Minutes and Accounts* i, pp. xxxi n.5, xliii and liv; iii, p. 97; iv, p. 56 n.1; v, pp. 20 n.2 and 31 n.2. Illustrations of inns contemporary with those at Stratford appear, for example, in Clark, in Keenan and on the website of Norton St Philip, near Bath, www.buildingconservation.com/articles/george/plans.htm, which shows a plan of the George Inn in its sixteenth-century guise, including a 'timber framed gallery running the length of the courtyard', rather as is thought was the case at the Guild Hall in Stratford (see below).

[40] See J. O. Halliwell's pamphlet, *An Inventory of the Furniture, Etc., of a Tavern at Stratford-on-Avon, Taken in the Time of Shakespeare*, (n.p., n.d.) presented to the Shakespeare Museum, March 1864. See also a report of a talk given by Edgar I. Fripp on 'The Bear' and 'The Swan', collected in the 'Summary of Papers read before The Shakespeare Club,

3. The Guild Hall courtyard at King Edward VI School. In the right foreground is Pedagogue's House, in the left foreground is the 'Chamber' with the Guild Hall beyond it, and in the background the tower of the Guild Chapel.

Performances could have taken place in the 'hall', the 'great upper chamber' or, one supposes, the yard. Inn yards such as those of the Bear and the Swan probably looked not unlike examples contemporary with them still surviving, physically or in detailed drawings, at Southwark, Gloucester, Cambridge and Norton St Philip, near Bath.

It is worth asking why the order to cease playing carried such weight – even if it was not invariably observed. The answer lies in the history of the Guild Hall itself. The Hall originated as the feast hall and business headquarters of the Guild of the Holy Cross, a religious and philanthropic organization similar to those in cities and towns across the country. Granted formal recognition in 1269 or 1270, the Guild, in addition to carrying out its primary religious functions, became the effective civic authority, accumulating wealth, providing employment, and managing the town's social security. The extant Hall was built in 1416–18, forming, eventually, part of a complex with the adjoining Guild Chapel, itself an ancient foundation that was undergoing renewal and restoration in the fifteenth century (illustration 3). The Almshouses next door may have been begun, it is now thought, in the first year or two of the sixteenth century, though

Stratford-upon-Avon, during the session 1924–1925', Shakespeare Centre Library, Shakespeare Club Papers 1920–8. Fripp's measurements of the wainscoting for the hall and chambers do not suggest very large rooms.

dendrochronology is awaited to confirm or modify this. In any case, they form part of what became eventually an extensive complex of Guild buildings. Pedagogue's House, for a period the schoolroom and headmaster's lodging, was, we now know, erected in 1503, to replace an earlier schoolhouse. With the coming of Reformation, the Guild was dissolved (1537). A civic charter, establishing the new borough and confirming the privileges of the school, was granted in the last weeks of the life of Edward VI (1545). The Guild complex served as the hub of the town's communal life, in religion (the Parish Church lay some distance from the centre of town), in law (law courts were established here), in government (the Borough Council met here until late in the nineteenth century), in commerce (the buying and selling of goods), in social care (the almshouses) and in education. Decisions taken within the Guild Hall carried, that is to say, both legal and moral authority conferred by history and custom.[41]

The Guild Hall has recently been the subject of archaeological and historical investigation, on behalf of King Edward VI School.[42] A scale drawing (illustration 4), prepared by Jonathan Clark and Kate Giles, shows the first floor of the Hall as it probably appeared in the sixteenth century, together with the 'Chamber' adjacent to it. Also included is the site of further chambers, now demolished, extending towards the Pedagogue's House, marked here as 'Schoolmaster's chambers of 1503' and 'Schoolroom of 1503'. The dotted line shows the location since the early eighteenth century of the Old Vicarage (or Headmaster's house), and marks the site of further half-timbered chambers, now demolished but occupied in the early period by priests serving the Chapel and the Parish Church. Across the northern boundary of the drawing, not marked here, runs the south wall of the Guild Chapel.

The feature of the drawing of immediate interest is the presumed configuration of the upper Hall (or 'over' Hall), as it may have appeared in the sixteenth century. There is clear evidence that the Hall was originally divided by partitions closing off two smaller rooms at its southern end to serve, probably, as buttery and pantry, with a corridor running along the eastern side giving access to the 'Chamber'. In the mid-1560s the interior partition of the buttery-and-pantry space was removed, probably at the time of the migration of the school from its earlier Schoolroom (1503) into the Guild Hall. At the dates on which the travelling players visited, the upper Hall would have had, that is to say, two distinct areas, one used by the Corporation (at the northern end) and the other by the School. It remains uncertain whether the players performed in the upper or lower Guild Hall. The upper Hall seems marginally more probable, chiefly on three counts, none of them decisive: if the players built a stage, which seems to have been a frequent if not invariable practice,[43] the lower Hall is altogether too low-ceilinged to permit this (illustration 5); secondly, any actor/producer/director, then or now, would prefer the commodious, bright and ample upper Hall (illustration 6) to the smaller, low-ceilinged Hall below; and, thirdly, some references in the documentary evidence suggest, though they fall short of proving, that the upper Hall was traditionally used in the relevant period for formal Guild occasions, including feasts, making use of the upper Hall for plays a natural development.[44] It

---

41 For a brief discussion of the Hall and its history, see Christopher Dyer, 'A Successful Small Town', in Bearman, *The History of an English Borough*, pp. 43–61. See also Robert Bearman, *Stratford-upon-Avon: a History of its Streets and Buildings* (London, 1988). The forthcoming report for the Heritage Lottery Fund will amplify and correct several aspects of existing histories (see below).

42 The archaeological research has been funded by the Heritage Lottery fund, and carried out by a team from Field Archaeology Specialists of York, led by Drs Jonathan Clark and Kate Giles.

43 We may ask, however, whether the expense, in both time and money, would have been justified for a single performance.

44 Jonathan Clark writes that 'the feasting references in the later 16th century accounts do not clearly differentiate between upper and lower halls . . . I think the most telling reference is from 1610–11, in which a new chimney is being erected for the hall. It was necessary to take up the boarded floor and to lay the "somers" (bressummers) and joists where the former "kyll" (presumably the former heating system) had stood in the hall (Shakespeare Birthplace Trust BRU 4/1/225). This work would only have been necessary at first floor level

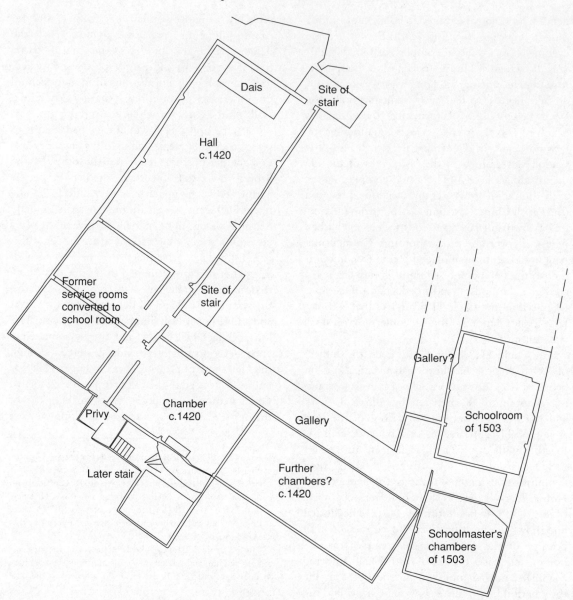

4. Scale drawing of the first floor of the Guild Hall, based on the provisional conclusions of Jonathan Clark and Kate Giles.

remains entirely possible, it has to be said, that the lower Hall was used instead. The partitions which had subdivided it in the medieval and immediately post-medieval period had gone by the late sixteenth century, clearing a possible performance space.

Where, assuming the upper Hall was used, did performance take place? One possibility is that in the upper hall. That it was felt necessary to upgrade the heating at this time would strongly suggest that the upper hall was still intended for relatively high status activities such as feasting' (private communication). It might be added that the discovery of a medieval kitchen on the first floor (a very rare survival) would tend to support this theory.

5. The lower Guild Hall. The Hall is now occupied by the library of King Edward VI School.

the actors performed with their backs to the schoolroom area, which they could use for a tiring room and for storage of stage properties. An audience would gather at the northern end of the Hall, probably seated on benches.[45] The 'Chamber' could also, or alternatively, serve for costume and stage-management purposes, except when it was occupied by the schoolmaster, as we know it was for a period in the 1580s. There is archaeological evidence for the existence of a dais in the upper Hall (see drawing). This measured approximately 11′8″ by 5′. It could be used as a stage, though a cramped one, if the players were to perform at the northern end of the room. It seems more likely, however, that the dais was occupied by the Bailiff (or Mayor) for his command performance, rather as, we know, a parallel arrangement was set up for Elizabeth (and James) on royal occasions.[46] If we

accept this suggestion, it is pleasing to reflect that John Shakespeare would have sat there during his term as Bailiff in 1568–9, with, we might like to think, four-or-five-year-old William by his side. William would have had subsequent opportunities to join his father as he grew older, when, after his term as Bailiff, John attended visiting shows as Alderman and civic leader.

---

45 The space available for performance in the upper Hall would be approximately 38′4″ by 21′8″, a fairly small area, but considerably larger than the upper chamber in Cambridge Town Hall (approximately 25′ by 17½′), where there is clear evidence of performance taking place, and not much smaller than the average size of civic halls as reported by Keenan: 20–25 feet in width and 45–50 feet in length (Keenan, pp. 28–9).

46 See, for example, the discussion in John H. Astington, *English Court Theatre, 1558–1642* (Cambridge, 1999), esp. ch. 2, pp. 35–74.

6. The Upper (or Over) Guild Hall looking north, as the players would have seen the space if they played with their backs to the area partitioned off for the School. The desks and master's chair are eighteenth century.

There is a final detail, for which we have to return to the banning order of 1602. The order specifies that 'there shalbe no plays or enterlewdes playd in the Chamber the guild halle nor in any p[ar]te of the howsse or Courte'. The Chamber referred to could be the 'Chamber c. 1420' shown on the drawing, especially if the minute-taker were thinking of its use as a green room when performances were taking place in the upper Hall – it is too small to serve as a primary playing space. Equally, 'Chamber' might be a name for the lower Hall. The *Minutes and Accounts* quite frequently use the term to refer to the Borough Council as a whole, and therefore by association to the Hall in which it met. The tantalizing feature of the order comes in the phrase 'any p[ar]te

of the howsse or Courte'.[47] A recent conclusion by archaeologists is that a gallery existed on the southern side of the outdoor space, immediately next to the Hall, and may also have extended along the eastern side of the courtyard – which at the time would have been an enclosed space of half-timbered buildings. The location of the gallery is indicated on the drawing. There is warrant in the Minutes of the Borough Council for January 1596 for use of the term 'the Chapell Courte' to refer to 'the court or quadrangle behind the Guildhall,

---

[47] A mistranscription of the *Borough Council Book* vol. B, 1593–1628, repeated in several sources, gives this entry as 'howsse and Courte'. Careful checking makes it clear that the correct reading is not 'and' but 'or'.

adjoining the Guild Chapel'.[48] It is possible, following this line of thought, that plays were performed, and were banned from future performance, not only within the building but also in the open-air courtyard, using the gallery as audience or performance space. This is a location used today by boys of King Edward VI School for the performance of Shakespeare and other plays, though without the facility of the long-dismantled gallery. The adaptable courtyard space, including the windows of the Upper Guild Hall which overlook it, may just possibly, on the analogy of contemporary inn yards, have served as an alternative performance location in Shakespeare's day.

There is a great deal that remains speculative about professional players in the Stratford of Shakespeare's time. It may be hoped that further archaeological discovery will tell us more about the spaces in which they performed, and that local history will further illuminate the social and commercial circumstances they encountered. Much, however, seems irrecoverably lost, a regrettable circumstance given the proportion of their acting lives the players of major companies spent on the road – and the influence their work may have had on the imagination of the greatest of English dramatists.

APPENDIX I

The orders for the cessation of playing in the Stratford Guild Hall. Transcribed from the Borough Council Book, vol. B, 1593–1628, held in the archives of the Shakespeare Birthplace Trust, Stratford-upon-Avon.

1602 (17 December)

At this halle yt ys ordered that there shalbe no plays or enterlewdes playd in the Chamber the guild halle nor in any p[ar]te of the howsse or Courte from hensforward vpon payne that whosoeuer of the Baylief Alderman & Burgesses of this boroughe (?) shall gyve leave or licence therevnto shall forfeyt for euerie offence x s.

1611/2 (2 February)

The inconuenience of plaies being verie seriouslie considered of with the unlawfullnes, and howe contrarie the sufferance of them is againste the orders hearetofore made, and againste the examples of other well governed Citties and Burrowes The companie heare are contented and there conclude that the penaltie of x s. imposed in mr. Bakers yeare for breakinge the order shall from henceforth be x l. vpon the breakers of that order: and this to holde vntill the nexte common councell, and from thencforth, for euer excepted, That [it] be then finally revoked and made voide.

The order for the cessation of playing at Chester (from Lawrence M. Clopper, ed., *Records of Early English Drama: Chester* (Toronto, 1979) pp. 292–3)

1615 (20 October) (Chester Assembly Books)

Moreover at the same Assemblie Consideracion was had of the Comon Brute and Scandall which this Citie hath of late incurred and sustained by admittinge of Stage Plaiers to Acte their obscene and vnlawfull Plaies or tragedies in the Comon Hall of this Citie thereby Convertinge the same, beinge appointed and ordained for the Iudicall hearinge and determininge of Criminall offences, and for the solempne meetinge and Concourse of this howse, into a Stage for Plaiers and a Receptacle for idle persons. And Consideringe likewise the many disorders which by reason of Plaies acted in the night time doe often times happen and fall out to the discredit of the government of this Citie and to the great disturbance of quiet and well disposed People, and beinge further informed that mens servantes and apprentices neglectinge their Masters busines doe Resorte to Innehowses to behold such Plaies and there manie times wastfullie spende thar Masters goodes ffor avoidinge of all which inconveniences It is ordered that from hensforth noe

---

[48] Levi Fox, ed., *Minutes and Accounts* v, pp. 73–5. It is just possible that 'Courte' could refer to the Court Room, probably at this period in the lower Guild Hall, or even to the building as a whole (a less probable interpretation, given the specificity of other items in this list).

Stage Plaiers vpon anie pretence or color What-soever shalbe admitted or licenced to set vp anye Stage in the said Comon Hall or to acte anie tragedie or Commedie or anie other Plaie by what name soever they shall terme hit, in the said Hall or in anie other Place within this Citie or the Liberties therof in the night time or after vje of the Clocke in the eveninge.

APPENDIX 2

VISITS OF PROFESSIONAL PLAYERS TO STRATFORD-UPON-AVON 1568–97 A CHRONOLOGICAL LIST

Transcribed in simplified form from the Borough Council Books, vols. A and B (1554–94 and 1593–1628) and the Chamberlain's Accounts 1590–7 and 1585–1619, held in the archives of the Shakespeare Birthplace Trust, Stratford-upon-Avon. Embold-ening added. The full list will appear in Alan Somerset, ed. *Records of Early English Drama: War-wickshire*, forthcoming.

1568–9   Item payd to the **Quenes Players** ix s. Item to the **Erle of Worcesters pleers** xij d.

1573–4   paid to Mr. bayly for the **earle of leces-ters players** v s. viij d

1574–5   geven my **lord of warwicke players** xvij s.
paid the **earle of worceter players** v s. vij d.

1576–7   Paid to my **Lord of Leyster players** xv s.
Paid to my **lord of Wosters players** iiij s. iiij d.

1578–9   paid to my **Lord Straunge men** the xi th day of february at the comaunde-ment of Mr. Baliffe v s.
Paid at the comaundement of Mr. baliffe to the **countye of Essex plears** xiij s. vj d.

1579–80   Paid to the **Earle of darbyes play-ers** at the comaundement of Mr. Baliffe viij s. iiij d.

1580–1   Paid to the **Earle of Worcester his players** iij s iiij d.
Paid to the **Lord Bartlett his players** iij s. ij d.

1581–2   Payed to Henry Russell for the **Earle of worcesters players** v s.

1582–3   Payed to Mr Berman that he layd downe to ye **lord Bartlite his players** & to a preacher v s.
payd to the **lord shandowes [Chandos'] players** iij s. iiij d.

1583–4   geven to my **lord of oxfordes pleers** iij s. iiij d.
geven to the **earle of worcester pleers** iij s. iiij d.
geven to the **earle of essex pleers** iij s.

1586   paide to Mr Tiler [Mr Bailiff] for the players [**? Sussex's**] v s.

1587   It paid for mendinge of a forme that was broken by the **quenes players** xvj d.
Item gyven to the **Quenes players** xx s.
Item gyven to my **Lord of Essex play-ers** v s.
Item gyven to **therle of leycester his players** x s.
Item gyven to **an other Companye** iij s. iiij d.
Item gyven to **my Lord of Staffordes men** iij s. iiij d.

1593   paid vnto **the Queenes players** xx s.

1594   payd to **the queenes players** xx s.

1597   payd to him ['a man at Mr. Lewes'] for **foure companyes of players** xix s iiij d.
paid p Mr. Bayliffe apoyntment to **play-ers** xj s.

[No record exists of payment thereafter, except for a payment compensating players for *not* playing: 1621/2 paid to the King's players 'fore not playinge in the hall', and a more shadowy 1633 record of payment 'to the players at Christtide by Mr Alder-mans appointment']

APPENDIX 3

PLAYING COMPANIES: THE THREE MAIN PROFESSIONAL COMPANIES VISITING STRATFORD-UPON-AVON, 1568–97.

EARL OF WORCESTER'S PLAYERS

Size of company

'Item paid by Consent to the Earle of Worcester his players the 14 of June [1577] beinge x of them'. Source: John Tucker Murray, *English Dramatic Companies 1558–1642* 2 vols (London, 1910) II.397, transcribing the *Liber de Finibus Ville Suthampton 1489–93*. Ten players also at Norwich and Leicester 1583/4.

Licence dated '14 of Januarye A° 25° Eliz. Re' [1583] lists a company of eight: Robt. Browne, James Tunstall [Dunstan], Edward Allen [Alleyn], Wm. Harryson, Tho Cooke, Ryc. Johnes, Edward Browne, Ryc. Andrewes. Murray adds two others for the visit to Leicester (6 March 1584), 'Wm. Pateson my lord Habards [Herbert's] man. Tho. Powlton my lord of Worcester's man'. Source: Murray, *English Dramatic Companies*, I.44–5; Gurr, *The Shakespearian Playing Companies*, pp. 42–3.

Worcester's Men visited Stratford in both 1576–7 and 1583–4.

Troubles with authority

Norwich 1583, the city authorities, being worried 'for fear of any infection as also for that they came from an infected place', banned their performance. The company defied the ban, playing 'in theire hoste his hows' (an inn?). The Mayor ordered 'that their Lorde [i.e. the Earl of Worcester] shalbee certyfyed of their contempt & that hensforth the sayd players shall never receive any rewarde of the citty whensoever they shall come agayn And that they shall presently depart owt of this citty & not to play uppon payn of Imprysonment'. This was apparently not reported to the Earl. Source: Gurr, *The Shakespearian Playing Companies*, 317, citing *REED Norwich* 65, 66

A similar dust-up with the Mayor of Leicester (6 March 1584) when the company defied the Mayor's order not to play by performing at their inn, giving him 'evyll & contemptyous words'. They repented, begged him not to write to their Master, and were permitted 'to play this night at there inn'. Source: Chambers, *Elizabethan Stage*, II.223–4

Worcester's Men played the Stratford Guild Hall in 1583–4.

EARL OF LEICESTER'S PLAYERS

Size of company

'Item paid [in Southampton] to my Lorde of Leycesters plaiers xii of them the xxiith of September 1577.' Source: Murray, II.397 transcribing the *Liber de Finibus* . . . Payment in Mayor's accounts at Bristol (1577) of 3s 6d for 'mending the borde in the yeld hall and dores there, after my lord of Leycesters players who had leave to play there'. Source: Gurr, *The Shakespearian Playing Companies*, p. 194.

Leicester's Men visited Stratford in 1576–7.

Personnel

Letter of 1572 asking to be upgraded to being the Earl's household servants (as against liveried players merely), in order to meet the proclamation of 3 January that year, is signed by James Burbage, John Perkin, John Laneham, William Iohnson, Robert Wilson and Thomas Clarke. Royal patent (10 May 1574) names the same players (except Clarke). Burbage 'a man of violent temper and not over-honest'. The Company visited Stratford in 1573–4 (as well as 1576–7 and 1587).

Source: Gurr, *The Shakespearian Playing Companies*, pp. 186, 187; Chambers, *Elizabethan Stage*, II.306.

QUEEN'S MEN

Size of company and personnel

Twelve players named at formation of company in 1583, including John Bentley, John Dutton, William Johnson, John Singer, Richard Tarlton and Robert Wilson. Probably divided into two companies, 1587/8.

Source: Gurr, *The Shakespearian Playing Companies*, pp. 196–211; McMillin and MacLean, *The Queen's Men*, *passim* esp. 194–7.

Trouble with authority

15 June 1583, an affray in connection with a performance at the Red Lion Inn, Norwich, occasioned by the reluctance of a would-be audience member to pay the entrance fee and leading to the death of a bystander, involving Tarlton, Singer and Bentley, the latter two of whom were committed to gaol. Source: Chambers, *Elizabethan Stage*, II.105; McMillin and MacLean, *Queen's Men*, pp. 42–3; Gurr, *The Shakespearian Playing Companies*, pp. 203–4; Keenan, *Travelling Players*, 99–106

The Company played Stratford in 1587, 1593, 1594.

Repertoire

Plays include *The Famous Victories of Henry V*, *King Leir*, *The Troublesome Reign of King John*, *The True Tragedy of Richard III*. Source: Gurr, *The Shakespearian Playing Companies*, p. 211; McMillin and MacLean, *The Queen's Men*, pp. 160–6.

RECONSTRUCTING THE ROSE: DEVELOPMENT OF THE PLAYHOUSE BUILDING BETWEEN 1587 AND 1592

JON GREENFIELD

The short period in which open-air playhouses were built holds a special interest for architectural historians. In a defined period of time, barely seventy years, this new building type developed and flourished, then disappeared. The playhouse period therefore provides a discrete sample to study, from its antecedents to its demise. It offers a sequence of development, in which old forms and construction methods were adapted, new elements prototyped and refined, to when the form lost favour and was comprehensively superseded by a completely different kind of theatre building. It also offers a building type that became wholly integrated with its use, that of dramatic entertainment, and at a time when the use itself was developing – playwriting and staging – and developing with the form and layout of each successive playhouse. This was an energetic period in playwriting, full of experiment in which many different forms and ideas were tried and discarded. The same is true of the playhouses.

To an architect, the relationship between the use and form of a building is fundamental. Individual buildings will often display this use/form correspondence; a group of buildings built in quick succession with progressive refinement, such as the open-air playhouses, will have the use and building form fundamentally entwined. A study of the use of the building will tell much about the form of the enclosure, as conversely the form of a building will tell us much about the use that the building served. For those less familiar with buildings the same relationship can be seen in everyday objects, a corkscrew or a teacup for example, where the shape of the object has been generated and refined so that it perfectly matches its intended use and the hands that will use it. To truly understand buildings, particularly vernacular buildings and particularly those for which the use has passed, it is necessary to study the building form in all its subtleties to find out all we can about the use it accommodated. Most particularly, when faced with an archaeological record like the one we have for the Rose, we must look at the areas that make the least sense, or that seem to be contradictory, for it is often in understanding the inconsistencies that we can gain a truer insight into the whole.

Some buildings loosely fit their use, such as houses, where people can adapt all sorts of structures to make a home, provided that they have some key basic facilities. Some buildings tightly fit their use, usually industrial buildings, particularly historic industrial buildings, where the building itself is largely a cladding to machinery or to a process. The playhouse fits somewhere between these two extremes. Actors are very adaptable, and can play in many different kinds of spaces. Siobhan Keenan's detailed study of the venues for travelling players gives an idea of the adaptability required:

London-based acting companies regularly toured the country in the Elizabethan and Jacobean periods, performing in many provincial communities and in a variety of spaces ranging from town halls and churches to large country houses.[1]

---

[1] Siobhan Keenan, *Travelling Players in Shakespeare's England* (Houndsmills, 2002), p. 2.

But, when given the chance to model and adapt a structure, the playing companies were keen to mould their buildings around their needs. Henslowe's record shows us that the Rose was subject to very major adaptations twice in thirteen years, with other minor modifications as well. These modifications were unusually frequent and unusually wide in their scope, which indicates that the process of moulding the playhouse to the actor's needs was a highly active one at the Rose and that we must therefore think of the Rose not as a perfect and finished playhouse in 1587 but as a *transitional* one.[2] If, as the record seems to show, there were no acting companies resident at the Rose during its first five years,[3] then the process of modification and adaptation is a particularly interesting one. Henslowe, in managing the Rose for letting out, would have been carefully studying his clients' needs and modifying the building to make it more attractive to them. There is a story to tell about how the actors came to know what were the vital elements of a playhouse, and the records of the story are embedded in the successive modifications of the Rose, if only we can decode them.

TRANSITION

Recognizing the Rose playhouse as *transitional*, particularly in the first five years, colours the way we interpret the archaeological and documentary evidence. Put simply, we need to be clear about what we think the Rose was when it was first built, and what it was changing into, rather than trying to make it fit the standard playhouse model. There are some fundamental questions that we need to answer when we look at the record. What was the particular antecedent (or antecedents) of the Rose? Why was the playhouse structure modified so often and why was it replaced with a new playhouse, the Fortune, after such a short period of time, just thirteen years? Gurr shares these concerns:

We do not know what use was made of the Rose from 1587 to 1592, when it was altered. But five years can hardly have been long enough to wear it out and justify such expensive refurbishing. Presumably the original design, only the fourth amphitheatre playhouse ever built in London, was found unsatisfactory in some way. Why else should Henslowe lay out so much money after only five years?[4]

There are many possible answers to these questions and all of them tend to reinforce the impression that, as a building, the Rose was not just another playhouse. I would like to examine aspects of the record that distinguish the Rose and could make it different to the other playhouses of the period. Unfortunately much of the evidence is inconclusive, so it is not possible to say with unquestionable certainty, one way or the other, on a number of key aspects of the Rose. Indeed, given the inconclusiveness of the evidence, it is essential that we keep in mind multiple interpretations and do not allow ourselves to close off alternative possibilities. To keep some shape to the argument here I have concentrated on just two particular elements of the playhouse, *how the Rose met the ground* and *how the Rose met the sky*, for I believe that there are alternative interpretations to the record that can be seen through these exemplars. I have also restricted the thoughts presented here to the first five years of the Rose, the playhouse as it was first conceived and built by Henslowe, and why it was necessary to modify the building.

EVOLUTION OR REVOLUTION?

Nine playhouses were built in London between 1567 and 1613,[5] and we can double count the Rose, because at least half of the structure was modified in 1592 generically changing the building, and we can double count the Globe, because it was burnt down in 1613 and, although rebuilt on the same foundations, the new Globe did contain some

---

[2] Even without record of any possible building modifications between 1587 and 1592, the additional modifications made in 1595, and the move to the Fortune in 1600 mean that the Rose was modified on average once every four years and four months.

[3] Andrew Gurr, *The Shakespearian Stage 1574 to 1642*, 3rd edn (Cambridge, 1992), p. 124.

[4] Gurr, *The Shakespearian Stage*, p. 124.

[5] Using the definition of 'Playhouse' as an open-air structure.

fundamental differences from its precursor. This interpretation gives a total of eleven purpose-built open-air London playhouses. The archaeological record of the Rose and Globe is therefore highly significant, for remembering that the Globe was rebuilt from the 'liberated' timbers of the Theatre, that there were two versions of both the Rose and Globe, these archaeological sites can tell us something about five of the playhouses (the Theatre, 1587 Rose, 1592 Rose, 1599 Globe and 1613 Globe). Five from a total of eleven is 45 per cent of the London canon. To come to this conclusion we have to ignore the few provincial playhouses, the medieval 'standings' that were still in use in many 'game places' in the medium-sized towns around the country and used by the players on their travels, and the overseas playhouses and the related animal baiting structures, as it seems that it was in London where the group effect was at work and the construction solutions adopted in one playhouse could inform the layout and features of another. Understanding the playhouses as a group allows us to place the Rose within the context of a developing trend.

When looked at in this way it is very tempting to construct a linear progression, from the earliest to the latest, from the crudest to the most sophisticated. The usual architectural classification of architectural periods into 'Early, High and Late' can be usefully applied to the playhouse-building era. Gurr has already used the classifications 'Early Amphitheatre Design' and 'Later Amphitheatre Design',[6] to which I have added the term 'high' for there is evidence of this building type reaching a kind of perfection before over-developing, although the sample size of eleven playhouses is very small and there is good evidence that the development was only occasionally on a truly linear evolutionary path. Indeed, if there were a clear linear relationship one would expect the Rose to be very similar to the Theatre, if a little more refined, and there is as much evidence to suggest that the playhouses were significantly different from one another. Despite misgivings, the Rose of 1587 usefully fits the classification of an 'early playhouse form', and the contention that the Rose was a transitional structure is supported by the evidence that by 1592 it was modified into a more recognizable 'high playhouse form', with a stage cover and heavens, features it did not have in 1587. The Globe of 1599 can be classified as 'high', but the rebuild of 1613 would be considered as a 'late playhouse form', displaying some tendencies to 'baroque', i.e. exuberant and highly decorated, a little overblown.[7]

One final point to bear in mind when studying the playhouses as a group is that the most information we have about any of them comes from the Fortune Contract. Therefore when we make a reconstruction, or build a mental picture of a particular playhouse, we have tended to use the Fortune Contract to fill the gaps. Since we have gained the large volume of archaeological information about the Rose as a result of the Museum of London's painstaking work,[8] which has also made it possible to make more sense of Henslowe's record, we now have enough information to look at the issues afresh and to examine the features of the Rose in some detail. However there remains a need to reach for the construction descriptions in the Fortune Contract to fill the many gaps in the records of the Rose.

HOW THE ROSE MET THE GROUND: THE LOWER GALLERY

The crucial argument here is presented in the accompanying diagrams (see illustrations 7 and 8), because it is derived from a consideration of the building construction as found by the archaeologists and what we can gather about the topography of the site from their notes. The cill height of the timber frame can be worked out from the highest ground level from the levels in their records.

---

[6] Gurr, *The Shakespearian Stage*, pp. 121–54.

[7] Gurr, *The Shakespearian Stage*, p. 142.

[8] It is a testament to the careful method of archaeological record keeping that we are able to look through the Museum of London Archaeological Service's excavation records, surveyed during the dig in 1989. Analysis of the records is now complete and will be published in a Museum of London Monograph, *The Rose and The Globe – Playhouses of Tudor Bankside, Southwark: Excavations 1988 – 1991* by Julian M. C. Bowsher and Pat Miller.

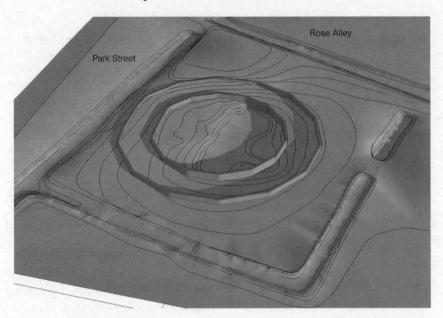

Park Street

Rose Alley

7. A contour model of the Rose site based on known features from 1587. Site levels were taken by the archaeologists (MoLAS and English Heritage Central Unit) inside and outside the playhouse on the western side, around the ditches and between Cholmley's House and the playhouse. Drainage ditches define the 94-foot square plot and the varying relationship between the height of the brickwork footings, the yard and the outside ground can be seen.

Contemporary good practice tells us that the timber cill would be at least twelve inches above the ground, set on a brick plinth, and the Fortune Contract stipulates fifteen inches of brickwork.[9] Quite how much the Rose followed the very best practice in building, and whether the height of the brick plinth was a little less at this point is debatable, however it gives us a good working hypothesis for setting a conjectural height for the timberwork. The plinth could have been as low as six inches, or less, and perhaps this is why the brickwork height is so carefully stipulated in the contract for the Fortune, the playhouse that would replace the Rose.[10] The highest ground outside the Rose was just adjacent to John Cholmley's house; all of the yard was lower than the outside.[11]

We can draw two conclusions from these levels:
• If the stage had been five feet above the yard, as stipulated in the Red Lion contract, and the brick plinth built only six inches above the highest point of the ground outside, then the top of the stage and the top of the lower gallery cill

would have been at the same level. This structural form has some constructional advantages.
• The floor in the lower gallery was set surprisingly high above the yard.
Concentrating on the second point, and the idea that the first gallery is set 'surprisingly high', it is important to look at the drawings of the ground levels outside the playhouse and those in the yard in comparison with the level of the gallery (see illustration 8). The issues come across better in

---

9 Fortune Contract, reproduced in J. R. Mulryne and Margaret Shewring, *Shakespeare's Globe Rebuilt* (Cambridge, 1997), pp. 180–2.

10 Phrases in the Fortune contract have led scholars to believe that everything stipulated about the Fortune describes a feature that was not found at the Globe. The same logic could also be applied to the Rose if one believes that Henslowe intended the contract clauses to ensure that the Fortune did not have the same defects as the Rose.

11 We have taken the trouble to plot the levels inside and outside the Rose and join them to form contours. This gives the best impression of the shape of the topography.

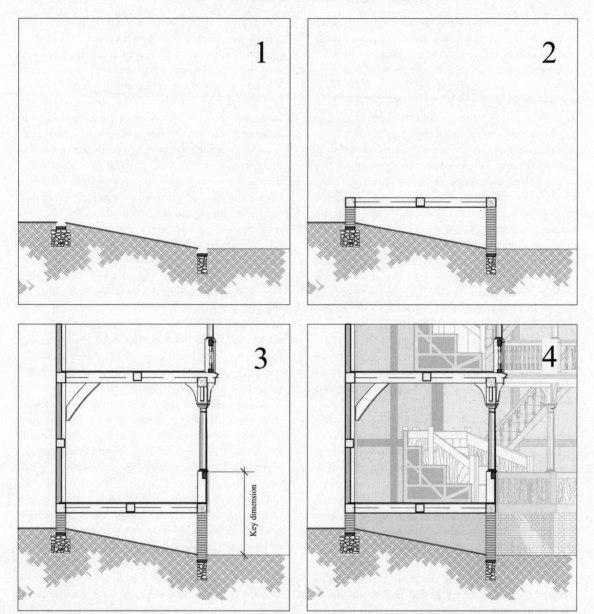

8. This sequence shows how the most probable construction of the galleries can be deduced from the archaeologist's findings, as can the height of the lowest gallery in relation to the yard. Inset 1: A typical gallery section showing the features discovered by the archaeologists: below ground foundations, occasional remnants of the 'robbed-out' brickwork and some key ground levels, both in the yard and outside the playhouse. Inset 2: A reconstruction of the probable timber cill levels, based on the lowest brick plinth acceptable and the highest outside ground levels found. Inset 3: A reconstruction of the probable playhouse frame, which reveals the surprising height of the lowest gallery in relation to the yard. Inset 4: Conjectured details of the Rose Playhouse interior.

drawings than in words, mainly because the ground levels outside the playhouse are varying so much, and the yard levels are varying too, making the relationship between them very complex. Put as simply as possible, the height of the gallery floor above the yard varies from 5′8″ (1.72 m) by the stage to 4′1″ (1.24 m) by the southern entrance.[12] Eye height of someone seated at the front of the gallery would have been about 4′1″ (1.24 m) above this, making the eye height of someone sitting at the front of the gallery 9′9″ (2.96 m) above the yard level by the stage and respectively 8′2″ (2.48 m) by the southern entrance. If we assume that the balustrade on the front of the lowest gallery is two foot five inches high, and that it was built like the one described in the Fortune Contract, i.e. finished on both sides with solid planking and not made as an open balustrade, it would have presented a wall to the yard that was over seven foot at its lowest (by the entrance) and nearly eight foot at its highest (by the stage). Surprising indeed. It is also possible that it had iron spikes on top of it, again like those referred to in the Fortune Contract. The step in levels from yard to first gallery is much greater than needed for those in the yard to look over the heads of the groundlings and constitutes a true separation between yard and gallery.

The separation between yard and lowest gallery, I believe, is central to our understanding of what kind of building was in Henslowe's mind before he built the Rose. The separation is one of those dissonant pieces of information that we have to explain, for, as we have already noted, it is by understanding such non-conformities that we gain the deepest insights. The high wall separating the yard from the first gallery, half made up of the step in levels that are indisputable, and half made up of the balustrading that is conjectured, is so singular that it cannot have been accidental. There must be something about the way Henslowe intended to use the building that brought about this peculiarity of form. Was Henslowe intending to make his new playhouse exclusively for showing plays? Or was he thinking of a building that could be used for a wider range of entertainments, including staging plays, but not exclusively? Or had he used

some other playhouse-like model for his structure, one that had a very strong physical barrier between the yard and first gallery, which he incorporated into his new playhouse without really needing to? We know that there were strong social divisions between the groundlings, those who stood in the yard, and those who had paid extra to sit in the galleries,[13] but this barrier at the Rose seems more than is necessary for pure social distinction. It is interesting that Henslowe had the yard filled when he made his adaptations in 1592, when, I believe, he was thinking of a building exclusively dedicated to staging plays, and he effectively raised the yard level by over eight inches, implying that the height relationship he had built in 1587 would not work in his re-invented playhouse.

To get an idea of what kind of structure Henslowe had in mind when he was planning the Rose it is useful to look at the agreement he made with John Cholmley, signed and sealed on 10 January 1586.[14] Much has been read into this document, but I interpret it as a *catering contract* and perhaps I need to digress from my main argument to explain why: Rutter states that the Deed 'includes sufficient detail to permit an estimation of the cost of the playhouse',[15] meaning the sum of £816, which is the final value of the annuity defined in the Deed of Partnership between Henslowe and Cholmley. This cannot be so; £816 was a huge sum of money in 1587, which, we will see, would have easily been enough to fund the construction of a playhouse and much, much more. Neither was Henslowe to receive Cholmley's money until a long time after he needed it to pay the builder. He was not to receive any of Cholmley's money straight away but was to receive payments four times a year, on the quarter days, over a period of eight years. These funds would not have helped

---

[12] Information taken from unpublished excavation records provided by MoLAS's Archive Department.

[13] Gurr, *The Shakespearian Stage*, pp. 215–22.

[14] At this point the new year still started on Lady Day, 25 March. We would call this 10 January 1587.

[15] Carol Chillington Rutter, *Documents of the Rose Playhouse* (Manchester, 1984), p. 36.

Henslowe fund the Rose. In development terms, and using the Fortune and Hope contract sums as a guide for when money would be due to a builder, Henslowe was in urgent need of several hundred pounds, even before 10 January 1587, the date on the Deed of Partnership. He must have already committed a lot of money on construction if the building could have been said to be 'in framing'. John Griggs, the carpenter, would not have started work without a substantial down-payment, and a high level of regular payments as the work proceeded.[16] Furthermore, this Deed of Partnership was to become valid after the playhouse was ready and open, so Cholmley was not due to make his first payment until five and a half months after the date on the Deed of Partnership, 'on the feast day of the nativity of St John the Baptist next coming',[17] 25 June 1587, by which time Henslowe would have had to have paid for the playhouse in full. The one payment Henslowe would have received from Cholmley of £25 10s 0d on 25 June 1587 would have helped a little, but not much; it would have been too little and too late to contribute to the construction cost, and it would not have 'pacified' the carpenter John Grigges very much.[18] In my view, Henslowe would have paid for the playhouse from his own resources, from another investment deal or from borrowing, and his income from Cholmley, set down in the Deed of Partnership, had nothing to do with the cost of constructing the Rose playhouse, possibly other than to help him pay off his borrowing. We therefore cannot use the value of the Deed of Partnership to help estimate the construction contract value of the Rose, or use it as a reliable record of construction features in the way we have come to rely on the Fortune Contract.

A better way to get an estimate of the cost of building the Rose is to scale it from the Fortune Contract, a document of 1600 which gives the dimensions and intended cost of the playhouse: £440 paid out for 4,557 square feet gives a rate of just under two shillings per square foot (23.17d).[19] The footprint of the Rose in 1587, measured from the archaeological outline, was 2,804 square feet which, when proportioned up, gives a total cost for the Rose of £270 15s (2,804 × 23.17d). The

Fortune may have been a more elaborate structure, with carved satyrs, heavens and columns 'wrought pilasterwise', so perhaps a better working construction cost is £250. The bigger Hope cost £360 twenty-six years later in 1613.

This digression is important because most scholars have hitherto concluded that the Deed of Partnership had something to do with the construction arrangements.[20] I see it as more to do with the 'facilities management', the running of the building once it had opened, and the construction arrangements are only referred to because construction completion triggers the start of the arrangements described in the Deed. However, although the language in the Deed is not precise in construction terms, it is of some use because it does convey something of Henslowe and Cholmley's enthusiasm for the new building. Returning to the consideration of what kind of structure was in Henslowe's mind when he commissioned the Rose, the Cholmley *catering agreement* is useful because it refers to the forthcoming building, and its use, on a number of occasions. For example, their financial arrangement is to have effect when the building is put to use:

by reasonne of any playe or playes that shallbe showen or played there or otherwysse howsoever.[21]

Henslowe and Cholmley are

---

[16] Both the Fortune and Hope contracts stipulate the precise timing of staged payments.

[17] Rutter, *Documents of the Rose*, p. 38.

[18] Henslowe, in notes made on the reverse of the Fortune contract records that he had to make a payment to Peter Street for construction of the Fortune 'to pacify him'.

[19] Mulryne and Shewring, *Shakespeare's Globe Rebuilt*, pp. 180–2, taken from the transcribed Fortune Contract. A more detailed analysis can be made separating the galleried footprint of the Fortune from the stage area, and comparing it with a two-galleried Rose. However the cost index noted here is sufficient at this point.

[20] For example Mulryne and Shewring reproduce it in the appendix of *Shakespeare's Globe Rebuilt*, referring to it as 'The Rose Playhouse Agreement', pp. 178–9. Although this is not inaccurate, it implies that it concerns the construction phases not the post-construction phase.

[21] Rutter, *Documents of the Rose*, pp. 37–9.

jointly to appoynte and permitte suche personne and personnes players to use exercise & playe in the saide playe house at theire wills[22]

and Cholmley can supply food and drink

when any playe or playes shall be played or showen in the saide playe howse . . .[23]

These phrases demonstrate clearly an intention to use the building for staging plays, but also that the building was intended for use 'otherwise howsoever' and that persons shall 'use and exercise' in the building 'at their wills'. The language could be transcribed to say that Cholmley is permitted to sell food and drink to anyone using the playhouse in any way whatsoever. Entertainments other than plays are included.[24]

Furthermore any thought that the use of the term 'playhouse' only referred to a house where plays were performed and therefore that the Rose was definitely used only for plays is erroneous. In the Hope Contract of 1613 the term 'playhouse' is used to describe a multi-purpose house, and implies that it is a term interchangeable with 'game place', as in the following extracts:

Vppon or before the saide laste daie of November newly erect, builde and sett vpp one other Same place or Plaiehouse fitt and convenient in all things, bothe for players to playe Jn, and for the game of Beares and Bulls to be bayted in the same

and

And shall new builde erect and sett vp againe the saide plaie house or game place neere or vppon the saide place, where the said game place did heretofore stande.[25]

The term 'playhouse' was used to describe a house used for many and varied entertainments and these comments do not exclude a broader spectrum of activity at the Rose just because it was referred to as a 'playhouse'. They certainly do not rule out the possibility that Henslowe had a multi-use arena in mind in 1587. One other explanation for this wall-like separation between the yard and first gallery, evidenced in the archaeology, is that the Rose was first intended as a multi-purpose playhouse, more like the Hope Henslowe built twenty-six years later

than Burbage's Theatre. It is an unfashionable idea, and one that we do not willingly wish to admit, but there is the possibility that the Rose, in its original form, was based on antecedent arenas that were set up for baiting fierce animals, bears and bulls, with dogs.

Professor Gurr has made the link between bears and players, through Henslowe:

Londoners in the late sixteenth century had two chief forms of public entertainment available to them, plays and the baiting of animals. Plays could be seen almost daily, baiting of bears and bulls by dogs only once a week, since they were based on the maiming and killing of their entertainers. These days, as readers of and audiences for plays, not animals, we tend to regard the two sports as culturally antithetical. Philip Henslowe, however, evidently did not, and against his career as a supporter of playing through nearly thirty years should be set his equally long-running support for bear-baiting. When we study Henslowe's involvement in the two activities, the rather fearsome conclusion seems to be that the bears and the players operated in much closer company that we like to think.[26]

A word of caution here, before I give too strong an impression that the Rose was a bear garden. My primary proposition is not that the Rose was necessarily used for baiting animals, but that the animal-baiting arenas provided Henslowe with his playhouse model. We do not know if Burbage used the same model for the Theatre, and it is possible that he did not. The similarity between the two structures, possibly from wholly different antecedents, implies that a kind of evolutionary convergence took place, particularly in 1592 when the Rose was modified to take on the features we more exclusively associate with staging plays.

---

[22] Rutter, *Documents of the Rose*, pp. 37–9.

[23] Rutter, *Documents of the Rose*, pp. 37–9.

[24] It would also be useful to make a study of the meaning of the term 'play' in 1587.

[25] Mulryne and Shewring, *Shakespeare's Globe Rebuilt*, pp. 183–4, taken from Greg's transcript of the Hope Contract.

[26] Andrew Gurr, 'Bears and Players: Philip Henslowe's Double Acts', *Shakespeare Bulletin*, 22 (2004), p. 31.

RECONSTRUCTING THE ROSE

THE PROVENANCE OF THE STAGE

The evidence against the Rose ever having been a truly multi-purpose playhouse like the Hope is the existence of a stage with permanent foundations within the 1587 area. It is a continuing frustration that the 1989 archaeological dig had to stop short of verifying whether the stage associated with the first phase of construction was built into the 'arena' foundations, or was separated from them.[27] It means that we have to carry three possible interpretations about this crucial feature of a playhouse and how the building was used in its earliest years. The uncertainty is increased because Henslowe's record, so good after 1592, is less helpful for the period 1587 to 1592, Rutter finding only Henslowe's Deed of Partnership with Cholmley (the Catering Contract) and six other documents that cover this period.[28] Also Gurr has pointed out that this was a very uncertain period for public playing companies, whose legality was in question and for whom the vital licence from the Master of the Rolls was highly restricted. No one acting company would have been able to take up residence at the Rose until 1592. If the stage foundations can be shown to have been built into the arena foundations then there would be no doubt that the Rose had been wholly conceived and built as a playhouse dedicated exclusively to staging plays right from the start and we will have to look for another explanation for the exaggerated separation between yard and first gallery. However, we have to bear in mind two other possible interpretations as well, such as:

- The permanent stage found by the archaeologists was built under a separate contract to the frame, as at the Red Lion, possibly by different builders, but it was constructed just after the frame so that the Rose opened with a permanent stage from the start;
- The permanent stage found by the archaeologists was built under a separate contract to the frame, possibly by different builders, and it was constructed some time *after* the Rose opened, after 1587 and before 1592.

If this last conjecture is correct then it raises the possibility that the Rose was used, in its first years, for many kinds of entertainments and that a temporary stage was set up for plays and that theatre was just one of a number of entertainments that Henslowe put on. It introduces the fascinating possibility that not only was the design of the Rose based on a bear garden model but possibly, for a short time, the Rose was used as a multi-purpose entertainment house as well. The idea of the playhouse as a multi-use arena includes its use for dancing, music and trials of combat, either in an open yard or on a temporary stage, and the inclusion of animals could only have been occasional. Henslowe could have had a house with an open yard or one with a temporary stage. Subsequently Henslowe grew to recognise that theatre was the most popular and profitable entertainment so he modified his playhouse to suit. Until it can be shown whether the stage was built into the arena frame, or separate from it, the question cannot be resolved, but there are no grounds for simply dismissing the possibility that the first permanent stage was built after 1587 because it is inconvenient.

HOW THE ROSE MET THE SKY: THE HEIGHT OF THE ROSE

Our mental picture of a playhouse is that it has a scaffold of three galleries. Two pieces of evidence suggest that the Rose could have had only two galleries. These are:
- Norden's depictions of the Rose
- An erosion line cut into the yard surface of the Rose by water dripping from the eaves.

Norden's Depictions of the Rose
It is not possible to get any objective dimensions from Norden's maps and panorama (*Civitas Londini* and *Speculum Britaniae*), but they do contain a lot of information about the comparative size of the Rose in relation to the other playhouses depicted, and the

---

[27] Julian Bowsher, *The Rose Theatre: An Archaeological Discovery* (London, 1998), p. 40: 'It is not known exactly how it [the stage] was attached to the inner walls of the main frame.'

[28] Rutter, *Documents of the Rose*, pp. 37–46, documents numbered 1–9.

surrounding domestic structures. Orrell noted that there is a general tendency for Norden to exaggerate the height of the buildings he draws, particularly the well-known public buildings:

In fact it was Norden's habit throughout the panorama, whether in the perspective of the north bank or the plan of the south, to exaggerate the height of buildings in order to give them a memorial celebratory quality. Bow Church is much too high, so is St Laurence Poultney, so are St Saviour's and St Olave's, and so of course are the theatres. The image of the Swan, seen almost in elevation, shows the frame to have been at most half as wide again as the height to the eaves, a maximum of, say, 50 ft to include the galleries, the internal yard and the stage. This is a manifest impossibility, and it would be absurd to claim that Norden offers a view of this playhouse that is intended to be taken as literally true. In the sketch of the building included in his scene design of 1638, Inigo Jones shows it some three or four times as wide as it was high to the eaves, proportions which agree with Hollar's reliable picture of the Hope, a playhouse building of the same dimensions as the Swan. In the panorama Norden renders all the playhouses much taller than other evidence (and common sense) suggests that they were.[29]

While this is true for the public buildings, the Swan and the Bear Gardens amphitheatres, it does not seem to be true about the Rose, or for that matter the Globe. Both are shown considerably smaller than would be expected for a three-storey building in relation to the surrounding buildings, and the other playhouses. On Norden's 1593 map the Rose is drawn at about twice the height of the surrounding houses, but it is drawn at only 87 per cent of the Bear Gardens in width and 75 per cent in height. On Norden's 1600 map the Bear Gardens and Rose are drawn the same width, but the Rose again is only 83 per cent of its neighbour's height. On the panorama the ridge height of the Rose is much the same as the ridge height of surrounding domestic buildings, but much lower than one of its very near neighbours. The Bear Gardens stands proudly about twice as high as its near neighbours. Is this significant? Was Norden trying to convey a diminished celebrity of the Rose, that the Rose was less popular? Or was the Rose a lower structure, two storeys rather than three?

Investigation of the windows depicted on Norden's map of 1600 leads to a similar conclusion. On the 1592 map the fenestration shown is very tentative, but it is clear, if sketchy, on the later map. There are two rows of windows on the Beargardens, but just one on the distinctly lower Rose. On his panorama Norden again shows one row of windows, but the base of the playhouse gets lost in the foliage of surrounding trees and so a second row of windows could be obscured as well (or a third, for that matter).

The Drip Line

It is almost certain that rainwater dripping from the roof created the erosion line found in the earliest floor of the mortar yard,[30] approximately 16 inches wide and 22 inches from, and parallel to, the inner line of the inner wall. This indicates that the roof was thatched and therefore the eaves did not have gutters. Examination of the Phase II surface also reveals a feature in the same line as the Phase I drip line, but here it was more of an even depression without the ragged edges of the Phase I feature.[31] It would seem that the Phase II feature was a purpose-made gully, formed as a dish in the yard surface. The Phase I feature could also have been a purpose-made gully, its deep erosion coming about because the earlier mortar surface was a more friable material. We have had a useful comparison at the reconstructed Globe, where the yard was laid with a mortar mix based on the Rose Phase II mortar surface. A very similar feature developed, 14 inches wide and 52 inches from the inner gallery plinth wall. If the impressions found at the Rose were from a three-storey structure, the Rose would have had two jetties of six inches each. The improbability of this jetty dimension, nine inches being the minimum jetty worth making, means it is necessary

[29] Orrell, *The Shape of the Globe*, p. 36; Mulryne and Shewring, *Shakespeare's Globe Rebuilt*, p. 58.

[30] Bowsher, *The Rose Theatre*, p. 39.

[31] Taken from unpublished excavation records provided by MoLAS's Archive Department when I was researching a reconstruction of the 1587 Rose for Shakespeare and Company in Lenox, Massachusetts with Peter McCurdy.

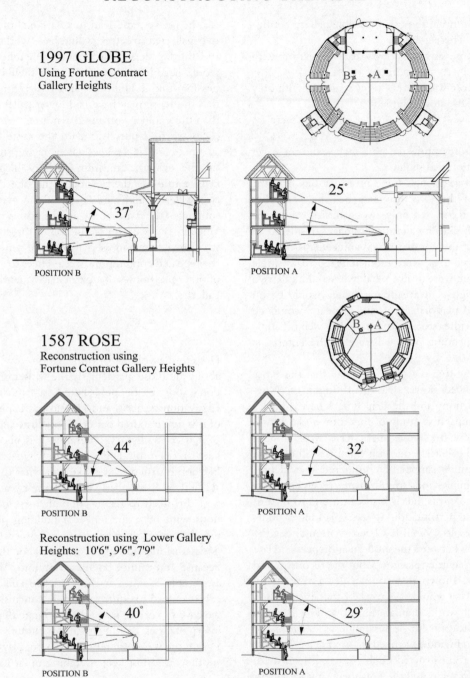

1997 GLOBE
Using Fortune Contract
Gallery Heights

1587 ROSE
Reconstruction using
Fortune Contract Gallery Heights

Reconstruction using Lower Gallery
Heights: 10'6", 9'6", 7'9"

9. The Rose in comparison with the reconstructed Globe, showing the effect that the diameter of the playhouse and the gallery height have on viewing angles. A two-gallery Rose seems plausible as a third gallery provides mostly compromised viewing angles.

to keep in mind the other possible gallery configurations. These are;

- The Rose was only a two-storey structure, with a single jetty of one foot
- The Rose was a three-storey structure with only one of the storeys jettied
- The eaves projected further and there were no jetties
- Each storey projected nine inches and the eaves projection was slight.

Inconclusive though these investigations into the height of the structure may be, the possibility that the Rose had only two galleries cannot be excluded. The medieval standings, considered to be one of the constructional antecedents of playhouse structures, were often referred to as single storey, but were really what we would call two storeys high. The wealthy audience would be on the raised platform level, and beneath would be used for either storage or for the less well off audience, depending on the nature of the entertainment.

To these two pieces of evidence that the Rose may have been lower than first thought, the Norden depictions and the drip line, I have added a short comparative study of the known playhouses to see how the Rose might have worked both with two galleries and with three (see illustration 9). This study cannot be considered as evidence, like the impressions found in the receiving earth by archaeologists, but it has been useful to try out the various permutations to see what kind of auditorium results. Much has been written about the differences between the modern audiences and late sixteenth-century playgoers, but the reconstructed Globe has shown that we can get a very useful sense of what would have worked dramatically then because it works dramatically now. The Fortune Contract is again our clearest guide, as it gives all the heights and widths we need to provide a comparator. The reconstructed Globe has also been used, although it again uses the Fortune Contract gallery heights, because it uses a carefully researched plan dimension and it is visitable, so that the viewing angles are not simply diagrams but can be verified in performances. Again the diagrams largely speak

for themselves, and lead us to a conclusion that a two-galleried structure would have worked well – the third gallery only adding an audience that would have been dissatisfied with their view, and possibly the audibility. It also raises the question that the Rose may have had lower gallery heights than the grander Fortune Playhouse.

So we find ourselves with the same dilemma as encountered earlier when trying to weigh up the evidence regarding gallery heights. We cannot rule out the possibility that the Rose was two galleries high and some of the evidence in support of the two-gallery proposition is very convincing. But we cannot rule out a three-galleried structure either, and we may be more convinced by the repeated contemporary references to a number of other playhouses that particularly mention three galleries.

CONCLUSION

Despite the volume of information now available about the Rose, particularly the Museum of London's soon to be published Post-Archaeological Excavation Analysis and Henslowe's Papers, none of it is one hundred per cent conclusive, and some of it is contradictory. Therefore it is necessary to keep an open mind about precisely what the Rose Playhouse structure was like and what took place at the Rose, particularly in the earliest years. I contrast this need to retain contradictory interpretations with my experience of building playhouse reconstructions,[32] when it is necessary to come down on one side of an argument or the other, because you cannot build two options. When we are simply looking at the evidence and have no external need to come to a single conclusion, then we have to keep in mind the full range of plausible interpretations. Rather than concluding that the 1587 Rose was definitely one kind of playhouse or another, we must keep weighing up at least three

---

[32] In my two chapters on construction research and practice for the Globe Theatre reconstruction in Mulryne and Shewring, *Shakespeare's Globe Rebuilt*, pp. 81–120.

possible kinds of playhouse, each of which, in my view, fit the evidence equally well.

However, one conclusion that can be drawn from the records is that there was a surprisingly high separation between the yard and first gallery in the first version of the Rose in 1587. I can see no better explanation than that Henslowe had a multi-purpose arena in mind when he built the Rose. There is proof that he did have to revise his thinking so that he could more comfortably accommodate the theatre players, and whether he did this during construction of the playhouse or some time later cannot be verified. It would be convenient to conclude that the Rose was dedicated only to staging plays right from the start, but there is a richer and more complex interpretation too, one that recognizes Henslowe's interest in multi-purpose arenas, exemplified by the Hope, and possibly in the first version of the Rose.

Indeed, if one is studying the development of the stage and the associated features of the playhouse structures, the rapid transformation of the Rose, possibly from multi-use arena to dedicated playing space, increases the value of the Rose to scholars and adds significance to the details and nuances of development seen at the Rose between 1587 and 1592. It means that we have a prototype to study, not the first production model. When the Rose site is opened up again, for excavation of the eastern third, the portion that could not be excavated in 1989, there are also some vital investigations that need to be carried out in the portion that was excavated. This would resolve some of the key issues, like the connection or separation of the first permanent stage foundations to the gallery foundations, and help us to greater certainty about the form of the Rose at each stage of development, and the uses it accommodated.

THE ROSE AND ITS STAGES

JULIAN M. C. BOWSHER

The archaeological discovery of the remains of the Rose playhouse in 1989 was a momentous revelation for the world of Shakespearian theatre studies. For the first time concrete evidence for the plan and layout of an Elizabethan playhouse was revealed. This immediately belied the tired documentary evidence hitherto used to create the image of a 'typical Shakespearian theatre'. A thorough study of those divergent documents should have revealed differences but the Rose remains forced the issue wide open: there was no 'typical Shakespearian theatre'.

As scholars came to visit the excavations, two questions were paramount: how many sides did the Rose have and where and what shape was the stage. A fourteen-sided polygon did indeed ruffle some feathers but nearly every aspect of the stage, the one essential component in a theatre, caused a surprise. I shall not only examine all its physical aspects but also emphasize its function. In particular I want to examine the views of Andy Gurr and Jon Greenfield that the Rose might have been used as a venue for animal baiting before being converted into a playhouse.[1] They acknowledge that their arguments were written before funding allowed a complete post-excavation analysis of the findings. This analysis is now virtually complete and should be referred to for full details on all aspects of the Rose (and Globe)[2] but the arguments presented here will concentrate on correcting some of the misapprehensions and suppositions in the articles in question and will present an alternative reasoning.

Philip Henslowe's papers relating to the Rose provide an almost unique account of contemporary theatres. The excavations then made the Rose doubly unique by locating the actual site to which those papers referred. Moreover the excavations have illuminated hitherto misunderstood references in the papers, the most notable of which was the 'carges as I haue layd owt a bowte my playe howsse in the yeare of o^r lord 1592'.[3] This can now be understood as the expenditure on altering and enlarging the building. This is, of course, something that happens to many buildings within their lifetimes, perhaps particularly in theatres where the

I am grateful to Kate McLuskie for inviting me to speak at the 2006 conference and to Peter Holland, and his colleagues on the *Shakespeare Survey* editorial board, for subsequently inviting me to write this paper for publication. I remain grateful of course, to Andy Gurr and Jon Greenfield for engaging in frank discussions on the subject of this paper. Their advice over the last seventeen years on the history and architecture of Elizabethan playhouses has been warmly appreciated.

[1] Andrew Gurr, 'New Questions about the Rose', *Times Literary Supplement*, 18 April 2003, 14–15; Jon Greenfield and Andrew Gurr, 'The Rose Theatre, London: The State of Knowledge and What We still need to Know'. *Antiquity*, 78 (2004), 330–40; Andrew Gurr, 'Bears and Players: Philip Henslowe's Double Acts', *Shakespeare Bulletin*, 22 no. 4 (2004), 31–41.

[2] J. M. C. Bowsher and P. Miller, *The Rose and the Globe – Playhouses of Tudor Bankside, Southwark: Excavations 1988–1991* (English Heritage / Museum of London Archaeology Service, Monograph Series, forthcoming).

[3] R. A. Foakes, ed., *Henslowe's Diary*, 2nd edn (Cambridge, 2002), p. 9.

latest fashions have to be continually catered for. This is also relevant to our topic today for these changes were, I believe, directly related to the stage.

Nevertheless, archaeology can only reveal so much and there is occasionally a difficulty with interpretation and mistakes are made. In my preliminary account of the building, undertaken before detailed post-excavation analysis began, there were indeed a couple of mistakes relevant to this discussion.[4] The polygonal frame of the Rose was thought to be an irregular one, albeit of fourteen sides. It has now been seen that this was based on faulty measurements and that it was entirely regular, with its southernmost bay parallel to Maiden Lane from which direct access was gained. Secondly, the attribution of the *ingressus* to our Phase 2 was wrong; it was in fact founded on earlier levels than had been initially thought. The dating of the timber drain at the northern end of the building is still uncertain though I am now inclined to think it may belong to Phase 2. Its association with ground levels will be discussed below.

For archaeologists the excavation and recording of a site provides the primary records used as a basis for subsequent analysis. The dating of the remains and the material finds then provide a chronological sequence. The distribution of those finds – within a chronological framework – can enhance a spatial analysis that is fundamental to the important question of function. Archaeologists will interpret differing remains as a Roman temple, a domestic house or a theatre as each will display differing characteristics of use.[5]

A unique aspect of dealing with, dare I say it, something as modern as a sixteenth-century playhouse is that relevant historical documents survive. More importantly perhaps, the plays that were performed there four hundred years ago are still being performed today. The performance of drama on the stage has undoubtedly developed over the years but actors remain particularly pragmatic and those that visited the Rose excavations were very helpful in discussing the 'use' of a playing space.

As I noted above, there is clear archaeological evidence for two main building phases at the Rose.

We have associated Phase 1 with its initial construction in 1587 and its Phase 2 with the alterations noted by Henslowe in 1592. I would argue that the regular and relatively simple layout of Phase 1 is better understood than that of Phase 2 which only affected the northern – stage – end of the building, where subsequent disturbance obscured many details. There is, however, no dispute about the function of the building from that date and this paper therefore will concentrate on the Phase 1 stage. Though not germane to the issues under discussion, I would mention that any tiring house area would appear to have been confined within the gallery frame behind the stage. Furthermore, the absence of any structural supports suggests that there was no permanent cover or roof over this stage. The presence of any awnings or even a small cantilevered cover cannot be determined by the archaeological remains.

LOCATION AND ORIENTATION OF THE STAGE

Our assumptions about stage orientation have for many years been dominated by its relationship to the afternoon sun and the question of shade or not to shade.[6] Thus the stage at the Rose was expected to be to the south or south-west and there was surprise at its appearance on the northern side of the building. Such a location prompted various questions and research into evidence for contemporary stages brought out conclusions entirely non-solar. The immediately obvious aspect about the Rose is

[4] Julian Bowsher, *The Rose Theatre, an Archaeological Discovery* (London, 1989).

[5] These issues are covered in Bowsher and Miller, *The Rose and the Globe*, but for directly addressing this issue at the Rose, see Julian Bowsher, 'Encounters between Actors, Audience and Archaeologists at the Rose Theatre, 1587–1989', in L. McAtackney, M. Palus and A. Piccini, eds., *Towards Diversity: Papers from CHAT 2003* (forthcoming).

[6] R. B. Graves, 'Orientation of the Elizabethan Stage', *Theatre Notebook* 34 (1980), 126–7; Andrew Gurr with John Orell, *Rebuilding Shakespeare's Globe* (London, 1989), p. 22.

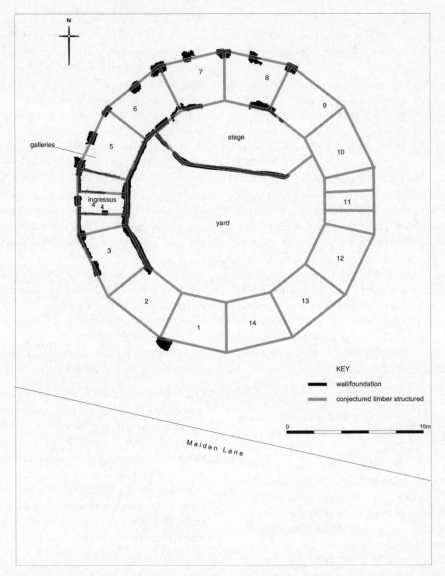

10. The Rose Playhouse Phase 1, 1587. Archaeological remains overlain by a timber superstructure proposed by Jon Greenfield.

that its stage was opposite the main entrance into the building, thus north of Maiden Lane.

It is true that John Norden's 1600 panorama shows an internal gable – thereby interpreted as being over the stage – at the northern side of what must be the Rose and the Globe.[7] His map inset into the panorama, however,[8] shows indeterminate

orientations for a hut at the playhouses (though that at the Swan is rather indistinct), and, interestingly, at the Bear Garden. It might be easy to dismiss this

_____

[7] Conveniently reproduced in R. A. Foakes, *Illustrations of the English Stage, 1580–1642* (London, 1985), p. 10.

[8] Foakes, *Illustrations*, p. 13.

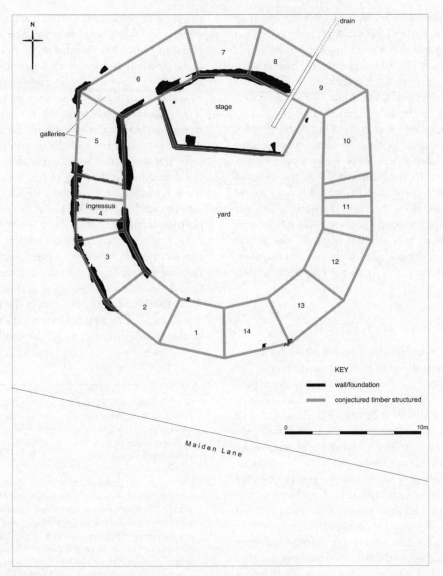

N

drain

7
8
6
9
stage
galleries
5
10
ingressus
4
11
yard
3
12
2
13
1
14

KEY

▬ wall/foundation

▬ conjectured timber structured

0 ———————— 10m

Maiden Lane

11. The Rose Playhouse Phase 2, 1592. Archaeological remains overlain by a timber superstructure proposed by Jon Greenfield.

as an artistic aberration but research has shown that the entrance to the Globe was from the north, or more likely north-east opposite Horseshoe Alley on Maiden Lane. What might be the more reliable views of Wenceslaus Hollar show the stage building of the second Globe to the south-west.[9] Unfortunately no traces of any stage structure were found at the Globe excavations, which were limited to its north-eastern part.

The cantilevered cover over the removable stage at the Hope is also shown by Hollar to the south.

---

[9] Foakes, *Illustrations*, pp. 29, 36.

This we know to be accurate because the entrance to the Hope, and its Bear Garden predecessor, was through the gatehouse built in 1606 to the north off Bankside.[10] The Swan appears on a map of 1627 whose topography suggests that any entrance was likely to have been made from one of the main roads lying to the north and to the east.[11] Little detail is known about the Theatre but it very clearly lay within ground opening on to a yard to the east from where an entrance would almost certainly be. To the rear, west, was the original curtain wall of Holywell Priory with only a private doorway from the fields beyond.[12] Though the stage of the second Globe may have been fortuitously in an area of even light, I believe that the greater argument was the location of the playhouse on land available for easy access by the paying public.

SHAPE AND SIZE OF THE STAGE

Of much greater variation has been the discussion of the shape and size of contemporary stages. The Phase 1 stage at the Rose was bound by the angled inner wall of the frame to the rear and a front wall against the yard and audience. The front wall had angles at its edges thus producing a shallow taper. This wall was not fully revealed but it was clearly a permanent feature with a brick footing and, at its ends, a lacing of stout timbers. It was relatively small, with an estimated maximum width of 8.20 m (26′ 10″) and a depth of 5 m (16′ 6″). This provided an area of some 46.4 m² (499.45ft²).

The obvious flaw seen in plan is that the front wall is not parallel to the flat face of the central stage bay behind, but appears to diverge by 4°. Without further excavation it cannot be known whether this was an eccentricity on the part of the builders, or a fault in our understanding of the geometry of an only partially revealed stage.[13] However, if it is a reality it makes little difference to the workings of that stage and it is unlikely that it was greatly noticed by the audience, except possibly those in gallery bays adjacent to it.

R. A. Foakes speculated that because, under close scrutiny, the written sources give no idea of the *shape* of the stages in other playhouses, tapered stages may have been in existence elsewhere.[14] Franklin Hildy has noted that the reconstruction of Elizabethan and Jacobean stages in the twentieth century has varied with fashion from tapered to rectangular.[15] After the discovery of the Rose, it was acknowledged that the fictionally derived tapered stage-fronts depicted in the *Roxana* and *Messalina* frontispieces of the seventeenth century were not as isolated as hitherto thought.[16] Only the overindulged drawing of the Swan appears to show something rectangular extending some way into the yard.[17] Hollar's view of the second Globe portrays what must have been a very large stage though details of its shape are unclear. Documentary sources do, however, suggest that contemporary stages were larger than those at the Rose. The Red Lion stage was recorded as 'fortye foote by thirty foot' (12 by 9.14 m), that at the Boar's Head was about 39 ft by 25 ft (12 by 7.6 m) and the width of the Fortune was 43 ft (13 m) with a breadth

---

[10] W. J. Lawrence and W. H. Godfrey, 'The Bear Garden Contract of 1606 and what it Implies', *The Architectural Review*, 47 (1920), 152–5. It might be noted here that the excavation of a small area of the Hope will also be included in a forthcoming MoLAS monograph.

[11] Foakes, *Illustrations*, p. 24.

[12] Julian Bowsher, 'Excavations at 86–90 Curtain Road 3–15 New Inn Yard, London EC 2: An insight into Holywell Priory and the Theatre', *London Archaeologist* (forthcoming).

[13] No obvious mistake can be found in the records – unlike the mistake found at the southern end of the building affecting the regularity of the frame. Jon Greenfield's ingenius solution to this problem, Greenfield and Gurr, 'The Rose Theatre, London', 337, is now rather redundant due to the correction of the regularity of the frame.

[14] R. A. Foakes, 'The Discovery of the Rose Theatre: Some Implications', *Shakespeare Survey 43* (Cambridge, 1991), p. 146.

[15] F. J. Hildy, 'Oppositional Staging in Shakespeare's Theatre', *The Re-Emergence of the Theatre Building in the Renaissance: Theatre Symposium* 4 (1996), 103.

[16] J. H. Astington, 'The Origins of the *Roxana* and *Messalina* Illustrations', *Shakespeare Survey 43* (Cambridge, 1991), pp. 149–69.

[17] The famous drawing of the interior of the Swan is reproduced in Foakes, *Illustrations*, p. 53.

extending to the middle of the yard (which calculates as 27′ 6″ (8.4 m)).[18]

HEIGHTS OF THE GALLERIES, STAGE AND YARD

The location, shape and size of the stage emerged in two-dimensional plan as foundations during excavation; calculating the third dimension, its height, was not initially thought possible. Jon Greenfield suggested that for architectural integrity, the level of the stage would be the same as the floorboards of the lowest gallery. Vertical measurements taken on archaeological excavations are related to Ordnance Datum and, from heights taken on surviving sixteenth-century ground levels at the southern part of the site, we can construct a hypothetical gallery level. This area was used for reconstructing measurements as it was one of the few areas where the contemporary external ground surface survived. Nevertheless, the timber construction will have been at a constant level throughout the building.

The outer wall of the galleries was built on a series of foundation pads; overlying these were brick piers flush with the ground level. These foundation pads and overlying piers would have supported the upright timbers of the frame. The maximum height found on the brick piers was 1.75 m OD. If to this we add a 12″ (0.30 m) brick plinth wall ('one foote of assize att the leiste above the grounde' attested in the Fortune Contract, though higher in the Hope Contract) it brings us to 2.05 OD. The timber cill beam over this can be conjectured at 9″ (0.24 m) square, as again attested at the Hope, thus bringing us to 2.29 m OD. The cill beams would have been at the same level as the cross beams and floorboards of one inch (0.02 m) over these would give a hypothetical gallery floor level of 2.32 m OD. A baluster fragment found during the excavations was used as a basis for reconstructing those fronting the galleries at the new Globe. This, with handrail and jetty rail, would provide a hypothetical handrail level fronting the lower gallery of 3.05 m OD.[19] It is possible that the frontage of the lowest gallery was boarded

in as shown in the drawing of the Swan and as appears to be specified for the lowest gallery at the Fortune.[20]

Our next step is to examine the floor levels in the yard whose depth has caused concern. It might be noted here that the notion that the yard was built around a 'natural hollow' or 'natural depression in the ground' has no basis in the archaeological evidence.[21] Indeed, the natural terrain and anthropomorphic ground surfaces associated with the playhouse were only ascertained in a few areas. Subsequent redevelopment and truncation of earlier levels destroyed much of the evidence.

The surface of the yard was a mortar screed and remains *in situ*; no further excavation was taken 'through' it. A modern truncation made in early 1988 by demolition contractors did allow a glimpse of the underlying strata seen in section. Here it could be seen that the floor surface had been either built in sandwiched layers or that it had been relaid; the lowest layer of mortar was a maximum of 0.20 m (8″) below the surface. The most striking thing about this floor is that it is raked; it is at an average level of 1.08 m OD in its southern half but then slopes down towards the stage where it is at about 0.60 m OD. The slight uncertainty is caused by severe erosion of the floor against the stage front; an

---

[18] On the Red Lion stage see J. S. Loengard, 'An Elizabethan Lawsuit: John Brayne, his Carpenter, and the Building of the Red Lion Theatre', *Shakespeare Quarterly*, 34 (1983), 15, n.2. For the Boar's Head see H. Berry, *The Boar's Head Playhouse*, (Cranford, NJ, 1986), p. 108. The Fortune measurements are included in its building contract, Foakes, *Henslowe's Diary*, p. 308.

[19] It is not known whereabouts in the building this baluster came from but it is assumed that handrail height was the same for all three galleries.

[20] The wording in the Fortune Contract is obscure on this point with mention of 'below' the lower storey of the said frame 'with inside' and of the same lower storey to be also laid over and fenced with strong iron pikes. Foakes, *Henslowe's Diary*, p. 308.

[21] Gurr and Greenfield, 'The Rose Theatre, London', 336, Gurr, 'Bears and Players', 34. Heights were, of course, recorded throughout but those at the lowest levels are not necessarily natural strata or original surfaces. Greenfield and Gurr, 'The Rose Theatre, London', Figure 7 is misleading because of differing heights of the 'outside ground level'.

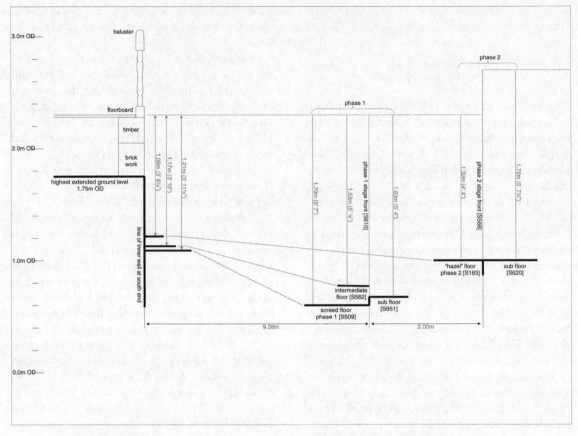

12. Archaeological levels across the site from south (left) to north (right) with conjectured heights of galleries and stage.

erosion caused, I believe, by the groundlings pressing up to the front of the stage. Another feature found in this yard floor was a conglomeration of stones laid in the mortar opposite the walls which we have defined as the ingressus. These we interpret as a threshold at the foot of steps leading up into the galleries.

Thus there is 2.45 m (8 ft) between the yard floor against the stage front and the handrail height of the lowest gallery. However, the height between the surface in the southern half of the yard and the handrail is lessened to 1.97 m (6′6″). A reduction of 0.73 m (2′4″) brings us to 1.72 m (5′8″) and 1.24 m (4′1″) below the gallery floor level.

The average height of an adult male human being at this period was 5′7¼″ (1.71 m) and a female 5′2½″ (1.59 m).[22] Thus they would have stood at

an average of 0.01 m and 0.13 m (5″) *below* the gallery floor against the stage but at an average of 0.47 m (1′6″) and 0.35 m (1′2″) *above* the gallery floor at the southern end of the yard.

For the stage to have had a floor level of 2.32 m OD, the same as the gallery floor, it will have been 1.70 m (5′7″) above the yard surface at its deepest point. This was clearly above eye level for the average man. Moreover, the only documentary reference for stage height is from the Red Lion of 1567 where it was five foot (1.52 m) high.[23] This is assumed to be its height above the level of the

---

[22] A. Warner, *London Bodies* (London, 1998), p. 108; C. Roberts and M. Cox, *Health and Disease in Britain* (Stroud, 2003), pp. 195, 248, 396.
[23] Loengard, 'An Elizabethan Lawsuit', 309.

yard. Certainly Thomas Platter in 1599 recorded that playing was on a 'raised stage' ('einer erhöchten brüge spilen').[24]

At some point between 1587, the original construction, and 1592, clearly defined in the excavated levels, an intermediate floor level was laid in the lowest, northernmost part of the yard. This was a more durable surface and was perhaps introduced to cover the erosion of the friable mortar floor. This new floor level was at an average height of 0.80 m OD, thus reducing that greatest difference by 0.20 m (8″).

It should be noted that the area below the stage also had a mortar surface. This was also sloped slightly down southwards and it abutted the front wall of the stage at about 0.60 m OD. This surface would indicate that the area below the stage was accessible, perhaps via a trap door, though no further excavation was undertaken in this area. A prominent feature uncovered in the excavations was a timber box drain at the rear of the building. This clearly drained down to the north into an irrigation ditch but where it drained from is still a puzzle. It cannot, however, have been the yard as Greenfield and Gurr had argued,[25] for it was at a higher level with its southern end much farther north. It may have been connected to a downpipe associated with the superstructure. Nevertheless, drainage of the building, in both phases, is still not fully understood.

These hypothetical levels for the galleries and the stage certainly have flaws associated with sightlines for the groundlings nearest the stage. It may be that the external wall foundations were lower than the twelve inches we have copied from later building contracts. Alternatively, the stage may have been at a lower level than the galleries, or even slightly raked towards the yard, as at the modern Globe. However, the rake of the yard surface must have been related to sightlines. Groundlings at the rear could clearly see over the heads of the groundlings who probably caused the erosion against the stage front. At the southern end, there was sufficient height for an audience seated there to have an uninterrupted view of the stage over the heads of the groundlings in the yard.

DATING THE STAGE

A key point in the argument about the early function of the Rose is whether the stage was an 'original feature' or a later addition.[26] In other words, what would the building have been used for without a stage?

The question arose because the actual junction of the stage wall and the inner wall of the frame was not revealed during the excavations. We do not know whether the two elements were structurally bonded together or whether the stage wall abutted the inner wall. Archaeologically this is actually of little significance as many buildings of this date are found with subsidiary but contemporary elements abutting rather than bonding. Only the lower parts of this stage wall were revealed, it being truncated by the rebuilding of Phase 2 in 1592. The wall was a solid construction of timber-laced brickwork though any foundation details were not revealed within the limits of the excavation. Thus, although it was a permanent feature rather than temporary trestles, the apparent absence of any stage roof precluded the need for deep or strong foundations.

It seems a clear constructional logic that the stage was built after the more solid frame had been erected. With our ignorance of the stage/gallery junction we might equally suppose that if the stage was just 'tacked on . . . after the galleries were completed'[27] it would probably have been days after, rather than years. Moreover, there are documentary sources from other playhouses which indicate that this is exactly what did happen.

The stage of the Red Lion was built by a different carpenter from the one who erected the main frame, but clearly as part of the same building programme.[28] There is no indication of any carpenter

---

[24] E. K. Chambers, *The Elizabethan Stage*, 4 vols. (Oxford, 1923), II.364.

[25] Greenfield and Gurr, 'The Rose Theatre, London', 336.

[26] Greenfield and Gurr, 'The Rose Theatre, London', 336; Gurr, 'Bears and Players', 32.

[27] Gurr, 'Bears and Players', 32.

[28] Loengard, 'Elizabethan Lawsuit', 301.

responsible for the Rose other than John Grigges and no need to assume that he did not oversee the different elements of the building.[29] Grigges was probably associated with the major alterations to the Rose of 1592 (our Phase 2) as well as work on other properties belonging to Henslowe. The Fortune Contract once had a plan or 'plott' attached and the wording suggests that it specified the stage and stairs.[30] This might imply again that the stage was a special structural consideration.

ARCHITECTURAL EVOLUTION

Andrew Gurr's view that Henslowe built the Rose 'markedly smaller than its playhouse predecessors to the north, more the size of the baiting houses' cannot be proved and is, moreover, unlikely to be the case.[31] We know nothing about the size of the Shoreditch playhouses save the notion that the Theatre was the same size as the Globe. This is a notion that is very far from certain though I have no space to discuss that particular chestnut here. It is more relevant to question the still common theory that playhouse design was based on the animal baiting arenas. In an argument largely – and rightly – directed against the assumption that the Swan drawing represented a 'typical Shakespearian stage', R. A. Foakes suggested its odd stage structure might have been a temporary insertion into an arena otherwise used for baiting.[32] I do not intend to present a history of animal-baiting arenas but the few facts we have are necessary to the argument in order to stress the differences and conclude that the influence appears to have worked in the reverse direction; from the playhouses to the baiting rings, as Oscar Brownstein demonstrated nearly thirty years ago.[33]

The early baiting rings on Bankside were single-storey scaffolds or standings. After William Payne's Bear Garden collapsed in January 1583 it was rebuilt 'larger in circuit and compasse' with 'galleries'.[34] Fragmentary walls tentatively identified as the inner walls of the rebuilt 'Payne's standings'[35] had an (internal) diameter of about 16 m (52'6''), only slightly larger than the Rose.[36] It was almost cer-

tainly this rebuilt Bear Garden that Lupold von Wedel visited in August 1584 and described as a round building three stories high.[37] Paul Hentzner's 1598 description of a bear-baiting arena (probably this one) described it as being built 'in the form of a theatre' (*Est et alius postea locus theatre quoque formam habens*), not, it will be noted, the other way around.[38] Finally, it might be remembered that the playhouses and the bear garden on Norden's maps and panorama appear to be the same size.

BAITING AT THE ROSE?

It might be argued that the evidence produced by the archaeological excavation of the Rose has thrown up more questions than answers. The documentary sources have also been questioned because although the 'partnership document' (certainly not a building contract) between Philip Henslowe and John Cholmley determined the date of construction as 1587, we have no accounts of

---

[29] Contra Greenfield and Gurr, 'The Rose Theatre, London', 337.
[30] Foakes, *Henslowe's Diary*, p. 308.
[31] Gurr, 'Bears and Players', 32.
[32] R. A. Foakes, 'The Image of the Swan Theatre', in A. Lascombes, ed., *Spectacle and Image in Renaissance Europe* (Leiden, 1993), pp. 357–61. The same arguments were reiterated in his 'Henslowe's Rose / Shakespeare's Globe' in Peter Holland and Stephen Orgel, ed., *From Script to Stage in Early Modern England* (Basingstoke, 2004), pp. 11–31. Despite the uncertainty behind the Swan drawing I remain uncertain about the baiting argument for the same reasons that I apply to the Rose.
[33] O. L. Brownstein, '"Why didn't Burbage lease the Beargarden?" A Conjecture in Comparative Architecture', in Herbert Berry, ed., *The First Public Playhouse. The Theatre in Shoreditch 1576–1598* (Montreal, 1979), pp. 81–96.
[34] TNA E134/18Jas1/Mich 10. The first Interrogatory and Depositions.
[35] So defined by W. W. Braines, *The Site of the Globe Playhouse, Southwark* (London, 1923), pp. 90–8.
[36] Anthony Mackinder and Simon Blatherwick, *Bankside. Excavations at Benbow House, Southwark, London SE1* (London, 2000), pp. 26–8.
[37] Chambers, *Elizabethan Stage*, II.455.
[38] Chambers, *Elizabethan Stage*, II.456.

activity at the Rose before Henslowe kept a (surviving) Diary from 1592. Thus there was conjecture that 'conceivably Henslowe was unsure what use to put it to'.[39] But, as far as I can see, Henslowe and Cholmley's partnership agreement signed 10 January 1587 was quite specific on what was being built for what purpose; they would 'permitte suche personne and personnes players to use exersyse & play in the said playe house'; 'any playe or playes that shallbe showen or played there or otherwysse howsoever'. The only activities specified within the building were to be plays or 'enterludes'.[40]

I can find no contemporary description written in English that uses the word *playing* to describe *baiting*.[41] The only document that *appears* to use the word play[house] in a baiting context is the Hope Contract of 1613:

newly erect, builde, and sett upp one other Game place or Plaiehouse fitt & convenient in all thinges, bothe for players to playe in, and for the game of Beares and Bulls to be bayted in the same.[42]

Here, both words, play and baiting, are used simply because both activities occurred within the one building. The two words are used separately and are certainly not interchangeable.

Descriptive accounts of the playhouses of Elizabethan and Stuart London mostly come from foreign visitors describing wonders not seen at home. Thus, the comments of Lupold von Wedel, Johan de Witt, Paul Hentzner and Thomas Platter were written in German or Latin. We might note therefore that the German word *spiel* has a wider meaning than (dramatic) play in English. Moreover, Platter's word *schauwplatz* was misleadingly translated by Chambers as 'playhouse'.[43] The Oxford English Dictionary defines 'enterlude' as 'An interval in the performance of a play; a pause between the acts, or the means (dramatic or musical) employed to fill this up.' They may also have been the 'variety of dances accompanied by excellent music and the excessive applause of those that are present' noted by Paul Hentzner in 1598.[44] The phrase

'otherwise howsoever' is a common legal term found in many contracts intended to embrace any ambiguity.

The partnership document notes that the 'framing' of the Rose had been started by early January 1587. Following the construction sequence described at the Fortune,[45] we might indeed conclude that the building had been completed by 25 June when Cholmley was to start paying for the catering franchise. Only four months later the Privy Council wrote to the Justices of Surrey to urge the 'restrayning of plaies and enterludes' that were being performed in the Liberty of the Clink on a Sabbath.[46] The only known venue for these activities in the area was the Rose. It can be no coincidence that it was precisely for the performance of plays and enterludes that Henslowe had built the Rose. In April 1588 the Surrey and Kent Sewers Commissioners referred to the Rose as the 'new plaie house'; it was still clearly a novelty but by March 1589 they referred to it just as 'the play house'.[47] The Rose is also clearly labelled 'The play howse' on John Norden's map of 1593 – which I suggest depicts the first Rose, being printed later than the actual survey.[48]

---

[39] Gurr, 'Bears and Players', 32.

[40] Foakes, *Henslowe's Diary*, pp. 304–6. Extracts from Dulwich College, Muniment 16.

[41] I cannot pretend to have made an exhaustive search of all sources but I have trawled through collections such as those made by Chambers, *Elizabethan Stage*, and now Glynne Wickham, Herbert Berry and William Ingram, *English Professional Theatre, 1530–1660* (Cambridge, 2000).

[42] Dulwich College, Muniment 49. Many published transcriptions mistakenly transcribe *Game* as *Same*.

[43] Chambers, *Elizabethan Stage*, II.456.

[44] Translation in Chambers, *Elizabethan Stage*, II.363.

[45] J. Orrell, 'Building of the Fortune', *Shakespeare Quarterly* 44 (1993), 127–44.

[46] 29th October 1587. Chambers, *Elizabethan Stage*, II.407; C. C. Rutter, *Documents of the Rose Playhouse* (Manchester, 1999), p. 41, Doc. 4.

[47] London Metropolitan Archives, SKCS/18 f147v; SKCS/18 f153v.

[48] Foakes, *Illustrations*, 6–7. The building shown is markedly different from that in Norden's 1600 edition.

Gurr suggested that 'Henslowe already had some business connections with the Beargarden's operators.'[49] No references were given and in fact Henslowe had no licence to bait bears before 1594.[50] However, we may explore what might have prompted this suggestion. The Sewer Commission's mention of the new playhouse in 1588 was in an order to 'Phillip Finchley [sic], Morgan Pope and John Napton and each of them' to clean out their sections of the ditch bordering their ground at the new playhouse totalling 10 poles (50.3 m) in length. Throughout the Sewer Commission's deliberations they frequently named adjoining landholders and tenants for adjacent stretches of sewers. There is no doubt that Pope and Napton held the Bear Gardens to the west of the Rose and the length of fifty metres precisely defines the Maiden Lane frontage of *both* properties. When the Commissioners fined the three for non-compliance in April 1590 the order referred to their *grounds* in the plural.[51]

The remarkable 'suspicion' that Henslowe's 'announced intention to make the arena a playhouse was there to disclaim any competition with the adjacent baiting house'[52] is a nonsense. There was no competition from any other playhouse on the Bankside in 1587 but there was from animal baiting, and we have seen that there was no business connection with the baiting industry. I cannot see any room for doubting that the new venture was indeed a playhouse. Finally, we might note the negative evidence of the sources. When John Taylor was called to give evidence in the 1620 Hope dispute, he listed the known baiting arenas, which formed a basis for W. W. Braines's authoritative listing of these monuments.[53] The Rose is conspicuously absent from such a list. Neither is there any record for the existence of the necessary stables, kennels, washing ponds and so on anywhere on the Little Rose Estate.

Whatever the depth of the Rose's yard, its rake would have been a most unlikely venue for animal baiting. Any suggestion that the rake was only introduced after the building was 'converted' to a playhouse belies the fact that it was its highest, southern, end that was undoubtedly the original level. Nevertheless, it may be instructive to look at the animals in use at the time.

The bones of the European brown bear have been found archaeologically at a number of sites in the vicinity.[54] If this was the species of bear baited, they could be large; adult males could be up to 5 ft (1.52 m) at the shoulder and if standing on hind legs would be nearly 6'6'' (1.98 m), weighing over 300 kg.[55] The Bear Garden west of the Rose had a 'house for white bears'. If these were polar bears, they are enormous; up to 8ft (2.44 m) at the shoulder.[56] The 'Schedule of Bulls and Bears' at the Bear Garden in 1590 included a young bear, a she bear, an old bear as well as a number of 'great bears' and three bulls.[57] Although they would be fastened by ropes or chains they are known to have broken loose on occasion. Henry Machyn recorded that at Bankside in 1554 a great blind bear broke loose and mauled a man so much that he died a few days later.[58]

Bulls, even tethered, provided another danger. There are records of them tossing dogs high up

---

[49] Gurr, 'Bears and Players', 32.

[50] As Edward Alleyn made clear, Foakes, *Henslowe's Diary*, p. 301. Bear-baiting was a royal prerogative, see S. P. Cerasano, 'The Master of Bears in Art and Enterprise', *Medieval and Renaissance Drama in England*, 5 (1991), 195–209.

[51] SKCS/18 f161. It should be noted that 50 m is also the length of the north–south sewer that lay between the properties on the line of the later Rose Alley.

[52] Gurr, 'Bears and Players', 33, acknowledging use of the word playhouse in the 1587 partnership document.

[53] TNA E134/18Jas1/Mich 10; Braines, *The Site of the Globe Playhouse*, Appendix E: The Sites of the Southwark Bear Gardens.

[54] The presence of bear, dog and horse bones at the Rose proves no other association than their inclusion as waste material in levelling dumps and fills.

[55] P. Ward and S. Kynaston, *Bears of the World* (London, 1995), p. 59.

[56] TNA E134/18Jas1/Mich 10, reproduced in C. Kingsford, 'Paris Garden and the Bear Baiting', *Archaeologia* 70 (1920), 175; Ward and Kynaston, *Bears*, p. 61.

[57] Kingsford, 'Paris Garden', p. 175.

[58] Kingsford, 'Paris Garden', p. 162.

into the galleries.[59] A loosened bull could jump great heights and anyone who has visited a Spanish bullring will see two sets of very high walls around the arena.

THE PHASE 2 STAGE

Before concluding, it may be useful to say a little about the stage of the Phase 2 building. It might be remarked that although in 1592 Henslowe still describes the building as a playhouse, there is no clue as to activity within! The accounts merely provide costs of building material and labour. Our analysis shows that little extra space was gained for an audience. Rather, we concluded that these alterations were to enhance the stage by providing greater dramatic potential – which may indeed have attracted larger audiences. It is interesting to note that the Theatre was also undergoing 'further building work and reparacions' in 1592.[60] Perhaps it is playhouse rivalry rather than conversions that should be examined.

The location, orientation and shape of the Phase 2 stage suggests that there was no dissatisfaction with its predecessor. There was only a small increase in the square footage of the new stage. This new stage and associated roof structure was now integral to the main frame. The presence of a stage roof not only explains the wider shape of the new plan, but confirms the absence of a stage roof in Phase 1. The widening of the gallery walls either side of the new stage was made so that sightlines from the upper galleries to the stage *below* the new roof could be maintained. Conversely, if the Phase 1 building had had a stage roof, the proximity of the upper galleries either side of it would have precluded any view of the stage. The construction of this Phase 2 involved the raising of the ground level in the yard by about 0.4 m (15″). It is uncertain whether the stage was also raised by this amount or whether the floorboard level of the whole northern half of the building was raised. The new stage maintained a tapered front though its increased depth also created more of a 'thrust' into the yard.

CONCLUSIONS

The point of this controversy over the Rose is not that it demonstrates that we know a lot about that playhouse, from documentary and archaeological sources, but that we know so very little about the other playhouses. Thus, stating that the Rose was so different is misleading. It may indeed have been different but we cannot compare the known with the unknown. That there are no records of what plays were performed, or by which company, at the Rose between 1587 and 1592 is no barrier to my argument: there are no such records for any other playhouse over much greater periods of time. Furthermore, the Victorian attitude towards Philip Henslowe – his arrival 'from nowhere', his ignorance and greed – still persists. We know no more about many other figures of the time without having to ascribe negative traits to them.

Bull baiting in England was traditionally undertaken within a convenient open space, such as the seventeenth-century 'bull rings' in Birmingham and elsewhere. Similarly bear-baiting, still happening illegally in far flung corners of the world, occurs on open ground. The construction of purpose-built venues ensured greater control over the animals as well as the collection of money from an audience. Further excavation on any identified bear gardens should be of comparative benefit to the study of the contemporary playhouses.

It may have been possible to have introduced a bear or bull into the Rose yard, though an appropriate entrance is not apparent. The depth of the yard cannot be denied but other

---

[59] Brownstein, 'Why Didn't Burbage', p. 87; see also the letter from Sir William Faunt to Edward Alleyn in G. F. Warner, ed., *Catalogue of the Manuscripts and Muniments of Alleyn's College of God's Gift at Dulwich* (London, 1881), p. 82, no. 38. In the later seventeenth century Samuel Pepys (14 August 1666) and John Evelyn (16 June 1670) both recorded such happenings in their diaries.

[60] Herbert Berry, 'Aspects of the Design and Use of the First Public Playhouse' in Berry, *The First Public Playhouse*, pp. 29–42, p. 32.

characteristics such as its rake and probable originality of the stage renders baiting most unlikely. I believe that combined with the documentary accounts, such usage can now be thoroughly dismissed and the Rose should be able to regain its rightful place in the history of English drama. The many discussions on Elizabethan staging practices, some specifically about the Rose, should be discussed afresh in the light of the archaeological evidence.

PHILIP HENSLOWE AND THE ELIZABETHAN COURT

S. P. CERASANO

At the opening of the well-known film *Shakespeare in Love* (1998) we are told that in 1593 'two [London] theatres were fighting it out for playwrights and audiences'. One of these was the Rose Playhouse, located on Bankside, south of the River Thames, a theatre owned by a dyer named Philip Henslowe. Tom Stoppard, who wrote the screenplay for *Shakespeare in Love*, described Henslowe as 'a man with a cash flow problem'; and Geoffrey Rush, who portrayed him in the film, depicted the theatre owner as a naive but lucky buffoon. As viewers of *Shakespeare in Love* are informed, Henslowe knows little about theatrical performance and even less about playwriting. In his words a good play is one that includes 'mistaken identities, a shipwreck, a pirate king, a bit with a dog, and love triumphant'.[1]

To some extent, early theatre historians depicted Philip Henslowe similarly, if more sympathetically – as a theatre manager whose primary interest was hearing the sound of pennies jingling in the collection box. Consequently, for some time now Henslowe has been identified as a 'banker', an 'entrepreneur', or simply a 'financier', impressions that grow naturally out of the extant evidence that has come down to us – most of it consisting of financial papers relating to Henslowe's businesses.[2] Of course, the terms by which Henslowe has been commonly identified are not, in themselves, mutually exclusive. Each characterizes some part of his life. However, the very list of terms – ranging from 'manager' to 'impresario' – points up our uncertainty about Henslowe's position vis-à-vis the playhouses he owned and the playing companies that

occupied them. But as it turns out, even such a lengthy list of terms is insufficient to suggest the many complexities of Philip Henslowe's life, or to explain how some of the seemingly disparate elements within his life actually complement one another.

One element of Henslowe's life has long seemed out of place within the general portrait of the playhouse manager. This concerns the relationship between Henslowe and the Elizabethan Court, particularly as this is defined by his appointment to two positions in the royal chamber previous to 1604 when he and the actor Edward Alleyn – who was married to Henslowe's stepdaughter – acquired the patent by which they became Masters of the Bears, Bulls, and Mastiff Dogs. In *The Elizabethan Stage*, E. K. Chambers noted that Henslowe held a 'watching livery' as a Groom of the Chamber in 1593. Then, some time in the next five years, Chambers thought that Henslowe was appointed a

---

[1] All quotations are from the film. I would like to thank Grace Ioppolo for chairing the session in which a version of this essay was delivered. I also owe grateful thanks to Reg Foakes for hours and hours of generous conversation, which have helped me to shape my ongoing work on Philip Henslowe.

[2] W. W. Greg's introduction to his edition of Henslowe's *Diary* (London, 1904) perpetuated the characterization of Henslowe as illiterate and mercenary, while R. A. Foakes takes a sympathetic view of Henslowe, noting that 'the idea of Henslowe as a kind of Scrooge, concerned only for profit, an unscrupulous mismanager in the mould of a later theatre owner, Christopher Beeston, has survived'. (See R. A. Foakes, ed., *Henslowe's Diary*, 2nd edn (Cambridge, 2002), p. viii.) All quotations in this chapter are from Professor Foakes's second edition of the *Diary*, abbreviated as *HD* hereafter.

Gentleman of the Privy Chamber.[3] Perhaps owing to Chambers's tentativeness, and because, subsequently, our primary interest in Henslowe has concerned the history of the early modern theatre, we have envisioned Henslowe's Court positions as being entirely peripheral to his work as a theatre owner or they have simply been ignored. However, it has now emerged that Philip Henslowe took up a position in the royal household around 1592, he retained a presence there through 1606 when he was granted a pension from the Crown, and he remained at Court even afterwards, to 1610 or 1611, after which time he apparently returned to London full-time and took on a more active role managing his many business ventures, only some of which were involved with the London theatrical scene.

Henslowe's status as a member of the Court circle is suggested by many manuscripts that vary in kind and purpose. Although these do not provide a seamless portrait of Henslowe's interactions with the Court, they allow us to chart his career there with a much greater understanding than we have possessed formerly. In turn, we can produce a more nuanced portrait than traditional characterizations provide. Moreover, this changed image of Henslowe encourages us to understand his ownership of theatrical businesses as related to a more ambitious personal project; and it simultaneously differentiates Henslowe from the other theatre owners of his time.

One piece of evidence relating to Henslowe's early Court career consists of a petition sent from the Watermen of Bankside to Henry Carey, Lord Hunsdon (written around July 1592) that refers to the restraint of a playhouse (probably the Rose) belonging to 'the saide Phillipp henslo[,] one of the groomes of her ma^ties Chamber'. Another – a letter from Edward Alleyn to Henslowe, written roughly one year later – is addressed to 'm[aste]^r hinslo, on[e] of the gro[o]mes of hir mai[e]st[y's] chamber'.[4] Both of these manuscripts suggest that as early as 1592, and certainly by 1593, Henslowe was being identified as a servant in the Royal Chamber, both by his son-in-law, and also by members of the business community who lived near to Henslowe

on the South Bank, and who would have been acquainted with him and the Rose Playhouse, to which the Watermen regularly ferried people from the north side of the Thames River.[5]

Other documents, written by administrative officers within the government, refer to the position with which Henslowe was identified later in the decade. For instance, Henslowe is listed as one of the Grooms of the Chamber in a warrant for payment drawn up for the use of the Lord Chamberlain's office in January, 1599, and signed by Sir Walter Ralegh, who was then Captain of the Queen's Guard. The manuscript is one in a series of such documents which list the Yeomen of the Guard, the Yeomen of the Chamber, the pages and grooms of the Chamber, and the officers of the 'robes and beds'. In addition to listing Henslowe, the document lists other grooms, some of whom appear amongst the Henslowe papers. (Valentine Harris, one of Henslowe's associates who appears in his *Diary*, is included.) Moreover, Henry Lanman, the owner of the Curtain Playhouse, is listed amongst the Yeomen of the Chamber.[6]

Not least of all, Henslowe's attendance at Court is confirmed in a series of Exchequer documents – called Certificates of Residence – which were drawn up to verify that the individuals named therein had paid their part of the lay subsidy taxes in some location other than their home. These certificates – which bear the annotation 'Cam*era* et hospice', the Latin for 'Chamber and Household' – verify that Henslowe was a member of the Royal Household at the time of the tax collection and

---

[3] E. K. Chambers, *The Elizabethan Stage* (Oxford, 1923), 1.358–9, note 1, abbreviated hereafter as *ES*.

[4] W. W. Greg, *Henslowe Papers* (London, 1907), pp. 36–7 and 42–3, abbreviated hereafter as *HP*.

[5] One of the signators of the Watermen's petition was Gilbert Rocket, a long-time friend of the Henslowe family, who appears at various points in the Henslowe papers and in Henslowe's *Diary*. (See, for example, *HD*, pp. 42, 247.)

[6] BL, MS Additional 5750, fos. 110–11, 112–13, and 144 is a series of warrants for the payments to Henslowe and others of the Grooms and Yeomen of the Royal Chamber (dated 1572, 1586, 1592 and 1599). Henslowe only appears in the latter two warrants.

testify to his presence at Court for substantial periods of time between 1598 and 1611.[7]

Additionally, three manuscripts from Henslowe's collection of personal papers suggest that his Court career was much more central to his ambitions than we have previously realized; and also, the manuscripts assist us in identifying some of the ways in which Henslowe's life was shaped by his interactions with the Court. The first manuscript is a letter – dated October 1603 – from Henslowe's stepdaughter, Joan Woodward, to her husband Edward Alleyn who was performing with the Lord Admiral's Men in Sussex. Following a report of the many plague deaths in the city of London, she wrote 'my father is at Court, but where the Court is I know not'.[8] In this way Joan established that Henslowe was travelling with the Court, which – as it turns out – was temporarily seated at Wilton House until the plague abated sufficiently to bring the new king into London.[9] Moreover, Joan's letter also suggests that there were times when her father's whereabouts were simply unknown, when the family might lack a fundamental sense of where he was or when he might return home. Consequently, as readers of Henslowe's manuscripts we must begin to consider the effects of Henslowe's movement, in and out of his London household, on the way in which we interpret his supposed 'management' of the various playhouses in which he invested.

The second manuscript from Henslowe's collection that attests to his court career is the draft of a petition from Henslowe to King James, written early in the new king's reign. Here, the author requested the grant of a lucrative office – 'Inspector to search, view, and seize all of the woolen cloths to be made within the counties of Kent and Essex'. In the preface to the petition Henslowe identified himself as 'one of the ordinary Grooms of your Majesty's Chamber' who had 'for many years spent his time in the service of the late deceased Queen'.[10] Although Henslowe seems not to have acquired the position he sought, the funeral book compiled by the Lord Chamberlain of the Household in April 1603 notes that Henslowe had, by that time, been promoted to the position of Gentleman Sewer (i.e., steward) of the Chamber, a title by which he continued to identify himself as late as 1611.[11] Nevertheless, Henslowe felt that he was deserving of more. As part of the rationale explaining why he deserved to be inspector of wools, Henslowe noted that 'the late deceased Queen' died 'before any recompense [could be] given unto him in lieu of his said service'.

The final Henslowe manuscript that assists us in defining his relationship to the Court is his well-known *Diary*, a folio-sized memorandum book of 242 leaves, which Henslowe started writing around the time of his first Court appointment. Among the *Diary*'s collection of play receipts, payments for costumes and play books, and miscellaneous personal annotations are entries suggesting that Henslowe was doing business at Court, and that he would have been an attractive addition to the Court circle, in part because of his financial resources. It is in Henslowe's memorandum book that we learn that William Paschall, Sewer of the Chamber, sold a horse to Henslowe.[12] Loans to some persons – which we have ignored previously, because they weren't associated with Henslowe's theatrical business – turn out to be loans to other servants of the Chamber.[13] Expenses recorded for messengers and other support help turn out to be fees for servants that Henslowe brought to Court for his personal use. Sums laid out to 'my Lord Chamberlain's man' are, possibly, personal loans to Lord Hunsdon, who sent one of his servants to Henslowe when he was short of cash.[14]

---

7 These include NA, E115/219/79 (10 October 1600), which identifies Henslowe as one of the Sewers of the Queen's Chamber.

8 *HP*, pp. 59–60.

9 *ES*, 4. 117.

10 Dulwich College, MS 5, no. 44, cited in George F. Warner, *Catalogue of the Manuscripts and Muniments of Alleyn's College of God's Gift at Dulwich* (London, 1881), p. 144.

11 *HP*, p. 18 (an abstract of Muniment 46, listed in Warner, *Catalogue*, p. 239).

12 *HD*, pp. 173–5, 195. The reference to Paschall's horse is on p. 173.

13 These include Valentine Harris (*HD*, p. 61) and John Palmer (*HD*, p. 65).

14 *HD*, p. 8.

Additionally, Henslowe's presence at Court emerges from a careful examination of the physical evidence supplied by the *Diary*, and principally from the observation that large sections of Henslowe's book lack the characteristics of a manuscript that was composed on a day-to-day basis. Rather, certain portions of the *Diary* were written in batches. As a result, it appears that receipts for play performances (which run from February 1592 through early November 1597) were copied from lists compiled by someone else, probably Edward Alleyn, who performed consistently at the Rose during this period, or by one of the other business managers of the company. And other details, hinting at Henslowe's presence at Court, are embedded in the series of theatrical loans that are recorded in the *Diary*. These tend to cluster around specific days of the week – frequently Sundays – suggesting that Henslowe only loaned money when he was actually at home in London; whereas profits could have been taken in at any time, by Henslowe's wife and daughter who had a hand in running some of his businesses when he was away from Southwark, and probably on tour with the Court.[15]

Other manuscripts – from the Henslowe–Alleyn papers, as well as other archives – corroborate the importance of Henslowe's Court career, as well as the significance of Alleyn's presence in that same setting. A few examples of these sources, which I will mention here, include a manuscript notebook produced by the Royal Exchequer (but now in the collection of the British Library), recording loans to the Crown in 1612, in which both Henslowe and Alleyn are mentioned prominently.[16] A diverse group of manuscripts, now housed in the Dulwich archive, establish the same case. For instance, there is a letter from one Richard Topping, tailor, to the Lord Chamberlain, asking for permission to arrest 'Philip Inchlow, one of the gromes of her Ma[jes]^tes chamber' when Henslowe offered to stand as security for the playwright Thomas Lodge who had borrowed money from Topping (1596?).[17] A note from Sir John Dorrington, Master of the Royal Game in 1600, requests that Henslowe bring the bears and dogs to the Court.[18] (Henslowe and Alleyn operated the Bear Garden

long before they acquired the patent for the office that Dorrington held in 1604.) Also, in pursuit of their interests at Court, sometime between 1597 and 1600 Henslowe (and perhaps Alleyn) purchased a manuscript copy of 'A Generall Collection of all the offices in Englande, with their ffees, in the queens guifte'.[19] And a warrant from Henslowe, written in 1611, identified as 'one of the sewers of his highness [King James's] chamber', commissions Thomas Radford to act as a deputy in taking up dogs, bears, and bulls 'for the King's service, and to bait in any place within his dominions'.[20] Furthermore, other manuscript evidence, attesting to the many interactions between Henslowe and Alleyn and the Court (as well as to their interactions with noblemen and other members of the gentry who served at Court), can be found throughout the Henslowe and Alleyn papers.

Needless to say, such evidence breaks significant new ground for biographers and theatre historians. If we examine our impressions of Philip Henslowe in this light our image of him is altered substantially; and, in turn, we must alter the ways in which we conceive not only of his career, but the careers of other so-called theatre 'owners' and 'managers' in early modern London. Let me suggest but a few of the many areas in which such changes become necessary.

At the most basic level, a more complex understanding of Henslowe's Court career allows us to clarify the relationship between his biography and the larger context provided by his family, a family

---

[15] I have discussed the manuscript evidence from Henslowe's *Diary*, and other supplementary sources, more fully in 'The Geography of Henslowe's Diary', *Shakespeare Quarterly*, 56 (2005), 328–53, pp. 338–40.

[16] S. P. Cerasano, 'Cheerful Givers: Henslowe, Alleyn, and the 1612 Loan Book to the Crown', *Shakespeare Studies*, 28 (2000), 215–19.

[17] Dulwich College, MS I, no. 21, described in Warner, *Catalogue*, pp. 13–14.

[18] Dulwich College, MS II, no. 3, in Warner, *Catalogue*, p. 67.

[19] Dulwich College, MS XI, noted in Warner, *Catalogue*, pp. 198–9.

[20] Dulwich College, Muniment 46, noted in Warner, *Catalogue*, p. 239.

that possessed a coat of arms and, having moved from Devon to Sussex, managed to establish ties with some of the local aristocratic families that were prominent at the Elizabethan Court.[21] As a result, it no longer seems unusual that Philip Henslowe's father was appointed Master of the Royal Game in Ashdown Forest or that his uncle, Ralph Hogge, was, at first, supervisor of one of the Sussex iron mines that was licensed by the Crown, and subsequently became prominent in arms manufacturing for the government.[22] Furthermore, acknowledging Henslowe's status as a servant within the royal household clarifies how he and Edward Alleyn – who was also armigerous by birth, and whose father served at Court as Gentleman Porter to the Queen – were, many years later, considered appropriate candidates to be appointed Masters of the Royal Game, a position that brought with it opportunities to generate a substantial income. Additionally, Henslowe's status as a servant of the Court – as he himself said, 'for many years' – clarifies why he managed the Royal barge house, under both Queen Elizabeth and King James, and why Henslowe was eventually designated a Gentleman Pensioner by King James. (In a little-known manuscript book located amongst the papers of Sir Julius Caesar (then Chancellor of the Exchequer) is a list of pensions granted for 1606. Among the honorees are the universities of Oxford and Cambridge, Winchester College, the Dean of Lichfield, and Gray's Inn. Near the bottom of the page, in a large clear hand, is the name 'Philip Henslowe'.[23])

Moreover, a clearer understanding of Henslowe's Court career raises significant questions regarding the ways in which we interpret individual manuscripts within the collection of Henslowe–Alleyn papers that have come down to us, many from Henslowe's theatrical businesses. Here, a reassessment of Henslowe's *Diary* is particularly called for since this manuscript can no longer be viewed as the record of a Scrooge-like playhouse manager who sat in the theatre and watched every penny cross his desk. Instead, as I have argued elsewhere, the *Diary* can be 'read in reverse', as an animated map of a man who used the Rose Playhouse as a venue through which to create a unique niche for himself at Court.[24] And also, it would appear that the Rose, as well as Henslowe's other businesses, were *funding* his career at Court, where the financial outlay could be daunting – especially in positions where the Court servants were given little or no money towards expenses for transportation to and from Court, or to offset the everyday expenses of having to pay for the maintenance of their servants, as well as themselves.

Not least of all, knowing that Henslowe's Court service was more than a sinecure encourages us to alter the model we have created of the 'theatre manager' or 'impresario'. These men – we have long imagined – were merely the natural outgrowth of a larger mercantile movement in which the emerging 'capitalist playhouse' (as it is sometimes termed) was a new phenomenon. Instead of pointing simply to the draper, grocer, joiner and the many actors who invested in London playhouses, we must now take into full account the Court servants, like Philip Henslowe and Henry Lanman, who saw the burgeoning entertainment industry as a venue through which they could become purveyors of entertainment to the Court, and for whom such businesses might – if they were fortunate – position them to make bids for other high-paying offices, for grants of property, or other royal favours.

And in rewriting this sector of the history of the Elizabethan theatre most importantly, perhaps, we need to recognize that none of the other theatre owners of the time were members of the gentry, as

---

[21] The Henslowe coat of arms was recorded in the Heralds' visitation of Sussex in 1530. It included a 'lion of England and a chief of France Ancient'. (See W. Bruce Bannerman, ed., *The Visitations of the County of Sussex* (London, 1905), p. 137.) The Henslowe arms were later incorporated with the Alleyn family arms as recorded in the Visitation of Surrey (1623). (See W. Bruce Bannerman, ed., *The Visitations of the County of Surrey* (London, 1899), p. 144.)

[22] For a fuller discussion of the connections between the Henslowe family and the Crown, see S. P. Cerasano, 'The Patronage Network of Philip Henslowe and Edward Alleyn', *Medieval and Renaissance Drama in England*, 13 (2001), 82–92.

[23] BL, MS Additional 14,313, fo. 21v.

[24] Cerasano, 'The Georgraphy of Henslowe's Diary', p. 340.

were Henslowe and Alleyn. James Burbage, a joiner by trade, never rose beyond the rank of 'gentleman', and this is a title he earned as a result of his status as a player who was patronized by the Earl of Leicester. His son, Richard, despite his status as one of the most celebrated actors of his day, acquired his status similarly, by being a servant of the Lord Chamberlain and, later, of King James. Francis Langley, the owner of the Swan Playhouse, was freed of the Company of Drapers, got his living by moneylending and other assorted businesses, and died in 1602, penniless, having failed at most of the endeavors that he had attempted.[25] By contrast, Philip Henslowe and Edward Alleyn came from privileged backgrounds, they managed to find a unique place for themselves as purveyors of entertainment, and, as a result, they rose to positions of status within the Royal Court. Although Edward Alleyn was said, by some contemporaries, to have been well positioned for a knighthood during his later years (an honorific he never acquired), yet one of the last glimpses we have of his service at the Court consists of a reference in a newsletter written by Dr Meddus to the Revd James Meade on 5 June 1623, describing how Alleyn, together with the Earls of Arundel, Pembroke, Montgomery, Carlisle, Sir Thomas Edmondes, Inigo Jones and others rode forth to Winchester and Southampton 'to take order for his majesty's entertainment with the prince and Lady Mary', a reference to arrangements for the intended marriage between Prince Charles and the Infanta of Spain (which never eventuated).[26]

Furthermore, when considered more broadly the nature and trajectory of Philip Henslowe's career requires us to reconsider the social boundaries that, we imagine, segregated the players and other theatrical personnel from the members of the Court circle. Despite the many studies which have demonstrated the Court's interest in and patronage of the theatre of Shakespeare's time, the interactions between the members of the Court circle and the theatrical personnel have not hitherto been illustrated in any detail. However, when we begin to re-examine such relationships, insofar as they can be traced, it appears that, in some cases, the borders between the two groups were more porous than we have previously imagined. If nothing else, glimmerings of cordial relations exist. Not only is it clear that Sir Philip Sidney was godfather to the actor Richard Tarleton's son, or that Robert Wilson seems to have demonstrated unusual loyalty to the Earl of Leicester, or that the Earl of Pembroke found himself unable to attend to a play performed by the King's Men, following Richard Burbage's death: 'I being tender-harted could not endure to see [a play] so soone after the loss of my old acquaintance Burbadg'.[27] And, occasionally, a player (perhaps with other connections?) left life in the theatre to take up a position at Court. One of these, George Bryan, left the Lord Chamberlain's Men after 1596 to take up duty as a Groom of the Chamber. Bryan apparently occupied that position in 1603, when he was listed in the Chamber Accounts for Queen Elizabeth's funeral, and retained the position as late as 1613.[28]

Finally, taking into consideration Henslowe's Court career necessitates that we re-examine former claims that Shakespeare and the King's Men served as Grooms of the Chamber in 1604 during the period when the Spanish ambassador stayed at Somerset House during the signing of the Spanish peace treaty. The evidence pertaining to this event was first reviewed by Ernest Law in 1910 in a short monograph entitled *Shakespeare as a Groom of the Chamber*, and Leeds Barroll later commented on

---

[25] William Ingram, *A London Life in the Brazen Age: Francis Langley, 1548–1602* (Cambridge, MA, 1978).

[26] BL, MS Harley 389, fo. 337.

[27] The relationship between Sidney and Tarleton's son can be found in *ES*, 2:343. Robert Wilson's relationship with Leicester is suggested by Wilson's career with Leicester's Men and his apparent return to that company in the late 1580s, during which time he carried letters to the Netherlands for Leicester. (See, for example, Sally-Beth MacLean, 'Leicester's Men: Patronage of a Performance Troupe' in Paul Whitfield White and Suzanne R. Westfall, *Shakespeare and Theatrical Patronage in Early Modern England* (Cambridge, 2002), p. 65, note 68, and Scott McMillin and Sally-Beth MacLean, *The Queen's Men and their Plays* (Cambridge, 1998), p. 20 and p. 201, note 7.)

[28] *ES*, 2. 304.

the situation in a different context.[29] In the course of his summary Law raised two key questions. First, were the King's Men given red cloth in 1604 so that he could march in King James's coronation procession? And second, were the King's players employed as servants at Somerset House when the Ambassador to the King of Spain stayed there during the summer of 1604?

In sorting out the first question – that related to the King's procession – Law, and others, have traditionally turned to a variety of dissimilar manuscript sources related to royal pageants in order to determine whether it was a matter of protocol for players to participate in such ceremonies. However, after a careful examination of these, and similar, manuscripts we can reasonably conclude that comparing such sources often proves inconclusive, primarily because there was no established precedent dictating the preparation of such lists. The list for a coronation or a funeral might be brief or lengthy, detailed or more generalized, comprehensive or partial depending upon the individual who prepared the list. (Their authors are frequently heralds from the College of Arms.) Some of these manuscripts, such as the Order of Precedence for the coronation of Edward VI (BL, MS Stowe 1047), runs a mere three folio pages, and stipulates only that the young Edward followed the Lord Great Chamberlain and a few other nobles in the formal procession to his coronation. 'Then', the writer continues, 'followed gentlemanne of the pryvye chamber/then all the nobles in their Robes of estate wth their/capes of estate and coronals one their heddes &c'. In this particular account there are no details regarding the precise order in which such 'gentlemen' walked. However, by contrast, BL MS Lansdowne 885 (the Order of Funeral for King James) runs for eight folio pages and provides a detailed description as to where the body would lie in state, and the order in which the many members of the royal household would line up to process before the casket on the way to the funeral. So detailed are these plans they include descriptions of the standards that were carried, where they appeared in the procession, and the names of the nobles who carried them. Also, it is clear

that the hundreds of individuals who participated in the procession were divided into small groupings and ordered (within each group) from the least important members of the household to the most exalted. In this instance, the Lord Chamberlain, staff in hand, walked at the end of the lengthy train, just before the king's casket, which was flanked by Gentleman Pensioners.

Also, and quite interestingly, theatrical personnel are named explicitly in two places within this manuscript. Midway through the procession (and placed just after the Standard of the Lion of Scotland) came the Masters of the Tents, Falcons, and Otterhounds, and then the Masters 'Of the Beares . . . of the Toyles . . . of the Revels . . . of the Roabes'. Next in line came the 'Artificer of ye Roabes' and 'Officers of ye great Wardrobe' followed by 'Actors & Comedians', 'Messeng[e]^{rs} of the Chamb[e]^r', 'all other Messengers . . . Herbingers' and 'Groomes of ye Chamber'. Further along came the standard of the dragon, carried by Sir Edward Villiers, followed by a group of Yeomen of the Robes, the Master of the Bears (who, at the time, was Edward Alleyn), and the Master of the Lions.[30] Therefore although we might learn little from comparing the order of precedence for the coronation of Edward VI with that of the funeral of King James, it *is* clear that certain officers and servants of the monarch participated regularly in royal processions, regardless of the nature of the procession. Consequently, while Law thinks that it is 'highly improbable that the players took any part in that day's proceedings', i.e. the king's procession of 1604, and states that the four manuscripts he examined were prepared 'without any mention of the King's Actors',[31] it seems equally probable that the Master of the Wardrobe would only have given cloth to the actors in 1604 if they *were* expected to participate in the procession. Especially because

---

[29] Ernest Law, *Shakespeare as a Groom of the Chamber* (London, 1910) and Leeds Barroll, *Politics, Plague, and Shakespeare's Theatre* (Ithaca, 1992), pp. 52–9.

[30] BL, Lansdowne 885, fol. 117r–118r.

[31] Law, *Shakespeare as a Groom of the Chamber*, pp. 9 and 11.

the procession was meant to be a ceremony in which the king was formally welcomed, it would make sense that the procession would include many individuals who depended upon his patronage, including virtually all of the members of the Royal Household and the King's Men.

In response to Law's second area of interest – the use of the King's Men as 'grooms' at Somerset House in 1604 – much is bound up in our sense of what a 'groom' was and what responsibilities attended such appointments.[32] For although Law wondered how it was that Shakespeare and eleven members of his company could be engaged in service for the Spanish Ambassador over a period of eighteen days, he was also attempting to understand how players might be asked to serve in an extraordinary capacity, one that, from all available evidence, appears to have been unique in the history of the acting company (even though it might well have been more common than we imagine). Here, we need to bear in mind that the term 'groom' (or 'grome' as it was commonly written), related (in this context) to an officer of the English royal household who held a position of middle rank. Moreover, within the Royal Household there were many 'kinds' of grooms – Grooms of the Chamber, Grooms of the Body, Grooms of the Stool, Grooms of the Stable, and so forth – who enjoyed different levels of status and attended to different responsibilities within the household.[33] Related to this, we also need to understand that players were merely termed 'servants' of their patron, a term which does not bring with it any sense of rank within the household.[34] Yet to be truly 'in service' at Somerset House, and *to be paid* for that service, required that the members of the King's Men be assigned some rank, if only temporarily, so that they could carry out their duties and receive the payment of £21 12s that they collected. This is, most probably, what occurred in 1604 when the King's Men were memorialized in a warrant for payment, made out to 'Augustine Phillipps and John Hemynges for th[']allowance to themselues and tenne of theire fellowes' that identified them as 'groomes of the Chamber and Players'. On this occasion the King's Men were not performing so they could not be

paid in their usual way, as players; rather, they were 'Wayting and attending on his ma*tes* service'.[35] The rank of 'Groom' (extraordinary) was a temporary honorific, specifying at what rank Augustine Phillips, John Heminges, and thier fellows had been 'Waytinge and attending on his ma*tes* service', as the account states.[36] Whereas when the company was paid for a performance at Court, the language of the payment was different. For instance, after the King's Men performed at Court during the Christmas season, 1603–1604, the record of payment was made out 'To Iohn Hemynges one of his ma*tes* players . . . for his paynes and expen*ces* of himselfe and the rest of his Company in p*re*senting of six interludes or playes before the king*es* ma*ty* and prince.'[37] Finally, it is also important to realize that the payments made to individuals who served at Court were determined *by rank*. Consequently, as fee books and other financial records of the Court would suggest, the King's Men needed to be assigned a rank so that they could be paid commensurate with their rank.

In considering all of this evidence it is clear that a new and complex portrait of Philip Henslowe emerges when we begin to take into account his

---

[32] Leeds Barroll decided that the King's Men were called in as supernumeraries for the Somerset House meeting. He argues, furthermore, that their status (as individuals or as members of an acting company) would not have been improved by these circumstances. He does not, however, take up the issues of the players' status as grooms or their participation in other kinds of formal Court festivities (Barroll, *Politics, Plague, and Shakespeare's Theatre*, pp. 52–9).

[33] See, for example, BL, MS Lansdowne 272, one of the many fee books which record what varying ranks of Court officers were paid, as well as any perquisites they were entitled to.

[34] The appointment of the King's Men was made by letters patent on 19 May 1603, over a year before the occasion at Somerset House, and refers to the players simply as 'theise our Servauntes' (*ES*, 2.208–9).

[35] David Cook, 'Dramatic Records in the Declared Accounts of the Treasurer of the Chamber, 1558–1642' in *Malone Society: Collections*, vol. 6 (Oxford, 1961), p. 38.

[36] The manuscript survives amongst the Declared Accounts of the Treasurer of the Chamber now housed at the National Archive (Roll 41, Bundle 388).

[37] David Cook, 'Dramatic Records in the Declared Accounts of the Treasurer of the Chamber', p. 38.

many years of service at Court. And this new portrait differs so completely from our traditional image of 'Henslowe-the-theatre-owner' that we must now read the Henslowe papers, including his great diary, in a radically different context. Amongst other things, this new knowledge should encourage us to adopt a completely different reading of 'theatre entrepreneurs' or 'theatre managers' when we are describing the evolving playhouse culture in the London of Shakespeare's time. Moreover, it begins to define the sharp division that would have separated Henslowe and Alleyn, who enjoyed a kind of genuine social privilege, from most of the other so-called 'playhouse owners' of the time, including William Shakespeare. For while it is true that Philip Henslowe joined the order of so-called 'new men' who became the driving forces behind the playhouse industry, it is equally true that his Court career – together with his family background – aligned him with the old established order. In this way he perhaps garnered the best of all opportunities that were available to him in his time. But also, as is becoming increasingly apparent, he *succeeded* by joining the pathways of ancient privilege with the emerging opportunities for new money. And fortunately, for us, in so doing Henslowe presents us with unexpected, even astounding possibilities for our interpretation of the roles that he performed in the history of two seemingly disparate but complementary worlds – the world of the Court, and the world of the capitalist playhouse.

FROM REVELS TO REVELATION:
SHAKESPEARE AND THE MASK

JANETTE DILLON

Shakespeare's late plays are often rightly said to be influenced by masque. The context for such influence is the sumptuous Jacobean masque, a series of performances particularly encouraged by Queen Anne from 1604, in which Shakespeare's company, the King's Men, usually took the speaking parts. This kind of masque is associated with the literary, classically inspired and often arcane writing of Ben Jonson and others, with the development of the scenic stage, the proscenium arch and perspective staging under the direction of Inigo Jones, and with the famous quarrel between Jonson and Jones as to whether poetry or picture should be considered the true 'soul' of masque. Its influence on Shakespeare is also often linked to the King's Men's move to the Blackfriars in 1609, an indoor theatre which may have encouraged a different approach to stage spectacle, though the late plays continued to be performed at the outdoor Globe as well as the newly acquired Blackfriars. To date, however, Tudor mask has been the poor relation both in Shakespeare studies and in studies of court theatre more widely. The distinction in spelling (mask versus masque) signals a widespread concern to mark a boundary between the two forms, implicitly suggesting that the later form is different, perhaps more grown-up, more sophisticated, more literary and certainly more worthy of critical attention, than its primitive forebear, despite the fact that the later form remains strongly indebted to the earlier. Yet the influence of Tudor mask on Shakespeare's Elizabethan plays cannot be denied, though it has traditionally been only grudgingly admitted, as in John Dover Wilson's expressed discomfort with the mask of Hymen in *As You Like It*: 'There is no dramatic necessity for this masque-business.'[1]

One reason for the continuing tendency to overlook the influence of Tudor mask on the early Shakespeare may be that masks at Elizabeth's court in the last decade of the reign were apparently infrequent and unlikely to have influenced popular dramatists in any direct way.[2] Though there is evidence in the Revels accounts of numerous masks early in the reign, there was no obvious way

---

[1] Dover Wilson is quoted by Agnes Latham in her introduction to the Arden edition of *As You Like It* (London, 1975, p. xxi), where the context is a discussion of the general critical dislike of masque-elements in Shakespeare's plays. Writing before the critical rehabilitation of Jacobean masque, the preference for the 'masque' spelling may represent an attempt to dignify a practice seen as primitive and childish by the critics concerned.

[2] Stephen Orgel summarizes and discusses the traditions of early mumming, disguising and masking in *The Jonsonian Masque* (New York, 1981), chs. 1 and 2. Orgel's summary, however, barely mentions the routine court masking of the early Elizabethan court, as evidenced by the Revels accounts and summarized by E. K. Chambers (*The Elizabethan Stage*, 4 vols. (Oxford, 1923), 1. 156–66) using Albert Feuillerat's indispensable printing of revels documents in *Documents Relating to the Revels at Court in the Time of Queen Elizabeth* (1908; rpt Vaduz, 1963). Since Revels accounts after 1589 are not extant, it is impossible to be certain how many masks may have been staged at court during that period, but the absence of other references to them (for example, in ambassadors' letters) is also suggestive of their decreasing frequency during this period. Holinshed, though he diligently reproduced all Hall's accounts of masks at the court of Henry VIII (see further below), described only the occasional Elizabethan mask (such as *The Four Foster Children of Desire*).

in which they were widely publicised beyond the court, with a few exceptions. In the latter part of the reign, Elizabeth's court tended to rely increasingly on inviting the adult companies to play at court, a much cheaper expedient than mounting a new mask. A fee of £10 to a company for performing at court scarcely dented the court purse by comparison with the cost of mounting a Jacobean masque, at sometimes two or three thousand pounds. The earlier Tudors, however, and above all Henry VIII, had staged masks and disguisings that, in terms of both spectacle and expense, as well as in several other important respects (the breaking down of the borderline between actors and spectators, the centrality of dance, the combination of formality and informality) matched the extravagant Stuart style of court masque[3] and these early Tudor revels, I want to argue here, had their effect on plays written and staged by the Elizabethan professional companies.

Their influence, however, unlike that of Jacobean masque, came not primarily through performance or spectatorship, but through printed texts, in particular popular histories of the reign of Henry VIII. The chronicles of Hall and Holinshed are best known to present-day literary critics precisely as sources for Shakespeare, in particular Shakespeare's history plays. What else Shakespeare might have found in them besides material for his history plays, however, has scarcely been investigated. The focus, furthermore, has been on Holinshed, Shakespeare's contemporary. Yet, while most critics know that Tudor historiographical practice was to rely on previous historians, not all of these critics realize that this often means incorporating vast chunks of earlier writing word for word, and that much of Holinshed's text for the reigns of kings up to and including Henry VIII, is exactly that: Hall's text word for word. The present paper thus seeks to reinstate two poor relations overshadowed by more famous descendants: Tudor mask and Edward Hall. Hall, like Holinshed, was often following his sources word for word; but it is Hall's organisation and sequencing of material that gives such prominence to the place of masks and revels in the reign of Henry VIII, and hence allows that material to

take the same prominence in Holinshed's text for the same reign.

Readers of Hall or Holinshed (it scarcely makes any difference in this context) on the reign of Henry VIII will know that the first half of the reign especially reads like a sequence of revels. History seems to be made up of banquets, music, dancing, jousting, receptions for ambassadors: one long run of spectacles, ceremonies and festivities. And though the list above implies that these were separate forms, within categories we now understand by these names, they should in fact be understood as elements that borrowed from one another's styles and were commonly mixed and matched to different degrees, depending on whether the entertainment lasted for minutes, hours or days. So, for example, a banquet might be interrupted by the sudden entry of masked dancers (and occasionally maskers might even leap out of a gigantic pie); the entry of a pageant-car might signal the start of an indoor disguising or of an outdoor tournament; a mock-castle might be besieged and defended by knights or might open to allow maskers to come out dancing; or a trip to the woods with music and feasting on May-day might encounter an allegorical

---

[3] The terminology is fraught here. Though the modern spelling distinction between mask and masque implies clear boundaries between different theatrical forms, the opposite is the case in practice. Different words ('mumming', 'mummery', 'disguising', 'mask') are used apparently interchangeably and even though Hall seems to be striving to identify the mask as something new and specific in 1512 (see extract 4 below), the use of the term among his contemporaries, including Richard Gibson, who wrote the Revels accounts, does not lend any consistent support to that notion of specificity. Orgel seeks to use the term 'revels' to describe dancing between maskers and spectators, but this diverges totally and misleadingly from early Tudor use, in which 'revels' is the broadest term of all. On the question of terminology and definition see further E. K. Chambers, *The Medieval Stage*, 2 vols. (Oxford, 1903), II. 390–402; Enid Welsford, *The Court Masque: a Study in the Relationship between Poetry and the Revels* (Cambridge, 1927), pp. 92–143; Sydney Anglo, 'The Evolution of the Early Tudor Disguising, Pageant, and Mask', *Renaissance Drama* ns 1 (1968), pp. 4–8; and Marie Axton, 'The Tudor Mask and Elizabethan Court Drama', in *English Drama: Forms and Development*, ed. Marie Axton and Raymond Williams (Cambridge, 1977), pp. 30–2.

ship leading the revellers back to a tournament. These forms of festivity and entertainment were understood all over Europe in the early sixteenth century. Italy led the way, but all the great European courts developed their own particular dialects of a spectacular language widely shared and understood as the discourse of magnificence. Ambassadors were expected to, and did, report to their kings on the receptions they attended, measuring each different court according to the design, cost and innovation of its revels. A letter of 1517 from Francesco Chieregato, the papal nuncio to England, to Isabella d'Este, Marchioness of Mantua, exemplifies the effect such spectacles sought to produce within the international courtly community: 'In short, the wealth and civilization of the world are here; and those who call the English barbarians appear to me to render themselves such. I here perceive very elegant manners, extreme decorum, and very great politeness.'[4]

Seven extracts from descriptions of masking in Hall's Chronicle are printed as an appendix to this article (pp. 68–71) to enable the reader to consider some of the most important aspects of mask in detail.[5] Before looking at how some elements of these revels are reworked in Shakespeare's early plays, I would like to explain the selection and emphasize certain features of Hall's descriptions. Extract 1 is selected as the first occasion on which the King himself participated in the disguising in order to highlight the extent to which this was a novelty. Henry VII had always been a spectator rather than a participant at disguisings and tournaments, but Henry VIII, not quite eighteen when he succeeded his father in April 1509, quickly demonstrated an active interest in both which was to dominate revels for the first eighteen years of the reign. The sudden and pseudo-impromptu nature of the event was also a novelty characteristic of the new reign. Though themed costuming was already established in earlier revels, the use of costume literally as a disguise, or quasi-disguise, to take an audience (here the Queen and her ladies in the Queen's chamber) by surprise, *is* new. This is why, on this first occasion, the recipients are 'abashed'. Typically for mask, however,

the boundary between spectators and participants is crossed at a given point, using dance as the means, and the revel continues with protracted dancing and 'pastime'. Dance, though often relegated to a passing phrase in Hall's descriptions, was an indispensable feature of mask, and from this point until the end of the Caroline period it was the dancing that evidently took up most of the time in such events. The second extract shows the disguising again themed, this time to compliment the Spanish ambassadors and guests from the Emperor Maximilian's court. The suddenness of the minstrels' entry parallels the suddenness of the irruption in the earlier Robin Hood disguising, and the participation of minstrels and torchbearers highlights the more elaborate format of a revel designed for full court performance. The dancers are masked as well as costumed on this occasion and the climax of the revel is the point at which the ladies take off the men's visors. The clearly gendered and hierarchical structure of the whole event is also very evident.[6]

The description of the Twelfth Night mask of 1512 is now the best known of all Hall's descriptions of masks, mainly because of the highly developed interest in Stuart masque and the search for origins of the form. This looks like the point of origin because Hall isolates the term 'mask' and stresses its novelty, but what constitutes its novelty has been much disputed.[7] The most persuasive argument, in my view, is that the new element is what Hall here calls 'common[ing] together'. The conjunction of extracts 4 and 6 together seem to emphasize that the novelty lies in the move from purely formal dancing to a more informal dancing that makes space for spontaneous, bantering and perhaps risqué conversation. In his account of the Newhall entertainment in 1519 (extract 6), Hall

---

[4] *Calendar of State Papers, Venetian,* ed. Rawdon Brown *et al.* (London, 1864–1947), vol. II, p. 400.

[5] Text is taken from my edition of selected material from Hall's Chronicle, *Performance and Spectacle in Hall's Chronicle* (London, 2002).

[6] See further Skiles Howard, *The Politics of Courtly Dancing in Early Modern England* (Amherst, 1998), ch. 1.

[7] See further Welsford, pp. 92–143, and other critics listed in note 3 above.

calls the first group of dancers 'maskers', but says that they 'daunsed with ladies sadly, and communed not with the ladies after the fassion of Maskers, but behaved theimselfes sadly'. It is the soberness, then, the failure to banter with the ladies, that marks out this part of the entertainment as unlike mask. But the event as a whole is one that sets youth in opposition to age, so that the seriousness of this group is deliberately planned to tie in with their age, and with the older, more traditional form of revelling, while the younger group, who come in second, spend a long time dancing and 'commoning' (or 'communing') as befits their youthfulness.[8]

The third extract is from a lengthy description of the Westminster Tournament of 1511. The point here is partly to show a very familiar element of Tudor revels, the pageant car, at the same time as emphasising the fact that it might feature in different kinds of revels, from outdoor tournaments to indoor disguisings. Large wheeled pageant cars, sometimes large enough to support casts of thirty people, and usually allegorically themed to represent familiar chivalric motifs (forest, castle, rock and fountain were especially popular) were characteristic of courtly disguisings all over Europe from the fifteenth century, following the fashionable lead of the Burgundian court. The description of the Twelfth Night festivities of 1513 (extract 5) is included not only because it illustrates the use of a pageant-car in an indoor revel, but also because it demonstrates that the new style of masking introduced in 1512, with its emphasis on informal interchange, did not immediately take over from the old-style spectacular and allegorical entertainment. The masked groups on this occasion do not mingle at all with the spectators but dance only with each other.

The last extract is included for four reasons. Firstly, it demonstrates the international currency of masking, since it takes place at Ardres before the French Queen Claude. Secondly, it shows the prominence of national costuming again, this time apparently not politically targeted but randomly chosen, presumably for the pleasure of new and exotic costume opportunities. Thirdly, it shows Hall using the term 'mask' for a revel that has very

little in common with the Twelfth Night 'mask' of 1512. And lastly, it shows the masked group going outside the palace precincts into the town. This is the only mask Hall describes in the reign of Henry VIII in which this happens, and it is probably not accidental that it takes place outside England. In order to explain this, and to elaborate on an aspect of mask-form with which Shakespeare was clearly familiar, it is necessary briefly to examine some aspects of revels in Italy, Hall's affirmed point of origin for the 1512 mask.

Two Italian forms were particularly influential on the development of Tudor masks and disguisings: the intermezzo and the masquerade. The intermezzo was a brief spectacular or musical show inserted into festivities, sometimes in between the acts of full-length plays, including Latin drama. It sometimes included a pageant car, often included the ascent or descent of gods and goddesses and showcased music and visual splendour. It was also associated with the morisco, a dance-form which, despite its popular associations (the word shares the same etymology as morris dancing), became increasingly sophisticated. Isabella d'Este expressed her boredom on an occasion when there seemed to her too little music and dancing interspersed through the performance.[9]

Masquerade was initially a less structured and formal entertainment than intermezzo, typically a relatively impromptu street activity involving bands of maskers out on the streets at carnival time, singing, dancing, joking and knocking on doors in costume and masks. Lorenzo de' Medici (d.1492) tried to give it respectability by turning it into a more formal, scripted and allegorical show.

---

[8] The younger group includes four French hostages and the so-called 'minions', who had been dismissed from court earlier that year and were now being forgiven and welcomed back. See further David Starkey, 'Intimacy and Innovation: the Rise of the Privy Chamber', in *The English Court: From the Wars of the Roses to the Civil War*, ed. David Starkey (London and New York, 1987), 71–118, and Greg Walker, *Persuasive Fictions: Faction, Faith and Political Culture in the Reign of Henry VIII* (Aldershot, 1996), ch. 1.

[9] Welsford, p. 88. I am indebted to Welsford, ch. 4, throughout my discussion of Italian dramatic practice.

Following his intervention, the masquerade could take one of two forms, with maskers either processing on foot or arriving in a pageant car with torch-bearers and musicians, and it eventually became typically a procession of pageant cars pausing in turn before the throne for the maskers on board to descend and perform a dance, song or recitation.

Popular masking on the streets, however, continued regardless, at elite as well as popular level, and masking, whether formal or informal, was widely understood as an activity incorporating 'a certaine libertie and licence'.[10] The phrase is from Castiglione's famous *Book of the Courtier*, and the context is a discussion of the kinds of dancing acceptable for a courtier. Certain kinds of dance, Castiglione is warning, are suitable only in private or at masked balls, because masking allows an unusual degree of social freedom. Thomas Hoby, Castiglione's English translator, who wrote an account of his travels in Europe, describes a mask at Shrovetide 1549 when the Duke of Ferrandine visited Venice. At night, he writes, 'The Duke cuming in a brave maskerye with his companions went (as the maner is) to a gentlewoman whom he most fansied . . . There cam in another companye of gentlmen Venetiens in an other maskerye: and on of them went in like maner to the same gentlwoman that the Duke was entreating to daunse with him, and somwhat shuldredd the Duke, which was a great injurie'.[11] The Duke was killed in the ensuing brawl, but the practice continued and spread in Italy. The Duke and Duchess of Mantua, visiting Ferrara in 1582, joined in the onstreet masking, wandering the streets masked and on foot, knocking on all the doors and, says the Italian writer describing them, doing other similarly juvenile and carnivalesque things. When they went back to Mantua they introduced the practice there.[12]

In England, however, masking of this kind was illegal. An 'Acte against disguysed persons and Wearing of Visours' passed in 1511 (*3 Henry VIII, c.9*) forbade the practice precisely on account of the disorder it caused and made the sale of masks illegal.[13] It is somewhat ironic to reflect that the King was encouraging the introduction of a courtly version of Italian masking at court within months of

passing this Act, though the social climate in which such an Act could be passed goes some way towards explaining the refusal of some of the ladies to take part.

Shakespeare's knowledge of masking could thus have come through a variety of written sources besides Hall, and may also have included anecdotal reports from those who had travelled in Europe, as English actors were beginning to do more frequently. Masking elements in the plays were sometimes also suggested by the play's immediate source, as in the case of *Romeo and Juliet*, for example. Certainly several of his Elizabethan plays show the impact of these courtly revels on his imagination. The scenes from Elizabethan plays which I propose to consider here are *Titus Andronicus*, 5.2, *Love's Labour's Lost*, 5.2, *Romeo and Juliet*, 1.4 and 5, *Merchant of Venice*, 2.5, *The Merry Wives of Windsor*, 5.5, *Much Ado*, 2.1, and *As You Like It*, 5.2 (here listed in chronological order, though not discussed in that order). These are not the only scenes in early Shakespearian plays to show the influence of

---

[10] Baldassare Castiglione, *The Book of the Courtier*, trans. Sir Thomas Hoby, introd. J. H. Whitfield, rev. edn (London and New York, 1974), p. 99. Welsford quotes from a letter of Castiglione's to Federico Gonzago describing Pope Leo X watching masking and moriscos in the palace courtyard from his window (p. 90).

[11] *A Booke of the Travaile and Lief of Me, Thomas Hoby, with Diverse things Woorth the Notinge*, ed. Edgar Power, *Camden Miscellany*, Camden Society, 3rd series, vol. x (London, 1902), p. 14, quoted in Welsford, pp. 101–2.

[12] Welsford, p. 101.

[13] Chambers, *Medieval Stage*, II.396. Chambers notes numerous earlier City of London edicts restricting varieties of masked practices. Later, however, in Shakespeare's lifetime, the Inns of Court mounted festive events that included processing through the streets in disguise, though the collective and organised nature of these entertainments distinguishes them from the more spontaneous and uncontrolled wandering described above. Masks retained the element of risk and unpredictability, however, partly because it offered a point of entry into the household for strangers. Kathleen McLuskie cites an instance from Holinshed of conspirators planning to gain entry to Windsor Castle 'under colour of a masque' in order to assassinate the King ('Shakespeare's "Earth-Treading Stars": The Image of the Masque in "Romeo and Juliet"', *Shakespeare Survey 24* (Cambridge, 1971), pp. 63–4).

mask (*Midsummer Night's Dream*, 5.1, for example, also displays features of mask), but they are sufficient to show the range of elements that Shakespeare exploits. Two of his early plays with Italian settings seem to reflect a direct knowledge of Italian practice which has come through neither Hall nor the English court. *Romeo and Juliet* presents Romeo and his friends on the street in masking attire with torchbearers in 1.4. Romeo, languishing for Rosaline, has no will for this kind of fun, and wants to be a torchbearer rather than a masker, but Mercutio insists that he must dance. The scene is full of foreboding, extended in talk of love and dreams (including Mercutio's dream of Queen Mab) and exploits the hint of potential trouble and violence inherent in masquerade to pave the way for the fatal meeting with Juliet in the next scene, which will indeed lead to a violent and tragic end. The mood shifts in 1.5 to the comic but wistful nostalgia of Juliet's father:

> I have seen the day
> That I have worn a visor and could tell
> A whispering tale in a fair lady's ear,
> Such as would please; 'tis gone, 'tis gone, 'tis gone.[14]
>
> (21–4)

The writing of masking and dance into this scene effectively provides the same kind of pleasure as an intermezzo in a serious Italian performance, allowing the audience to enjoy music and dancing inserted in between speeches. The emphatic association of masking with youthfulness, however, also links this scene to the ethos underpinning Hall's descriptions of the playful 'commoning' of mask, and in particular with his description of the Newhall mask, in which only the young men indulge in this frivolity. The playfulness is summoned up through Capulet in Shakespeare, however, precisely so that the abrupt and ironic change of tone when Romeo sees Juliet is highlighted. At that point the declaration of love moves the scene from the different kinds of playful banter that characterize both the previous scene and the early part of this scene to sudden and utter seriousness, while the threat of violence lightly hinted at in Romeo's earlier unwillingness to participate is intensified as

Tybalt recognizes Romeo. Shakespeare thus draws on both the playfulness and the potential for violence associated with mask-form to give shape and emphasis to this first fateful meeting between the lovers. The suddenness with which Romeo can touch Juliet's hand also seems to indicate that their first encounter is as their hands come together in the formality of dance, thus allowing the audience to experience the pleasure of that first sensuous touch through the controlled 'measure' (the word is a recurrent one in Shakespeare's mask-scenes) of formal dance, and allowing the kiss to grow out of, but also break free of, that orderly but tempting restraint. Clearly the ladies who refused the invitation to dance in the 1512 mask Hall describes well understood the potential sexual frisson of combining the physical closeness of dance with the intimate conversation of masked 'commoning'.

The introduction of masking in *The Merchant of Venice* has several parallels with its introduction in *Romeo and Juliet*. The first mention of it is in a scene where Shylock, like Romeo, is expressing vague foreboding by association with his dreams the night before. When Launcelot Gobbo mentions masking as a likely pastime in the Christian household where Shylock is invited for supper, Shylock pours scorn on the practice and warns Jessica to protect herself from it:

> What, are there masques? Hear you me, Jessica:
> Lock up my doors, and when you hear the drum
> And the vile squealing of the wry-neck'd fife,
> Clamber not you up to the casements then,
> Nor thrust your head into the public street
> To gaze on Christian fools with varnish'd faces;
> But stop my house's ears, I mean my casements;
> Let not the sound of shallow fopp'ry enter
> My sober house.[15]
>
> (2.5.28–36)

As Romeo is unwilling to take part in masking, so Shylock is resistant to going out to supper

---

[14] Quotations from Shakespeare, unless otherwise indicated, are taken from *The Riverside Shakespeare*, ed. G. Blakemore Evans, 2nd edn (Boston, 1997).

[15] The spelling is consistently 'mask(e)' in the Quarto and Folio texts. 'Masque' reflects post-Jacobean editorial practice.

and revels; and, as with Romeo, his fears prove well founded. In the next scene Lorenzo and his friends steal Jessica away under cover of a mask. Jessica's own willing male disguise fits easily into the 'libertie and licence' of mask as she becomes Lorenzo's torchbearer. Once again, mask covers for deceit, danger and illicit practice, setting up the parameters for anger and vengeance to follow.

Anger and vengeance are also central to its use in *Titus Andronicus*, one of only two other tragedies besides *Romeo and Juliet* to incorporate mask-form. (The other is a later, Jacobean tragedy: *Timon of Athens*, discussed below.) Here the mask, with its pageant car and allegorical framework, in which Tamora poses as Revenge and her sons as Rape and Murder, more closely resembles the old-style Tudor disguising than the Italian masquerade. Yet despite the formal difference, the event again brings with it a sense of foreboding that proves to be well founded. Here too emerges a variation on classic mask which is to become regular in Shakespeare's adaptations. Where, in Hall, the mask usually culminates in the maskers unmasking or allowing themselves to be unmasked, Shakespeare's maskers are often perceived through their masks for who they are by their spectators. Thus here, Titus, while pretending to be taken in by the representation, in fact recognises Tamora's deceit but does not reveal his perception, so that, while he sees through her, she does not see that he does. The power positions of masker and spectator are thus reversed, so that the spectator is in the position of superior knowledge. Titus uses another traditional form of festivity, the banquet, to disguise and formalize his own revenge, so that both he and Tamora use the pretence of revelry with intent to deceive and do violence to each other. The stylized entry of Titus and Lavinia bearing a knife and a basin represents a further grim variation on the masking form, in its aestheticized formalization of violent action; while the serving up of Tamora's sons, though it has an obvious classical source, is also faintly reminiscent of those devices at spectacular banquets in which maskers burst out of a pie to entertain the guests.

With *Love's Labour's Lost* we reach the kind of mask that directly parallels the classic form in Hall, where the King and a group of companions, masked and costumed, typically come upon the Queen and the court 'suddenly', seeking to dance with them, and perhaps 'common' with them. The most obvious difference, of course, is that Shakespeare turns the whole event here into a conscious parody of the form, allowing the ladies, who in Hall are usually passive recipients, surprised, embarrassed, or politely feigning surprise, to take control of the whole event and make the men look like fools. Every aspect of the form is undercut, not least by Boyet's laughter as he first ruins the traditional surprise entry by forewarning the ladies not only of their coming, but also of their costume and purpose. They are dressed as 'Muscovites or Russians', says Boyet, and

> Their purpose is to parley, to court, and dance,
> And every one his love-feat will advance
> Unto his several mistress, which they'll know
> By favors several which they did bestow.
>
> (5.2.121–5)

The ladies thus have time to make their subversive plans, which strike at the three roots of the form: disguise, dancing and love-talk. They will mask themselves, so that the gallant wooers will 'woo contrary', and swear love to the wrong woman; they will refuse to dance; and they will turn their backs on any set speeches.

When the men arrive, their costume and bearing seem so predictable as to be ridiculous. Their Russian costumes recall earlier masks in a very deliberate and hackneyed way (the mask of 1520, presented in extract 7, employs Russian costumes, and the fiction underlying the Elizabethan *Mask of Proteus* (performed in March 1595, probably very close in time to *Love's Labour's Lost*) takes the mock-Prince on an imaginary visit to the Emperor of Russia). To cap the cliché, they even have Moors with them. Moorish disguise first figures in Hall (alongside Russian and Turkish costumes) in a disguising of February 1510, and the notion that Moors are already a virtually indispensable feature of mask is evident from Titus's joke to Tamora and her sons in *Titus Andronicus*, when he says, playing on the absence of Aaron, 'Well are you fitted, had you but a Moor' (5.2.85). The disguised men never have the satisfaction of unmasking which usually constitutes a climactic moment in Hall's masks; instead, the women have unmasked them without their knowing it, while they have been entirely taken in by the women's disguises. All they know is that they have been mocked.

The Merry Wives of Windsor, like *Love's Labour's Lost*, also works through mask as parody. The mask has a dual function, however, working to further as well as to mock illicit love. Thus Falstaff is mocked at the same time as Fenton steals away Anne Page; and the deceits are more than double, since, besides the two plots designed to achieve these ends, there are also two further plots which don't succeed: Page's plot to marry his daughter to Slender and Mistress Page's plot to marry her to Doctor Caius. The play's multiplicity helps to construct its parodic aspect: three plots are underway to steal the same young woman, while a fat old lecher is to be exposed wearing a costume with horns by the very women he has failed to tempt and the very husbands he has failed to cuckold. Like Bottom, in another play which has strong elements of mask (and which shares with *Merry Wives* an outdoor setting for some of its mask-like elements), Falstaff is 'made an ass' (5.5.119). But where the fairies retain some otherworldly aspect in *Midsummer Night's Dream*, in *Merry Wives* these potentially more fantastic and ethereal elements are allied to a bathos that renders them absurd. We see behind the scenes of this mask that the fairy dancers are local children directed by a Welsh parson whose pronunciation of English makes him a figure of fun; these 'fairies' form a ring around a fat knight (a parody of the honoured addressee who might often be the King in Hall's masks) only in order to pinch him; and the 'Welsh fairy' (5.5.81), far from keeping to the peripheral position of a torchbearer, deliberately uses his torch to burn Falstaff's fingers. Thus the classic elements of both disguise and threatened violence are made comically grotesque.

Much Ado About Nothing incorporates the element of planned manipulation into its masking

in darker vein than *Merry Wives*. Both men and women are masked here, and both groups are being manipulated by the malicious Don John. Here the loose talk associated with mask is filtered through Don John's claim to have overheard Don Pedro betray Claudio by wooing Hero for himself rather than his friend. Whereas, in *Love's Labour's Lost*, the scene works on the simple basis that the women can see through the men's disguises but the men are taken in by the women's, there is much play with the uncertainty of who can see what in *Much Ado*. Ursula knows Antonio, she claims, 'by the waggling of your head' (2.1.115), and is not remotely taken in by his claim to be performing Antonio's mannerisms; Beatrice's mockery of Benedick demonstrates that she sees through his mask, but he cannot be certain that she does; and when Don John and Borachio recognize Claudio 'by his bearing' (159–60), they deliberately exploit that knowledge to pretend that they take him for Benedick. As always in the early Shakespeare, formal mask is a cover for deceit, and, as in all the plays so far discussed except *Love's Labour's Lost*, that deceit carries with it a significant threat to life or happiness.

This underlying violence or danger is one of two very consistent features in Shakespeare's use of mask in his early plays. The other is an aspect of scenic form: an interest in developing a formally patterned shape that gives pleasure through the measured pacing of its playing out. Mask most commonly presents a symmetrically costumed group or groups, either dancing or enacting a formal encounter reminiscent of dance through an interchange that involves individual couples tracing variations on the same theme. This is at its most obvious in *Love's Labour's Lost* and *Much Ado*, though part of the pleasure in the more violent and unpredictable scenes in tragedy is in feeling the threat of that possible surge of violence pushing against the constrained fixity of formal shapes. The sonnet that Romeo and Juliet speak in the ball-scene derives its force by retaining its visible shapeliness to the end within a scene that threatens to disrupt it; and the allegorical device in *Titus* similarly holds its shape against an encroaching fear that it may not. Shakespeare's consciousness of cultivating measure, formality and precision finds further confirmation, too, through the fact that variants on the word 'measure' keep recurring in these scenes. Both *Love's Labour's Lost* and *Romeo and Juliet* foreground it through wordplay, the former in an especially long sequence that passes the word back and forward between different speakers, the latter merely in passing (*LLL*, 5.2.184–222; *R&J*, 1.4.9–10); and Evans in *Merry Wives*, as he directs his maskers to close in on Falstaff, bids them 'lock hand in hand; yourselves in order set; / And twenty glow-worms shall our lanterns be, / To guide our measure round about the tree' (5.5.76–8).

Mask changes its shape in *As You Like It*, the latest of these early plays. The last act scripts Silvius, Phebe, Orlando and Rosalind into a sequence of patterned exchanges that resembles nothing more than dancing measures and again highlights the idea of 'measure' through both wordplay (5.4.175–80) and the wording of Jaques's prominent refusal to follow the pattern of the others: 'I am for other than for dancing measures' (5.4.193). Though not literally conceived as a mask, the symmetry of the writing here owes much to the formal figurations of mask. It brings together this formal and balletic encounter, however, with the other aspect of mask so far treated only once and ironically in *Titus Andronicus*, the entry-tableau. By combining these two aspects of mask, the symmetrical disposition of characters (in dance or otherwise) and the spectacular entry of an allegorical or mythological figure or figures, *As You Like It* points the way to a different use of mask, anticipating the late plays in subordinating dance and conversation to tableau, spectacle and resolution. Commoning, with all that that implies of easy and spontaneous banter, gives way to formal and musical monologue, and informal interaction is concluded with the imposition of higher authority as mediated through overwhelming, godlike or divine spectacle.

On the other hand, the very fact that *As You Like It*, an Elizabethan play, already contains the germ of the later, spectacular form indicates that there can be no absolute separation between 'mask' and 'masque', between the Elizabethan and Jacobean

forms of this court entertainment, or between Shakespeare's early and later uses of the form. Two of Shakespeare's Jacobean plays, both probably jointly authored, help, together with *As You Like It*, to unpick the overlap between forms and periods. *Timon of Athens*, written *c.* 1605, just as the great sequence of Jacobean masques was beginning (Daniel's *Vision of the Twelve Goddesses* was performed in 1604 and Jonson's *Masque of Blackness* in 1605) was probably co-authored with Thomas Middleton. It is a play strongly structured on the opposition between two banqueting scenes, the first of which, thought by many to be authored by Middleton, includes a lavish mask (or masks), including Cupid (the presenter), the five senses and a group of Amazons, '*with lutes in their hands, dancing and playing*' (2.126).[16] This is a particularly spectacular mask, very much in the classic form we find represented throughout Hall's chronicle of Henry VIII's reign, and both Cupid and Amazons are familiar and recurrent figures in the form. It is a mask arriving as it were by chance, as did so many of Henry's masks, representing its performance as a gift to an honoured host. It is, however, if not parodic, as in some of the comedies we have looked at, certainly framed and ironised by Apemantus, whose comments continue throughout its performance:

> What a sweep of vanity comes this way!
> They dance? They are madwomen.
> Like madness is the glory of this life
> As this pomp shows to a little oil and root.
> . . .
> I should fear those that dance before me now
> Would one day stamp upon me.
>
> (2.128–40)

The import is clear. The spectacle of this mask, with its '*much adoring of Timon*' (2.141), exemplifies the hollowness of such shows, representing them less as forms of deceit enabling such plots as the elopement of lovers than as deceitful by definition, by virtue of being mere shows. The second banquet

---

[16] Quotations from *Timon of Athens* are taken from John Jowett's edition (Oxford, 2004), which has no act divisions.

scene, with its parodic feast of stones and water, performs Timon's own recognition of the empty flattery of what has gone before it, which reaches its highest and most vacuous point of excess in this mask.

Between *Timon of Athens* and *Henry VIII*, co-written with Fletcher *c.* 1613, Shakespeare develops the epiphanic form of mask heralded in *As You Like It* and currently developing in ever more technologically sophisticated ways at the Jacobean court. As Tudor mask moves away from the sudden irruption of a masked group of dancers and the orderly measures of dance formations to the different kinds of emphasis and stage-picture of Jacobean masque, with its divine interventions and spectacular revelations, so Shakespeare's dramaturgy partly reflects that development. What Shakespeare presents in *Cymbeline*, *The Winter's Tale* and *The Tempest* is close to what Jacobean masque presents: spectacular and conclusive moments of clarity and confirmation, shown in the descents of gods and goddesses or the seeming resurrection of the dead. There is, in sum, a move away from revels and towards revelation. At the same time, however, we should note that there is no clear break with the older forms of masking, either in Jacobean masque or in Shakespeare's late plays. Jacobean court masques retain many elements of Elizabethan mask, including the entry of formal groups of exotically costumed dancers; and *The Tempest* scripts a mask of nymphs and reapers alongside the descent of Juno.

Henry VIII is especially interesting in the way it brings elements of the Tudor and Jacobean forms of masking together. It not only has a strong ground-bass of recurrent mask-like ceremonial, deriving from the ceremonies and entertainments of Henry VIII's reign itself, from the opening description of the Field of Cloth of Gold to the closing christening of Elizabeth; but it also contains two scenes that respectively mark out the earlier and later traditions of masking very prominently within the same play. Both scenes are generally held to be by Fletcher, so they cannot be used to make too much of developments in Shakespeare's dramaturgy; but as a collaborator Shakespeare must have at least endorsed, if not revised, these scenes, as well as contributing to the strongly spectacular bias of the play as a whole. The scene of Tudor masking (1.4) is lifted straight out of the chronicles, with one major change, and straightforwardly based on the life of Henry VIII, as recorded by Holinshed.[17] Henry, in disguise alongside the other maskers, brings a mask of shepherds to Wolsey's house; and as the maskers take out the ladies to dance, Henry chooses Anne Bullen. As in *Romeo and Juliet*, and in Hall's Italian masking, the occasion creates the space for a kiss. The mask is thus a key moment, as it usually is in Shakespeare's Elizabethan plays, in changing the course of events. On this occasion it is to change the shape of the nation. In fact Henry met Anne Boleyn much earlier than this, and Holinshed does not mention her presence on this occasion, but Shakespeare and Fletcher choose to make the mask into the moment of first meeting.

The later scene, 4.2, borrows more strongly from the tradition of divine dream or revelation and goes quite outside Holinshed and the historical record to create this visionary moment, which is described in a very full stage direction following 4.2.82. Where the earlier mask was courtly, sensual and secular, this extended dumb-show is spiritual, full of biblical imagery and effectively Katherine's apotheosis.[18] Where the earlier mask was followed by a banquet of wines and sweetmeats, the banquet to which Katherine is invited in this vision is a banquet of angels promising 'eternal happiness' (4.2.90). Here the appearance of angels is kept quite separate from,

---

[17] Shakespeare draws on Holinshed to create this scene, but on this occasion Holinshed is not following Hall (who does not describe this 1527 mask). The ultimate source for this occasion was George Cavendish's *Life of Wolsey*. Shakespeare is unlikely to have known this directly, as it was not printed during his lifetime, but Judith Anderson has argued that he was influenced by the version of Cavendish incorporated by John Stow into his *Annals* of 1592, a version significantly different from the second edition of Holinshed (*Biographical Truth: The Representation of Historical Persons in Tudor-Stuart Writing* (New Haven, Conn., 1984), p. 136, cited in Gordon McMullan, ed., *King Henry VIII* (London, 2000), p. 169, n.1).

[18] McMullan, ed., *King Henry VIII*, p. 380. McMullan notes that Howard Davies's production for the Royal Shakespeare Company in 1983 'quite specifically choreographed this vision as a redemptive version of the dance at Wolsey's party'.

and deliberately contrasted with, the secular pleasures of earthly feasting and dancing. The dream thus recalls and distances itself from the mask of shepherds, the point of origin for Katherine's sufferings, here produced as leading to celestial reward. This latest of Shakespeare's plays, then, draws on the full extent of the masking tradition to create a productive tension between secular revels and divine revelation.

APPENDIX: EXTRACTS FROM HALL'S CHRONICLE (1550 EDITION)

1. Disguising in Queen's Chamber, January 1510
The kyng sone after, came to Westminster with the Quene, and all their train: And on a tyme beyng there, his grace, therles of Essex, Wilshire, and other noble menne, to the numbre of twelve, came sodainly in a mornyng, into the Quenes Chambre, all appareled in shorte cotes, of Kentishe Kendal, with hodes on their heddes, and hosen of thesame, every one of theim, his bowe and arrowes, and a sworde and a bucklar, like out lawes, or Robyn Hodes men, wherof the Quene, the Ladies, and al other, there were abashed, aswell for the straunge sight, as also for their sodain commyng, and after certayn daunces, and pastime made, thei departed.

2. Disguising, November 1510
The second night were divers straungers of Maximilian the Emperours court, and Ambassadours of Spaygne with the kyng at supper: when they had supped, the kyng willed them to go into the Quenes chamber, who so dyd. And in the meane season, the kynge with .xv. other, appareled in Almayne Jackettes of Crymosyn, and purple Satyn, with long quartered sleves, with hosen of thesame sute, their bonettes of whyte Velvet, wrapped in flat golde of Damaske, with vysers and whyte plumes, came in with a momery, and after a certayne tyme that they had played with the Quene and the straungers, they departed. Then sodenly entred syx mynstrels, rychely appareled, plaiyng on their instrumentes, and then folowed .xiiii. persones Gentelmen, all appareyled in yealow Satyne, cut

lyke Almaynes, bearyng torches. After them came .vi. disguised in whyte Satyne and grene, enbroudered and set with letters and castels of fyne golde in bullion, the garmentes were of straunge facion, with also straunge cuttes, every cutte knytte with poyntes of fyne golde, and tassels of thesame, their hosen cutt and tyed in lykewyse, their bonettes of clothe of sylver, wounde wyth golde. Fyrst of these .vi. was the kyng, the erle of Essex, Charles Brandon, Sir Edward Hawarde, syr Thomas Knevet, and syr Henry Guylforde. Then part of the Gentlemen bearyng torches departed, and shortly returned, after whome came in .vi. ladies, appareled in garmentes of Crymosyne Satyn enbroudered and travessed with clothe of gold, cut in Pomegranettes and yokes, strynged after the facion of Spaygne. Then the sayed .vi. men daunced with these .vi. ladies: and after that they had daunced a season the ladies toke of the mens visars, whereby they were knowen: Whereof the Quene and the straungers muche praysed the kynge, and ended the pastyme.

3. First day's jousting at the Westminster Tournament, February 1511
A place in the Pallayce was prepared for the kynge, and also the Quene, rychely hanged, the inner parte with cloth of golde, and the utter with ryche clothe of Arras. These Justes beganne the .xiii. daye of February. After that, that the Quene with her trayne of ladyes had taken their places, into the Palays was conveyed a pageaunt of a greate quantitie, made like a forest with rockes, hylles and dales, with divers sundrie trees, floures, hathornes, ferne and grasse, with six forsters, standynge within thesame forrest, garnished in cotes and hodes of grene Velvet, by whome lay a greate number of speres, all the trees, herbes, and floures, of thesame forrest were made of grene Velvet, grene Damaske, and Silke of divers colours, Satyn and Sercenet. In the middes of this forrest was a castell standing, made of golde, and before the Castell gate sat a gentelman freshly appareiled, makyng a garlande of Roses for the pryce. This forrest, was drawen, as it were by strength of twoo great beastes, a Lyon and an Antelop, the Lyon florished all over

with Damaske golde. The Antelop was wrought all over with sylver of Damaske, his beames and hornes and tuskes of golde: these beastes were led with certayne men appareiled like wildemen, or wood-houses, their bodies, heddes, faces, handes, and legges, covered with grene Silke flosshed: On either of thesaied Antelop and Lyon, sate a ladye rychely appareiled, the beastes were tied to the pageaunt with greate chaynes of golde, as horses be in the carte. When the pageaunt rested before the Quene, the forenamed forsters blew their hornes, then the devise or pageant opened on all sydes, and out issued the foresaied foure knyghtes, armed at all peces, every of them a spere in his hande on horsebacke with great plumes on their heddes, their basses and trappers of clothe of gold, every of them his name enbroudered on his basse and trapper: on the other parte with great noyse, aswell of Trompettes as of Drommes entred into the fielde: The erle of Essex, the lord Thomas Hawarde with many other cleane armed, their trappers and basses all of Crymosyn Satyn enbroudered with braunches of Pomegarnettes of golde, and posies with many a freshe Gentelmen, rydyng before them, their fotemen also well appareiled: And so the Justes beganne, and endured all that daye.

4. Mask, Twelfth Night, 1512

On the daie of the Epiphanie at night, the kyng with a .xi. other wer disguised, after the maner of Italie, called a maske, a thyng not seen afore in Englande, thei were appareled in garmentes long and brode, wrought all with gold, with visers and cappes of gold, and after the banket doen, these Maskers came in, with sixe gentlemen disguised in silke bearyng staffe torches, and desired the ladies to daunce, some were content, and some that knewe the fashion of it refused, because it was not a thyng commonly seen. And after thei daunced, and com-moned together, as the fashion of the Maskes is, thei toke their leave and departed, and so did the Quene, and all the ladies.

5. Disguising, Twelfth Night, 1513

The kyng after this Parliament ended, kept a solempne Christmas at Grenewiche to chere his nobles, and on the twelfe daie at night came into the hall a Mount, called the riche Mount. The Mount was set full of riche flowers of silke, and especially ful of Brome slippes full of coddes, the Braunches wer grene Sattin, and the flowers flat Gold of Damaske, whiche signified Plantagenet. On the top stode a goodly Bekon geving light, round aboute the Bekon sat the king and five other, al in cotes and cappes of right Crimosin velvet, enbroudered with flatt gold of Dammaske, their coates set ful of spangelles of gold, and foure wood-houses drewe the Mount till it came before the quene, and then the king and his compaignie dis-cended and daunced: then sodainly the Mounte opened, and out came sixe ladies all in Crimosin satin and plunket, embroudered with Golde and perle, with French hoodes on their heddes and thei daunced alone. Then the lordes of the Mount toke the ladies and daunced together: and the ladies reentred and the Mount closed, and so was con-veighed out of the hall. Then the kyng shifted him and came to the Quene, and sat at the banquet which was very sumpteous.

6. Newhall mask/disguising, September 1519

This yere in September the kyng laie at his manour of Newhall in Essex, otherwyse called *Beaulieu*, where the kynge had newly buylded a costly man-cion, and there to welcome the quene and the Lordes, and the Frenche gentlemen, he made to them a sumpteous banket, and all a long the cham-ber sat a ladie and a lorde, or a knight, which were plenteously served. And after the banket ended, with noise of minstrelles entered into the cham-ber eight Maskers with white berdes, and long and large garmentes of blewe satyn pauned with Sipres, poudered with spangles of Bullion golde, and they daunsed with ladies sadly, and communed not with the ladies after the fassion of Maskers, but behaved theimselfes sadly. Wherefore the quene plucked of their visors, and then appered the duke of Suffolk, the erle of Essex, the Marques Dorset, the lorde Burgainy, sir Rychard Wyngfeld, sir Robert Wyngfelde, sir Rychard Weston, sir Willyam Kyngston: all these were somwhat aged, the youngest man was fiftie at the least. The ladies had good sporte to se these auncient persones Maskers. When they were departed, the kyng and the foure hostages of fraunce, and the erle of Devonshire with sixe other young Gentelmen entered the chamber, the whiche sixe were all in yelowe Sattyn, hosen, shoen, and cappes, and sixe other were in like maner in Grene: the yelowe satyn was freted with silver of damaske, and so was the grene very rychely to behold: and then every Masker toke a ladie and daunsed: and when they had daunsed and commoned a great while, their visers were taken of, and the ladies knewe them, and there the king gave many broches and proper giftes to the ladies. And after this done, the quene made a banket to the kyng and his lordes and the other strangers.

7. *A mask given by Henry VIII for Francis I's queen at the Field of Cloth of Gold, 1520*

After diner the ladies dressed them to daunce, the king the more to glad the quene and thesayde ladies, departed secretly and put hym self with .xxix. persons more in maskers apparel, fyrst .x. young honorable lordes apparelled after the maner of Ry and Revel in Ruselande or farre Estland. Fyrst theyr hosen of rych goldsatten called Aureate satten, overrouled to the kne with skarlet, and on theyr fete, shoen with litle pykes of white nayles after the Estlande guise, theyr doublettes of ryche crimosin velvet and cloth of gold with wide sleves lyned with cloth of gold, over thys they had clokes of crymosyn velvet short, lyned with cloth of gold, on every syde of the clokes ringes of silver with laces of Venice gold, and on their heades thei had hattes made in the toune of Danske and Purses of Seales skynnes, and gyrdles of thesame: all these yong lordes had visers, on their faces and their hattes were drawen lyke hatbondes full of Damaske gold.

Other .x. lordes were apparelled in long gounes of blewe Satten of the auncient fashion embrodered wyth reasons of golde that sayd *adieu Junesse* fare well youthe: they had typpettes of blacke velvet and hattes hangynge therby, and on their heades, high violette standyng cappes and girdelles

of silke, and Purses of cloth of golde after the auncyent maner, with visers, their faces of lyke auncyentie.

Then was ther another compaignie of .x. lordes in whiche maskery the king was hym selfe, apparelled all in longe garmentes of estate all pale riche clothe of golde, all these had rych gounes which were lyned with grene Taffata, and knit with poinctes of Venice silver wherwith the rychclothe together was fastened [o]n their faces visers, and al the berdes were fyne wyer of Duket golde, the Drunslad plaiers and other minstrels arayed in whit, yelow, and russet Damaske, these mynstrels blew and played, and so passed throughe the citie of Arde. All these noble revelers came into the French court and put them in presence of the French Quene and ladies: and when the Quene had them beholden, these revelers toke ladies and daunsed, in passynge the tyme right honorably. Then at thinstaunce of the French quene and her ladies these maskers and revellers them disvisered, shewinge them what persons thei wer. Then spices, fruites, jelies and banket viandes wer brought, that done and ended, the king toke his leave of the French quene and ladies and in secret places every one visered him selfe, so that they were unknowen, and so passed through the French court, to whome were brought .xxx. horses trapped in Damaske, whyte and yelowe, and so in maskeler passed the toune of Arde, into the felde or campe.

Select glossary

abashed confused, confounded
Almayne German
auncyentie antiquity
cleane properly, completely
commoned mixed and talked together
disvisered unmasked
Duket golde fine gold (as in a ducat)
florished adorned
flosshed made to resemble floss-silk
freted interlaced
maskeler, (in) masked
overrouled encased
plunket a woollen fabric of grey or light blue

poinctes laces
posies emblematic devices
pykes gold or silver trimmings
Ry game, sport
sadly seriously
sercenet very fine silk

travessed crossed
typpettes long hanging pieces of cloth worn loose like scarves, or attached to hoods or sleeves; garments covering the shoulders, often with trailing ends
utter outer

BRIDE-ING THE SHREW: COSTUMES THAT MATTER

BARBARA HODGDON

I recall a single, memorable moment of looking: Alexandra Gilbreath as Katherina in Gregory Doran's 2003 *Taming of the Shrew*, kitted out for her wedding. Absorbed in her costume's artifice – a paradise of ribbon rosettes, its skirt distended by a huge flat-topped farthingale – actor and character receded into the background: she was 'all clothes'. In performance, this was a wedding dress that mattered. But when, much later, it surfaced in the archive on a mannequin, Kate's costume bore little resemblance to my memory of what I had seen – a parody of the dress worn by Elizabeth I in the Ditchley portrait (illustration 13). It is, of course, always surprising to see a costume's theatrical life frozen on display, missing the intimacy of the body and, in this case, the farthingale. That I had mapped one gown over the other points not just to the tricksiness of looking and memory – one dress shadowing or haunting the other (ghosts on both sides) – but also to how fashion and theatre, avatars of one another,[1] compose subjects as well as histories. 'Speak, clothes, for me', says the actor-as-character, says the play's written language of costume. So what costume plot does Shakespeare write for *Shrew*, and especially for the actor who plays its title role? And how do Kate's clothes – those worn by Gilbreath and by other Kate-actors – play with the most serious theme of human, and theatrical, consciousness – *Who am I?* – to perform the double dream of identity and play which lies at the heart of *Shrew*'s theatrical self-fashioning? The story that emerges from these questions involves double looking. First, setting *Shrew*'s written language of clothes

alongside early modern social customs, I imagine how costume *acts out* and supports historical and cultural meanings;[2] then, I explore how theatre's fabrications have invited spectators to look at (and listen to) Kate's speaking body in performance. This strand of my story, which returns to Gilbreath's Kate, is and is not about that absent farthingale.

Among Shakespeare's plays, *Shrew* makes a major investment in wardrobe, especially in second-hand clothes, which constitute its stock in theatrical trade, performing their own suppose-ings. The play even makes an in-joke about it: when, about to set out for Padua, Petruccio instructs Grumio, 'bring our horses unto Long-lane end' (4.3.182), the action suddenly swerves from fictive Italy to the Elizabethan London locale where brokers and second-hand clothes dealers hawked their wares.[3]

With deep thanks to David Howells, Carol Chillington Rutter, Rowan Rutter, Yvonne Gilbert, Peter Kirwan, Michael Cordner, Bill Worthen, Helen Hargest, G. B. Shand, the Women of the RSC's Hire Wardrobe and Richard Abel.

[1] I draw on Herbert Blau, *Nothing in Itself: Complexions of Fashion* (Bloomington, 1999), p. 22.

[2] Roland Barthes, *The Fashion System*, trans. Matthew Ward and Richard Howard (New York, 1983), p. 289. Writes Barthes: 'Written clothing is at once institution ("language") on the level of clothing, and action ("speech") on the level of language. This paradoxical status is important: it will govern the entire structural analysis of written clothing' (p. 18); his purely semiotic analysis, however, is a schematic which elides a deeper reading of clothing's histories.

[3] Long Lane was a 'Place of Note for the sale of Apparel, Linen, and Upholsters Goods, both Second-hand and New, but chiefly for Old, for which it is of note'. John Stow, *A Survey of the Cities of London and Westminster . . . Corrected,*

13. Wedding costume for Katherina displayed on mannequin; worn by Alexandra Gilbreath in *Taming of the Shrew*. Director: Gregory Doran. Royal Shakespeare Company, 2003.

In a play where metamorphosis is not just a piece of plot machinery but also part of the costume plot, clothes, obeying early modern culture's sumptuary codes, label their wearers by gender, class, occupation and station. So, too, do theatrical clothes.[4] Overall, it seems less than accidental that *Shrew* features a Tailor and a Haberdasher. In the Induction, the Lord orders that 'Some one be ready with a costly suit' for Sly and that Bartholomew the Page be 'dress'd in all suits like a lady' – presumably borrowed clothes (Ind.1.57, 104).[5] So attired, Bartholomew anticipates Katherina, mirrors the transformation of boy actor in drag to boy actor 'becoming' the woman's part. *Shrew*'s male wardrobe is remarkably full, if occasionally generally described, such as 'the habit of a mean man' (Lucentio's disguise as Cambio) or 'brave' – Tranio's showy Lucentio-dressing (2.1.38SD; 1.2.216SD).[6] In this play, which from its initial moments evokes touchstones of the 1590s theatrical repertoire, one

might conjecture an early modern performance in which, when Lucentio offers Tranio 'my colour'd hat and cloak' (1.1.207), its colour matches that of the Company's patron. For both Lucentio and Tranio first appear as *players*: and as 'household Servants and dailie wayters', players wore their patron's livery and bore his badge; at James I's coronation procession (15 March 1604), for instance, the Great Wardrobe furnished each of the King's Men with four and a half yards of red cloth.[7] A further hint of that possibility appears when the true Vincentio mentions Tranio's 'bravery' in his disguise as

Improved, and very much Enlarged by John Strype (London, 1720), Book 2, p. 122. See also Ann Rosalind Jones and Peter Stallybrass, *Renaissance Clothing and the Materials of Memory* (Cambridge, 2000), pp. 192–3.

4 The 'Homily on Excess of Apparel' mandates that 'every man behold and consider his own vocation, inasmuch as God hath appointed every man his degree and office, within the limits whereof it behoveth him to keep himself. There fore all may not look to wear like apparel, but everyone according to his degree . . .' *The First Book of Homilies* (1547), ed. John Griffiths (Oxford, 1859), p. 310. In practice, such restrictions were not followed religiously: Stubbes railed against the 'confused mingle-mangle of apparrell' that unfixed the dress codes marking social identities. Philip Stubbes, *The Anatomie of Abuses* (1583), C1v–C2v.

5 All citations to Shakespeare's text are from the Arden 2 *The Taming of the Shrew*, ed. Brian Morris (London, 1981).

6 In terms of dress, *The Taming of A Shrew* (1594) contains more precise hints than *The Shrew*. Sly appears (Sc. 2 SD) '*richly appareled, and the music playing*'. When Ferando arrives for his wedding, he is '*basely attired and a red cap on his head*' (Sc. 4, 107SD); Scene 6 mentions an old jerkin and a 'pair of canvas breeches down to the small of his leg'. Ferando's argument for dressing down is that 'if [he and Kate] should once fall out / She'll pull my costly suits over mine ears'. Speaking in Marlovian terms, he claims ownership of 'as many suits /Fantastic made to fit my humour so / As any in Athens, and as richly wrought / As was the massy robe that late adorned / The stately legate of the Persian king'. Once Alfonso's three daughters appear, they are described only as 'bright of hue', with eyes 'brighter than the lamps of heaven'. Ferando promises Kate that 'garments wrought of Median silk / Enchased with precious jewels fetched from far / By Italian merchants that with Russian stems / Plows up huge furrow in the Terrene Main–', yet, as in *The Shrew*, what arrives (Sc. 10) – a curtailed cap, round-compassed cape, large trunk sleeve and loose-bodied gown – is less ornate.

7 E. K. Chambers *The Elizabethan Stage* (Oxford, 1923), 4 vols., I. 311; II. 86, 211.

Lucentio: a silken doublet, a velvet hose (breeches as well as stockings), a fashionable copintank hat – shaped like a 'sugar-loaf' and often trimmed by a band, a small plume or a large jewelled ornament – and a scarlet cloak (5.1.58–9).[8]

Some references to clothes function like promissory notes, arousing anticipation only to counter it, as with Petruccio's promise of 'fine array' for Kate once the wedding date is set (2.1.316). But when it comes to Petruccio's own wedding clothes, Shakespeare writes precise instructions: 'a new hat and an old jerkin; a pair of old breeches thrice turned; a pair of boots that ha[d] been candle-cases, one buckled, another laced' – there is, of course, even more about his horse (3.2.41–4). Similarly, Grumio wears 'a linen stock on one leg, and a kersey boot-hose on the other, gartered with a red and blue list' – poor motley-wear topped with 'an old hat, the humour of forty fancies pricked in't for a feather' – a simulacrum ornament (3.2.64–7).[9] Then, at Petruccio's, Grumio asks whether the servingmen are in their 'new fustian' – a cheap cotton velure with the silky look of velvet and probably sky-blue, customary dress for servants – whether they have white stockings, and whether 'every officer [has] his wedding-garment on'; later, he tells Petruccio that 'Gabriel's pumps were all unpink'd i'th' heel' – a style of pinking or 'picking' that varied considerably, moving up and down the class ladder (4.1.120).

In a theatre of male performers, perhaps it is no surprise that the men get fully stocked closets to enhance their performances. Yet what this demonstrates irrevocably is that the play really is about looking at (as well as listening to) men: whether dressed up (Sly) or down (Petruccio's outrageous attire) they are the centre of Shrew's fashion spectacle. As in Henslowe's inventories, which detail men's doublets, shirts, cloaks and hose, Shakespeare-the-designer mandates masculine fashion, looks at (early modern) men behaving badly, yet pays scant attention to feminine apparel. How, then, does Shakespeare dress Shrew's women? What is the Bianca-look? The Katherina-look? The single *material* hint of Bianca-dressing occurs when she is 'bound' and harassed by Katherina over the very 'goods' she wears – tokens, perhaps, from her suitors, badges of her conquests – a scene that begins, as Carol Rutter notes, with Kate binding Bianca and concludes with Kate bound to Petruccio (2.1.3–4).[10] In stark contrast to the men, the Minola sisters are constructed by language and the look – the base and pillar of Shakespeare's theatre – 'coloured' and clothed by men's voices, eye-ings and opinions. Just as 'maid's mild behaviour and sobriety' initially dress Bianca, Katherina is fashioned as a 'stark mad wench', ready for carting through Padua (1.1.71, 69, 55): her first appearance is 'about' how the town looks at her, takes her on. Although H. J. Oliver conjures up an early modern stock 'shrew' costume that immediately identified her figure, it is primarily behaviour, not clothes, which 'character' Kate.[11] Only later, from her wedding forward, does the narrative arc of her costume begin to tell her story.

The play dramatizes the stages of Kate's and Petruccio's wooing, winning and wedding, from a courtship based on the proverbial 'Love is potent but money is omnipotent' that marks the mercenary 'Smithfield match'[12] to the church door.

---

[8] The copintank (or copatain) hat's name derived partly from 'copped', meaning sharp and high; it fell out of fashion with the introduction of a small hat or flat cap – which may be Ferando's 'red cap': such caps were worn exclusively by citizens and apprentices. See M. Channing Linthicum, *Costume in the Drama of Shakespeare and His Contemporaries* (Oxford, 1936), pp. 41, 228.

[9] Kersey was light-weight wool cloth that came in many colours, usually worn by lower-class persons; apparently Grumio wears the pretence of poverty. The *OED* suggests that the feather is picked out in a design. See also Linthicum, *Costume*, pp. 79–80.

[10] Carol Chillington Rutters, *Clamorous Voices* (London, 1989), p. 9.

[11] H. J. Oliver, ed., *The Taming of the Shrew* (Oxford, 1982), p. 49.

[12] In such marriages, the prime negotiator was called a cattle-dealer. See John Cordy Jeaffreson, *Brides and Bridals*, 2 vols. (London, 1872), 1. 309. Bianca's marriage also is a 'Smithfield match'; there were heavy fines for such clandestine marriages; pardons for them cost less than the license to marry. See Emily S. Holt, *Ye Olden Time: English Customs in the Middle Ages* (London, n.d.), p. 23. In *Shrew*, this transgression is summarily excused by both fathers' pardons.

Although Bianca leaves her suitors to 'dress [her] sister's chamber up' (3.1.81), that scene of women's community is not, as it is in *Romeo and Juliet* and *Much Ado About Nothing*, staged: by and large, Kate is on her own, surrounded by men. Shakespeare does, however, dramatize the spectacle of her arrival for her wedding, which reprises her first entrance: coming on with family, guests and attendants, she again is put on show to both onstage and offstage spectators, made the object and subject of public attention to onlookers who may or may not share the shame ('No shame but mine' (3.2.8)) she takes on herself when Petruccio does not arrive on time.

And when the town looks, what do they see? Thomas Deloney's *Jack of Newbury* (1780) envisions such an early modern scene of looking. There, the bride,

in a gowne of sheepes russet [symbolizing steadfastness][13] and a kertle of fine worsted, [with her hair down, signifying her freedom – the last time a woman would be seen bare-headed in public][14] . . . was led to church between two sweet boys, with Bride laces and Rosemary tied about their silken sleeves . . . [and] a fair Bride-cup of silver and gilt carried before her, wherein was a goodly branch of Rosemary gilded very fair, hung about with silken Ribands of all colours . . . [N]ext was there a noyse of Musicians that played all the way before her: after her came all the chiefest maydens of the countrie, some bearing great Bride Cakes, and some Garlands of wheate finely gilded, and so she past unto the Church.[15]

As for the bridal gown, the one colour that it was pretty certain *not* to be was white, for white, worn by widows immediately upon bereavement, denoted death; nor would it be black, associated with lighter mourning. Any other colour or mixture thereof was possible: Henry I's queen was married in crimson; Richard II's Isabelle of France in blue; Anna of Cleve, Henry VIII's fourth wife, in cloth of gold; and Queen Mary in gold brocade.[16] Thus any of three dresses for women specified in Henslowe's inventory – an 'orange tawney velvet gown with silver lace', a gown of cloth of gold, and a yellow satin gown embroidered with silk and gold lace – might serve as wedding attire.[17] But rather than writing what Kate wears, *Shrew*'s

rhetoric of costume gives the over-performance of dress to Petruccio: it is he, not she, whose monstrous apparel and behaviour offend the town – and it is he who introduces the metaphor of value that henceforth will govern the play's law of spectacle as well as the relationship between bodies, clothes and identities: 'To me she's married, not unto my clothes' (3.2.115).

From this point forward, as the play begins to burrow beneath surface appearances, it purposefully deconstructs and reassembles the customary order of things. The wedding itself is not staged but reported by Gremio, who catalogues Petruccio's antics – swearing, cuffing the priest, throwing sops at the sexton, kissing Kate with 'a clamorous smack' – and interprets what he has seen as a 'mad marriage' (3.2.180). However much his account may depart from any expectation or prior interpretation of what a wedding should be, perhaps this ceremony's most significant omission – call it early modern, or Shakespearian madness? – is the sermon on the duties of husbands and wives, prescribed in the Elizabethan *Book of Common Prayer* as well as in the *Homily on Matrimony*.[18] Petruccio, of course, also preaches a sermon – on

---

13 Linthicum, *Costume*, p. 30.

14 The bride's wedding veil comes later, perhaps as a substitute for the long tresses. See Jeaffreson, *Brides and Bridals*, 1. 201–2, 175, 177.

15 See *The Novels of Thomas Deloney*, ed. Merritt E. Lawless (Bloomington, 1961). Suckling's 'Ballad upon a Wedding' mentions that, after the bridal dinner, the young men and women of the wedding party catch the ribbons and laces that held the couple's clothes together, effectively undressing them. For other customs, see David Cressy, *Birth, Marriage, and Death: Ritual, Religion, and the Life-Cycle in Tudor and Stuart England* (Oxford, 1997), pp. 363–4.

16 See Holt, *Ye Olden Time*, pp. 30–2.

17 Henslowe's inventory for the Lord Admiral's Men (March 1598) lists Juno's coat, hood for the witch, Dido's robe and three dresses; Henslowe also details costumes for 'Alice Peerce'. See *Henslowe's Diary*, ed. R. A. Foakes, 2nd edn (Cambridge, 2002), p. 323.

18 The Elizabethan *Homily on Matrimony* decrees that 'if there is no sermon declaring the duties of the man and wife, the minister shall read as followeth' and then provides further instruction. Edward VI instituted the sermon. Jeaffreson, *Brides and Bridals*, pp. 262–4.

continency – but, like the wedding, that is reported (briefly), not spoken. Although, according to scripture, he may have the ideological upper hand, *Shrew* puts the last word(s) on those matters into a woman's mouth. Just as the wedding itself appears to substitute a Petruccian taming regime for church ritual (or jams the two together in a radical rewriting), so also is the sermon not only delayed but doubly displaced, occurring at the play's close and – in an equally radical rewriting – spoken not by a male priest and not in church but by Kate, ex cathedra, so to speak, at Bianca's wedding feast. And, given the sentiments expressed in Kate's sermon and the imaginative range it evokes in spectators, who very well may imagine – and hear – her words differently, that sermon cannot be enclosed entirely within its early modern historical moment.

Insofar as unsettling customs and rearranging church ritual contributes to violating social as well as generic expectations, *Shrew*'s narrative also registers how the usual 'festive comedy' knitting up is undone, both by the antic ceremony and by what follows it: two unconventional feasts and the shredding of Kate's clothes. By tradition, the wedding banquet took place at the groom's lodgings, since the bride is now his 'goods, [his] chattels' (3.2.228). In *Shrew*, however, not only is it staged at Baptista's but it also is a broken feast. And when, about to spirit Kate away, Petruccio instructs the company to 'revel and domineer / Carouse full measure to her maidenhead, / Be mad and merry' (3.2.222–4) – his allusion would have resonant echoes with prevailing opinion concerning the 'barbarous customs' and 'public and disorderly banquets' that marred the 'great and serious matter' of marriage.[19] Heinrich Bullinger, for one, strongly disapproved of dancing: 'Then there is such a lyftinge up and discoueringe of damsels clothes and of other wemens apparel / that a man might thinke / all these dauncers had cast all shame behind them'.[20] Whereas folklore custom decreed that the bride should always buy something as soon as she is married and before the bridegroom can make a purchase, so that she will be master for life,[21] Kate has no chance to shop but is carried off by a 'mad-brain rudesby' (3.2.10) to yet another

(parodic) wedding feast in that space which earlier editors call Petruccio's country house – the semi-Sade-ean locale of the taming school. Although *Shrew*'s poetics of fashion promise her the Tailor's 'ruffling treasure' – a 'loose-bodied gown' with 'a small-compassed cape', trunk sleeves – and a cap (4.3.60, 133, 130, 137), once Petruccio re-launches his clothing metaphor – 'For 'tis the mind that makes the body rich, / And as the sun breaks through the darkest clouds, / So honour peereth in the meanest habit. / What, is the jay more precious than the lark / Because his feathers are more beautiful?' (4.3.169–73) – Kate is dressed, not with silken coats, ruffs and cuffs, farthingales, scarfs and fans (4.3.55–7), but with philosophy. Writes Sonia Rykiel: 'To give one's body to the fantasies of another, . . . to surrender to a stranger who would adorn the skin with his *idées fixes*, his dreams . . . Aren't we mad to let them push us around?'[22] Like Christopher Sly, who has 'no more doublets than backs, no more stockings than legs' (Ind. 2.7–10), according to the logic of the jay and lark, Kate remains 'bemoiled' (4.1.67), her history – and her performance – hangs on the dirty threads of her wedding dress.

And on the cap, which defines the wedded woman: 'I am', brags the Bride in Samuel Rowlands's poetic dialogue to the maidens who attend her, 'your better now by *Ring* and *Hatt*'.[23] Both Kate's claim that 'gentlewomen wear such caps as

---

[19] Erasmus, *Guide to Christian Matrimony*, cited in *Social Life in Britain from the Conquest to the Reformation*, G. G. Coulton, comp. (Cambridge, 1938), pp. 439–40.

[20] Henry (= Heinrich) Bullinger, *The Cristen state of Matrimonye*, trans. Miles Coverdale (London, 1541), cited in Jeaffreson, *Brides and Bridals*, p. 24.

[21] *Notes on the Folk-Lore of Northern Counties of England and the Borders*, cited in Edward Westermarck, *The History of Human Marriage*, 3 vols. (London, 1922), II: 493–4.

[22] Sonia Rykiel, 'From *Celebration*', trans. Claire Malroux, in *On Fashion*, ed. Shari Benstock and Suzanne Ferriss (New Brunswick, 1994), 102.

[23] Samuel Rowlands, *The Bride* (1617), 3, l.29. Trimming for such hats often included an elaborate brooch or a bunch of feathers. Elizabeth I wore a hat to Cambridge in 1564 that was spangled with gold and trimmed 'with a bush of feathers'; Linthicum, *Costume*, p. 221.

these' and Petruccio's repeated taunts about this 'lewd and filthy' velvet dish (4.3.65) echo elsewhere in the early modern drama. Fearful of being cuckolded, *Every Man in His Humour*'s Kitely remarks: 'Our great heads, / . . . never were in safety, / since our wives wore these little caps' . . . [M]ine shall no more / Wear three-piled acorns, to make my horns ache'.[24] If Petruccio alludes to the idea that the 'curtailed' cap, no longer completely covering the head, makes a woman sexually available, the nuanced relation that once burred onto it has been lost. All present-day readers and spectators are likely to read off this performance and, more especially, from Petruccio's last-scene command – 'Off with that bauble, throw it underfoot' (5.2.123) – is that, by reiterating the logic of the jay and lark, it builds into the string of continuities and discontinuities tracking through the play. Petruccio's gesture may, of course, read as yet another instance of dominance, yet if, for instance, Bianca and the Widow wear similar caps, his request also might invite Kate to be unlike them, to be someone else.[25] Yet, given its position as prelude to Kate's radical re-speaking of the postponed sermon on the marital duties of husbands and wives, the point where all the play's ambiguities become most dazzlingly available, both object and gesture may well be invested with meanings so far unimagined in our (post)modern philosophies.

Whatever the case, the cap offers only one instance of how clothes invite spectators to read different stories, different histories. 'What *is* Katherina's theatrical substance, whereof is she made / That decades of strange fashions on her tend'?[26] My account of the narrative logic of Kate-dressing in the theatre – a realm of immediacy and plenitude where clothes, arousing expectancy, mediate the sense of what the body is and may be – begins in 1887, with Ada Rehan (illustration 14), a quintessential Kate-the-Shrew: chin held high, arms defiantly crossed, her splendidly intractable presence enhanced by her brocaded dress and train. Blending clothes and theatrical costume, its design is wedded to late nineteenth-century high fashion and so appeals to two sites and sightings, to onstage and offstage looking: in

14. Ada Rehan as Katherina in Augustin Daly's *Taming of the Shrew*, 1887.

motion, Kate and this dress would take up considerable stage space. Most significantly, however, Rehan's dress is red. And whereas in the early modern period, some hues of red were reserved for nobility while others, as with Judas's red beard and hair, signified evil, more recently, red evokes transgression, the scarlet woman, defying conventions. In the case of Kate-dressing, red equals 'visual fact as argument, a social gestus';[27] it is the colour which releases all the labels attached to her figure,

---

[24] Ben Jonson, *Every Man in His Humour*, 3.3.34–9, ed. Gabriele Bernhard Jackson (New Haven, 1969).

[25] Reading Petruccio's gesture as not intended to humiliate her 'but rather to convince his skeptical friends', R. W. Bond saw it as 'a needless affront to her feelings . . . offered at the very moment when she is exhibiting a voluntary obedience . . . I feel it as a case where the poet has failed to reconcile the dramatic with the psychic requirements'. R. Warwick Bond, ed., *The Taming of the Shrew* (London, 1904), lvii–lviii.

[26] This phrasing derives from the sonnet to Silvia in *Two Gentlemen of Verona*, 4.2.38–42.

[27] Roland Barthes, *Critical Essays*, trans. Richard Howard (Evanston, 1972), p. 50.

and it does good shrewish – and shrewd – work. Costume is seldom 'pure' archaeology: even when it does ferret out 'authentic' *Shrew*-history through simulacra or historical pastiche, red fabric rather than that quintessential Elizabethan signifier, the ruff, marks Kate by contagion. Making her a highly visible spectacle, the red dress has a long performative afterlife as part and parcel of *Shrew*'s formulaic taming. Amanda Harris's Kate (1992) wore red for her initial costume, her wedding dress and the skirt she wore in the sun–moon scene, its visual energies softened there by a white blouse; Josie Lawrence (1995), also in red, sported a vaguely Elizabethan dress, its neckline and silhouette tweaked and eased to a crisply tailored modern look.

In *Sartor Resartus*, Thomas Carlyle writes: 'Clothes present us, place us, show us, make our case, and sometimes make the case we're not sure we want'.[28] For Sinead Cusack (1982) and Fiona Shaw (1987), living archives of Kate-opinion, Kate-dressing, and the difficulties of negotiating her narrative during feminism's high moment, costume was a contentious matter. What, each asked, is the meaning of my dress? What does a performance say about Kate by putting her in pale pink silk, lace and pearls (Cusack) or giving her a softened silhouette in gold satin (Shaw)? Each actor resisted her clothes. When Cusack first saw her costume ('Elizabethan Zandra Rhodes'), she knew that the person she had discovered during rehearsal would not wear it: slashing it with scissors, she wore Wellingtons under it; suspecting she should be wearing a rather dull tapestry, Shaw showed her distaste for glamorous gold.[29] Paola Dionisotti, who played Kate in Michael Bogdanov's 1978 production, remarked that 'someone as angry as Kate would have been at the forefront of the women's movement and would not have behaved as the play requires her to'.[30] As though echoing her, during the run and for some years after, a chalked-up graffiti on the Royal Shakespeare Theatre's backstage wall read: 'Shrew Kills'.

Whether suiting the historical moment or evoking the past, wedding attire for theatrical Kates moves in and out of style. In 1939, hints of Russian orientalism pervaded Vivienne Bennett's panniered silhouette, the energy and menace of its coiling embroiderie softened by lace at the sleeves, feathers and a veil. Sprouting raven's wing feathers at neck and head, Cusack wore black, became a vampire bride; Sian Thomas (1985) threw a second layer and a veil over her previous dress: tatty and messy, framed in a Brechtian landscape, she looked like second-hand Kate. Up to date in exquisitely tailored cream brocade, Josie Lawrence served primarily as a foil to Petruccio's eclectically gawdy peacock. Following the wedding, late twentieth-century performances have tended to map Kate's move from church to Petruccio's interruptive feast onto her clothes. Once there, the physical and psychological abuse deriving from folklore (and travelling into critical history) gets played out, in performance, not on bodies, but on dress. Yet one of the few photographic traces of Petruccio's fashion-attack on the Tailor's creation occurs in Angus McBean's still of John Barton's 1960 *Shrew* – a staged moment that, like most of McBean's work, may not represent performance: stripping Peggy Ashcroft's Kate down to her shift, Peter O'Toole's Petruccio illustrates his idea that externals don't matter (illustration 15). Here, too, image becomes anecdotal, creating a moment of cultural anamnesis which not only remembers an early modern all-male theatrical world but also replaces it with one where women play women, dramatizing theatre history as well as criticism. That moment travels into later performances: Shaw, her travelling clothes confiscated, also was stripped to her shift, then put into the Tailor's dress and set on a platform, like a tailor's dummy; Harris's dishevelled, smock-dressed Kate seemed infantilized. In a play where false and true identities can be worn, discarded, and taken up again simply by changing clothes, late twentieth-century theatre looks at what Kate is to learn – that outsides don't matter – and fabricates one metamorphosis beyond early

---

[28] Carlyle cited in Blau, *Nothing in Itself*, p. 224.

[29] John O'Connor, *Shakespearian Afterlives: Ten Characters with a Life of Their Own* (London, 2003), p. 262.

[30] Rutter, *Clamorous Voices*, p. 13.

15. Peggy Ashcroft as Katherina, Peter O'Toole as Petruccio in *Taming of the Shrew*. Director: John Barton. Shakespeare Memorial Theatre, 1960.

writes the narrative of her transformation from shrew to not-shrew by stitching her into a glamorous dress. At times, she wears a version of the costume Petruccio dismantles earlier – a story that bows less to his schema of value than to how commodity capitalism inevitably makes Kate everybody's material girl. There are some exceptions or quirks in the pattern. Putting on Petruccio's hat, Vanessa Redgrave (1962) blurred gender-dressing, took up (part of) the man's part; paying homage to a literary icon of perfect obedience, Susan Fleetwood (1973) wore Griselda-grey. But in most cases, Kate's final dress – however stunning, however visually seductive – marks her redemption: Cusack gave up wedding black for a sculptural white gown; Harris also discarded dark colours and the heavy sobriety of damask for a lighter palette, wore a feather in her billiment-like cap, strings of pearls – and a smile. When theatre looks, what it sees is A Big Dress for a Big Speech. Implicitly assuming that no one in the audience hears Baptista, theatre's Big Dress blanks out his words, says it all: Kate 'is chang'd, as she had never been' (5.2.116).

'In the Renaissance', writes Roland Barthes, 'as soon as one got a new costume, one had a new portrait done'.[33] Countering – and critiquing – those of her theatrical forebears, the clothes Alexandra Gilbreath's Kate wore in Doran's 2003 *Shrew* paint that portrait. It is, however, not entirely 'new'. For, arguably, it shadows the portrait Shakespeare limns, one tied to the deep structure of the play's narrative, the one that mines early modern marriage ceremonies and customs, runs riffs on them, displaces and parodies them, ruptures and rearranges their ordering. Gilbreath's first

modern theatrical practice. At the role's most abject moment, modern (even post-feminist) Kates wear some form of un-dress.

Evoking Shakespeare's costume logic, Shaw remarks that, when Kate goes to Bianca's wedding dinner, 'She should be in her muddy wrecked wedding dress . . . And she should have the hat – the hat they rowed over.'[31] However, except for the cap, which usually though not always appears, what emerges is a whole fake history of Kate-dressing which routinely, though not religiously, either defies or undermines the logic of Shakespeare's costume plot. Indeed, it is at this point that *Shrew* – and Kate – become most like a fashion show, composed from a mélange of stage traditions and charged in performance by 'the presence of the now'.[32] There also is a shadow plot going on here, one that engenders carnal fancies of shrew-presence about which only theatre dreams. As though anxious to give Kate a pretty frock that atones for playing the shrew-part, theatre over-

[31] Rutter, *Clamorous Voices*, p. 21.

[32] Walter Benjamin, 'Theses on the Philosophy of History', in *Illuminations*, ed. Hannah Arendt, trans. Harry Zohn (New York, 1977), p. 263.

[33] Barthes links fashion to the '*neomania* which probably appeared in our civilization with the birth of capitalism'. *Fashion System*, 300, n.16. On how early modern portraits hide the sitter's 'self' in material ornament, see Patricia Fumerton, *Cultural Aesthetics: Renaissance Literature and the Practice of Social Ornament* (Chicago, 1991), pp. 77–85.

costume – white drawstring top, petticoat, blue-grey dress and cream stockings – fabricates the 'plain Kate' Petruccio labels her when they first meet (2.1.185). Her next change is to her wedding dress. Here, however, the curatorial lens has reordered – and reinterpreted – its appearance: as archived, the dress resembles a memorially reconstructed text in which some speeches are remembered and others aren't. For according to Yvonne Gilbert, Gilbreath's dresser, her hooped farthingale was so large that it took up all the space in the quick-change room; the dress also had a large bumroll, even more rosettes adorned the neck, lace drooped from the cuffs, and multiple strands of ribbons ran down the sides and back of the head-dress. As though remembering *Taming of A Shrew*'s Kate, who voices her consent to marry and 'match' Ferando in an aside, Gilbreath remarked that what Kate wants is to be a bride,[34] but her dress – which, according to Alistair Macauley's costume bible, was patterned after one in an (unidentified) Renaissance portrait – said that she got it all horribly wrong. Most of the wedding party tried not to stare at this caricatured creature and her distended farthingale, but Bianca's look – you're wearing *that?*[35] – gave it away: clearly, her sister not only lacked fashion sense but also had no idea of what it meant to be a bride – or even a 'woman'.

Later, at Petruccio's, Kate appeared, dirty and wet, in a broken-down version of her wedding dress with a tiered rather than hooped petticoat; but by the Tailor Scene, the dress had gone: she wore only the petticoat, a white slip, thick wool socks and a rat-coloured cardigan called The Peggy – because it was first worn by Peggy Ashcroft as *All's Well*'s Countess. Gilbreath was wearing performance memory, perhaps with the image of Ashcroft's Kate, her flame-coloured dress matching her fiery behaviour, in mind.[36] Pulled from stock, the Tailor's creation was very fancy and very dark red. Although Yvonne Gilbert does not remember more precisely, in my fantasy I want this to have been a Big Dress worn by a previous Kate. For it is the only time in my memory that Kate appears, in the final scene, *without* a Big Dress: instead, having discarded her muddied wedding dress, she

wears only its under-dress, tucked up, to show knee-length brown trousers under it, little brown boots – and the cap – of red velvet with small gold studs and feathers at the side, now turned inside out to reveal a dirty beige lining (illustration 16). Cracking theatrical codes, Gilbreath's Kate did not, like her predecessors, 'mak[e] to the world a pecocke showe'.[37] Rather, she appeared as a 'Kate [like] other household Kates' (2.1.271), but not *quite* like she was before.

How, then, does Gilbreath's costume, rubbing together the sticks of tradition and transgression, play into the theatre of *Shrew*'s final scene and especially its centrepiece, where she performs the displaced, delayed sermon on the duties of husbands and wives? Just as The Peggy is inherited costume, the sermon is inherited discourse: remembering language from the *Book of Common Prayer*, the *Homily on Matrimony* and the *Homily against Disobedience and Wilful Rebellion*, it is structured like a man's speech. Copious, filled with *sententiae*, it is not just didactic but also *affective*, designed, like its precedents, to instruct and to *move*, to effect a metamorphosis upon both speaker and listeners.[38] Is a Kate-actor conscious of her radical role as preacher – or, given the play's pedagogical bent, as teacher? An early modern

---

34 Yvonne Gilbert, private communication, 15 May 2006. O'Connor, *Shakespearian Afterlives*, pp. 271–2. See *The Taming of A Shrew*, Sc. 3, 169–71; the aside travels into David Garrick's *Catherine and Petruccio*, the most popular *Shrew* play in England from 1754 to 1844 and in the United States until 1887.

35 I evoke the title of Deborah Tannen's *You're Wearing That?: Understanding Mothers and Daughters in Conversation* (New York, 2006).

36 See Hodgdon, 'Shopping in the Archives: Material Mnemonics', in *Shakespeare, Memory and Performance*, ed. Peter Holland (Cambridge, 2006).

37 Rowlands, *The Bride*, 36, line 628.

38 See Walter J. Ong, *Rhetoric, Romance, and Technology: Studies in the Interaction of Expression and Culture* (Ithaca, 1971), pp. 25, 29–30. The speech resembles that of another Kate, Kate Percy, whose 'O yet, for God's sake, go not to these wars' (*2 Henry IV*, 2.3.9–45) offers an example of a rhetorical exercise that persuades by emotion as well as proof, eliciting Northumberland's 'You do draw my spirits from me'.

16. Alexandra Gilbreath as Katherina in the final moments of *Taming of the Shrew*. Director: Gregory Doran. Royal Shakespeare Company, 2003.

Kate-actor might have known that she – or he-as-she – was invading the domain of masculine biblical interpretation by preaching, a potentially transgressive act associated with Lollardy.[39] But, like the early modern meanings surrounding Kate's cap, those associations, as well as the social (and theatrical) power the sermon accords to Kate, suiting the outspokenness of the shrew figure, are lost and gone, written over by another (more recently inherited) discourse in which 'sermon' has been replaced by 'speech of submission'. For what she's wearing – her petticoat tucked up to reveal her leggings – a substitute for breeches, one sign for the shrewish woman,[40] and the cap, flipped inside out as though to overturn being seen as Kate-the-tamed – offers a material complement to the ambiguities of the sermon and its surrounding socio-theatrical context. In the case of Doran's *Shrew* – performed in tandem with Fletcher's *The Woman's*

Prize, or the Tamer Tamed – it is tempting to read Gilbreath's 'breeches' as travelling costume, moving from *Tamer Tamed*'s recalcitrant wives ('Let's all wear breeches', says Livia (1.2.)[41]) back into *Shrew*, a

---

[39] Lollardy constituted a vaguely defined set of beliefs, but since the movement espoused the idea that all faithful persons were effectively 'good priests', it often was associated with women preaching. Women figures do preach in medieval verse drama (in, for instance, the Digby *Mary Magdalene*), but a difficult distinction pertains between preaching and teaching: in the early modern period, the authority women could claim to preach not only was limited but also was considered transgressive. See, for instance, Alcouin Blamires, 'Beneath the pulpit', in *The Cambridge Companion to Medieval Women's Writing*, ed. Carolyn Dinshaw and David Wallace (Cambridge, 2003), pp. 141–60.

[40] See, for example, Linda Woodbridge, *Women and the English Renaissance: Literature and the Nature of Womankind* (Urbana, IL, 1984), p. 217.

[41] John Fletcher, *The Tamer Tamed* (London, 2003), p. 12.

proleptic sign of Maria's role and as (just one more) marker of the inversions, reversals and suppose-ings that track throughout the play. It's a Janus-faced costume: a gift from one theatre, one figure of woman, to another: the past remembered in the present, the present using the past.

Yet, like so much else about theatrical *Shrews*, Gilbreath's dress also reads as a hybrid in more than one way. For, so dressed, she is neither one thing nor the other: neither the obedient wife of masculine desire nor the shrewish woman, bent on achieving what the Wife of Bath calls 'maistrie'. Being neither one nor the other also swerves back to remember not only the early modern boy actor of her role but also Bartholomew, the Lord's Page, recruited to play Sly's 'Madam Wife' (Ind. 2.13). Indeed, Gilbreath's costume invites reading her as a learned metamorphosis, puts that on her back. Remembered and embedded as costume image and silhouette, the story her dress re-enacts traces and retraces memory *and* metamorphosis. Saluting both patriarchy and anarchy, that dress speaks a kind of patranarchy: viewing rhetorical and theatrical inheritance as though through an anamorphic lens, both turn askance or awry, inviting spectators to see what they have not seen before. As Sonia Rykiel writes, 'Woman is institution and what's good about institution is to be able to break away from it'.[42] And Gilbreath's Kate did. For as the sermon proper concluded, with the words 'bound to serve, love, and obey' (5.2.165) and she then went on to ventriloquize the culture's prerogatives on her own terms, the play landed back in her hands.[43] In Doran's *Shrew*, obeying Shakespeare's costume logic remembered – and re-generated – an ending other than the (by now, overly familiar) one that can't forget the psychic destruction of the woman. The ring and the cap were all Gilbreath's Kate needed: she and Petruccio left the stage cheek by jowl.

EPILOGUE: ON BEHALF OF KATE AND THE ARCHIVE

At first, I mistook Gilbreath's wedding dress for a parody of Elizabeth I's – a dress fashioned for

and bespeaking a theatre of extraordinary political power. Yet in taking a deeper look, this time at Gilbreath's dress and under-dress, what surfaced was not a parodic knock-off but a costume fashioned in part from inherited apparel and past embodiments which opened up a space, an attitude and a history that offered access to another theatre of power. When a costume performs, it becomes material for interpretation: in this, it resembles a written text. In the case of Gilbreath's Kate-dressing, reading her costume worked, in tandem with Shakespeare's words, to discipline previous critical and theatrical performances. Yet, though obviously related, costume as written – what I have called Shakespeare's costume plot – and as performed, observed, interpreted, are not the same. As with the still troubled and troubling relationship between text and performance, one never *is* the other. Just as the dresses worn by Kate-actors differ, so do performances of her wedding sermon: each dress, each utterance enables but does not dictate interpretation. That's also, I think, the logic that drives *Shrew*'s ending. Speaking the words of the marriage ceremony is one thing, but the marriages generated from those words constitute quite different, often decidedly ambiguous, performances. If I were to inhabit Kate's last-scene space, my sermon would take as its text, 'Looking back'. Look closely at Shakespeare when, contravening generic conventions, he makes space for a wedding smack in the middle of a play. Something mischievous is going on. Look even more deeply when, breaking apart the narrative order of a sacrament, he puts the priest's sermon in a woman's mouth – and then, shrewdly, gives her even more to say.

On that note, a final word for archivists of Kate-fashioning:

Derrida writes that the archive is not just about the past but can structurally determine the very

---

[42] Rykiel, 'From *Celebration*', p. 108.
[43] Shaw sees the journey that both have undergone as being 'almost medieval . . . like all those journeys of people who go through a terrible ordeal . . . It's her play at the end. It's a very serious play'. Quoted in Rutter, *Clamorous Voices*, pp. 24–5.

question of the future.[44] Although what the archive currently saves is Kate's Big Dress – or her wedding dress – what it should be saving, to mark both past *and* future, is her broken-down wedding dress, still filthy dirty, Gilbreath's petticoat and brown trousers – and her (borrowed) cap, flipped inside out. None, perhaps, might celebrate the designer's artistry. Yet they would serve not just to take another look at one embodiment of Katherina Minola but also to tell the story of a woman who mistook herself for a shrew – a shrew in search of a hat who put on a surprising performance while dressing down her audience.

---

[44] Jacques Derrida, *Archive Fever*, trans. Eric Prenowitz (Chicago, 1995), pp. 90–1.

'WHEN MEN AND WOMEN ARE ALONE': FRAMING THE TAMING IN INDIA

RUTH VANITA

In this chapter, I argue that *The Taming of the Shrew* shows Kate being tamed not by her husband alone but by society's active collusion with him.[1] A man and a woman never are truly alone, as Petruccio's grammatical slippage in the phrase, 'when men and women are alone' inadvertently indicates. Through a close study of language, especially pronouns, singulars and plurals, I argue that the play represents and critiques 'men and women' – the weight of material conditions that structure gender and the power politics that uphold male domination – as always present in every particular male–female interaction, however private it may seem. I thus differ both from those who read the play as a celebration of a companionate marriage, and also from those who read it as a misogynist reinforcement of patriarchal ideology.[2] Through an examination of Elizabethan marriage manuals, I demonstrate that both Petruccio's taming methods and Kate's unquestioning obedience violate contemporaneous ideals of a good Christian marriage.

My reading evolved from a student production that I co-directed at Delhi University, India, in 1992, which cross-dressed the sexes, with women playing male parts and men female parts. In my work on Mariological images in *The Winter's Tale* and *Henry VIII*, I began to notice connections and verbal echoes between Shakespeare's representations of his first Kate and his last, which I explore at the end of the essay.

[1] All citations are from the Arden2 Edition of *The Taming of the Shrew*, ed. Brian Morris (London, 1981), and the Arden Edition of *King Henry VIII*, ed. R. A. Foakes (London, 1957).

[2] Among those who see the play and the taming of Kate as reflective of Shakespeare's concurrence with masculinist ideology are Linda Woodbridge, *Women and the English Renaissance: Literature and the Nature of Womankind, 1540–1620* (Urbana, 1984), pp. 221–2, n.22; Kate McLuskie, 'Feminist Deconstruction: The Example of Shakespeare's *Taming of the Shrew*', *Red Letters*, 12, 33–40; Lynda E. Boose, 'Scolding Brides and Bridling Scolds: Taming the Woman's Unruly Member', *Shakespeare Quarterly*, 42 (1991), 179–213; Leah Marcus, 'The Shakespearian Editor as Shrew-Tamer', *English Literary Renaissance*, 22 (1992), 177–200; and Emily Detmer, 'Civilizing Subordination: Domestic Violence and the *Taming of the Shrew*', *Shakespeare Quarterly*, 48 (1997), 273–94. A majority of critics (and an overwhelming majority of directors) view Kate and Petruccio's marriage as evolving into a loving and companionate mutuality. See, for example, Brian Morris, Introduction to the Arden2 Edition of *The Taming of the Shrew* (London, 1981), pp. 1–149; George R. Hibbard, '*The Taming of the Shrew*: A Social Comedy', in *Shakespearian Essays*, ed. Alwin Thaler and Norman Sanders (Knoxville, 1964); Robert Miola, 'The Influence of New Comedy on *The Comedy of Errors* and *The Taming of the Shrew*', in *Shakespeare's Sweet Thunder: Essays on the Early Comedies*, ed. Michael J. Collins (Newark, 1997); Margaret Lael Mikesell, '"Love Wrought these Miracles": Marriage and Genre in the Taming of the Shrew', in *The Taming of the Shrew: Critical Essays*, ed. Dana E. Aspinall (New York, 2002), pp. 106–29. A variant of this view involves the idea that the taming is an educative game in which Kate learns to participate. See Cecil C. Seronsy, '"Supposes" as the Unifying Theme in *The Taming of the Shrew*', *Shakespeare Quarterly*, 14 (1963), 15–30; John C. Bean, 'Comic Structure and the Humanizing of Kate in

'TRAGICAL-COMICAL'

Twentieth-century critics tend to assume that because *Taming* is classified as a comedy, generic convention requires the ending to be, in some sense, 'happy' – happy either for chauvinists or for feminists or perhaps even for both. Readings of Kate's last speech are heavily influenced by this notion of generic convention: if the ending is to be happy, the reasoning goes, Kate must speak the speech cheerfully, whether her pleasure arises from having learnt the art of capitulation or that of manipulation.[3]

As Amy Smith points out, the play's 'consistently unfavorable labelling of Petruccio's actions makes it more and more difficult to see the play as somehow supporting the dominance he claims'.[4] Nevertheless, many critics continue to appeal to the conventions of comedy; for example, Emily Detmer claims, 'To enjoy the comedy of the play, readers and viewers must work to see domestic violence from the point of view of an abuser – that is, they must minimalize the violence and, at the same time, justify its use', and Lynda Boose argues that Petruccio's misbehaviour at the wedding is 'dramatically arranged so as to make Kate's humiliation seem wildly comic'.[5]

When played for an audience familiar, from everyday experience and observation (as a modern Indian audience is), with the ways bridegrooms routinely humiliate brides and their families in the course of marriage negotiations, during weddings and after marriage, Petruccio's behaviour at his wedding seems darkly foreboding rather than 'wildly comic'. So also, Petruccio's soliloquy ('Thus have I politic'ly begun my reign') and the play's ending can be staged as grim without rendering the wooing scene or the rough-and-tumble between the servants, the tailor and Petruccio any less funny.[6]

Our 1992 production was staged at two Delhi University colleges – Miranda House, the women's college where I was then teaching, and Hindu College, where my co-director, Leela Gandhi, was then teaching. The audiences were mixed, ranging from large numbers of students for whom

English is a second language, to the faculty of Delhi University, including Renaissance scholars of international repute. Since we had retained Shakespeare's language throughout, adding nothing and subtracting little, we were pleasantly surprised to find that sections of the audience to whom this was an unfamiliar idiom were enthralled by the play, and even laughed at the right moments. This may be in part because the story of a father anxious to marry his daughters, of educated young women under tremendous pressure to marry, and of young men eager to marry from mercenary motives comes close to the lives of many Indians today.

Even though a number of exegeses have demonstrated how the play critically frames the taming through a range of devices, such as metatheatricality, irony and choric commentary ('he is more

---

The Taming of the Shrew' in *The Woman's Part: Feminist Criticism of Shakespeare*, ed. Carolyn Ruth Swift Lenz, Gayle Greene and Carol Thomas Neely (Urbana, 1980), pp. 65–78; Marianne L. Novy *Love's Argument: Gender Relations in Shakespeare* (Chapel Hill, 1984).

3 If enjoyment of comedy required adopting the point-of-view of one character or even a group of characters, and if comedies had to be consistently funny, little enjoyment could be had from such plays as *Measure for Measure* or *Troilus and Cressida*, also classified as comedies. The pleasure derived from such plays depends precisely on viewers' awareness that one person's comedy may be another person's tragedy. An awareness of that type led some editors to classify such plays as tragicomedies or dark comedies. Although the first folio divides the plays into tragedies, comedies and histories, Polonius's reference to 'tragical-historical, tragical-comical-historical-pastoral' (*Hamlet* 2.2.389) suggests that the division was not rigid even in the seventeenth century.

4 Amy Smith, 'Performing Marriage with a Difference: Wooing, Wedding, and Bedding in *The Taming of the Shrew*', *Comparative Drama*, 36 (2002), 289–320, 305.

5 Lynda Boose, 'Scolding Brides and Bridling Scolds', 193, and Emily Detmer, 'Civilizing Subordination', 274.

6 Gary Schneider argues that 'the theatre becomes transformed into a site of social control' because audience 'participation' is encouraged by such devices as Petruccio's soliloquies. 'The Public, the Private, and the Shaming of the Shrew', in *Studies in English Literature, 1500–1900*, 42 (2002), 235–58, 252. This ignores the fact that Kate also has a soliloquy lamenting the injustice done to her; furthermore, if audiences always sympathize with soliloquies, are we to assume that all audiences sympathize with Iago rather than Othello and Desdemona?

shrew than she'), critical and popular opinion has not yet crystallized into a full recognition of the play's presentation of the taming as a tragic social reality. This is perhaps in part because material conditions for women in the West have changed so drastically since Shakespeare's time that it is psychologically difficult for viewers or scholars in the West to jettison modern ideas of individual choice when assessing Kate's last speech.

DOWRY AND THE DYNAMICS OF FAMILY-ARRANGED MARRIAGE

With the virtual disappearance of dowry and family-arranged marriage from the modern West, most Euro-Americans do not have first-hand experience of marriage as a nakedly monetary transaction. The increased privatization of domestic life among most segments of the population means that the brutal realities of wife- (or girlfriend-)beating and murder, though still widely prevalent, are not visible in daily life to most of those who study and watch Shakespeare, except perhaps in television melodramas, ranging from the occasional O. J. Simpson trial to police shows like 'Law and Order'.

In modern India, though, members of the college-educated public routinely participate in the drama of family-arranged marriage and the exchange of dowries, and often witness male violence against women, either in their own extended social circles or among the poor who work as domestic help in almost all middle-class homes. Petruccio's behavior, therefore, did not seem to our students at Delhi University to require elaborate explanations. His repeated announcements of his desire to marry a wife with a large dowry is similar to that of many well-bred, highly educated young men in modern India. The dynamic of Petruccio's relationship both with Kate and with her kin is admittedly at the more extreme end of the spectrum of bridegroom behaviour, yet is not unfamiliar to people living in a society where dowry remains normative.

Nor does Baptista appear to Indians an especially oppressive father, as some critics have made him out to be. Middle-class Indian fathers of daughters live in great anxiety lest they be unable to fulfil their duty to marry their daughters well; they also make efforts to endow their daughters with whatever degree of education and accomplishment the marriage market demands for their class, and to display these endowments to the world. Education, however, must be accompanied by the more solid endowments of a dowry, which usually includes a cash component. Also, like Baptista, most fathers insist that older daughters marry before younger daughters do (and older sons before younger sons). This social convention puts considerable emotional pressure on older siblings to marry unsuitable spouses; this is especially the case if their younger siblings are already in love and anxious to marry.

Conversely, young men often seek out girls who have no brothers, hoping not only to acquire dowry but also to inherit all of the girls' parental property. Petruccio is not the only dowry-seeker; Hortensio points out, 'there be good fellows in the world, and a man could light on them, would take her [Katherine] with all faults, and money enough' (1.1.129–30). All of Bianca's suitors (except the wholly unsuitable Gremio) also discuss the dowry question with Baptista. Informing Vincentio of his son's marriage to Bianca, Petruccio assures him that the girl 'is of good esteem, / Her dowry wealthy' (4.5.64–65). The suitors' offers of large marriage settlements are balanced by their expectations of land and money to be acquired in dowry and inheritance.

Petruccio's behaviour on his wedding day is calculated to shame Katherine and also to humiliate her family and friends. It reinscribes not only the man–woman hierarchy but also the derived hierarchy between husband's and wife's families. In India today, where weddings usually take place at the bride's home, the bridegroom and his kin frequently humiliate her family by behaving inappropriately at the wedding – getting drunk, insulting her relatives and criticizing the wedding arrangements. Indian newspapers report occasional cases of a bride protesting such behaviour by rejecting the groom at the altar. More commonly, the bride and her family silently endure the mistreatment, fearing disgrace if the marriage is called off.

This pattern of endurance continues after marriage, when women's families pressure them to put up with mistreatment and deprivation. The fear of having a divorced daughter return to the natal home leads women's parents and kin to pander to unreasonable sons-in-law. This often results in escalating violence against the woman, which may or may not culminate in her death. Kate's lament that she is 'starv'd for meat, giddy for lack of sleep' (4.3.9) is one that I often heard from married women in India, when I worked for thirteen years at *Manushi*, a women's organization in New Delhi, of which I was a co-founder. Women complained that their food was strictly rationed out, was insufficient and of poor quality, that they were sleep-deprived and were not permitted to communicate with their natal families. Such women yearned for brief visits to their parental homes, where they obtained respite from suffering, and would do much to be permitted those visits. Petruccio's flinging away of food and breaking the dishes that contain it is also reminiscent of a standard type of bullying behaviour by husbands, attested both in real-life cases and in Indian literature and cinema.

It is important, though, to emphasize that such behavior is not normative for men. That men can get away with bad behavior demonstrates their power; however, this conduct continues to be socially disapproved of and condemned by religious authorities as misbehaviour. I argue that this was the case even in Shakespeare's England, and I demonstrate, later in this chapter, that Elizabethan marriage manuals unequivocally condemn both husbandly discourtesy and wifely obedience to husbands' unrighteous commands.

HIGHLIGHTING POWER

Traditional theatre in India, like Shakespeare's theatre, is often acted by all-male casts, and women's schools and colleges frequently stage plays with all-female casts. Our decision to cross-dress the sexes, enlisting four men from two predominantly men's

colleges (Hindu and St Stephen's), was unprecedented and had the effect of the male actors being outnumbered by female actors. The power dynamics within the cast collided with the power dynamic between the characters they played.[7]

The young woman who played Petruccio was under five feet tall, and the best of our actors. She had tremendous energy and dominated the stage like a small dynamo. Contrasted with the height of the male actors, this generated a dynamic that foregrounded gender as based on social power, not on physical strength. By visually detaching gender from sex, it highlighted the absurdity of gender-based roles.

We made no attempt to have the actors 'pass' — the men wore bonnets but not false hair so their short hair showed as did Petruccio's ponytail. Petruccio and other major male characters did not wear fake facial hair (the two old men wore beards to indicate their age). This defamiliarized the social subordination of women and the macho swaggering of Petruccio, making both appear simultaneously ridiculous and horrifying. Since the men playing women were much taller than the women playing men, the female 'weakness' to which Kate refers in her last speech came across not as physical weakness but as the powerlessness of women in male-dominated society.

We staged the taming scenes as they are written, showing Kate tortured by starvation and sleep deprivation. We did not play these scenes for laughs as they are often played, but demonstrated Kate's

---

[7] The male actors initially felt somewhat uneasy at having to enter an all-women environment (women's colleges in India have an all-women faculty too) for rehearsals. This discomfort was heightened by having to play female roles. But as the production progressed and the cast cohered, this discomfort almost disappeared in the fun they all had together. The young men seemed even to enjoy the opportunity they had to wear pretty clothes and make-up. The first time I actually understood the much-discussed beauty of young men was at the dress rehearsal, when I saw these boys as brides in the wedding scene. The bridal attire highlighted the awkward vulnerability of male youth in a way that made me understand Shakespeare's and Barnfield's use of the epithet 'sweet' for their beloveds. The girls on the other hand thoroughly enjoyed the situation from the start.

anguish and isolation in her marital household after her kin have virtually abandoned her. Petruccio's soliloquy, where he gloats over his plan to tame Kate, was played on a darkened stage with one highlight, and his shadow was lengthened to emphasize its sinister effect. The sun and moon scene where Kate capitulates was similarly stylized, with all four actors in a row, backs to the audience, in a dim blue light. They spoke their lines in a monotone, and moved a step at a time, in a synchronized fashion.

FRAMING THE TAMING

Historically, most directors have chosen to drop the Prologue, although, in recent years, this trend has been partially reversed. Dropping the Prologue gives the taming story normative status, whereas retaining the Prologue renders the taming story a farce staged in the course of an elaborate practical joke. The Lord who plays the joke on Sly is probably the only character in Shakespeare who arranges a cross-dressing incident with the intention of creating sexual confusion. He presents his cross-dressed Page as the befuddled Sly's wife and enjoys the ensuing flirtation. A patron of theatre, he himself flirts with the male actors, and is given to hedonistic enjoyment with an all-male entourage. Our retaining the Prologue in its entirety framed the story of gendered power within a story of same-sex flirtation that highlights the performativity of gender.

Although the text does not mark an exit for Sly, directors who retain the Prologue often have Sly exit or fall asleep after his last lines at the end of Act 1, scene 1.[8] We chose to keep Sly onstage and awake throughout the play. He became increasingly interested in the action, and increasingly sympathetic to Katharina, conveying his sympathy through gestures. Finally, in Act 5, we had him don a bonnet and skirt onstage and stride into the play as the Widow who marries Hortensio.

Sly was played by a big boney young man, a talented actor whom the audience loved, and whose gestures encouraged them to sympathize with Kate. His metamorphosis into the Widow was greeted with cheers from the audience. Hortensio was played by the same actor who played the Lord. Thus, his wedding to the obstreperous Widow who was also Sly, had the double effect of fulfilling the homoerotic suggestiveness of the Lord's and Sly's desires in the Prologue, and also making clear, as the text itself does, that the Widow and Bianca actively resist the taming to which Kate succumbs.

Before this production, I had never been able to reconcile *Taming* with my understanding of the rest of Shakespeare's oeuvre; the production helped me grapple with and appreciate the play's complexity. It was through this production that I first noticed how syntax works to undercut and complicate the surface meaning of speech in this play; later in this chapter, I return to this dimension of the play's critique of the taming. However, the critique can work only if the taming violates social and cultural ideals, as I believe that it does.

IS THE TAMING NORMATIVE?

There appears to be a critical consensus that the tenor of the play and of Kate's last speech conforms to the marriage manuals. Some defenders of Petruccio justify his behaviour as warranted by Kate's conduct and argue that his antics are carefully planned to educate her for her own good.[9] They claim that Petruccio's educational strategies exemplify the norms that Elizabethan marriage manuals uphold. On the other hand, some critics argue that Petruccio's adherence to the marriage manuals shows that the play conforms to dominant Elizabethan beliefs about male–female relations that Shakespeare endorses.[10]

---

[8] Margie Burns suggests that the Induction characters 'become *lost in the play*'. She and others speculate as to which actors doubled parts in the Induction and the play. See Margie Burns, 'The Ending of The Shrew', in *The Taming of the Shrew: Critical Essays*, ed. Aspinall, pp. 84–105.

[9] A typical example is Anne Barton's Introduction to *Taming* in *The Riverside Shakespeare*, ed. Blakemore Evans (Boston, 1974), pp. 106–9.

[10] See John Bean, 'Comic Structure and the Humanizing of Kate', and Marion D. Perret, 'Petruccio: The Model Wife', *Studies in English Literature, 1500–1900*, 23 (1983), 223–35.

Such critics have been unjust to the marriage manuals. While the manuals do uphold an ideal of gendered hierarchy within companionate marriage, Petruccio's behaviour consistently violates the norms of husbandly conduct and Christian mutuality constructed in the manuals.

Petruccio's violations of appropriate conduct begin at the wedding. *The Christian State of Matrimony*, by Heinrich Bullinger, issued in 1541 and reprinted several times through the rest of the sixteenth century, describes the quiet and pious way in which the couple and their guests should conduct themselves at the wedding:

And let them take theyre honest kynfolkes and neyghbours with them, and in good season, soberly, discritly, lowly, as in the sight of God, without pomp, manerly, and in comely honest raiment, without pride, without drumming and piping, let them go into the house of the Lord, and there heare the Lords word, make their faythfull prayer unto God with feruentnes, and stedfast beliefe receaue the blessing, and then manerly and with silence to go home againe.[11]

Petruccio curses, swearing by God's wounds, knocks the vicar and his book to the ground, throws wine in the sexton's face, and creates a ruckus that embarrasses guests into leaving the church. His raiment is neither comely nor honest, and is an insult to the church, as is his violent behaviour. Remarkably, modern critics are so busy disputing whether or not his behaviour is justified as a taming method that they ignore its blatantly unchristian and impious aspects.

Critics tend to cite those portions of the manuals that stress gender inequality, such as the injunction that the wife should comply with her husband's moods. However, the manuals also stress that each partner should be sensitive to the other's state of mind. Thus, Bullinger advises: 'let ech one learne to be acquainted with the nature and condicions of the other, and to apply him self according to the same, in as much as they must needes dwel together, one enjoy another, & the one dye and live with the other'.[12] He criticizes husbands who, like Petruccio, are merry when their wives are sad: 'Sometyme when the wife is sad and disquieted, then wyll the husband haue to much sport and pastime of her.'[13] Likewise, *A brefe and a playne declaratyon of the dewty of maried folks*, issued in English in 1553 and again in 1588, reproaches husbands, who, 'when the wyfe is sadde and disquieted then with spiteful wordes & wanton fashions, so provoking hir to anger'.[14] Petruccio is spiteful in precisely this way: 'The more my wrong, / The more his spite appears' (4.3.2).

Bullinger warns that the first cohabitation after marriage is crucial to conjugal happiness: 'For if at the beginning of mariage there chaunce such rudenes and uncomely discord, then wyll it always be breakyng out.'[15] He advises each to do what pleases the other, to express displeasure rather than foster it in secret, and to listen patiently when the other expresses displeasure: 'there is no maner of thing that more strongly kepeth and increaseth love matrimonial, then doth curtesy, kindnes, plainnes, & gentlenes, in wordes, maners and deedes'.[16] *Counsel to the husband: to the wife instruction* (1608), by Ste B, states: 'The husband also must not disdaine to bee counselled by his wife, to heare her reasons, and to waigh her words.'[17]

The manuals insist that order and quietness are the qualities of a Christian home, and patience, gentleness and humility those of a good husband.

Perret goes so far as to argue that Petruccio models for Kate the way an ideal wife should behave, by serving her food and giving instructions to the servants. She does not say whether an ideal wife was required to beat up servants and tradesmen, or prevent her husband from eating and sleeping.

[11] Heinrich Bullinger, *The Christian State of Matrimony* (London, 1575), fo. 59.

[12] Bullinger, *Matrimony*, fo. 63.

[13] Bullinger, *Matrimony*, fo. 70.

[14] *A brefe and a playne declaratyon of the dewty of maried folkes: gathered out of the holy scriptures, and set forth in the almayne tonge by Hermon archbyshop of Colayne, whiche wylled all the housholdes of his flocke to haue the same in their bedchambers as a mirror or glasse dayly to loke in, wherby they might know and do their dewties eche vnto others, and lede a godly, quiet and louing life togethers, and newly translated into ye Englishe tonge by Hans Dekyn* (London, 1553), fo. 8.

[15] Bullinger, *Matrimony*, fo. 62.

[16] Bullinger, *Matrimony*, fo. 70.

[17] Ste B, *Counsel to the husband: to the wife instruction* (London, 1608), p. 85.

Even Petruccio's best friend could not call him patient, gentle or humble. Indeed, some of his actions shock his admirer Hortensio while his servants consistently describe him as a raging terror.

Most important, the manuals do not permit a husband to behave tyrannously even towards a wife who misbehaves, nor do they advocate food and sleep deprivation as educational methods. Although the manuals view the husband as ruler and the wife as subject, they carefully distinguish between good rule and tyranny:

even as Christe norisheth and techeth hys churche, so oughte everye oneste husebande (also) lovyngly and gentlye to informe and instructe his wyfe.

For in manye thynges (saith saynte Peter) God hath made the men stronger then the women, not to rage upon them & to be tyrans unto them, but to helpe them and bere theyr wekenes. Be curtes therefore (sayth he) and wynne them to Christe, and overcome them with kyndnes that of loue they may obey the ordynans that GOD made betwene man and wyfe.[18]

One manual even modifies this metaphor by pointing out that if the husband has the powers of a ruler the wife has the rights and freedoms of a citizen: 'She is a free Citizen in thine owne house, and hath taken the peace of thee, the first day of her marriage, to hold thy handes till she release thee agayne.'[19]

Kindness is the hallmark of the Christian husband, as of Christ:

But to the intent that the husband shal not turne his autority unto tiranny, therfore doth Paul declare after what maner and how the husband is the wives head. The husband (saith he) is the wives head, even as Christ is the head of the congregacion . . . Therfore must the husbands be head unto the wives in like maner, to shew them like kindnes, & after the same fashion to guide them, and rule them with discretion for their preseruation, & not with force and wylfulnes to entreate them.[20]

Petruccio mocks this Christian rhetoric of kindness when he boastfully claims that he has found a 'way to kill a wife with kindness', and compares her to domestic animals and household commodities. In contrast, the manuals compare women to

precious, delicate vessels made of glass and gold, which must be gently handled precisely because they are fragile: 'As we do not handle glasses like pots, because they are weaker vesseles, but touch them nicelie, and softely for fear of crackes, so a man must intreate his wife with gentelenesse and softnesse . . .'[21] Using the same metaphor, Ste B instructs men not to 'oppresse' their wives.[22]

The manuals insist that, in accordance with Biblical injunctions like 'A soft answer turneth away wrath', an angry wife must be addressed with patience and mildness: 'Let us therefore have humylytye in our heartes: for as a wyse man loketh well to hys owne goinges, even so pleasante are the wordes spoken in due season, whyche moueth the woman in hir wrath unto pacyence.'[23] Petruccio's behaviour as a husband constitutes an outright contradiction of the norms of husbandly behaviour in companionate marriage.

IS KATE'S OBEDIENCE 'GOOD, ONESTE AND COMELY'?

Elizabethans knew that several wives, both Catholic and Protestant, had chosen to be martyred for their faith, in disobedience to their husbands' wishes, just as many subjects had chosen to disobey monarchs' religious instructions and to suffer death as the consequence of this disobedience. They were aware that obedience, whether a wife's or a subject's, ought not to violate Christian virtue. Indeed, for a husband or a king to require obedience in doing evil, such as lying or blaspheming, was defined as

---

[18] *A brefe and a playne declaratyon of the dewty of maried folks*, fo. 8.

[19] Henrie Smith, *A preparatiue to mariage The summe whereof was spoken at a contract, and inlarged after* (London, 1591), p. 54.

[20] Bullinger, *Matrimony*, fos. 65, 66.

[21] Henrie Smith, *A preparatiue to marriage*, p. 53.

[22] 'Our most pretious vessels (whether glasse or gold) are commonly the weakest, by reason either of nature or workmanship, & these we most precisely order, not roughly or carelessely . . . shew not your rough and manlike courage (like Lamech) to your wife, but to your enemie. You are the couering of her eies, which shall defend her, not oppresse her.' Ste B, *Counsel to the husband: to the wife instruction*, p. 94.

[23] *A brefe and a playne declaratiue of the dewty of maried folks*, fo. 8.

tyranny, which a wife or a subject would be justified in resisting.

Obedience to the husband 'as unto the Lord' was consistently interpreted to mean that the wife was to obey only in doing good, not in wrongdoing. *A brefe and a playne declaration* states, 'the wyfe muste be obedyent unto hyr husbande as unto Christ hym selfe, whereoute it foloweth that the sayde obedyens extendeth not unto anye wyckednes or euyll, but unto that whyche is good, oneste and comely'.[24] Ste B says that if he 'shall command her things unlawfull and uncomely, she is not bound to obey herein, neither can he restraine her, or if he shall do it by violence, she is excused'.[25]

Petruccio requires Kate to act in discourteous and socially inappropriate ways and he also requires her to lie, a clearly unchristian act. Not surprisingly, twentieth-century critics have failed to take this violation seriously. I suggest that the sun and moon scene is constructed to demonstrate the dangerous consequences of exacting and acceding absolute obedience.[26]

In Elizabethan poetic rhetoric, the sun and the moon retain some of the divine qualities attributed to them by the Greeks and are among the most important visible signs of God's power.[27] Associated with divine glory and saintly perfection, they had not long before served as tropes to celebrate the Virgin Mary's splendour, and the sun in particular was also a trope associated with Christ. These associations with royalty and divinity are found in other plays: thus, Cleopatra compares Antony's face to the heavens and his eyes to the sun and moon, and in *Henry VIII*, the dying queen has a vision of angels whose faces cast a thousand beams upon her, 'like the sun'(4.2.89).

Petruccio pits himself against the natural and the sacred order of things when he tries to control the meaning of the sun: 'Now by my mother's son, and that's myself / It shall be moon, or star or what I list' (4.5.6–7). The near-blasphemous nature of this claim and of his arrogation of the son/sun pun, normally used to glorify Christ, is highlighted by his reference to God in the opening line in this scene, 'Come on, a God's name, once more toward our father's' (4.5.1). Petruccio's attempts to play God begin with his insisting that he will control time: 'It shall be what o'clock I say it is' (4.3.192), and Hortensio's choric closing comment points to the Phaethon-like presumptuousness of this: 'Why, so this gallant will command the sun' (4.3.193).

The sombre rhythms of the initial exchange in the sun and moon scene foreground the seriousness of what is going on. Petruccio compels Katherine to perjure herself deliberately, and even draws attention to the perjury lest the audience miss it: 'Nay, then you lie. It is the blessed sun' (4.5.17).

The moon, being conventionally feminine, was associated with female fickleness as well as lunacy. Even as she submits, Katherine comments, 'the moon changes even as your mind' (4.5.20). This contemptuous choric comment (Petruccio does not object to it, which suggests that it is for the audience's rather than his benefit) undercuts Petruccio's much-vaunted manliness, and alerts the audience to the fact that Katherine, submitting to the 'half lunatic' she has married, is acting under compulsion, not from a change of heart.

OBEYING GOD OR THE DEVIL?

Katherine's obedience, then, is not 'honest' as it leads her to tell lies, not 'good' since it serves no useful purpose, and not 'comely' insofar as it is socially disruptive and foolish. Her participation in Petruccio's insulting of Vincentio by addressing him as a young marriageable woman anticipates the violent mistreatment to which other young people will later subject Vincentio. As Hortensio notes,

---

[24] *A brefe and a playne declaratyon of the dewty of maried folks*, fo. 4. *The Christian State of Matrimony* uses almost identical words, when discussing the apostle's injunction of wifely obedience: 'And addeth thereto, that they must esteeme this obedience none otherwise, then if it were shewed unto God hymselfe. Whereout it foloweth that the said obedience extendeth not unto wickedness and euil, but unto that which is good, honest, and comely' (fo. 65).

[25] Ste B, *Counsel to the husband: to the wife instruction*, p. 65.

[26] The play departs from its folk sources in using the sun and the moon rather than animals in this reality test.

[27] For Hindus, both are Gods.

'A will make the man mad, to make the woman of him' (4.5.35).

Henry Smith, whose manual was developed from a wedding sermon and issued twice in 1591, goes so far as to say that if the wife obeys the husband in wrongdoing, she obeys him not as the Lord but as the devil: 'Paul saith, *Wiues submit your selues unto your husbands as to the lord*. Shewing that she should regard his wil as the Lords wil, but withal as the Lord commandeth only that which is good & right: so she should obey her husband in good & right, or else she doth not obey him as the Lord, but as the tempter.'[28] This recalls the post-wedding exchange between Gremio and Tranio, where Gremio, who has witnessed the wedding, points out that Petruccio is 'a devil, a devil, a very fiend'; Tranio, who was not at the wedding, retorts that 'she's a devil, a devil, the devil's dam', and Gremio insists that she is 'a lamb, a dove, a fool to him' (3.2.153–5).

Petruccio and Kate's contemptuous treatment of the old mirrors the violence that other vulnerable beings, such as Kate and the servants, suffer at Petruccio's hands, and the violence to animals that Petruccio boastfully describes as manly behaviour. It is certainly not 'comely' for a woman to insult an elderly man of her father's age in the way that Kate, at Petruccio's behest, does. This is a continuation of Kate's earlier rudeness to her own father, which was mirrored by Petruccio's rudeness to him.[29] Her later rudeness to Bianca also continues her earlier ill treatment of her. Her flinging down her cap at Petruccio's command is, as the other women comment, 'silly' and 'foolish'. It is socially inappropriate, serves no purpose and is thus not 'comely'. Petruccio does not cure Kate's 'devilish spirit' (2.1.26); he merely uses it to his own ends, much as a vicious trainer may teach a ferocious dog to attack at command.

ARE 'MEN AND WOMEN' EVER ALONE? SINGULARS AND PLURALS

A grammatical oddity in one of Petruccio's speeches first suggested to me the way rhetoric pulls against itself in this play. After the wooing scene,

Petruccio gives Kate's father and others a wholly fictional description of how Kate, when they were alone, hung about his neck, giving him kisses and vows of love, till she won him to her love. He continues: ''Tis a world to see / How tame, when men and women are alone, / A meacock wretch can make the curstest shrew' (2.1.304–6). The language begs the question: a man and a woman can be alone together, but in what sense can 'men and women' be alone? Does not the plural preclude aloneness?

Petruccio here appeals to the stereotype of women's (hetero)sexual voraciousness. He claims that women pretend to be sexually modest in public, even enacting that modesty through pretended aversion to marriage but when left alone with a man, even the most apparently man-hating woman becomes tame simply because she is overcome with uncontrollable desire for him. Petruccio slips up, though, when he says that this taming occurs 'when men and women are alone'. From this plural, he proceeds to singulars: 'meacock wretch' and 'veriest shrew'. As the audience, who witnessed the wooing scene, knows, Kate was finally tamed and silenced not by her desire or even his desire, but by Petruccio's declaration of men's social power, embodied in the agreement between her father and himself: 'Thus in plain terms: your father hath consented / That you shall be my wife; your dowry 'greed on; / And will you, nill you, I will marry you' (2.1.262–4).

Kate and Petruccio are not alone in the wooing scene, any more than a modern Indian young couple is alone in the living room when the families who arrange the match briefly retreat into the next room. They are hedged in by gendered

---

[28] Henrie Smith, *A preparatiue to marriage*, p. 66.

[29] Some critics read this ill treatment of the old as an anti-paternalist strain in the play: Marianne L. Novy, 'Patriarchy and Play in *The Taming of the Shrew*', *English Literary Renaissance*, 9 (1991), 264–80; Karen Newman, 'Renaissance Family Politics and Shakespeare's *The Taming of the Shrew*', in *English Literary Renaissance*, 16 (1986), 86–100; Thomas Moisan, '"What's that to you?" or Facing Facts: Anti-Paternalist Chords and Social Discords in *The Taming of the Shrew*', in *The Taming of the Shrew: Critical Essays*, ed. Aspinall, 255–76.

expectations and compulsions, most visibly incorporated in Kate's father and in Bianca's impatient suitors who intrude into the supposedly private conversation without warning and whose collusion is crucial to Petruccio's success.

The audience's presence itself reinforces this societal permeation of supposed aloneness. The presence of 'men and women' when a man and woman are alone strengthens the man but weakens the woman. When Katherine is alone with Petruccio in the wooing scene, the assumed presence of all 'women' constrains her; she can expect no support from women – there is no love lost between her and the one other woman we have seen. Petruccio, however, is boosted by the presence of all 'men', and specifically by the hovering presence of Baptista and of Bianca's suitors who have provided him with financial backing.

When Baptista appears and asks him how he has fared, he accurately answers, 'How but well, sir? How but well? / It were impossible I should speed amiss' (2.1.275–6). Since 'wealth is burden of [his] wooing dance', (1.2.67), male privilege embedded in the marriage system makes it 'impossible' for him to fail.

'OUR WEAKNESS': PRONOUNS AND THE BATTLE OF THE SEXES

The way pronouns are used in this play works against the opinion, popular today, that Kate and Petruccio's marriage evolves into loving intimacy. Petruccio uses first-person plural pronouns, 'we' and 'us', a dozen to fifteen times, to refer to himself and Kate as a couple. This usage, almost always, functions to impose his will on an unwilling Katherine by subsuming them both in a unit wherein, to apply Blackstone's notorious phrasing, 'husband and wife are one, and that one is the husband'.

His first use of the first-person plural is a barefaced lie, told to Baptista, and is symptomatic of his later uses of the first person plural: 'And to conclude, we have 'greed so well together, / That upon Sunday is the wedding day' (2.1.290–1). Kate immediately contradicts him, splitting up his 'we'

into the first and second person singular: 'I'll see thee hang'd on Sunday first' (2.2.292). Petruccio, then, as noted above, tells a lie to construct himself and Kate as a heterosexual couple inhabiting a private sexual space that no one else can witness. This fiction enables him to silence Kate's 'I'.

However, in the long soliloquy where he outlines his taming strategy for the audience, Petruccio nowhere mentions love and nowhere uses the matrimonial 'we'. Instead, he uses the first person singular 'I' throughout this brutal speech, and the third person singular 'she' for Kate. In this speech, he never mentions her name; she has become an undifferentiated 'wife' and 'shrew' who is to be tormented into submission, like the unfortunate birds used in hunting. In this soliloquy, 'we' is used only to address men as a collective entity: 'Another way I have to man my haggard . . . to watch her, as we watch these kites' (4.1.180–2). Here, the wife is the tormented bird, and men who torment both wives and birds constitute the self-confident 'we'.

Petruccio uses the matrimonial 'we' only to bully Kate, but when he is alone that pretence drops away. Kate sees through this pretence of conjugal love, as is clear in the series of first and third person singulars in her answering near-soliloquy that opens the next scene in Petruccio's house: 'The more my wrong, the more his spite appears . . . / And that which spites me more than all these wants, / He does it under name of perfect love' (4.3.2, 11–12).

Kate uses the first-person plural only twice in the play in a way that includes (but is not restricted to) herself and Petruccio. Both times, she does so to request Petruccio to allow her and the others in the group to proceed with an action in which she has an interest. The first time is in the sun and moon scene, when Petruccio threatens to abandon the trip to her father's house (where she is anxious to go, to get some food and sleep). Hortensio uses the first person plural, referring to the whole group, to advise Kate to lie, 'Say as he says, or we shall never go' (4.5.11). Kate agrees, 'Forward, I pray, since we have come so far, / And be it moon, or sun, or what you please' (4.5.12–13). Here, the 'we,' referring to the group, not the couple alone, is framed by herself as the pleading 'I' and him as the bullying 'you'.

The second occasion is very similar and occurs at the end of the next scene, when Kate wants to proceed towards her father's house: 'Husband, let's follow to see the end of this ado' (5.1.130). The 'us' in 'let's' includes herself, Petruccio, Grumio and the other servants. Petruccio threatens to make them all return home unless she kisses him in the street, which she is embarrassed to do. Kate has now learnt the lesson of the preceding sun and moon scene, and acquiesces, 'Nay, I will give thee a kiss. Now pray thee, love, stay' (5.1.136). This is the only occasion in the play when Kate uses a term of endearment to address Petruccio, and those who argue that the marriage develops into a loving companionship rely heavily on it. I do not contest the fact that affection can develop in a relationship based on compulsion and domination (as it may in a master–servant relationship like that of Petruccio and Grumio), and that this line suggests that this type of affection may be developing between Kate and Petruccio (although it is also possible to read her behavior here as manipulative). But this one very brief exchange, itself resulting from a battle of wills, is not sufficient to counter the entire weight of the play's representation of Petruccio as a dowry-seeking bully who flies in the face of the marriage manuals' ideal of a Christian husband as a gentle, patient and courteous protector of his wife.

KATE'S 'WE': WOMEN AND THE FIRST-PERSON PLURAL

Kate's last speech is notable for its complete avoidance of the first-person plural 'we' to refer to herself and Petruccio.[30] It throughout divides women and men, constructing them as two separate orders of being who are compelled to enter into a transaction, either peacefully or with hostility. In the gendered economy as she constructs it, women can choose either to wage futile battle or to acknowledge their inevitable defeat.

Since the speech is addressed to the other women, our 1992 production had all three women (acted by men) come to the front of the stage and face the audience, with the lights on them, while the men (acted by women) sat in the background under dimmer light. The speech was dramatized as the expression of a pragmatic philosophy of survival in a society where the only other option offered to Kate – that of being a despised old maid – is less attractive than the one of subordinated wife that she accepts. Towards the end, Kate assumed a crucifixion posture, her outstretched arms supported by the other two women.

It is now well established that the status of single women declined in post-Reformation England, after the respectable alternative to married life provided by convents was violently repressed and marriage came to be exalted as the highest type of existence for all, especially for women. Virginity, once a jewel, was now a liability, to be traded in a buyers' market. Earlier, religious advisers had assured women that virginity, unlike physical beauty, retained its value forever; now, young women were warned that virginity was a commodity that rapidly grew stale. As Rosalind tells Phebe, 'Sell when you can, you are not for all markets' (*AYLI* 3.5.60). That Kate knows and fears the humiliations of being an old maid helps explain her acceptance of her lowly status in marriage.

Much has been made of the way Kate's last speech echoes the marriage manuals and conventional Elizabethan wisdom about marriage. But the speech is radically different from the marriage manuals in at least one respect – while the manuals emphasize the natural mutuality of love between husband and wife, Kate constructs love entirely as a transaction. The wife's love is mentioned twice, both times as something the wife owes her husband, along with obedience, as part of the transaction that constitutes marriage. This is very different from the love propounded by the marriage manuals, which follow the Bible in adjuring the husband to love the wife as his own flesh, and insist on

---

[30] As Margie Burns points out, 'little serious analysis has been devoted to the language of the speech itself; most criticism has its starting point in the supposed tenor of the speech and then addresses itself to justifying or debunking the supposed message' (90). I agree, though my examination of the language leads to a different conclusion from Burns's.

the naturalness of this love, holding up animals as examples.

The first time Kate mentions a woman's love, she defines it as a 'tribute' and an inadequate payment of the 'debt' a wife owes her husband for working to maintain and care for her: 'Thy husband is thy lord . . . / one that cares for thee, / And for thy maintenance. . . / And craves no other tribute at thy hands / But love, fair looks, and true obedience; / Too little payment for so great a debt' (5.2.147–55). The second time she mentions love, the element of constraint is even clearer, since she says wives 'are bound to serve, love and obey' (5.2.165). In this formulation, a wife's love is not freely given but is enforced by the marriage contract.

Ste B is one of the few manual writers to acknowledge, as Kate does, that, in the last analysis, the wife's obedience depends not on love or duty but on the husband's power. In his 1608 manual, having held up the ideal of a husband and wife who truly love one another and strive to anticipate each other's desires, he admits that there are, nevertheless, some 'unreasonable men and women' – men who will 'rule tyrannouslie' and women who will 'liue contentiouslie'. In such cases, the husband may insist that he will love his wife only if she first obeys him, and she may say she will obey only if he first loves her. Ste B concludes that, in such unfortunate cases, the woman will have to give in because

as we say in our proverbe, the wrong end of the staffe will be her parte; that is, it is in vaine (in this case) for the wife to striue with the husband, which is the weaker with the stronger; the horse (pardon me good wiues to use so base a similitude) the horse (I say) with him that hath the bridle and is able to sit fast.[31]

Considering the question of whether a woman can dissuade her husband from doing unlawful things or can persuade him to do good, he concludes, in terms very similar to those of Kate's speech, that though she may try, she really is powerless to influence him if he chooses not to be influenced:

hee will do whatsoeuer list (lawfull, honest, and indifferent) and shee cannot hinder him. So that looke how

vaine a thing it is, for one to striue with another, that is bound hand and foote, and cannot wagge a finger; so vaine a thing it is for the wife (who for every thing must depend upon her husbands will) to striue and wrestle with him.[32]

It is this bleak view of heterosexual coupledom that many modern critics and directors find hard to swallow at face value. It is a much grimmer view than the overall view propounded by the marriage manuals, wherein the natural and loving oneness of husband and wife is stressed along with gendered hierarchy. Kate's speech realistically assesses the social gulf between men and women, and does not balance this out with any sense of husband and wife being 'one flesh'. Indeed, in her speech, the flesh divides men and women instead of uniting them – women's soft, weak bodies are in conformity with their soft hearts and lie comfortably at home, while men's bodies are subjected to 'painful labour' far away. This may constitute a type of wishful thinking. She envisions the husband 'watch[ing] the night in storms, the day in cold' (5.2.151) while the wife sleeps peacefully at home, whereas we know, from Petruccio's soliloquy, that he compelled her to 'watch all night' (4.1.192), staying awake himself only to prevent her from sleeping.

This distancing between men and women builds up to her inclusion of herself with the other women in a collective 'we', when she contrasts the past Kate who had 'a spirit to resist' (3.2.219) with the present Kate who 'may be made a fool'(3.2.218), trampling on her bonnet in public at her husband's whim: 'My mind hath been as big as one of yours . . . But now I see . . .' (5.2.171–4).

The pathos of the speech peaks in the plangent rhythms of the lines in which Kate uses the first person plural, for the first time in the play, to figure women as a collective 'we':

> But now I see our lances are but straws,
> Our strength as weak, our weakness past compare,
> That seeming to be most, which we indeed least are.
> (5.2.174–6)

---

[31] Ste B, *Counsel to the husband: to the wife instruction*, p. 55.

[32] Ste B, *Counsel to the husband: to the wife instruction*, pp. 63–4.

Nowhere in her speech does Kate use either the first person plural 'we' or even the second person plural 'they' to construct the married couple as a unit. She throughout refers to husband and wife as 'he' and 'she'. Even the famous last line is not addressed to her husband in the second person; it distances him through the third person singular: 'In token of which duty, if he please, / My hand is ready, may it do him ease' (5.2.179–80). The distance between the 'I' and the 'he' here is countered by her new perception of women as a collective 'we'. Since Kate, unlike most other Shakespeare heroines, has no female friends or confidantes and throughout seems to dislike other women, this shift suggests not sisterly solidarity but an acknowledgement of her participation in collective victimhood.

THE TRAGI-COMIC ENDING

In the critical battle over the meaning of the last speech, the ranks seem to be divided into those who read the speech as an enforced performance, satirical or otherwise, and those who read it as a joyful, even self-assertive, sign of self-transformation.[33]

I suggest that Kate is not being sarcastic in the last speech (even though the text contains situational ironies, such as the description of the toiling husband) nor is she joyful in proclaiming her allegiance to the ideology of women's innate weakness. To use the rhetoric of matrimonial wisdom taught to couples, especially to women, in India today, she has learnt to 'adjust', that is, to change her behaviour because she has no other viable option.

Let us consider her much-disputed description of women's resistance, 'That seeming to be most which we indeed least are' (5.2.176). Critics tend to read this either as ironic (Kate is suggesting that her submission is fake) or as evidence of Shakespeare's subscription to patriarchal ideology (he and his audience think that women are innately weak and their resistance is a foolish performance lacking substance), or a combination of both. I suggest another possibility – Kate, from her experience of the way her society works against women (her family's eager abandonment of her to Petruccio's mercy, his servants' and friends'

collusion with him in torturing her, his ability to deprive her of food and sleep and keep her away from her kin, and his threats of physical violence) now realizes that women's resistance, however rational ('my reason haply more') and courageous ('my heart as great') is really very weak because it depends wholly on the husband's or father's willingness to put up with it.

The law is on men's side, as Petruccio pointed out when he graphically described Kate as his property, and society is on his side too. Bianca and the Widow can put up a fight only as long as their husbands do not assert their power to its full extent. Their strength is thus only an appearance and their lances indeed are straws. The power dynamic could alter at any moment if their suitors change after marriage, as suitors are wont to do.

Brian Morris suggests that at the end of Kate's speech of submission, the actor playing Petruccio 'should show him as perilously close to tears, tears of pride, and gratitude, and love'.[34] Conversely, in the 1992 production of *Taming* at Delhi University, the male actor who played Kate almost always, even during rehearsals, came close to tears or even shed tears during the last speech. The experience of being bullied and tormented throughout the play, perhaps more agonizing for him as a male, culminating in the humiliation of the last speech, had the effect of gradually pushing him to an emotional edge.[35] The actress playing Petruccio, on the

---

[33] Among those who read Kate's last speech as either playful or sharply ironic, and Kate as something of a free agent, are Harold Goddard, 'The Taming of the Shrew' in *The Meaning of Shakespeare* (Chicago, 1960), I, pp. 68–73; Coppélia Kahn, 'The Taming of the Shrew: Shakespeare's Mirror of Marriage', *Modern Language Studies*, 5 (1975), 88–102; Peter Saccio, 'Shrewd and Kindly Farce', *Shakespeare Survey 37* (Cambridge, 1984), pp. 33–40; Valerie Wayne, 'Refashioning the Shrew', *Shakespeare Studies*, 17 (1985), 159–87; and Amy Smith, 'Performing Marriage with a Difference'.

[34] Brian Morris, ed., *Shrew*, p. 149.

[35] While I agree with Juliet Dusinberre's brilliant analysis of how the fact that a boy played Kate on Shakespeare's stage would denaturalize and foreground gendered role-playing, I do not entirely agree with her conclusion that the speech represents a seizing of power. See Dusinberre, 'The Taming of the Shrew:

other hand, remained as cocky as his closing lines, addressed to the other men, suggest: "'Twas I won the wager, though you hit the white, / And being a winner, God give you good night!' (5.2.187–8). Nothing in these lines suggests tearfulness to me.

Taming is now recognized as a problem play, and it can be viewed and played as a tragi-comedy. Like most of Shakespeare's comedies, except the last plays, it is a comedy for the male protagonist but at least a tragicomedy, if not a tragedy, for the female protagonist. The play is complex enough to elicit many laughs and still sustain the weight of a sombre ending.

'I KNOW NOT WHAT TO SAY': COLLUDING IN PETRUCCIO'S ABUSE OF LANGUAGE

The taming of Kate crucially depends on the collusion of society, including her natal family, with Petruccio. Modern critics and directors mirror this collusion when they justify the taming, both by downplaying the many ways the play critically frames Petruccio's conduct, and by reading romantic love into the Petruccio–Katherine marriage, with Katherine as a 'beloved wife' who is 'tenderly in love' with her husband.[36] In the play, it is Kate's father who first adopts the strategy of reading love into a marriage of convenience.

Aspiring to be a good father at a time when parents were being advised against tyranny and companionate marriage was being idealized, Baptista does not wish to force his daughters into marriage; he is anxious for Petruccio to win Kate's 'love'. In this, he is similar to many middle-class Indian parents today, whose self-image as good parents requires both that they arrange their daughters' marriages and also that they be able to tell themselves they have made their daughters happy by doing so. Many middle-class arranged marriages in India involve leaving the prospective couple briefly alone, as Petruccio and Katherine are left, in the hope that they may decide to fall in love with one another. After discussing the dowry and dower, Baptista tells Petruccio that the marriage contract

can take place only 'when the special thing is well obtain'd, / That is, her love; for that is all in all' (2.1.128–9).

Petruccio, who is less given to romantic self-delusion than the fond father is, responds, 'Why, that is nothing' (2.1.130). And, throughout the play, he sticks to this view of Katherine's interiority as 'nothing'. What he wants, as he goes on to tell her father immediately thereafter, is not that she love him but that she 'yield' to him: 'so she yields to me, / For I am rough, and woo not like a babe' (2.1.136–7). To Petruccio, Katherine's emotions are 'nothing' and her actions everything.

Words, however, fall like a shadow between emotions and actions. When Baptista returns after the wooing scene, Katherine angrily reproaches him for wishing to wed her to 'one half lunatic, / A madcap ruffian and a swearing Jack' (2.1.280–1). Baptista now has a problem: he wants to get Kate off his hands but he does not want to appear, to himself or to others, as the kind of father who forces his daughter into a marriage she does not want. Petruccio immediately solves the problem, by assuring Baptista that Kate does not mean what she says. His praise of her has an ominous ring: 'For patience she will prove a second Grissel, / And Roman Lucrece for her chastity' (2.1.288–9). While Lucrece ended up dead, Grissel suffered deprivation and humiliation without her husband laying a hand on her. Several critics have waxed eloquent in their praise of Petruccio for not hitting Katherine; in this, Grissel's husband is Petruccio's illustrious forebear.

Katherine, however, explicitly refuses the proposal to marry Petruccio the following Sunday: 'I'll see thee hanged on Sunday first' (2.1.292). Though Gremio and Tranio take note of her refusal, Baptista remains silent, as if waiting for some pretext to marry her off anyway. Petruccio

---

Women, Acting and Power', *Studies in the Literary Imagination*, 26 (1993), 67–84.
[36] The first phrase is Margaret Mikesell's, 'Love Wrought these Miracles', 121; the second is from David Danell, 'The Good Marriage of Katherine and Petruccio', in *The Taming of the Shrew: Critical Essays*, ed. Aspinall, p. 81.

provides that pretext, with his blatant lie regarding Kate's attempted seduction of him. Although Baptista chooses to collude with Petruccio's misuse of language, it is clear that he has doubts: 'I know not what to say, but give me your hands' (2.1.311).

That his agreement is driven by the mechanics of the marriage market is evident in his subsequent remark: 'Faith, gentlemen, now I play a merchant's part, / And venture madly on a desperate mart' (2.1.319–20). Tranio's reply clarifies the term of the bargain, ''Twas a commodity lay fretting by you, / 'Twill bring you gain, or perish on the seas' (2.1.321–2). In other words, Baptista has gotten rid of a burden, though the risk is that Katherine may 'perish'. Many modern Indian parents make this type of bargain, when, in their anxiety to marry off daughters perceived as a financial and social burden, they put those daughters at risk, marrying them to men with dubious credentials who show signs of being unkind or even violent.

THE WIDOW AND BIANCA: SIGNS OF HOPE?

Widowhood represented a type of empowerment for some women in medieval and early modern England. It could provide them with a measure of economic autonomy as well as physical mobility that was not easily available to unmarried girls, and was accessible only to those wives who had liberal husbands. It is not coincidental that the only women among Chaucer's pilgrims are two nuns and a widow. In this context, a semi-comical line early in the play may provide a clue to Kate's possible liberation. Petruccio, discussing her marriage settlement, says, 'And for that dowry I'll assure her of / Her widowhood, be it that she survive me, / In all my lands and leases whatsoever'(2.1.123–5). Although the word 'widowhood' here refers to the estate he will settle on her, the construction of the sentence and the pause after the word is likely to raise a somewhat uneasy laugh. John Fletcher's *The Woman's Prize, or The Tamer Tam'd* constructs a happy ending of sorts by showing a second wife reforming Petruccio after his peculiar brand of

kindness brings about Kate's untimely death. A happier ending for Kate might involve her rather than his widowhood.

The unnamed Widow, who is referred to by that title even after she remarries, embodies that possibility. Her sudden appearance in the last scene somewhat redresses the number imbalance in this play, which is singular in its lack of women – there is not even a woman servant. The Widow chooses and pursues Hortensio not for money but because she falls in love with him, and her marriage is thus, in several respects, very different from Kate's.

Though Bianca has received short shrift from nearly all critics of every persuasion, Mikesell has rightly termed her 'the only rebel to patriarchy in the play'. Mikesell, however, goes on to argue that, 'the play does not endorse Bianca's rebellion' because her personality elicits audience disapproval.[37] I would argue that this is not a foregone conclusion and depends largely on how the character is played. Baptista does not consult Bianca when he arranges her marriage; in fact, he is more concerned to obtain Kate's consent than Bianca's because he expects Kate to rebel. While Lucentio may be, to some extent, a target of mockery, as several critics suggest, Bianca's choice of him over Hortensio shows remarkably good judgement, as close consideration of the two men's language in the wooing scene shows. When the two men, disguised as tutors, woo Bianca, she first insists on her own right to direct how her education should proceed, and then warns Lucentio that she cannot trust him because she does not know him.

She decides against Hortensio only after he presents his suit in words that inadvertently give away his Petruccio-like ambitions: 'Bianca, *take him for thy lord* . . . that loves with all affection' (3.1.73–4). In contrast, Lucentio introduces himself as 'disguised thus *to get your love*'(3.1.33) (emphases mine). She chooses the man who echoes

---

[37] Margaret Lael Mikesell, 'Love Wrought these Miracles', 111, 112.

Baptista's notion that getting the woman's love is 'all in all' rather than the one who wants to lord it over her.[38] Later, Lucentio addresses her as mistress of his heart (4.2.10), while the jealous Hortensio echoes Petruccio in terming her a 'haggard' (4.2.39). When Tranio tells her that Hortensio plans to tame the widow, Bianca ironically comments, 'He says so, Tranio' (4.2.53).

I disagree with Mikesell's claim that Lucentio's assumption of disguise and his secret marriage are unnecessary contrivances by an overly busy Tranio, and thus undercut the positive significance of the New Comedy romance and marriage plot. Lucentio's assumption of disguise is necessary to enable him to woo Bianca and obtain her consent, since Baptista was ready to bargain away her love to the highest bidder: 'he of both / That can assure my daughter greatest dower / Shall have my Bianca's love' (2.1.335–7). The secret marriage is also necessary because Lucentio could not be sure that his father would agree to such a huge marriage settlement, and Baptista insists on the father's agreement because if Lucentio were to die before his father Bianca would be left dowerless. As Gremio is quick to point out, it is highly unlikely that any sensible man would settle his entire estate on his daughter-in-law and become wholly dependent on his son: 'Sirrah, young gamester, your father were a fool / To give thee all . . . / An old Italian fox is not so kind, my boy' (2.1.393–6). It is in response to this situation that Tranio plots to find a fake father for Lucentio, so that the real father will be presented with a *fait accompli*.

Bianca's marriage elicits what is arguably the play's most romantic line, 'Love wrought these miracles', which Mikesell unaccountably annexes to the Kate–Petruccio marriage. That she does not degenerate into mindless obedience at the end is not a sign that the marriage is a failure; rather, it suggests that the 'miracle' of love is more complex than the mechanical 'wonder' of a woman playing a robot.

The Widow's presence is crucial in the last scene because she and Bianca outnumber Kate two to one. They both declare, in different but related contexts, that they are not afraid of men, and they concur in the opinion that Kate's mindless obedience in throwing off her cap is foolish. Bianca picks up the bird metaphor that Petruccio and Hortensio have used in other contexts to refer to women, and describes herself as able to elude the hunter who pursues her. In these two women's refusal to come when called, the play presents two Vashtis to one Esther. But, unlike Vashti, who is divorced and disappears, Bianca and the Widow cannot be wished away. Bianca accurately points out to Lucentio that his loss of the bet is the consequence of his own folly in placing such a bet.

Like Isabella's famous silence at the end of *Measure for Measure*, Bianca's and the Widow's silence at the end of Kate's speech speaks volumes. What is not said may be as significant as what is said. Just as Petruccio does not mention love in his soliloquy, and Kate does not mention the 'we' of conjugality in hers, Bianca and the Widow are not made to concur in Kate's analysis. Kate's use of the 'we' for all women is another tragic mistake on her part. Not all women are the same – this fact constitutes the fatal loophole in facile generalizations about men and women.

Petruccio acknowledges that Kate's speech has not worked a miraculous conversion when he tells Lucentio and Hortensio that they are 'sped', and he perhaps suggests in his final line ('And being a winner, God give you good night', 5.2.188) that he prefers to leave the gaming table before his luck turns and Kate does something to show that she is not as tamed as she seems to be.[39] Lucentio underscores this with the play's last line, expressing incredulity in response to Hortensio's praise of Petruccio for taming the shrew: ''Tis a wonder, by your leave, she will be tam'd so' (5.2.190).

---

[38] Karen Newman ignores this dynamic when she claims that Bianca's words in the wooing scene are 'as close as possible to the silence we have come to expect from her' (Newman, 'Renaissance Family Politics', 88).

[39] R. Warwick Bond, editor of the 1904 Arden edition of *Taming*, annotates Petruccio's last line as 'alluding to the natural wish of successful gamesters to leave the table before their luck turns'. Brian Morris reproduces the note in his 1981 Arden edition, p. 298.

SHAKESPEARE'S LAST KATE: WHAT HAPPENS WHEN ESTHER GROWS OLD

Both in *The Taming of the Shrew* and in *Henry VIII*, a Katherine, called Kate by her husband, makes a riveting speech about the duties of a good wife, and kneels to her husband. Shakespeare's first Kate, newly wed, declares her intention of being obedient to her husband, as a subject is to a king, and expects this to result in a happy marriage. His last Kate, Queen Katherine, has been a devoted, unquestioningly obedient wife and subject to her husband, the king, for more than twenty years, a fact the king himself confirms, yet we see her mercilessly discarded. At the end of his career, Shakespeare demonstrates, through one of the most notorious exempla of his times, that Katherine Minola's assumptions and expectations were ill founded.

Katherine was a very common name in sixteenth-century England. As Laurie Maguire points out, 'the name Kate assumes an almost generic quality and becomes a synecdoche for "woman"'.[40] The shared powerlessness of women across the social spectrum emerges when we compare Queen Katherine's trial with Katherine Minola's.

Katherine Minola advises women to be meek and submissive, because men are more powerful than women. Queen Katherine, however, has been just the kind of submissive wife Katherine Minola and the marriage manuals praise. She has been true and humble, always obedient to her husband's slightest whim, and has adjusted her moods and her likes and dislikes to his.[41] She even goes so far as actively to promote the type of self-isolation that Petruccio imposes on his wife – she retains only her husband's friends as her own, and dismisses those of whom he disapproves. She kneels at the outset of her speech as Katherine Minola does at the end of hers; this humility results, in both cases, in the husband praising the wife. However, where Katherine Minola, the young wife, is raised up, kissed and taken to bed, Queen Katherine, the old wife, is discarded.

Henry, depicted as similar to Petruccio in his rough and ready manner as well as his arbitrariness, confirms his wife's account of herself. He terms her 'saintlike', full of 'meekness', 'gentleness' and obedience (2.4.135–7); she is what Petruccio predicted his Kate would become, 'a second Grissel / and Roman Lucrece for her chastity'. According to Petruccio, this type of virtue and obedience in a wife was an indicator of peace, love, and a happy married life, 'An aweful rule, and right supremacy, / And to be short, what not that's sweet and happy' (5.2.109–11). But Petruccio, it turns out, was wrong. Queen Katherine's obedience and her husband's 'rule and right supremacy' result not in sweetness and happiness but in her being cast off against her will.

Katherine Minola declares that no man will deign to touch an angry quarrelsome woman. Queen Katherine reports that despite her patience, love and obedience, her husband hates her and will not touch her: 'hates me / Alas, 'has banished me his bed already, / His love too long ago' (3.1.118–20). Having been discarded in favour of a younger woman, her only relationship with him now is that of obedience: 'I am old my lords, / And all the fellowship I hold now with him / Is only my obedience' (3.1.120–1).

The conclusion of Queen Katherine's trial ironically echoes the ending of *Taming*. In *Taming*, Katherine, considered by all to be the worst of the three wives, proves she is the best by coming when her husband calls. Conversely, Queen Katherine, universally deemed the best of wives, ends her

---

[40] '"Household Kates": Chez Petruccio, Percy and Plantagenet' in *Gloriana's Face: Women, Public and Private, in the English Renaissance*, ed. S. P. Cerasano and Marion Wynne-Davies (Detroit, 1992), pp. 129–65, esp. 130.

[41] A typical statement of this requirement: 'If she saw her husband to be merry, then was she merry: if he were heavie or passionate, she would indeavore to make him glad: if he were angrie. She would quickly please him: she would never contrary him in any thing.' Philip Stubbes, *A Crystal Glass for Christian Women, Containing the Most Excellent Discourse of the Goodly Life and Christian Death of Mistress Katherine Stubbes* (London, 1592), sig. A3r.

trial by walking away and refusing to come when her husband calls. Henry says, 'Call her again' and the Crier calls out, 'Katherine Queen of England, come into the court' (2.4.123–4). Katherine does not answer but rebukes the usher and says to herself, 'Now the Lord help, / They vex me past my patience' (127–8). She declares that she will not return and will never appear again in any of their courts.

After Kate proves her obedience, Petruccio tells her to kiss him and go with him to bed; both Hortensio and Lucentio admiringly say to Petruccio, 'Go thy ways.' Using the same phrase, Henry declares, as his wife disobeys him and walks away, 'Go thy ways Kate / That man i'th'world who shall report he has / A better wife, let him in nought be trusted / For speaking false in that' (2.4.131–4). The best of all wives ends up disobeying her husband yet still compelling his respect and admiration.

If Katherine Minola is a Vashti turned Esther, Queen Katherine is an Esther turned Vashti. Cardinal Campeius criticizes her behaviour: 'The queen is obstinate / Stubborn to justice, apt to accuse it, and / Disdainful to be tried by't; 'tis not well, / She's going away' (2.4.119–22), but the king disagrees, declaring Katherine the best of wives. Yet he does not want her in bed – she stands as the warning symbol of what may happen when Esther grows old.

Queen Katherine also represents the literalization of Katherine Minola's (and the marriage manuals') metaphor: 'Such duty as the subject owes the prince / Even such a woman oweth to her husband' (5.2.156–7). Throughout *Henry VIII*, we see how the prince mistreats dutiful subjects; the apotheosis, though, is his treatment of Katherine, which thus becomes the archetype of the unjust relationship dynamic set in motion by absolute obedience. As the obedience exacted by Petruccio forces his wife to lie, the obedience exacted by Henry sends his wife (and, as the audience well remembered, several wives thereafter) to death.

Both Katherine, Queen of England, daughter of a King, and Katherine Minola, daughter of Baptista, in their different ways, represent Everywoman. G. Wilson Knight notes of Queen Katherine, '[h]er every phrase comes direct from her woman's soul, her typical woman's plight. She is universalized, not by abstraction, but rather by an exact realization of a particular person only lately dead.'[42] Just as we never see Kate and Petruccio alone after marriage, we never see Queen Katherine and her husband alone either. Both cases starkly dramatize how women are socially besieged and isolated; the wonder, in the case of Shakespeare's last Kate, is that, though a perfect wife, she will not be tamed.

---

[42] G. Wilson Knight, *The Crown of Life: Essays in the Interpretation of Shakespeare's Final Plays* (London, 1947), p. 296.

THE CROWN AND THE PILLOW:
ROYAL PROPERTIES IN *HENRY IV*

STEPHEN DICKEY

THE TAVERN

This is a meditation on two objects, a crown and a pillow, and what they might be made to mean on stage. Their juxtaposition in two scenes of Shakespeare's *Henry IV* plays contributes to the complex staging of Hal's career, to the enormity of Falstaff's character, and to the enormously complex formal relationship between the two plays. The first of these scenes is Act 2, scene 4 of *Henry IV, Part 1*, wherein Prince Hal and Sir John Falstaff jest with and against each other on several topics: Falstaff's behaviour at the Gadshill robbery, the fearsome Percy rebellion, the shapes of their own bodies, and Hal's disrepute in the eyes of his father, the king. Knowing that Hal 'must to the court in the morning' (2.4.334–5), they decide to prepare him for the royal dressing down by staging a royal dressing up.[1] In this impromptu play Hal will 'practice an answer' (375) to his father, and so he and Falstaff take turns acting the roles of prince and king in front of the tavern audience. 'Do thou stand for my father and examine me upon the particulars of my life' (376–7), orders Hal. At this point, Falstaff places a cushion upon his head, and in this position I leave him for a moment.[2]

Theatrical properties starkly exemplify the onto-logical paradoxes of drama, as an audience watches real people and fictional characters simultaneously manipulating real objects that are subjected to the demands of make-believe. When placed on stage, the inert property begins to function both mimetically and symbolically. Consider one of the more spectacular examples in drama: Yorick. In the fiction of the play *Hamlet*, the prince holds the skull of his late father's late jester. Along with the diverse cups, swords and papers that are manipulated by actors in various roles in *Hamlet*, the skull thus assists the representational illusion of the performance. But on stage, as Martin Esslin says, 'the object is raised to the status of a sign',[3] and so in performance this transaction between the actor playing Hamlet and the prop-skull of Yorick forms a symbolic tableau that depicts, both efficiently and profoundly, several of the play's most important motifs: individual death and human mortality; burial and the afterlife (such as it is); remembrance and oblivion; something rotten; comedy with its jaw broken by tragedy; silence. It is notoriously unclear whether the macabre reunion with Yorick propels Hamlet toward 'readiness' (*Hamlet* 5.2.222), but it does appear that a prop, and the symbolic energies that flow through it, can have a kind of agency within the world of a play, instigating action and characterizing (or re-characterizing) those who handle that prop, wear it, or even – as Hamlet does

---

[1] All references to Shakespeare's works follow *The Riverside Shakespeare*, 2nd edn, ed. G. Blakemore Evans *et al.* (Boston, 1997). Editorial brackets have been silently removed.

[2] While acknowledging that pillows and cushions are distinct items with, at times, different domestic, ornamental and ceremonial functions, I will be treating them similarly throughout this essay, using whichever term seems most apt to the moment under discussion. See note 45, below, for an instance of a contemporary witness, Thomas Middleton, using the terms interchangeably.

[3] Martin Esslin, 'The Stage: Reality, Symbol, Metaphor', *Themes in Drama* 4 (1982), 1–12; see especially p. 6.

with Yorick's skull – smell it.[4] Theatrical properties both deliver and acquire meaning, and what they mean is subject to the unfolding process of performance, to the ways they are put into play.

For his part, Falstaff puts a cushion into play: an improvised self-coronation characteristically stuffed with meaning. Most immediately, the cushion looks silly – a lampshade, as it were, attesting to the frivolity, excess and even drunkenness of the scene. Beyond that, Falstaff's appearance may activate iconographical associations with one or more of the Seven Deadly Sins.[5] A pillow or cushion is an obvious emblem of Sloth, both physical idleness and (by implication) spiritual indolence:

I shall be out of heart shortly, and then I shall have no strength to repent. And I have not forgotten what the inside of a church is made of, I am a peppercorn, a brewer's horse. The inside of a church! Company, villainous company, hath been the spoil of me. (3.3.6–10)

Articulating his spiritual plight with customary imagery of food and drink, Falstaff reminds us that the wearing of a pillow could connote those other, mutually encouraging sins of the appetitive flesh embodied by (or attributed to) him: Gluttony and Lechery.[6] (Indeed, the words 'pillow' and 'cushion' also functioned in the sixteenth and seventeenth centuries as slang for women's sexual parts, or for women as sexual objects.)[7] Yet let us also consider the most obvious, thoroughly mundane use for a cushion in a theatrical context. Thomas Platter, a Swiss tourist who visited the Globe in 1599, describes the playgoer's options as follows:

Whoever cares to stand below pays only one English penny, but if he wishes to sit he enters by another door and pays a second penny, while if he desires to sit on the most comfortable seats with a cushion he pays yet another English penny at another door.[8]

Falstaff's relocation of this prop therefore manifests some of his carnivalesque energies, especially so if he crowns himself with what he had just sat upon. In placing above that which is ordinarily beneath, Falstaff becomes an emblem of the topsy-turvy state – a diversely recurring image in the play as various characters remark nostalgically

upon Richard II's reign, now newly defined as the good old days by a collective, convenient failure to remember instances of Richard's misrule. Describing the miserably polluted and impoverished conditions of his lodgings, one of the carriers observes 'This house is turn'd upside down since Robin ostler died' (2.1.10–11), a remark that records in microcosm the state of the realm under Henry IV. With the cushion on his head, Falstaff shrinks the microcosm further from nation to inn to body 'turn'd upside down', as if to say 'Bolingbroke is crowned! Bottoms up!'

Falstaff's other royal properties work similarly toward a political critique of the present regime of Hal's father: his throne is a tavern chair, his sceptre a dagger.[9] Insofar as Henry IV came to the crown

---

4 Such a process is made vivid in one of Pirandello's broadest metatheatrical jokes in *Six Characters in Search of an Author* when the collected hats and cloaks from the rehearsing actors magically summon Madame Pace, a seventh character, into material being: if the family of characters never satisfactorily locates an author for its melodrama, at least the various garments manage to create a character to adorn.

5 See, e.g., Samuel C. Chew, *The Pilgrimage of Life* (New Haven, 1962), p. 75, p. 343 n.7, and fig. 70, Jan David's 'The World, the Flesh and the Devil assault the Soul' (1601) which depicts a bare-breasted Flesh, pillow on head, as one of the Soul's assailants. In *The Virtues Reconciled* (Toronto, 1947), pp. 15–17, Chew links this iconographical tradition to Falstaff in the tavern scene, as does William S. Heckscher, 'Shakespeare and the Visual Arts', in *Art and Literature: Studies in Relationship*, ed. Egon Verheyen (Baden-Baden, 1985), pp. 370–1.

6 For more on the symbolic association between the cushion and sin, especially sloth and luxury or lechery, see Erwin Panofsky, *Studies in Iconology* (New York, 1939), p. 88, n.72, and fig. 66 on Bronzino's 'An Allegory with Venus and Cupid', and *The Life and Art of Albrecht Dürer* (Princeton, 1955), pp. 71–2, figs. 98 and 103, treating 'Dream of the Doctor'.

7 Gordon Williams, *A Dictionary of Sexual Language and Imagery in Shakespearian and Stuart Literature* (London, 1994), vol. 2, pp. 1030–1.

8 Quoted in Andrew Gurr and John Orrell, *Rebuilding Shakespeare's Globe* (New York, 1989), p. 54.

9 For a treatment of Falstaff's choice of props emphasizing their political satire, see Roy Battenhouse, 'Falstaff as Parodist and Perhaps Holy Fool', *PMLA*, 90 (1975), 32–52. Though concurring with Battenhouse's attention to these details, I reach different conclusions about Falstaff's dramatic and symbolic function in the *Henry IV* plays.

through popular support and the military assistance of powerful allies like the Percys, Falstaff's staging is apt and to the point. The dagger-sceptre, though leaden, is a particularly sharp image of a king who must now rule by force rather than awe, and who will spend the better part of his reign – that is, the better part of two plays – preoccupied with armed rebellions that have been enabled by, and to some extent are modelled on, his own act of usurpation. Working in close collaboration with his cousin, Richard II, Henry IV has effectively drained the symbolism of the crown, reversing Esslin's formulation, so that the sign of divinely sanctioned royalty is now merely an object up for grabs. This desacralizing process underscores the arbitrariness of the crown itself as a symbol of royal power, especially when other objects begin to stand for the crown. Paradoxically, such false crowns set off the king's crown as authentic while simultaneously threatening the stability of that crown as a symbol *per se*: if, in theory, any object will do, then why not wear a cushion?

This line of thought is in many ways absurd, but not on stage. Hal's reply, 'Thy state is taken for a join'd-stool, thy golden sceptre for a leaden dagger, and thy precious rich crown for a pitiful bald crown' (2.4.380–2), explicitly notes that the props Falstaff uses are just that: props. Moreover, Falstaff's particular choice of the cushion elicits a profoundly ambiguous assessment from Hal, whose phrase 'bald crown' blurs the distinction between authentic king and imposter subject. If Falstaff adorns himself with a 'bald' cushion, then Hal is commenting on the shabby upholstery of the Boar's Head Tavern and, beyond that, the threadbare claim of his father to the kingdom.[10] But because the word so much more obviously could describe Falstaff's aging head – with, perhaps, additional implications of venereal disease[11] – Hal has rhetorically rendered the cushion-crown temporarily invisible. Anyone who has a head has, in this sense, a crown, and thus one need not have any prop, finally, to play a king who is 'taken for' a subject. Corollary moments of demystification occur elsewhere in the tetralogy, as when Henry IV refers to the throne as 'mine empty chair' (2H4, 4.5.94), or when

Henry V's speech on 'ceremony' (H5, 4.1.266) defines royalty as little more than the possession and management of certain props, an argument mirrored – that is, both reflected and reversed – in the Chorus's persistent derogation of the drama as a medium by which to represent heroic kingship.

Far from rebutting Falstaff's critique of Henry IV, then, Hal merely furthers it in different terms. Although Hal implies that the crown his father wears is the one that matters, by denying these objects any symbolic potential he opens up the possibility of endless audience skepticism about the artifices of performance. On stage, to adapt Peter Handke's formula, a cushion is both itself and a cushion pretending to be another cushion.[12] Either way, it is an object one might find useful when removed from theatrical space and placed in the real world offstage, such as on a bench at the Theatre, Curtain or Globe. But a stage crown offstage is not a handy item; its significance lies only in its significance, and it is invested with meaning only within the fiction of the playworld.[13] When that fiction

---

[10] Similarly, Hal's reported comment in *Richard II* – 'His answer was, he would unto the stews, / And from the common'st creature pluck a glove / And wear it as a favour' to his father's coronation (5.3.16–18) – reveals not just the prince's 'dissolute spirit', as Sandra Billington observes, but 'that he is aware of the hollowness of his father's coronation' and that 'the pomp is prostituted'. See *Mock Kings in Medieval Society and Renaissance Drama* (Oxford, 1991), p. 154.

[11] The mercury 'cure' for syphilis resulted in hair loss, thus associating baldness with venereal diseases in numerous jocular insults of the age: see, e.g., *A Midsummer Night's Dream* 1.2.97–8, *Measure for Measure* 1.2.27–35. And see notes 5–7, above, for the association of lechery with the pillow or cushion.

[12] *Offending the Audience* in *Kaspar and Other Plays*, trans. Michael Roloff (New York, 1969), p. 10. I was led to this quotation by Bert O. States, 'The Dog on the Stage: Theatre as Phenomenon', *New Literary History* 14 (1983), 373–88, an important treatment of phenomenology and the semiotics of theatrical properties. See also James Calderwood's discussion of the 'stool' where only Macbeth sees Banquo's ghost: *Shakespearian Metadrama* (Minneapolis, 1971), pp. 12–13.

[13] An audience thus could be said to reproduce the ideological manoeuvre performed by subjects within a monarchy, suggesting that to move the crown from a palace to a stage is not to move it very far. As Stephen Greenblatt writes,

deploys the crown as an icon of power only to undermine that meaning, we are reminded that, on stage, all crowns are fake, a fact *1 Henry IV* exploits repeatedly to convey the problems of Henry's reign. The crown thus serves as an obvious emblem not of royalty but of the acting or pretense of royalty.[14] 'What art thou / That counterfeit'st the person of a king?' (5.4.27–8) asks the Earl of Douglas, in a rare moment of lucid inquiry among the rebels, when faced with yet another soldier who is wearing the king's clothing. Although (or rather because) in this particular case it *is* the king, Douglas's question remains a good one. Indeed the question has been implicit ever since *Richard II* 4.1, if not before, and inevitable ever since the tavern skit of *1 Henry IV* 2.4.[15]

However much the cushion-crown exemplifies Falstaff's improvisational skill while exposing the arbitrariness of royal power, the juxtaposition of these objects is not itself entirely a random accident. It was routine for the crown, when not on the monarch's head, to rest upon a 'state cushion' of some kind.[16] The anonymous *Look About You* (1599?) has Lancaster enter with a 'Crowne Imperiall on a cushion'.[17] Act 5 of Dekker's *Lust's Dominion* (1600) begins with another processional entrance, including 'Baltazar bearing the Crown on a cushion'.[18] Barnabe Barnes's play of 1606, *The Devil's Charter*, has the following stage direction at the start of 1.4: 'Alexander in his study with bookes, coffers, his triple Crowne upon a cushion before him.'[19] And the allegorical pageant scene (4.3) of James Shirley's *The Coronation* (1635) includes the stage direction 'Enter Honor with the Crown upon a mourning cushion.'[20] Some modern filmed performances have followed this convention of coronal storage and transport. Laurence Olivier's *Richard III* (1955), for example, contains the following bit of business: after Edward's coronation at the very start of the film, Olivier's Duke of Gloucester places his coronet on a cushion held by an attendant. It then falls awkwardly between them in a comic foreshadowing of the unsettling of the English crown by Richard. Likewise in the deposition scene from the BBC production of *Richard II* (1978, dir. David Giles), the crown is brought in upon a cushion

for Richard to hand over to Bolingbroke: 'Here, cousin, seize the crown' (*R2* 4.1.181). I will have more to say about the historical – as partly distinct from theatrical – collocation of these objects but, for now, let us simply note that Falstaff's selection of props is neither random nor arbitrary, but a pointedly comical manoeuvre. It is as if he chooses exactly the wrong object for his head: the cushion will remind his audience not only of a crown but, even more perhaps, of its absence.

The nuances of Falstaff's cushion-crown are thus both inversive, as one object substitutes for the other, and subversive, for on this cushion rests a critique of kingship in the world of these plays, a critique therefore, inevitably, of Henry IV and, by extension, of Hal himself. Though disguised

---

'theatricality . . . is not set over against power, but is one of power's essential modes' (*Shakespearian Negotiations* (Berkeley, 1988), p. 46). While its power may be 'merely' iconic, and may emerge from largely unexamined cultural and political traditions, the crown nonetheless tangibly expresses something like the consent of the governed, at least in the agreement that the very wearing of the crown is a claim to power, a claim that itself has real consequences for the state.

[14] 'The very act of a player putting a crown on his head to represent a historical figure turned him, and, by association, the character he portrayed, into a mock king even before the text gave greater definition as to the type he portrayed' (Billington, *Mock Kings*, p. 6). For a thorough assessment of the 'mock' or 'counterfeit' royalty on display here, see James L. Calderwood, *Metadrama in Shakespeare's Henriad* (Berkeley, 1979).

[15] As Kenneth S. Calhoon notes, 'deposing Falstaff, Hal assumes the role of his not-yet-dead father, creating a redundancy of regal representation that privileges the role over the body' (104–5). See 'Emil Jannings, Falstaff, and The Spectacle of the Body Natural', *Modern Language Quarterly* 58 (1997), 83–109.

[16] An association recorded by numerous English hotels and pubs named 'The Crown and Cushion'.

[17] *Look About You* (London, 1600), sig. k3[r]. Dates and speculative dates for plays mentioned in this study are drawn from the Chronological Table in *The Cambridge Companion to English Renaissance Drama*, ed. A. R. Braunmuller and Michael Hattaway (Cambridge, 1990), pp. 419–46.

[18] *The Dramatic Works of Thomas Dekker*, ed. Fredson Bowers, 4 vols. (Cambridge, 1961), vol. 4.

[19] *The Devil's Charter by Barnabe Barnes: A Critical Edition*, ed. Jim C. Pogue (New York and London, 1980).

[20] *The Coronation* (London, 1640), sig. G4[v].

as camaraderie, the incessant, jabbing ironies are hard to miss in Falstaff's references to Hal as the 'true prince' (2.4.272) and 'not of the blood royal' (1.2.140–1) unless he participate in highway robbery, or in his greeting 'a bastard son of the King's' (2H4 2.4.283), or in his mockingly incredulous 'Depose me?' (1H4 2.4.435) when, in the tavern scene, Hal takes over the part of his own father and Falstaff steps down to play Hal. In these and other speeches Falstaff calls attention to the fundamental flaw in the Lancastrian line, and may indeed articulate some of Hal's own ambivalence about his prospective kingship, inherited not just by blood but by bloody usurpation. This is the fact and basis of Hal's power that haunts him even into *Henry V* when, before the battle of Agincourt, he prays that God 'think not upon the fault / My father made in compassing the crown' (4.1.293–4).[21]

THE DEATHBED

The second scene involving the crown and the pillow occurs in Act 4 of *2 Henry IV*. Having received news of the latest royal victory, the dying king asks to be carried into another chamber, to hear soft music, and then gives his last and most explicit order: 'Set me the crown upon my pillow here' (4.5.5). This detail comes to Shakespeare straight from Holinshed's *Chronicles*, where we read of the king that 'During this his last sickness, he caused his crowne (as some write) to be set on a pillow at his beds head', a placement the French chronicler Monstrelet calls the custom of the country in England.[22] At this point, Prince Hal enters and keeps solitary watch, remarking 'Why doth the crown lie there upon his pillow, / Being so troublesome a bedfellow?' (21–2). Assuming his father to be dead, Hal takes the crown and exits. While it is usually Hal himself who controls the deceptions of his various audiences throughout the tetralogy, this is, in fact, the second time he is fooled by someone playing possum. As Falstaff had risen to claim Hotspur's body at Shrewsbury, so the king rises to reclaim the prize Hal had thought his own. Upon waking from his death-like sleep, Henry IV asks, 'Where is the crown? who took it from my pillow?' (57).

The crown itself, and all it stands for, is clearly the focus of the scene, but the script insists that we notice the thrice-mentioned pillow too in the staging, for both props are needed to bring the prince face to face with the emblems of his own personae: tavern Hal and court Hal. On the bed, the pillow: the mock crown representing holiday sport, Falstaffian carnival, the power of parody (indeed, of theatre), 'father ruffian' Falstaff himself, the sleep and sloth of Hal's past. And on the pillow, the crown: representing not just royalty but responsibility, political power, the father's ruffian crime of usurpation, the wars and work of Hal's future. These props do not, let me stress, convert the scene into a princely psychomachia, for they do not confront Hal with a genuine choice between the 'real' crown and its Falstaffian variant. We know, from as long ago as *1 Henry IV* 1.2, that the prince has always already rejected Falstaff. Though an audience may be startled (or even amused) when Hal takes the crown from beside his father, at no time, I assume, does it expect him to try on the cushion instead. Nonetheless, the moment registers that action as the ghost of a chance, the road not taken. The scene in the king's bedroom in *Part 2*, then, is yet another rehearsal of a choice Hal has already made, with props similar to those of the tavern

---

21 'In compassing the crown': a phrase that can be heard to mean not just 'obtaining' or 'seizing' but something more like 'encompassing' (with, perhaps, the subterranean nuance of 'passing on' (i.e., to an heir)). Each of these meanings pertains to different aspects of the consequences of Henry IV's reign for Henry V. Indeed, virtually all of *OED*'s definitions for the verb 'compass' are in play here, including 'to contrive, devise, machinate (a purpose). Usually in a bad sense' (I.2) and 'to form a circle about, surround, with friendly or hostile intent' (III.6), to cite two that might illuminate some of Henry's specific actions in *Richard II*. If Henry IV then compassed that which will uneasily compass his own head, Falstaff lives 'out of all compass' (1H4 3.3.20, 22) and cannot be contained by any authority or rule; hence his eventual banishment from any courtly circle.

22 Geoffrey Bullough, ed., *Narrative and Dramatic Sources of Shakespeare*, 8 vols. (London, 1957–75), vol. 4, p. 277. Monstrelet's observation from *Chroniques d'Enguerrand de Monstrelet* is quoted in *Shakespeare's Holinshed*, ed. W. G. Boswell-Stone (London, 1896; rpt. New York, 1966), p. 158, n. 2.

scene of *Part 1*, in advance of its final, public performance at the end of the play.

In putting on the crown prematurely, Hal paradoxically bequeaths to his own father the prop of counterfeit, parodic kingship: the pillow. Henry IV's waking speech elaborates the juxtaposition of these objects from his own paternal perspective:

> How quickly nature falls into revolt
> When gold becomes her object!
> For this the foolish over-careful fathers
> Have broke their sleep with thoughts, their brains
>   with care,
> Their bones with industry;
> For this they have engrossed and pil'd up
> The cank'red heaps of strange-achieved gold.
>
> (4.5.65–71)

Beyond the generic mutterings of the aggrieved *senex* lie some specific references to the king's immediate situation. At this moment there can be little doubt that the 'gold' in question is not merely the profit of an industrious life but the missing crown itself, 'strange-achieved' by Henry when he himself quickly fell 'into revolt' in *Richard II*.[23] (Perhaps this is the reason the king seems averse to naming the object.)[24] That crown, moreover, had been not simply 'pil'd' but, as it were, 'pillowed up' just previously. Indeed, the quarto text of *2 Henry IV* (1600) has 'pilld' where the Folio prints 'pyl'd'. Either word enables the pun that further links the hypothetical father's wealth to this particular father's crown, though 'pilled' is obviously closer in pronunciation to 'pillow' and, cognate with 'pillage', has a stronger sense of the theft which, Henry implies, 'cank'r[s]' or tarnishes the gold.[25] As with most of the king's speeches, there is an arresting combination of self-exoneration and self-blame here as the image metamorphoses from selfless labour to something more like miserliness betrayed, or even (as at Gadshill) robbery robbed.[26] Thus provoked by the pillaged pillow, Henry pursues yet another comparison of fathers and workers:

> When like the bee tolling from every flower
> The virtuous sweets,
> Our thighs pack'd with wax, our mouths with
>   honey,

> We bring it to the hive, and like the bees,
> Are murd'red for our pains. This bitter taste
> Yields his engrossments to the ending father.
>
> (4.5.74–9)

The king's peculiar stress on the term 'engrossed'/'engrossments' links this speech competitively to Hal's self-defense in *1 Henry IV* when he had promised his father that he intended to use Hotspur as a 'factor . . . / To engross up glorious deeds on my behalf' (3.2.147–8), and registers yet again that the crown is now subject to the language of bookkeeping as well as bee-keeping. (It will be left to Canterbury in *Henry V* to attempt to restore the apian simile to its more conventional use: the depiction of an orderly society.)[27] More to the point, though, the king's deathbed speech as a whole is haunted by diverse Falstaffian associations, exemplified by the two 'gross' words and reference to the theft of the king's gold (the 'crowns' (*1H4* 1.2.132) taken at Gadshill were 'going to the King's exchequer'

---

[23] 'Rebellion lay in his way, and he found it' (*1H4* 5.1.28) – Falstaff's wry assessment of the Percy uprising – seems to apply with equal if not greater force to Henry IV. The swiftness with which Hal shuts Falstaff up – 'Peace, chewet, peace!' (29) – testifies to the comment's potential offence, especially as this is the only time king and knight share the stage.

[24] See Robert N. Watson, *Shakespeare and the Hazards of Ambition* (Cambridge, MA, 1984), p. 47, on the way Henry IV thus 'conveniently evades acknowledging the justice of his having to endure disobedience' by Hal.

[25] See Giorgio Melchiori, ed., *The Second Part of King Henry IV* (Cambridge, 1989), 4.2.200 n. Buried somewhere within this pile of associations may be another link between the gold of the crown and the fabric of the pillow. In a dense series of puns in *Measure for Measure* 1.2.32f, 'pil'd' is made to mean both 'covered with pile' and its opposite, 'bald' (among other things). Henry IV's piled/pilled/peeled crown thus draws ever closer to Falstaff's 'pitiful bald' pillow-crown.

[26] See Harry Berger's treatment of 'Henry's relation to the interplay of the donor's, victim's, and sinner's discourses' in his 'Uneasy lies the head that wears a crown' soliloquy in 3.1. Berger's depiction of the king as 'afraid to commit himself to the bad faith of playing donor and victim yet equally afraid to confront his self-despite head on' seems equally pertinent to his soliloquy in 4.5. *Making Trifles of Terrors: Redistributing Complicities in Shakespeare* (Stanford, 1997), p. 248.

[27] *H5* 1.2.187–204.

($1H4$ 2.2.55)).[28] Perhaps appreciating Richard II's achievement of martyrdom, Henry IV now tries to appropriate that kind of power by rhetorically hammering the crown's gold into hard-won income, laboriously gathered pollen, the honey therefrom, and finally into a series of paradoxes that combine sweet and bitter, sustenance and death. In complementary acts of devouring, the returning bees yield their sweetness to the murderous hive and filial betrayal yields its bitterness to the dying father. In the economics of martyrdom, after all, loss is profit, and the more conspicuously one gets consumed, the better. The prince's theft of the crown, like the heir's of the estate, like the hive's of the food, 'yields' a bitterness to the king who, already embittered, finds it sweet and who therefore eats, being eaten.[29]

THE CHILDBED

Of course the *Henry IV* plays contain another 'foolish' and 'ending father' with an appetite for martyrdom and only a pillow for his head.[30] Returning to the Falstaffian milieu, we find that Shakespeare is not yet done with this most adaptable prop or, more precisely, with the idea of the cushion as a prop. Toward the end of *2 Henry IV*, after Pistol brings news to Falstaff of the old king's death, Sir John busies himself with fantasies of advancement and revenge against the Lord Chief Justice. Falstaff cannot know, however, what the audience has witnessed in the previous scene – the new king has retained the Lord Chief Justice in his office – nor what we are to witness in the following scene, where the first consequences of Henry V's rule appear as a legal clampdown. 'The laws of England are at my commandement' (*2H4* 5.3.136–7), asserts Falstaff, but they are at that moment being executed by his opposite, an emaciated beadle, who arrests Doll Tearsheet over the protestations of Hostess Quickly. Accused of involvement in a man's death, Doll pleads pregnancy to mitigate the violence of her arrest: 'and the child I go with do miscarry, thou wert better thou hadst strook thy mother'. The Hostess then adds her dire prayers that 'the

fruit of [Doll's] womb miscarry', to which the Beadle replies, 'If it do, you shall have a dozen of cushions again; you have but eleven now' (5.4.8ff). So is Doll with child or with cushion? If truly pregnant, is it possible that the child she carries was conceived during some diseased and melancholy union with Falstaff? Is there to be a bastard prince of the carnival king's? A sobering thought indeed, though surely it is genetically appropriate that a child of the doublet-stuffed, cushion-crowned Falstaff and the onomastically bedridden Doll Tearsheet should turn out to be a pillow.

Although expectant mothers had been represented before on the English stage, and although Gill in *The Second Shepherd's Play* memorably feigns pregnancy to conceal the sheep stolen by her husband Mac, it may be that Doll offers the earliest theatrical example of the use of a cushion to simulate a simulated pregnancy. A number of prop-assisted false pregnancies do appear in later Stuart plays, however. In a subplot of Thomas May's *The Heir* (1620), Luce appears to be pregnant ('gravida' as the stage direction at 1.3.0 has it), but this is part of an elaborate trick she plays with Francisco, her

---

[28] As the crown melts, via the king's simile, into fatal honey, we may recall the association of honey and murder in the Hostess's malaprop epithets/endearments for Falstaff: 'honey-suckle villain' and 'honeyseed' (*2H4* 2.1.50ff) for, presumably, 'homicidal' and 'homicide' respectively.

[29] The prince shortly returns the crown to the king, but so compelling are these appetitive paradoxes to the king that he soon imposes them upon Hal via a peculiarly mixed Falstaffian metaphor: 'Dost thou so hunger for mine empty chair?' (*2H4* 4.5.94). Implicit here is the king's oft-repeated insinuation that Hal desires Henry's death, that Hal wants not the chair so much as the emptiness of the chair – and the sooner the better. Yet the question also encodes a threat: Hal may 'hunger' for the 'chair', but the throne, too, is 'empty' and may devour the prince. The centrepiece of Hal's subsequent self-defence is perhaps all the more effective to the king because it uses his own vocabulary, accusing the crown of having 'fed upon the body of my father' (159) and of having 'eat thy bearer up' (164).

[30] James Winny tracks further analogies between the physical bulk of Falstaff and the figurative corpulence of Henry IV, especially from the point of view of the Percys who 'durst not come near' the appetitive king 'for fear of swallowing' (*1H4* 5.1.63–4). See *The Player King* (London, 1968), p. 115.

true love, against her rich father and Shallow, the man her father has chosen for social and monetary advantage to be her husband. Persuaded that he has fathered the child while drunk and thus has no memory of the event, Shallow attempts to go through honourably with the marriage. At this point, among other revelations of trickery and disguise, Francisco (who has already wed Luce) oversees the 'birth': 'behold her yet an untouch'd virgin, Cushion come forth, here Signior Shallow, take your child unto you, make much of it, it may prove as wise as the father'. The stage direction follows: 'He flings the cushion at him.'[31] John Fletcher's *The Noble Gentleman* (1623?) shows a cushion-bearing Maria secure marriage to Bewford when she claims to be with child from an anonymous assignation with him (4.5). That she is visibly pregnant but twelve days after the alleged conception does not seem to raise his suspicions.[32] And Richard Brome's *The Sparagus Garden* (1635) concludes somewhat similarly to *The Heir* when Annabel pretends to have conceived premaritally so as to avoid a match with Sir Arnold Cautious and, instead, to secure parental blessing for her desired union with Samuel Touchwood. 'My supposed stain thus I cast from me', she then announces while hurling the prop forth, and another character marvels, ''znails, a cushion. How warm her belly has made it' (5.12.115–16).[33]

Since nothing in the text of *2H4* necessarily calls for a cushion to be produced from beneath Doll's clothing and her trickery displayed, we might take Doll at her word. Yet we cannot extend this trust to the Elizabethan actor beneath the costume. He is not pregnant. The beadle's retort, rather like Hal's derisively literal-minded assessment of Falstaff's tavern props or Henry IV's sharp reference to his 'empty chair', again makes explicit the material reality beneath the theatrical fiction. Indeed, like Falstaff with his cushion-crown, his dagger-sceptre, and his pistol of sack, Doll here darkly parodies an issue of considerable significance to the monarchy: namely, the concept of lineage and legitimate or, in this case, illegitimate succession to power. The mock-crown is now a mock-heir, and if women in the tetralogy are, in the words of a recent study,

the 'custodians of dynastic legitimacy', Doll can be seen as a threat, however merely symbolic, to the hopes both Henrys have placed upon a resumption of patrilineal succession.[34]

Doll's arrest thus furthers a pattern of action that has been developing since *Richard II*, where Henry IV effectively orders the assassination of Richard II who, though deposed and imprisoned, remains a 'living fear' (*R2* 5.4.2) to the new king. In *1 Henry IV*, in turn, those of the nobility who would be kings are defeated by Henry's forces. Moreover, at Shrewsbury, the Earl of Douglas kills all of Henry's troops who have strategically disguised themselves as the king and is rewarded with his freedom by Prince Hal.[35] In *2 Henry IV*, now

---

[31] Thomas May, *The Heir* (London, 1620) sig. H2^v. I am indebted to Alan C. Dessen and Leslie Thomson, *A Dictionary of Stage Directions in English Drama, 1580–1642* (Cambridge, 1999) for this reference.

[32] *The Noble Gentleman*, ed. L. A. Beaurline in *The Dramatic Works in the Beaumont and Fletcher Canon*, gen. ed. Fredson Bowers, vol. 3 (Cambridge, 1976).

[33] *A Critical Edition of Richard Brome's The Weeding of Covent Garden and The Sparagus Garden*, ed. Donald S. McClure (New York and London, 1980). Other versions of, or references to, this kind of ruse may be found in Chapman's *Chabot, Admirall of France* (1612?: ed. G. Blakemore Evans in *The Plays of George Chapman*, gen. ed. Allan Holaday (Woodbridge, Suffolk, 1987)) 3.2.159–63; Middleton and Rowley's *The Old Law* (1618: ed. Catherine M. Shaw (New York and London, 1982)) 4.1.148ff; and Webster's *Appius and Virginia* (1624?: *The Works of John Webster: An Old-Spelling Critical Edition*, ed. David Gunby, David Carnegie, and MacDonald P. Jackson, vol. 2 (Cambridge, 2003)) 4.1.91ff.

[34] Jean E. Howard and Phyllis Rackin, *Engendering a Nation* (London, 1997), p. 26. See also p. 64:

Political authority based on hereditary right required the repression of women for the same reason that it could never do without them. The necessary medium for the transmission of patrilineal authority, women were also the only custodians of the dangerous knowledge that always threatened to dishonor the fathers and disinherit the sons and in so doing, subvert the entire project of patriarchal history.

[35] My phrasing is, admittedly, tendentious, but all the other rebel leaders are to be executed. That Douglas survives is a matter of the historical record in Holinshed, of course, but *1 Henry IV* places his enfranchisement in the context of numerous complex acts of political and military manipulation. It is almost as if, having served his rebellious function for the king by

king by succession, Hal extends this project by imprisoning or banishing any who would wear a false crown or bear a rival claimant – the cushion of tavern royalty or of pregnancy – any who would turn civil rebellion into a tavern brawl by carrying a bottle of sack into battle, any who might turn dynastic struggles into a pillow fight.[36] Those who might remind us of Hal's 'madcap' times (*1H4* 1.2.142, 4.1.95), indeed those who mimic or satirize either Henry in any way, are doomed.

From such a pattern of action, as well, emerges a frankly paranoid reading of *Henry V* which finds that the new king undertakes a war not so much against France as against Francis, not so much to bar the Dolphin's claim but to claim the life of Bardolph. Whatever else the king achieves abroad, by the end of *Henry V* he manages to complete the destruction of nearly everyone who shared the stage with him in Eastcheap – from the fully complicitous, like Falstaff, to an innocent bystander like the Page. Assuming that the Page of *2 Henry IV* becomes the Boy of *Henry V*, then his slaughter by the French must be laid directly to Hal's actions as both prince and king. Hal assigns the child to attend Falstaff in *2 Henry IV* (1.2.12–20), thus bringing him into the corrupting circle of Pistol, Bardolph, *et al.*: "A had him from me Christian, and look if the fat villain have not transform'd him ape' (2.2.70–2), Hal himself observes to Poins. Disgusted by the taverners' cowardly thieving, the Boy twice, and at length, expresses his desire to escape their company (*H5* 3.2.28–53; 4.4.67–77) but, unlike Hal, never has a chance to do so. First seen 'bearing [Falstaff's] sword and buckler' (*2H4* 1.2.0), weapons we know to be rarely used except for false shows of bravery, and last seen following his duty to 'stay with the lackeys with the luggage of our camp' (*H5* 4.4.74–75), the Boy is killed defencelessly at Agincourt. Insofar as he is a surrogate to Hal himself in *2 Henry IV*, keeping company with Falstaff when the prince no longer does, the French atrocity may thus be considered roughly analogous to Douglas's killing of the disguised kings at Shrewsbury: in each case the king's enemies destroy not the king himself but a royal doppelganger. The king has twice placed the boy in harm's way: once comically, so

to speak, and once historically, but the outcome is tragic and surely tests the king's thesis that 'war is [God's] beadle, war is his vengeance; so that here men are punish'd for before-breach of the King's laws in now the King's quarrel' (*H5* 4.1.169–71).[37]

By annihilating his own past and, as it were, giving birth to himself, Hal paradoxically proclaims his authentic patrimony as the true and loyal son of Henry IV by fulfilling the dying king's exhortation to 'busy giddy minds / With foreign quarrels, that action, hence borne out, / May waste the memory of the former days' (*2H4* 4.5.213–15). Henry IV's advice is usually and aptly cited to demonstrate the political cunning of father and son, but the other advice, the other burden, is interior and psychological and clearly extends to Henry IV himself, whose repeated attribution of patricidal urges to his son (e.g. *1H4* 3.2.122–6; *2H4* 4.5.106–8) tacitly endorses the necessity of his own removal to legitimize Henry V's reign. Thus Henry IV also joins the parade of false or surrogate kings to be purged on behalf of Henry V. For his part, Hal presumably hears both components of his father's injunction, the political and the personal. From this perspective, then, the 'foreign quarrel' is but the means to a more important end, giving Henry V the chance to 'waste . . . memory': to erase vestiges of his

---

purging the kingdom of imposters, having been driven off by Hal ('*Douglas flieth*' reads the stage direction at 5.4.43), deluded by Falstaff, and finally captured in flight (when 'falling from a hill' he was 'bruis'd' ignominiously (5.5.21)), Douglas is so impotent a threat that he can be lavished with praise and set harmlessly free.

36 For an example of a literal pillow-fight in performance, see Barbara Hodgdon's description of the tavern scene (2.4) in Trevor Nunn's 1982 production of *2 Henry IV*, featuring Doll and Francis jumping onto a bed, Pistol throwing a bedcover over Falstaff (in premonition of Falstaff's death, as reported in *Henry V*?), and 'the revengeful Francis bash[ing Pistol] over the head with a pillow' (*Shakespeare in Performance: Henry IV, part 2* (Manchester, 1993), pp. 107–8).

37 Pistol presents another awkward test case for Henry V's concept of war as retroactive divine justice. The only figure from Hal's past to survive *Henry V* (albeit in a humiliated state), Pistol was complicit in a fatal beating (*2H4* 5.4.16–17) and eventually resolves to 'steal' home to England as a 'bawd' and 'cutpurse' (*H5* 5.1.85ff).

dubious past, his dubious title, his dubious father, and to affirm his right to rule. 'No king of England, if not king of France!' (*H5* 2.2.193) conceals this logic in its battle cry.

SLEEP

The most personal of Henry V's famous victories over his unkingly past occurs at the end of *2 Henry IV*, when the new king banishes Falstaff from his presence in a speech at once astonishing and predictable. Indeed predicted, for when Falstaff had encouraged Hal to 'practice an answer' to Henry IV in the tavern play, that was not the only answer Hal practised. 'I do, I will' (*1H4* 2.4.481) concludes the royal improvisation with an explicit promise of banishment for Falstaff. Now, at the end of *2 Henry IV*, Henry V does not even use Falstaff's name but instead redefines him as a licensed fool whose office, ironically, has ended as the new court begins. The king elaborates this judgement with a metaphor contrasting sleep and waking:

> I know thee not, old man, fall to thy prayers.
> How ill white hairs becomes a fool and jester!
> I have long dreamt of such a kind of man,
> So surfeit-swell'd, so old, and so profane;
> But being awak'd, I do despise my dream.
>
> (5.5.47–51)

'Prince Hal' is now retroactively designated a condition of sleep. To become king is to wake up and, on the evidence of the tetralogy's royal insomniacs, it means one can never sleep again. Richard II counts the tedious minutes of his prison clock. Henry IV frets wakefully all night, echoing his predecessor by comparing 'the kingly couch' to 'A watch-case or a common 'larum bell' (*2H4* 3.1.16–17) and, in confirmation of this anxiety, discovers that the moment he falls asleep, someone takes his crown.[38] ('Depose me?' (*1H4* 2.4.435) mocked Falstaff in the voice of Henry IV, and Hal does so, at least temporarily.) Staying awake all night before Agincourt, deriding the 'proud dream' of ceremony 'that play'st so subtilly with a king's repose' (*H5* 4.1.257–58) and claiming to envy the sleep of a 'wretched slave' (268), Henry V performs espi-

onage on his own troops, implicitly affirming his earlier observation: the crown is indeed a 'troublesome . . . bedfellow' (*2H4* 4.5.22), especially when it leads one to the hard ground of war. It is much easier to sleep on 'a good soft pillow' of the kind he wishes for Sir Thomas Erpingham, and not the 'churlish turf of France' upon which, Erpingham jokes, he himself lies 'like a king' (*H5* 4.1.14ff.). Falstaff's removal is not just the physical space of ten miles, then, but the much further distance between sleep and waking, fiction and history, or, one might say, *2 Henry IV* and *Henry V*. Banished to the realm of the new king's old nightmares, Falstaff resumes his association with sleep, hollowly hoping to 'be sent for soon at night' (*2H4* 5.5.89–90). At the end of the tavern scene in *1 Henry IV*, he is discovered to have fallen asleep, 'snorting like a horse' (2.4.529) (or so he pretends, anyway; one can never be sure), and conceivably the very first speech he utters – 'Now Hal, what time of day is it, lad?' (1.2.1) – is made upon waking.[39] The association of this

---

[38] The precariousness of Henry IV's reign is sharply rendered by an episode in Holinshed, unused (perhaps for obvious reasons) by Shakespeare, where even the preparation for sleep leaves the king vulnerable:

> One night as the king was going to bed, he was in danger to have beene destroied; for some naughtie traitorous persons had conveied into his bed a certeine iron made with smiths craft, like a caltrop, with three long prickes, sharpe and small, standing upright, in such sort, that when he had laid him downe, & that the weight of his bodie should come upon the bed, he should have beene thrust in with those pricks, and peradventure slain: but as God would, the king not thinking of any such thing, chanced yet to feele and perceive the instrument before he laid him downe, and so escaped the danger.

Holinshed concludes that 'perils of death crept into his secret chamber, and laie lurking in the bed of downe where his body was to be reposed and to take rest'. Quoted from Bullough, vol. 4, p. 181.

[39] As in J. Dover Wilson, *The Fortunes of Falstaff* (Cambridge, 1943), p. 37, or in Orson Welles's *Chimes at Midnight* (1965) where, in one of the many small brilliances of that film, Falstaff feigns sleep to disrupt an attempted prank by Hal. Assured (by lines imported from 2.4) that Sir John is fast asleep and that Poins has picked his pocket, Hal prepares to pour ale on the snoring Falstaff, who promptly kicks the mug from his hands and then carries on as if just waking up. This business

character with the cushion or pillow thus comes full circle, because to banish Falstaff is also, in some sense, to murder sleep, to admit that it is no longer available to Hal as king, to push away the pillow and to put on the crown. Hal's last private words to Sir John before the public rejection are 'Falstaff, good night' (*2H4* 2.4.366). In *Henry V*, we learn that Falstaff dies in bed, fumbling with the sheets, asking for more covers, and hallucinating.[40] Enter Falstaff, asleep? Exit Falstaff, abed, a-dream, a dream.

King Henry V's treatment of Falstaff had been predicted in another way as well, for it is striking how its basic features are anticipated in the portrayal of Falstaff/Fastolfe in *1 Henry VI*. In the earlier play, the first mention of Fastolfe (as, for clarity, I will refer to the character here) notes that he 'play'd the coward' (1.1.131) and 'cowardly fled' the battle, 'not having struck one stroke' (134). Such behaviour leads to Talbot's refusal to be 'so pill'd [F1: pil'd] esteem'd' (1.4.33) as to be part of a prisoner exchange with the unworthy Fastolfe. Confirming this judgement, Fastolfe's first entrance is an exit, deserting Talbot 'in such haste' while stating frankly his intention 'to save myself by flight' (3.2.104–5). In his only other appearance, intruding upon the newly crowned Henry VI, Fastolfe claims that he 'rode from Callice, / To haste unto' the coronation and delivers what turns out to be yet more treason in the form of a letter from the Duke of Burgundy (4.1.9–10). (In *2 Henry IV* Falstaff claims that his poor appearance, 'stain'd with travel, and sweating with desire', will advertise his own haste to the new king, 'the zeal I had to see him', 'my earnestness of affection,' and 'my devotion' (5.5.14ff).) Fastolfe is promptly silenced, humiliated by Talbot for his treachery in battle and stripped of his garter of knighthood, then banished by the king who turns his attention to consolidating his French claims: 'Henceforth we banish thee, on pain of death' (*1H6* 4.1.47). Henry V's sentencing of Falstaff – 'Till then I banish thee, on pain of death' (*2H4* 5.5.63) – shares some of the prefabricated iambics of royal pronouncement, but it is both more personal ('I' not 'we') and technically more lenient in the promise of 'competence of life' (66). Of course the emotional weight of this moment

is infinitely greater than that of Henry VI's executive dismissal of Fastolfe, but the dramatic contours of the scenes match closely. Hasting to his king, a cowardly knight interrupts and profanes – the word attaches to both characters (*1H6* 4.1.41, *2H4* 5.5.50) – the ritual of coronation and is then himself ritually demoted and abjured. It is in just this context, then, that I wish to discuss another scenario in which crowns and cushions are brought together.

THE THRONE ROOM

The English coronation ceremony consists, in brief, of several parts: procession of regalia, royal procession, recognition, oath, anointing, investiture and crowning of the new sovereign. Stressing the role of cushions within these rites is rather like making a close study of the music stands during an orchestral performance: they are necessary, ubiquitous and ideally unnoticeable in their merely supportive functions, yet I will now notice them. The Great Wardrobe accounts from 1483–4, for example, reveal that expenses for the coronation of Richard III included a sum of 23s 4d paid to one 'Thomas Lawford, for the makying and covering of xxxv cushions, some covered in tissue cloth of gold, some in damask cloth of gold, some in velvet and some in baldekyn [silk embroidered with gold thread]'.[41] Some of these would have been used, perhaps, for the regalia, and some for the king, newly arrived at the 'King's Bench' in Westminster Abbey, to sit upon 'under clothe of estate in the marble chaire appareled with clothes and quisshons of gold bawdekyn'.[42] The accounts for Richard

---

foreshadows not only Falstaff's counterfeit at Shrewsbury, which allows him to subvert Hal's victory over Hotspur, but also King Henry's waking from apparent death in *2 Henry IV*, which disrupts Hal's seizure of the crown. More generally, too, we are alerted to the impossibility, with Falstaff, of ever making stable distinctions between being and acting.

40 See the Hostess's account at 2.3.9ff.

41 *The Coronation of Richard III: The Extant Documents*, ed. Anne F. Sutton and P. W. Hammond (Gloucester, 1983), p. 136.

42 The language of the *Little Device* for Henry VII, quoted in Jocelyn Perkins, *The Coronation Book* (London, 1911), p. 168.

III also requisition twenty-one other cushions of specific lengths and materials, including 'A longe quysshon covered in crymsyn tisshue cloth of gold for the anoynting of oure said souverain Lorde the Kyng'.[43] The need for these is explained by the fact that, just before anointing, the new monarch is to approach the area in front of 'the high altar worshipfully arrayed with carpets and cushions' where 'the King shall there lie down *grovelling* whiles the said Cardinal as Archbishop sayeth upon him *Deus Humilium*':[44]

God the visitor of the humble who consoles us with the shining forth of the holy spirit, extend your grace over this your servant so that through him we may feel that you have come to us.

Nichols's account of Elizabeth's coronation in 1559 confirms the practice: 'and there was a carpet with kussyns of golde spread before the aulter . . . The Queenes Majestie being new apparelled came byfore the aulter and leand upon the kussene and over her was spread a reed silken cloth.'[45] Indeed, English monarchs through James I knelt for the anointing rite itself, presumably upon the kind of 'longe quysshon' described above.[46]

The ceremonial function of such cushions may make their first appearance in Shakespeare in the following lines from *2 Henry VI*, where the ambitious Duchess of Gloucester exhorts her husband to consider his chances for the crown:

> Why are thine eyes fix'd to the sullen earth,
> Gazing on that which seems to dim thy sight?
> What seest thou there? King Henry's diadem,
> Enchas'd with all the honors of the world?
> If so, gaze on, and grovel on thy face,
> Until thy head be circled with the same.
>
> (1.2.5–10)

Although the action of crawling on the ground might refer to the quest for supernatural aid,[47] in the context of the Duchess's subsequent speech about her own dream of the diadem (35–40) these lines more likely refer to the coronation ritual itself. To understand the causal link in the Duchess's logic – grovel *until* crowned – and to see that her advice is not merely sarcastic, we can consult the

German *ordo* of 961. This, the paradigmatic coronation script for the English monarchy, makes explicit that the king is to lie in front of the altar, prostrate and in the shape of a cross, before his oath and anointing. (The 'Lytlington' *ordo* or *Liber Regalis*, used for Richard II's coronation in 1377, adds the direction 'super tapetis et quissinis'.)[48] Although the 'grovelling' described in medieval and early modern ceremonies evolves into something far less ostentatious, kneeling, it remains a remarkable image of royal ascendancy achieved by and through humility. The coronation script thus demands a particular performance with prescribed props, including cushions and crown, and such a performance may lie behind the juxtaposition of these objects in the *Henry IV* plays.

I do not, nor need not, claim that Shakespeare had personally observed any such ceremony by

---

43 *The Coronation of Richard III*, p. 156.

44 Again from the *Little Device*, in *English Coronation Records*, ed. Leopold G. Wickham Legg (Westminster, 1901), p. 229. Wickham Legg notes more generally that 'mediaeval and Tudor descriptions tell us' that the king '"lies groveling" upon the cushions and carpets that are spread about the area' (p. xxvii).

45 John Nichols, *The Progresses and Public Processions of Queen Elizabeth*, 3 volumes (London, 1823), vol. I, pp. 61–2. See also, e.g., Thomas Middleton's description of 'Prince Charles his Creation' in *Civitatis Amor* (London, 1616), sig. B3ᵛ:

the Prince made lowe obeisance to his Maiestie three times, and after the third time, when hee was come neere to the King, hee kneeled downe on a rich Pillow or Cushion, whilest sir *Ralph Winwood* principall Secretarie, read his Letters Patents: then his Maiestie, at the reading of the words of Inuestment, put the Robes vpon him, and girded on the Sword, inuested him with the Rodde and Ring, and set the Cappe and Coronet on his head.

46 Percy Ernst Schramm, *A History of the English Coronation*, trans. Leopold G. Wickham Legg (Oxford, 1937), p. 108.

47 As glossed in *The First Part of the Contention* 1.2.9, in *The Norton Shakespeare*, gen. ed. Stephen Greenblatt (New York, 1997). Such a meaning is far clearer in the later conjuring scene: 1.4.10–11.

48 Schramm, p. 106. See also William Jones, *Crowns and Coronations: A History of Regalia* (London, 1902), pp. 202–3: 'The offering being finished, the king bowed himself upon the pavement before the altar, being before prepared by the king's officers, with clothes and suitable cushions of velvet'.

the time he writes the second tetralogy, though an awareness of its details is strongly suggested by *Richard II* 4.1, a scene which dramatizes the process through which Richard becomes 'unking'd' (220) by staging 'the precise reverse of the order of investiture'.[49] But I do suggest that our own awareness of the ceremony allows us to see yet one more way in which the relationship between Hal and Falstaff follows a ritual paradigm. That relationship has been variously construed and profoundly illuminated as, for example, the trial and expulsion of Carnival,[50] a 'Return of the Prodigal Son' scenario,[51] the production and containment of 'subversive perceptions',[52] or as part of a political analogy to Christ's Harrowing of Hell.[53] To these I would add yet another analogue, yet another performance – the historical and material pageant of the coronation ceremony in several of its documented particulars – in part to suggest that some of Falstaff's force as a character comes from his ritual function in an event that is always being staged in a displaced, indirect or anticipatory way: the crowning of Hal as Henry V.

THE TIRING HOUSE

To work out this possible connection, let us return to the centre of the plays' comic gravity: Falstaff's body. The same cushion that theatrically signifies pregnancy for a woman can also assist an actor in the presentation of obesity, especially for a character who refers to his belly as 'my womb, my womb, my womb' (*2H4*, 4.3.22) and who compares his appearance, while walking beside the much smaller Page, to 'a sow that hath overwhelm'd all her litter but one' (1.2.11–12).[54] No direct evidence survives telling us what the first Falstaff, probably Will Kemp, wore to pad out his costume. The plays themselves suggest some, admittedly unlikely, possibilities: a 'bolting-hutch' or 'bombard' as Hal says (*1H4*, 2.4.450–1); 'a huge full hogshead' as Doll says (*2H4*, 2.4.62–3); 'straw' as Shallow implies (*2H4*, 5.5.82); or even 'puddings', the opinion of Mrs Page (*MWW* 2.1.32). Yet other phrases could be heard as literal descriptions of the actor's costume. As David Wiles observes, some of Hal's

epithets – 'wool-sack', 'creature of bumbast', 'stuff'd cloak-bag' (*1H4* 2.4.135, 327, 451–2) – call attention to the fact that 'Falstaff is an actor with stuffing inside his doublet.'[55] (It is no accident that these references are clustered within the intensely metatheatrical tavern scene, showing Falstaff to be false stuff in so many senses.) One could add Ford's 'a bag of flax' (*MWW* 5.5.151) to a list that, again, underscores the *Henry IV* plays' persistent project of demystifying theatrical illusion, whether by crowns that display their status as props, by a throne that is, after all, just a chair, or by clothing that is advertised as costume.

Inigo Jones gives us a tantalizing but, finally, not very informative reference to a Falstaffian costume. In 1634, Jones designed the production of Davenant's *Temple of Love*, a masque featuring 'certaine Magicians' described in the Argument as 'enemies

---

49 Naomi Conn Liebler, 'The Mockery King of Snow: *Richard II* and the Sacrifice of Ritual' in *True Rites and Maimed Rites*, ed. Linda Woodbridge and Edward Berry (Urbana, 1992), pp. 220–39; see especially p. 231.

50 C. L. Barber, *Shakespeare's Festive Comedy* (Princeton, 1959), pp. 192–221.

51 Harry Berger, Jr., 'The Prince's Dog: Falstaff and the Perils of Speech-Prefixity', *Shakespeare Quarterly* 49 (1998), 40–73.

52 Stephen Greenblatt, *Shakespearian Negotiations*, pp. 21–65, and see especially 56.

53 Beatrice Groves, 'Hal as Self-Styled Redeemer: The Harrowing of Hell and *Henry IV, Part 1*', *Shakespeare Survey* 57 (Cambridge, 2004), pp. 236–48.

54 The feminization of Falstaff is accomplished rhetorically at several points in these plays, as when Hal hopes to cast Falstaff in the role of Lady Percy (*1H4* 2.4.108–110) and when, though a self-proclaimed 'sow,' Falstaff is implicitly rendered a ewe in Pistol's reference to Hal as 'thy tender lambkin' (*2H4* 5.3.116). See also *The Merry Wives of Windsor*, where Falstaff is transformed into 'the fat woman of Brainford' (4.2.75–6). For a psychoanalytic reading of Falstaff in the Henriad, with special attention to his figurative femininity, see Valerie Traub, *Desire and Anxiety: Circulations of Sexuality in Shakespearian Drama* (London, 1992), pp. 50–70.

55 *Shakespeare's Clown* (Cambridge, 1987), p. 126. Wiles notes that doublets were ordinarily stuffed out with bombast, a custom that predictably incited the loathing of Philip Stubbes whose *Anatomie of Abuses* (1583) deplores 'these doublets with great bellies, hanging down beneath their pudenda, and stuffed out with four, five, six pound of bombast at the least' (quoted in Wiles, p. 204, n.19).

17. Falstaff and the Hostess. Detail from Francis Kirkman, *The Wits* (1672).

to chaste Love'.[56] Jones stipulated that one of these lecherous figures should wear a shirt 'girt low with a great belly with naked fat sleeves' and 'buskins to show a great swollen leg', noting that the overall effect should be 'like a Sir John Falstaff'.[57] Indeed, whereas Falstaff describes himself as the 'fellow with the great belly' (*2H4* 1.2.146), Fluellen recalls him as the 'fat knight with the great belly doublet' (*H5* 4.7.48), virtually redefining him as a specific costume.[58] The Falstaff depicted in the familiar frontispiece to Francis Kirkman's *The Wits, or Sport upon Sport* (1672) looks very much as though he has simply tucked a small pillow into his shirt and buttoned it up, preferring to distress the Hostess with the size of his goblet as an emblem of his appetite.

Some nineteenth-century Falstaffs, like Stephen Kemble and Julia Glover, evidently required no

[56] William Davenant, *The Temple of Love* (London, 1634), sig. A2ʳ.

[57] Martin Holmes, *Shakespeare and His Players* (New York, 1972), p. 54.

[58] Fluellen, being an Elizabethan stage-Welshman, tends to pronounce his initial 'b's' as 'p's,' which makes me hear him saying 'great pelly doub(p)let', bringing 'belly' within pun's reach of 'pillow'; but neither the Folio nor Quarto texts will let me do this. (Cf. also Fluellen's countryman Evans at *MWW* 5.5.140–1, who tells Falstaff 'Seese is not good to give putter; your belly is all putter', transforming the initial 'b' of 'butter' to 'p', but leaving the 'b' of 'belly' as is.) *The New Pelican Shakespeare*, gen. eds. Stephen Orgel and A. R. Braunmuller (Harmondsworth, 2002), does print 'pelly', though, in Fluellen's speech.

special effects to play the part. The prologue for Kemble's performance even called attention to the actor's size, while implying the conventional use of pillows to pad out actors in the role: 'A Falstaff here tonight by Nature made / Lends to your favorite Bard his pond'rous aid. / No man in buckram he! no stuffing gear! / No feather bed, nor e'en a pillow-bier'.[59] The American actor James Hackett, who performed the role before Abraham Lincoln three times in 1863 and later dined with him to discuss the theatre and Shakespeare's history plays specifically, revealed that he played the role 'with stuffing of india rubber', justifying his choice by claiming that 'Shakespeare refers to it when he says "How now, blown Jack!"'[60] Lincoln's response to this argument is not recorded, though he did wonder why performances of the tavern scene routinely cut the playlet between Falstaff and Hal.[61]

Sir Ralph Richardson, by consensus the greatest, most complexly moving Falstaff of the twentieth (or perhaps any) century, was bulked out with layers of quilting and toweling to protect him from an outer layer of horsehair that he compared to 'an attack from a swarm of bees'.[62] More recently, in the San Diego Old Globe Theatre production of 1995, the role of Falstaff was performed by John Goodman.[63] Entering 1.2 in modern street clothes, Goodman carried a pillow which he then, in plain view of the audience, placed under his shirt as though he were trying it on, or as though it were an ordinary part of his daily attire. Three scenes later, at the Gadshill robbery, Falstaff (along with the rest of the cast) was beginning to acquire a historical costume, but, preposterously, the pillow was now strapped to the outside of his shirt, quite visibly, perhaps to absorb any blows or sword thrusts he might receive during the ambush. The prop was thus simultaneously out of and in character. It was not until 2.4, the tavern scene, that Goodman appeared in full costume, having, as it were, internalized the pillow and become Falstaff.

I do not cite this performance as decisive to my argument, but as a convenient image for my last, admittedly impressionistic point. Namely, it

is Falstaff himself – 'stuffing and all', as Maurice Morgann's famous essay puts it – who is a kind of cushion.[64] Shakespeare's second tetralogy shows us an interrupted coronation ceremony (Henry IV's by Carlisle in *Richard II* 4.1) followed swiftly by a

---

[59] Quoted in William Winter, *Shakespeare on the Stage*, 3rd Series (New York, 1916), p. 341. Winter seems to take special pleasure in noting which actors, male and female, were physically apt for the part.

[60] Tyler Dennett, ed. *Lincoln and the Civil War in the Diary and Letters of John Hay* (New York, 1939), p. 138. In his first appearance in the role, in 1832, opposite Charles Kean's Hotspur, Hackett wore 'a heavy padding or stuffing of curled hair'. See James Hackett, *Notes and Comments upon Certain Plays and Actors of Shakespeare* (New York, 1863), pp. 313–14. Hackett was especially associated with this role, as Edwin Booth wryly noted: 'You know the old gentleman [Hackett] always carried his *Falstaff* belly with him, on all his hunting and fishing tours – by mere chance, of course!' (Quoted in Winter, p. 352.)

[61] Arthur Colby Sprague, *Shakespeare's Histories: Plays for the Stage* (London, 1964), pp. 62–3.

[62] Garry O'Connor, *Ralph Richardson: An Actor's Life* (London, 1982), p. 124. Elsewhere, Richardson was more complimentary about his costume: 'My costume was wonderful, it was Al[i]x Stone who designed it. She created a complete anatomy for me in padding, I had two or three stomachs, two or three chests, and two huge arms. And over this she put a very light, revealing flannel material, so that you could see the anatomy of the creature; in other words, he wasn't a puffed-up football, as he has often been. This was entirely Miss Stone's work and it helped me a great deal.' (Quoted in *Great Acting*, ed. Hal Burton (London, 1967), p. 69.) O'Connor notes that Richardson himself contributed to the costume: 'The bulky gnarled and varicosed legs were, on Richardson's prompting, sculptured in silk quilting . . . and covered in light red stockings' (p. 124).

[63] This was a single play, thoughtfully adapted by Dakin Matthews from the two parts of *Henry IV*, directed by Jack O'Brien, with costume design by Lewis Brownlee.

[64] *Morgann's Essay on the Dramatic Character of Sir John Falstaff*, ed. William Arthur Gill (London, 1912), p. 127. On this point, it is striking how Falstaff is repeatedly entangled in matters of clothing, from his debts to the Hostess for a dozen shirts (*1H4* 3.3.68) to his concealment in Mistress Ford's laundry basket (*MWW* 3.3) and subsequent disguise in the gown, 'thrumm'd hat and . . . muffler' (4.2.78–9) of the fat woman of Brainford, to his promise to Doll of a cap and a kirtle of 'what stuff' she desires (*2H4*, 2.4.274). Falstaff's material being is surely part of his overwhelming verisimilitude, and yet more ironic given his fictive status in the history plays.

systematically inverted coronation (the deposing of Richard II), then by various parodies of the ritual. Among these are Hal's two acts of self-crowning: the first, following Falstaff, with the tavern cushion – perhaps the same cushion Doll will thrust beneath her dress – and the second with the crown of the still-living Henry IV. The tetralogy then stages Henry V's own (and finally official) coronation procession and, in the last play, as Henry V achieves a second crown for his head, we hear his sustained contemplation of 'thrice-gorgeous ceremony' (*H5*, 4.1.266) with its almost obsessive inventory of the trappings of royalty (259–65). In all of this, 'plump Jack' (*1H4*, 2.4.479) has one more part to play. Padded out, 'fret[ting] like a gumm'd velvet' (*1H4*, 2.2.2), wishing to be covered expensively in 'two and twenty yards of satin' (*2H4*, 1.2.43–4) from Master Dommelton,[65] invited to dine with Master Smooth the silk-man (2.1.28–9), Falstaff it is upon whom Prince Hal 'grovels' before assuming the throne. Far from polluting or profaning the thrice-gorgeous royal ceremony of Henry V, then, Falstaff's presence is absolutely necessary to it. For two plays, Hal has wilfully subjected himself to a coronation ritual of self-abasement precisely so that he may stage his rise to kingship as the sun above the clouds, Henry V above Falstaff, and, as the property crew might put it, the crown above the pillow.[66]

---

[65] The sumptuary laws under Henry VII and Henry VIII, which continued with some modifications and occasional disregard into Elizabeth's reign, correlated the length of gown to the rank of the wearer. Knights were limited to five yards of material, and even dukes could not exceed sixteen yards. (See Cumberland Clark, *Shakespeare and Costume* (London, 1937), pp. 14–15.) Falstaff's request for twenty-two yards (for whatever garment he intends it) records the unruly size of both his body and his social aspirations. Furthermore, as Barbara Hodgdon (*Shakespeare in Performance: Henry IV, Part 2*, p. 5) points out, 'the price of the short cloak and slops (£30–60) he has ordered from Master Dommelton' is a large sum, comparable to Shakespeare's purchase price of New Place (£60).

[66] As C. L. Barber puts it, 'Hal's final expulsion of Falstaff appears . . . to carry out an impersonal pattern, not merely political but ritual in character' (*Shakespeare's Festive Comedy*, p. 206). Not merely ritual either, I would add, but politically ritual. On this point, too, we might recall that the historical Henry V was crowned – as were all English monarchs since Edward I – in St Edward's chair in Westminster Abbey. Beneath its seat lay the stone of Scone, by legend the very stone that Jacob had set up as an anointed pillar to commemorate his dream of the ladder signifying heavenly ascent and the continuance of divine blessing (see Genesis 28:10–22). Before acquiring its symbolic heft, however, the stone of kings had a humbler function on the plain of Luz: it was Jacob's pillow.

HUMANITY AT STAKE: MAN AND ANIMAL IN SHAKESPEARE'S THEATRE

ANDREAS HÖFELE

I

John Foxe's account of the life of Thomas Cromwell, Lord Chancellor to King Henry VIII, includes an episode which, 'though it be somewhat long, with the circumstances and all',[1] Foxe deems worth our attention. It is the story of how Cromwell helped Cranmer's secretary. In 1540, the twenty-first year of his reign, King Henry pushed the so-called Six Articles through Parliament, 'much agaynst the mind and contrary to the consent of the Archbishop of Canterbury Thomas Cranmer, who had disputed three daies agaynst the same in the Parliament house, with great reasons and authorities'.[2] Henry asked to see Cranmer's objections in writing, presumably without the slightest intention of being swayed by the Archbishop's opinion but because of 'the singular favour which he ever bare to Cranmer, and reverence to his learning'. Whereupon Cranmer 'collecting both his arguments, authorities of Scriptures, and Doctors together, caused his Secretary to write a fayre booke thereof for the king, after his order' (1185).

Complications ensued, and with them the story proper begins. Due to a series of trivial mishaps involving a locked closet, a missing key and a visiting father from the country, the secretary, instead of having deposited the book in a safe place, finds himself in a wherry on the Thames with his precious and, of course, highly incendiary parcel 'thrust [. . .] under his girdle'. With him in the boat, bound from Westminster Bridge to St Paul's Wharf, are four yeomen of the guard. As it happens, the King himself is in his barge on the river as well, 'with a great number of Barges and boates about him' (1185), watching a bear being baited in the water. The guardsmen, overriding the secretary's wish to make directly for St Paul's Wharf, decide to stop and watch. Using their poleaxes, they manoeuvre the wherry so far into the throng, 'that being compassed with many other whirryes and boates, there was no refuge if the Beare should break loose and come upon them; as in very deede within one pater-noster' the bear does. The guardsmen rather unheroically abandon the boat – 'Talle yemen but ill keepers', says the note in the margin – leaving the poor secretary trapped (1185).

The Beare and the doges so shaked the whirry wherein the Secretary was, that the boate being ful of water, soncke to the ground, and being also as it chanced an ebbing tide, he [the secretary] there sate in the end of the whirry up to the middle in water. To whom came the Beare and all the dogges. The Beare, seking as it were aide and succor of him, came back with his hinder parts upon him and so rushing upon him, the booke was losed from his girdle, and fell into the Thames out of his reach (1185).

The King, highly displeased with his pastime turned to mayhem, calls it off: '[A]way away with the Beare, and let us go all hence' (1185), he cries.

---

[1] John Foxe, *Actes and Monuments of Matters Most Speciall and Memorable* [1583], Facsimile edition on CD Rom, ed. David G. Newcombe and Michael Pidd (Oxford, 2001), p. 1185.
[2] Foxe, *Actes and Monuments*, p. 1185.

The secretary's plight, however, is not relieved. '[P]erceiving his booke to fleete away in the Thames, [he] called to the Beareward to take [it] up' (1185). But the bear warden, though a servant of the young princess Elizabeth, is an 'errant Papist'. No sooner does he lay hands on the manuscript than he delivers it to a priest of his own persuasion, who conveniently happens to be 'standing on the bancke' (1185). Before the secretary manages to scramble onto dry land, the priest examines the book, 'made much a doe, and tolde the Beareward, that whosoever claymed the booke, should surely be hanged' (1185). When the secretary does claim the book, the bear warden, who 'seemed rather to be a Beare himselfe, than the Maister of the beast' (1186), refuses to hand it over. Not for love nor money can he be dissuaded from wanting to see both the secretary and his master, the Archbishop, hanged.

In the end, after yet further complications, it is only Cromwell's personal intervention that saves the day. 'It is more meter', he tells the bear warden, 'for thee to medle with thy Beares than with such writing and were it not for thy maisters sake, I would set thee fast by the feet, to teach such malapert knaves to meddle with Counceliers matters' (1186). The book is restored, the bear warden put in his place. Cromwell and Cranmer exchange amicable jests about the danger now luckily past. 'And so after humble thanks geven to the Lord Cromwell, the said [secretary] departed with his booke, which, when he agayne had fayre written, was delivered to the kinges Maiesty' (1186).

II

Foxe's story predates the Elizabethan theatre by several decades. But the ingredients it draws into the hurly-burly of its central incident look oddly like the parts of a Shakespearian drama assembly kit. There is a disrupted court entertainment and a king rising in anger; there is a faithful retainer pursued by a bear and another, saucy one put in the stocks (well, almost); there is a viciously misappropriated object used to ruin its owner and a book (again, almost) drowned. All this is brewed into a plot of potentially fatal consequence but then rerouted into a romance-like pattern of loss and eventual recovery. So full of quasi-Shakespearian motifs is Foxe's tale that it seems almost impossible, quoting Duke Senior, *not* to find tongues in trees, books in the running brooks, and Shakespeare in everything. But even setting aside such figments of Shakespearian tunnel vision, the story is of interest for the traces of early modern performance in it.

First, and most obviously, the story provides a record of bear-baiting performed in one of its more unusual forms. This particular variety was evidently not new, 80-odd years later, when James I had one of his famous white bears baited in the Thames for the entertainment of the Spanish ambassador.[3] But bear-baiting is not the only public spectacle evoked. The secretary faces the prospect of hanging. Actual execution is averted here but not, of course, in the larger narrative, 'The history concernyng the lyfe, actes, and death of the famous and worthy Counsailour Lord Thomas Cromwell, Earle of Essex'. This history, in which the story of the secretary serves as an exemplary illustration of the wit and goodness of the future martyr, has its predictable *telos* in the final scene on the scaffold. And likewise, Foxe's life of the secretary's master, Archbishop Cranmer, moves towards its inevitable conclusion in the graphically described, and indeed graphically illustrated, public burning at the stake in the town ditch at Oxford (illustration 18). The story, thus fraught with images of violent death, serves as a prelude to the horrendous grand final 'act' on the scaffold or at the stake in which Foxe's lives of Cromwell and of Cranmer culminate, as do all his other tales of Protestant martyrdom. Dramatically intersecting with the disrupted spectacle of bear-baiting, the story of the secretary itself forms an episodic intersection of the lives of two martyrs on their trajectory to spectacular death.

In Foxe's Christian world view, the saint and the beast would seem to be conceivable only as polar opposites, but in drawing them together, the story

---

[3] For a discussion of this see Barbara Ravelhofer, 'Beasts of Recreation: Henslowe's White Bears', *English Literary Renaissance*, 32 (2002), 287–323; p. 291.

The burning of Tharchbishop of Cant. D. Tho. Cranmer, in the town dich at Oxford, with his hand first thrust into the fyre, wherwith he subscribed before.

L. Receiue my spirit.

Frier John.

18. The burning of Cranmer from Foxe's *Actes and Monuments* (1563).

serves as a reminder that the drama of public torture, both of humans and of animals, was a show in much the same arena. The spectacle of execution and the spectacle of bull- and bear-baiting share the same basic type of performance space: an arena, a scaffold, stake or platform surrounded by spectators. It is of course the same as that of the Elizabethan public theatres on the northern outskirts of the city and on Bankside, the former right next to the gallows at Shoreditch, the latter close to the Beargarden and indeed close to the stretch of river where the bear is baited in Foxe's story.

What is even more important than their physical proximity is a sense of the connection between these forms of public spectacle and their mutually reinforcing affective energies in what we might call the perceptual topography or, to use a term coined by the Russian structuralist Yuri Lotman, the semiosphere of early modern London.[4] The similarity of the two spectacles, animal torture and public execution, creates semantic spill-over, *synopsis*, that is, 'seeing together'. The staging of one performance is always framed by, always grounded in, an awareness of the other. If heretics, like baited bears, were tied to the stake, this would on the one hand signify their demotion to a level below the human. But on the other hand it would also suggest the Christian iconography of the sacrificial

---

4 Yuri M. Lotman, *Universe of the Mind: A Semiotic Theory of Culture* (London and New York, 1990), pp. 123–4.

lamb of God, with the stake a typological analogue of the Cross.

In joining martyrs with a bear and thus evoking the spectacle associated with their respective suffering, Foxe's story traces out a tableau in which the stage is set for Shakespeare – the wings of a triptych, as it were, in which the centrepiece remains to be inserted. With the establishment of the public playhouse, the dyadic interplay between the scapegoating rituals performed on the bodies of saint and beast becomes a triadic arrangement. To speak of theatre as the centrepiece in this arrangement is not, I would claim, just another effect of Shakespearian tunnel vision. The human stage of the playhouse does indeed mark a middle position between saint and beast. Horizontally linked with the other contemporary forms of public spectacle and vertically placed on a sliding scale between heaven and hell, Shakespeare's stage thrives on an economy of endlessly fungible signifiers which this symbolic order of space offers. And it is within this economy that it negotiates the place of the human.

III

No story without incident, no incident without a border crossing. At the most elementary level, this is, according to Lotman, what defines narrative, what distinguishes plot from description. The breaking loose of the bear in Foxe's story is such an incident. It brings about the secretary's plight and ultimately Cromwell's intervention, from which the story derives its title. Lotman speaks of *'the shifting of a persona across the borders of a semantic field'*[5] (italics Lotman). Although the label 'persona' is usually reserved for humans, its use for the bear in Foxe's story is curiously apt.

Crossing the boundary that separates the stage from the audience and thus guarantees the containment of the spectacle, the bear invades the space of the spectators. Confusion ensues, distinctions collapse. Those who had come as safely distanced spectators to watch an animal show find themselves involuntarily drawn into the show as co-actors thrashing about with the dogs and the bear in the river. But the worst part is obviously that of the secretary transfixed in panic-stricken dignity as the wherry sinks to the shallow river bottom and the beasts close in. Bear-baiting, it has often been remarked, is an enactment of man's ascendancy. It is a demonstration of wild, brutish nature released but under control and thus, for all its brutal uncouthness, a fitting entertainment for a monarch. Not only Henry VIII and James I, but Elizabeth too is reported to have been particularly fond of bear-baiting. At the other end of the social scale, bear-baiting provided the one domain where those at the bottom, those who in their daily lives had to cringe under the whip and scorn of their betters, were given the opportunity to lash out at a creature below even themselves.[6]

The central moment in Foxe's narrative, the moment when human control over animal nature breaks down, is all the more striking because it elides not just the distinction between spectators and actors. As the bear joins the secretary in the swamped boat, the distinction between man and beast all but collapses too. The text registers this in a single image, that of '[t]he Beare seking as it were aide and succor of him'. Granting the bear intentionality, the text makes him momentarily indistinguishable in kind from the man in the same boat. Briefly, for the span of half a sentence, an odd, perhaps comical, but perhaps also oddly touching companionship in distress is established across the suspended species boundary, bear and man, suddenly fellow creatures. But only for a fleeting moment. Instantly the boundary is re-established through a vanishing act. The bear simply disappears. Unlike the secretary – a footnote in some editions of Foxe's work informs the reader that his name was Morris and that he was alive and well at the time of publication – the bear has neither name

---

[5] Jurij Lotman, *The Structure of the Artistic Text* (Ann Arbor, 1977), p. 233.

[6] And, not to be forgotten, bear-baiting offered an ever-ready store of abusive metaphor for the assertion of male dominance over women. Terence Hawkes, 'Harry Hunks, Superstar', *Shakespeare in the Present* (London, 2002), pp. 83–106: p. 151 n.22) quotes Joseph Swetnam's tract *The Arraignment of Lewd, Idle, Froward and Unconstant Women* (London 1645) for particularly graphic illustration.

nor further story. How many more mastiff attacks he survived we do not know. Nor do we know whether the dogs did not eventually bite or scratch out his eyes so that his only further use to his human masters was to be whipped by their customers in the popular pastime of 'whipping the blind bear'.

Such considerations certainly go against the further drift of Foxe's story, in which the dangerous bear is instantly supplanted by the even more dangerous Papist bear warden, who 'seemed rather to be a bear himself, than the master of the beast'. We can of course swathe the moment of species confusion and category breakdown in layers of contextualization. We could, for instance, relate the humanizing of the bear to the age-old tradition of animal fable where it is a matter of course that animals think, act and even speak like humans. Or we could refer to the symbolic zoology of the bestiaries and *The Physiologus* with their perpetual recourse to anthropomorphism. But this would defuse the special strangeness of the moment in which the bear escapes enclosure, the moment in which the order of representation that keeps man and beast apart is overrun by the bear's sheer uncontainable presence. Foxe's story not only marks the precise slot which the theatre in due course filled within an ensemble of semiotically interacting forms of spectacle; its central incident also highlights a resistance to representational closure which the theatre inherits and shares.

In the remaining part of this chapter I want to explore the three aspects I have highlighted in Foxe's narrative with reference to Shakespeare. The three aspects are: the collusion between theatre and bearbaiting,[7] the permeability of the species boundary between humans and animals, and the interaction of presence and representation. My contention will be that these three aspects converge in Shakespearian drama.

IV

The early modern theatre is an exemplary site of the transition from a culture of presence to a culture of representation, or, as Hans Ulrich Gumbrecht puts it in his recent book,[8] from a culture

of presence to a culture of meaning. Like others before him, Gumbrecht takes the contrast between the medieval, or Catholic, and the early modern, or Protestant theology of the Eucharist, the contrast between the doctrine of Real Presence and the doctrine of commemorative representation, as a central indicator of this transition.[9] Applying this distinction to the theatre, Gumbrecht writes:

As the substance of Christ's body and the substance of Christ's blood were being replaced by body and blood as meanings in Protestant theology, so the attention of the spectators at theatrical performances switched from the actors' own bodies to the characters that they embodied.[10]

Citing Hamlet as such a complex character, Gumbrecht writes that, increasingly, 'the actors' bodies became removed [. . .] from the spectators'

---

7 Recent research on bear-baiting and the theatre includes Andrew Gurr, 'Bears and Players: Philip Henslowe's Double Acts', *Shakespeare Bulletin*, 22 (2004), 31–41; John R. Ford, 'Changeable Taffeta: Re-Dressing the Bears in *Twelfth Night*', *Upstart Crow*, 24 (2004), 3–14; Jason Scott Warren, 'When Theatres Were Bear-Gardens; or, What's at Stake in the Comedy of Humors', *Shakespeare Quarterly*, 54 (2003), 63–82; and my own 'Sackerson the Bear', *REAL*, 17 (2001), 160–177.

8 Hans Ulrich Gumbrecht, *Production of Presence: What Meaning Cannot Convey* (Stanford, 2004).

9 Gumbrecht's historical watershed closely resembles what Heidegger conceived of as the beginning of 'the age of representation'. As Heidegger argues in his essay on 'The time of the world-picture', the Middle Ages did not see objects inherently related to their perception by man. The world was not placed before man, it was not 'pictured', and man did not have to relate to it. Everything in existence was seen as *ens creatum* and received its meaning from precisely the fact that it was part of creation and specifically from the idea that as part of creation it was analogous to the creative cause (*analogia entis*). This axiom, that by virtue of being its creator God was present in everything, rendered the question of representation irrelevant. There was no place, and no need, for further enquiry into the nature of God's presence, let alone for enquiry into the structure of reference or signification. According to Heidegger, it was for modernity to introduce the question of *repraesentatio* and to create what antiquity and the Middle Ages could not develop: a world-picture, a sense of the world-as-picture. Martin Heidegger, 'Die Zeit des Weltbildes' in: Martin Heidegger, *Holzwege*, 4th edn (Frankfurt, 1963), pp. 69–104.

10 Gumbrecht, *Production of Presence*, p. 30.

reach' and 'whatever is tangible, whatever belongs to the materiality of the signifier, becomes secondary, and indeed removed from the early modern signifying scene, as soon as the meaning in question is being deciphered'.[11] All this is, of course, very sweeping and in need of careful differentiation as one comes to look more closely at specific historical material. But positing a neat historical divide is not Gumbrecht's main concern anyway. More important is the recognition of a simultaneity and productive tension between presence effects and meaning effects[12] and the potential for (quoting Gumbrecht) 'provocative instability and unrest'[13] that this tension generates. Gumbrecht urges that we renew our engagement with the neglected or even repressed aspects of the tangible, the material – of that which we experience with our senses before the mind's analytical reflexes kick in. Perennially strong in poetry – 'even the most overpowering institutional dominance of the hermeneutic dimension could never fully repress the presence effects of rhyme and alliteration, of verse and stanza'[14] – the tension between presence effects and meaning effects is manifested with particular force in early modern drama. Straddling the divide between conceptual orality and writing, and thriving, as Robert Weimann has shown, on the interplay between *platea* and *locus*, Shakespeare's theatre of course attests to the emergence of the modern regime of representation. But its impact derives from its capacity to disturb this very regime through moments which not only (quoting Weimann) 'exceed the bounds of representational closure'[15] but seem to lie outside it, belonging to a different order altogether.

V

Returning to the bear whose uncontainable presence led into these observations, and looking now for Shakespearian exemplars of his species, one has to admit that the real physical presence of animals on the Shakespearian stage is scanty at best. According to *Shakespeare in Love*, Lance's dog Crab was a real live creature; and according to a minority vote on *The Winter's Tale*, so was the bear at the end of

Act 3.[16] But even if bears, or any other live animals for that matter, are rare birds on Shakespeare's human stage, their imaginative presence can be overwhelming. The world of *Lear*, of *Timon* or of *The Tempest* virtually teems with them. Can we put down this teeming multitude to 'representation'? Does the Prologue of *Henry V* apply here? Must we think, when we hear of bears, serpents, spaniels or 'the wolf and owl' (*Lear* F 2.2.382), that we see them? The effect of Shakespeare's clusters of animal 'images', I would suggest, is very often not so much mimetic or visual as affective, even visceral. Perhaps it is misleading to speak of animal '*imagery*' at all. The term seems rather too closely associated with the overconfident assertion of meaning by an older school of criticism, as expressed in the title of Caroline Spurgeon's *Shakespeare's Imagery, and What It Tells Us*. The imaginary range of animals in Shakespeare's plays goes well beyond classifiable signification. Its impact may result precisely from a refusal to tell us what it 'means'. And this is hardly surprising. What is designated as 'animal' or 'bestial' in Shakespeare's culture – and, of course, not just in *Shakespeare*'s culture – is a sphere beyond the reach of rational control and discursive order, no less strange and unfathomable than the so-called supernatural, but perhaps even more uncanny because it is closer to us. The *super*-natural lies *outside* nature, whereas man and beast are in it together. The condition of natural being that they share entails a troubling propensity towards convergence. This convergence, which also always undermines the representational order of things, may account for the special affinity of animal nature to presence effects in Shakespearian theatre. This is

---

[11] Gumbrecht, *Production of Presence*, p. 30.
[12] Gumbrecht, *Production of Presence*, pp. 106–7.
[13] Gumbrecht, *Production of Presence*, p. 108.
[14] Gumbrecht, *Production of Presence*, p. 18.
[15] Robert Weimann, *Author's Pen and Actor's Voice: Playing and Writing in Shakespeare's Theatre* (Cambridge, 2000), p. 199.
[16] The minority vote is Barbara Ravelhofer's ('Beasts of Recreation'). Neville Coghill ('Six Points of Stagecraft in *The Winter's Tale*', *Shakespeare Survey* 11 (1958), pp. 31–41) opposes the idea of a real bear on the stage, a view endorsed in Stephen Orgel's edition of *The Winter's Tale* (Oxford, 1996), pp. 156f.

nowhere more evident than in the first scene of
Macbeth.

VI

Thunder and lightning. Enter three Witches

FIRST WITCH	When shall we three meet again
	In thunder, lightning, or in rain?
SECOND WITCH	When the hurly-burly's done,
	When the battle's lost and won.
THIRD WITCH	That will be ere the set of
	sun.
FIRST WITCH	Where the place?
SECOND WITCH	Upon the heath.
THIRD WITCH	There to meet with
	Macbeth.
FIRST WITCH	I come, Grimalkin!
SECOND WITCH	Paddock calls.
THIRD WITCH	Anon.
ALL	Fair is foul, and foul is fair,
	Hover through the fog and filthy air.

Exeunt   (1.1.1–11)

This unique opening addresses the usual questions
the exposition of a play is expected to answer:
When? Where? Who? But it does so in a way that
baffles normal expectation. The here and now of
a represented fictitious situation like, for example,
that on the battlements of nocturnal Elsinore in
the first scene of *Hamlet*, is and is not established at
the beginning of *Macbeth*. 'Thunder and lightning',
says the stage direction, but thunder, lightning and
rain are at once transported, quoting Lady Macbeth, 'beyond the ignorant present' (55f) so that we
are disconcertingly made to feel 'the future in the
instant' (1.5.57). The distinction between present
and future, between the place where we are and the
place where we will be is elided, landing us simultaneously in both. Time and place, instead of being
reliably fastened down, acquire the hovering indeterminacy of the weird sisters themselves. While
strongly drawing us into the play, the opening scene
does not provide us with a clearly identifiable fictitious *locus*. As representation it remains diffuse. Its
presence on the unlocalized *platea*, however, is all
the more powerful.

This is largely due to the 'presence effects of
rhyme and metre' (Gumbrecht), the incantatory
trochaic rhythm. The words register as magically
performative, their ritualistic function dominates
over the discursive production of sense. The jarring logic of line 4, 'When the battle's lost, and
won', is driven home by the inexorable cadence of
the verse. Some of this strangeness can, no doubt,
be defused through rationalization. Battles, some
commentators have pointed out, unless they end in
a draw, *are* actually lost *and* won, if not by one and
the same party.[17] (The line would thus signal not
so much the suspension of binary logic as an attitude of indifference.) But, feasible though it may
be, such rationalization flattens rather than captures
the effect of the scene. The 'or' in line 2 ('In thunder, lightning, or in rain') is arguably even stranger
than the 'and' in line 4. By simply exchanging the
two words we would be semantically back in the
normal world, but the point is precisely that we are
not.

If the presence effect of the scene is crucially
linked with the undoing of distinctions, the name
of Macbeth turns up at the very core of this undoing. After the 'when' and the 'where', the 'who'
follows as the necessary third step in a sequence
whose endpoint is made all the more inevitable by
the awkward fit of the rhyme, 'heath'/'Macbeth'.
But the eerie flow of the witches' chant, once it has
closed in on its target, immediately takes off again.
The seamless transition to Grimalkin and Paddock
in lines 8 and 9 enrols Macbeth in a trinity of bestial familiars. As comrade with the cat and toad, his
'single state of man' is shaken before he even enters
the stage.

From the first scene on, the play continues
to probe one of the foundational distinctions of
Western culture, that between man and beast,
human and non-human. As Stephen Booth said
of *Macbeth*: 'Categories will not define. Words,

---

[17] Unless, of course, that party happens to be King Pyrrhus of
Epirus.

notably the word man, . . . will not define.'[18] Definition entails separation, the demarcation of a border between A and non-A. But it is in the logic of borders that their very existence generates the impulse to cross them, to smuggle, to transgress. Such border-crossing is at the core of the play's insistent questioning of the human. It surfaces in those instances where terms are shifted across the species boundary; in Lady Macbeth's remark about the messenger, for example, 'The raven himself is hoarse / That croaks the fatal entrance of Duncan / Under my battlements' (1.5.37–39).

Or when the First Murderer's assertion, 'We are men, my liege', triggers Macbeth's casual slip into a taxonomy of dogs whose inflationary differentiation of canines elides the much more momentous difference between dog and man.

> Ay, in the catalogue ye go for men,
> As hounds and greyhounds, mongrels, spaniels, curs,
> Shoughs, water-rugs, and demi-wolves are clept
> All by the name of dogs; the valued file
> Distinguishes the swift, the slow, the subtle,
> The house-keeper, the hunter, every one
> According to the gift which bounteous nature
> Hath in him closed – whereby he does receive
> Particular addition from the bill
> That writes them all alike; – and so of men.
>
> (3.1.93–102)

Most horrendously, this shifting of epithets across the species divide shows up in the murder of Lady Macduff and her son. After Macbeth's visionary 'pity, like a naked new-born babe' (1.7.21) and the numerous other references to babes in the play, the murderer's 'What, you egg!' (4.2.84), instantly followed by the brutal killing of the boy, is all the more horrifying.

All these instances are orchestrated around the central figure of Macbeth. In him, the questioning of the boundary between human and in-human becomes obsessively intense. It culminates in the agitated dialogue before the killing of Duncan:

MACBETH   I dare do all that may become
            a man, Who dares do more is
            none.

LADY MACBETH   What beast was't then
                That made you break this enterprise to me?
                When you durst do it, then you were a man;
                And to be more than what you were, you would
                Be so much more the man.

(1.7.46–51)

Amid the tense haggling over the proper relation between the terms 'man' and 'more', it is the word 'beast' that catches the ear. The single most strongly stressed syllable in the whole passage, it virtually bursts out from its semantic frame, a suppressed truth finally coming out into the open. The 'beast', these lines declare, is no intruder from outside, but always already lurking within. In this, the play endorses and anatomizes the Renaissance, or Humanist, notion of man.

In his recent book on *Shakespeare's Humanism*, Robin Headlam Wells has offered a timely reminder that sixteenth-century notions of human nature were probably somewhat less postmodern than we have come to take for granted.[19] But that does not mean these notions were comfortably stable or harmoniously unified. Pico della Mirandola's famous oration known under the title 'On the Dignity of Man' may be, as Jakob Burckhardt enthused, 'one of the noblest of that great age'[20] but its neo-Platonist celebration of unlimited human perfectibility is also the record of a fundamental aporia and as such, according to the Italian philosopher Giorgio Agamben, 'anything but edifying'.[21] Rather than giving substance to the notion of man, Agamben argues, it 'verifies the absence of a nature

18 Stephen Booth, *King Lear, Macbeth, Indefinition and Tragedy* (New Haven, 1983), p. 97.
19 Robin Headlam Wells, *Shakespeare's Humanism* (Cambridge, 2005). Cf. also Kent Cartwright, *Theatre and Humanism: English Drama in the Sixteenth Century* (Cambridge, 1999).
20 Jacob Burckhardt, *The Civilization of the Renaissance in Italy* [1860] (London, 1990), p. 229.
21 Giorgio Agamben, *The Open: Man and Animal* (Stanford, 2004), p. 29.

proper to *Homo*, holding him suspended between a celestial and a terrestrial nature, between animal and human – [a] being always less and more than himself'.[22] The relevant passage from Pico reads:

We have made you neither celestial nor earthly, neither mortal nor immortal, so that, freely choosing and for your own honour, as it were the moulder and maker of your self, you may form yourself in what pattern you choose. You will be able to degenerate into the lowest ranks, which are those of the brutes. Through the judgement of your soul you will be able to be reborn into the highest ranks, those of the divine.[23]

In placing *homo*, not between animal and divine, but between 'animal and human', Agamben obviously misreads Pico. But he does so in a way that clarifies rather than distorts. In Pico's *Oration*, the category of the 'human' is not the middle part of a triadic symmetry, equidistant between two poles, but always already predicated on the exclusion of animal nature.

As early as Pico man emerges as 'a field of dialectical tensions always already cut by internal caesurae that . . . separate . . . "anthropophorous" animality and the humanity which takes bodily form in it'.[24] This is also borne out by Carolus Bovillus's *De Sapiente* (1509), in the words of Ernst Cassirer, 'perhaps the most peculiar and in some respects most characteristic creation of Renaissance philosophy'.[25] Bovillus illustrates his anthropological system with a diagram (illustration 19). At first glance, it looks reassuringly innocuous – a ladder of degree to please a Tillyard. But the solid-looking architectural symmetry actually enforces a logical paradox: A equals non-A. While the left side distinguishes the mineral, vegetable and animal stages from man, the right side includes them all within him. While the left construes man as a separate entity, the right dissolves this entity, inadvertently revealing (quoting Agamben once more) 'the aporias of this body that is irreducibly drawn and divided between animality and humanity' (12).

When Macbeth braces himself for the murder, it is as if he were trying to overcome this aporetic disjunction by replacing it with his own deliberate dissociation of hand and eye:

> Stars, hide your fires,
> Let not light see my black and deep desires,
> The eye wink at the hand – yet let that be
> Which the eye fears, when it is done, to see.
>
> (1.4.50–3)

The Oxford editor, Nicholas Brooke, glosses line 54 'let the eye not see what the hand is doing'. Since antiquity the hand has ranked high among the distinctive criteria of the human. Anaxagoras held that it was the possession of hands which made humans the most intelligent of animals. Aristotle, conversely, claims that 'it is because they are most intelligent that human beings are given hands'.[26] The hand, it is safe to say, is distinctively human, 'the instrument of instruments',[27] as Aristotle calls it, but an instrument it is nonetheless and as such it is relegated to the merely physical, or animal side of the fundamental binarism Greek philosophy has bequeathed to Western culture. In seeking to cut the connection between eye and hand, Macbeth is attempting to rid himself of the fetters of human self-perception; he is trying to become an *unconscious* doer of deeds, which is how we first encounter him in the battle report of the 'bloody man' in scene 2 where the grammatical confusion about who unseams whom 'from the nave to th' chops' (1.2.22) bestializes both the celebrated butcher and his quarry.

The same severance of doing and seeing recurs in Lady Macbeth's soliloquy in the following scene – evidence of the couple's almost telepathic rapport at this stage. The dissociation is even more extreme when the hand, now 'keen knife', is driven by its own volition and hidden from the view of watchful Heaven:

---

22 Agamben, *The Open*, p. 29.
23 Giovanni Pico della Mirandola, 'Oration: On the Dignity of Man', Stevie Davies, ed., *Renaissance Views of Man* (New York, 1967), pp. 65–82; p. 67.
24 Agamben, *The Open*, p. 12.
25 Ernst Cassirer, *Individuum und Kosmos in der Philosophie der Renaissance* [1926] (Darmstadt, 1969), p. 93.
26 Aristotle, *On the Parts of Animals*, trans. with a commentary by James G. Lennox (Oxford, 2001), p. 98 (=687 a).
27 Aristotle, *De Anima*, 423a 1–3.

MINE RALE · VEGE TABILE · SENSI BILE · RATIO NALE · VIR TVS · LVXV RIA · GV LA · ACE DIA ·

PETRA · ARBOR · EQVS · HOMO · STVDIOSVS · SENSVALIS · VITALIS · MINERALIS ·

INTEL LIGIT · INTEL LIGIT ·

SENTIT · SENTIT · SENTIT · SENTIT ·

VIVIT · VIVIT · VIVIT · VIVIT · VIVIT · VIVIT ·

EST · EST · EST · EST · EST · EST · EST · EST ·

19. Carolus Bovillus's anthropological ladder of degree (1509).

> Come, thick night,
> And pall thee in the dunnest smoke of hell,
> That my keen knife see not the wound it makes,
> Nor heaven peep through the blanket of the dark
> To cry, 'Hold, hold'.
>
> (1.5. 49–53)

Frederick Engels, founding his anthropology on the centrality of work, turned from the idealist tradition to the materialist Anaxagoras and the hand as evolutionary key factor in the 'Menschwerdung des Affen', the anthropogenesis of the ape.[28] The work mentioned in *Macbeth* is of two kinds. It is 'this most bloody piece of work' of which Banquo speaks after the murder of Duncan (2.3.127) and the 'work' Macbeth commissions the murderers to perform

on Banquo and Fleance (3.1.135). This is the work where the eye winks at the hand. But there is also the work directed against Macbeth, the campaign expressly ratified by 'Him above' (3.6.32), that 'may again / Give to our tables meat, sleep to our nights, / Free from our feasts and banquets bloody knives' (3.6.33–5). And even more sharply contrasted with Macbeth's handiwork is the 'most miraculous work in this good King' (4.3.148), the work of 'touching' performed by Edward the Confessor with his

---

[28] Friedrich Engels, 'Der Antheil der Arbeit an der Menschwerdung des Affen' (='The Part Played by Labour in the Transition from Ape to Man'), Karl Marx and Friedrich Engels, *Werke* vol. 20 (Berlin, 1962), pp. 444–55, p. 444.

healing hands: 'but at his touch, / Such sanctity hath Heaven given his hand, / They presently amend' (4.3.144–6).

By this time in the play (Act 4, scene 3), Macbeth's inner dissociation has come to the surface and hardened into an image of total bestialization. While his struggle with himself had revealed the 'mobile border within living man' over which, according to Agamben, 'the very decision of what is human and what is not'[29] is – always inconclusively, always provisionally – fought out, he is now perceived as unambiguously inhuman. What was dual has become single. The play has given us no cause to assume that Macbeth is particularly 'luxurious' or 'avaricious' but in Malcolm's verdict in 4.3 these and all the other 'multiplying villainies of nature . . . swarm upon him' (1.2.11f) – all the vices, in fact, which Christianity and Humanism classify as 'animal':[30]

> I grant him bloody,
> Luxurious, avaricious, false, deceitful,
> Sudden, malicious, smacking of every sin
> That has a name.
>
> (4.3.58–61)

This radically simplified view of Macbeth is held by his victorious enemies at the end of the play. Macduff's 'Turn hell-hound, turn' (5.10.3) sounds an ironic echo of the dog catalogue of Act 3 which includes, among other breeds, the category of the 'house-keeper'. As 'hell-hound' Macbeth would now register as 'house-keeper', too, though of a rather dismal kind of abode. Macbeth endorses this bestialized version of himself: 'They have tied me to a stake, I cannot fly, / But bear-like I must fight the course' (5.7.1f).

With the end of the play we return to the triadic collusion[31] I described at the beginning of this paper. The playhouse, the beargarden and the site of public execution – stage, stake and scaffold – generate a powerfully synoptic vision. Each of the three implies the absent-presence of the other two, a presence never quite erased and sometimes, as in the last scene of *Macbeth*, emphatically foregrounded. As the tyrant is cornered, the stage of the Globe converges with the bear garden. And when,

only a few moments later, Macduff re-enters from the final combat, displaying, as stage tradition has it, the head of the slain Macbeth on a pole, the executioner's scaffold is brought into play as the third perceptual frame of action. The most palpable effect of this collusion is mutual reinforcement. The 'sweet violence' (to use Terry Eagleton's term) of the stage incorporates, and is sustained by, the competitive co-presence of the other spectacular blood rituals of the period.

But the border traffic between the human stage and its animal counterpart is not a one-way system. When the playwright Thomas Dekker visits the Bear Garden he sees a moral drama in which the animals perform the parts of human actors:

No sooner was I entred [the Bear Garden] but the very noyse of the place put me in mind of *Hel*: the beare (dragd to the stake) shewed like a black rugged soule, that was Damned and newly committed to the infernall *Charle*, the *Dogges* like so many *Diuels*, inflicting torments vpon it. But when I called to mind, that al their tugging together was but to make sport to the beholders, I held a better and not so damnable an opinion of their beastly doings: for the *Beares*, or the *Buls* fighting with the dogs, was a liuely represe[n]tation (me thought) of poore men going to law with the rich and mightie.

At length a blinde *Beare* was tyed to the stake, and in stead of baiting him with dogges, a company of creatures that had the shapes of men, & faces of christians (being either Colliers, Carters, or watermen) tooke the office

---

[29] Agamben, *The Open*, p. 15.

[30] An interesting alternative to the humanist position can be detected in Malcolm's rather ambiguous testing of Macduff. It has been argued (Barbara Riebling, 'Virtue's Sacrifice: A Machiavellian Reading of Macbeth', *Studies in English Literature 1500–1900*, 31 (1991), 273–86) that Malcolm proves himself a dexterous disciple of the anti-idealist humanism of Machiavelli and his essentially positive view of man's animal capacities.

[31] I am appropriating a term here which was coined by the theatre historian Klaus Lazarowicz to describe the interplay between playwright, actor and spectator. Klaus Lazarowicz, 'Der Zuschauvorgang', Christoper Balme and Klaus Lazarowicz, eds., *Texte zur Theorie des Theatres* (Stuttgart, 1991), pp. 130–7.

of Beadles vpon them, and whipt monsieur *Hunkes*, till the blood ran downe his old shoulders: It was some sport to see Innocence triumph ouer Tyranny, by beholding those vnnecessary tormentors go away w[ith] scratchd hands, or torne legs from a poore Beast, arm'd onely by nature to defend himself against *Violence*: yet me thought this whipping of the blinde *Beare*, moued as much pittie in my breast towards him, as y[e] leading of poore starued wretches to the whipping posts in *London* (when they had more neede to be releeued with foode) ought to moue the hearts of Cittizens, though it be the fashion now to laugh at the punishment.[32]

Dekker's response registers a gradual progress from presence to representation. He is overwhelmed by the sheer impact of the spectacle. It 'puts him in mind of Hell'; in other words, it is the spectacle which imposes the presence of Hell on him without his being actively engaged in construing this vision. Rational activity and, with it, affective detachment from the terror sets in once Dekker 'calls to mind' what the scene might signify. The progression is similar to that in *Macbeth* where the disconcerting irrational presence of the opening is subsequently absorbed into the representational frame of the dramatic plot. Even though in Macbeth's case, rational activity does not lead to detachment but creates its own Hell, 'the torture of the mind' that keeps him awake 'in restless ecstasy' (3.2.23–4).

If the representational structure of a play such as *Macbeth* is always liable to break up into moments of intense presence and if, under the basically non-mimetic conditions of a baiting show, blind 'monsieur *Hunkes*' can become a figure of Aristotelian terror and pity, such slippage between *representational* and *presentational* modes of early modern spectacle reinforces the slippage of the species boundary. Just as blind 'monsieur *Hunkes*', blood running down 'his old shoulders', assumes the tragic pathos of a Gloucester, Shakespeare's Gloucester becomes the baited bear. 'I am tied to th' stake', he exclaims, as Goneril, Regan and Cornwall close in on him, 'and I must stand the course' (3.7.52). The words of Gloucester the victim are almost the same as those of the cornered tyrant, Macbeth ('They have tied me to a stake, I cannot fly, / But bear-like I must fight the course' 5.7.1f). The one scene bestializes the attackers, the other bestializes the speaker himself and is thus fully in keeping with how the 'hell-hound', the 'rarer monster' (5.10.25), the 'butcher and his fiend-like queen' (5.11.35) are seen by their righteous enemies. But when the beast is bagged and Macduff presents Macbeth's severed head as a hunting trophy this final image hardly captures the complex response evoked by the play's two central characters. Lopping off Macbeth's head is a drastic reaffirmation of the species boundary, a triumphant gesture of exteriorization. The beast is expelled, the reign of humanity re-established. However, as Alan Stewart observes, 'the borders of the human are never marked solely by the threat of the non-human beyond them'.[33] Malcolm's concluding speech thus seems glibly reductive, because the play has so hauntingly impressed on us a sense of the humanness of the bestial couple. Of all the play's dramatis personae, they are the most fully realized human beings. The transgressive 'more' that pushes Macbeth beyond the bounds of the human paradoxically also offers us a 'more' of humanness. Disturbingly, then, the play's conclusion leaves us not with the satisfaction of new-found wholeness but with the recognition of inescapable duplicity. If the early modern theatre provided the stage for what a popular book title calls 'the invention of the human', it could not have found itself a better accomplice than the bearpit.

---

[32] Thomas Dekker, 'Worke for Armourours', *The Non-Dramatic Works*, ed. Alexander B. Grosart, vol. 4 (New York, 1963), pp. 97–9.

[33] Alan Stewart, 'Humanity at a Price: Erasmus, Budé, and the Poverty of Philology' in Erica Fudge, Ruth Gilbert and Susan Wiseman, eds., *At the Borders of the Human: Beasts, Bodies and Natural Philosophy in the Early Modern Period* (New York, 2002), pp. 9–25; p. 9.

POPULAR SHAKESPEARE IN JAPAN

YUKARI YOSHIHARA

This chapter examines two pieces of popular Shakespeare in Japan, 2006. The first is the adaptation of *Julius Caesar* by the Takarazuka Revue (directed by Shinji Kimura), and the second is Shinkansen RS's adaptation of *Macbeth*,[1] titled *Metal Macbeth* (script by Kankurô Kudô, directed by Hidenori Inoue). In the former, *Julius Caesar* is appropriated as a means to express populist nationalism in today's Japan, and in the latter *Macbeth* is turned into sci-fi to express the *fin-de-siècle* pessimism which Japan in the twenty-first century has not yet succeeded in overcoming.

The two are 'pop' in different registers. Takarazuka, with a longer history, is a theatre for devoted female fans who are constructed as 'ordinary people', while Shinkansen RS has affinities with recent 'geeky' 'nerdy' postmodern cultures such as *manga* (Japanese graphic novels) and computer games. Both display, in different degrees and manners, ambivalence towards the cultural authority of 'proper' Shakespeare, of avant-garde Shakespeare performances and academic Shakespeare. They audaciously appropriate the original works and are unabashedly proud of their 'pop' quality.

At the same time, both Takarazuka and Shinkansen have high status. Takarazuka is a highly respected theatrical institution with a long history (more than ninety years), even though, because of its 'pop' quality, it is sometimes derided as a theatre suitable only for unsophisticated women. Shinkansen RS's *Metal Macbeth* includes an acting 'aristocracy' of stars who have played in Ninagawa Shakespeare productions, or who come from top Kabuki families. Because of their ambivalent status, the two are most suitable for my purpose in this article to examine the blurring boundaries between pop culture and high culture in Shakespeare productions in Japan.

Arguably, these popular productions, which draw audiences of thousands, are Shakespearian kitsch, but, as Douglas Lanier argues, 'what is often dismissed as Shakespearian kitsch ought to be taken seriously',[2] in order that we may re-examine the cultural authority of 'authentic' or 'proper' Shakespeare in an age of globalization when the simplistic dichotomy of the 'global' and the 'local', of the 'authentic' and the shallow, of 'high' art and 'pop', cannot be easily maintained.

JULIUS CAESAR IN THE TAKARAZUKA REVUE

In 2006, the Takarazuka Revue produced an adaptation of *Julius Caesar*, titled *Rock Opera: Akatsuki no rooma* (*Rome at dawn*). All roles were played by Takarazuka actresses, clad in gorgeous costumes combining Roman togas and rock'n'roll outfits, singing and dancing to rock music. It was in true Takarazuka style, spectacular, stunningly pop; a melodramatically emotional musical entertainment version of *Julius Caesar*.

---

[1] 'Shinkansen' means 'new line of feelings', with a pun on the official name of a network of high-speed railway lines called 'Shinkansen' ('new trunk line'; written with a different Chinese character). 'RS' stands for 'rock' and 'Shakespeare'.

[2] Douglas Lanier, *Shakespeare and Modern Popular Culture* (Oxford, 2002), p. 3.

Visiting the Takarazuka Grand Theatre in Takarazuka City is quite an experience. The theatre is part of an expansive entertainment complex, comprising a theatre arts museum, a photo gallery where you can have your picture taken in gorgeous Takarazuka costumes, and souvenir shops with endless lines of Takarazuka goods. At the time when the adaptation of *Julius Caesar* was performed, the souvenir shop was stuffed with *Julius Caesar* merchandise: *Julius Caesar* paper holders, *Julius Caesar* mouse pads, a variety of stage pictures, and *Julius Caesar* cakes. The translation of *Julius Caesar* by Tsuneari Fukuda, a respected scholar-director, was displayed in an inconspicuous corner of a shelf, almost hidden by mountains of cute Takarazuka goods. Takarazuka is pop – both in the sense of popular and commercialized. What does it have to do with Shakespeare?

The all-female Takarazuka Revue (*Takarazuka kageki*) was founded in 1913 by Ichizô Kobayashi (1873–1957).[3] From the outset, Takarazuka was designed to be a commercial 'popular' theatre for 'ordinary people' (*taishu engeki*). Kobayashi was the immensely wealthy Hankyu railway and department store tycoon, who, by building up inter-urban railroads and department stores, established the new consumer culture of salaried workers in the early twentieth century. The Revue was successful enough to build its own 3000-seat Takarazuka Grand Theatre in 1924, the largest Japanese theatre of its kind at the time, in the city of Takarazuka at the terminus of a Hankyu line leading up to Osaka. Conveniently situated and popular for its hot springs, Takarazuka City was the ideal spot to open up commercialized entertainment venues for 'wholesome family entertainment', at a time when new conceptions of family life and leisure activities were emerging.

In the Revue, all parts are played by women, who, before becoming Revue members, undergo two years of intensive training in a school specifically designed to train Takarazuka players. The women who play male parts are referred to as *otokoyaku* (literally 'male role') and those who play female parts are called *musumeyaku* (literally 'daughter role'). Most of the audience is female: of the

2.5 million fans Takarazuka attracts every year, about 90 per cent is said to be women. Regrettably, it is undeniable that there is a tendency to look down upon the Takarazuka Revue as 'nylon Kabuki', 'Kitsch Heaven' or a parking spot for 'the adolescent girls' chewing gum'[4] suitable only for intellectually unsophisticated women.

The Revue has a long history of Shakespeare production. The earliest Shakespearian work by the Revue, titled *Death of Ophelia*, was performed in 1926. The official list of Shakespeare performances in Takarazuka style shows that twenty-eight Shakespearian plays were performed between 1926–99, of which *Hamlet*, *A Midsummer Night's Dream* and *Romeo and Juliet* are the most popular. Earlier Takarazuka Shakespeare performances include an adaptation of *Midsummer Night's Dream* (1940) in which, according to Jennifer Robertson, the whole story and settings were 'japanized', Japanese names being given to the various characters and Japanese fairies replacing English fairies in the original.[5] Noteworthy is the year 1999, called 'the Shakespeare Year', when eight adaptations of Shakespeare's plays[6] were performed successively by the younger members of the Revue at Bow Hall

---

[3] The most comprehensive book about the Revue written in English is Jennifer Robertson, *Takarazuka: Sexual Politics and Popular Culture in Japan* (Berkeley, 1998). Kim Longinotto and Jano Williams's documentary film, *Dream Girls* (1994; distributed by Women Make Movies) offers deep insights into the life of Takarazuka players and the gender politics of Takarazuka.

[4] Robertson, *Takarazuka*, p. 26.

[5] Robertson, *Takarazuka*, p. 94.

[6] *The Winter's Tale* (set in the Kabuki world of the feudal Edo Era), *Much Ado About Nothing* (set in America in the 1950s), *Romeo and Juliet '99* (which refers to the political situation in Yugoslavia in the late 1990s), *Twelfth Night* (directed by Shinji Kimura), *Yume Shakespeare* (an adaptation of *A Midsummer Night's Dream*, set in contemporary America), *The Tempest in Kowloon* (set in Hong Kong in 1947, two years after the end of the Japanese occupation), *Say It Again* (an adaptation of *The Two Gentlemen of Verona*; set in New Orleans at the beginning of the twentieth century), and *Epiphany* (an adaptation of *Twelfth Night*, set in the Kabuki world of the late nineteenth century; the Viola figure disguises herself as her twin brother and makes her debut as a Kabuki actor).

Theatre (a smaller theatre adjacent to the Grand Theatre).

It is generally said that the Takarazuka Revue is a theatre for dream-like fantasy, set widely apart from the political and ideological concerns in the real world. However, Shinji Kimura, the director of the *Julius Caesar* adaptation, challenges the tradition of the Revue's professed apoliticalness. Kimura's controversial works include *Song Dedicated to the Royal Family* (2003), based on Giuseppe Verdi's opera, *Aida*, where Kimura compares Egypt in his work to the United States after 9/11. Another example is *Susano'o* (2004), based on a Japanese myth. Susano'o, a god, is sent out to a neighbouring country to rescue his people abducted by the charismatic leader of the adjacent country. This was unmistakably a reference to the abduction of Japanese nationals by North Korea.[7] Furthermore, Susano'o, forbidden to use violence by his sister, the goddess Amaterasu, symbolizes Japan, which renounced war in the 1947 constitution.[8] Kimura declares that Shakespeare's *Julius Caesar* is a superb political play and implies that this is the very reason he chose the play. According to him, *Julius Caesar* shows that, just as monarchy can turn into tyranny, democracy can degenerate into mob-rule.[9]

Generally speaking, the absence of significant female roles and the relative insignificance of the heterosexual love plot are some of the drawbacks of *Julius Caesar*, Shakespeare's most 'womanless' play, for the Takarazuka Revue.[10] Kimura, commenting on the original play as a 'men's story', adds two significant female roles: Cleopatra (Caesar's mistress) and Servilia (Caesar's mistress and Brutus's mother). Cleopatra and Servilia are openly materialistic strong-willed women who pursue Caesar for the political power he possesses. According to Servilia, it is a woman's honour to be a mistress of the great hero, Caesar, and he proves his manliness by being a master of numerous mistresses, while her son, she suggests, lacks true manliness by being a devoted husband to his wife Portia. She sings: 'A man is not a man if he cannot seduce at least ten or twenty women. Women love strong men; they love Caesar because he is powerful!' (Scene 4).[11]

In stark contrast to them, Portia in the adaptation is an ambitionless, domestically orientated housewife who stays at home to wait for her lord's return. She is proud to be the daughter of Cato the Younger; yet she is little interested in her father's or her husband's political commitments to republicanism. Just once she asserts herself to Brutus demanding that, if he truly loves Caesar and Rome, he should declare his opposition to Caesar for his suspected monarchical ambition. Her arguments do not derive from her political convictions or interests, however, and she expresses herself in 'feminine' terms of love, not of political antagonism and ambition. She argues that, as she is Brutus's wife, not his servant, slave nor mistress, she has the right and duty to advise her husband when he is in trouble. Astonishingly, her first words when she meets her husband after the assassination of Caesar are 'I must wash your garment.' She is frantic at the thought that Brutus's garment is stained with Caesar's blood. Obviously intended to remind the

---

[7] In 2002, when Japanese Prime Minister Koizumi Junichiro visited North Korea to meet North Korean leader Kim Jong-il, Kim admitted his country had abducted thirteen Japanese citizens in 1977–83. In 2004 when *Susano'o* was performed, North Korea–Japan relations were highly strained, media coverage in Japan fanning nationalistic and xenophobic emotions.

[8] In 2004, the Japanese government sent a contingent of the Japan Self-Defense Forces to Iraq to help in its reconstruction. As article 9 of the Constitution of Japan prohibits Japan from using force, this intervention is considered to be unconstitutional by many.

[9] 'A note on the history of *Julius Caesar* in Japan' in the production's programme. In the 1880s, at the peak of the Movement for Civic Rights and Freedom in Japan (*Jiyu'u minken undô*), the figure of Julius Caesar was often employed as a symbol of tyranny. In Kutsuzan Komuro's *Song of Liberty* (1882), Caesar is condemned as a tyrant who destroys the Roman people's historical struggle for freedom and republicanism, while Brutus is glorified as a hero who tries to defend people's rights. Shôyô Tsubouchi, the first to translate the complete works of Shakespeare into Japanese in 1928, translated *Julius Caesar* in 1883 in this political context of the 1880s.

[10] Michael L. Greenwald, 'Multicultural and Regendered Romans: *Julius Caesar* in North America, 1969–2000', in Horst Zander, ed., *Julius Caesar: New Critical Essays* (New York, 2005), p. 325.

[11] Shinji Kimura, 'Akatsuki no rooma', *Le Cinq* 83(6) (Tokyo, 2006). All translations from Japanese are mine.

audience of the hand-washing scene of Lady Macbeth, Portia makes movements to wash Brutus's garment with her hands and dies immediately thereafter, as if taking responsibility for her presumption in influencing her husband's political choice. It must be said that her housewifely devotion to her husband is almost ridiculous in the scene, and her sudden death in the adaptation is not convincing either. On the other hand, Servilia blames her daughter-in-law, saying that she must have instigated Brutus to assassinate Caesar, for she, as a daughter of Cato, must hate Caesar. Both Portia and Servilia are represented as politically unsophisticated, narrow-minded women who can conceive of state matters only in private terms.

It might be surprising, but the male-centred plot of *Julius Caesar* is not in itself a drawback for a Takarazuka Revue production, for in Takarazuka, where those playing male roles (*otokoyaku*) have more prestige than those playing female roles, plays in which the *otokoyaku* can show off their virtuoso performances of idealized manliness are preferred.[12] If Servilia and Portia lack some lustre in comparison with the *otokoyaku* players performing Caesar, Brutus and Cassius, it could be argued that they serve only to highlight the idealised masculinity of the *otokoyaku*. Hence it can even be argued that Takarazuka is heterosexist theatre dominated by the *otokoyaku* who merely reproduce patriarchal gender hierarchy.

The homosocial bond between men, rather than heterosexual love, is the central theme of the adaptation. Furthermore, the homosocial bond in the adaptation is highly eroticized. Kimura refers to the adaptation as 'a story of men attracted [*hikareru*] by other men' (production programme). The expression '*hikareru*' has a strong hint of sexual attraction, and I believe the choice of the expression is a deliberate one. In the assassination scene, when Caesar recognizes Brutus among the assassins, he gazes lovingly into Brutus's eyes, and expires, saying 'Et tu Brute? (*Smiling*) Then that's fine.' Two female players playing the parts of men for the pleasure of an audience mostly consisting of women: this is one excellent example of the Revue's particular charm, where, thanks to its convention of female to male

cross-dressing, it can raise vertiginous gender-bending ('queer' if you like) effects to counter heterosexist notions of gender and sexuality.[13]

Kimura states about the original play '"Monarchy or republicanism?" This is the central theme.' However, the adaptation itself is not a straightforward affirmation either of monarchy or republicanism. In the last but one scene, the chorus appear on stage to say that there is no definite conclusion to be drawn from the tragedy of Caesar and Brutus, for some adore Caesar as a hero who established the basis of Roman Empire, while others admire Brutus as a hero who tried to defend Roman republicanism. The adaptation glorifies heroic figures like Brutus and Caesar regardless of their political belief, while it condemns their followers as a mob without any integrity or principle: Brutus's

---

[12] In the adaptation of *Twelfth Night* (1999) directed by Kimura, the Orsino figure becomes far more charismatic and sexy than Shakespeare's Orsino, and the scenes where he interacts with the Cesario/Viola figure are endowed with highly homoerotic overtones. But in no scenes would the audience forget that both roles are played by young women. In *The Tempest in Kowloon* (1999) directed by Yoshimasa Saitô, the Prospero figure, a mafia boss in Hong Kong, is husband to the Miranda figure, and the Ferdinand figure is her former lover. The story develops around the male homosocial rivalry between the two men over the Miranda figure.

[13] The Revue, in its highly eroticized scenes between men played by actresses, has some affinities with what is called 'yaoi' culture. One of the Japanese pop culture phenomena in recent years, 'yaoi' culture would be a loose equivalent to 'slash fiction' culture in the US, which describes secret or forbidden romantic couplings, often homoerotic, between characters. See Johan A. Lent, ed., *Themes and Issues in Asian Cartooning: Cute, Cheap, Mad, and Sexy* (Bowling Green, 1999), p. 116. A variety of slash Shakespeares can be found on the net, such as 'Shakespeare Slash' (http://community.livejournal.com/bard_slash/, accessed 8 October 2006). 'Yaoi' culture is often, but by no means exclusively, created by women for women. As for 'slash fiction' in Shakespeare fan fiction, see Lanier, *Shakespeare and Popular Culture*, p. 82. One of the earliest examples of 'yaoi' Shakespeare is Yasuko Aoike's *manga* for girls, titled *Ibu no musuko tachi* (Sons of Eve, Tokyo, 1978), in which Shakespeare, Lear, Hamlet and Romeo appear as male gay characters. One excellent example of an adaptation of *Hamlet*, with strong affinities with 'yaoi' culture, is Azusa Noa's *Kyo-tenshi* (Evil Angel. Tokyo, 1986), in which Hamlet is in love with Horatio.

20. Brutus (left) and Caesar (right).

followers sing, 'Every man wants to be a king / If I cannot be a king, I will not allow anyone else to become one' (scene 5). The adaptation in its call for stronger leadership accords with the recent rise in populist demand for strong leadership (both domestic and international) in Japan.

Just as homosocial bonding is eroticized, patriotism is described in the words of passionate love. In the last scene, all the characters, including anonymous Roman citizens, appear on stage and sing 'I love Rome' together happily, in spite of their differences in political belief and party interest. The song is sung several times on stage: first, it is sung as emblematic of Brutus's love for his wife and his country; next, its emphasis is shifted to express the conflict between his love for Caesar and for Rome; finally, it is a song of love predominantly for country, in which everyone, overcoming the differences in their political philosophy, class and gender, joyously joins. The song has the effect of blurring the boundaries between heterosexual love, homosociality and patriotism. In the last scene where they sing 'I love Rome' in typ-

ically flamboyant Takarazuka mode, no one raises a questioning voice about the nature of love for one's country so lavishingly glorified in the song. The authority of 'Shakespeare' is appropriated in order to naturalize, dehistoricize and universalize patriotism. In this way, the adaptation reflects populist nationalism prevalent in today's Japan.

I would like to end this part by referring to another, 'top of the pops', 'girlie' stage play with the quasi-Shakespearian theme of a girl disguised as a boy directed by Kimura. In August 2006, just one month after his *Julius Caesar*, Kimura directed *Ribon no kishi* (*Princess Knight*), starring the members of an all-female pop group, *Morning musume* (morning girls). In *Princess Knight*, Sapphire disguises herself as a prince as her country's laws forbid girls to succeed the throne. While Kimura's *Julius Caesar* is about the homosocial world of men, his *Princess Knight* depicts a girl's struggle against patriarchal gender hierarchy.[14]

---

[14] Kimura's *Princess Knight* belongs to a longer tradition of a girl-in-boy's clothing in Japanese 'girlie' pop culture, especially

Kimura manages to smuggle some elements of *Hamlet* into his *Princess Knight*. An evil minister suspects that Sapphire might be a girl pretending to be a boy. He (played by a woman) sets up an occasion in which Sapphire fights with Prince Franz (her future husband) in a practice fencing bout, and anoints Prince Franz's sword with poison, reminiscent of the sword play scene in *Hamlet*. Furthermore, the 'confession drug' the evil minister administers to the queen is evidently designed to make the audience associate it with the poisoned 'potion' Gertrude drinks. The queen questions the justice of the kingdom's laws: 'This country's laws, forbidding girls to ascend to the throne, are the cause of our misery' (Act 8).[15] The fact that Kimura's adaptation of *Julius Caesar* and his *Princess Knight* were produced in close succession invites us to consider the queen's condemnation of the male-only succession law as a comment on the male-centred world of the *Julius Caesar* adaptation in which women are excluded from participating in the political struggle, and in which a song with a line 'every *man* wants to be a king' is sung (Act 2: emphasis mine).[16]

A SCI-FI *MACBETH* IN A DYSTOPIAN FUTURE

Which is more global, Shakespeare's *Macbeth* or Katsuhiro Ohtomo's *manga*/animation *Akira*?[17] *Metal Macbeth*, a retro-futuristic sci-fi adaptation of *Macbeth*, provocatively challenges us to relate the two. It is 'Shakespop', unabashedly catering to a mass-market audience, implicitly criticising academy- and art-oriented Shakespeare in Japan.[18]

To the deafening sound of metal rock played live on stage, characters appear on Harley-Davidsons, wearing black leather jackets studded with shiny silver metal spikes and high-heeled black leather shoes. They race their 'Easy Rider'-style motorcycles through a post-apocalypse high-tech slum to where an enormous iron gate stands, reminiscent of the castle gate in Kurosawa's film, *Throne of Blood*. The dead-tech jungle is explicitly designed to look like the post-apocalypse worlds of *Mad Max 2*

(1981, directed by George Miller) and Ohtomo's *Akira*.

shojo manga (*manga* for girls). It is based on Osamu Tezuka's *manga* (1953–6) of the same title. It is widely known that Tezuka, the 'god of *manga*', was inspired by the themes and styles of the all-female Takarazuka Revue, which Tezuka had watched in his youth. The popularity of Shakespearian plays such as *Twelfth Night* and *As You Like It* in Japan might partially be attributed to the gender-bending 'tradition' in the Takarazuka Revue and *manga*.

15 Citations of Kimura's *Princess Knight* are from a booklet sold at the theatre.

16 The queen's condemnation of the male-only succession law could be an allusion to the lively debate at that time whether the Imperial Household Law should be changed from that of male primogeniture to non-gendered primogeniture, which would allow Aiko, the sole daughter of the Crown Prince, to succeed to the throne after her father. About ten days after *Princess Knight*'s last performance, Kiko, wife to the second son of the Emperor, gave birth to a son, whose birth would exclude Aiko from succession.

17 *Akira* is a Japanese cyberpunk sci-fi serial *manga*/animation by Katsuhiro Ohtomo (*manga* version: 1982–1990). The scenes are set in 2019, where juvenile delinquents roam a New Tokyo that has been rebuilt from ruins after a failed secret-weapons experiment in 1988. *Akira*, inspired partly by *Star Wars*, became a cult phenomenon in Japan, and, in translation, a worldwide phenomenon. Since the publication by Marvel in the United States, thirty-eight paperback volumes have appeared in English, selling a total of two million copies. Worldwide sales, excluding Japan, have totalled seven million copies. See Mark Schilling, *The Encyclopedia of Japanese Pop Culture* (New York, 1997).

18 *Metal Macbeth* is the second Shakespearian work that Hidenori Inoue, the director of *Metal Macbeth*, has directed. The first was *Shakespeare in the Year Tempo 12* (2002), written by Yasushi Inoue (1973), which is set in feudal Edo era Japan, and which reduces Shakespeare's thirty-seven works to just one play. Hidenori Inoue produced it as a world where feudal gangsters with brightly dyed yellow hair and dressed in a postmodern remake of *kimonos* belt out rock songs. The last scene, equivalent to the scene of Richard III's death, is directed as a parody of the scene of Christ's death in *Jesus Christ Superstar*. The absurd combination of Shakespeare, Japonesque dress and rock suggests that Shakespeare, as well as Japonism, is 'foreign' to Hidenori Inoue. One character even appears in a *kimono* with Shakespeare's face printed on it. For unknown reasons, Hidenori Inoue omitted these lines in the original play (with Yasushi Inoue's permission), 'If it were not for Shakespeare / There would have been a lot of scholars without PhDs / There would have been a lot of bankrupt publishers', which Yasushi Inoue intended as satire against

21. Poster for *Metal Macbeth*.

Metal Macbeth is a work which begins with the end of history. The scenes are set in two parallel worlds: Tokyo in the 1980s of the Japanese Bubble Economy, and Tokyo in the early twenty-third century after an apocalypse. The 1980s story is about the rise and fall of a heavy metal rock star named Macbeth Uchino, and the twenty-third century story is about Randomstar, a warrior lord of the ESP kingdom in the post-apocalypse future, a reincarnation of Macbeth Uchino (both played by Masaaki Uchino).[19]

In 2206, Randomstar appears on stage with his fellow warrior, Explorer (Banquo), on their way back to their king, Les Paul (Duncan), to report their victory. From their conversation, we learn that the Third World War occurred in 2006. In a desolate field full of war debris and massacred corpses, they are greeted by the three witches. They refer to Randomstar as Macbeth. Randomstar is puzzled, for he does not have any reason to be called Macbeth (nor does he know anything about Shakespeare's *Macbeth*). The witches hand him a CD produced by the heavy metal band Metal Macbeth

in the 1980s. Seeing the CD jacket, Randomstar learns that the band's Macbeth Uchino (vocals and guitar) looks exactly like himself. As in some cyberpunk sci-fis such as *The Matrix*, Randomstar downloads the contents of the CD directly to his brain, only to learn that it contains songs prophesying his future. The CD contains songs titled 'Fair is Foul, and Foul is Fair', 'Full of Scorpions is My Mind', 'None of Woman Born' and 'The Night is Long that never Finds the Day'. As if to draw the audience's attention to the fact that *Metal Macbeth* (both the play and the CD) is a pop consumer commodity, the CD was sold in the theatre foyer. *Metal Macbeth*'s

blind admiration for the Bard in Japan. When Yukio Ninagawa produced the play in 2005, this time the lines were not omitted.

19 He made his stage debut as Sebastian in *On'na tachi no ju-ni-ya* (*Twelfth Night* in an almost all female cast, 1995), played Pericles in Ninagawa's *Pericles* (2003), and Macheath in John Gay's *The Beggar's Opera* (2006). Appearing in various TV dramas in leading parts, he makes a two-way cross-over between high culture and pop culture.

retro-futuristic styling conforms to the aesthetics of postmodern commodity culture.[20]

Macbeth Uchino climbs to the top of stardom in the early 1980s. The stage names of band members come from the character names of *Macbeth*: Macbeth Uchino, Banquo Hashimoto and Macduff Kitamura. The president of their music corporation, the Duncan figure, intends to make the band a flagship commodity as part of his grand design to make his company a global one through mergers and acquisitions of American music corporations. However, Macbeth Uchino cannot keep up with the rapid changes in the popular song market governed by fickle fans (played by an actor in drag and two actresses who play the three witches in the twenty-third-century plot). He becomes a homeless alcoholic, desperately trying to make a comeback to stardom. Rose (Takako Matsu),[21] his manager and wife, becomes a heavy drug-user. He ultimately ruins himself in 1989 (I shall later examine the importance of that year).

The director, Hidenori Inoue (1960–),[22] and the script writer, Kankurô Kudô (1970–),[23] hold highly ambivalent attitudes towards the authority of 'authentic' or 'essential' Shakespeare. In a metatheatrical scene at the beginning of *Metal Macbeth*, the three witches appear on stage with several *Macbeth* translations in their hands, including the translation by Kazuko Matsuoka,[24] on which *Metal Macbeth* is based. They compare several translations of the line 'Fair is foul, and foul is fair' in order to examine which translation is most faithful to the original but immediately declare that they must be more faithful to the intentions of Inoue and Kudô than to Shakespeare. 'Authenticity' does not count. At the very beginning, with transgressive glee, Shakespeare and his translators are declared to be far less authoritative than the appropriators.

In a production interview, Kudô, one of the most popular contemporary television and movie scriptwriters, pretends that he had never read any of Shakespeare's works before he became involved in the *Metal Macbeth* production project and declares that he does not have any particular attachment to or admiration for Shakespeare's works. The director, Inoue, says that inasmuch as he greatly admires Yukio Ninagawa, the greatest virtuoso of Shakespeare production in Japan, he is afraid that, if he

---

20 The liner-notes for the CD have on one side lyrics of the songs and on the other side a group portrait of the band, Metal Macbeth. The songs are credited as written and performed by the band Metal Macbeth – for example, the song 'Of Woman Born' is credited as written and sung by Macbeth Uchino – but actually, the lyrics are by the script writer, Kankurô Kudô. Various *Metal Macbeth* commodities were sold at the theatre, making the occasion look more like a rock concert where various star goods are sold. *Metal Macbeth* subsidiary and spin-off goods include production programmes in the CD jacket design, *Metal Macbeth* silver rings, *Metal Macbeth* key chains, and *Metal Macbeth* T-shirts. Furthermore, the *Metal Macbeth* players produced a metal rock concert in which actors playing the principal roles in the play appeared in the roles of the band members (e.g. Masaaki Uchino as Macbeth Uchino) to perform their *Metal Macbeth* numbers.

21 The leading actress of this populist production comes from the acting world's elite in Japan. She appeared in the role of Ophelia in Yukio Ninagawa's *Hamlet* (with Hiroyuki Sanada as Hamlet, 1995 in Tokyo, 1998 at the Barbican). Her father is a prominent kabuki actor, Kôshiro Matsumoto, who played all the leading roles in Shakespeare's four best-known tragedies, including *Othello* (1994, directed by Ninagawa) and *Macbeth* (1996, directed by David Levaux). Her brother is Somegorô Ichikawa, a kabuki actor, who played the triple role of Ophelia/Hamlet/Fortinbras in a kabuki adaptation of *Hamlet*, titled *Hamuletto yamato nishiki-e* (Hamlet drawn in the style of Japanese colored woodblock print; Tokyo Globe and Mermaid in London, 1991); he often performs leading roles in what is called '[Hidenori] Inoue kabuki' (see n.22) as a part of an effort to make kabuki more popular among young people.

22 Director of the Shinkansen troupe (established 1980). His works are said to be qualitatively close to *manga* in their styles, storylines and sentiments, using numerous references to pop youth culture and absurd gags. Being an ardent fan of metal rock and the sword fights in *jidaigeki* (Japanese period costume drama), he successfully combines those to form an idiosyncratic style, known as the *Inoue Kabuki style*, juxtaposing elements from Japanese myth and history with postmodern Japanese pop culture.

23 He is also an actor and script writer in another theatre troupe, *Otona keikaku* (plan to become adults). He has proved his unique talent for appropriating canonical works in his adaptation of Japanese eighteenth-century *rakugo* stories (comic monologues), which he morphed into stories of contemporary Tokyo youth in a television drama series, *Tiger and Dragon* (2005).

24 She declares herself to be a self-appointed public relations spokesperson for Shakespeare in Japan. Her project of translating the complete works of Shakespeare started in 1996, and

directs Shakespeare's work, it will turn out to be merely an inferior imitation of Ninagawa Shakespeare. Ten years after he first conceived the idea of *Metal Macbeth*, he finally plucked up the courage to produce it. Somewhat contradictorily to his deferential tribute to the authority of Ninagawa, however, Inoue impertinently implies that what is called 'proper' Shakespeare is no fun. By using the same actor (Uchino) and the same actress (Matsu) who had worked with Ninagawa in *Pericles* and *Hamlet*, Inoue can underline this idea. He argues that even though he does not have particular attachment to Shakespeare's works, he is confident that *he* is able to make Shakespeare's work fun with his idiosyncratic style, combining the old and the new, the classy and the postmodern, the serious and absurdly comic.

Another *Macbeth* virtuoso is, needless to say, Akira Kurosawa. *Metal Macbeth* alludes to the authority of Kurosawa's *Throne of Blood* in three oblique ways. The first is in the iron gate of Macbeth's castle, Metal Castle, which is designed to look like the gate of Castle of the Spider's Web in Kurosawa's film. The second is in the *Metal Macbeth* castle's coat-of-arms, a skull with spider's legs. This can be taken to be a reference to the original title of Kurosawa's film, *The Castle of the Spider's Web* (*kumonosu jô*). The third is in the sweaters the witches wear, with the logo of 'MIKI MOUSE' written on them. There are three levels of allusions here: (i) to the MIKI HOUSE designer brand, a Japanese clothing manufacturer popular in the 1980s especially among middle-class suburban housewives; (ii) to Mickey Mouse, Miki and Mickey being pronounced alike in Japanese; (iii) to Miki, the Banquo figure in Kurosawa's film, whose house is favoured by the witches. Thus, through the simple device of the sweaters, *Metal Macbeth* pays tribute to Kurosawa and to Shakespeare, at the same time as suggesting that 'Shakespeare', Kurosawa's film and *Metal Macbeth* itself are commercialised commodities for mass consumption like MIKI HOUSE sweaters or, on a grander scale, Disney merchandise.[25]

In spite of audacious changes in settings, the basic plot of *Metal Macbeth* is surprisingly faithful to the original. Obviously, the language is different: not only is *Metal Macbeth* in Japanese, it is in contemporary youth slang. As Dennis Kennedy points out, this is an example of the relative freedom from the 'accustomed linguistic approach to Shakespeare' in Japan where 'the postmodern delight in eclectic transtemporality has been given free rein'.[26] At the same time, 'Shakespeare' given in contemporary, direct, simple and colloquial Japanese can be seen as a means to implicitly criticise high-art or academic Shakespeares in Japan with their loyalty to Shakespeare's sophisticated, verbose, archaic, difficult language. In the scene just after Duncan's death, the Porter figure cannot understand what happened to Duncan, because the elite warriors, including Macbeth, talk in a dignified 'Shakespearian' language that he cannot comprehend.[27] He protests: 'Don't speak in such difficult words. I am a dumb fool. I cannot understand.' His protest caused a sympathetic giggle among the audience. *Metal Macbeth* is proud to be 'a dumbed-down Shakespeare rewritten in the idiom of mass culture'.[28]

Another example of reducing Shakespearian language into the prosaic language of today's youth

---

most of Yukio Ninagawa's recent Shakespeare productions at Sainokuni Theatre are based on her translations.

[25] Through the 'MIKI HOUSE' reference, the play invites the audience to connect Lady Macbeth in the adaptation with Ms. Masumi Hayashi, a Japanese woman sentenced to be hanged for indiscriminate murder, killing 4 people and poisoning 63 others with an arsenic-laced curry dish in 1988. Ms Hayashi was often photographed in a MIKI HOUSE sweater. One of the witches is sometimes called 'Hayashi' by other witches. The witches' cauldron is compared to the curry hotpot at a community festival that Ms Hayashi is said to have poisoned. The actress who plays Lady Macbeth appears as one of the witches wearing a MIKI MOUSE sweater in one scene. Lady Macbeth as Ms Hayashi could be a suggestion that the crime of Lady Macbeth is that of a housewife whose ambition cannot be satisfied by her husband, for it is said Ms Hayashi turned murderous because of her disillusion with her husband.

[26] Dennis Kennedy, ed., *Foreign Shakespeare* (Cambridge, 1993), p. 15.

[27] Shakespearian lines are sometimes made into songs with the lyrics projected on a giant screen at the centre-top of the stage.

[28] Lynda E. Boose and Richard Burt, 'Introduction', in Boose and Burt, eds., *Shakespeare, the Movie: Popularizing the Plays on Film, TV, and Video* (London, 1997), p. 2.

comes up when Macduff tells Macbeth the circum-stances of his birth. In the original, he announces 'Despair thy charm, / And let the angel whom thou still hast served / Tell thee Macduff was from his mother's womb / Untimely ripped' (5.10.13–16); in the adaptation, he says simply 'I was [born through] Caesarean section.' The reaction of the audience? A great roar of laughter. They laughed presumably because the simplistic solution to the Second Apparition's mysterious prophesy, 'none of woman born / Shall harm Macbeth' (4.1.96–7), sounded lacking in grandeur and solemnity, being too down-to-earth, mundane and almost vulgar. In fact, some of the audience took the lines to be an invention by Kudô, the scriptwriter, known for his expertise in producing ridiculously comic effects out of serious situations and would seem not to have believed that it was in Shakespeare.

Of two cultural authorities, 'one conferred by Shakespeare and professional scholars, the other conferred by the mass media and popular subcul-ture', it is evident that *Metal Macbeth* puts more weight on the latter, though, at the same time, using the former.[29] However, the adaptation also seduces the academic Shakespearian by subtly dropping hints that the creators have esoteric knowledge about details of the original work and its historical backgrounds. One example is a scene[30] just after the intermission, where a character demonstrates his deep knowledge about the stage history of *Mac-beth*. An old man[31] explains that, as *Macbeth* was per-formed at a banquet to which a foreign king was invited, some scenes were necessary to which the audience did not have to pay much attention, like the one he is appearing in. He pleases the academic Shakespearians among the audience by referring to the context of the possible first performance of *Macbeth* in 1606 when the King's Men performed the play before Christian IV of Denmark. Another instance concerns the end of Randomstar, Macbeth in the twenty-third century. He confines himself in the cellar beneath the Metal Castle to fire weapons of mass destruction hidden there. This could be an oblique allusion to the Gunpowder Plot (1605) in which the conspirators smuggled barrels of gun-powder into a cellar beneath Parliament.

In this way, the *Metal Macbeth* creators enter-tain academic Shakespearians by referring to the intricate details of the original and its historical backgrounds, in acknowledgement that their sub-versive adaptation must, in part at least, depend on the cultural authority of 'Shakespeare'. Even so, they appropriate the original play in ways that make it unmistakably apparent that 'Shakespeare' is a usable cultural commodity in so far as it can seduce both ways to suit contemporary cultural and political concerns. For instance, the weapons of mass destruction beneath the Metal Castle are more directly related to the poison gas attack in the Tokyo Subway by Aum Shinrikyo in 1995, North Korea's nuclear weapons and the alleged existence of weapons of mass destruction in Iraq. In terms of popular culture, the weapons are also reminiscent of the secret weapons that destroyed Tokyo in the film *Akira*.

The adaptation touches on what are regarded as social maladies caused by the long depression since the early 1990s. Lady Macbeth accuses his husband, who confines himself in the basement, of being a '*hikikomori*'. The term refers to the phenomenon of reclusive young adults who have chosen to with-draw from social life. The '*hikikomori*' phenomenon is sometimes attributed to a decade of flat economic indicators and a shaky job market in Japan, and a majority of '*hikikomori*' are said to be absorbed in the fantasy worlds of *manga* and computer games. Macbeth Uchino is killed by deliquent youths in

---

29 Lanier, *Shakespeare and Popular Culture*, p. 13.

30 This scene is a loose equivalent of the interpolated scenes where Hecate appears (3.5 and 4.1).

31 It should be added that, as this man is clumsily comic, his words about the first performance of the original work lack an authoritative ring. It is worth pointing out that this character looks like a figure in an enormously popular *manga* in the 1970s titled *Ashita no joe* (*Tomorrow's Joe*), about a juvenile delinquent in a slum who succeeds as a boxer but meets a sad end by dying in the ring, for the opening scene of *Metal Macbeth* had a line 'Let's be honest: *Tomorrow's Joe* is much more fun than *Macbeth*.' Even though the line was omitted in actual performances, it shows the creators' impertinence towards (and fear of) the authority of Shakespeare and their commitment to the cultural authority of their subculture.

punk fashion, reminding us of recurrent violence against homeless people since the 1980s. The childlessness of the Macbeths is also underlined, which reminds the audience of the declining birth rate of Japan (1.25 as of 2005).

The ending of *Metal Macbeth* is totally desolate. Malcolm (Mirai Moriyama)[32] goes up to the top of the Metal Castle to cut off the castle's electricity so that Randomstar cannot ignite the weapons of mass destruction hidden underneath, while Macduff pursues Randomstar in the basement. The scene is designed to look like the final stage of a role-playing computer game. Macduff kills Randomstar, Malcolm is electrocuted, and Metal Castle is burnt to the ground. Fleance is then chosen to be king, quite arbitrarily and with no enthusiasm on his part.

Metal Macbeth is a parable about pessimism and claustrophobia in Japan since the 1990s. The year 1989, when Macbeth Uchino dies, has a particular importance. 1989 was, globally, the year of the Tiananmen 'Incident', the dismantling of the Berlin Wall and the beginning of the end of the Cold War. Locally, it was the year of the death of Emperor Hirohito, and the beginning of Japan's long economical recession after the bursting of the economic bubble.

THE LATEST CULTURAL COMMODITIES IN TOKYO 'BARDMART'

Both the Takarazuka *Julius Caesar* and *Metal Macbeth* are variations of what Gary Taylor calls 'Walmart Shakespeare' that appropriate the 'flagship commodity of the world's most powerful culture', Shakespeare.[33] The adaptations are cultural commodities manufactured specifically for the Tokyo 'Bardmart'. Both adaptations are unabashedly commercial, and they make it apparent that 'Shakespeare' is a usable cultural commodity in so far as it can be appropriated to give expression to contemporary concerns, namely, populist nationalism in today's Japan (*Julius Caesar*) and *fin-de-siècle* claustrophobia (*Metal Macbeth*). *Metal Macbeth* and the Takarazuka *Julius Caesar* challenge us to re-examine the cultural authority of 'authentic' Shakespeare in today's globalised 'Bardmart', a world in which even authentic Shakespeare is 'available' for adaptation and reinterpretation, as Kathleen McLuskie argued in her 2006 lecture to the Shakespeare Society of Japan conference in Sendai, Japan.[34] We should not forget that William Shakespeare was once a young populist playwright.

---

[32] He made his film debut in the epoch-making popular film, *Crying out for Love, at the Centre of the World* (also known as *Socrates in Love*, 2004), a story about a boy whose first love passes away. The film's catchphrase is 'I am a Romeo who survived his Juliet.'

[33] Dominic Dromgoole and Gary Taylor, 'Welcome to Bardworld', *The Guardian*, 13 July 2005.

[34] Kathleen McLuskie, '"Enter the ghost in his night-gowne": the corpus or corpse of Shakespeare now'. The abstract is available at wwwsoc.nii.ac.jp/sh/ (accessed 5 December 2006).

'PHILOSOPHY IN A GORILLA SUIT': DO SHAKESPEARIANS PERFORM OR JUST PERFORM-A-TIVE?

SHARON O'DAIR

At the Thirty-Second International Shakespeare Conference, held in Stratford-upon-Avon, at the Shakespeare Institute, in August 2006, Andrew Lavender and Simon Shepherd offered 'A Presentation in 13 Bits' about Shakespeare performance in a postdramatic theatre, a twenty-first century theatre of digitization, effect, and affect.[1] Appearing together, Lavender and Shepherd alternated in addressing the audience of Shakespearians, with Lavender at the podium and Shepherd elsewhere, a bit to the side, sometimes near or on, and sometimes roving around, a table, which, it later became apparent, housed some props. Lavender and Shepherd told the Shakespearians that today's theatre increasingly depends upon the kinesthetic and the phenomenal; a significant source of an audience's engagement with the onstage action, they contended, is the ability of visual stimuli directly to affect the bodies of the audience.

The Institute had prepared for presentations requiring digital projection, and a large screen loomed behind the podium. Many speakers availed themselves of technology, showing photos or data or offering up summaries of their major points, but the screen was in use even when a speaker read a paper and presented nothing more: the speaker's head and shoulders were projected onto the screen behind him or her, somewhat disconcertingly in my opinion, for I never knew where to focus my attention, large head or small. Of all the speakers, Lavender and Shepherd made best use of the available technology when, late in their presentation, Shepherd began to discuss *Macbeth* and slowly revealed his hands to be covered in blood. Scooping

up a video camera, Lavender began to film Shepherd, circling him as he spoke, so that a close-up of the bloody hands projected onto the screen. In the next of the thirteen bits, again thanks to Lavender's camera, we watched on the screen and in person as Shepherd undid the effect – slowly, he poured bottled water on his hands, washing them carefully to avoid getting the blood on his nicely tailored and very pale linen suit, and then drying them on the sheets of paper from which he had just read.

If one of Lavender and Shepherd's aims was to challenge Shakespearians to think about the possibilities of a postdramatic theatre oriented around visuals and affect, another was to challenge them to think about what it is that they themselves are doing when reading a paper: are they performing and, more importantly, are they performing well, sticking to time limits, eyeing their audiences, looking dapper rather than dishevelled, articulating words with grace and ease? Do they even perceive what they are doing to be a performance, an activity with which they ought to be concerned? In the question period following the presentation, this latter challenge was taken up and with more gusto, I believe, than was the case with the former (because, perhaps, the notion of 'postdramatic' theatre is less shocking than the notion of performing Shakespearians?). A few in the audience agreed we do perform when we present a paper – everything

---

[1] Andy Lavender and Simon Shepherd, 'Affects: Early modern *mise en scene* and postdramatic process. A presentation in 13 bits', presented at the Thirty-Second International Shakespeare Conference, 8 August 2006, Stratford-upon-Avon.

is a performance, after all! – and a few bemoaned the fact that in the main we perform badly. Still others challenged the challenge; one person complimented Lavender and Shepherd's *performance*, making it clear, in a polite way, that she did not consider what she had just seen and heard to be a presentation, a lecture or (most certainly) an argument. Discussion continued in the garden, over glasses of wine and bits of cake, and it was clear to me that what we were doing was contesting and defending a disciplinary boundary, or more accurately, perhaps, a sub-disciplinary boundary, as well as a particular notion of a disciplinary or sub-disciplinary performative. Lavender and Shepherd's paper – or presentation – or performance – had called attention to meaningful, even significant, differences among Shakespearians.

And Shakespearians do come in many shapes and sizes. A Shakespearian can find herself located in a number of academic departments – English or theatre, of course, but also film, television, communications or humanities – all of which impose on her certain norms for performance, as well as certain norms for performativity, for what constitutes a performative. (Lavender and Shepherd, for example, are affiliated with the Central School of Speech and Drama in London, not a department of English.) More important than institutional location in determining these norms, however, is the kind of object the Shakespearian takes for her study. Is the Shakespearian an actor, a performance critic, a literary critic or a textual scholar? Does she think about how to embody a Shakespearian character? Does he think about the history of set design? Does he think about the meaning of love in Shakespeare? Does he think about who has access to Shakespeare? Does she think about establishing a reliable text? Does she wonder about early modern practices of warfare? Each of these Shakespearians thinks differently about Shakespeare, about academic performance and, more importantly, about the academic performative, the norms by or form(s) in which those thoughts will be disseminated to others and that reinscribe the social or institutional – in this case, the professional – order.

A paper by a historian of set design, for instance, requires the analysis of many photographs and drawings, but one by a critic concerned about access to the plays now, in the twenty-first century, requires hard-hitting but elegantly formed prose, since his goal is to move his readers or auditors to some sort of action. Each of these emphases in turn affects the way the Shakespearian will present the paper, whether orally or in writing, to a group of her peers, as well as, of course, the way that audience will respond to the paper.

To the extent that one of these kinds of Shakespearians dominates the larger group of Shakespearians – let us say for the sake of argument that the scholars do so dominate – tensions inevitably arise about legitimacy and authority. Thus it should not surprise that when Lavender and Shepherd offered a challenge to the performative authority of the scholars, one of these scholars engaged immediately in a shoring up of that authority and a policing of the disciplinary boundary it secures, labelling Lavender and Shepherd's work a 'performance' rather than a 'presentation', 'lecture' or an 'argument'. After all, would the scholar still be engaged in the presentation of research if she had to 'perform' the results of her archival investigations into the sixteenth-century book trade, having dipped her hands in blood? Could she even do so? Or, to put these questions as does the poet Charles Bernstein, in thinking about a lecture he once heard on Hollywood melodrama by philosopher Stanley Cavell: 'Can you do philosophy in a gorilla suit or a white tuxedo and still be responsible to the profession and to the activity of philosophy (which is not the same thing)?'[2]

Later in this chapter, I will return to these questions of responsibility – of disciplines, subdisciplines, and the boundaries between them – and of the relationship between (academic) performance and (academic) performativity, but first I want to lay some groundwork for that

---

[2] Charles Bernstein, 'A Blow is Like an Instrument', *Daedalus*, 126, (1997), 177–200; 177–8.

discussion by considering two other realms of performance and performativity, sports and acting.

During the last Olympiad, in Athens, I watched from Alabama, usually while wishing wistfully that my satellite provider offered access to the Canadian Broadcasting Corporation, whose coverage would allow me to focus more on the performance of the athletes and less on that of the network itself. One evening, I tuned the television to watch NBC's coverage of the team competition in men's gymnastics. Unusually, both the men's and the women's teams from the United States expected to place highly in the competition, perhaps even to take the gold medal. The American men were about to perform on high bar, and in telling us about the upcoming performances, commentator Tim Daggett, himself a former Olympian in the sport, noted that, in a highly unusual move, two of the Americans were putting up routines that had been changed, just two days before. Having learned that certain elements in their routines no longer held a degree of difficulty sufficient to compete with the Chinese, Japanese and Romanians, the Americans would attempt several moves they had not practised. Doing so was risky, the likelihood of failure in the new moves very high, because, in order to compete in this arena, on this particular night, Daggett judged, each athlete had put in 'about a year of practising an exact routine'.[3] The performance in the Olympics was supposed to be the final iteration of moves that had been performed maybe several thousand times in concert, in precise order. To achieve a flawless performance, a peak performance, Daggett implied, the athlete would have had to make the routine *routine*, so that it might be performed automatically, without conscious thinking. Without the thousands of iterations, Daggett implied, the athlete's conscious mind, as the philosopher Fred Dretske puts it, would not be able to 'go . . . elsewhere while the body performs'.[4] And if the conscious mind is not 'elsewhere' when the athlete performs, he lowers his chances of achieving a superior athletic performance. As Kevin Costner's Crash Davis says in *Bull Durham* to Tim Robbins's Nuke LaLoosh,

who cannot understand why he is serving up fat pitches and wild ones, too: 'Don't think, Meat.'[5]

In this 1988 film, the implication is clear: the clueless pitcher, Nuke LaLoosh, holds the blazing talent that will take him to stardom in the major leagues, while the cerebral catcher, Crash Davis, holds nothing but the minor league record for home runs in a career – well, that and the sexy junior college English teacher. But *Bull Durham* plays to the crowd in suggesting that superior athletic performance is a 'no-brainer' – the result of instinctive talent only. The experience of the gymnasts suggests otherwise: in addition to talent, such performance is 'the result of intelligent planning and diligent practice', as Gerald Graff puts it, in using sports to comment on America's ambivalence about the intellect.[6] But what Graff does not pursue in his discussion of the intellectualism lurking in athletic performance, is this: the intellectualism is directed towards making conscious intellect irrelevant to the performance and thus, to some extent, to the performative as well. Through the planning and the practice, through iteration after iteration after iteration, the athlete builds or works or, to use metaphors familiar to us, writes or programs the moves into his muscles (although, as Hans Ulrich Gumbrecht points out, 'recent research in cognitive science' suggests this actually to be 'an empirical description rather than just a metaphor');[7] and he does so in the hope that when the competition occurs, the muscles will remember and not one conscious decision will need to be made. The athlete hopes she will achieve what Marianne Moore

---

[3] 'NBC News Transcripts: Olympics Coverage: Athens 2004', National Broadcasting Company, Inc., 14 August 2004, p. 12. http://web.lexis-nexis.com/universe/document?_m=f28dad4dbd3391136e3e4d07ca94876.

[4] Fred Dretske, 'Where is the Mind when the Body Performs?', *Stanford Humanities Review*, 6 (1998), 84–8; p. 84.

[5] *Bull Durham*, directed by Ron Shelton, Orion Pictures Corp., 1988.

[6] Gerald Graff, *Clueless in Academe: How Schooling Obscures the Life of the Mind* (New Haven, 2003), p. 99.

[7] Hans Ulrich Gumbrecht, *In Praise of Athletic Beauty* (Cambridge, MA, 2006), p. 170.

cherished in professional baseball players, an 'accuracy that looks automatic'.[8]

Achieving the look of the automatic, what Gumbrecht calls 'this complex, dehumanizing impression',[9] requires an athlete to clear her mind at the moment of performance – not just of thoughts extraneous to the task at hand but even of thoughts about it. Thoughts may cause the body to miss the boat; as Dretske observes, 'it has been shown . . . that athletes react to starting signals before they become aware of them. A runner will start to run, at least the motor commands to initiate running will be sent to leg muscles, before the starter's gun is actually heard . . . The athlete's body – almost literally – leaves the athlete's mind behind at the starting line.'[10] This is why athletes develop rituals they must accomplish before attempting a particular kind of manœuvre – a putt in golf, a free throw in basketball, getting set in the blocks in track, facing the pitcher and swinging at the ball in baseball. Like the near interminable iterations in practice, these rituals help the athlete clear the mind and they suggest, too, how difficult it is for the athlete to separate the body from the conscious mind, to achieve an accuracy that looks automatic, that looks, in fact, like what the body and not just the brain is actually or, rather, mostly doing, which is to say, processing data – unconsciously, at almost unmeasurable speed and in ways still mostly mysterious to science – to accomplish the proprioceptive control that results in superior athletic performance.[11]

An engrossing example of this difficulty – of separating body from conscious mind and, perhaps more importantly, of how difficult it is for us to say what we mean (or not) by 'instinct' or 'improvisation' or 'judgement' or 'decision-making' within the moments of athletic performance – occurred during a play in the American League Championship Series between the New York Yankees and the Boston Red Sox, in October 2004. In the eighth inning of game six, with the Yankees trailing 4–2, though still leading the series they would lose the next day, Alex Rodriguez came to bat with one out and Derek Jeter on first base. The star third baseman of the Yankees and the highest paid player

in the game (then and still today),[12] Rodriguez dribbled a grounder about 50 feet up the first base line. Pitcher Bronson Arroyo fielded the ball and went to tag Rodriguez, who was running up the line toward him and first base. But when Arroyo's glove approached his chest, and with first base still many feet away, Rodriguez suddenly slapped at the glove, releasing the ball, which rolled into short right field, and allowing Jeter to score. Moments later, however, after a protest from the Red Sox's manager, Tony Francona, the umpires conferred and ruled Rodriguez out for interference. Jeter was returned to first base and the Yankees did not score again that night.

What happened? What was Rodriguez thinking, or did he think at all, when he reached out his hand and slapped the ball from Arroyo's glove? Rodriguez claimed afterward, 'I don't know what I was trying to do.' But, whether thinking or not, why slap the ball away from the pitcher rather than run him over? Arroyo was a leaf, tall and lanky; his blonde hair skirted out in corn rows from under his cap; and Rodriguez outweighed the Boston pitcher by thirty-five pounds. According to the *New York Times*, Rodriguez admitted that 'he would have been better off barreling into Arroyo . . . "when I tried to reach the ball, the rule goes against me"'.[13] Better off indeed: even had Arroyo held onto the ball after a collision, Jeter would have been on second base, in scoring position and Rodriguez would have been spared a skewering in the press for his

[8] Marianne Moore, *The Complete Prose of Marianne Moore*, ed. Patricia C. Willis (New York, 1987), p. 686.

[9] Gumbrecht, *Beauty*, p. 169.

[10] Dretske, 'Mind', p. 88.

[11] E.g., Dretske, 'Mind'; Alain Berthoz, 'General Introduction', *Multisensory Control of Movement*, ed. Alain Berthoz (New York, 1993), 1–4; Michael S. A. Graziano, 'Where Is My Arm? The Relative Role of Vision and Proprioception in the Neuronal Representation of Limb Position', *Proceedings of the National Academy of Sciences*, 96 (1999), 10418–21.

[12] Christopher Young, 'Are baseball's highest-paid players earning their keep?' *Sporting Eye*, The Phoenix.Com, 6 July 2006. www.thephoenix.com/SportingEye/PermaLink.aspx?guid=dedfc714-9f46-4590-b72f-496cc66817dd.

[13] Jack Curry, 'A Play Boston Won't Let Rodriguez Forget', *New York Times*, 21 October 2004, pp. C15, C19; p. C19.

dubious behaviour, behaviour that revealed him to be either a cheat (if, while running up the base path, he *decided* to break the rules) or unmanly, a coward (for not bowling the pitcher over, whether or not he decided to break the rules or just instinctively slapped at the pitcher's glove).

Female sportswriter Selena Roberts was merciless in *The Times*, slurring Rodriguez's manhood in order to exemplify the 'hollowness' of Rodriguez and other 'mercenaries' on the Yankees. Accusing Rodriguez of 'Jeter-envy', Roberts suggested that New York was getting the best of Rodriguez, discomfiting him, undermining him, so that he was getting

a little scared of inconsequence. And this is why Alex Rodriguez looked so desperate to be significant in Game 6 . . . With . . . an opportunity to deliver an incandescent hit for a Yankee team fading into the night, Rodriguez dribbled a weak grounder to tough-guy pitcher Bronson Arroyo. Out of frustration or star petulance, Rodriguez all but cat-scratched Arroyo as the pitcher in cornrows tried to tag him down the first-base line, a calculated slap by A-Rod that dislodged the ball and sent a shot of euphoria through Yankee Stadium as Jeter scored. For a moment, while he stood on second base after the play, A-Rod must have felt a prankster's high. He had gotten away with one, hadn't he? He had gotten a whiff of attention in a pivotal moment on the sly? But once the umpires convened, they correctly called interference on A-Rod, sending Jeter back to first, adding to Rodriguez's collection of big-moment disappointments.[14]

Roberts held no doubt about Rodriguez's intent – the slap was calculated – and she offered a nicely bitchy back story to justify the imputation. But I think Rodriguez answered honestly when he claimed he didn't 'know what [he] was trying to do'. As Dretske might say, he left his mind in the batter's box. Rodriguez's conscious mind likely was not directing his body to slap at Arroyo's glove; his body was doing what it was trained to do, to adapt its movements in face of the demands of the situation. Training – repetition and iteration, slowly writing the moves into the muscles, into the body – does not produce that which is 'fixed, rote, mechanical, or unintelligent' but that which is 'both flexible and adaptive'.[15] Unfortu-

nately for Rodriguez, as for all of us in far less public situations, sometimes those flexible and adaptive responses of the body, what Dretske also calls 'the intelligence of the body', lead to less than satisfactory results, results one might not have willed, or consciously chosen, results that allow others to attribute undignified motive to what one has done.

In light of the press's pillorying of Rodriguez, one might be tempted to think the athlete damned if he does and damned if he doesn't. To perform at the top of his game, the athlete trains herself not to think, to clear her conscious mind at the point of performance; but when a crucial moment arrives in the performance, requiring instantaneous judgement, spectators expect him to think like Einstein. Or Hamlet. Yet Hamlet has been pilloried in criticism – and by himself – for 'thinking too precisely on th'event',[16] for letting his conscious mind get in the way of performing the part he has been assigned by the ghost of his father. Shakespeare spends a good deal of time emphasizing this point, the debilitating effect of thought on action, and puts it into the mouths of three characters: Hamlet, in his soliloquy in 3.1, as well as the one in 4.4, alluded to above; the Player King in the 'Mousetrap'; and Claudius in conversation with Laertes, in 4.7. As the Player-King says to his wife:

> I do believe you think what now you speak;
> But what we do determine oft we break.
> Purpose is but the slave to memory,
> Of violent birth but poor validity,
> . . .
> What to ourselves in passion we propose,
> The passion ending, doth the purpose lose.
>
> (3.2.168–71, 176–7)

---

[14] Selena Roberts, 'Yankee Mercenaries Are Searching for Meaning', *New York Times*, 21 October 2004, p. C19.

[15] Dretske, 'Mind', p. 87.

[16] William Shakespeare, *The Tragedy of Hamlet, Prince of Denmark*, quoted from *The Norton Shakespeare*, ed. Stephen Greenblatt *et al.* (New York, 1997), 4.4.9[31]. Subsequent references to the play appear in the text. Passages from Q2 only are indicated by superscript lineation, as above.

In each instance, the implication is clear: accomplishing 'an enterprise of great pith and moment' (3.1.88) requires an immediate giving over to passion, what Hamlet will later describe as 'rashness' (5.2.7). Counsels Claudius: 'That we would do, / We should do when we would: for this "would" changes / And hath abatements and delays as many / As there are tongues, are hands, are accidents' (4.7.95$^{5-8}$).

I do not wish here to equate Shakespeare and Ron Shelton, or Hamlet, Claudius or the Player King and Crash Davis – 'Don't think, Meat' – but I do wish to suggest that in *Hamlet*, Shakespeare asks us to contemplate theatrical analogies, to plumb the similarities and differences or even, perhaps, the continuum between acting on stage and acting in life, in order to understand or think through the moral and intellectual problems central to this play. Hamlet does this himself, in the soliloquy in Act 2, brooding on the Player's ability, 'in a fiction, in a dream of passion', to 'force his soul so to his whole conceit / That from her working all his visage wanned, / Tears in his eyes, distraction in's aspect, / A broken voice, and his whole function suiting / With forms to his conceit' (2.2.529, 30–4). What would the Player do, Hamlet wonders, 'had he the motive and the cue for passion / That I have?' (538–9). Answering that question, the Prince assumes 'real life' passion to be more intense, more of a motivator, than that of 'fiction': the Player, he contends, would perform much better in such circumstances, with such a motive and cue. He would 'make mad the guilty and appal the free, / Confound the ignorant, and amaze Indeed the very faculties of eyes and ears' (541–3). In contrast, Hamlet laments, he himself rests in Elsinore, 'like John-a-dreams, unpregnant of my cause', able to 'say nothing', not even 'for a king, / Upon whose property and most dear life / A damned defeat was made' (546–8).

Hamlet is an astute critic, one of the 'judicious' (3.2.24), and he is talented enough to pen a scene that would, he thinks, 'get [him] a fellowship in a cry of players' (255), but here he forgets what he knows about the actor's craft, mistakenly asserting that acting is fundamentally about 'speech' and

that 'real life' passion creates a stronger (theatrical) effect than does a passion practised and rehearsed. As Hamlet later explains to the players, actors must 'acquire and beget a temperance' that can give 'smoothness' to their passions, passions that flow from them in a 'torrent, tempest, and . . . whirlwind'. Actors, and specifically clowns, should not improvise, should 'speak no more than is set down for them' (3.2.5–7, 35). Hamlet thinks this latter a matter of not interfering with the audience's attention (lines 37–8), but actors know that it is also and, from their point of view, more fundamentally a matter of acting. Like athletes, actors know they may fail when they think too precisely on the event; they do not, in the middle of a performance, say to themselves, 'About, my brain[s]' and improvise a plot to 'tent . . . to the quick' their adversaries (2.2.565, 574). Such self-consciousness is risky and potentially debilitating; the actor can suffer a 'complete loss of perception and rehearsed function'.[17] The actor with stagefright, says one psychoanalyst, is 'like a surfer' who loses her 'radar . . . You can ride a ten-foot wave with confidence, not thinking about it, just doing it. Then all of a sudden, you become too self-aware. You think too much. You get wiped out.'[18]

It is tempting to claim that Hamlet gets wiped out, is struck with stagefright, when he finds himself in 3.3 with an easy opportunity to kill Claudius, who is kneeling in prayer. Certainly, Hamlet fails to act because he becomes too self-conscious, thinks too precisely on the event, scanning the implications of killing Claudius in this setting and then concluding, arrogantly, that his sword should and will 'know . . . a more horrid hint' (3.3.88). And Shakespeare emphasizes Hamlet's mistake; the reasoning by which he comes to this decision is proved false immediately, when Claudius acknowledges the futility of his prayers: 'words without thoughts never to heaven go' (3.3.98). Furthermore, the predicament of the actor in performance mirrors that of the athlete (or the musician or ballet dancer),

---

[17] Donald Kaplan, quoted in John Lahr, 'Petrified', *The New Yorker*, 28 August 2006, pp. 38–42; pp. 38–9.

[18] Christopher Bollas, quoted in Lahr, 'Petrified', p. 39.

as a number of acting theorists and teachers point out, particularly, though not exclusively, those who are concerned with movement or who think the body is the actor's expressive instrument.[19] In common parlance, after all, we speak of the acting 'coach', someone who might remind us, like John Harrop, that 'it is not in the mind but in muscular memory that a performance is stored'[20] or, like Richard Schechner – and in words anticipating Dretske's cited above – that actors should enter into 'a constant state of training so that when a situation arises one will be ready to "do something appropriate" to the moment'. Such training, Schechner adds, 'is what a good atheletic [sic] team does'.[21]

Nevertheless, and temptation notwithstanding, it is more accurate to claim that Shakespeare alludes to stagefright here in order to force attention again on the continuum between 'acting' on stage and 'acting' in life, the similarities and differences between the two. Even if an actor or a psychoanalyst might identify what happens to Hamlet at this moment as stagefright – he is there, he knows what to do, he starts to think about it, and he freezes – Hamlet by definition cannot experience 'stagefright', because he is not immobilized by fear just as he is about to 'do the very thing [he is] trained to do'.[22] He is immobilized by fear, or fails to act, because he is about to do something he has not trained to do, a significant act of dubious moral quality, a cold-blooded murder. Hamlet has not trained for this part, nor does he train for it in the course of the play, as he trains for the fencing match with Laertes – 'Since he went into France', he tells Horatio, 'I have been a continual practice. I shall win at the odds' (5.2.148–9). And he does not train for this part because, if I may be a bit facetious, Hamlet was not written by Mario Puzo, and the play does not chronicle the struggles of a hit man or assassin. What Hamlet can and does do is think through the need sometimes to be rash, to (re)act without thinking. Discovering on the seas that 'our indiscretion sometime serves us well / When our dear plots do pall' and realizing in the graveyard that 'imagination [may] trace the noble dust of Alexander till a find it stopping a bunghole', Hamlet is able, finally, to 'let be', to stop

'consider[ing] too curiously' the situation he is in and the action he should take (5.2.8–9, 5.1.190). He is able to allow himself to (re)act, if not to 'act': 'The readiness is all' (5.2.168). Thus, the difference, here, between Hamlet and the actor or the athlete is that Hamlet clears his conscious mind in order to (re)act, which leaves him without control of his situation and leaves Elsinore a mess, littered with bodies, including his own. The actor or the athlete clears his conscious mind to 'act' or to 'perform' in a way that, because of years of training, offers the illusion, and sometimes the reality, of being completely in control of his situation – the 'accuracy' that the poet Moore cherished for looking 'automatic'.[23]

At this point, you may be thinking, 'fine, but what has all this to do with academic performance and academic performativity, the subject of your performance today?' Or, more accurately, perhaps, since this paper is no longer, strictly speaking, being performed but is being read, you may be thinking, 'fine, but what has all this to do with this bit of academic performativity, your argument in this essay?' And if you are thinking this, you have every right to do so, for the promise implied by being in a room together at a conference or reading this essay in this journal is that I will say something interesting about academic performance and academic performativity. Such a promise, whether in the conference room or in the journal, is one of the norms of our profession, to which I should, indeed must, submit. Perhaps I have confounded your expectations or merely tried your patience by devoting so much time to sports, even a discussion of sports that morphed into a discussion of *Hamlet*,

---

[19] E.g. John Harrop, *Acting* (London, 1992); Richard Hornby, *The End of Acting: A Radical View* (New York, 1992); Phillip B. Zarrilli, ed., *Acting (Re)Considered*, 2nd edn (London, 2002).

[20] Harrop, *Acting*, p. 22.

[21] Richard Schechner, 'From Ritual to Theatre and Back', in *Ritual, Play, Performance: Readings in The Social Sciences / Theatre*, ed. Richard Schechner and Mady Schuman (New York, 1976), pp. 196–222; p. 222 n. 27.

[22] Lahr, 'Petrified', p. 38.

[23] Moore, *Prose*, p. 686.

but I hope the next move I make, a discussion of performativity in the work of Judith Butler, will bring the gymnastics arena in Athens and the base paths of Yankee Stadium, not to mention the court at Elsinore, closer to the concerns implied by my title, that is, to concerns about academic performativity.

Sports have never been paradigmatic for our understandings of performance and, while dramatic performance used to be so, it no longer is, being merely 'a small slice' of a field that has globalized massively, as W. B. Worthen put it recently.[24] For most academics today, including those in theatre or performance studies, performance means something related to the non-literary or the non-theatrical, to the social construction of reality and thus to the quotidian, to something called performativity, which, in the work of Judith Butler, is a model of gender structuration that weds Nietzsche to Foucault via Derrida. Some may lament this fact, because Butler's work is dense and, in addition, has confused many of her readers but, in fact, Butler is not the first to appeal to theatrical role performance to understand 'real life' role performance, nor is she the first to insist upon differences between the two. One might cite as Butler's forerunners in this regard certain sociologists and philosophers, such as Erving Goffman or George Herbert Mead, but I hope the discussion of *Hamlet* above indicates the long history of such thinking: Shakespeare, too, thought deeply about issues like these.

What is necessary to emphasize, however, is that for Butler 'performativity' derives from discussion in philosophy or linguistics, not from literature, theatre or literary or theatrical history: 'within speech act theory', she writes, 'a performative is that discursive practice that enacts or produces that which it names'; for Butler, then, a performative of gender is 'always a reiteration of a norm or set of norms'; it involves the 'power of discourse to produce effects through reiteration'.[25] For this reason, and it is a good one, Butler insists upon a distinction between 'performance' and 'performativity'. The latter 'is neither free play nor theatrical self-presentation, nor can it be simply equated with performance'. Indeed, 'the reduction of per-

formativity to performance would be a mistake'.[26] Not all gender performances, then, are performative of gender, yet when they are, when gender 'performance . . . is performative, gender is an "act", broadly construed', which '*draws on and covers over* the constitutive conventions by which it is mobilized . . . the accumulating and dissimulating historicity of force'.[27] As such an 'act', the performance of gender must necessarily occur *in medias res*: 'the act that one does, the act that one performs, is . . . an act that has been going on before one arrived on the scene'.[28] The crucial component in the performativity of gender, in contrast to the performance of gender, whether physical or verbal, is one's citational iteration of legal and social norms, which iteration then reproduces those norms. (This is a point, ironically, Butler found it necessary to repeat, repeatedly, in *Bodies that Matter* and elsewhere.) And a crucial component in any sort of subversion of those norms is recognition that one is 'implicated in that which one opposes'. The 'question of subversion' is a question of 'of *working the weakness in the norm*'.[29]

Butler has identified athleticism as a 'technolog[y] . . . of the body', which, like surgery or hormone therapy, may 'generate new forms of gender'.[30] Such technologies, I think it safe to say, are ways of 'working the weakness in the norm'. And yet, athleticism works the weakness in the norm differently from the way surgery or hormones do, because athleticism is itself performative: as we have already seen, athleticism depends on the citational iteration of legal and social norms,

---

[24] W. B. Worthen, *Shakespeare and the Force of Modern Performance*, (Cambridge, 2003), p. 1.

[25] Judith Butler, *Bodies That Matter* (New York, 1993), pp. 13, 12, 20.

[26] Butler, *Bodies*, pp. 95, 234.

[27] Judith Butler, 'Performative Acts and Gender Construction: An Essay on Phenomenology and Feminist Theory', in *Performing Feminisms: Feminist Critical Theory and Theatre*, ed. Sue-Ellen Case, (Baltimore, 1990), p. 279. See also Butler, *Bodies*, p. 227.

[28] Butler, 'Performative', p. 272.

[29] Butler, *Bodies*, pp. 241, 237, 241.

[30] Judith Butler, *Undoing Gender* (New York, 2004), p. 203.

what Butler calls 'a prior and authoritative set of practices',[31] which, in this case, are the rules of the game and the accrued wisdom of coaches, trainers and mentors about how best to perform moves necessary to it. As Butler put it in an essay on athletes, published in 1998, 'what we appreciate by way of shape and form is the labored effect of a ritualistic exercise', and this laboured effect finds its best or, at least, most public manifestation in sites of competition. Such a site is composed not simply 'of the various bodies by which it is inhabited; it is, rather, a set of rules, norms, and relations by which a body assumes its bearings and its shape'.[32]

But by subsequently calling athleticism a 'technolog[y] . . . of the body', and coupling athleticism with hormones and surgery, which in themselves are not performative (except, perhaps, for the medical personnel involved), Butler may imply that to call athleticism performative may be controversial or odd. What is at stake in acknowledging the performativity of athleticism? Perhaps we can get at this by taking the theoretical road alluded to by Butler in 'Athletic Genders'. In this essay, Butler wishes to make two points. First is one familiar to those who know her work: 'ideals of gender are not only imposed retrospectively on athletic activity by photography or by the media, but they form part of its meaning and structure, such that no athletic activity can proceed without some reference to these ideals'. Second is the point that women's sports have the power to 'call into question what we take for granted as idealized feminine morphologies' or, to put it a bit more baldly, to challenge 'the categories by which we sort men from women'.[33] And in fact, as Butler takes great pleasure in describing, through the example of Martina Navratilova,

women's sports . . . has shown us in the last few decades just how radically gender norms can be altered through a spectacular public restaging . . . Martina may not have known that her emergence on the international scene would precipitate a crisis in the category of 'women' as it is used in the field of 'women's sports' and its public perception. But this is a crisis that only makes us more capable as the imagining beings that we are, as those who must live the very genders that we seek to understand . . .

Martina produced the crisis that allowed us, in turn, to love her accomplishment all the better.[34]

As important as these points are, particularly the notion that gender norms do change, and that 'a more capacious and imaginative set of gender norms' is possible, Butler points at the end of her essay to the difficulty of such changes, suggesting that there 'is no simple passage from regarding a given body as abject, anomalous, or monstrous, as outside of gender as we know it, to regarding that same body as ideal'. In fact, the 'reconsideration of what we claim to know or imagine as gendered life can take place only by passing through an unstable and troubled terrain, a crisis of knowledge, a situation of not-knowing'.[35]

It is here that we may wish to follow the road alluded to but not taken: in pointing out that for the 'likes of Martina and her athletic progeny' and 'in the labored crafting of the athletic body, certain ideal feminine morphologies come into crisis', Butler observes that these feminine ideals 'come into conflict with other competing culturally elaborated ideals'.[36] Concerned as she is about the potential for crisis in and thus transformation of gender norms, Butler does not consider what these other ideals might be, or how they might be structured or situated in society or culture, or even related to gender. But I would like to develop the gesture Butler makes here: what happened when Martina got athletic on the tennis court was not just that feminine ideals came 'into conflict with other competing culturally elaborated ideals' but more specifically that one arena of performativity, that of athleticism, came into conflict with another arena of performativity, that of gender. And what happened when Martina made a body like hers

---

[31] Judith Butler, *Excitable Speech: A Politics of the Performative* (New York, 1997), p. 51. See also Butler, *Bodies*, p. 227.

[32] Judith Butler, 'Athletic Genders: Hyperbolic Instance and/or the Overcoming of Sexual Binarism', *Stanford Humanities Review*, 6 (1998), 103–11; pp. 104, 105.

[33] Butler, 'Athletic', pp. 104, 111.

[34] Butler, 'Athletic', pp. 108, 111.

[35] Butler, 'Athletic', p. 110.

[36] Butler, 'Athletic', p. 110.

acceptable for women on tennis courts was that she helped make such bodies acceptable for women in society everywhere. What happened was that one arena of performativity, sports, affected and changed yet another, gender.

Butler is correct to suggest that there 'is no simple passage from regarding a given body as abject, anomalous, or monstrous, as outside of gender as we know it, to regarding that same body as ideal';[37] the passage is difficult and laboured and time-consuming. Butler does not describe the mechanisms of that passage, though we may be sure she would argue it is neither voluntaristic nor theatrical, some 'fabrication of the performer's "will" or "choice"'.[38] I would like to suggest that one such mechanism is a(nother) structured arena of performativity. That is, in this case, a subversion of received gender categories, or the proliferation of constitutive gender categories, occurs not because one person works the weakness in the norm – voluntaristically or theatrically – but because many, many persons operating in a 'culturally elaborated' environment do so. In the case of athletic performativity, persons submit, willingly and willfully, to regimes of discipline far more controlling, if far more limited in scope, than those that structure gender. Martina, for example, did not just 'emerge . . . [one day] on the international scene'. She and doubtless dozens of other people had been working for years and years to effect this emergence, and Martina was, in fact, already a seasoned professional before she engaged in the weight and endurance training that resulted in the body that would precipitate a crisis in the category of 'woman' on the tennis courts and elsewhere. Further, since athletic performativity requires persons to accept as an ideal of performance a situation in which conscious thinking is less than pertinent, we are faced with the irony that citational repetition, which dulls the mind and makes what is arbitrary seem natural, is perceived here to be a positive or a good, something worth achieving, rather than a constraint to which one must submit, as is the case for gender performativity *per se*. Finally, and perhaps most importantly, these groups of persons must submit, willfully and suc-

cessfully, to the constraining force of received athletic performativity even as they are resisting – or more accurately – while they are submitting, less wilfully and successfully, to the constraining force of received gender performativity, that is, when they are children, adolescents and young adults. It does not stretch the imagination to hypothesize that the structured arena of athletic performativity gives some of those children, adolescents and young adults the emotional wherewithal to withstand the competing pressures of structured gender performativity.

What I hope all this helps us to see is that, as Worthen also suggests, social life is constituted in many arenas of performativity; dramatic performativity, to take another example, consists not in the citing of texts but 'in reiterating its own regimes of performance . . . the disciplined application of conventionalized practices – acting, directing, scenography'.[39] These arenas can relate to or affect one another in significant ways or not at all. Performances may or may not result in performativity and performances can vary crucially, in terms of the performer's willingness or ability to subject herself to regimes of discipline, in terms of the performer's goals in accomplishing citational iterations and in terms of the performer's need to cite effectively or rigorously any given set of prior and authoritative practices. For example, when an academic, when a Shakespearian, delivers a paper, must she cite the authoritative practices of, say, the professional actor? And if so, what are her goals in doing so? Are they the same as, similar to, or different from those of the professional actor? Looking at the question from another angle, it is a fact that throughout the composition of this academic performative, I usually spent an hour each day running, during which time I thought about the ideas I was trying to hone. Occasionally, though, I'd lose concentration and my thoughts would turn to the irony of doing this thinking while 'performing' a run I did not have to think about, a run that even had a certain formal

---

[37] Butler, 'Athletic', p. 110.

[38] Butler, *Bodies*, p. 234.

[39] Worthen, *Force*, p. 9.

style but that also had very little, if any, relation to a citation of the authoritative practices of the professional long distance runner. Does the amateur athlete engage in, was I, while running, engaging in, athletic performativity? Does a Shakespearian giving a paper engage in dramatic performativity? Within a professional theatrical company, who so engages? An actor? A director? The production's designers? And are these persons engaged in the same dramatic performativity?

As the questions above suggest, defining the authoritative practices relevant to a given arena of performativity poses problems of great difficulty. For instance, academic performance occurs – we perform – in many settings, though mostly, as Worthen points out, we perform in the classroom and in the conference room.[40] But which of our performances may we say constitute disciplinary or professional performativity? Can we identify a set of such performances? A hierarchy? If performativity works to reproduce, hegemonically, the social or institutional order, one might say that administrative performances rank highly. Or teaching performances. Alternatively, if one's professional identity was formed in an elite PhD programme, then one would have to say that one's intellectuality – one's research and thus the conference paper and the journal publication – ranks highly, too. Further, as I have already observed at the beginning of this paper, even the set of practices associated with research and intellectuality varies between disciplines and even between sub-disciplines. Without doubt, the relationship is vexed among these possible sites of academic performativity – for instance, does the citational iteration of intellectual practices constitute a citational iteration of institutional bureaucratic practices and vice-versa? Or not? But my guess is that most of us concern ourselves not much at all with such vexed relationships.

Some people do think about it, however, and have concluded that argument is the keystone of the 'prior and authoritative set of practices' associated with the academic profession, and certainly with professional intellectuality. 'Making arguments is the name of the game in academia', says Graff;[41]

'conflicts are the lifeblood of the intellectual world', says sociologist Randall Collins.[42] (This may be why athletes and artists fit uncomfortably within the academy, and why they provide me an excellent counter-example; they are accomplished at what they do, and strongly competitive about it, but they tend not to argue.) But attention, too, is necessary for success in the academy, even for those with good arguments, because our profession is also competitive and rivalrous. And, as the academic world has expanded, attention has become more difficult to obtain and preserve, because the traditional means of gaining attention – affiliation and pedigree – no longer guarantee that people will attend to you. As a result and to be competitive, academics sometimes turn theatrical in their performances, focusing attention *on the performance rather than the performative*, indulging in a bit of a costume either to underscore an argument or simply to stand out – witness Michael Bérubé's electric blue suit, Jane Gallop's skirt of men's ties, or Richard Burt's 'loser' combo of sunglasses, gray hoodie, Doc Martins and shorts. Some academics go further in their theatricality, beyond the merely sartorial: as we have already seen, Lavender and Shepherd brought stage effects to the stage of academic performativity in Stratford and, several years ago, a Shakespearian stripped to the music of David Rose during her seminar at the Shakespeare Association of America, a performance that indeed garnered attention, finding its way into the blogosphere.[43]

Rest assured: even when I read this paper at a conference, my next move was not to strip. Rather, as in this performative, I suggested then that whatever strategies an academic uses to garner attention, to get us to listen to him or her, academic performativity is not even modestly about blue suits, gray hoodies, skirts of ties, stage blood or stripping. Nor is it about how smoothly you

---

[40] Worthen, *Force*, p. 15.
[41] Graff, *Clueless*, p. 3.
[42] Randall Collins, *The Sociology of Philosophies: A Global Theory of Intellectual Change* (Cambridge, MA, 1998), p. 80.
[43] 'Like *Circus Ponies*?' *Invisible Adjunct*, 21 November 2003: www.invisibleadjunct.com/archives/000360.html.

deliver your paper or whether you use powerpoint or stick religiously to twenty minutes of reading time. Academic performativity is not about muscle-memory, the kinesthetic or the short-circuiting of the brain, making the brain appear not to be part of the performance; no one would advise a young academic as Crash Davis advises Nuke LaLoosh or as Claudius advises Laertes. Nor, presumably, is academic performativity about creating an affective rather than intellectual response in one's audience. Academic performativity is, finally, about coming out on top – or, at least, about coming out well, close to the top – in argument, and one achieves this not through the quality of one's oral performance but through the quality of one's archival research and data, if one is a scholar, or the quality of one's insightful, even purple or punchy prose, if one is a critic. (These are all reasons why I find over-laboured Worthen's attempt to distinguish, via 'its insertion into orality', the conference paper from its printed and published heir. Whether a conference paper 'work[s] like a theatrical script' or looks like one is irrelevant, and even Worthen admits not everyone's conference papers do;[44] the point of a conference paper, of a conference performance, unlike that of a theatrical performance, is to make a point, an argument.)

The contours of our academic performativity are shaped by the institutions in which we work or, as Butler puts it, by 'a prior and authoritative set of practices'. Thus, explains Stanley Fish, for a literary critic 'to produce something that would count as a reading, [she would have] . . . to pose questions that are recognizably literary and give answers in terms that would make sense to literary actors, even if those answers [are] contested by some of [her] peers'.[45] 'Performances in the academy', writes Fish, 'must take a certain obligatory form', precisely because, like other professions, ours is constructed 'such that those who enter its precincts will find that the basic decisions, about where to look, what to do, and how to do it, have already been made'.[46] When performances do not so conform – when, metaphorically, someone does literary criticism in a gorilla suit – we sit up, take notice

and police the boundary, as the Shakespearian in Stratford tried to do, in response to Lavender and Shepherd's presentation, calling what they did a 'performance'. For this Shakespearian, and for many others in the audience, their paper was not performative but a performance. Their paper violated norms of the discipline (or the sub-discipline) and, perhaps even worse, their paper suggested that these norms should be changed. Of course, as a profession, we could change them: if Lavender and Shepherd's call were taken up by others and made repeatedly, or if Lavender and Shepherd's call itself were so compelling that other scholars began to pack their own stage blood, then the violation might be legitimized and smooth performance, performance as an end in itself, would become part of our performative norm. But until then, as they say in the Westerns, Lavender and Shepherd's words will remain 'fightin' words!' And as such, they tend to bring out the (stage) blood!

Butler and Fish, then, agree: we begin our performances, our performatives, *in medias res* and we end them there, too, however much we may contribute to tweaking or even changing significantly the norms that govern us, that give us meaning. Thus, even though I spent a significant number of pages during this performative talking about gymnasts and baseball players, I spoke about them in ways that were recognizably literary, or, at least, recognizably theoretical. But had I not provided a recognizable context for my discussion, had my performative instead consisted of a compilation of baseball statistics from the year 1947, or even from the American League Championship Series in 2004, I would have operated outside what Fish calls the 'immanent intelligibility' of the discipline.[47] In offering a compilation of baseball statistics, I would have offered you a gorilla suit or a strip show that could not even be construed as providing emphasis

---

44 Worthen, *Force*, p. 18.
45 Stanley Fish, *Professional Correctness: Literary Studies and Political Change* (Cambridge, MA, 1995), p. 50.
46 Fish, *Professional*, p. 44.
47 Fish, *Professional*, pp. 20–3, 23, 73.

for, as Fish notes, 'one can . . . bend, stretch, violate, and extend the rules [of literary criticism] in
all kinds of ways, but not in any old way'.[48] It is
tempting, of course, to see if, in conclusion, I might
violate the rules of the academic performative, perhaps by offering those baseball statistics from 1947
or, better yet, some recipes from a cookbook. But
I would rather conclude in a conventional way,
by gesturing toward the implications of this discussion for further research, by gesturing, that is,
toward the place where Butler and Fish disagree,
where, indeed, so many of us disagree: the ways
we respond, personally and theoretically, to the fact
of social construction, to having to begin – and
end – *in medias res*. Does this fact imply constraint?
Deviance? Normalcy? Opportunity? Risk? All of
the above?

I have some answers, and I am sure you do, too,
but exploring them will have to wait for another
academic performance or, rather, another academic
performative.

---

[48] Fish, *Professional*, p. 44.

SUDOKOTHELLOPHOBIA: WRITING HYPERTEXTUALLY, PERFORMATIVELY

ROB CONKIE

If you are an adventurous (or hypertextual, perhaps performative) reader I invite you to skip this introduction and go straight to the puzzle (you can always come back); what follows here is an orientation, a way into and around the main body of this article. If, as Umberto Eco writes, 'A title must muddle the reader's ideas, not regiment them',[1] then the next few pages aim to (slightly) un-muddle, though certainly not regiment, access to the puzzle through explanation of my title and method. I feel, at once, that I should apologize for this title and perhaps I would have abandoned the initial monstrosity altogether had its tripartite awkwardness not so neatly encapsulated the method. Writing about (Shakespearian) performance often involves such apologies, especially when the writing is deliberately methodological rather than descriptive of performance itself – I mean not writing about performance, but writing about writing about performance – and this is perhaps a tacit acknowledgement that writing cannot hope to reproduce a given production, neither its materiality nor ephemerality. Mike Pearson and Michael Shanks, to whom I will return, defend their discrete disciplines of theatre and archaeology with 'Apologia' before less apologetically and less obviously bringing them together into a fruitful interdisciplinary blend.[2] Michael Dobson begins his reflection on 'Writing about [Shakespearian] Performance' most deferentially (which is not always the way he writes about Shakespearian performances): 'I should apologize first of all for starting this chapter thus in the first person' and then he further excuses the arti-

cle, which is 'purely personal' and 'very cursory and simplistic'; he also defends a title about which he feels uncomfortable.[3] Broken down, my title reveals an attempt to create a form of writing which thickly describes Shakespearian production – in this case an adaptation of *Othello* I directed in 2003/4 called *Othellophobia* – and to weave together the most pressing textual and contextual concerns. Thus: the **form** of the writing is (post)structured by the number puzzle *sudoku*; the **content** is Shakespeare's *Othello* – the text itself, its more recent production history and the way that my production shaped the play; and the **analysis** of the content, which is facilitated by the form, is represented by *phobia*, which signals my concern here with (sub)textual and cultural anxieties generated and sustained by the play in performance.

My role not just as director of *Othellophobia*, but as facilitator of a wide-ranging collaborative process, focused my thoughts on wanting to document far more than what actually and finally happened on the stage (on any given night, or as recorded onto DVD). I developed a goal akin to that expressed by Ric Knowles, which 'is to articulate and apply a method for achieving a more precise and more fully contextualized and politicized understanding of how meaning is produced in the

---

[1] *Reflections on The Name of the Rose* (London, 1985), p. 3.
[2] *Theatre/Archaeology* (London, 2001), pp. 14, 29, 53–67.
[3] 'Writing about [Shakespearian] Performance', *Shakespeare Survey 58* (Cambridge, 2005), 160–8, p. 160.

theatre'.[4] Knowles's excellent book, to my mind, certainly achieves this via his various analyses, but his skilful readings of the materials of these theatres, are, for the most part, 'readerly' and confirmed as opposed to the 'writerly' and open text/s that I was hoping to produce. In searching for this Barthesian[5] multivalence I imagined a kind of hard-copy hypertext, whereby, to some extent, the freedom to cross-link, as on the internet, would be available to the reader of the following pages. George Landow defines hypertext as 'text composed of blocks of words (or images) linked electronically by multiple paths, chains or trails in an open-ended, perpetually unfinished textuality'.[6] Though not linked electronically, the blocks of words, what Barthes calls 'lexia', enable such paths through the juxtaposition and interplay of, for example, aspects of the rehearsal process with the way the production was received in the press. The documentation of performance/art offers a further methodological precedent for this type of interaction: such work has attempted to incorporate documentation within the work itself and thus to deconstruct product-centred analyses by making process a visible priority.[7] The form of sudoku foregrounds precisely this type of deconstruction and incorporation through the post/structure of nine pages with nine blocks (of words/images) to each page: though the box in the top left corner of the first page and the box in the bottom right corner of the last page ostensibly appear as starting and finishing points, entry to, exit from and movement within the article is not bound by conventional linearity.[8]

Whether this sense of open-endedness actually produces a 'perpetually unfinished textuality' is another matter; you can obviously read all of the boxes, although perhaps you could continue to find new resonances between them and to other external texts. Marvin Carlson's seductive notion that 'Performance by its nature resists conclusions, just as it resists the sort of definitions, boundaries, and limits so useful to traditional academic writing and academic structures'[9] might appear strategically apposite for my project given its implicit encouragement to test performative boundaries through challenges to 'traditional

academic writing' but (Shakespearian) performance seems to me to embrace conclusions, if not a conclusion: the final line of a text, a curtain call, Othello is noble, Othello is a monster. Also helpful here is Pearson and Shanks's observation that 'Rather than pretending to be a final and complete account of things, a closure, the performance document, an equivalent of the dramatic text, might be in itself equally fragmentary, partial and encouraging of interpretation.'[10] This text is exemplary of my method: in fact, in attempting to demystify those processes, practical and theoretical, which co-create the meaning of *Othello* as it is staged as *Othellophobia*, less of the actual production is revealed than might be by a more traditional theatre 'review'; instead, this space is ceded to other priorities and the performance document becomes increasingly fragmentary and partial and, hopefully, more 'encouraging of interpretation'. It is this notion of the reader being what Barthes calls 'a producer of the text', of choosing how to read it and how to make meaning of it (or, Hawkes-like, mean through it[11]) which constitutes the writing/reading as performative. For just as J. L. Austin characterises performative speech acts as those utterances which also enact, which say *and* do something, this article offers writing which actively encourages, perhaps

---

4 *Reading the Material Theatre* (Cambridge, 2004), p. 9.
5 These oft-rehearsed ideas come from Roland Barthes, *S/Z*, trans. Richard Miller (New York, 1974), pp. 3–16.
6 Cited in Gabriella Giannachi, *Virtual Theatres: An Introduction* (London, 2004), p. 13.
7 I am indebted to Synne K. Behrndt for steering me both through this discourse and towards Matthew Goulish, *39 Microlectures: in proximity of performance* (London, 2000) and Tim Etchells, *Certain Fragments: Contemporary Performance and Forced Entertainment* (London, 1999).
8 Indeed, the puzzle represents an ironic reversal of the commonplace observation of documentation of Shakespearian theatre: that the writing palely and partially reflects the performance. In this case the documentation is perhaps more interesting and layered and provocative than the performance (or its DVD recording) itself.
9 *Performance: A Critical Introduction* (London, 1996), p. 189.
10 *Theatre/Archaeology*, p. 13.
11 Terence Hawkes, *Meaning by Shakespeare* (London, 1992).

demands, interpretation, a critical performance on behalf of the reader.[12]

Published within a year of each other, two seemingly independent – neither cites the other (though each is in the other's acknowledgements) – and yet strikingly similar articulations of this idea help further to explicate the notion of performative writing as I am here practising it:

'Meaning' in a given performance situation – the social and cultural work done by the performance, its performativity, and its force – is the effect of all these systems and each pole of the interpretative triangle [of performance text, conditions of production and conditions of reception] working dynamically and relationally together.[13]

. . . the work of scripted drama and its performance, what we might call 'dramatic performativity' – the relationship between the verbal text and the conventions (or, to use Butler's term, 'regimes') of behaviour that give it meaningful *force* as performed action.[14]

Both texts are concerned with performativity, with inter-relationships, meaning and force but there are subtle differences: the first, by Knowles, characterizes performativity as a result or effect; the performance, through the conjunction of a series of material factors – including, for example, script, design, the actors, working conditions, auditorium, audience amenities, ticket prices, cultural moment of reception – produces a performative force, its meaning. The second, by W. B. Worthen, expresses performativity more as a process, whereby a series of citations – to 'regimes' such as modes of performing identity or subjectivity, historical reconstruction and authenticity or globalization – produces the meaning/s of performance. Thus, I am concerned with the way both *Othello* and *Othellophobia* generate/d meanings as a result of their material construction and with how their citation of various discourses, historical and contemporary, enabled this meaning. Allow me to summarize this as simply as I can: this article documents an adaptation of Shakespeare's *Othello* which is hypertextual in the way it weaves together the different narratives and discourses which shaped its production and reception. The hypertextuality

facilitates the article as performative in that it: one, reveals a thick description of the production in action; two, explores the effect of that action, how the play means; and three, demonstrates how that meaning is contingent upon a series of citations, the recognition of which might otherwise be elided or occluded.

The puzzle of sudoku requires that every row, every column and every 3 × 3 box contains the numbers 1–9.[15] As I have adapted the puzzle for this article, the nine boxes concern different aspects of the production, some of which inevitably overlap, and given that every row, column and box (in this case, a single page of the puzzle) must contain each of the numbers 1 through 9 only once, the form of the puzzle affirms the notion that each of these spheres, narratives, discourses and practices is equally (or near-equally) as important as any of the others in (in)determining the meaning of the play. The boxes have ghosted numbers and the numbers decode as follows:

1. **textual** – the text of the production was heavily filleted in order to play through 90 minutes without an interval and to leave space for the physical dimension of the production; these boxes provide an edited selection of those parts of the text which were most relevant to the overall conception of the production.
2. **theoretical** – much of the theoretical underpinning of the production was drawn from literary or theatre studies; the practice of the production – including martial arts, dance and clowning – was far more interdisciplinary.
3. **anecdotal / personal / cultural** – this is a testimony of how personally invested I (and others) was/were in the work and how the play shaped the participants' personal lives throughout the production; John Russell Brown writes that 'any full account of performance must go

[12] See Jonathan Culler, *Literary Theory: A Very Short Introduction* (Oxford, 1997), chapter 7.
[13] *Reading the Material Theatre*, p. 19.
[14] W. B. Worthen, *Shakespeare and the Force of Modern Performance* (Cambridge, 2003), p. 3.
[15] www.sudoku.com/, accessed 10 January 2006.

beyond mere quotation or factual description and call upon impressionistic and very personal reconstruction.'[16]

4. **rehearsal processes** – this process was extremely collaborative so that I became almost a facilitator of the production, as much as a director: the other creative authors included; the designer/producer, choreographer, bouffon director, composer, voice/text coach, assistant director and, of course, the actors.

5. **production history** – this was predominantly the recent stage history of the play and there were many to choose from in 2003/4 in the UK as post-colonial Britain continued to wrestle with its own phobias.

6. **finished production** – there were two versions of the production, as outlined in the puzzle.

7. **critical reception** – the production was reviewed by *The Bath Chronicle*, *Times Educational Supplement*, *The Stage* and *Time Out*, and by colleagues, mostly from The University of Winchester.

8. **pedagogical** – this mainly concerned a second-year class at The University of Winchester called 'Shakespeare and Ideology', which ran concurrently with the production of the play.

9. **visual/photographic** – these are images taken from the DVD recording of the production and contemporary and historical paintings and photographs which inspired or influenced the work.

The nine pages are arranged, in no particular order of importance, according to themes:

1. sexuality
2. emotion
3. history
4. stereotypes/binaries
5. animals
6. nightmare/monsters
7. race/blackness
8. stupidity
9. Desdemona

Though it can be read perfectly acceptably one page after another, to see the puzzle as conceived, the pages should be laid out thus:

1	2	3
4	5	6
7	8	9

This pattern, on the wall or on the floor, will allow the reader to make connections along lines, vertical or horizontal, or from page to page. Here are some ways, according to degree of difficulty, the puzzle might be read:

1. Easy: thematically – a whole page at a time, perhaps according to the reader's interest, for example, the Desdemona and then the Sexuality page.

2. Moderate: follow a number – again by interest, you might prioritize the production history (5) and develop an overall sense of those production moments that most impacted upon the production of *Othellophobia*.

3. Difficult: chronologically (roughly) – you might want to attempt to reconstruct an approximate chronology of the production's conception, creation and reception; this would mean reading (perhaps) the text boxes (1), followed by the theoretical (2) or production history (5), then onto the anecdotal, rehearsal, pedagogical and visual (3, 4, 8, 9), followed by the finished production (6) and then critical reception (7).

4. Fiendish: resonances – there are deliberate connections between boxes, sometimes on the same page and sometimes across pages: you might attune your reading to discovering such connections; for example, boxes 2.6 (by which I mean the box with the ghosted number six on page 2), 8.9 and 9.5 are linked by the trope of smudged make-up and also, less obviously, connect to 1.3 and 3.2.

A final deferral – if you didn't heed my initial advice – before moving to the puzzle, and continuing apologetically, I conclude with what I'm not doing through this article. I am not trying to persuade anyone to adopt my somewhat radical reading of *Othello*, which for some will seem unhelpfully ideological and for others obvious good sense; in

---

[16] 'Writing about Shakespeare's Plays in Performance', in *Shakespeare Performed: Essays in Honour of R. A. Foakes*, ed. Grace Ioppolo (Newark, 2000), p. 151.

part, the catharsis of putting on the production has (almost) cured me of such proselytising ambitions. I am not, either, advocating a new form of writing about Shakespeare in performance. I doubt that I shall ever repeat this experiment and a collection of articles in sudoku form would be obviously excessive, perhaps somewhat ridiculous. And I am not making any startling conclusions, open-ended or otherwise; the main conclusion of the article, and you really should not read this before the puzzle itself, is that the meanings of the play and the production were hopelessly beyond my authorial desire to control them (though this is perhaps especially the case given the collaborative nature of the project); I can proclaim with Sebastian of Messaline that 'My determinate voyage [was] mere extravagancy' (*Twelfth Night* 2.1.10). Though the death of the author may have been exaggerated, the suggestion that a production's meaning exceeds the designs of those authors is hardly groundbreaking. I am, however, offering a consistent, if biased, and deliberately self-invested, view of the play for early twenty-first-century Britain; I am making a challenge to find new and creative structures for the documentation of (Shakespearian) performance, including, for those more able than me, the creation of actual hypertexts on e-journals such as *Borrowers & Lenders*, which encourages 'contributors to use the online format to its best advantage, in particular, by imagining how to enhance or illustrate their essays with multimedia (screen captures, sound clips, images, and so on)';[17] and I am emphasizing the hypertextual and performative as the organizing apparatus by which unfixed and multi-layered meaning might be, at least for a moment, grasped. Now, complete the puzzle.

---

[17] See *Borrowers and Lenders: The Journal of Shakespeare and Appropriation*, at http://atropos.english.uga. edu/cocoon/ borrowers/, accessed 4 May 2006. As far as I can tell, the 'and so on' has yet to be fully explored.

I was teaching a Shakespeare and race class in parallel with the production of *Othellophobia*. After several weeks of theoretical discussions, we split the class into two groups who worked on edited productions of the play, one as a tragedy and the other as a comedy, and with the shared brief of foregrounding the ideological implications of staging the text. The comedy group was largely devoid of sexuality, excepting Iago's homoerotic/phobic desire for Othello; the tragedy group started with the murder - and with the young black actor topless - and then constructed a sexually assertive and promiscuous Desdemona.

I saw Ricky Fearon's Othello for Concentric Circles at the Haymarket in Basingstoke with a large group of women. Their chief topic of conversation was of waiting to see Othello naked. The production's publicity did not disappoint; at the beginning of 3.3 Fearon started stripping to his fetishised white boxer shorts and muscular body and then took a shower as Iago began to reel him in: more exemplary Othellophilia I have not seen. Making not quite the same point a local review decided, 'His vulnerability was highlighted in a highly original shower scene, when he stripped down to his underpants.'

Adi Bloom, reviewing *Othellophobia* for the *Times Educational Supplement*, focused on the production's use of the death / desire dynamic as outlined by Jonathan Dollimore. Bloom picked up that the murder was troublingly bestialised and eroticised and, as in the play, inextricably linked to her father: 'When Brabantio discovers the betrayal of his daughter, Desdemona, he glares like a wild-cat about to pounce... [her] murder is a culmination of animal baseness. Declaring "I would kill you and love you", Othello pulls her to him, her writhing death throes a reflection of his lust.'

This is a text saturated by sex, and nasty sex at that. Iago warns Brabantio that 'an old black ram/Is tupping your white ewe' (1.1.89-90), and that 'you'll have your daughter covered with a Barbary horse' (111-12), images which prefigure the tupping / covering / smothering of the final bedroom act. Emilia complains that 'when they are full,/They belch us' (3.4.99-100) but advises reciprocal treatment: 'The ills we do, their ills instruct us so' (4.3.99). This threat, however, is idle; the women have no means by which to return the violence enacted on them, let alone to resist it.

My first idea for Desdemona's murder, according to the strategy of exploding and exposing the play's stereotypes through grotesque exaggeration, was to have Othello beat her to death with a six foot phallus; the cast didn't go for it... What evolved through rehearsals, in collaboration with the designer, was that the tie around Othello's waist, and which could be read as phallic, was used to strangle her. The Brabantio figure was on stage throughout this, and later made a noose from the tie with which to hang Othello - obviously a horrible historical image - and prevent him taking his own life.

Othello and Desdemona's sexual union in Cyprus was represented far more poetically; this was the one moment in the production where the sexuality was healthily unpolluted. The consummation took the form of an improvised dance which happened upstage throughout the drinking scene; thus the apparent health was physically juxtaposed with the ensuing sickness. Brabantio watched both scenes, impotently unable to interrupt the love-making, but enabled to oversee and endorse Iago's machinations with Cassio's drinking - and soon the dance was halted by a screaming, Artaudian siren.

I met up with one of the actresses in the show to discuss elements of the production. It was a fine hot day so we sat outside at a local pub. The outdoor furniture meant that she had to sit, perfectly demurely, with her legs either side of a slightly obtrusive pole. When I returned with drinks she reported the comments of near-by male drinker: 'Stay out here much longer and you'll turn dark, love. Still, you've got a mighty shaft between your legs there.' Is it merely fanciful to connect this kind of comment to *Othello* in a manner similar to that of Bloom's connection of *The Merchant of Venice* to the Holocaust?

Celia Daileader coins the term 'Othellophilia' to describe overt, if sometimes unconscious, sexualisation of the black classical actor; this cultural process approaches 'biracial porn [and] functions to exploit both white women *and* black men.' It is defined by dramaturgies which foreground 'violence, physicality, sexuality, the demonic; black leather, leopard skin, black nudity against white dishabille.' Though she lauds the casting of black actors in non-black Shakespearean roles she laments the all-too-common 'pageant of black fantasy flesh, the fruits of allegedly colour-blind casting.'

Rosenberg begins his exhaustive chronicling of *Othello*'s various social, literary and theatrical histories with a biblical echo; 'From the beginning, men wept at *Othello*.' Emotional responses form the spiritual core of this history, which Bristol argues 'signals a chronic unwillingness amounting at times to outright refusal to participate in the performance of a play as the ritual or quasi-ritual affirmation of certain social practices.' I think this is perhaps an optimistic, carnivalesque reading: as often as not, such responses might express (latent) sympathy with Brabantio, if not Iago.

Perhaps *Othello* is the Shakespeare play which has elicited the most involved (and recorded) emotional responses from both readers and spectators. Iago says 'I will wear my heart upon my sleeve' (1.1.65) but it is Othello who, Tom Cruise-like, speaks of his 'soul's joy', such that he 'cannot speak enough of this content' (2.1.176, 188). His young bride continues to be the locus of the emotional 'rack' Iago ties him to, and, having murdered her, he describes himself as 'one whose subdued eyes, / Albeit unused to the melting mood / Drop tears as fast as the Arabian trees / Their medicinable gum' (5.2.344–8).

When I went to the cinema to see *Far From Heaven*, a story of prohibited love between a white woman and a black man, there was a poster for the Australian film, *Rabbit-Proof Fence*. Its warning about the narrative of Aboriginal assimilation, in this case the removal of 'half-caste' children from their families for institutional instruction, read 'mild emotional content'. It made me so mad I went back with a permanent marker and scrawled next to it, 'white English perspective'. The poster for *R-PF* eerily re-images Parker's *Othello* poster, with an over-sized Branagh looming over the three girls / Fishburne + Jacob.

Like *Shakespeare in Love* (1999), *Stage Beauty* (2004) trebles the emotional impact of the play (*Othello*) it stages: the tragic ending of the play itself is played; so is the audience's intense involvement in, and euphoric/cathartic response to, the tragedy; and, the characters playing the parts are romantically involved and their parts reveal their characters. Crudup playing Kynaston playing Desdemona (& Othello) seeks the emotional truth of the death scene. This can be read as an attempt to kill his 'feminine side', which the film suggests is the result of abuse, and once achieved allows him to embrace heterosexual love.

My emotional reactions to this play have changed over time. Reading it for the first time at 20 I was shattered by the destruction of what appeared to be an ideal romance; on the page Othello's blackness did not register with my yet-to-be-politicised eyes and my response was of an essentialised despair at love destroyed. Maybe ten years later I noticed the first signs of othellophobia: unease reading the play; a focus on the sexualised/bestialised construction of Othello; further unease sitting in the naturalistic (white audience) theatres; a nauseous inability to watch any contemporary adaptation of the play. Is it just me?

At a Sunday afternoon rehearsal, with opening night fast approaching and much still to be worked on, Oni turns up. Oni is Olu's very beautiful baby daughter. She is the physical reality of the Brabantio's nightmare of miscegenation, a brown baby. She is here an hour before the scheduled close of rehearsal, I suspect, because her mum quite rightly wants to make clear her prior claim to her over-worked husband. So Oni walks in and out of scenes, a haunting presence disrupting all around her by her beguiling smile and curls - chaos is come again - and I feel powerless as a controlling figure of the production's meaning.

At the end of the production Brabantio was very much involved in Desdemona's death. At different moments he held them, ambiguously either trying to prevent the murder or facilitate it. Othello struck Desdemona and then pulled her up onto him using his waist-tie. Her strangulation as she sat astride him was disturbingly sexual and at the end he invariably had her white makeup smudging his face. Then, farce; Brabantio breathed life back into Desdemona so that Othello had to keep cartoonishly killing her. All the reviews singled out the murder as harrowing; several were upset about the too-immediate comedy.

Of the two student productions, the tragedy group sought to provoke emotional responses to the play by turning Othello into a victim of domestic abuse (and cuckolding). This was tied to universalised notions of character which largely attempted to erase race as a central consideration of the production. The comedy group totally resisted any sort of emotional engagement with the narrative. The characters were represented as very broad stereotypes and even the serious actions of the play - Iago still tricked Othello into murdering Desdemona - were mocked as not worthy of serious attention.

Olu's agenda was recuperative; like many black actors he wanted fiercely, and entirely justifiably, to resist a white-constructed Othello and to affirm a black identity which was powerful and autonomous. His chief means for this were historical and cultural: for the former he did extensive research into Moorish history and used this to inform his characterisation; for the latter he developed a British/Nigerian accent as a way of focusing otherness. My agenda, contrarily, was 'explosive': I wanted to expose what I saw as pernicious (trans-historical) white constructions of the part; we were on a collision course...

Here is Ben Kingsley historicising his appearance via the Moorish Ambassador to Elizabeth I, and yet offering a rather ugly universalism: 'Thus from the beginning of rehearsal a being emerged who, if provoked at a primal level, would react with the violence of a psychopath.'

The senate's questions to Othello about his elopement was played as a bear-baiting, which, as described by Hawkes, involved 'the chaining to a stake and the whipping of a blinded bear... The use of specially trained dogs to tear the bear's flesh... guaranteed violent mutilation and plenty of blood, guts and noise'. More often connected to Macbeth's end, Othello defines himself when referring to Desdemona's powers of musical placation; 'O, she would sing the savageness out of a bear!' (4.1.186). His statement is a kind of performative fortification against such an appeasement, a renewed commitment to savagery.

Newman outlines some of the early modern explanations for blackness, in particular George Best's late sixteenth-century theory, extrapolated from the birth of a black baby to a black father and white mother, that 'it seemeth this blacknes proceedeth rather [as opposed to the previous notion of exposure to the sun] of some natural infection of that man'. This infection is given a scriptural aetiology which confirms, according to Newman, 'the link between blackness and the devil, the myth of black sexuality, [and] the problem of black subjection to authority'.

We aim, in the Shakespeare class, to develop a cultural materialist theatre practice. Part of this process is attempting to historicise any text which we study - in this case with particular reference to Newman and Vaughan - and analysing its relationship to a present context. The students are often quite reluctant to let slip the security blanket of universalism, preferring to connect themselves to the play's themes of love, jealousy and honour. We steer them towards a specific contextualisation of the universal theme: what are the material factors which produce Othello's, as opposed to OJ's, jealousy?

Two historical and anecdotal accounts of the play's emotional impact:

... Desdemona killed before us by her husband, although she always acted her whole part extremely well, yet when she was killed she was even more moving, for when she fell back upon the bed she implored the pity of the spectators by her very face.

During a performance in Baltimore in 1822, a soldier on guard duty, seeing Othello about to strangle Desdemona, drew his gun and fired at the stage, breaking the arm of the actor playing the Moor.

One of the actors who was later cast in Max Stafford-Clark's enormously successful 'African' *Macbeth* came to see the first version of the production. He was extremely generous about the show and he was especially complimentary about Olu's citation of Africa - specifically Yoruban Nigeria - through accent and gesture, and saw this as a means of taking ownership of the role and moving it away from white authority. A colleague of mine - white, European, female - took an opposite view, supposing that it 'felt too much like "cultural tourism" rather than subverting or asking questions of the content.'

Sello Maake ka-Ncube, the black South African actor who played Othello for the RSC in 2004, revealed to the *Times*'s Gore-Langton that 'Basing the whole thing on race is a bit ridiculous... It's the emotional/psychological landscape that interests me.' His descent into madness, however, was a journey from civilised poise to African barbarism. As Carnegy's review lamented, 'his fall is all too swift. As he works himself up into a paroxysm, [pre-epilepsy] he grotesquely reverts to the stamping war dance of some tribal beast within'. Sher's Iago did a monkey-dance, but that, at least, was on the surface.

Just as Olu's characterisation of Othello was informed by Moorish history, Othello's character is similarly defined by his/story. His (perhaps unintended) courting of Desdemona involves recounting his 'disastrous chances', of being 'sold to slavery' and 'all my travels history' (1.3.133, 137-38). That relationship is symbolically sealed (and later undermined) by the handkerchief, which has 'magic in the web of it' (3.4.65). Dying, Othello recalls an incident in Aleppo where he, in an act of Christian and Venetian alliance, and in appropriating an alternative history, smote a traducing and turbaned Turk (5.2.349).

In rehearsal we started with the following stereotypes as a way of developing distinct and non-naturalistic ways of moving and of breaking down traditional modes of characterisation:

Othello - monster
Iago - devil
Desdemona - doll / whore
Emilia - nagging wife
Bianca - hysteric
Cassio - ladies man
Brabantio - dotard
Roderigo - fool
Montano - soldier
Lodovico - messenger

There were two incarnations of *Othellophobia*. In the first the real and the nightmare worlds were mixed, the natural and animal physicalities interwoven. I came away from the first night of this show thinking I had perpetuated/confirmed a racist nightmare. In version two the scenes up until the end of the senate were a real, modern world, with much of Iago's animal images filleted out. The remainder of the play was Brabantio's nightmare, when these images were re-inserted, and during which he roamed as spectator: he occasionally influenced the action and he unleashed the uncontrollably destructive Iago.

I gave a lecture to our Theatre & Society class entitled 'Monsters and black cool', in which I traced the 'coalescence' of early modern and postmodern stereotypes of blackness. I argued that modern Othellos, who begin according to black cool - eg. gangsta rap or Samuel L. Jackson - and then, as their script demands, turn into monsters, further consolidate (and even exacerbate) the nasty binary which sustains the role. Leo Wringer (Nottingham Playhouse) and Ron Cephas Jones (Greenwich Playhouse) were especial agents/victims of this with their initially unflappable demeanours and subsequent monstrosities.

Honigmann's optimistic reading - 'Shakespeare's determination to question "the normal" emerges from the large number of stereotypes that he sets up only to knock them down... each one fails to conform to our expectations' - is countered almost directly by Loomba's - 'But the play goes on to show us that, despite his seeming different from other Moors, Othello ultimately embodies the stereotype of Moorish lust and violence - a jealous, murderous husband of a Christian lady'. My position is that Shakespearean stereotypes carry such weight (and threat) because they seem (and are so-oft portrayed) as real people.

One day during a break in rehearsals (for some reason) the conversation turned to Viagra (for some reason). One of the actresses turns to Olu and says 'well, you wouldn't need that.' At a staff meeting the topic of sexual discrimination is raised; 'I vote Olu to be the rep' smirks an older Marxist colleague. Both remarks were intended as compliments, endorsements of Olu's physical beauty, but tied, I would suggest, to the stereotypical problems of:

othellophobia
othellophilia
negrobilia
brabantioddities.

It is, though, a fine performance by Wringer - a fluent and accomplished Shakespearean actor whose soft and honeyed tones lapse into a raw, almost primitive utterance as he descends into madness.
The manner in which Jones allows his cool two-star general to become a caged animal pacing in ever smaller orbits to something crouched, reptilian [and] cowering...
The first, eclectic + contemporary, jarred because Othello went from Zen contentment to monster in a flash; the second, a US general in WWII, made Othello's investment in magic seem ridiculous.

If I were to stage the play again (God forbid), I would take on board Ray Proctor's vehement defence of the poetic Othello. I would have two actors playing the part, one playing the 'noble Moor', those incredibly progressive characteristics Shakespeare creates, and one playing the stereotype, the fool, the buffoon. My fantasy casting for this production would be Hugh Quarshie - a very serious Shakespearean - and Lenny Henry - a genius with comic racial stereotypes. The production would be a struggle between the two for priority with perhaps one (alternately) killing the other.

Iago is in charge of the stereotypes which drive the play - 'these Moors are changeable in their wills' (1.3.336) and 'I know our country disposition well:/In Venice they do let God see the pranks/They dare not show their husbands' (3.3.202-4) - and Othello internalises them (in the seduction / temptation / capitulation scene, 3.3) - 'And yet how nature erring from itself-' (229) and 'O curse of marriage,/That we can call these delicate creatures ours/And not their appetites!' (270-72). Question: to what extent are these stereotypes 'internalised' by the text itself, as opposed to the characters it represents?

The latter (1997) National Theatre *Othello* defined himself by reference to the former (1964). Of Olivier, Harewood says, 'You can see the technique: the relaxed hands, hung low, the open mouth with the tongue stuck out',[34] and yet as he gives into Iago he falls to his knees, rolls his bass Rs and beats his chest - Harewood, not Olivier. Then, the murderer, he grunts (16 times) like an animal.

John Ray Proctor - black American actor, scholar and martial artist - and I explored the possibility of staging Othellophobia in the US. His response to version 1: 'Your production makes Othello an animal, on so many levels, but it is not clear that Othello's animism is caused by... the white society in which he exists... your production repeats a cycle of ideology which posits that black men are thick tongued, aggressive and bestial... Making Othello an animal; I think I understand the impetus but I am absolutely positive that I cannot participate in this tradition.' He was right, about version 1 at least.

Neill writes that 'Iago locates their marriage in that zoo of adulterate couplings whose bastard issue... are the recurrent "monsters" of the play's imagery'. MacDonald locates the transference of the monstrous to (include) the women in the play: they are 'racialized as black, assigned a set of negative sexual characteristics associated with Africa'. Bianca is described as a fitchew, which, along with monkeys 'were thought to have particularly strong sex drives. Indeed, many early modern travellers gave credence to the notion that black Africans were the product of cross-species breeding between humans and apes'.

Kenneth Muir's New Penguin introduction to the play lists, like a perverse rendition of Old McDonald's Farm, some of the text's animal references -

'ass, daws, flies, ram, jennet, guinea-hen, baboon, wild-cat, snipe, goats, monkeys, monster and wolves'

- spoken especially by Iago in the first three acts and then, almost as if accepting the baton, by Othello in Acts 3 and 4. To this list can be added, of course, the particularly sexualised and racialised references to the 'old black ram' and the 'Barbary horse' (1.1.89, 111).

Perhaps surprisingly, the RSC's Education website is intent on demonstrating the historically constructed nature of discourses which underpin their universal author's works. The resources for teachers of *Othello* include this assistant director journal entry: '*Othello* is teeming with images of animals and beasts. Day Two: Text work, language, imagery. We discussed [Iago's] use of beasts and animal imagery to describe people and his consistent desire to reduce men and their actions to that of beasts'. Following this is an extensive list of the play's animal imagery and connections made to sexuality and jealousy.

In version 2 of the show we introduced more animals and more animal-like movements in order to better distinguish the 'real' world from the nightmare world. So not only did Othello move, at various times, like a bear, a tiger, and even the ape-like creature, but there was also a snake, meercat, peacock, barracuda (actors!), cat and owl. On the soundtrack for the show were dogs barking and various other roars and screeches (directors!). However, whilst these additions added to the Goya-like disturbance of the staging, they muddied the notion that the text's obsession with animals is most expressly tied to Othello.

Olu comes out of the rehearsal room at the Janacek Academy of Music and Performing Arts, Brno, Czech Republic. Suddenly he is surrounded by a group of skinheads. They menacingly start mimicking monkeys, the gestures and the all-too-familiar 'ooh-ooh' sounds an obscene parody of the choreographic work he has just been doing on an intercultural production of *The Wizard of Oz*. Some people watching from the outside laugh at the spectacle. He wants to tear them apart, all of them, and he is physically capable of it, but he just waits until the 'performance' ends.

The teen adaptation *O* (2001) follows Shakespeare's structure with one very disturbing interpolated scene; in the grip of Hugo's lies, Odin, who is linked to a predatory hawk, begins his first sexual encounter with Desi tenderly but then, having imagined Michael in his place, brutishly thrusts into her until orgasm though she repeatedly shouts 'no'. Like the 2001 TV adaptation, Iago's temptations begin a third of the way into the film, but this 'spreading' of 3.3, though an acknowledgment that the capitulation is unjustifiably quick, at least in a contemporary version, fails, in both cases, to rationalise Othello's monstrosity.

Olu and I had a big argument in rehearsal. I was pushing, in accordance with what we had talked about, or so I thought, about doing a literal monkey for the scene where Lodovico arrives (4.1.230ff). 'I can't do it. I won't do it', he said. 'We've got to find a compromise.' I pushed further. He stormed out. After a while I went out and apologised. Then we did some work on the tiger and he was brilliant. The monkey eventually evolved into a movement he had learned from Australian Aborigines, an unnerving and performative glare at the audience, a very brave and confronting compromise.

This painting by Henry Fuseli perfectly encapsulated my idea for the production (a nightmare): the devil (Iago) sits atop the damsel (Desdemona), drawing her life from her; complicit and menacing, the Barbary horse (Othello) awaits his turn.

My best friend at high school was an Aboriginal kid - black mum (a legend), white dad (not qite so impressive) - called Jeff. One day, coming home on the bus, I casually called him a 'black cunt'. He spat in my face and I wept for the entire trip (and never spoke of it). It was 'forgotten' but I had a recurring nightmare that I had gotten into heaven and that he had not (because he scored 7/10 on a test). During the rehearsals, whilst I was having dreams about Olu and I reconciling our friendship after the extreme tensions of the production, I received news that, back in Australia, Jeff had committed suicide.

IAGO
Awake! What, ho, Brabantio!
Brabantio sits bolt upright, as if waking from a nightmare, eyes staring.

INT. CASTLE – FLASHBACK FANTASY – NIGHT
Desdemona's arm is stretched over the bed, fingers splayed as in their earlier love-scene.
Groans of pleasure. A hand reaches out to grasp her (as Othello did). This hand is white.

INT. BEDROOM – NIGHT
Othello's eyes flash open and he drops her hand in shock. He gets up.

Brabantio has the nightmare - 'This accident is not unlike my dream' (1.1.141) - and Iago is the (subconscious, if you like) instrument through which the nightmarish devils and monsters are conjured. He says, 'Hell and night/Must bring this monstrous birth to the world's light' (1.3.385-86). Othello is right in supposing of Iago that there is 'some monster in his thought/Too hideous to be shown' (3.3107-8), a thought which turns him, Hulk-like, into 'the green-eyed monster which doth mock/The meat it feeds on' (3.3.168-69), 'Begot upon itself, born on it-self' (3.5.156).

Proctor's response to version 1 of the production was astute, and what I was hoping for, but in general white audiences did not respond this way. One of the problems was that Othello's animalism was, ironically enough, presented in a too naturalistic, and not sufficiently performative, manner. Thus, it was nightmarishly racist, to a certain viewer, but not enough for less (or differently) politicised viewers to be disturbed by an animal-like black man. One of my colleagues wrote; 'I thought [it] was going to be more exploratory than it was... I'm not sure what it was about the story that you found exciting or controversial.'

Artaud's manifesto on cruelty was a key text for our shaping of the nightmare. In version 2 we had a blind man figure, mostly made up from Lodovico, who trampled all over both Cassio's wounding and Emilia's discovery of the murder. This expressed Quarshie's notion that 'Shakespeare's attempts to tie up the loose plot threads at the end of the play invite derision'. The blind man (and everyone else) kept accidentally bumping into Cassio's wound and then he looked in completely the opposite direction when Emilia pointed to the lamentable evidence. Perhaps needless to say, the actors with hitherto big moments were miffed.

One of the key themes of the nightmare was of being out of control: Iago goes out of control and wreaks havoc; the production itself was a monster that got away from me; the meanings I sought to generate mocked me and took on grotesque shapes. I explained this to a class, that I had attempted to do something with the play and that it had turned into a monster, a nightmare. A few years ago a group of boys had played the ending as a riotous comedy; a 17 stone hairy man played Desdemona, who when attacked by Othello, retaliated with a series of devastating world wrestling moves - the play gave me the pile-driver.

Iago was the instrument of the nightmare, Brabantio's subconscious unleashed. When the old man's nightmare began he simultaneously spoke some of Iago's words to Roderigo: 'An erring barbarian... she will find the error of her choice... I hate the Moor; let us be conjunctive in our revenge against him' (1.3.339ff). From this point, Brabantio watched Iago carry out his demonic charivari. The problem, for Brabantio, was that Iago's menace could not be contained and thus not only was the marriage destroyed but everyone else with it. In version 2, Brabantio awoke, shocked, lights down.

In the documents Newman uses to contextualise *Othello*, she finds 'always... the link between black-ness and the monstrous, and particularly a monstrous sexuality'. In a *Cheers* episode from 1983 Rippy critiques the perpetuated Othello myth in the representation of an occasional character: 'a widening of the eyes, opening of the mouth, and general depiction of the stereotype of mental instability that recalls racial stereotypes from minstrel performance'. This reading puts the US on the psychoanalytic couch and unpacks a nightmare of 'the black sexualized beast threatening a white female victim'.

Othellophobia

i. A dread of watching Othello's stupidity and savagery.
ii. A series of fears related to stereotypical racist representation.

The production exploits the text's obsession with beastliness and the demonic by exposing these images through grotesque physical caricature.

I first noticed this fear / discomfort watching contemporary adaptations of the play; the teen film *O* and a TV film set in the London police department. When it got to the temptation scene (3.3), and Othello's impending credulity, I just couldn't watch any more.

Quarshie argues that *Othello* endorses 'a racist convention'; he invents the word 'negrobilia' to 'describe the representations of black people commonly made by white people' which depict 'grinning "darkies" with woolly hair, thick lips and cavernous nostrils' and he suggests that *Othello* might be just such a representation. Thus he asks, 'if a black actor plays Othello does he not risk making racial stereotypes seem legitimate and even true?' and concludes that such an actor further risks 'personifying a caricature of a black man, giving it credence.' I agree with him but I cast a black man as Othello.

Michael Ray Charles's artwork, controversial and negrobiliac, also influenced the production. He writes: 'a lot of blacks have accused me of perpetuating stereotypes, and I think there's a fine line between perpetuating something and questioning something. I like to get as close to it as possible in order… to create that tension… to have people question how they deal with these images.' He discusses an anxiety about responses to his art which label the subjects of his paintings as real people, not as images or representations. This problem is doubly resonant for the stage where the image is embodied by a real person.

'I hope it's not so unbearable on screen that people want to switch it off!… I actually went to the filming on the day they were doing that scene [the murder], and it was really distressing to watch… When they'd finished, Eamonn was in floods of tears, and poor Keeley was a physical wreck.' Davies's reflection on adapting a contemporary *Othello* (2001) reveals elements of othellophobia, but the uneasiness I am describing is more explicitly tied to the speed of 3.3, in particular, to Othello's too-immediate capitulation - which is spread out in the film from the 40th minute - rather than the (consequent) violence of 5.2.

Sometimes provincial reviewers comment most acutely. A local critic sardonically observed of the Concentric production that 'the decision to have Othello strip down and take a shower offered more beef to his cake than anyone expected.' For *Othellophobia* the city reviewers offered universalised praise, but found little offence in what was intended to be an offensive production; it was a scathing local critic who indirectly found me out: 'Olu Taiwo cuts a dash as the noble Moor, until he lapses into barely credible Black - and - White Minstrel parody.' Here, as a colleague observed to me, is a black man blacked up.

Iago speaks (of) the 'blackest sins' (2.3.318), Emilia calls Othello a 'blacker devil' (5.2.132) and Othello himself internalises these ideas, supposing Desdemona's name as 'begrimed and black/As mine own face' and summoning 'black vengeance' to destroy her (3.3.388-89, 448). But worse than references such as 'thicklips' is Desdemona's description of Othello in the last scene. The text invites/invokes centuries of grotesque minstrelsy:

…I fear you, for you're fatal then
When your eyes roll so…
why gnaw you so your nether lip?
Some bloody passion shakes your
very frame (5.2.37-44).

Can you identify the odd one out?

The students who had opted to turn *Othello* into a comedy explained to me that they didn't want their piece to be about race; it was to be about comic misunderstandings in relationships. On the spur of the moment I clutched at an analogy, not knowing where it would lead. *Titanic* (which I've not seen) is a film, I said desperately, about love, jealousy and betrayal but it's all about the iceberg. *Othello* is also about all of those things but race is its iceberg: not just because of the racism in the world of the play, but because race shapes who the people are and how they act; it's the fucking iceberg!

Start neologising and it's difficult to stop. How about this? Brabantioddities: old white men misjudging the cultural climate (with reference to *Othello*). Eg.1. After Quarshie had delivered his 'second thoughts' for the Shakespeare Centre (1998) an elderly gent apologised for the way *Othello* had been ruined by racism. Eg.2. Ernst Honigmann's lecture at the Bath Shakespeare Festival (2003), in which he spelt out Desdemona's injudicious and corrective-inviting behaviour: Juliet Dusinberre followed this lecture with the remark, 'if your husband smothers you, don't forget it's your fault.'

'Ulrich Wildgruber, his face obviously blackened in Negro Minstrel fashion, wearing a parody of an Emperor Jones jacket, deliberately played Othello on the surface, underscoring the cliche and therefore deconstructing it...

Ridiculously, and yet most movingly, as Wildgruber kissed and hugged her dead body, his black make-up smeared more and more on his cheeks, rubbing off onto Desdemona's white face.'

Two commonplace observations about *Othello*'s double-time scheme: **1.** It's brilliantly conceived. **2.** You don't notice the inconsistencies watching it on stage. But 'To my mind, it happens too quickly', writes Quarshie of Othello's speedy capitulation to Iago's lies, which is the reason Parker's film splits 3.3 to different locations to imply the passing of time. This scene deserves the same ironic *Guardian* scorn offered to the hit TV show *24*: '10.0 24 Kim continues her most-kidnapped girl world record bid.' This show's real-time scheme requires a day's action packed into every hour: farcical, but mostly overlooked.

This review (of version 1) from a colleague casts me as the Roderigo-like fool - this was *Othello* for idiots:

'It was very simplistic-it reminded me of a 4-hander version of *Macbeth* that I did many years ago, for 5 to 11 year olds ... There seemed to be nothing new about this production - no new angles, explorations, takes, etc. - but almost the opposite. The black / white issue was so blatant and stereotypical, that the complexities were not even touched upon. I find this rather worrying in this complex multi-racial world that we live in.'

Olu's Othello was the fool at the end of the play described by Emilia. The aftermath of the murder was a clown trio with Desdemona playing 'straight', Othello the inept, and Emilia the reprimanding boss. First he had wearily (and in exasperation) to keep re-finishing the murder. Then, as Emilia entered he stood in front of the body, went this way and that to prevent its discovery, and when discovered, feigned shock that there she was (shoulder shrug, 'gosh'). When Emilia could not register that Iago was the villain, Othello almost throttled her - '*He*, woman... Dost understand the word?' (5.2.151). It's all there.

The comedy Othello was a masterstroke. Originally, a black student had been cast to play the part but he had to decline for reasons outside the class. The group's first response to having to have a white actor play Othello was to erase race but then they conceived of a wigga Othello, something like an Ali G character. He had convinced himself that he was black, his simple bride had believed him, and the regiment went along with the fiction because of his prowess as a soldier. Othello constantly said 'innit', did some of the world's worst rap dancing to prove himself to the senate and generally behaved like a total dolt.

Bristol, like Zadek, is more interested in the play's surface than its apparent depth: 'To think of Othello as a kind of black-faced clown is perhaps distasteful, although the role must have been written not for a black actor... To present Othello with a black face, as opposed to presenting him as a black man, would confront the audience with a comic spectacle of abjection rather than with the grand opera of misdirected passion.' Part of my problem in turning this theory into practice was in casting a black man; I thought it could be negotiated but the various depths kept breaking the surfaces.

Honigmann notices that perhaps Othello is short-sighted, but it might be more accurate to say that he is an idiot; described by Iago whilst in the trance as a 'credulous fool' (4.1.43), his credulity, trance-like throughout, is capacious. After first calling him a devil and then realising he has been duped, Emilia chastises Othello for his stupidity:

'O gull! O dolt!/As ignorant as dirt... O thou dull Moor... O murderous coxcomb, what should such a fool/Do with so good a wife?' Othello agrees:
'O fool, fool, fool!'
(5.2.162-63, 223, 231-32, 319).

One of the rehearsal techniques we used was of the *bouffon* as practised by Cuming (who played Brabantio in version 1) via Gaulier via Lecoq. Lecoq writes that the *bouffon* made fun 'not only of what the person did, but also of his deepest convictions... when *bouffons* appear on stage, it is always to depict society.' We applied this to the epileptic fit, where all of the other players came on stage as various grotesque and lewd beasts and mocked the enthralled general. Othello is just such a *bouffon* in the last scene as described by Desdemona; uncontrollably rolling, quivering and gnawing.

Zadek's *Othello* (1976) was a key influence on *Othellophobia*:
'The method, intended to affront and shock, also proved a supple means of connecting the audience to the 'hidden' play, going beyond traditional psychology into the realm of cultural myth and cultural fear... The director was most outrageous at the end, treating the last scenes in an overtly sexual manner... The murder became a parody of a sex crime. When the audience laughed and shouted at him, Wildgruber shouted back, then recovered enough to continue the scene - five minutes or so of pandemonium, a pandemonium of comic terror.'

Desdemonas have been dubbed and daubed: Potter describes the 'fate of Suzanne Cloutier, [in Welles's film] who was cast as Desdemona entirely on the basis of her looks and sometimes literally deprived of voice and identity by being dubbed and doubled by other women actors.' Maggie Smith was famously daubed by Olivier's meticulous makeup, perhaps prompting Honigmann's editorial note on the lover's encounter in Cyprus; 'two gestural kisses, perhaps without physical contact, as Othello's make-up might blacken Desdemona's face.' Historical, if not hysterical.

Brabantio fashions his daughter as perfectly virginal and dutiful: 'A maiden never bold;/Of spirit so still and quiet' (1.3.94-95). From such an elevated position is her virtue inevitably turned to 'pitch' (2.3.327), inscribed as she is as 'whore', 'subtle' and 'cunning' (4.2.20,70-71,88). The latent readiness of this transition is signalled by the juxtaposition of the two ideas within Othello's wailing, 'be sure thou prove my love a whore' (3.3.360). She may have trouble saying the word but Desdemona must hear it repeatedly, first from her husband and then from Emilia, who comically and incredulously repeats it.

The comedy group's Desdemona was played as broadly as possible and in total defiance of unified characterisation. Her entrance to the senate meeting was bottom-first through the curtain and with her skirt tucked into her pants. She had uneven pigtails, boots, pink and purple tights and she spoke in a slow, uncomprehending drawl. She was so parodied, so thick, that she believed her deranged husband when he said that he was black. The tragedy Desdemona offered an opposite representation; here was a consistent character, but instead of the naivety being overly amplified, her supposed sexual duplicity was taken seriously.

On *White Girls Are Easy* Adebayo finds a black man who 'has capitalised on the notions that eternally surround black masculinity.' On *Forbidden Fruit*, David Dabydeen connects 'plantation and slavery' ideas about the size of a black penis with a prevailing attitude that 'with a black male you [can] have vigorous, passionate, brutish sex.' Both documentaries interview women intent on pursuing the black cock fantasy, and Reginald D. Hunter's comedy show 'White Women' tells the story of 'two stereotypes fucking each other': he, giving in to being constructed as a predator; she, capturing/subduing a black man.

We explored patriarchal constructions of femaleness: 'Underneath the dichotomization of women into virgins or whores, *Othello* implies, lies the belief that women may be simultaneously appear as virginal and yet *be* promiscuous.' I can accept an argument that Desdemona makes sense, that her change from active to passive is justifiable, but I cannot reconcile her response to being struck - 'I have not deserved this' - with her response to being called a whore - 'Tis meet I should be used so' (4.1.231, 4.2.106). This discontinuity emerges from the virgin / whore binary which is unable to sustain consistency.

Desdemona pops out of her box

'child-like in her innocence'

'He called her whore'

'O monstrous act'

Desdemona first appeared from out of an on-stage box like a doll, complete with white face and rosy red cheeks. Her movements were similarly marionette-like, sometimes dependent on others for motion. In 3.4, when Othello, duped by Iago, demanded to see the handkerchief, Desdemona changed from being the doll into a vixen. She moved sensuously, produced the wrong handkerchief from a garter belt, and turned his inquisition into a sex game. Enraged he picked her up and placed her on a spot; she turned back into the doll and flopped forward, inanimate until Emilia came and straightened her.

Building on Belsey and Sinfield's exploration of female character discontinuity as represented by early modern play-texts, Werner shows how rehearsal methods perpetuate and occlude such discontinuities: 'By reading a play's language as revelatory of a character's feelings..., voice work ignores the representational and dramaturgical strategies of the text and withholds from actors the tools to deconstruct patriarchal character readings. It focuses on character at the expense of the play.' Our tools to disrupt character were a juxtaposition of contrary subject positions; how the actor clings to consistency...

One colleague wrote, 'I realised what a dismal part Desdemona is, but by Jo playing it as this luminous archetypal character it worked as a perfect foil to Iago.' The reviews focused on her being 'child-like in her innocence and naivety', 'movingly innocent' and having 'simple trust'. This was another characterisation which 'got away' from me; we had not intended to create an idealised and passive victim, but the way we attempted to sexualise Desdemona, at least in the nightmare, was ignored. Another colleague did notice, however: 'her change to temptress in the handkerchief scene made so much sense.'

PAGE 1 SEXUALITY

Box 1.2, Celia R. Daileader, 'Casting Black Actors: Beyond Othellophilia', in *Shakespeare and Race*, ed. Catherine M. S. Alexander and Stanley Wells (Cambridge, 2000), pp. 179, 185, 196.

1.3, Harold Bloom, *Shakespeare and the Invention of the Human* (London, 1999), p. 190.

1.5, Jane Meredith, 'Deadly Game of Consequences', <www.newburytheatre.co.uk/archive/200302d.htm> accessed 9 June.

1.7, See Jonathan Dollimore, 'Desire is Death', in *Subject and Object in Renaissance Culture*, ed. Margreta De Grazia, Maureen Quilligan and Peter Stallybrass (Cambridge, 1996), pp. 369–86.

1.7, '*Othello* takes a Fearless Turn', *Times Educational Supplement*, 12 March 2004.

1.9, Ray Fearon (Othello) and Richard McCabe (Iago), Royal Shakespeare Company, 1999, photograph by Donald Cooper, courtesy of the Royal Shakespeare Company Collection; David Harewood (Othello) and Claire Skinner (Desdemona), Royal National Theatre, 1997, photograph by Mark Douet, courtesy of ArenPAL (illustration 22).

PAGE 2 EMOTION

2.2, Marvin Rosenberg, *The Masks of Othello: The Search for the Identity of Othello, Iago, and Desdemona by Three Centuries of Actors and Critics* (Newark, 1961), p. 5.

2.2, Michael Bristol, 'Race and the Comedy of Abjection in Othello', in *Shakespeare in Performance*, ed. Robert Shaughnessy (Basingstoke, 2000), p. 165.

2.9, Screen captures from DVD recording of version 1 of *Othellophobia* (5.1, Desdemona's murder) (illustration 23).

PAGE 3 HISTORY

3.2, Karen Newman, '"And Wash the Ethiop White": Femininity and the Monstrous in *Othello*', in *Shakespeare Reproduced: The text in history and ideology*, ed. Jean E. Howard and Marion F. O'Connor (New York, 1987), pp. 146, 147.

3.3, See Gāmini Salgādo, *Eyewitnesses of Shakespeare: First Hand Accounts of Performances 1590–1890* (London, 1975), p. 30.

3.3, Kyle Brenton, 'Three faces of Othello', www.amrep.org/othello/threefaces.html, accessed 23 May 2003.

3.5, Robert Gore-Langton, 'Black and White Moor Show', *Times*, 19 February 2004.

3.5, Patrick Carnegy, *Theatre Record* 12–25 February 2004, p. 243.

3.6, *Shakespeare in the Present* (London, 2002), p. 85.

3.8, See Virginia Mason Vaughan, Othello: *A Contextual History* (Cambridge, 1994).

3.9, Ben Kingsley, 'Othello', in *Players of Shakespeare 2*, ed. Russell Jackson and Robert Smallwood (Cambridge, 1988), p. 173.

3.9, Abd el-Ouahed ben Messaoud ben Mohammed Anoun, Moorish Ambassador to Queen Elizabeth I, 1600, image courtesy of The University of Birmingham Collections; Ben Kingsley (Othello), Royal Shakespeare Company, 1985, photograph by Reg Wilson courtesy of the Royal Shakespeare Company Collection (illustration 24).

PAGE 4 STEREOTYPES/BINARIES

4.1, Shannon Jackson writes in *Professing Performance: Theatre in the Academy from Philology to Performativity* (Cambridge, 2004), p. 183, that 'Performativity names the iterative processes that do the "institutionalizing" in institutional racism and that do the "internalizing" in internalized oppression. Racism is thus the ultimate performative.' Though I've not the space to argue it here, perhaps the category of 'Shakespeare' could be substituted for racism in this sentence; thus Shakespeare becomes an 'ultimate performative', for example, in the way various iterations of *Romeo and Juliet* – pedagogical, theatrical, cultural, quoted and misquoted – construct romantic subjectivities.

4.2, William Shakespeare, *Othello*, Arden 3, ed. E. A. J. Honigmann (London, 2001), p. 61.

4.2, Ania Loomba, *Shakespeare, Race and Colonialism* (Oxford, 2002), p. 95.

4.5, *The Stage*, 13 November 2003.

4.5, Posting on BBC e-feedback; www.bbc.co.uk/northamptonshire/stage/2003/othello/othello_review.shtml, accessed 10 July 2004.

4.8, Bruce R. Smith, *Shakespeare and Masculinity* (Oxford, 2000), pp. 131–61.

4.9, See Kyle Lawson, 'That's Moor like it; Royal National Theatre does right by Othello', *The Arizona Republic*, 25 September 1997. Screen capture from *Othello* (1965), directed by Stuart Burge (original stage production directed by John Dexter) – Laurence Olivier (Othello) and Frank Finlay (Iago). David Harewood (Othello) and Simon Russell Beale (Iago), Royal National Theatre, 1997, photograph by Mark Douet, courtesy of ArenPAL (illustration 25).

PAGE 5 ANIMALS

5.1, William Shakespeare, *Othello*, New Penguin, ed. Kenneth Muir (London, 1968), p. 22.

5.2, Michael Neill, 'Unproper Beds: Race, Adultery, and the Hideous in *Othello*', *Shakespeare Quarterly* 40 (1989), 383–412, p. 410.

5.2, Joyce Green MacDonald, 'Black Ram, White Ewe: Shakespeare, Race, and Women', in *A Feminist Companion to Shakespeare*, ed. Dympna Callaghan (Oxford, 2000), p. 196.

5.8, See www.rsc.org.uk/othello/current/home.html, accessed 26 August 2005.

5.9, This composite image was created by the production's designer, Alexandra Hoare: the base image is Francisco Goya's 'The sleep of reason produces monsters' (1797–98); Photo: akg-images, London (illustration 26).

PAGE 6 NIGHTMARE/MONSTERS

6.2, '"And wash the Ethiop white"', p. 148.

6.2, Marguerite Hailey Rippy, 'All our Othellos: Black Monsters and White Masks on the American Screen', in *Spectacular Shakespeare: Critical Theory and Popular Cinema*, ed. Courtney Lehmann and Lisa S. Starks (Teaneck, 2002), pp. 39, 27.

6.4, Hugh Quarshie, 'Second Thoughts About *Othello*', International Shakespeare Association Occasional Paper No. 7 (Chipping Campden, 1999), p. 19.

6.5, Screenplay for *Othello*, dir. Oliver Parker (Columbia Pictures, 1995) obtained from www.geocities.com/thelunalounge/site/sections/screenplays/screenplays.html.

6.9, Henry Fuseli, 'The Nightmare' (1781); Photo: akg-images, London (illustration 27).

PAGE 7 RACE/BLACKNESS

7.2, 'Second thoughts', pp. 3, 5, 18.

7.4, See 'Art:21', www.pbs.org/art21/artists/charles/clip1.html, accessed 27 November 2005.

7.5, 'An Interview with Andrew Davies', www.pbs.org/wgbh/masterpiece/othello/ei_davies.html, accessed 27 January 2003.

7.7, See mandanajones.net, accessed 9 June 2003.

7.7, Peter Patston, 'Tragedy Lies in the Treatment of Shakespeare', *Bath Chronicle*, 9 March 2004.

7.9, Michael Ray Charles, courtesy and copyright Cotthem Gallery, Brussels-Barcelona; Screen capture from *Othello* (1965); Laurence Olivier as Othello (illustration 28).

PAGE 8 STUPIDITY

8.1, *Othello*, Arden 3, pp. 17–19.

8.2, 'Race and the Comedy of Abjection in *Othello*', pp. 151–52.

8.3, 'Second Thoughts', p. 8.

8.4, Jacques Lecoq, *The Moving Body: Teaching Creative Theatre* (London, 2002), pp. 117–25.

8.5, Dennis Kennedy, *Looking at Shakespeare: A Visual History of Twentieth-Century Performance* (Cambridge, 1996), p. 269.

8.9, *Looking at Shakespeare*, p. 269.

8.9, Ulrich Wildgruber (Othello), Hamburg, 1976, photograph by Roswitha Hecke, courtesy of the Deutsches Theatre Museum (illustration 29).

PAGE 9 DESDEMONA

9.2, Catherine Belsey, *The Subject of Tragedy: Identity and Difference in Renaissance Drama* (London, 1985), pp. 149–221.

9.2, Alan Sinfield, *Faultlines: Cultural Materialism and the Politics of Dissident Reading* (Oxford, 1992), pp. 52–79.

9.2, Sarah Werner, *Shakespeare and Feminist Performance: Ideology on Stage* (London, 2001), p. 34.

9.3, Screened on Channel 4 (in the UK) on 30 May 2003.

9.3, Screened on Channel 4 (in the UK) on 4 December 2003; see www.bfi.org.uk/filmtvinfo/ftvdb/ for details on both documentaries.

9.3, See Fiachra Gibbons, 'Sexist and Racist but Certainly not Surreal', *Guardian*, 14 August 2003.

9.4, Valerie Traub, *Desire and Anxiety: Circulations of Sexuality in Shakespearian Drama* (London, 1992), p. 34.

9.5, Lois Potter, *Othello*, Shakespeare in Performance (Manchester, 2002), p. 142.

9.5, *Othello*, Arden 3, p. 175.

9.9, Screen captures from DVD recording of version 1 of *Othellophobia* (1.3, Desdemona's entrance; 3.3, the napkin; 4.2, false comfort; 5.1, murdered).

LIVING MONUMENTS: THE SPATIAL POLITICS OF SHAKESPEARE'S ROME ON THE CONTEMPORARY STAGE

BRIDGET ESCOLME

Upon a close view of this story, there appear'd in some passages, no small resemblance with the busy faction of our own time. And I confess, I chose rather to set the parallel nearer to Sight, than to throw it off to further Distance.

> Nahum Tate, *The Ingratitude of the Common-Wealth; or the fall of Caius Martius Coriolanus*[1]

What is the city but the people? – William Shakespeare.
Sign on hoardings covering the City Center Shopping Mall, Minneapolis, during its refurbishment, 2006.

In the California Building Gallery in South Minneapolis, Aidan, a nine-year-old boy is trying to get the attention of the actor playing his father, in a workshop production of Shakespeare's *Coriolanus*. The actors are having a break and are discussing the end of the presentation: how will the company leave the playing space once Martius has been killed? F1 has the Volscians leave the stage 'bearing the dead body of Martius'. If we have Jim Bovino, who is playing Martius, carried off stage, it must be through the audience, as they surround the action throughout the piece. No one is taking much notice of Aidan. He starts to mould his onstage father into a monumental pose, right arm curved in front of him, fist clenched, left arm up as if brandishing a sword. Having studiously ignored this activity for a while, it occurs to Bovino that Aidan's idea for a human sculpture is something of an inspired one, and the *Coriolanus* that I directed for Flaneur Productions in the California Building Gallery, Minneapolis, and Rochester Art Center, Rochester, Minnesota in April 2006, ended as the Volscians hauled Martius onto his feet, onto the block where he has just been killed and on which he had stood to receive the citizens' vote in his gown of humility in 2.3. At the end of each performance, Martius' son climbed onto the block, pulled from his father the Volscian shirt Martius had acquired when he left Rome for Actium and moulded him into a monument to Roman *virtus*. Or Mother Russia. Or Saddam Hussein. Or the Statue of Liberty, perhaps. When the boy was satisfied with the monument he had made of his father, he left the playing space.

When workshops for this, the first stage of a practical research project, began, I had partly intended it as an exercise in finding alternatives to analogy in Shakespeare production – alternatives to the explicit, visual assertion that Shakespeare has always miraculously prefigured the present.

My thanks to Queen Mary University of London, Aldo Moroni, John Kremer and Jennifer Young at the California Building Gallery, Scott Stulen at Rochester Art Center and Paul Shambroom for permission to use his images.

Credits for the Flaneur Productions *Coriolanus*:

Rich Barlow: Sound, graphic design; Jim Bovino: Coriolanus; Jeff Broitman: Aufidius; Bridget Escolme: Director; Christian Gaylord: Menenius; Kit Gordon: Dramaturg, Servingman, Officer, Volsican Lord; Aidan Haarman: Coriolanus' Son; Robert C. Hammel: Citizen, Soldier, Aedile, Conspirator; Tracie Hodgdon: Valeria, Citizen; Ben Kreilkamp: Cominius; Scott Reynolds: Citizen, Messenger, Officer, Soldier, Watch, Conspirator; Jillia Passenda: Virgilia, Citizen; Don Mabley-Allen: Brutus; David Schneider: Titus Lartius, Servingman, Volscian Lieutenant, Conspirator; Cristopher Tibbetts: Sicinius; Jim Westcott: Senator, Volscian Lord.

[1] Nahum Tate, Dedicatory epistle, *The Ingratitude of a Common-Wealth* (London, 1682). p. 2.

Nevertheless, this final image was instantly analogous to any number of allegorical and monumental figures ancient and modern, and the questions underpinning the project had shifted somewhat by the end of our month's work. In this chapter, I make a critique of what I perceive to be some of the limitations of visual analogies in Shakespeare production, but I am certainly not presenting this work as some sort of magnificent corrective to those limitations. The Minnesota *Coriolanus* has rather been an exploration of the ways in which we might permit and provoke audiences both to make analogies and not make them, to find the early modern drama both familiar and strange. By the end of the workshop, the project was primarily exploring the role of space, and performers' and spectators' bodies in space, in the production of Shakespeare.

My resistance to modern analogy in Shakespeare production crystallized in response to the critical reception of Deborah Warner's *Julius Caesar* at the Barbican Theatre, London, in 2005. Here is Paul Taylor's preview article in the *Independent*:

Plainly the driving force behind the project is a passionate and freshly pondered belief in the play and in the political timeliness of reviving it now in a world where, after the dubiously motivated toppling of a somewhat different dictator, analogous bloodshed and appalling waste of human life ensued.[2]

I was irritated by Taylor's determination to find analogy between bloodshed in *Julius Caesar* and bloodshed in Iraq, where I saw simply bloodshed, in both cases. There is a utilitarian specificity here that reached its nadir in an editorial in the same newspaper just before Shakespeare's birthday of the same year. Entitled 'An Inspiration for Ever and a Day', and again referencing Warner's production, this editorial warns us against complacency in the face of an erosion of Shakespeare teaching in schools:

Are [there] indications that the reverence with which we treat 'The Bard' is fading? Let us hope not, because the work of Shakespeare remains vitally important to our national life.

The editorial goes on to assure us of Shakespeare's relevance, his

genius for dramatising the human condition. Who could argue that *Julius Caesar* – a tale of conspiracy, ambition and the mob – has nothing to say to our own times, especially since we are in the midst of an election campaign? Caesar suspects Cassius because he 'has a lean and hungry look; He thinks too much: such men are dangerous'. This could describe any number of New Labour rivalries.[3]

Here, Shakespeare is immortalized as monument, while his genius for dramatizing the human condition reduces all human experience to a psychological sameness, for despite Taylor's determination to draw attention to highly specific political resonances in *Julius Caesar*, the Warner interview overall gives the impression that it is psychologically constructed character where our universals are to be found. Published accounts of rehearsal process contain post-Stanislavskian exercises devised to produce psychological back story: hot-seating exercises in which Cassius is revealed to have been thinking of suicide since the age of eight, discussions of the school days of the central figures.[4]

The play has clearly struck Deborah Warner as relevant to recent events, specifically the war in Iraq. 'I was knocked sideways by it', she says to Kate Kellaway in the *Observer*,

This is a moment to look at issues of power and whether democracies can survive. In a time of crisis, we go to the strong texts – well, I certainly do. This is not a time for TV-style documentaries about politics. We need insights, important truths about the human condition.[5]

It would be something of a cultural materialist commonplace to point out that 'important truths

---

2 Paul Taylor, 'Breaking the Rules – Again', *The Independent*, 15 April 2005.
3 Editorial, 'An Inspiration for Ever and a Day', *The Independent*, 21 April 2005.
4 See Taylor, 'Breaking the Rules – Again'; Benedict Nightingale, 'Friends, Romans and Warner Men', *The Times* 18 April 2005.
5 Warner in Kate Kellaway, 'Power Play', *The Observer*, 10 April 2005.

about the human condition' are ideologically and historically contingent, but this interesting slip on Warner's part from the more specific political question, of 'whether democracies can survive', to something more vague and essentialist is an interesting one for an analysis of the production. What Warner wants from 'strong texts' is clearly a challenge to the national political interests of current Western leaders. However, the way in which the rehearsal process and costume choices produce character – encouraging actors' imagined psychological back-story, dressing Cassius as a politician in a sharp, conservative suit on the battlefield, the plebeians as highly individualized 'characters' – finally produces a 'truth' central to Western postmodern apathy regarding the political process. Perhaps this is the point. But though Carol Chillington Rutter is right to point out that 'Warner didn't bid for glib comparisons' between characters in *Julius Caesar* and players on the contemporary political stage, I would take issue with Rutter's detailed and lucid review article where she asserts that 'by directing with such textual clarity, [Warner] allowed us to hear the speech craft of this play as utterly topical'.[6] I would rather argue that, at the Barbican at least, the energy of textual clarity was directed towards psychological subtext, while illustrative scenography and programme photographs do the work of producing topicality. Warner's *Caesar* was a starting point for the *Coriolanus* project, however, more than merely in terms of a productive irritation. The project was partially inspired by the ways in which I perceived *Julius Caesar* occupying, and being reproduced by, theatrical space when it left the naturally pictorial Barbican Theatre. Warner's production played in Madrid, Paris and Luxembourg, and I will move from London to Minneapolis via Madrid.

SPATIAL POLITICS

As the audience entered the Barbican Theatre for *Julius Caesar*, the wide proscenium at the Barbican Theatre had a fine white curtain drawn across it. Behind it, someone could just be seen with a large bunch of helium balloons. Once the house

was closed, more figures, in rainproof jackets with fluorescent stripes, began to arrange crash barriers around the playing area. A space was being prepared for some kind of state-controlled celebration, or a celebration that the state was at least keen to control. Members of the audience had been looking at their programmes, which contained a number of images from current wars and war zones, including one of George Bush beaming at some marines, and an Iraqi prisoner, his head covered, on a bombed battlefield. The partially transparent curtain was drawn, to reveal a staging of the postmodern turn in architecture: the pastiche ancient in the form of marble steps and truncated pillars was framed by the self-consciously new in Perspex screens and a bright yellow cyclorama. We saw the Iraq war and other current conflicts illustrated in the programme; we saw the cultural and political landscape in which the Iraq war was conceived illustrated on stage. To use the word 'illustrated' here is not to suggest that there was anything of box-set naturalism in Tom Pye's set. This was a public arena in which domestic space was produced by lighting, reinforcing the production's foregrounding of the public import of private friendship in the play. But as the much-publicized, unusually large crowd filled the space between the Perspex screens and the yellow cyclorama, they gave the disconcerting impression of flies behind glass. We were offered frames within the frame of the Barbican proscenium through which to view the contemporary through Shakespeare. The effect was distancing and separating, allowing the spectator to have already discovered the links between Shakespeare and 'our world'. If it was Warner's intention that we should 'unknow what we already know',[7] this scenography was in danger of working against against such an alienation, producing the comfortable separation of the knower and the known rather than the productive disruption of Brechtian distanciation.

---

[6] Carol Chillington Rutter, 'Facing History, Facing Now: Deborah Warner's Julius Caesar at the Barbican Theatre', *Shakespeare Quarterly*, 57 (2006), p. 83.

[7] Warner, in Taylor, 'Breaking the Rules – Again'.

As their first scene progressed and the crowd moved downstage, it became clear that this was no undifferentiated proletarian mass. Costumes and casting suggested a range of age and social background here – and each plebeian 'acted', in carefully considered, individuated fashion, their reactions to the speeches of the patricians.

'Crowds are of course a problem', said Margo Heinemann twenty years ago, in the cultural materialist collection, *Political Shakespeares*:

You can't present the crowd in Shakespeare's Rome as if they were the modern, organized industrial working class . . . The fickleness of this mob, which is the main thing Shakespeare shows about it, is a real characteristic of a pre-industrial city crowd, united only temporarily to riot over a specific grievance.[8]

There was neither the homogeneity of the 'organized industrial working class' nor that of the 'pre-industrial city' about Warner's postmodern plebeians. Multi-racial, cross-class, dressed individually, one cannot imagine the specific grievance that would unite them – unless it were the February 2003 protests against war in Iraq evoked by the programme photographs. The problem with this analogy is that that the 2003 crowd stuck with its stance and was ignored, whilst Shakespeare's is fickle and manipulated to violence. These individuated costumes and performances offered a highly conservative analysis of postmodern consumerism – beneath the superficial impression of individuality produced by choice of clothing lies the aggressive human animal, easily manipulated by politicians.

Very much to the fore in the crowd scenes was a figure in punkily torn tights and a fake fur coat. The death of Cinna the Poet was a highly sexualized act by this figure. Another Iraq reference perhaps? Post-Lynndie England it would be naive to object to the image on the grounds that women do not commit acts of sexual abuse in violent circumstances. Here, though, the act seemed all of a part with a portrayal of the plebeians as a mix of decadent and cynical, naive and stupid postmoderns whose rapacious ids are only superficially contained by consumer society.

The Madrid crowd scenes worked differently with a new crowd of locally recruited extras. They appeared less cynically aggressive, more ebullient and enthusiastic. Paradoxically, they read as less stupid than the British crowd, because they seemed more genuinely persuaded by each speaker in 3.2. Perhaps they were listening harder, as English was not their first language. But their persuasive persuadability was, I would argue, in part produced by the Teatro Español in which they were playing. This theatre's auditorium consists of gently raked stalls in a long, narrow hall and a horseshoe of three galleries. Though nothing remains of its eighteenth-century incarnation but the façade, its nineteenth-century rebuild and refurbishments were not designed for the modern stage lighting that allows the audience to be plunged into complete darkness. Its shape and size – narrow and tightly packed with a far smaller stage than the Barbican, its galleries looking precipitously down over the stage – creates an illusion of presence that the Barbican cannot, a sense of being in the same space as the action which produces the spectator as participant. As a spectator here, I was less inclined to judge the plebeians, as I was closer to them and to those attempting to inspire and persuade them. I was, after all, part of a theatre crowd, being persuaded of all kinds of things myself. The rapacious woman with her balloon and tights produced a jarring alienation effect in Madrid – I asked myself, could I become part of a crowd that would do that? In London her actions somehow seemed par for the course: as Rutter suggests, a logical extension of the behaviour of the crowd which can't keep its hands off Antony in 1.1.[9]

The different modes of affect and involvement produced by *Caesar* at the Barbican and at the Teatro Español were significant for the *Coriolanus* project. Flaneur Productions are a politically engaged company, concerned with the political

---

[8] Margo Heinemann, 'Brecht and Shakespeare' in Jonathan Dollimore and Alan Sinfield, eds., *Political Shakespeares* (Manchester, 1985), p. 250.

[9] Rutter, 'Facing History', p. 83.

place of the arts in the USA. Until this point, the group had produced new work by a pool of writers, along with a range of other arts and music events on Minneapolis's alternative arts scene, but were feeling, I think, a similar urge to Warner's to look at issues of power in and through a powerful historic text when they began to discuss the *Coriolanus* project. As we began the month's workshop, we were concerned to explore how being witness to the events of *Coriolanus* might become immediately rather than analogously 'political', and to avoid the mere illustration of the connections an audience might make between the 'busy faction of our own time' and Shakespeare's Rome. To implicate an audience in the power politics of *Coriolanus* feels, however, politically uncomfortable. A play much loved in Nazi Germany, Brecht had to rewrite it to make it speak socialism,[10] and one Minneapolis theatre director had told Kit Gordon, dramaturg and performer with the Flaneur project, that it felt too much like a fascist play for him ever to tackle. I had some sympathy with the American student I overheard leaving the 2006 Globe production of the play, saying to his friend 'I thought Coriolanus was kind of great . . . did I learn the wrong lesson there?' An initial concern for the workshop was how heroic we might permit our Minneapolis Martius to be.

Before the workshop began, we discussed Martius's notorious contempt for words, and the direct comparisons that might be made with the way in which the Bush government privileges (or wishes to be seen to privilege) 'proceeding' over 'speaking' – this both literally, in terms of foreign policy, and figuratively in the rhetoric that styles liberals as obfuscating, wordy and elitist, and the right as down to earth men of action. 'Come, come we'll prompt you' says Cominius to Martius (3.2.106), when Martius insists he will be incapable of speaking 'mildly' to the citizens, and we were reminded of the suspicious lump in the back of Bush's jacket in his 2005 election debate with Kerry. 'They'll sit by the fire and presume to know / What's done i'th' Capitol, who's like to rise, / Who thrives and who declines . . .' (1.1.189–91) spits Martius, and might evoke, for a modern audience, Neocon

contempt for the 'chattering classes' of liberalism. The analogy game is fun – and can be justified given the openness of ancient Rome to early modern analogy for Shakespeare and his audiences. Eventually, however, direct analogy will tend to fall apart in production and the audience are in danger of being left wondering who can possibly represent who, as the cracks begin to show. After all, in terms of Bush Regime analogies, central to Martius's tragedy is his absolute refusal of political spin. His contempt for the populace is openly expressed to them. He is at war with a city perhaps a day's march away rather than with an abstract noun and, though he is up for a position in civil government, he fights that war himself. John Hirsch's Old Globe production in San Diego in 1988, on a stage backed with TV screens pumping out game shows and news of the Iran-Contra scandal, solved the challenge of representing the army man in government by presenting Martius as Oliver North – but the analogy breaks down when he is banished and leaves Rome for a Latino Antium. The effect, says one online critic in retrospect, 'is as if Oliver North got fed up at our lack of appreciation for his anti-Communist crusade and signed up with the Sandinistas'.[11]

MONUMENTS AND SCULPTURES

Exploring an aesthetic for the presentation of our work in Minneapolis, we shifted from early analogy discussions to a consideration of the shapes and forms of contemporary politics and how they might inflect the production of meaning in *Coriolanus*. Working in gallery spaces inflected the kinds of exercises we used to explore the text from the outset. The California Building Gallery, in which we both rehearsed and performed, is, at a first glance, an awkward shape for performance: a misshaped oblong with a wall jutting out into one part

---

[10] Though he did later speculate as to whether it would be 'possible to stage [the first scene] without additions . . . or with very few, just by skilful production'. Unpublished note by Bertolt Brecht, in John Willett, ed., *Brecht on Theatre* (London, 1964), p. 265.

[11] www.donshewey.com/theater_reviews/coriolanus.html.

of it, dividing the space to facilitate the hanging of paintings rather than live performance. There was no part of the room that suggested a natural playing space with exits and entrances for actors. Enter from the foyer through the narrow door and one's natural inclination is, unsurprisingly, to drift around and across the space, looking at what is on the walls. Our first reading of the play took place over two days, and the initial exploration was of meaning produced by the juxtaposition of text and space, rather than textual exegesis around a table. Some performers' instincts were to behave, during this 'active' reading, as the ideal promenade audience, shifting from one space to create another according to what the public or private nature of the text seemed to demand. They would become citizens or soldiers where required and create little end-on spaces for more intimate performance where appropriate. Others experimented with breaking these unspoken laws, standing as voyeurs against the pillar in Volumnia's 'home' as the women sewed or behind the wall to hear rather than see the action. Still others were drawn to remaining 'in character' for a number of the scenes in which they did not appear. Jillia Pessanda as Virgilia was particularly inclined to this, so that one was continually reminded, by her presence, of the spaces in the play from which women are excluded; thus female gender was continually seen to be both producing and excluded from space.

Working in the gallery space produced the performers as three-dimensional objects that the viewer was continually being asked to place him or herself in relation to – the space produced the performers as live sculptures. It seemed a nightmarish place for an intensely anti-theatrical figure like Martius – worse for him, even, than a theatre. I was drawn to moments in the text when Martius must stand or sit still and be looked at, and the focus seemed to produce a Martius of, paradoxically, both complete subjective emptiness and intense agency. Watching Martius, watching Martius looking, watching Martius being looked at, drew attention both to Martius as social construct and to Martius as a violent resistor of anyone who might wish to determine his social role. Through

the workshop, he repeatedly emerged as the empty subject of critical commonplace, the unmade stone from which a monument to or a critique of a war-mongering culture could be hewn – but paintings and sculptures are there to be looked at, and Martius recalcitrantly refuses the admiring and the critical gaze. Aidan's sculpted Coriolanus was a living monument to warmongering and refused that construction utterly.

In 3.1, we placed Martius as Coriolanus-monument in Volumnia's domestic space, a space created in a corner made from the main wall and the jutting, temporary one. Thus the Martius of his mother's imagination was present to the audience when she spoke the lines

> Me thinks I see him stamp thus and call thus
> Come on you cowards! You were got in fear
> Though you were born in Rome.
>
> (1.3.34–6)

Jillia Pessanda's Virgilia almost succeeded in pulling the monument into life at this point, by taking Bovino's hand and drawing Martius into individual relationship with her. We also had him lifted into the centre of the space before the surname Coriolanus was to be conferred upon him, so that as Volumnia and Menenius discussed the number of wounds he might have acquired in his latest battle, Martius became both absolute materiality and absolute allegory – a material object whose wounds can be counted – nine, twenty-five, twenty-seven – and a figure whose arm alone figures death, monumentalized by rhyming couplet:

> Death, that dark spirit, in's nervy arm doth lie,
> Which being advanced, declines, and then men die.
>
> (2.1.157–8)

In both of these moments, Virgilia was the figure who appeared to 'see' the potentially deathly meanings in the live Coriolanus monument. Her response to the excitement around her husband's prospective wounds – 'O no, no, no' (2.1.118) – is spoken as she sees her husband hefted onto his block to be praised, a reaction all of a part with Pessanda's productive inclination to remain as a characterful presence at the periphery of scenes in which she had no role. No one else 'sees' this image of Coriolanus dead – they are too preoccupied with the monumental wounds that later he refuses to show the citizenry.

I had been struck by Rebecca Schneider's analysis of monuments in American culture, and the suggestive possibilities of paying attention to that which passes by the monument. Her article 'Patricidal Memory and the Passer-by' contains photographs she took of tourists looking at American monuments, and she interrogates the political implications of 'passing by' the monument, marking the spectator's unwitting implication in their meaning:

I gathered [images] while thinking about Patricidic Culture . . . culture that depends on the production of Dead Dads – dads that must die to insure that dead dads remain. Patricidic culture is . . . invested in insuring that the dead remain and the live pass by.[12]

What we made of Shakespeare's Rome was a culture at a liminal point in the production of the patricidic. On the one hand, presenting the wounded Martius as a monument to his own already mythologised deeds and *Romanitas*, always already dead, suggested a patriarchy in complete control of its monumental Dead Dads. The living – represented at the end of the production by Aidan – not only pass by, they construct the monuments that will render themselves, in Schneider's terms, always passing and comparatively ephemeral. But whereas Schneider points to the Barthesian *punctum* in the modern monument – she includes, for example, an image of a sculpture of Lincoln with a hole in its head – the live monumental figures of Shakespeare's Roman and English history seem often to have partially reappropriated breaks and fissures, incorporated them into monumentality. The wounds on the corpse of Henry VI open and ooze blood on the way to his funeral; Caesar's statue pours forth blood in Calpurnia's dream, Pompey's statue (according to Antony) runs blood as Caesar is stabbed; Antony makes a monument of the corpse of Caesar while the holes in his garment are still fresh with blood. The dead, when dead, continue to signify very literally and with seeming intentionality. The

reappropriation is never entirely complete however, as this living monumentality appears physically and semiotically both powerful and helpless. Henry's body bleeds when Richard comes near, yet Anne marries Richard nonetheless; Decius Brutus's interpretation of Calpurnia's dream is upheld over Calpurnia's and Caesar dies for it. The memory of Caesar conjured by Antony via the 'poor dumb mouths' of Caesar's wounds may succeed in monumentalizing every tiny scrap of Caesar's remains in the minds of the plebeians, as Antony intends,

Let but the commons hear this testament . . .
And they would go and kiss dead Caesar's wounds,
And dip their napkins in his sacred blood;
Yea beg a hair of him for memory,
And dying mention it within their wills
Bequeathing it as a rich legacy
Unto their issue.

(*Caesar* 3.2.131, 133–8)

but the monument he makes of Caesar's body speeds a violent descent into civil war rather than producing acquiescent passers by. In *Julius Caesar*, Rome cannot politely or apathetically pass by the monument; it bleeds and demands Rome's engagement – though there is still this semiotic vulnerability to the monument's tendency to signify from the dead.

Schneider's monuments in postmodern America appear both more and less vulnerable to semiotic analysis by the passer-by, more vulnerable, in the sense that these Dads seem really Dead: they don't actively signify by bleeding, and their intended significance can be subverted by academics in the age of electronic reproduction – Schneider has snapshots taken of her sitting on Lincoln's knee and putting a finger in a hole in his head. They are less vulnerable, in that the quotidian passing by of the monument by today's 'citizens' suggests unconscious acceptance of its public significance. A live Coriolanus monument in a Minneapolis gallery

---

[12] Rebecca Schneider, 'Patricidal Memory and the Passerby', *The Scholar and Feminist Online*, vol. 2, no. 1, 2003 (Barnard Center for Research on Women), www.barnard.columbia.edu/sfonline/ps/schneide.htm.

space recalled, perhaps, both the live/dead monument of Shakespeare's Rome and the passed-by monument of contemporary America. However, Bovino's Martius appeared reluctant to accept the semiotic vulnerability of either.

The monumental underpins Martius's social construction as a constant Roman who is always already a monument to himself, thinks 'brave death outweighs bad life' (1.7.71), assumes his son will live and fight as a memory to him, 'like a great sea mark, standing every flaw / And saving those that eye thee' (5.3.74–5). Yet he also hates to be the object of public commemoration, does not want to stand still and be 'eyed' himself, and he has very little time alone on stage to be subject to the exposing gaze of the audience. Martius seemed aware that the monumental Coriolanus we made of him, and which we hefted several times onto his wooden block of glory and humiliation, was always in danger of looking faintly ludicrous. This was particularly the case when he was surrounded by audience members, who inevitably tended to stand around, rather like Schneider's passers-by, understandably lacking the energy of theatrical intentionality (with the exception of a few enthusiasts who enjoyed joining in with the citizens' cries against Martius). As the herald began to announce his victory in Corioles, Bovino relaxed his sculptural stance, shifted awkwardly upon his pedestal on hearing himself named and renamed, then stepped down and tried to rush from the playing space on 'No more of this, it does offend my heart' (2.1.165).

Martius's determination not to become the monumental body Rome wants to make of him became central to his paradoxical theatrical attraction. Whilst it may be exhilarating to be included in a group of Plebeians rioting over corn prices, it seemed even more thrilling to be insulted by a man who seems to be able to hush and divide those rioters with his contempt – and then to be included, albeit momentarily, in a conspiracy of the contemptuous rather than a crowd of the contemptible, when Martius tells us it is better to die or starve, than '[t]o beg of Hob and Dick that does appear / Their needless vouches' (2.3.116–17). Plutarch marks as Coriolanus's problem

that which Plato called 'solitariness'; as, in the end, all men that are wilfully given to a self-opinion and obstinate mind and who will never yield to others' reason but to their own, remain without company and forsaken of all men.[13]

But such men don't, I would argue, remain forsaken by the audience. In the day- or candle-lit auditorium, where a key theatrical pleasure is the moment of direct address, he that joins us to stand outside the fiction – physically, by coming away from a marked fictional locus or by refusing the social norms of the fictional world – is theatrically compelling even when morally repulsive. We found that a look from the man who, for most of the play, refused to look or be looked at, had a tremendous seductive charge. Such an attraction is one the women of Rome appear to experience too: they are, to the tribunes' frustration, 'spectacled to see him' (2.1.203), 'clambering the walls to eye him'(207), 'all agreeing / In earnestness to see him' (209–10). 'Seld shown flamens' (habitually withdrawn priests) come out to see him, exposing themselves to the pressure of common flesh (210–12), and women who usually fear to expose themselves to the sun 'commit the war of white and damask in / Their nicely guarded cheeks to the wanton spoil / Of Phoebus burning kisses' (212–15). The figurings of sight and exposure to sight tumble over one another like the people trying to view the war hero, and Martius ironically increases his theatrical charge by refusing to stand still and be looked at for long.

MEETINGS AND PHOTOGRAPHS

If the shape of heroism is the monumental figure with his 'nervy arm' aloft, the shape of peacetime government is less easy to imagine – and we wanted to give some aesthetic attention to the Tribunes. Before the workshop, I was introduced by Rich Barlow, a Flaneur artistic director who composes and designs for the company, to the work of

---

[13] Plutarch, 'Life of Caius Martius Coriolanus', trans. North, in Geoffrey Bullough, *Narrative and Dramatic Sources of Shakespeare*, vol. 5 (London, 1964), p. 519.

31. Fairplay, Colorado (population 576) Board of Trustees, June 4, 2001 (L to R): Tim Gibson, Marie Chisholm, Nancy Reed (Mayor), Rachael Edwards, Tammy Quinn.

32. Markle, Indiana (population 1,228) Town Council, 21 July 1999 (L to R): Wayne Ridgley, Jay Fox (President), Jeff Stockman.

Minnesota photographer Paul Shambroom, and a series called 'Meetings'. Shambroon photographed council meetings in a variety of small towns across the US and published his work alongside the minutes of each of these meetings (see illustrations 31, 32 and 33). For us, they captured how supremely unglamorous the workings of government are, how hedged about with contingency and tedium, and how unused we are to seeing artistic images of them. The huge size of the originals, the theatricality of the set-ups and the painterly quality of the colour shots – 'the photos seem to approach the impressive seriousness of Salon-style history paintings' reads one review[14] – read, to us, ironically.

---

[14] Jessica Ostrower, 'Paul Shambroom at Julie Saul', *Art in America*, January 2004.

33. Marshfield, Missouri (population 4,508) Board of Aldermen, 23 May 2002 (L to R): Jack Watters, Jim Downing, C. R. Clark (Mayor), Talt Greer, Tom Owen.

Yet the images also potentially dignify and endear the viewer to these small-town figures, and on Shambroom's website, alongside reviews that recognize humour in the work, are archived those that recall the *Independent*'s grandiose humanism regarding Warner's *Caesar*:

Paul Shambroom confers [on these figures] the human nobility of democracy.[15]

The warm humanism that celebrates such down-home individuality is rare in an art world that seems to thrive on irony.[16]

In Shambroom's pictures, the simple, actual event is revealed as a marvelous and beautiful enactment of the highest democratic ideals of equality, dialogue and representation. They are pictures not just of rituals, but of the real-life practice of self and community empowerment.[17]

It is easy enough to play the tribunes as sinister, self-interested schemers; at the Globe reconstruction they were clearly the villains of the piece and, at one performance I attended there, they were booed when they entered after Martius's banishment. The Flaneur workshop was keen to avoid tipping the political scales so far in Martius's favour. However, we had no ambitions to confer upon the tribunes the Human Nobility of Democracy. We had a long table of just the sort common to so many of Shambroom's photographs in our first rehearsal and performance space, the California Building Gallery,

then, in the Rochester Art Center, a more pristine version in a dedicated conference room. The conferral of the patricians' approval of Coriolanus as consul took place behind the table.

The scene in illustration 34 (2.2), with figures of government confined in a meeting space suggestive of some kind of discursive democracy, was a highly Shambroom-like set up. It was an improbable space for the rhetoric of Cominius (Ben Kreilkamp), whose resonant voice and impressive bearded presence seemed more appropriate to the battlefield, his words to be obeyed or resisted rather than discussed. Kreilkamp performed the obliteration of the fragile emerging democracy confined behind its table, by coming out from behind it, physically and vocally reconfiguring the quotidian setting; Coriolanus is a sea, a meteor, who wipes out all before him and, though this is the conferring of a peacetime office, it is the nervy arm of war-heroism that is dignified. Cominius turns the fragile democratic space back into a patrician space, one that might contain a Coriolanus statue. The

---

[15] Stephen Doyle, 'Reviews: Democracy in Action', *Creative Review*, November 2004.

[16] Fred Camper, 'Paul Shambroom: Evidence of Democracy', *Chicago Reader*, 28 November 2003.

[17] Diane Mullin, 'Democratic vistas', *Art Review*, October 2003.

34. *Coriolanus*, Flaneur Productions, Rochester Art Center, Act 2 scene 2. At table: Don Mabley-Allen: Brutus; Jim Westcott: Senator; Christian Gaylord: Menenius; Ben Kreilkamp: Cominius; Cris Tibbetts: Sicinius; Kit Gordon: Officer. Standing: Jim Bovino: Coriolanus.

living Coriolanus has absented himself from the scene rather than hear himself monumentalized.

Imprisoned behind a table, the Tribunes' manipulation of the citizens in 2.3 read as thankless work in the face of the glamour of the monumental figure Cominius makes of Coriolanus. The table is the place where they appeared to be safest and most assured in their dealings with Christian Gaylord's deceptively affable Menenius, the place from which they were able to persuade the citizens to rescind their vote for Martius. But finally, in order to achieve Coriolanus's banishment and the peacetime world of 4.6, they had to rely on demagogy not discussion. Cris Tibbetts's Sicinius appeared to accept this more readily than Don Mabley-Allen's Brutus. The former was the more manipulative and self-interested of the tribunes, the latter the more exhaustedly determined that the people should understand for themselves where their democratic interests lay. Leaning across the table in the California Building, now an uncrossable bureaucratic barrier between people and representatives, Brutus

exasperatedly questioned the citizens' reading of the unwilling Coriolanus monument they had encountered in the market square:

> Did you perceive
> He did solicit you in free contempt
> When he did need your loves; and do you think
> That his contempt shall not be bruising to you
> When he has power to crush?
>
> (2.3.119–203)

In Rochester, this scene took place in a large freight lift between floors. The audience had been chivvied from the large, ground-floor public space into this lift, to travel to the conference room for the Patricians' approval of Martius as Consul, then drawn out into a corridor of television sets to become part of the crowd of citizens offering their votes. The presence of these television sets was entirely fortuitous: they were part of an artist's installation on display at the Art Center at the time of the *Coriolanus* project and were switched off during the time of the performance. They sat blankly on white plinths, reminders, perhaps, of the ways in which our audience might be used to seeing their politicians – through screens rather than in market squares. Playing the tribunes' appeal to the citizens of 2.3 back in the lift produced the effect of politicians desperately working behind the scenes; Brutus and Sicinius trap the audience in a non-theatrical space and tell them, along with the citizens, what they must do when they get back onto the political stage.

But, *pace* the critical commonplace that Martius is a heroic anachronism in peacetime Rome, it was the tribunes behind their table or crammed in their lift who read anachronistically here. It was not simply that the time for democratic discussion had not come – indeed, to figure the play thus would be to paint too optimistically Whiggish a picture of emergent political progress. When Sicinius screamed his demand that Martius be hurled from the rock Tarpeian, and undercut another potentially monumentalizing speech about Martius from Cominius – 'We know your drift, speak what?' (3.3.120) – he appeared to want to topple the monument. But the image of Martius being hurled from the rock presaged not the short-lived peacetime idyll of 4.6, a market square full of happy equals, but a momentarily empty plinth for Aufidius, finally, to step onto.

Jeff Broitman's Aufidius established himself from the beginning of the performance as a figure who both understood the significance of choosing his position in the gallery, of looking and being looked at. He entered the California Building Gallery behind the audience, and positioned himself as an onlooker from the outset, as if deciding where his scenes might take place to best advantage. In the performance at the Rochester Art Center, this decision was more clearly in evidence. The Center is structured as a series of balconies around a central atrium, with a large, social space stretching away at ground floor level towards a wall of glass windows through which a stretch of grass and trees runs down to the Zumbro river. Broitman became a competing monument to the one the Roman patriarchy was determined to make of Coriolanus. He gazed down at Menenius's encounter with the citizens, fortuitously backed by the American flag outside the Arts Center (see illustration 35), or stared across the atrium at Martius being confirmed as consul in the glass-walled conference room.

Aufidius was never exposed to public gaze as Martius was; he seemed not to find the public gaze exposing. Even when his status is threatened by his soldiers' tendency to 'fly to the Roman' (4.7.1), he appeared perfectly at ease with the audience as he offered his analysis of Martius's inability to shift from 'casque' to 'cushion' (4.7.43); he even addressed a baby in his mother's arms, who gratifyingly confirmed his charisma by stretching an arm out towards Aufidius as he moved away. Martius finds himself constructed as monument and dislikes the experience; Aufidius understands the worth of choosing his own plinth.

A consummate controller of space to equal Aufidius was Volumnia (Kym Longhi), who took control of each space into which she stepped, to the point where the performatives that were spoken there appeared to be instigated by her. Volumnia created Martius, both literally in the fiction and figuratively on stage; she made him into the monumental Coriolanus of her imagination by, seemingly unselfconsciously, raising Bovino's 'nervy arm' aloft as she describes him in 3.1. When he was 'made' Coriolanus by the Roman patriarchy, Longhi turned the scene into Volumnia's party, smiling and greeting Romans and audience expansively. When Martius's choler seemed in danger of preventing him from being re-made as consul, she stormed across a space that had been masculinized by the conflict between patriarchs and tribunes, to pull him by the hand like a naughty boy, back into her domestic space, to be moulded back into acquiescence again. This Volumnia understood that in order to save Rome, the gallery must be changed into a performative as well as a performance space, one in which Martius might be called to a change, remolded from the 'thing of blood' she had been party to producing. She made a slow, ceremonious procession through the space in 5.3 with Virgilia, Valeria and Martius's son, entering through the door to the space, as no one but the audience had done thus far, singing and

35. *Coriolanus*, Flaneur Productions, Rochester Art Center: Act 1 scene 1.
Jeff Broitman: Aufidius; Robert C. Hammel: First Citizen.

pulling the rest of the cast into the ceremonial – the cast who eventually dropped to the ground at the audience's feet, one by one, as Volumnia shows Martius Rome's fate. The final unmoulding of the *Romanitas* that has been ironically upheld for Antium is able to take place because Volumnia has transformed a sculpture gallery into a space for ritual. Martius's admission to the spectators standing close to him that he has forgotten his part like a dull actor (5.3.40–2) thus produced not so much the universalizing trope of *theatrum mundi*, whereby the hero acknowledges that all is mere theatre then takes his final step towards his tragic end, so much as a sense of performative transformation, awkward and unfinished, and a fleeting sense of being in the presence of a subject making a decision, rather than a living monument whose decisions are prescribed by *virtus*. Volumnia makes a sculpture of Martius in 1.3 and tells Virgilia she would rather have a glorious dead son than many voluptuously surfeiting out of action. In 5.3, she momentarily reversed the

patricidic and produced the paternal, persuading Martius to spare Rome by drawing him into a ritual space with Virgilia, a pregnant Valeria,[18] and his son, played by a nine-year-old boy.

This chapter opened with Nahum Tate's admission that he foregrounded the resemblance he saw between the story of *Coriolanus* and the 'busy faction' of his own time and a fairly blatant example of the decontextualized use of Shakespeare to legitimate the social production of space (I wonder how many people walking past the scaffolding covering the City Centre shopping mall in Minneapolis knew that the cry 'What is the city, but the people?' incites the banishment of a war hero). What was sought in the *Coriolanus* workshop was a

---

[18] Tracey Hodgdon, who played Valeria, was seven months pregnant at the time of the workshop. I should add that the lines about her being 'The moon of Rome, chaste as an icicle / That's curdied by the frost from purest snow' (5.2.65–7) were cut.

performance process by which audience might be brought into conscious relationship with the social production and reproduction of text and space. Thus, I hoped, each moment of looking and being looked at, each shift from passing by to standing and gazing, might produce its own political analogies and significant opposites in each spectator. Like Schneider, we wanted to mark the political significance of passing by the monument – the monument of the war hero, the monument that is Shakespeare. Unlike the creators of Warner's programme, we did not want to predetermine the nature of that significance pictorially, but to produce meaning in the live encounter between performer and spectator as that encounter shifted about the playing space. This

might seem to imply a conclusive preference for promenade performance – but I am not suggesting the abandonment of theatre seating. Making *Coriolanus* in two gallery spaces in Minnesota has not suggested to me that a rough-hewn, site-specific Shakespeare should somehow replace high budget, beautifully designed productions in conventional theatre spaces. I do want to argue, though, that foregrounding the live encounter between text, space, human figures acting and human figures recalcitrantly being themselves is one productive way of bringing historic play texts, which were undoubtedly intended to provoke 'analogous' thinking, into productive relationship with our own political crises and concerns.

'IN WINDSOR FOREST AND AT THE BOAR'S HEAD': THE 'FALSTAFF PLAYS' AND ENGLISH MUSIC IN THE EARLY TWENTIETH CENTURY

JULIE SANDERS

Let the sky rain potatoes, let it thunder to the tune of "Greensleeves"

Merry Wives 5.5.18–19

The history of Shakespeare's work in musical adaptation is one in which composition and performance is driven not simply by its Shakespearian source but one in which the music has proved central to, indeed constitutive of, our understanding, interpretation and subsequent stagings of Shakespeare. In a recent edition of *The Merry Wives of Windsor*, Giorgio Melchiori observed that the position of this particular play in the canon, not least as a 'Falstaff play', one that can be placed alongside the two parts of *Henry IV* in this regard, is largely a product of the sustained attention of operatic adaptors and in particular of the phenomenal success in the late nineteenth century of Giuseppe Verdi's *Falstaff* (1893).[1]

Despite its recent rightful reclamation by critics who have argued persuasively on behalf of the local detail and specificity of the play's representations of domesticity and female agency, few scholars would argue that *The Merry Wives of Windsor* is central in the performative or literary-critical canon of Shakespeare.[2] Yet a history of opera and musicals would tell a very different story. There were ten major operatic versions between 1761 and 1929, ranging from eighteenth-century French and German adaptations – *Les Deux Amies, ou le Vieux Garçon*, with music by Louis August Papavoine, now lost, performed in Paris in 1761; *Herne le Chasseur* set by P. A. D. Philidor in 1773; and two musical settings of *Die Lustigen Weiber von Windsor*, a German libretto by Georg Christian Romer, by Peter Ritter in 1794 and Karl Ditter von Dittersdorf in 1796 – to Antonio Salieri's *opera buffa* or comic opera for the Austro-Hungarian imperial court at Vienna in 1799, *Falstaff, o le tre burle*, which created a soprano role for the character of Anne Ford, to Otto Nicolai's *Die Lustigen Weiber von Windsor* (1849). This cluster of examples, when placed alongside Verdi's late masterpiece and Ralph Vaughan Williams's archetypical English pastoral, first performed in 1929, *Sir John in Love*, is proof that opera has found recurring reasons to visit the green environs of Windsor.[3] Musical and operetta versions include J. P. Webber's *Falstaff* (New York, 1928), C. S. Swier's *When the Cat's Away* (Philadelphia, 1941), and James Gilbert's *Good Time Johnny* (Birmingham, England, 1971); a list augmented in 2006 with the Royal Shakespeare Company's staging of a newly commissioned musical adaptation of the play by Paul Englishby as part of their Complete Works Festival.

Patterns of interest in the domain of music and musical theatre can, then, serve to challenge the

---

This article is dedicated to the memory of Sasha Roberts.

[1] Giorgio Melchiori, ed., *'The Merry Wives of Windsor'* (London, 2000), pp. 93, 101.

[2] See, for example, Richard Helgerson, 'The Buck Basket, the Witch, and the Queen of Fairies: The Women's World of Shakespeare's Windsor' in Patricia Fumerton and Simon Hunt, eds., *Renaissance Culture and the Everyday* (Philadelphia, 1999), pp. 162–82; and Phyllis Rackin, *Shakespeare and Women* (Oxford, 2005), pp. 62–71.

[3] See Melchiori (ed.), *The Merry Wives*, pp. 90–103.

mainstream canon of Shakespeare as established by conventional theatre histories. A history of Shakespeare and opera or Shakespeare and musical adaptation more generally not only subverts rigid canon formations, however; it also reveals that the musical works are themselves deep responses to their own moment of production, reflective of movements, fashions and reactions within their specific generic categories, and that they have a precise intertextual framework of their own, one which can be historicized and contextualized. Operatic composition after Verdi, for example, not least in the field of Shakespearian adaptation, is either influenced by or consciously offering an alternative to his aesthetic and dramatic practice. In a related field, productions of *A Midsummer Night's Dream* since the nineteenth century, on stage and screen, feel compelled to acknowledge – in acts either of direct allusion or conscious eschewal – that play's almost inextricable relationship in the popular imagination with the overture and incidental music created for it by the German composer Felix Mendelssohn.

Musical adaptations are, then, as subject to the contingencies of their moment of creation, historical and political, as Shakespeare's playtexts were to theirs. It was a complex combination of all these factors that fostered the particular atmosphere and conditions in which three major British musical variations on the 'Falstaff plays' were composed and first performed in the early twentieth century: Edward Elgar's symphonic or tone poem *Falstaff* (1913), Gustav Holst's single-act chamber-opera, *At the Boar's Head* (1924), and Vaughan Williams's previously mentioned full-scale opera *Sir John in Love* (composed between 1924 and 1929). As this article will outline, this trio of musical interpretations of the 'Falstaff plays' were strongly shaped, and indeed partly determined by, the literary-critical and intellectual accounts of the plays that were current at this time.

All three of the composers under discussion here regularly attended lectures on literary and artistic themes, not least Shakespearian, and were therefore readily exposed to contemporary critical debate. Elgar made this clear in his analytical essay on his symphonic study of the *Henry IV* plays (Opus 68;

its full subtitle is 'Symphonic Study in C Minor'), which was first published in *The Musical Times* just prior to the premiere of his composition in 1913. That article acknowledges the influence of Maurice Morgann's 1777 *Essay on the Dramatic Character of Sir John Falstaff*. Morgann had aimed to prove that Falstaff was not a coward and to relocate him as something like the tragic centre of the history plays in which he appeared. Jonathan Bate has described Morgann's brand of character-criticism as akin to 'mythmaking' and in this respect we can see Elgar's work responding to a particular 'myth' of Falstaff, one in which the character, and by extension the plays in which he appeared, were rendered iconic by literary-critical attention.[4] The focus of Morgann and his contemporaries on specific character psychologies proved hugely influential both on the Romantic movement and subsequent Shakespearian scholars, not least Edward Dowden and A. C. Bradley, whose quasi-tragic interpretations of Falstaff were available in print when Elgar came to compose his symphonic study (and to the title of which in a gift copy of the score presented to Alice Stuart-Wortley on the occasion of its premiere he tellingly added the label of 'tragedy' in parentheses).[5] Critical context is, then, key to a full comprehension of the motives behind musical adaptations of Shakespeare.

A further historical layer of meaning to the musical interpretations of the Falstaff plays discussed here can be provided by means of a more detailed recognition of the ways in which the Shakespearian scholarly industry in the early twentieth century was complemented by, even running in tandem with, a movement to identify and curate 'native English' culture. This interest was partly influenced by the new social sciences of folklore and anthropology, which had been steadily gaining ground in the academy since the 1870s. Particularly interested

---

[4] Jonathan Bate, *The Genius of Shakespeare* (London, 1997), p. 253.

[5] I am grateful to Daniel Grimley for this information and for permission to use material from his '*Falstaff* (tragedy): Narrative and Retrospection in Elgar's Symphonic Study' prior to publication.

in ritual and customary practice, English exponents of these disciplines discovered a surprisingly comfortable match between an interest in past rituals of kingship and their particular version of 'English History', one linked to notions of monarchy and imperial identity, and the values and ethics that the 'Age of Empire' was keen to advance. Shakespeare's work and times proved central to this project.[6]

Quasi-anthropological interpretations and justifications of English culture proved to have considerable staying power and fed directly into later twentieth-century versions of the 'English myth', not least in literary-critical circles in the work of F. R. Leavis and others as it appeared in influential journal publications such as Scrutiny (which was founded in 1932). The harnessing of Tudor and Stuart literature and in particular the works of Shakespeare to the notion of an indigenous 'English culture' was strongly linked to the emergence and consolidation of English Literature as a university subject and academic discipline in the late nineteenth and early twentieth centuries. Ideas such as these helped to shape the canon of texts that was taught and analysed on literature syllabuses, a canon in which Shakespeare was predominant. Leavis was a significant inheritor of all these developments and regarded Shakespearian drama both as a crucial mediator between the folk past and the present and as a vital product of it.[7]

The movement to explore 'English origins' and the kind of conceptual geography it evoked found perhaps its most overt apotheosis in the English Folk Revival and the activities of the English Folk Song and Dance Societies (founded in 1898 and 1911 respectively). As Terry Eagleton has noted, Leavis's, and Scrutiny's, notion of Englishness was less one 'of imperialist flag-waving than of country dancing', that is to say the values promulgated by the Folk Song and Dance societies in the early decades of the twentieth century.[8] These societies, presided over at various times by Cecil Sharp, were groupings to which all three of my focus composers had affiliations, although in Elgar's case these were more combative than supportive in tone.[9]

Georgina Boyes has rightly located the ideological and artistic impulses of the Folk movement in seeking the regeneration of a 'traditional English culture' (those terms were deeply contested, then as now) in a moment of cultural crisis in the years leading up to the Great War (1914–18) and its aftermath. She also suggests that the notion or concept of 'England' and 'Englishness' which these movements promoted was itself a mythical construct, one that offered an image of a 'fantasized rural community', of maypoles, harvest homes and social harmony, alongside an idealized landscape of cob cottages and hedgerows.[10] This version of 'Merry England' was a 'remarkably pervasive myth', one whose presence was felt 'in the words of leading politicians, the policies of educational authorities, the works of "serious" composers and across the whole spectrum of intellectual movements', as well as finding a particular outlet in a penchant for town and village pageants, community dramas which recreated versions of English history, in the early decades of the twentieth century.[11]

Both Shakespeare and the particular patriotisms and mythic constructs of Englishness located in his playtexts, not least his history plays, proved central to these movements. One of the most high-profile pageant organizers, for example, was Louis N. Parker, who also collaborated with Herbert

---

[6] See a related discussion in Georgina Boyes, *The Imagined Village: Culture, Ideology, and the English Folk Revival* (Manchester, 1993), p. 30.

[7] F. R. Leavis, 'Literature and Society', *Scrutiny*, 12:1 (1943).

[8] Terry Eagleton, *Literary Theory: An Introduction* (Oxford, 1983), p. 37.

[9] Elgar was, by invitation, a member of the Folk Song Society, but he rejected the influence of folk music on his compositional style; see Ernst Newman, 'The Folk-Song Fallacy', *English Review*, 5 (1912), 267–8.

[10] Boyes, *The Imagined Village*, p. vii.

[11] Boyes, *The Imagined Village*, pp. vii, 35. The 'southern' identity of this landscape is notable in terms of the geopolitics of England at this time. On the pageant tradition, see Anthony Parker, *Pageants: Their Presentations and Production* (London, 1954). This tradition lies behind Virginia Woolf's creation of Miss La Trobe's historical village pageant in *Between the Acts*, her 1941 novel, which is itself studded with Shakespearian reference and allusion; see Gillian Beer's introduction to the Penguin edition of *Between the Acts*, ed. Stella McNichol (Harmondsworth, 1992), p. xix.

Beerbohm Tree on commercial theatre productions of Shakespeare, including *Henry VIII*, for which he acted as assistant producer at Her Majesty's Theatre in 1910. Cecil Sharp, veritable patriarch of the Folk Revival, was involved in Shakespearian theatre too, composing and arranging incidental folk music for productions by Harley Granville Barker, not least of *A Midsummer Night's Dream* at the Savoy Theatre in 1914, which was regarded by contemporaries as notable for its rejection of the Germanic influences of Mendelssohn's incidental music in favour of folk-tunes of a distinctively English provenance.[12]

The impact of these active versions of 'Englishness' can be registered not just in the association of Shakespeare and folk music in the productions of his plays staged at this time but also in specific interpretations of the plays. Perhaps unsurprisingly in this context of wider investigations of national identity and a backdrop of warfare, national trauma and social transition, Shakespeare's history plays found a particular purchase. The *Henry IV* plays, with their scenes of English taverns and orchards juxtaposed quite deliberately with the more establishment settings of court and church and the horrors and barbarities of the battlefield, were one particular focus of intense artistic activity.

The Merry Wives of Windsor may have been established in the canon as a 'Falstaff play' by the specific attentions and embellishments of Verdi's Italian opera but its comedy found new resonance on the English stage in this period precisely because of its detailed portrait of an English locale and community, the neighbourhood of the town of Windsor and its forested environs, depicted by Shakespeare in the playtext in terms of a vividly created Elizabethan milieu. Shakespeare, Falstaff, ideas of 'History' and of Englishness all combined together in a heady mix at this particular moment in British history and culture. When Elgar, Holst and Vaughan Williams turned to the *Henry IV* plays and *The Merry Wives of Windsor* in the early decades of the twentieth century for their musical inspiration, then, they were consciously situating themselves in the context of this wider series of debates about theatrical and musical tradition, academic practice and English identity.[13] In turn, for schol-

ars of Shakespeare listening to the music of these composers who turned to and adapted his work at this specific moment in time, reactivating this context tells us much about both the reception of his plays in the early twentieth century and what was current politically, as well as in terms of literary theory, at the time of their adaptation. Working backwards in chronological terms, this is what this article will do, situating the specific compositions of Vaughan Williams, Holst and Elgar in this wider context and exploring what this can tell us about early twentieth-century ideas of Shakespeare and 'Englishness'.

At the start of the twentieth century the disciplines of history, anthropology, literary criticism, musicology and performance came together to provide a strikingly coherent account of 'Englishness' and 'English history', one in which the re-staging of Shakespeare's plays proved to be key, as well as something in which the Folk Revivalists frequently played a major role. As Georgina Boyes notes, 'Turn-of-century historicism was . . . supportive of the emerging movement's interests. The culture of the newly fashionable Tudor period could be directly linked with the Revival through the performance of recently discovered folk dances as part of Shakespeare plays in London and at the Stratford-upon-Avon Shakespeare Festival.' The new interest in 'authentic' stagings of Shakespeare promoted by the likes of Lady Gomme, William Poel, the London Shakespeare League and the Elizabethan Stage Society provided a 'productive reinforcement of the relationship'.[14] As an indication of that mutual reinforcement, as well as

---

[12] This score was published, originally with a preface by Sharp justifying his choice of folksong; see Stanley A. Bayliss, 'Music for Shakespeare', *Music and Letters*, 15 (1934), 61–5; p. 62. On the perceived national significance of selecting folksong for the incidental music for this production, see Edward J. Dent, 'The Musical Interpretation of Shakespeare on the Modern Stage', *The Musical Quarterly* 2 (1916), 523–37; p. 536.

[13] For a comparable argument, see Robert Stradling, 'England's Glory: Sensibilities of Place in English Music, 1900–1950', in Andrew Leyshon, David Matless and George Revill, eds., *The Place of Music* (New York, 1998), pp. 176–96.

[14] Boyes, *The Imagined Village*, pp. 70, 88 n. 17.

providing incidental music for his productions, Cecil Sharp produced a programme of folk dances at the Savoy Theatre when Granville Barker had a season of Shakespearian plays in the repertoire. He also judged the country dance competition at Stratford-upon-Avon during the Shakespeare festival which took place annually at the Memorial Theatre for several years running, as well as participating in numerous summer schools there.

In any account of versions of English identity and 'conceptual geography', Shakespeare's birthplace is a crucial site. Since David Garrick's high-profile involvement in productions and processions in the town in the eighteenth century, Stratford had become the repository of deep-seated notions and performances of Englishness and intellectual and cultural heritage that persist to this day.[15] It is not just Cecil Sharp's career which interacts with the symbolic spaces of Stratford-upon-Avon and the Memorial Theatre. Ralph Vaughan Williams worked for the director Frank Benson during the 1913–14 theatrical seasons, significantly producing incidental music for productions of *Richard II*, *The Merry Wives of Windsor*, *Henry V* and the second part of *Henry IV*. Reflecting the interest in English folksong and ballad traditions, not least in his own work, Vaughan Williams included settings of 'Greensleeves' in the incidental music for both *Richard II* and *The Merry Wives of Windsor*. The latter proves particularly significant since in the late 1920s when he composed his opera based on the latter play he returned to that tune for a set-piece moment in Act 3.

'Greensleeves' is, famously, referred to directly twice within the playtext of *The Merry Wives of Windsor*. At 2.1.58–60 Mistress Ford, describing Falstaff's false declarations of love, observes: 'But they do no more adhere and keep place together than the hundred and fifty psalms to the tune of "Greensleeves"', and at 5.5.18–19, Falstaff cries out 'Let the sky rain potatoes, let it thunder to the tune of "Greensleeves"'. David Lindley observes that these easy references indicate how well known this folk-ballad was when *The Merry Wives of Windsor* was written and performed at the turn of the sixteenth century, although he rightly cautions against

any intertextual readings that merely reapply the methodology for understanding classical or literary allusions in early modern drama, suggesting that there is an 'intertextual dialogue' in operation, but one that is far less precise in its references.[16] In Vaughan Williams's opera, however, a multi-layered 'intertextual dialogue' is clearly operating. 'Greensleeves' is sung by Mrs Ford, to the accompaniment of a lute, towards the beginning of 3.3, while she awaits Falstaff's arrival at her home for the misguided purposes (on his part) of seduction. She is joined in the delivery by Falstaff (a baritone part to her mezzo-soprano), initially offstage, although he actually makes his entry during the song. The moment is one of several beautiful examples of counterpoint in both song and staging in Vaughan Williams's opera. In an earlier scene, at the close of Act 1, Mrs Ford duets, largely from an offstage position, with Mrs Page on a song derived from another Shakespearian play-source, 'When daisies pied', the song of Spring from the closing sections of *Love's Labour's Lost*. What audiences witness onstage in the opera at this point is Ford's jealous assumption that the song's lyrics of the cuckoo refer to him as a cuckolded husband. Vaughan Williams's opera often seems to work in this knowing way, able to assume the working knowledge of 1920s audiences of the songs and tunes he is adopting and adapting and allowing that knowledge to contribute further layers of meaning to the opera's unfolding action. As well as the traditional English folk airs and recognized settings of Shakespearian songs from the plays, Vaughan Williams raided the wider early modern canon for lyrics and settings. *Sir John in Love* includes lyrics by Thomas Middleton, Thomas Campion, John Fletcher, Sir Philip Sidney and Ben Jonson among others.

But the 'Greensleeves' moment goes beyond providing mere 'early modern colouring' for the production's *mise-en-scène*. It is a ballad that had and

---

[15] On Garrick and the Memorial Theatre, see Stanley Wells, *Shakespeare: For All Time* (London, 2002), p. 224.

[16] David Lindley, *Shakespeare and Music* (London, 2006), pp. 144–5.

continues to have specifically English elite cultural significances, linked as its history is to the court of Henry VIII and the history of Tudor courtly music more generally. Vaughan Williams, an erudite reader of early modern poetry and context throughout his career, brings all of these resonances to bear when he includes it in his self-consciously 'English' operatic version of *The Merry Wives of Windsor*. He is attempting to mobilize both the 'folk tradition' and the national and historical significance of 'Greensleeves' when he accords it a prime location in the opera's dramaturgy.[17]

The significance of Verdi's *Falstaff* in the history of operatic adaptations of *The Merry Wives of Windsor* has already been noted and it is a precedent that Vaughan Williams was acutely conscious of. In the preface to the published score of *Sir John in Love* he noted: 'To write yet another opera about Falstaff at this time of day may seem the height of impertinence, for one appears to be entering into competition with three great men – Shakespeare, Verdi, Holst.'[18] The particular grounds for the encounter with Holst will be discussed shortly, but it is the encounter with Verdi that will detain us for a moment longer.

It has already been noted that the neighbourhood setting of *The Merry Wives of Windsor* is unusual in the Shakespearian canon. In stage productions of the play we witness the quotidian friendships and rivalries of this community and, in the accompanying discourses of gossip, exchange and slander, the fact that women play a vital role. The women's network of friendship and exchanges of confidence, which enables them to play practical jokes on the egotistical and bombastic Falstaff, in turn provides several rich roles for the sopranos and mezzo-sopranos of any operatic community. Verdi's *Falstaff* is a fine example of these ideas in operation. The opera's dramaturgy is built around a structure of contrast and juxtaposition between male and female voices and different environments. The 1.1 setting of the Garter Inn consciously emphasizes the male voice, in particular the power of the baritone Falstaff. The scene is one of noise, tumult, male banter, rivalry and invective and quickly establishes a tone of jealousy and competi-

tion that will be important for the rest of the opera. By contrast, 1.2 takes place in the pastoral calm of a garden and offers a distinctly female alternative, not least in vocal register. Here the orchestration is far more delicate and creates an atmosphere of gossip, chatter and intimacy, a world of shared confidences rather than egotistical rivalry. It is the female willingness to share that immediately punctures Falstaff's plot since Alice and Meg readily confer over the love letters he has sent them. The result is a beautiful echoing duet as they read the letters aloud and uncover Falstaff's multiple infidelities; this in turn develops into the wider shared grouping of the quartet in a dialogic pattern of stichomythic exchange and interlinked lyrics:

MEG	Gli stessi versi.	[The same verses.]
ALICE	Lo stesso inchiostro.	[The same ink.]
QUICKLY	La stessa mano.	[The same writing.]
NANNETTA	Lo stesso stemma.	[The same crest.][19]

---

[17] Vaughan Williams subsequently introduced an orchestral refrain of 'Greensleeves' at the end of 4.1 for the full public staging of the opera in Bristol 1933 (the 1929 performance had been privately sponsored). This is usually retained in modern performances (the opera was re-staged by the English National Opera to considerable acclaim in 2005). Cecil Sharp had also used 'Greensleeves' in his previously discussed arrangement of incidental music for a production of *A Midsummer Night's Dream* directed by Harley Granville Barker in 1914 (see Bayliss, 'Music for Shakespeare', p. 63). Interestingly, the song, and Vaughan Williams's particular setting of it, retained a resonance in Shakespearean productions for several decades. In 1946, it was used for the scene in Imogen's bedroom in a production of *Cymbeline* staged as part of the Stratford-upon-Avon Shakespeare Festival (see Wilfred Mellors, 'Shakespeare Festival Music', *Tempo*, 1 (1946), 13–15; p. 15, for a less than favourable review of this decision). In further acts of aesthetic recycling, Vaughan Williams himself reworked parts of *Sir John in Love* for the cantata 'In Windsor Forest' (1928) and in 1934 Ralph Greaves arranged the version from *Sir John in Love* as the *Fantasia on Greensleeves*.

[18] Cited from the CD liner notes by Michael Kennedy to The Sinfonia Chorus and Northern Sinfonia's 2001 recording of *Sir John in Love*, conducted by Richard Hickox, Chandos Records, CHAN 9928(2).

[19] The translation used is that provided in the booklet that accompanies the 2001 recording of the opera, conducted by Claudio Abbado and performed by the Berliner Philharmoniker and the Rundfunkchor Berlin, Deutsche Grammaphon 471 194 1.

The wit, humour and inventiveness of the women as they describe Falstaff variously as a wineskin, a barrel, a cannon and a whale, sets the tone for their agency and the impact of female intelligence in the drama that follows.

Verdi's female protagonists were directly influenced by Salieri's equally active depiction of femininity in his comic opera version of *The Merry Wives of Windsor*. Not only is Salieri's Mistress Ford an independent-minded and inventive individual whose thought patterns we see clearly presented in bold assertions to her female friends and in numerous telling asides to the audience – 'Ohibò, ohibò! Senz'entrare in processi, senza metterei in man di tribunali, l'aggiusterem da noi' [Now, now! There's no need for trials and courts, we can do things ourselves][20] – but he is careful to create a perfect gender balance in his presentation of two witty servants: Bardolf, the put-upon assistant to Falstaff, and Betty, who serves the Windsor women. The pair (conventional in *opera buffa*) has a central role, serving as linking narrators of sorts for the audience.

It is in these balancing acts both of dramaturgy and the disposition of character and action that we clearly see the gender consciousness of opera at work. In all these regards, Vaughan Williams's *Sir John in Love* would appear to follow in a traditional operatic line, one that acknowledges both Salieri's and Verdi's contributions to the field. Yet in his feminocentric choice of Shakespearian play for adaptation and in the set-piece moments he accords his female characters in terms of song, let alone his notably unindulgent deployment of the great baritone part of Falstaff – who is offstage for large parts of the opera and made to play an equal role with the witty, self-aware Windsor women – we might identify another far more overtly English line of influence on Vaughan William's opera, what could be described as the 'operatized' production history of Shakespeare in the English nineteenth-century theatre.

The early part of the nineteenth century, not least in the productions of Frederick Reynolds, displayed a marked tendency for introducing songs, arias, musical pieces and dance into Shakespeare performances, especially of the comedies. As part of this tendency it became common stage tradition to cast female actor-singers – sopranos on the whole – to play those parts which required a considerable amount of singing, including male roles such as Oberon in *A Midsummer Night's Dream*. One of the best-known of these performers was actor-singer-manager Madame Lucia Elizabeth Vestris, who played Oberon in 1826 and 1840 productions of the *Dream*, as well as being a significant singing Desdemona. Vestris was also Mistress Page in an 1824 production of *The Merry Wives of Windsor* for Reynolds in which she sang not only lyrics introduced from *A Midsummer Night's Dream* but songs from other Shakespearian plays and poems.[21] This provided a direct template for the work of opera-composers in England in the early part of the twentieth century, not least Holst and Vaughan Williams. One might argue that Vaughan Williams is consciously pitting his operatic work in opposition to Verdi, positioning it in the public consciousness as one whose dramaturgic practice and musical aesthetics stem from English performance traditions and cultural inheritances rather than continental European ones. This nationalistic positioning of his opera goes beyond Vaughan Williams's use of the English language for the libretto and drills right down to the aesthetic core of his production, its use of traditional English folksong and pastoral, and its incorporation of songs from other Shakespearian and early modern plays and poetry.

When he composed *Sir John in Love*, Vaughan Williams – as his previously quoted preface to the published score acknowledged – had the

---

[20] The translation used is that provided in the booklet that accompanies the 1998 recording of the opera conducted by Alberto Veronesi and performed by The Madrigalists of Milan and the Orchestra Guido Cantelli of Milan, Chandos Records, CHAN 9613(2).

[21] *A Midsummer Night's Dream* and *The Merry Wives of Windsor* were linked for the nineteenth century by their 'fairies' and forests, even though, as Phyllis Rackin has recently noted, in *Merry Wives* 'the fairies who appear in the woods outside the town are town children in masquerades' (*Shakespeare and Women*, p. 63).

significant precedent of an English chamber-opera based on Shakespeare written by his friend and collaborator Gustav Holst. *At the Boar's Head* is conceived on a far smaller scale; Holst himself labelled the one-act piece a 'musical interlude', and it is based not on *The Merry Wives of Windsor* but, as its title suggests, is an extrapolation from the Eastcheap tavern scenes of the two parts of *Henry IV*.[22] Holst's choice of chamber-opera in the 1920s was another self-consciously 'English' compositional act. In recent years the composer had begun experimenting with a number of hybrid forms of music theatre, including ballet and semi-opera. In 1911 he had prepared the first full performance since 1697 of Henry Purcell's *The Fairy Queen* (another Shakespeare-inspired 'opera') and he shared Vaughan Williams's interest in seventeenth-century masques. These hybridized dramatic forms, a combination of text (libretto), dance, music and visual spectacle, appealed to Holst's fascination – partly derived from an interest in Eastern mysticism – with the relationship between music, dance and ritual. It was Vaughan Williams who encouraged Holst to experiment further with the incorporation of English folk music and melodic structures into his work.[23] In 1911, Holst was commissioned by the English Folk Dance Society to score music for morris dances and, like Vaughan Williams, he experimented with combining folk music traditions with more élite Tudor and Stuart influences.

At the Boar's Head is a striking example of this latter practice. Recuperating from depression at his home in Thaxted in 1923, Holst had been reading the *Henry IV* plays in close proximity to studying musical arrangements for traditional songs by Cecil Sharp. He realized how beautifully lines from the Shakespearian dramas would work when placed in conjunction with traditional melodies and arrangements. He set to task converting the tavern scenes from the plays into his chamber-opera, deploying tunes and dances from Sharp's anthology, but also many more from John Playford's *English Dancing Master* (1651). The resulting work is a remarkable achievement challenging simplistic notions of 'original' composition, then as

now. Only three tunes in the entire piece are 'by' Holst; what we are hearing in action, however, is a brilliant musical amalgam of Shakespeare with other definitively 'English' and 'traditional' forms of musical expression to create a work that nevertheless directly engages with its 1920s context. In that respect, Holst is more than 'original', he is groundbreaking.

At the Boar's Head is a studied adherence to the classical unities in that its events unfold on stage in real time in a single place on a single day. The chamber opera is both a remarkable interpretation of the Shakespearian history plays that provide its source and a work that dances to the music of its own time. The dates of composition are telling enough: Holst turns to Shakespeare's histories in the post-Great-War era of residual patriotism, a period also defined by a deep-seated and traumatic sense of loss following devastating battles such as those at Paschaendale and the Somme. The curtain rises on a drunken exchange of traditional song lyrics between Bardolph and Peto in an upper room of the Boar's Head Tavern in Eastcheap. Holst's stage directions tell us that it is late afternoon. Presumably the temporal setting of the scene could have been established through lighting and a sense that the tavern drinkers have been sat in their places for some time. The theme of belatedness overarches the entire opera as the scene gradually darkens to its candlelit finale, including *en route* a highly resonant sunset (also specified in the stage

---

22 In his Oxford World's Classics edition of *1 Henry IV*, David Bevington notes that although the tavern is never directly called 'The Boar's Head' it has long been presumed that the 'old place' referred to by Bardolph in the exchange with Hal where he refers to Falstaff as an 'old boar' is a coded allusion to the well known tavern on the north side of Great Eastcheap. Other local references in the play clearly rest in the association between Falstaff and food, butcher's cuts and meat, since Eastcheap was a place renowned for butchers and cooks' shops (Oxford, 1998 [1987]), pp. 28–9.

23 For full details of both men's careers, see the separate entries on Vaughan Williams and Holst in the *Oxford Dictionary of National Biography* (Oxford, 2004–6), authored by Alain Frogley and John Warrack respectively.

directions).[24] It serves as a poignant metaphor for the trajectory of Falstaff's own life and character – he is in a permanent state of belatedness, past his best, not least physically, and persistently holding out for false hopes of a better tomorrow, saying at one point to Doll: 'What stuff wilt thou have a kirtle of? I shall receive money o'Thursday; shalt have a cap tomorrow', followed poignantly by 'A merry song, come: it grows late. Thou'lt forget me when I am gone.'[25] But it also, like the use of folk music allusions, stands for the wider world of England (both that of the opera and Holst's own society).

Audiences are constantly reminded that what lies just beyond the parameters of the stage and the Eastcheap tavern is a world of *realpolitik* and war. The stage setting draws attention to this wider reality in a number of ways, not least through the inclusion of a window through which characters communicate and connect with the outside (Bardolph, for example, seeing Ancient Pistol down in the street but also the troops of soldiers marching past to war), and through that classic stage device of the knock on the door, here less the occasion of farce (though Pistol's entry brings a kind of comedic chaos onto the stage, a temporary distraction from the talk of war and conscription) than a reminder of Hal's worldly duties when a messenger comes from the court. In *1 Henry IV*, as David Bevington has noted, 'The knock at the door . . . defines stage space: beyond the tiring-house wall lies the outside world with its demand for maturity, while for a time the stage is transformed into a magical world'.[26] Holst's opera takes this same idea and compresses it beautifully into the single space and forty-five minutes of his chamber-piece.

As in Vaughan Williams's *Sir John in Love*, a work which we can see was strongly influenced by this earlier experimental operatic venture by Holst, 'noises off' prove deeply important to the production of meaning, from the soldiers' songs which reach up to the tavern interior to the cheers of commoners in the street that greet Hal's 'return' to the world – an action he has himself foretold in the chilling certainties of his soliloquy at 1.2: 'I know you all, and will a while uphold / The unyoked

humour of your idleness' (lines 192–3). Hal's soliloquy, delivered in *1 Henry IV* in the privacy of his royal apartments, is rendered in the chamber opera as a tavern aria, affecting an age-old equivalence between the operatic genre and its dramatic literary sources, not least Shakespearian. But there is an additional layer of reference both in Shakespeare's soliloquy and Holst's compositional treatment of the tenor part of Hal. Shakespeare underscores the cool control of his feelings by Hal at this point by having this soliloquy move effortlessly into a perfectly measured and rational fourteen-line sonnet at its close:

> If all the year were playing holidays,
> To sport would be as tedious as to work;
> But when they seldom come, they wished-for come,
> And nothing pleaseth but rare accidents.
> So when this loose behaviour I throw off
> And pay the debt I never promisèd,
> By how much better than my word I am,
> By so much shall I falsify men's hopes;
> And like bright metal on a sullen ground,
> My reformation, glitt'ring o'er my fault,
> Shall show more goodly and attract more eyes
> Than that which hath no foil to set it off.
> I'll so offend to make offence a skill,
> Redeeming time when men think least I will.
>
> (*1 Henry IV* 1.2.201–14)

---

[24] Verdi's *Falstaff* also features a metaphorical sunset and may have been a direct source for Gustav Holst. Vaughan Williams was only too aware of the Verdian precedent although he expressed a personal preference for Nicolai's *Merry Wives* opera (see the CD liner notes to Northern Sinfonia's 2001 recording of *Sir John in Love*, cited at note 18).

[25] The libretto quoted is that provided in the booklet that accompanies the 1981 recording of *At the Boar's Head* performed by the Liverpool Philharmonic Choir and the Royal Liverpool Philharmonic Orchestra, conducted by David Atherton, EMI Classics, CDM 5 65127 2, 1995.

[26] Bevington, *1 Henry IV*, p. 67. On the staging of the tavern scenes, Bevington observes: 'The tavern furnishings – tables, joint-stools, cushions, leaden dagger – become stage props in their revels, hinting at wider emblematic significance and helping to invoke a graphic sense of place on the otherwise unfurnished Elizabethan stage' (p. 67). Holst's opera is equally alert to the significance of performance, role play and metatheatricality.

Holst continues another English musical tradition of setting sonnets to music when, taking his cue from this embedded sonnet in Hal's 1.2 soliloquy, he accords the prince two further arias which are settings of sonnets from the Shakespearian sequence.

The connecting theme in these arias is undoubtedly time: in disguise as a tapster, Hal sings Sonnet 19, 'Devouring Time, blunt thou the lion's paw' and later still – at the end of a sequence which includes a remarkable polytextual and contrapuntal ensemble where Hal seems to sing deliberately against the grain of the nostalgic chivalric ballad duet of Falstaff and Doll Tearsheet – Sonnet 12, 'When I do count the clock that tells the time'.[27] These themes of temporality and ephemerality are key to comprehending Holst's particular interest in reworking the Falstaff scenes of Shakespeare's histories into a one-act chamber opera at this particular juncture in English history, and why he was less drawn than many of his contemporaries to the comedy of *The Merry Wives of Windsor*.[28] Certainly the ending of *At the Boar's Head*, which sees all the male characters heading off to possible death in the wars, would have been a resonant topic for the post-war generation of the 1920s, many of whom would have lost loved ones in the Great War, but it also proved troublingly prescient of further warfare to come.

In thinking about the Falstaff plays as material for musical adaptation, Holst, unlike Vaughan Williams, looked specifically not to the Windsor comedy but to the *Henriad*. This undoubtedly alters the gender balance of his Falstaff opera by comparison with *Falstaff* or *Sir John in Love*. Phyllis Rackin has recently described the *Henry IV* plays, especially *1 Henry IV*, as ones 'in which female characters are most marginalized' and inevitably there is a concern with codes and practices of masculinity in Holst's opera, with its themes of roistering and military and political conscription.[29] Nevertheless, the roles of the female characters in *At the Boar's Head* prove both insightful and central to Holst's method.

There are just two parts for female voices in this tightly scripted piece: the Hostess (Mistress Quickly from the plays) and Falstaff's prostitute companion, Doll Tearsheet (who does not appear until *2 Henry IV*). While the women are undoubtedly subjected to the onstage misogyny of Hal and Poins (something which scarcely endears them or their world-view to audiences) their sung dialogue invariably introduces a new tone and tempo into the scene. As well as being a practical reminder of the world outside (the Hostess feels obliged to answer the urgent knocking on her tavern door), it is the women who feel acutely the sense of emptiness and loss that will remain behind once the men of the tavern have departed for London and the wars. Doll may sound flippant in her comments to Falstaff, 'Come, I'll be friends with thee, Jack; thou art going to the wars; and whether I shall see thee again or no, there is nobody cares', but the tragic undertones are registered by the instrumental oboe accompaniment that often conjoins with the women's voices.

The women are also crucial to the opera's finale. Holst's brilliant understanding of scenic orchestration and dramaturgy is best demonstrated by the remarkable denouement to *At the Boar's Head*. Following the rampaging chaos of the Pistol sequence, Bardolph briefly exits the stage to see the ejected Ancient out into the street below. The tone switches once more as Falstaff returns to the by-now familiar theme of the swiftly fading day and the alternately mortal calls of war and age: 'Now comes in the sweetest morsel of the night, and we must hence, and leave it unpicked. Farewell, hostess, farewell, Doll. You see my good wenches how men of merit are sought after: the undeserver may sleep, when the man of action is called on. Farewell good wenches. If I be not sent away post, I will see you again ere I go.' This is, of course, a brilliant telescoping of 2.4 of *2 Henry IV*. In this way, the dominant stage presence of 'Sweet Jack Falstaff' appears to leave the stage for good and the

---

[27] See Paul Edmondson and Stanley Wells, *Shakespeare's Sonnets* (Oxford, 2004), p. 175.

[28] On the sonnets and time, see John Kerrigan, ed., *The Sonnets and Love's Pilgrimage* (Harmondsworth, 1986), pp. 33–45.

[29] Rackin, *Shakespeare and Women*, p. 49.

light – operating emblematically as it has throughout the opera – appropriately goes out.

The stage direction here tells us '*The stage is almost dark*' and yet Bardolph's surprise return with his candle, peeping through the curtains and the promise of Falstaff's carnivalesque bodily presence just offstage proves a brilliant *coup-de-théâtre*. The promise is, of course, of one last sexual assignation with Doll, a final, joyous act of resistance to the *realpolitik* world outside and a fantastic alternative redemption of time to that promised by Hal in his first dark, determined aria. The hasty monosyllables of the Hostess as she pushes Doll towards the bedchamber and the abrupt ending of the opera are, however, double-edged in their impact. There is a brilliant urgency in her final line and her repetition of the word 'run', an expansion of the line in the Shakespearian text, and there is a wonderful death-, age- and war-defying optimism in all of this, and yet the tragic undertow never quite subsides. Holst does not choose to show us 5.4 of *2 Henry IV* where with Falstaff's protection gone Mistress Quickly and Doll are under arrest and face a beating and, perhaps, even the gallows, but for Shakespeare-aware audiences in 1924 he did not need to. That suggestive world beyond the stage space provided all the 'dark colours' that Orson Welles so rightly identified in the *Henriad*.[30]

If Vaughan Williams was partly drawn to the comic lightness and reassuringly English domesticity of *The Merry Wives of Windsor* as both a response to the trauma of the 1914–18 war and a reclamation of that work's long history of continental European operatic adaptation and appropriation, Holst appears drawn to the alternatively tragic shades of the *Henriad* for directly comparable reasons. The shadow-text for both these men working in the 1920s was a non-operatic composition of the previous decade, the aforementioned symphonic study of the *Henry IV* plays created by Edward Elgar in 1913. Elgar's *Falstaff* evinces the concerns of its own time as much as the two operatic interpretations we have been discussing. In focusing on the central figure of Falstaff and rejecting what he described as the 'caricature' of that character in *The Merry Wives of Windsor*, as well as creating an

undoubtedly tragic hue around Falstaff's persona, Elgar was reflecting a distinct trend in early twentieth-century literary criticism. As part of the previously mentioned resurgence of interest in Tudor and Stuart literature, and in particular in Shakespeare's English history plays 'at this time of day', as Vaughan Williams so eloquently put it, there was not only an interest in the opportunities for pageantry and national assertions of identity these occasioned but also an unavoidable fascination with their potential for tragic interpretation. Filtered in Elgar's account through Morgann's reading of Falstaff's character in tragic terms, the contemporary writings of A. C. Bradley – in particular his article for *The Fortnightly Review*, 'The Rejection of Falstaff', published in 1902 – make their influence felt in the remarkable closing moments to this symphonic study.[31]

Daniel Grimley indicates that Elgar was unsure what to do with his ending until very late in the compositional process. Elgar's ultimate decision underscores the tragic reading of Falstaff offered. Although on the surface the final section depicts the progress of the newly crowned King Henry V, the melodic refrain of the clarinet that signifies Falstaff (an intriguingly 'feminized' instrumental interpretation of his character) returns us to his rejected friend and colleague ('I know thee not, old man', 5.5.47):

This is a classic Elgarian device: the music offers a snatch of a faintly-remembered tune (never heard in its full actuality), that inspires thoughts of melancholy, loss, and nostalgia, as well as the sense of a singing presence . . . Set off from the main body of the work, and isolated within

---

[30] Quoted in Bevington, *1 Henry IV*, p. 85.

[31] John Bayley suggests that Bradley may not have known the work of his amateur eighteenth-century predecessor Morgann; see A. C. Bradley, *Shakespearean Tragedy* (Harmondsworth, 1991 [1904]), p. 6. However, Morgann's essay on Falstaff had been published in 1902 as part of a collection of *Eighteenth-Century Essays*, edited by D. Nichol Smith and published by James Maclehose, which at least raises the possibility that Bradley had direct contact with Morgann's arguments, and Elgar with both.

its own other-worldly context, the melody is a graphic representation of the moment of Falstaff's death.[32]

The coda to the piece is, however, even harsher in the tragic experience it offers. The ending of the final eight bars returns us briefly, suddenly, but also seemingly incontrovertibly, to the *realpolitik* of the new king's reign – Elgar's commentary in his analytical essay clarified the point: 'the man of harsh reality has triumphed'.[33]

In 1913 Elgar was working on the cusp of the supposed 'war to end all wars' but he was working in the tragic aftermath of another conflict, the Boer War (1899–1902). These external factors shape his remarkable symphonic study as much as the Great War makes its presence felt in Holst's and Vaughan Williams's Falstaffian operas of the following decade. Like Holst and Vaughan Williams, whose own interpretations he would influence deeply, in his choice of musical form

Elgar is presciently aware of the potential for an assertion of a very English aesthetic in his work. Instead of opera he re-imagines a different set of musical inheritances through his tone poem, ones filtered through the continental European examples of Franz Liszt and Richard Strauss. This stylistic choice is, however, an equally active engagement by Elgar with concepts of Englishness and national, not least martial, identities 'at this time of day'. In all three examples of musical 'Falstaffs' offered here, then, we, as contemporary interpreters of Shakespearian musical adaptations, must attend to their own highly specific contexts of production – musical, political, and literary critical – if we are to hear them fully and in all their remarkable shades.

---

32 Grimley, '*Falstaff* (tragedy)', p. 5.
33 Grimley, '*Falstaff* (tragedy)', p. 8.

MICHAEL BOGDANOV IN CONVERSATION

JOHN DRAKAKIS

The following conversation took place on a number of occasions beginning on Friday 3 September, 2004 and ending on 4 February 2005, in Cardiff, where Michael Bogdanov's Wales Theatre Company has its administrative base. It has often been the case that discussions of literary and artistic matters have historically taken place against backdrops of national politics or crises. Dryden's *Essay of Dramatick Poesy* was cast in the form of a dialogue that was conducted against the backdrop of an Anglo-Dutch trade war, and these interviews with Bogdanov were no exception: on the day of the first interview the siege of the school in Beslan, North Ossetia, that was to end in massive loss of infant life, was in its third day; the aftermath of the war in Iraq continued, with President Bush of the USA announcing an aggressive foreign policy directed at 'changing the world', and declaring the USA to be 'liberty central'. At the same time as being sensitive to larger global issues, Bogdanov's theatrical endeavours are also firmly rooted in a strong sense of community; indeed the two are integrated at a fundamental level in his own thinking.

MB You cannot ignore the war in Iraq, the siege in Chechnya, two hundred and fifty children injured and others dead, the planes that crash, the trains that are blown up, and pretend that these events have nothing to do with Shakespeare. You can't close your eyes to plays that deal with Elizabethan brutality and terrorism and pretend that it all happened in a bygone era. Unless you make links with what is happening today, on the street and in the rest of the world, I do not understand how you can do the plays at all.

JD This awareness of what is happening on 'the world stage' coincides with your interest in the community aspect of theatre and the projects that came from that. What prompted the move that resulted in *The Tempest in Butetown*, a production mounted with mostly amateur actors, people who occupied prominent positions in Cardiff's Tiger Bay community?

MB Let me answer the second part of your question first: *The Tempest in Butetown* with reference to *Shakespeare on the Estate* on the Ladywood estate in Birmingham. It has always been my belief that you could take ten people off the street, and seven could act well in conventional terms – maybe all ten. The problem is that most people start by having a tremendous imagination – just look at children at play – but then go on to do something else, whereas some carry on playing. Generally, by the time you're eleven years old a lot of this capacity for imaginative play has been driven out of you. Those who want to continue to play end up acting or working in the interpretative and imaginative field; then there are those who go off into some other area, and don't exercise their creativity at all, or at least not in the 'acting' way. Only those who then go on to train end up working in the acting profession. But you can release the dormant, latent talent that is there in all of us by pressing the right button. If you take those people off the street and work with them and enthuse them, and give them the confidence to use language in a certain way, you can create an actor out of anybody. To the acting profession this sounds like heresy, because actors like to think that they are part of a profession that is chosen. Of course, in terms of advancing your technique over a period of years that is fundamentally true, but it is because they choose to do it day in day out, like the Derek Jacobis or the Ian McKellens. For those people who haven't or can't possibly acquire that level of expertise, you can, nevertheless, find a way of animating them that surprises both them and anybody who watches them. It has always been my contention that people who have grown up in deprived circumstances need to show that they *have* got what it takes to be creative when measured alongside those who have been the beneficiaries of privilege and access. So when I went on to the Ladywood estate in Birmingham, funnily enough, it was precisely to do the opposite: it was to prove that in that kind of environment Shakespeare was totally irrelevant to 95 per cent of the population. In the process of proving that, I also proved that you could take people who couldn't care less whether Shakespeare lived or died and excite them with Shakespeare in a way that surprised them. Initially, they couldn't understand one word in ten, and some hadn't even heard of *Romeo and Juliet*, let alone *Timon of Athens*, or *Coriolanus*. But with encouragement they came to understand what the speeches meant, and I found that I could present them in a form that made sense to them. And it wasn't just a question of making sense of Shakespeare's language, but also of finding something inside particular speeches that communicated meaning absolutely fundamentally and accurately. Residents on the Ladywood estate – battered wives, mothers whose children had been taken into care,

36. Uli Tukur as a pensive Hamlet contemplating the source of his discontent (*Hamlet* 1.2).

alcoholics, drug addicts, the homeless, the unemployed, people to whom normally you wouldn't give a chance – handled some of this text coherently and meaningfully; and so I realised that I was proving to myself, and to the world, that Shakespeare is not the mystery the profession would have him be. He can be made accessible to everybody and anybody if you only actually unlock the right box and release the talent.

When I came to do *The Tempest in Butetown* the same thing applied, but with this difference. In Butetown, a former dock-land area of Cardiff Bay, there is a very deep-rooted culture, completely different from the rootless culture of the Ladywood estate, so I was already dealing with a kind of aestheticism and intellectual appreciation that is completely different. There was, and is, a well of understanding in the multi-cultural society of Cardiff that didn't exist on the Ladywood estate. I'm not making great claims for *Shakespeare on the Estate* or *The Tempest in Butetown*, but the desire to engage and work with people who, for all their faults, irrespective of whether they turned up or didn't turn up or whether they could or couldn't remember their lines, the desire to actually help them come to terms with Shakespeare, was a genuine one, and I never rejected anybody. In order to get *The Tempest in Butetown* off the ground, I had *five* Prosperos; I had *three* Mirandas and *two* Calibans because I couldn't rely on people being there all of the time! I was actually creating a concept on the hoof because I'd be ready to shoot a scene and somebody hadn't turned up, so we had to find somebody else. The money wasn't there to give us the means to adjust to this fact of life, and so we had to keep going regardless.

JD Your *Tempest in Butetown* was a re-visitation because you've done *The Tempest* before. What you reject in traditional readings of the play is the idea of Prospero as the artist in the twilight of his career asking forgiveness for what he has done. This is something you've also written about, but you feel strongly that the traditional reading misses the social and political centre of the play by relegating it to what you call 'the realm of soporific romanticism'. A characteristic feature of *The Tempest in Butetown* was that, at the time of the production, Butetown was in the middle of a massive political upheaval: there was the whole of the Cardiff Bay development, with people coming in and taking over, in precisely the same way, presumably, that Prospero takes over Caliban's island. What you did was to take Shakespeare's play, and while using the language that is Shakespeare's, injecting it with a political urgency that anybody who was familiar with the internal politics of Cardiff would have recognized immediately. And not only that, you actually had as actors, people who were

themselves politically active in the community – I'm thinking particularly of local old-style Labour councillors like Dai Richards (Antonio).

MB Yes, I cast the lords in the roles of developers who were usurping the island. In fact that little Loudon Square area, the centre of the old Tiger Bay, is like an island, an oasis in the midst of this massive awful retro development that is now the Bay with no stylistic continuity whatsoever. They even paid Harry Ramsden to set up down there in the beginning because they were frightened that nobody would want to develop the area, and they gave him one of the best sites in the Bay. So the lords were the developers and Butetown was the island. It was a very simple premise, and of course it was very difficult to sustain for the whole of the ninety minutes. But for two-thirds of the time it worked. I had difficulty, as I said, with preserving continuity in the production, but the area I had the most difficulty with was the Stephano–Trinculo–Caliban episodes. This was partly a problem of performance, but I also had difficulty in trying to jam it into the concept. I was trying to look at the incestuous, lustful longings that Prospero has for his daughter, Miranda, and to see how it might fit in, but I didn't manage to pull it off really.

JD In the last theatre production of the play that you did in 1994, and in your book, you put forward the thesis that Caliban is the suppressed sexual side of Prospero. This proposes a much more energized version of Caliban than the one to which we have been recently more accustomed, Caliban the victim of colonization. Now when you returned to the play in *The Tempest in Butetown* your concern was to foreground a real political conflict. This wasn't a case simply of authority versus the victim. Rather there was a real tension between the two forces. You see 'colonialism' in a much more politically dynamic way in that it energizes and politicizes the victim.

MB Yes, but you can see that in Iraq at the moment or in Afghanistan. That is what happens when you are colonized. Some people sit down and let it steamroller them, but others take up arms and there subversion is the name of the game.

The Tempest is the most difficult and most mystifying play of the lot because it doesn't owe very much of its origins to anything other than Shakespeare's imagination. And this is one of the reasons why it lends itself to so many different interpretations. No two productions of The Tempest are alike, and there is no other play in the Shakespeare canon about which you can actually say that. The play yields itself up to dozens of interpretations, but there is a centre around which everything revolves and unless you hit that centre then you can't make sense of all the other pieces. So the play can be about colonialism, it can be about the artist in society. But unless you nail those lords down to the ground for the pragmatic, usurping, greedy, power-hungry bastards that they are, you can't get anywhere near the revenge that Prospero is plotting in his head, and you can't get near to the fact that there is no solution because it is in his head. The man who dreams all of this up is impotent because he was always impotent; this is just the kind of wish-fulfilment dream of revenge that we all have.

JD This would suggest then that, moving towards Caliban, he replicates at a different level, precisely the same energies that characterize Prospero's dream of revenge. Caliban repeats this dream but in a different linguistic register. Is that what you are saying?

MB Certainly. I contend that all these things that take place do so within that framework, and what you have to do is to lasso that dream, and see how everything works within that framework. Derek Jarman's film of The Tempest did the same thing. In fact it was, I think, Miranda's dream: she's asleep in bed

and she dreams the play. For me it matters not whether we think of the play as a daydream or not; into it we have to put Caliban, to make sense of everything. Within that framework you can have an analysis of imperialism or colonialism or you can have an analysis of the artist asking forgiveness. But it has to be within the context of impotence, that Prospero the man is powerless, not powerful. That is the key to the play. He is powerless to do anything about the situation that he finds himself in because he was not strong enough in the first place. And no matter how many times in his head he humbles his enemies, the truth of the matter is that when he wakes up he is going to be in exactly the same position as he was before. If you buy that, then the play makes absolute sense.

JD This seems to me to add another dimension to that moment at the very end when Prospero says that 'Now all my charms are here o'erthrown.' He remains onstage and can't be released until the audience releases him, and of course, the audience can only release him by their applause. Now if we extrapolate your view of Prospero as ultimately powerless, then he's powerless at the end of the day as an actor who is at the mercy of his audience. What you are offering us is the possibility of a subtly nuanced reading of the end of The Tempest which aligns the social and political aspects of the play with the role of the actor within the theatre.

MB That's absolutely right; everything takes place between the hours of 2 and 6, which is basically what the performance span of the play would have been. The actor at the end is reduced to what he was before he took on the role of Prospero, but he can't leave the stage because he doesn't have the power to do so. The idea of the artist asking forgiveness at the end seems to me to be such a trite view of a dramatist who wrote 37 or 38 towering plays. It's as if he's saying '37, 38 plays, please forgive me if there's anything you don't like. I'm trying my best!' And of course the point is that *The Tempest* wasn't his last play.

JD The idea of taking *The Tempest* and giving it a specific geographical location literally in what Shakespeare would have called 'The Marches' (the margins), leads me to ask (aside from the consideration of your own Welsh background) about your specific interest in Welshness, because your recent interest in 'Welshness' has much more to it than simply a matter of coming back to your own roots.

MB Sure. I was very interested when we were doing *The Wars of the Roses* with the English Shakespeare Company how much Welshness there is in the plays. And then I began to wonder about when the disparaging view of the Welsh came into being. Was it at the start of the Industrial Revolution, or was it through coal? When did the rest of the nation start to belittle the Welsh when it was clear that in Shakespeare's day they were held in a fair amount of esteem, and by Shakespeare himself? So what had happened in between, from the point when arguably the world's greatest writer had an humanitarian view of Welsh culture and wrote one of the greatest scenes about racial and linguistic tolerance ever – the scene in *1 Henry IV* between Mortimer and Glendower's daughter (3.1.185ff)? Where did it go wrong? It was that that set me going. When I looked at *Cymbeline*, suddenly Wales became the civilizing force of nature away from the autocratic fascism of the English court – let's call it Westminster – and its stifling autocratic ethos. The liberating force of Wales, the Welsh countryside, and the exercise in primitive democracy that Belarius, Guiderius and Avirargus experience represents a changing order that isn't hierarchical: one day one is the best hunter and the others servants and the next day they swap. In a nutshell,

Shakespeare's view of the perfect society. The fact that you have to go to Wales in order to practice democracy leads on 400 years later to the problem we now have with the committee concept of communitarianism in Wales. This is what started me into looking at the whole way in which Shakespeare related to the Welsh. He obviously had a couple of actors in his company who were Welsh-speaking – *1 Henry IV* requires two Welsh speakers – and then in *Henry V* you have Fluellen and characters like Gower and Williams (who has the pacifist argument in *Henry V*) appear – both Welsh names – so that the play is pervaded by Welshness. Three times Henry claims that his origins are Welsh; he's from Monmouth, and proud of it.

JD I take your point, but there's an ambivalence there too. You have Glendower's daughter playing the scene in the English Shakespeare Company version of *1 Henry IV* in Welsh dialogue and then she sings in Welsh, and the result is a very tender scene between her and Mortimer. Isn't the lyricism here undercut because it's played in the rebel camp where the ethos is one of discord? But then, as Shakespeare does with Shylock, you are given a character who technically you are expected to disapprove of, but who engages our sympathies. It is a problem in *1 Henry IV* because Mortimer has been nominated as successor to the throne by the dead Richard. I sense that you yourself are fascinated by this ambivalence in Shakespeare too, by this counter-movement that undermines the direction in which things seem to be going on the surface.

MB I don't agree with your reading of this scene. First of all it's not the rebel camp, it's Glendower's house in North Wales. Mortimer has been held captive there and he falls in love with his daughter. But when you look at Hotspur here, he represents the extreme view of the perfect English philistine, just as Glendower represents the perfect view of a Welsh wind-bag. The two are pitted together and get driven further and further apart. Glendower gets more irate and Hotspur gets more blunt, but there is a jealousy attached to Hotspur. When Lady Mortimer sings he wants his wife to sing as well, and she won't. Basically he becomes a kind of lager lout; he gooses his wife and makes dirty jokes. Shakespeare juxtaposes a kind of lyricism with a kind of football thuggery, pointing out that there is one culture that believes in language and imagery and another culture that operates at the level of the street. And surprisingly, it is in Wales that the belief in linguistic resource and imagery reside, not in England. Hot-spur's problem is that he is so stubborn that he just drives himself into a corner.

But coming back to the scene in Welsh, the only thing you have extant in the quartos and the Folio is 'The lady speaks in Welsh' or 'The lady speaks again in Welsh', or 'Here the lady sings a Welsh song.' Now, you have to piece together from Glendower's comments what she has said. And unless you want the actress to speak in short five-word sentences, then you have to create *some* sort of scene. This I did by taking an anonymous twelfth-century poem for the song, and bits and pieces from Welsh poetry of the eleventh and twelfth centuries, and constructing a scene in Old Welsh which we then worked back into contemporary Welsh. If the stage direction says that 'The lady speaks in Welsh' then you might as well have her speaking in Welsh in order to justify Mortimer saying that he doesn't understand what she's saying. The real nub of the scene is when Mortimer says 'But I will never be a truant, love, / Till I have learnt thy language, for thy tongue / Makes Welsh as sweet as dit-ties highly penn'd, / Sung by a fair queen in a summer's bow'r / With ravishing divisions to her lute' (3.1.200–4). Suddenly, an heir

to the throne wants to learn Welsh. Here you have this wonderful plea for linguistic and cultural tolerance. Mortimer's 'This is the deadly spite that angers me, / My wife can speak no English, I no Welsh' (3.1.186–7) anticipates by almost four centuries the substance of Brian Friel's play *Translations*. Here in *1 Henry IV* you've got a nugget of a scene that really says everything that needs to be said about racial, cultural, linguistic tolerance.

JD So if we extrapolate that line right the way through the tetralogy, it allows us to think differently about the Katherine–Henry V dialogue in the later play, in which things move in precisely the opposite direction. Here Hal can't speak French and she can't speak English.

MB Absolutely. But Katherine is saying OK, if I have to speak English to this guy, by God I'm going to make him sweat for it. There's also a link here with Caliban's learning of 'lan-guage' in *The Tempest*: 'You taught me lan-guage and my profit on't is / I know how to curse', and Katherine does exactly that. So these strands seem to emanate from a preoc-cupation with Welshness as an alien culture to be embraced but then moves into other areas. In *Henry V* Hal says he loves France so much that he wouldn't part with a piece of it, and he claims to be no good at mak-ing speeches. Bollocks! We've had nothing else but Hal making speeches for three plays. What he engages in is an exercise in manip-ulation. The point is that Hal as king has to prove to himself that he can conquer this girl like he's conquered France. But he doesn't *really* conquer her; she *has* to give in. It's no love match.

JD Obviously this is an historical matter, but your own sense of history is vibrant and dynamic. This leads me to your idea of 'real' theatre, a concept that you mention in the introduction to your recent book, *The Director's Cut* where you talk about your production of *Romeo and Juliet* in 1973–4. You described how you began with a straightforward production in Renaissance costume that was dull, and then at the end you decided to cut part of the final scene, and to bring the play up to date, and suddenly people responded. Could you say something about that connection between Shakespeare and 'real theatre'?

MB The interesting thing was not the switch at the end of *Romeo and Juliet* into modern dress, and a press conference around the golden statues of Romeo and Juliet. The whole play was re-assessed by the audience, not by everybody, by any means, because there were many who booed and walked out, but others suddenly thought back to the relationships between the characters that they had seen at the beginning and those at the end of the play. The thing about modern dress at that stage of my life, as opposed to now – modern dress is more the norm than the exception in Shakespeare production nowadays – is that it made people look at the play in one way if it was in Elizabethan or Renaissance costume, and look at it another way if it was in modern dress. And yet the actors were saying the same words, delivered in the same manner. So the perception was in the eyes and ears of the audience, and not in what I was actually doing. You think that you are being modern, whereas what you are doing is stripping away the accoutrement of expectation and supplying something that forces the audience to think in a contemporary fashion. I am making a blanket generalization here because obviously there are those, like you or I, who would look at them no matter what costume they were in and identify their political content. But for an audience, some of whom are not accustomed to reading the plays in any political light, then you force that confrontation on them.

Interestingly enough, I was just about to reply to an apoplectic letter as a result of my production at the Ludlow Festival that said, how dare I put Malvolio in *Twelfth Night* in a black hood and tie him up, and turn a scene that is essentially comic into something grotesque. I say, What? Locking somebody in a dark room, tying them up, and trying to convince them that they are mad is comic? I'm sorry, I think I have a good sense of humour, but I don't see the comedy in that. And I've just replied to a similar objection from a newspaper critic, Sam Marlow, of *The Times*. Actually, back in 1973, just after the *Romeo and Juliet* experience, I did an experimental version of *Twelfth Night*, cut it down to about an hour, focusing on the cruel elements in the play, and Malvolio there had a paper bag over his head. Now, a couple of years later, we were looking at pictures of IRA prisoners with paper bags over their heads. Actually what I did preceded that but, obviously, in my own sub-conscious the image had come from somewhere, because I didn't think that the device of the paper bag was original. But then, thirty years later I put Malvolio in a black hood, and because it immediately lifted *Twelfth Night* out of the realm of the parochial – a rather nice little festive (Feste) celebration of self-indulgent love and rampaging drunkenness. When I confronted the audience with an image that they had seen that very day, suddenly I was accused of being outrageous, anarchic, gratuitous and gimmicky. All I did was actually follow what the text says and find a theatrical way of showing it. I added the rope that is held by Maria in order to emphasise that it is she who is the instigator of the events that lead to Malvolio's imprisonment. And so you immediately get that image of the American female soldier (Lynndie England) who was recently photographed with Iraqi prisoners in the prison of Abu Graibh in Baghdad. But theatre is about making you think, 'Well, what did they really do to Mavolio? Did he really deserve that treatment? What is funny about the way that they treat him?' Then, in asking people to confront themselves, you fulfil what I believe to be the prime motive of theatre: that is, a quest for how we can make this world better to live in by analysing our actions and the consequences of those actions.

JD This is a dynamic and interactive view of theatre; 'entertainment' isn't a diversion that distracts an audience from the tensions and the demands of ordinary life. Also, you are saying that in terms of your own practice, then, what you deal with is a kind of dialogue between the play, your audience and the contemporary situation, whatever images you might find there, or whatever images you think are appropriate and that the text will withstand. Obviously, the purists are going to object to that, aren't they? And, of course, many of them have done, not only in terms of your *Romeo and Juliet*, but also in relation to your 1978 RSC production of *The Taming of the Shrew*. Could you tell us a little about the RSC production, that did cause something of a stir at the time, firstly, in relation to what you wanted to do with the play, and secondly, the kind of reaction you got and your view of it?

MB It was because of the review that I received earlier in the summer for *Twelfth Night*, and because I recently received a request from a student who wanted to write a thesis on my production of *The Taming of the Shrew*, that I dug out all the old notices. And almost to a critic, – with two exceptions – they were saying the same thing: 'gratuitous and gimmicky', and so the language of the critics, over a period of almost thirty years, in their approach to a Shakespeare performance that was overtly political and challenging hasn't changed. That isn't to say that critics of today are as conservative as the critics of thirty years ago; by and large I don't believe they are, because they are exposed now to far more productions from abroad and from the fringes of theatre, from experimental groups, than they ever were then. But that production of *The Shrew* got up people's noses because, possibly for the first time on one of the two of the big stages, i.e. the RSC and the National Theatre, the places where ideology is made, a production challenged the view that the play is a chauvinistic play.

Michael Billington said in his review of my production that it was 'a play that should be put back on the shelf, and never be performed again' because I took a feminist view. He accused me of changing the ending and, of course, I didn't; I basically staged it in a way that made it much more accessible and understandable to people whose consciousness of feminism was growing in the late 70s and early 80s. So the guiding principle was not to look at whether Katherine was not a 'shrew', because she patently is. The interesting thing is *why* she is: she is being held hostage to a dowry that her father Baptista requires for the younger daughter, Bianca. She is termed 'the prize' in the list of characters, and Katherine is totally frustrated by the whole repressive male world that surrounds her. And then a man comes along, in the form of Petruccio who beats the shit out of her. But the key to the play lies in the Induction in which a tinker, who is the lowest of the low, a mender of pots and pans, is slung out of the pub for being drunk and for breaking the glasses; and he threatens the landlady who throws him out. He falls asleep and dreams a wish-fulfilment dream of male revenge. Out of the dark come a bunch of huntsmen – a symbol, if you like, of wealth and power, who bet on their dogs in the same way that the men bet on the women at the end of the play – and they find Christopher Sly asleep on the ground. They decide to play a trick on him by convincing him that he is a Lord. So, in his dream he becomes a Lord, and the point about the tinker, the lowest of the low, and who wishes he could take revenge on society, is that he *can't* take revenge unless he is, himself, in a position of power, where power equates class and wealth. From that point of view the play *is* about male chauvinism, but the play then turns itself on its head, because at the end it is a moot point as to who is the winner: Kate or Petruchio. Kate has an embarrassingly long speech at the end that is twice as long as any other speech in the play. There she goes on and on about being subservient to the point where you can't help but be shuffling by the end of it, if it is played in the way that I think it should be played. This woman says: 'Right, if you want subservience, I'll give you subservience. Take a load of this!' Kate has been bashed and beaten and yet she still finds a way to win. The other two female characters (Bianca – butter wouldn't melt in her mouth when she is single, but as soon as she's married she's giving her husband hell – and the Widow – as soon as she's got the ring on her finger she's giving Hortensio hell) take a different path and expose some of the hidden assumptions of power as it is presented in the play. In other words, for women, power is equated in the play with marriage to power. That is the only way. We know that from the example of Queen Margaret in *Richard III*, who loses power as soon as her husband is dead. Then there is Gertrude in *Hamlet* who manages to hang on to her power by marrying not one king but two. You're not going to tell me that *that* woman doesn't know what she's doing! So, empowerment for a woman in Elizabethan terms equates being married to power. Kate still retains her individuality right to the end albeit she finds a different way to cope with it, but the one who loses out is Petruchio.

At the end of the anonymous *The Taming of A Shrew*, which people now think may be an early version by Shakespeare, there is a little scene at the end in which the action returns to the Tinker asleep on the ground. The Tapster comes out of the pub at dawn, wakes him up and says 'Hey, you've been asleep all night', and the Tinker says 'Ha! I've had this most wonderful dream; I dreamt how to tame a shrew!' And the Tapster says 'Really!' And the Tinker says, 'Yeh, I'm gonna go home and show my old lady what for!' And the Tapster says, 'This I gotta see!' And, of course, when he gets home, I'll bet he gets smashed about the head with a rolling pin because, actually, it has all been in his imagination. If he wants to find a place in society then there would have to be a much more egalitarian approach to the whole hierarchical structure. That basically is the line that I took.

JD But one of the problems that some members of the audience at that RSC production had was that they seemed to want to identify with Kate, but because you had the actress playing Kate, Paola Dionisotti, at the very end, speaking that long speech as though she had been really battered into submission, in fact, that she had become more of a zombie than anything else, they were alienated from that position. Can I ask you to compare that ending of the play, as you directed it in 1976, with the various endings that you experimented with in the TV series of workshop performances, *Shakespeare Lives*, where you went back to the ending of *The Shrew* with Daniel Massey as Petruccio and Suzanne Bertish as Kate? There you offered two alternative endings with one in which Bertish played the role as a completely subservient Kate, constrained and contained, and the other, a much more ironical ending in which she actually wins and is empowered by appearing to accept her husband's superiority.

MB Let me go back to the original production because it would depend on what night you saw it as to how that speech was performed. The problem with Paola Dionisotti is that she is a very wilful actor who will take her cue from the mood according to what happens on the night. For example, if she tripped over in a scene, the whole scene would then be played on the ground as though she had hurt her foot, asking for sympathy. In the early stages I had a problem because she refused to behave as the text indicates. This is why I said earlier that you have to accept as a given that Katherine behaves as a shrew and that there can be no argument about that. But Paola wanted to be meek and mild. This forced Zoe Wannamaker (Bianca) into the position of behaving like a shrew herself; the meeker and milder that Paola got, the more dominant and angry and shrewish Bianca became, which, of course, produces a completely wrong balance in the play and you cannot then follow the story through properly. I was at continual loggerheads – and so was Jon [Jonathan Pryce, Petruccio] – with Paola over the line that we were taking on the play, so that when we came to the end, it was a toss-up as to whether Paola that night was a zombie, or a cheerful cheer-leader, so I can't answer for that. This is rather like a debate I had with [the critic] Nicholas de Jonghe over my interpretation of *Henry V*, because there were two actors as Henry V: one was Michael Pennington and on some days John Dougal. When John Dougal took over, try as I could, I could not stop him playing the last scene of the courtship and the subduing of Katherine (of France) as romantic. When Michael was onstage it was an exercise in male power, but John played it like Olivier used to play it, so when de Jonghe came up with his criticism, I then said: 'I'm very interested because you are so accurate when you say this is an old fashioned interpretation *if* you saw it with John Dougal as Henry.' Sure enough, he had. So the problem you have as a director is always that, no matter what you think, and how you shape a play, and whatever comes out on the rehearsal floor,

because a performance is live and because it only happens *once* at any particular point in time, and one audience sees it one way, and another audience sees it another way, you are – and I say this not with any sense of criticism actually – at the mercy of the actor in terms of the interpretation, which is why directing is such a bastard art. There is also a problem with the English rehearsal process inasmuch as rehearsals are *so* short in England that actors tend to do in performance the work that they should have done in rehearsal. If you leave a production for two or three weeks, it becomes like a team of wild horses going in twenty different directions, which you then have to pull back. I've been in continental Europe where you get eight, ten, maybe twelve weeks rehearsal and where this doesn't happen. A first night in English theatre is usually a very uneasy truce between the audience, the director, the text and the actors, and you are lucky if that truce holds for a short period of time: a couple of weeks or so, at least, before it starts to break down.

JD That is one of the most concise and frank descriptions that I have heard of the various elements of the theatrical process, in which there is a tension between all of the elements and they all change, and they continue to change, and this is an important point if we consider the difference between a video performance and a genuinely live performance. But can I return to the rehearsal process. Could you take us through what *you* do in rehearsal when you start with a Shakespeare text. What are the first stages and how do you develop the process?

MB I don't come to a Shakespeare *text* – this is a paradox, really – fresh. In other words, I never do a Shakespeare play until I think I know what it's about. That is *me* personally knowing what it's about. There are some of the plays that I have not yet fathomed out, and a couple of times I've gone into rehearsal and found out that I didn't know what the play was about. Something clicks in my mind. I see a production on television, or in the theatre, or I read something in the newspaper and something happens. Then I read the play to see whether what I think is actually consistent with what is there in the text. If it is, then the next thing I do is to look at how that story can be best told dynamically. Now, that often involves cutting and, sometimes, readjusting. With a play like *Timon of Athens* which was a first draft, not performed in Shakespeare's lifetime, you have got to do a lot of re-shaping. Take a play like *Cymbeline* in which there is a fifth act that defies belief in terms of its dramaturgy and you have to do something about it. In my production I rewrote the whole thing and half the lines are something that we might call 'Bogspeare' and the other half is 'Shakespeare'. I also straighten up lines that I think are unintelligible because sometimes you get one of those sentences where Shakespeare gets verbal diarrhoea and doesn't know where to stop: you can't take 'a flower is like . . .' or 'My love is like . . .' for too long, and so you strip them down. If you've got, in a ten-line sentence, a word that is totally unintelligible and by substituting it for something more comprehensible you can unlock the meaning of those ten lines, then you change it. I treat the text like a piece of organic living material. I don't butcher the text, to the extent that I make them new plays; *Hamlet* in its entirety is about five hours, and I reckon that if you can get it down to about three and a half – which involves cutting a quite large amount – it is possible to retain the dynamic story of the piece. But even in *Hamlet* there are inconsistencies of scene juxtaposition; for example, is the 'To be or not to be' in the right place? I believe that it was inserted, and that it actually comes after the 'Nunnery' scene [3.2]. Also I believe that the Horatio–Marcellus dialogue in which Horatio

describes the exploits of Old Hamlet [1.1.83ff], is problematic. Can we believe that a student who has spent most of the time in Wittenberg and just returned to Denmark knows exactly what is going on, when the captain of the guard doesn't? I think the speech is badly positioned, perhaps because the actor playing Horatio wanted something to say. It's rather like the actor playing Mercutio in *Romeo and Juliet* who probably got jealous of all the speeches that everybody else was given and says 'I want a monologue too!' So Shakespeare says: 'You want a monologue? Cop hold of this!' And the result is the Queen Mab speech [1.4.53ff]. It comes from nowhere, out of the blue, an undigested chunk of wonderful writing, but it isn't germane to the action (some would say).

JD But what about speeches that convey 'information' that an audience might need? I'm thinking of the instance at the beginning of *Henry V* where the Archbishop of Canterbury goes on and on about Salic Law [1.1.33ff]. This is an important speech but we find it rather dull, and so it tends to attract comic attention in performance as in the Olivier film. This speech encapsulates the very condition upon which war is declared. We are talking here about dramatic structure but I think that you and I think differently about this. The question I want to ask is: when you are thinking about a Shakespearian structure, do you think about the structure in the same way as a literary critic might?

MB First of all let me say that the *Henry V* example is an important moment in the play that has to be treated seriously. On the question of 'structure' my answer is no. When I did the *Henrys*, for example, I reversed the last two scenes in *1 Henry IV* knowing that *2 Henry IV* was going to follow instantly. At the end of *1 Henry IV* as it stands, it appears that Hal is reconciled with his father. But at the beginning of *2 Henry IV* he's not. So, therefore, when I directed it with one following on from the other in a matinee performance an hour later, I had to find a way in which Hal finished on a sour note with his father after the battle, after Falstaff has claimed to have killed Hotspur, in order that things made sense when you start *2 Henry IV*. When I did the *Henry VI* plays, I started the cycle with a prologue performed by John Price, who tragically died during rehearsal. He was a wonderful actor and he sat there with a glass of whisky and a cigarette, like the Irish comedian Dave Allen, with crossed legs (he looked very much like Dave Allen), and he started off with the explanation of royal lineage beginning with Edward I: 'Edward I had eight sons', and then he says 'Are you with me so far?' [a catch-phrase that Dave Allen used frequently]. He then goes on to enumerate them, so that the audience has that information up front. Using the idiom of Dave Allen worked very well.

Whatever I do with a Shakespeare play, I always try to give the audience time to settle down before somebody speaks important lines. When a speech is unintelligible, I re-write the thing, because it is absolutely vital that the audience gets a springboard for the rest of the story; when somebody coughs at a crucial moment, for about five or six rows around a vital bit of information is gone. Once I have this framework, then I lasso the production, within which the actors mill around, improvise, throw out ideas and gradually that lasso gets pulled tighter and tighter till nothing can move. It means that everybody is within the same framework; every single scene, every single line, each actor onstage knows exactly what they are saying and why and how it relates to everything else. I never ever let a line go by without challenging it in terms of the full story. There are so many inconsistencies in Shakespeare sometimes that you have to find a way round them.

JD When you think of a play like *Hamlet* that has accumulated a theatrical tradition, when you decide to mount your own production, do you familiarize yourself with previous productions, particularly those that have stamped themselves on the theatre-going public's imagination. Or do you lay these aside and decide on your own strategy based on what *you* think the play is about?

MB I wipe my mind clean of those productions, really, except where something strikes me as being right. Of course there are plays that I have been asked to direct that I have refused because I considered that there have been productions that have said everything there is to say about them. I can't say that about a Shakespeare play, incidentally, though there are other plays that fall into this category. I've no qualms about taking other people's ideas and trying to make them work in the way that I think they should work, and I have no problem with other people taking my ideas either.

JD Can we push our discussion on a little more because you have already indicated that when you want to get from one point to another in a performance you actually interpolate some lines, that you've labelled 'Bogspeare'. The point about this is that what you are doing is making the text available to a modern audience and bringing it up to date. One of your objectives here, it seems to me, is to assert that Shakespeare *has to be* our contemporary, and that you are not engaged in an historical exercise or producing costume drama. This raises the question, in relation to some of your other work, of precisely what kind of audience there is for Shakespeare. Recently, as we've seen, you've moved away from Shakespeare as a representative of 'high culture' and into a much more community-based version of Shakespeare. Can you say something about how that is developing?

MB This goes back to something I was saying earlier. There's no point in doing a play unless people can understand it. I don't believe that any artist creates a work of art to baffle. He or she wants that work to be understood, whether it's a piece of music, a poem, a sculpture or a play. However complex or convoluted it may seem, there is always something that informs a very clear point of view that is embedded in an artist's work. Sometimes, inadvertently an artist creates something outside of what they imagine and doesn't even know until other people say 'It's about this', 'It's about that' or 'It's about something else.' But the fact is that the moment of creation of that work has been informed by an attitude and a view about which the artist is totally clear. I believe that Shakespeare started out with a totally clear view of what he wanted to say in his plays; irrespective of the fact that he was able to put together extraordinary combinations of words and juxtapose them in iambic pentameter, words connected to each other in extraordinary ways, still means to me that he wanted an audience to understand fundamentally where he was going with the story. All I ever try to do, and all I have ever tried to do from the beginning, since I was baffled by the Shakespeare productions that I saw because I couldn't fathom what was going on, was to try and assume that nobody in the audience had ever seen the plays before, had ever read them, had never been to the theatre before, couldn't care less whether Shakespeare lived or died, and actually would rather not be in the theatre that afternoon or that evening, or would rather be involved in karaoke or drag or strip or football or pop music or whatever. That way I could start to tell a story without being encumbered by the baggage of four hundred years of inherited views, which weigh down on you so heavily. So when you accuse me of moving away from 'high art' or upper-class elite approaches to Shakespeare, it's not that I've moved away, it's just that I've never subscribed to them because I never thought that that was what theatre, or Shakespeare, was fundamentally about. Shakespeare is about communication. I don't believe it's about Aristotelian catharsis; I believe it's about engagement. I don't believe it's about Brechtian alienation; it's about engagement. In other words, arousing passions in people that make them want to shout, stand up and be counted, go out into the street still arguing, boo, cheer, but at some point make contact between their lives as they live them now and what is being said onstage. The best theatre does that all the time, and I believe that Shakespeare at his best did and he does that. All I have ever tried to do is to go back to what I think is Shakespeare's engagement with an audience, not in the sense that the New Globe in London does it, which offers an appalling distortion of audience participation of the most embarrassing kind. That is a real middle-class approach to how the plays should be done: audiences shouted out in Shakespeare's day, so we must imitate them by shouting out today. You don't shout out at performances because you are asked to do so; you react to something.

One of the great experiences of my life was taking a seven-person *Macbeth* to Africa with four black actors and three white actors. There were audiences of 4–5,000 on beaches, we went to secret villages, playing to people with no knowledge of Shakespeare or of Western culture or Western theatre whatsoever. Here we were, with a seventy-minute version of *Macbeth*, relying very heavily on mime – no invisible dagger but a real dagger held by actor Carlton Chance, drawing Macbeth along – watching the way that people were mesmerized by the sound of the language and the visuals of the story, talking to each other, pointing out things that were happening, and understanding fundamentally what the conflict was between this 'bad' man and what was happening elsewhere in the play. This

37. John Woodvine in the Porter's scene (2.3) in *Macbeth*.

what we might call 'the Globe experience' is that the audience is invited to become a set of actors, so, for example, in a recent production of *The Merchant of Venice* they were encouraged to hiss Shylock. No modern audience would do that spontaneously.

MB No, you're right. You do it, of course, if you set the production up as a pantomime. But then it becomes a Pavlovian reaction because you are expected to hiss the villain. I find hissing Shylock appalling. It's so embarrassing. I had a row with Susannah Clapp the *Observer* critic about this. She found it terrific but I said, 'I'm sorry, this is patronizing middle-class behaviour encouraged by wishy-washy Globe ideology.'

JD During the past ten years you have directed stage performances of Shakespeare, numerous workshops on the plays, and a modern dress film of *Macbeth* in which the Weird Sisters are bag ladies who melt into the detritus of a rubbish tip. But I want now to turn to your most recent projects that you've been involved in with the Wales Theatre Company, particularly the *Twelfth Night* (we've already said something about the *Cymbeline*) and, of course, *The Merchant of Venice*. You set the *Twelfth Night* in a festive country-house but you alter the ending by giving Malvolio the last word. His 'I'll be revenged on the whole pack of you' is spoken by Paul Greenwood, dressed in a black leather raincoat, directly to the audience, in what is a superb moment in the theatre. How did you arrive at that arresting reversal?

MB I arrived at it through a combination of things. Just around the corner, historically, the theatres will be closed, and Malvolio is a Puritan, the group who ultimately closed the theatres down. All I did was to shift that moment to the end of the play itself so that Malvolio's revenge is one that includes the theatre audience as well. It elevates Malvolio to a higher status than that of a steward of the house, but he is a forerunner of those early seventeenth century neo-conservatives who

was an oral, a listening, culture, and the quality of listening was astonishing. The quality of listening seems to me to be a fundamental part of how you engage an audience and the only way you do that is by telling the story. Now if people feel angry enough or excited enough to shout something out spontaneously as a result of something that is happening onstage, then that's terrific. In the days when I grew up in theatre in Dublin the audience used to talk all the time, members of the audience used to tell each other what was happening on the stage, because the stage had a reality as it did for the Africans that we played to because they listened and watched something that mesmerized them. Now British audiences can't supply that.

JD This is peculiar, because in the case of the listening audience you are talking about, it is mesmerized, but it is also perfectly aware of its own identity and is quite comfortable with it. The point that you are making about

38. A demonstrative Andrew Jarvis playing Richard III, astonished at his own audacity (*Richard III* 1.3).

closed the theatres down in the name of liberty and freedom. In the modern world, the invasion of Iraq looks likely to be extended to Iran; that American bunch of neo-cons are so dangerous that they frighten me; they have no morality and yet they profess to have 'the word of God' on their side. Of course all their actions belie that; they are determined to conquer and rule the world by force, by aggression, by deprivation. So really, the moment at the end encompassed all of that, and harks back to the image of Malvolio bound and with the hood over his head, led in on the end of a rope, earlier in the production. A lot of people hated that image in the production and I got lots of letters, and the critics were hostile as well. I suspect that, if I did this now, then it wouldn't be as contentious, but at the time it actually came hard on the heels of the Abu Ghraib incident. I had, as I said earlier, used a similar device years ago but the context for that was the Northern Ireland conflict. This rep-

etition, although it came after the Iraq scandal broke, sort of linked back to the earlier image.

JD You do deliberately de-romanticize the play, don't you?

MB But, it's *not* a romantic play. When people wrote to me saying how could you do what you did to what is essentially a comic scene, I had to ask them to explain what was comic about tying somebody up and locking them in the dark and driving them mad. It may have been comic in 1600 but it isn't now. But I don't think Shakespeare wrote comedy in that way. I think that the play is a cruel play.

JD You also alter the beginning of the play. You reverse the two opening scenes, so that the play begins not with the lovesick Orsino, but with Viola being cast upon the shore after having almost been drowned. This clear depiction of danger establishes a mood for the play that the events concerning Malvolio sustain.

MB Yes, though I think quite a few directors do that. Trevor Nunn did it in his recent film of the play. The beginning does make sense to me. In my production of *The Tempest in Butetown* I discovered that by splitting the opening scene with Miranda and by splitting the long scene with the lords, you add a much greater dynamic to the play, and audiences are able to concentrate on the action much better.

JD The other thing I wanted to raise with you in relation to *Twelfth Night* is Bill Wallace's performance as Feste. Feste is at the centre of the play, but you had Wallace play Feste as a sardonic hanger-on.

MB He's an old fool who used to be in the service of Olivia's father, and he's tolerated in a household that is actually poor compared with the rich household of Orsino. He is a cynical, sardonic old bugger but too often you see him played in a much lighter vein. I've just seen a terrible *King Lear* where the Fool has cap and bells, and you miss all that bitterness that there is in Shakespeare's Fools, particularly in Feste who's like an old dog who has an itch that he has to scratch. Things that he says to the other characters are quite tough sometimes. For example the first scene that we see him in with Maria establishes that unless he behaves himself he'll be thrown out. Also, the enmity between him and Malvolio is intense, and he loses no time in getting his own back on him.

JD The reason I raise the issue of Bill Wallace's performance is because I'd like to get your view on how you use particular actors from one production to another. For example, you have Wallace in *Twelfth Night* as the cynical Fool figure, and you cast him as Tubal in *The Merchant of Venice*. There Tubal is usually regarded as the figure who sympathises with Shylock, but not in this case. The figure that you create in *The Merchant* seems quite happy to pick away at whatever is going on.

MB Well, he only has one scene in *The Merchant* really, but in that scene he does wind Shylock up with the good and the bad news about Jessica. Whatever there is in Tubal's nature he's not sympathetic in that respect because he likes seeing the knife going in. Tubal is rich and he's happy to live off the Christians in Venice.

JD It's even more interesting when we think about Paul Greenwood, who plays Malvolio in *Twelfth Night* and Antonio in *The Merchant of Venice*. His Malvolio is completely besotted with his own fantasies, and yet there are some brilliant small touches: like the comic tripping over the hem of his gown when he exits after he's castigated Sir Toby, Sir Andrew and Feste, while at the same time repressing a kind of Fascism that explodes at the end when he assaults the audience. Then you cast Greenwood as a not quite so repressed gay man in *The Merchant of Venice*. The kiss that he shares with Bassanio in the trial scene provokes a very disapproving look from Portia, and you explore the tension between Portia, Bassanio and Antonio. Is there any carry-over from one production to the other? Are you suggesting that even in *Twelfth Night* Malvolio is a repressed gay man?

MB Well, if there is a connection it's an unconscious one on my part. The two plays were done a year apart, and therefore the link was not made from one year to the next. Now when I put the plays together in repertory, and cast Paul as Antonio I was exploring different aspects of social behaviour in a middle-class sense and wasn't looking at how they linked in that way.

JD We have to conclude with *The Merchant of Venice*, and of course we can't really do that without talking about Shylock. You have a very strong view of the play, in which you say that although the play is anti-Semitic, it is anti-racist. You have Philip Madoc play Shylock initially as an amiable, tolerant and very avuncular character; he gets on with the

Christians in Venice, he isn't too disturbed by their treatment of him, but then gradually, as he finds himself in difficulty, you have him retreating into his Judaic faith. For example, it is only at the moment when he discovers that Jessica is gone that he drapes his prayer-shawl over his shoulders. And it is only when he is finally cowed in the trial scene, when the Christians knock his yarmulke off his head, and force him to his knees, that he actually speaks in Yiddish. Madoc said that he had taken some advice from a rabbi friend, and at this point in the play he wanted to say something that a Jew at the nadir of his fortunes might say. You have your Venetians, rather like you had your Montagues and your Capulets in your 1976 *Romeo and Juliet*, as louts – the marriage between Gratiano and Nerissa doesn't look as though it's going to last because you've already depicted him and his mates shagging around –

MB Yes, but Gratiano is the key to the kind of guy that Bassanio is. He's a bit of East End rough, a wide boy who's made a lot of money on the stock market and who swigs champagne. When I went back to the play to look at it afresh two things struck me immediately. One, Shylock hates Antonio because he's a Christian, but more because he lends out money gratis; and the other thing is: what exactly are the chances of him actually exacting the conditions of the bond? He isn't a gambler, he is very cautious with his money, so why does he gamble on such a wild improbable chance that *all* of Antonio's ships will not come home within three months? Why doesn't he just lend Antonio the money? Well, just lending him the money is playing exactly the game that Antonio wants him to play, and he's not going to do what Antonio expects him to do – charge him a massive interest on the capital sum. That would be playing into Antonio's hands, so he thinks up some ridiculous, improbable bet that he doesn't

think he is going to win. And even when he gets news of the first ships not coming back he's not concerned to get his pound of flesh, but that he'll lose his money. It's not until Jessica disappears, taking with her all that cash, and his precious ring that he would never have sold – (she gives it away for a monkey!) – that he says he wants to meet Tubal at the synagogue where he will take an oath. Now he takes that oath and when he is asked in court to renege on the conditions of the bond, he can't do so because his faith is total. But the Christians break oaths all the time, they make marriage vows that they can't keep. Now that's the kind of social behaviour that fascinates me in Shakespeare because if we look at the way in which he presents both sides of this issue, then he's clearly not anti-Semitic. Quite the reverse, he's actually supporting the Jewish position of faith and fidelity and constancy and consistency, whereas the Christians are just profligate wild braggarts and gamblers who end up on the right side of the sheets by chance without having much in the way of a consistent morality.

JD Is that why, at the very end of the production – you explore the problematical ending of the play, and as far as you're concerned the problems are all with the Christians – you have Jessica leaving the stage on her own? Then you have Bassanio, and then Gratiano and Nerissa leave and Antonio is left onstage alone. The letter Portia gives him and the news of the return of his ships are no consolation. He's lost his man and the money is not enough. The ending you construct is a very disturbed one and what you do is to suggest very powerfully that the play is a 'problem' play.

MB There's no reconciliation at the end, but then I don't support the Victorian view that these are romantic comedies with ultimate reconciliation and harmony restored. People don't read the texts closely enough; it is a dark and bitter ending; even the music is sour and the moon is clouded, and then there's the dialogue between Lorenzo and Jessica that is bitchy, bitter and is getting closer and closer to the knuckle. Here there's a row in the making, as all of the classical allusions suggest, that's only interrupted by the entry of Lancelot. All this is about betrayal, infidelity, bitterness. So you can't play it as a romantic interlude.

JD The recent Michael Radford film of the play indicates clearly in the final shot that Jessica has not given her father's ring away. The story of the monkey in this version is a malicious rumour but in Radford's film she is still the outsider.

MB I haven't yet seen the film but the idea of Jessica as the outsider is important. She crosses over, she wants to join the Christian crowd, but actually she isn't part of the crowd and Lorenzo is only after her for the money that she brings, in just the same way that Bassanio is only after Portia for her money. Of course Portia ends up wearing the trousers whereas Jessica doesn't. I still think that Tubal's recounting of the exchange of the ring for a monkey leads to one of the great lines of the play: 'I would not have given it for a wilderness of monkeys.'

JD But it's also a line that works against itself. It suggests that Shylock's marriage is an imitation of a Christian marriage, in just the same way that a monkey imitates human behaviour.

MB I think that's a fanciful academic interpretation. But I'd like to have a go at *The Merchant* again because there are still areas that I'm unhappy with. I'm happy with the general thrust of the story but I know I can develop it further and make it clearer.

JD Have you got one example of what you would do differently?

MB I think the handling of the whole area of the Venetian 'boys'. The whole Gratiano-Solanio-Salerio areas of the play are things

that I can develop in a much bigger style. The evening of the festivities and the masque offers a big opportunity to see exactly what it is that the Christians get up to. As it is I had somebody puking into a handbag and pissing up against a wall, examples of the gross behaviour that Shylock warns about. In the face of this misbehaviour Shylock is actually a responsible parent. He doesn't just say to Jessica that he will lock her in; he gives her his keys and asks her to make sure that the doors are locked. There are all sorts of clues as to Shylock's humanity, such as when he agrees that Lancelot can go off to serve in Bassanio's house. He doesn't spit at the Christians, the Christians spit at him.

JD The final question: what next?

MB I'm doing *Hamlet* again, which will be for the sixth time but I'm doing a Welsh language version and an English language version, back to back and with the same twenty actors. I've had a translation commissioned from Gareth Miles which I worked on with him, so it's a version rather than a translation. We've re-ordered some of the scenes and made some cuts, and transposed a few of the speeches between Horatio and Marcellus because I believe that they are the wrong way round in terms of the dynamic of the story. That's going into rehearsal in September 2005 and it will open in Swansea and then it will go to Cardiff, and then on tour in Wales, and then I'm hoping to bring it to London for a short season before going off to international festivals. It'll be a major event because a Welsh-language *Hamlet* — or indeed Welsh-language Shakespeare — is unusual, and back-to-back is a fascinating thing to do because of the different rhythms of the two languages. It will be interesting to see what happens because there is a definite way that Welsh actors act in Welsh as opposed to acting in English, and I want to see how all that stacks up.

THE MOUSE AND THE URN: RE-VISIONS OF SHAKESPEARE FROM VOLTAIRE TO DUCIS

MICHÈLE WILLEMS

We cannot surely but sympathize with the horrors of a wretch about to murder his master, his friend, his benefactor . . . Yet this sentiment is weakened by the name of an instrument used by butchers and cooks in the meanest employments; we do not immediately conceive that a crime of any importance is to be committed with a *knife*; or who does not, at last, from the long habit of connecting a knife with sordid offices, feel aversion rather than terror?

Dr Johnson's impatience with Shakespeare's style is well known and this is but one of his numerous remonstrances against it, taken from a 1751 article in *The Rambler*. The present subject of his indignation (which probably caused him to confuse husband and wife) was the speech in which Lady Macbeth calls upon the night to hide her black thoughts and deed:

> Come, thick night,
> And pall thee in the dunnest smoke of hell,
> That my keen knife see not the wound it makes
> Nor heaven peep through the blanket of the dark,
> To cry 'Hold, hold!'
>
> (*Macbeth* 1.5.49–53)

The critic's reprobation of Shakespeare's incongruous choice of words does not stop at *knife*: while *dun* is described as 'an epithet now seldom heard but in the stable', *the blanket of the dark* is singled out as a generic mistake:

Who, without some relaxation of his gravity, can hear of the avengers of guilt *peeping through a blanket*? I can scarce check my risibility when the expression forces itself upon my mind.[1]

Interestingly, if we look up the same passage in Sir William Davenant's revision of *Macbeth*, first published in 1674, we discover that the adapter seemed to have foreseen every one of Johnson's objections.

> Make haste dark night,
> And hide me in a smoak as *black* as hell;
> That my keen *steel* see not the wound it makes:
> Nor Heav'n peep through *the curtains* of the dark,
> To cry, hold! hold!
>
> (1674, p. 11, my italics)

This coincidence between practice and theory, even at a century's distance, is not really surprising: throughout the Age of Reason, both re-writing and critical censure ostracize Shakespeare's everyday words and 'low' style, banishing metaphorical language at the same time. This, in itself, signals the change in literary modes of representation which Erich Auerbach investigates in his seminal book aptly entitled *Mimesis*[2] in which the close analysis of representative passages leads him to distinguish between the 'single' style of the classicists influenced by Antiquity and the 'mixed style' inherited by the Renaissance from the Middle Ages. Auerbach's categories may serve to throw a new light on the incompatibilities between Shakespeare's drama and the French model of tragedy which then

---

[1] *The Rambler* 168, 26 October 1751. *Dr Johnson on Shakespeare*, ed. W. K. Wimsatt (Harmondsworth, 1969), p. 45. In this and the following quotation, the italics are mine.
[2] Erich Auerbach, *Mimesis: The Representation of Reality in Western Literature*, trans. Willard R. Trask (Princeton, 1953).

prevailed on both sides of the Channel (they may also reveal the often ignored similarities between the history of Shakespeare reception in England and in France). Approached from this angle, re-visions of Shakespeare in the eighteenth century can be fruitfully studied as the outcome of a clash between the dramatist's mixture of styles and languages and the Neo-classicists' demand for a strict separation of styles. It is significant that in the article on 'Taste' which he contributed to the seventh volume of Diderot's *Encyclopédie* in 1757, Voltaire compares the man of taste to the gourmet who rejects mixtures and blending of styles. In France, the tyranny of Taste, complicated by the change of language, induced specific revisions, sometimes more complex than the replacement of *knife* by *steel*. Two cases, taken from *Hamlet*, will illustrate this: the tribulations of Francisco's mouse through critical censure, correction or omission, offering a straightforward example of linguistic revision from which to explore Jean-François Ducis's drastic re-vision of Shakespeare's play and particularly his 'translation' of Old Hamlet's ghost into an urn, a creative way of making Shakespeare's drama 'fit' the classical vision of tragedy.

The liberties taken with Shakespeare's text in France throughout the eighteenth century, and well into the nineteenth, are not mainly due to the difficulty of translating Shakespeare into French; they often are, in themselves, symptomatic of a change of vision. In the opening scene of *Hamlet*, Francisco's apparently insignificant reply to Barnado, 'Not a mouse stirring' (1.1.8), can hardly be defined as a translation crux. Nothing like Hamlet's taunt to Claudius 'a little more than kin and less than kind' (1.2.65), or even 'Seems, madam? Nay, it is. I know not seems' (1.2.76). Yet the mouse would have to wait until 1821 and François Guizot's revised edition of Pierre Le Tourneur's 1776 translation to be granted an accurate equivalent in French; in the meantime this harmless – and absent – animal elicits censure, indignation and theoretical confrontations. From Voltaire and the Abbé Le Blanc to Madame de Staël and even Chateaubriand, remonstrations against Shakespeare's mingling of genres and styles were recurrent and *Hamlet*

(Shakespeare's best-known play at the time) offered a textbook example of sublime tragic style debased by low popular language. The gravediggers' jokes, the prince's quibbling or Ophelia's mad scenes were repeatedly quoted as unacceptable features of those 'monstrous farces to which the name of tragedy is given', as Voltaire defined Shakespeare's drama in his famous *Letter on Tragedy*, first published in English in 1733.[3] Gertrude's shoes were also singled out for reprobation; but the attacks levelled at the mouse seem to me more instructive, because Shakespeare's objectionable half-line is often quoted in contrast to Racine's admirable way of evoking the silence of the night in the opening scene of his 1674 *Iphigénie*: 'Mais tout dort, et l'armée, et le vent, et Neptune' (1.1.9). This beautifully balanced alexandrine is delivered by Arcas, a character described in the list of dramatis personae as one of Agamemnon's servants and, like Francisco's allusion to the mouse which did not stir whereas a ghost soon will, it is fraught with anticipatory irony: in Aulide, the army, the winds and Neptune will only stir once Agamemnon has sacrificed his daughter. But irony held no interest for the commentators of the time; their only concern was with the propriety of the descriptions given by two secondary characters on a stage. The opposition between the two representations of the night seems to occur for the first time around 1744, in a letter written by the Marquis d'Argens, a great traveller and theatregoer, to his fiancée, Mademoiselle Cochois, an actress famous at the time; the mouse here appears in a critique of *Hamlet* as an example of Shakespeare's undignified imitation of nature.[4] After this, we find the comparison bandied about in patriotic sparring on both sides of the Channel with such regularity that one may be tempted to consider this nationalistic competition between Neptune and the mouse as the first sign of the

---

[3] Known as 'Letter 18', it was first published in *Letters concerning the English nation*. References to Voltaire will be to Theodore Besterman's edition of *Voltaire on Shakespeare*, (Geneva, 1967), p. 44. Hereafter referred to as *VS*.

[4] *Lettres philosophiques et critiques par Mademoiselle Co *** avec les réponses de Monsieur d'Arg****. (The Hague, 1744), Letter 14.

battle between waning classicism and nascent romanticism which is epitomized in the title of Stendhal's 1825 manifesto: *Racine et Shakespeare*.[5]

Voltaire first mentioned the mouse in his 1761 *Appel à toutes les nations de l'Europe des jugements d'un écrivain anglais*, an anonymous appeal to the impartial taste of Europe to choose between Shakespeare and the French masters. This was written in reply to an anonymous article, supposedly translated from English and entitled 'Parallèle de Corneille et de Shakespeare', which was published on 15 October 1760 in the *Journal encyclopédique* (100–5) and proclaimed its author's preference for Shakespeare over Corneille. Voltaire's demonstration of Shakespeare's lack of art and taste includes a seemingly objective synopsis of *Hamlet* which reduces the play to a senseless disconnected story beginning with a mouse and a ghost (*VS*, 63–76). Neptune is not here summoned in contrast to the mouse but the opposition reappeared a few years later in a review of Lord Kames's *Elements of Criticism* which Voltaire published in *La Gazette littéraire* on 4 April 1764: here, he commented ironically on the bad taste of this Scottish critic who considered Arcas's allusion to Neptune unnatural in the mouth of an officer compared to Francisco's mention of the mouse (*VS*, 87–8). What Voltaire judged sublime had been pronounced 'ridiculously pompous' by Lord Kames; what he rejected as improper had been praised for being natural. But for Voltaire as for Boileau before him, nature can only be viewed through the lenses of taste; it is only acceptable as *la belle nature*. Propriety and nobility are prerequisites in Voltaire's representation of reality (the words *décence* and *noblesse* occur several times in this review). Significantly, Voltaire now referred to 'Gilles' Shakespeare (instead of Will), Gilles being a name for a traditional clown in popular theatre: 'Gilles, in a village fair, would express himself with more nobility and propriety than prince Hamlet', he commented, after giving a literal translation of the 'solid flesh' soliloquy.[6]

Voltaire's objections to the dramatist's mixed styles were even more clearly and forcibly expressed in the (in)famous *Lettre à l'Académie française* which his friend d'Alembert, then Secretary to this noble body of French critics, read out in his name in August 1776. This long chauvinistic diatribe was part of his avowedly 'patriotic' campaign against the foreign barbarian, at a time when the French defeat in the Seven Years' War induced him to consider England as both a literary and military enemy;[7] but its main trigger was the immediate success of Pierre Le Tourneur's 20-volume translation of Shakespeare's plays. In this text which accumulates instances of the dramatist's licence and lack of taste, the mouse logically reappears, along with the jokes cracked by the cobbler in *Julius Caesar*. And yet Le Tourneur had had the good taste not only to omit Gertrude's shoes but also to transform the mouse into an insect, an effort to make Shakespeare decent and proper which was obviously wasted upon Voltaire. His objections to the mouse, again contrasted with Neptune, are clearly motivated this time: 'A soldier may speak like this in a guardroom, but not on a stage, in front of the elite of a nation, who use elevated language and before whom one should do the same.'[8] In other words, the language used on the stage must be filtered in order to conform to decorum, propriety and taste; tragedies could only be written in the elevated style adapted to the Court. Conversely, and logically since he repeats that Shakespeare wrote for 'the dregs of the people' [*la lie du peuple*], Voltaire explains the success of *Hamlet* by its appeal to the taste of sailors, cab-drivers, butchers and the like, people, he goes on, who throng to see cock-fights, bull-baiting and ghosts.[9] Whatever his enlightened

---

[5] This is actually a politico-literary pamphlet which contains few precise references to Shakespeare's plays but which does use the English dramatist as a positive 'romantic' pole opposed to the French outdated 'academic' theatre.

[6] 'Gilles, dans une foire de village, s'exprimerait avec plus de noblesse et de décence que le prince Hamlet' (*VS*, 86–7).

[7] In a Letter to Condorcet, dated 7 September 1776, he refers to Le Tourneur as 'a deserter' (*VS*, 213).

[8] 'un soldat peut s'exprimer ainsi dans un corps de garde, mais non pas sur le théâtre, devant les premières personnes d'une nation, qui s'expriment noblement, et devant qui il faut s'exprimer de même', *Lettre à l'Académie française* (*VS*, 201).

[9] 'Les porteurs de chaises, les matelots, les fiacres, les courtauds de boutique, les bouchers, les clercs même, aiment beaucoup

views in other domains, Voltaire never envisaged that a theatre audience could include groundlings. His demand for *bienséance* and propriety of style proceeded from an aristocratic conception of the theatre which banned gravediggers and porters from tragedies, excluded butchers and sailors from their audiences and proscribed everyday language on the stage. The all-inclusiveness (in terms of audience, social characters, genres and language) which Shakespeare had inherited from medieval drama and made his own was alien to the representation of reality founded on exclusion and restrictions which was favoured by French classicism. It would take more than the social Revolution of 1789 for dramatists (and Shakespeare translators) to start calling a mouse a mouse. Yet, if we are to believe Victor Hugo, the linguistic revolution on the stage also had to do with class, as he implies in a poem entitled 'Réponse à un acte d'accusation' in which he vindicates his own use of *mots roturiers* (plebeian words – as opposed to aristocratic). Provocative and self-complacent as ever, Hugo derides the formalism that prevailed on French stages until he came along, topped the old dictionary with the legendary red cap worn by revolutionaries and decided to call a pig a pig;[10] and when François-Victor, his son, later published his translation of Shakespeare's *Complete Works*, Victor, the father, proclaimed that, at long last, Shakespeare had been 'unmuzzled': 'c'est Shakespeare sans muselière'.[11] One sign of this was the presence of Francisco's mouse.

The quest for linguistic propriety, an avatar of the demand for *bienséance*, may be one way of explaining why and how the ghost of old Hamlet came to be 'translated' (Bottom-wise) into an urn in which his disconsolate son carries the ashes of his dead father. This major re-vision occurs in Jean-François Ducis's *Hamlet, tragédie imitée de l'anglois*, which was performed for the first time on 30 September 1769, twenty years before the French Revolution. A ghost certainly posed an acute problem of representation, since there was no reality to be imitated and such a character was, in any case, incongruous in a rational age. Writing to Garrick a few months before his *Hamlet* was first performed, Ducis dis-

missed the ghost, along with the players and the fencing match, as 'dramatic mainsprings totally unacceptable on the French stage'. The Abbé Le Blanc considered ghosts as dangerous because they could strike weak imaginations. Yet, he also wrote of the 'terror and force' of Hamlet's scene with the ghost.[12] This is typical of the paradoxical reactions to Shakespeare's drama in eighteenth-century France. From Voltaire onwards, the dramatist was perceived as both a genius and a barbarian, *Hamlet* as his most famous play is a fascinating monster, and the ghost, though an irrational ingredient in a tragedy, as a powerful stage-effect. Voltaire himself was so conscious of the character's potential theatrical impact that he introduced one, first in his *Eriphyle* in 1732 and then again, in 1748, in *Semiramis*;[13] but the fact that his ghosts had to thread their way through the rows of young fops encumbering the stage was not conducive to their success. Although the stage had been cleared of spectators by 1759, Ducis confined his ghost offstage and replaced him by an urn, a metonymy for the dead father.

Altogether, this *Hamlet* was a drastic revision, if only because Ducis, unlike Voltaire and many of his contemporaries, could not read English; as he wrote in his Foreword, he had to turn for his source to the only existing 'translation' of *Hamlet*, the abridged and sometimes approximate version published by Pierre-Antoine de la Place as part of his 1746 anthology of *Théâtre anglais*. This short adaptation which alternated paraphrases of speeches and

---

ces spectacles; donnez-leur des combats de coqs, ou de taureaux. . . . des gibets, des sortilèges, des revenants, ils y courent en foule.' *Appel à toutes les nations*, 1761. (*VS*, 73).

[10] 'Je mis un bonnet rouge au vieux dictionnaire: / Je nommai le cochon par son nom; pourquoi pas?' This 'answer to an indictment' was published in *Les Contemplations* in 1856.

[11] François-Victor Hugo's complete translation of Shakespeare's Works in 15 vols. was published from 1859 to 1865. It was promoted by Victor Hugo in his *Shakespeare*, published in 1864 for the tercentenary.

[12] *Lettres d'un Français concernant le gouvernement, la politique et les moeurs des Anglais et des Français* (Paris, 1747), vol. 2, p. 77.

[13] Here the ghost of Ninus was presented in the preface as appearing in similar circumstances to that of Hamlet's father.

synopses of situations was meant for a reading public, which may explain why La Place, in the midst of his many cuts and omissions, retained the ghost.[14] He even granted him some of his few alexandrines (the hero's famous soliloquy receives only a prose equivalent) and lines which seem to come straight out of Corneille's *Le Cid*: 'Frappe, venge ton père et montre-toi son fils' (strike, avenge your father and prove a worthy son) sounds like an echo of Don Diègue's famous injunction to his son: 'Va, cours, vole et me venge' (Go, run, fly and avenge me).

A revision inspired by a previous revision raises interesting questions as a palimpsest, especially as Ducis must have been submitted to other intertextual influences, if only unconsciously. As a result of Voltaire's agitation and of the ambivalent reactions of other less influential critics, Shakespeare's play had become literary news: three translations of Hamlet's monologue had been made available for the reader in 1733 alone, one of these by the Abbé Prévost (another cleric attracted by England), who later published a long, accurate narration of the play in his journal *Le pour et le contre*.[15] The general line of the story in which the hero is pursued by a ghost calling for revenge was well known: indeed, some features, like the prince's melancholy, are treated as a given from the start. But as Ducis wrote in the same letter to Garrick, the original was so full of 'wild irregularities' that he had to create a new play.[16] From the dramatic action relayed by La Place, he fashioned an orthodox tragedy, adapted to the taste of his audience, a Frenchified *Hamlet* which is Shakespeare's and not Shakespeare's, and which nowhere mentions his name. This may explain why this imitation of *Hamlet* at second remove has been of little concern to Shakespearians. However, it is sobering to remember that Ducis's adaptation was the only *Hamlet* performed at the Comédie-Française for eighty-two years (with 208 performances before 1851), that it enjoyed considerable success both on the stage and with the reading-public, the 1770 edition being reprinted seven times (I shall refer to the 1789 reprint),[17] and that, more importantly, while *Hamlet* was being acted in a more or less original form in England, it was through Ducis that many countries in, and even outside Europe, discovered this play and five other tragedies,[18] a fact that John Golder, in his exhaustive study of Ducis's adaptations, *Shakespeare for the Age of Reason*, mentions only in his conclusion.[19] Yet it is the global resonance of this local *Hamlet* which intrigues me most. The paths that lead to the sacralization of Shakespeare's text are full of twists and turns and the major detour taken by Ducis's *Hamlet* (travesty or profanation for some) must, somehow, have allowed some Shakespearian images to transcend time and place.

The play, as such, has more to amuse than to arrest a present-day reader, who is often reminded of Victor Hugo's sarcastic description of classical tragedy in his 1827 *Préface de Cromwell*: the action

---

[14] These were meant to spare Shakespeare 'our compatriots' criticism for passages they might consider as weak, ridiculous or improper', as La Place wrote in a preliminary *Discours* largely borrowed from Pope.

[15] This was in vol.19, published in 1738.

[16] This letter, in which he regrets 'des irrégularités sauvages' as well as 'des ressorts dramatiques totalement inacceptables sur notre scène' (vide supra), was written on 14 April 1769 (Pierre Albert, *Lettres de J. F. Ducis*, vol. 8 [Paris, 1879]).

[17] A scanned image of this fifth reprint of the Gogué edition (Paris, 1789) can be consulted on www.hamletworks.org. A new version of the play, written in collaboration with Talma, who took over the part of the prince in 1803, ran to two editions in Paris in 1815 and 1816. Mary B. Vanderhoof reproduces the 1770 edition with variants (collected from the manuscript, from the 1809 and 1813 editions, and from the reprintings) which are printed in footnotes and appendixes. See Mary B. Vanderhoof, '*Hamlet*: A Tragedy Adapted from Shakespeare (1770) by Jean-François Ducis: A Critical Edition', *Proceedings of the American Philosophical Society*, 97 (1953), 88–142.

[18] Between 1769 and 1793, Ducis wrote 'imitations' of *Hamlet*, *Romeo and Juliet*, *King Lear*, *Macbeth*, *King John* and *Othello*. Apart from their direct influence at a time when French was the language of European culture, most of these plays were translated, or freely adapted, into Italian, Spanish, Dutch, and even into the languages of Latin America: see José Robert O'Shea's essay 'Early Shakespearian Stars Performing in Brasilian Skies' in *Latin American Shakespeare*, ed. B. Kliman and R. J. Santos (Madison, 2005), 25–36.

[19] *Shakespeare for the Age of Reason: The Earliest Stage Adaptations of Jean-François Ducis 1769–1792* (Oxford, 1992).

mostly takes place offstage and is reported on stage. As Hugo puts it graphically: 'we are only shown as it were the elbows of the plot on the stage, its hands are somewhere else'.[20] Following the rules of orthodoxy, everything happens inside the palace of Elsinore, within twenty-four hours. The single plot involves only eight characters, including Voltimand, who is hardly ever heard, and excluding the ghost who is only heard about. They all speak in rhyming alexandrines, the trademark of French appropriation. Ducis achieves the transfer from action to narration by flanking his main characters (Claudius, Gertrude, Hamlet and Ophelia) with confidants (Polonius, Elvire, Norceste/Horatio), to whom they can relate past events and reveal future plans. Claudius (who is not the brother of the old King, which eliminates the incest) plots with Polonius the usurpation of Hamlet's throne; Gertrude reveals from the start that she has poisoned Old Hamlet at her lover's instigation (decorously, with a cup of poisoned 'infusion' placed beside his bed) and she proceeds to pour out her remorse into Elvire's breast; as for Hamlet (who makes his first entrance in 2.4, preceded by many allusions to his sorry state), he relays to Norceste the ghost's call for revenge – on both Claudius and Gertrude. Norceste rationally explains that the apparition was an hallucination, and he suggests using the urn containing his father's ashes to test his mother. The hero's doubts and hesitations are clearly justified, especially as he is discovered to be in love with Ophelia who happens to be Claudius's daughter. And so Ducis's prince, like La Place's, finds himself caught between duty and love in true Cornelian fashion. The situation is neatly summed up by Ophelia in a couplet of rhetorically balanced alexandrines when Hamlet reveals to her that her father murdered his:

> Mon devoir désormais m'est dicté par le tien:
> Tu cours venger ton père et moi sauver le mien.
> (4.2)
> (My duty is now prescribed by yours:
> You rush to avenge your father, I to save mine)

But the love-interest central to classical tragedy is here displaced by a focus on family relationships more characteristic of bourgeois domestic drama, a popular genre at the time (Molé, who first took the part of the prince, was then also playing in Diderot's very successful *Père de Famille*). Gertrude, the guilty but immediately repentant mother, is given almost as many lines (most of them didactic) as her son (314 to his 400), and appears in more scenes (thirteen to his twelve); and Ophelia, a forceful and vocal character (the only one without a confidant), is prone to disquisitions on filial love and regal duty. Both Laertes and Fortinbras having been ousted, the prince is the only model of filial piety, intent on avenging his father but reluctant to punish his mother (which nicely explains his procrastination) and prepared to forgive her as soon as she confesses and repents. In the 1770 edition, Gertrude is killed offstage by Claudius; in other versions she commits suicide;[21] but in any case morality and poetic justice are safe. Although repeatedly described as dying [*mourant*], the prince suddenly proves worthy of the throne by killing Claudius and sacrificing his love for Ophelia who lives on. Hamlet too lives on because, although tempted by suicide, he responds to the call of duty:

> Privé de tous les miens dans ce palais funeste
> Je t'adore et te perds. Ce poignard seul me reste.
> Mais je suis homme et roi. Réservé pour souffrir,
> Je saurai vivre encore et fais plus que mourir. (5.7)

> (Bereft of everyone in this dismal palace
> I both love and lose you. This dagger is all I have
> left.
> But I am man and king. I was born to suffer
> And will go on living, which is worse than dying.)

---

[20] 'Nous ne voyons en quelque sorte que les coudes de l'action sur le théâtre, ses mains sont ailleurs.' Victor Hugo, *Cromwell* (Paris, 1949), p. 36.
[21] Throughout its theatrical life, the play (and particularly its last Act) was in a permanent state of revision, especially under the influence of Talma who knew English perfectly (he had lived in London for eight years as a child) and had studied Shakespeare in the text. The actor was responsible for the introduction, in the 1809 version, of an equivalent to the 'To be or not to be' monologue, copied out from La Place. He enjoyed great popularity in the title-role, both in France and abroad, until his death in 1826.

And so the adapter keeps the play both within the rules and within the bounds of *bienséance*, having also dispensed with Hamlet's antic disposition, with Ophelia's mad scenes and with the gravediggers. By paring down Shakespeare's intricate plot to a single crisis, he could concentrate on the passions of a small number of characters. But Ducis is no Racine, either in the exploration of the human soul or in the writing of alexandrines; his most common expression of human dilemma is through formalistic opposition. This is sometimes dramatically effective as when the two lovers share an alexandrine which sums up their now divided loyalties:

Oph. Vous, massacrer mon père?
Ham.   Il m'a privé du mien (5.2)
(You, murder my father? He deprived me of mine).

But some of his antithetical lines defeat even their didactic purpose as when Gertrude justifies her refusal to marry Claudius:

Si par un crime affreux je l'ai privé d'un père,
Il est bien juste au moins qu'il retrouve une mère
    (1.2).
(Though my foul murder deprived him of a father
'Tis only fair he should at least regain a mother.)

Such a candid conception of expiation (expiating the murder of the father by being a good mother – in effect, making sure that the son sits on the throne) does not improve the character's credibility. Nor is Ducis's pompous academic style conducive to the expression of individualized feelings. All the characters speak the same stereotyped language which does not incline them to introspection (unsurprisingly, Hamlet is only given 26 lines of soliloquy). Inner and outer conflicts, interrogations about love and revenge are all expressed through the conventional clichés of poetic diction, through predictable associations of epithets and nouns: lovers are *cruel*, criminals *perfides* and errors *funestes*. (I suspect that the main reason for transforming Horatio into Norceste was that the name could rhyme with *funeste*.) Added to the exigencies of rhyme, the necessities of metre, which are often met with padding, bring some lines to the verge of parody,[22] as in the revelations of the ghost which Hamlet relays for Norceste's benefit:

Ta mère, qui l'eût dit? Oui, ta mère perfide
Osa me présenter un poison parricide.
(Your mother, who would have thought it? Yes,
    your perfidious mother
Dared offer me a parricide potion.)

The unexpected description of poison administered by a wife as *parricide* is probably a side-effect of the use and abuse of poetic diction. Systematic periphrasis and euphemism commonly translate even the most common vocabulary into far-fetched or fastidious equivalents worthy of Molière's *Précieuses Ridicules*: Ducis draws on a whole lexicon of linguistic embellishments in which *les flambeaux de l'hyménée* stand for marriage, *les feux* or *la flamme* for love, *forfait* for murder, *trépas* for death, *courroux* for anger, etc.

His re-vision of the ghost seems to me to proceed from a similar transposition, perhaps an unconscious linguistic transfer originating in his taste for periphrasis, for linguistic decorum. In his letter to Garrick, Ducis insisted that, regrettably, 'an out-and-out ghost who is given long speeches' ('le spectre tout avoué qui parle longtemps') was totally unacceptable on the French stage: a ghost could not be both seen and heard, like a full-fledged character. This explains why he kept him offstage and invented the urn, mostly referred to as the ashes of the dead father: Hamlet says to Ophélie: 'De mon père en ces lieux j'entends gémir la cendre.' (In this place, I can hear the ashes of my father groan. 4.2); later he calls the urn *cette cendre plaintive et chère* (these dear plaintive ashes) or *la poudre des tombeaux* (the powder of graves), a periphrasis also used by Norceste in 5.3. The urn, a metonymy of the dead father, is the ghost's delegate on stage, a

---

[22] For instance, Racine sometimes creates the illusion that action is caught *in medias res* by opening an Act or a speech with *Oui*. Similarly, Ducis opens his play with Claudius's confidences to Polonius: 'Oui, cher Polonius, tout mon parti n'aspire, / En détrônant Hamlet, qu'à me livrer l'Empire.' ('Yes, dear Polonius, my party's dearest wish / Is, by ousting Hamlet to give me the kingdom.') He then does the same thing for four acts out of five. One can have too much of a good thing.

glossed-over representation of Shakespeare's offensive character, something like a politically correct equivalent.

And it mostly fulfils the same dramatic function as the ghost in the original: when Hamlet, following Norceste's suggestion, confronts his mother in a closet-scene with no bed but with an armchair to swoon on, the urn replaces both the play-within-the-play as a device to arouse remorse, and the ghost appearing to remind his son of his mission. Whereas Shakespeare's ghost is several times seen and heard (and not only by Hamlet), Ducis's urn transforms his *spectre* into an absent-yet-present character who is, from the start, banned from the stage by the hero himself, in his very first words uttered offstage:

> Fuis, spectre épouvantable,
> Porte au fond des tombeaux ton aspect redoutable.
> (2.4)

> (Away, horrid ghost,
> Go hide in some dark tomb your frightful face.)

A stage-direction then indicates that Hamlet rushes in 'comme poursuivi par un phantôme' (as if pursued by a ghost). The ghost now works as a metaphor for the hero's terrifying mission; though absent, he is hovering about, both in Hamlet's imagination and through his reported speeches: the prince relates for Norceste's benefit the two apparitions of his father and then relays the narration of his torments and his call for revenge. Here we find some echoes of Shakespeare, via La Place, but, with a glance at Sophocles, Ducis also legitimates his invention of the urn by presenting revenge as the only way of appeasing the ashes of the murdered father, who has revealed to his son whose blood is to be shed:

> Je viens enfin t'apprendre
> Quel sang tu dois verser pour appaiser ma cendre
> (2.5).

> (I come at last to tell you
> Whose blood you must shed to appease my ashes)

The religious references are unclear: though the call for revenge appears to come from heaven ('c'est le ciel qui parle'), yet Ducis also increases the unchristianity of his ghost who, unlike his precedent in Shakespeare (followed in this by La Place), insists from the start that his son should shed his mother's blood. In the first performance, in which the confrontation between mother and son concluded the fourth act, the ghost was even heard to shout *Frappe* (Strike), when Gertrude had swooned over the urn and Hamlet was drawing his dagger.[23] This attempt to give the ghost a voice was apparently never repeated: even though Hamlet resisted the call to kill his mother, Ducis, as was reported in a retrospective published in the *Journal de Paris* on 17 April 1803, had to 'weaken his play in order to make it more reasonable'. This appeal to reason was probably all the more necessary as the same article mentioned that 'the shade of the murdered king speaking in a sinister voice the death sentence of his murderer' had appeared briefly on stage in the very first performance.[24] 'Monsieur Ducis' may have been trying to see how far he could go; perhaps he was running ahead of his public, as when he later attempted to have his Hédelmone (Desdemona) killed on the stage in his 1792 *Othello*. But at the end of the very first performance, the public rose as soon as Talma raised his dagger and Ducis later changed his ending.

The urn, which was immortalized in a portrait of Talma as Hamlet, exhibited by Lagrenée at the 1810 *Salon*, was certainly popular, more so with the public than with some critics, who preferred the original play and its ghost.[25] Yet, for a long time, the impact of the actors impersonating Hamlet was greater than that of the text, even with those who could read the original; we seem to know nothing

---

23 This is presented as a variant in the 1789 reprint of the 1770 edition, and, according to Mary B. Vanderhoof, it also appears in somewhat altered form in the MS kept at the Comédie-Française, 'but has been crossed out', p. 137.

24 'M. Ducis fut obligé d'affaiblir sa pièce pour la rendre plus raisonnable'; 'L'ombre d'un roi assassiné paraissait dans le 4ᵉ acte et prononçait, d'une voix lugubre, l'arrêt de mort de ses meurtriers', *Journal de Paris*, 17 April 1803.

25 Diderot reviewed the play unfavourably in '*Hamlet*, tragédie de M. Ducis', *Œuvres Complètes*, vol. 8 (Paris, 1969–72), pp. 239–45. Other critics like Collé or Fréron considered that if a ghost was to be used, it should have been seen by the audience; see Golder, *Shakespeare in the Age of Reason*, p. 45ff.

about Molé's commerce with the ghost but several testimonies indicate that the performance of Talma, who starred in the play from 1803 to 1826, managed to make this absent character present, as when the sight of the offstage apparition was reflected on his face, a moment greatly praised in 1810 by Mme de Staël who, like most early nineteenth-century critics and spectators, still associated *Hamlet* with Ducis's play.[26]

The magic of acting could thus bridge the gap between the onstage urn and the offstage ghost, confirming the subversive presence of his absence and, up to a point, of the absent Shakespeare. The ambivalence of Ducis's present–absent character, part ghost part urn, part metonymy part metaphor, seems an apt response to the ambivalent reactions to the ghost which epitomize the age's ambiguous reception of Shakespeare. Ducis's astute re-vision of this controversial character manages to reconcile stage-decorum and stage-effect, orthodoxy and innovation, rationality (represented by Norceste) and tormented imagination (one of the hero's sur-

viving features). Thus Ducis's *Hamlet*, though alien to its original in so many ways, mediates between antinomic dramatic traditions and cultures. This is the too often despised function of adaptations which, throughout the centuries, have bridged many gaps between Shakespeare and the general public, sometimes paving the way for the original plays. While Diderot professed to prefer 'Shakespeare's monster', audiences flocked to see what he called 'Ducis's scarecrow'.[27] In another century, Ducis might have directed popular films based on Shakespearian plays. There are many different ways of serving Shakespeare, but posterity is not kind to them all: Voltaire is remembered more as the deprecator of the Bard than as his discoverer; as for *le bonhomme Ducis*, as Napoleon would call him, he is hardly remembered at all.

---

[26] *De l'Allemagne*, 2 vols. (Paris, 1968), vol. 2, p. 37.
[27] Diderot preferred 'le monstre de Shakespeare à l'épouvantail de Monsieur Ducis'. See '*Hamlet*, tragédie de M. Ducis'.

'I COVET YOUR SKULL': DEATH AND DESIRE IN *HAMLET*

GRAHAM HOLDERNESS

O skull! O skull! O skull! I hold thee out . . .
Was here the brain that wrought some forty plays . . .
And brought forth endless comments everywhere?'[1]
    Belgrave Titmarsh, *Shakspere's Skull* (1889)

You interest me very much, Mr. Holmes. I had hardly expected so dolichocephalic a skull or such well-marked supra-orbital development. Would you have any objection to my running my finger along your parietal fissure? A cast of your skull, sir, until the original is available, would be an ornament to any anthropological museum. It is not my intention to be fulsome, but I confess that I covet your skull.[2]
    A. Conan Doyle, *The Hound of the Baskervilles* (1902)

I am Hamlet the Dane
Skull-handler, parablist . . .
Seamus Heaney, 'Viking Dublin: Trial Pieces' (1975)[3]

I

In July 1648 John Evelyn, early and influential member of the Royal Society, sat for prolific portraitist Robert Walker.[4]

1st July. I sate for my picture, in which there is a Death's head, to Mr. Walker, that excellent painter.

The painting was designed to accompany *Instructions Oeconomique*, a treatise on marriage written for Evelyn's (very) young wife. He had hoped to have it executed as a miniature 'by Peter Oliver, Hoskins or Johnson', but with Oliver dead and the other two unavailable, Evelyn 'could meet with none capable'.[5] This context of marital intimacy now seems out of keeping with the image, which displays Evelyn with one hand embracing a human skull,

and is annotated by a Greek motto ('Repentance is the beginning of Philosophy') and a quotation from Seneca on the importance of preparing for death.

As a whole the portrait condenses a wide range of semiotic codes. The figure is pensive and romantic, dressed in the chiaroscuro costume of Renaissance melancholy, a sighing lover, cheek on hand. The introduction of the skull and the accompanying hortatory text subsumes the image into the tradition of *memento mori*, where the skull functions as a ghastly or salutary reminder of mortality.

But when the portrait was displayed at the National Portrait Gallery in 2000 as part of an exhibition of 'Scientific and Medical Portraits 1660–2000',[6] alongside Herschel and Faraday and

---

Thanks to Dr Carol Banks and Dr Ruth Richardson for their help with this paper; and to Dr Bryan Loughrey for resurrecting my interest in skulls.

[1] Belgrave Titmarsh, *Shakspere's Skull and Falstaff's Nose: A Fancy in Three Acts* (London, 1889), p. 25.

[2] Arthur Conan Doyle, *The Hound of the Baskervilles* (London, 1902), p. 13.

[3] Seamus Heaney, 'Viking Dublin: Trial Pieces', *North* (1975), from *New Selected Poems 1966–1987* (London, 1990), p. 60.

[4] John Evelyn, *Diary and Correspondence*, vol. 1, ed. William Bray (London, 1883), 255. See also Nigel Llewellyn, *The Art of Death: Visual Culture in the English Death Ritual 1500–1800* (London, 1991), p. 12.

[5] W. G. Hiscock, *John Evelyn and his Family Circle* (London, 1955), pp. 20–1. See also Oliver Millar, *The Age of Charles I: Painting in England 1620–1649* (London, 1972), p. 102.

[6] See the associated book by Ludmila Jordanova, *Defining Features: Scientific and Medical Portraits 1660–2000* (London, 2000).

39. John Evelyn by Robert Walker.

rapprochement of opposites: love and death, marriage and bereavement, romance and science, desire and thought. The hand that took a young bride in marriage now caresses a death's head; the effete pose of a melancholy lover mocks the stern spirit of scientific inquiry. Yet as we shall see, this image, which is both traditional and modern, takes us deep into the early modern love-affair with death, which is as inseparable from seventeenth-century thought as it is from modern post-Freudian philosophy. Everywhere in seventeenth-century culture, and classically in Shakespeare's *Hamlet*, we will find the marriage of Eros and Thanatos, the union of love and death. And at the heart of this mystery lies the human skull.

II

The most famous theatrical prop in the history of drama, possibly in the history of Western culture, is a human skull, that which appears in the fifth act of Shakespeare's *Hamlet*.[8] It is one of a number of skulls unearthed from Ophelia's newly dug grave. Multiple occupancy of graves in the sixteenth century was nothing unusual, as David Cressy notes: 'Gravediggers . . . often encountered the remains of previous burials. Fresh bodies were superimposed on those who had gone before'.[9] The skull is named as '*Yoricks* Scull, the Kings Iester' (3369). The skull is the one part of the human skeleton immediately recognizable as human bone; and among the remains of the grave's

Jenner, the pose was read as typical of 'men of learning':

The supporting hand indicates the weight of learning, and the skull is a *memento mori*.[7]

Here the skull remains a token of mortality, but in a context of scientific inquiry and medical knowledge; while the 'melancholy' pose has less to do with love and more (as in Dürer's famous engraving *Melancolia*) with learning. Skulls were often depicted in this period as seamless and uniform, and with the mandible attached, hence presumably not drawn from what we ironically call 'life'. The skull in the portrait is realistically delineated, clearly showing the coronal and squamous sutures and the left temporal bone, so that as an anatomical specimen it was not out of place in that scientific pantheon.

In its overdetermined totality the portrait presents us with what now seems an incongruous

---

[7] Christopher Martyn, Review of National Portrait Gallery exhibition 'Defining Features: Scientific and Medical Portraits 1660–2000', *British Medical Journal*, 320 (2000), 1546.

[8] All references to *The Tragedy of Hamlet Prince of Denmark* are to *The Norton Facsimile: the First Folio of Shakespeare*, edited by Charlton Hinman (New York, 1968), and cite Hinman's 'Through Line Numbers' (TLN).

[9] David Cressy, *Birth, Marriage and Death: Ritual, Religion and the Life Cycle in Tudor and Stuart England* (Oxford, 1999), p. 466. John Donne anticipated encountering this practice post-mortem in 'The Relic': 'When my grave is broke up again / Some second guest to entertain'. *Poems of John Donne*, ed. E. K. Chambers, vol. I (London, 1896), pp. 66–7.

various occupants, Yorick's skull is evidently identifiable by some obvious physiognomic characteristics. In Kenneth Branagh's film version the skull is identified (not just to the cast but potentially to the audience as well), by its grotesque teeth, as belonging to the comedian Ken Dodd, who then plays Yorick in two interpolated flashback scenes where we see him playing with the young Hamlet and entertaining the court.[10] Hamlet holds the skull to camera, and a dissolve fills in Dodd's face around it, much as Hamlet imaginatively reconstructs the remembered face in his mind's eye.

Hamlet uses the other excavated skulls as props for a generalized satire on human frailty and corruption.[11] But when faced with Yorick's skull, his response is much more personal and intimate.

Alas poore *Yorick*, I knew him *Horatio*, a fellow of infinite Iest; of most excellent fancy, he hath borne me on his backe a thousand times: And how abhorred my Imagination is, my gorge rises at it. Heere hung those lipps, that I haue kist I know not how oft. VVhere be your Iibes now? Your Gambals? Your Songs? Your flashes of Merriment that were wont to set the Table on a Rore? No one now to mock your own Ieering? Quite chopfalne? Now get you to my Ladies Chamber, and tell her, let her paint an inch thicke, to this fauour she must come. Make her laugh at that . . . (3372–82)

Knowing whose skull he is addressing, Hamlet undertakes a forensic reconstruction of the object, restoring its features ('heere hung those lipps'), reawakening its voice ('That Scull had a tongue in it, and could sing once', 3267).[12] Revulsion from the horror of human decomposition ('my gorge rises at it') co-exists with desire for the flesh that has gone ('lipps, that I haue kist'). Vivid recollections of the comedian at work ('Ieering') contrast with an awed contemplation of his present dumbness, mandible misplaced ('Chaplesse', 'chopfalne'), lost for words. The imagination that dwells on death is both nostalgic and abhorrent. Making way for Ophelia's remains (a circumstance Hamlet does not know, but the audience does), Yorick's skull also has the versatility to double as the true features underlying the painted face of a woman: 'to this fauour she must come' (3381–2). Echoing the well-known

'Death and the Maiden' motif, which Gertrude also elaborates with her metaphors of the grave as a marriage bed, the death's head is held up to female vanity as a compelling image of 'the skull beneath the skin'.[13]

We can see what is implicit in *Hamlet* more fully and extravagantly fleshed out in Middleton's *The Revenger's Tragedy*. Vindice addresses Gloriana's skull:

> Thou sallow picture of my poison'd love,
> My study's ornament, thou shell of death,
> Once the bright face of my betrothed lady,
> When life and beauty naturally fill'd out
> These ragged imperfections,
> When two heaven-pointed diamonds were set
> In those unsightly rings: then 'twas a face . . .[14]

The skull is both object and effigy, an empty 'shell of death' but also a 'picture' of Gloriana. It is both a decorative exhibit in the *memento mori* tradition ('my study's ornament') and the relic of a living body (indeed what Jeremy Bentham would have called an 'auto-icon'). As such it suggests both presence and absence, and Vindice reconstructs the life that 'fill'd out' its hollow bareness, the bright eyes that once adorned its 'unsightly rings', just as Hamlet, in Michael Neill's words, '(like a milder Vindice) immediately adorns [Yorick's] pate with the dress of memory'.[15] When Vindice passes off the skull as a living woman in order to poison the Duke, the grotesque simulation of vitality again draws attention to the true lifelessness of the remains:

[10] *Hamlet*, dir. Kenneth Branagh (Castle Rock, 1996).

[11] Roland Mushat Frye was among the first to define the tradition in 'Ladies, Gentlemen and Skulls: *Hamlet* and the Iconographic Traditions', *Shakespeare Quarterly*, 30 (1979), 15–28.

[12] These words are addressed of course to another previously exhumed and anonymous skull, not to Yorick's.

[13] T. S. Eliot, 'Whispers of Immortality', *Collected Poems 1909–1962* (London, 1963), p. 55. Modern technology can reconstruct the skin from the skull, the face from the facial bones.

[14] *The Revenger's Tragedy*, 1.1.14–20, in *Thomas Middleton: Five Plays*, ed. Bryan Loughrey and Neil Taylor (London, 1988).

[15] Michael Neill, *Issues of Death: Mortality and Identity in English Renaissance Tragedy* (Oxford, 1997), p. 235.

here's an eye
Able to tempt a great man – to serve God;
A pretty hanging lip, that has forgot now to
    dissemble,
Methinks this mouth should make a swearer
    tremble

(3.5.54–7)

Just as Hamlet is painfully conscious of the extreme contrast between his imaginative reconstruction of Yorick and the object itself – 'This?' – so Vindice also voices a similarly disgusted awareness of ironic discrepancy – 'For *thee*?':

Does the silkworm expend her yellow labours
For thee?

(3.5.71–2)

Both Hamlet and Vindice are playing out what Douglas Bruster called 'variations on a single rhetorical question concerning the lack of fit between the object at hand and a complex set of memories and truths separate from it'.[16]

They are also both to some degree adhering to the ancient *memento mori* tradition, and more specifically recuperating a century of the *Danse Macabre*, which travelled quickly from the walls of Les Innocents in Paris to St Paul's, and thence to the Guild Chapel in Stratford-upon-Avon, where it was observed by John Stowe, and noted in a manuscript addition to his copy of Leland's *Itinerary*, in 1576. It was there for the young Shakespeare to see, complete with a representation of 'a King Eaten by Worms', and an image showing a coffin or grave with a shrouded and vermiculated corpse; two skulls and three scattered bones; and two men positioned on either side, pointing to a *contemptus mundi* text.[17] The basic trope of the Dance of Death is to demonstrate the interlinking of life and death by showing skeletons of the dead seizing the living in indiscriminate rapture: young and old, rich and poor, men, women and children.[18] In the Stratford representation the figures of death are walking corpses, complete with skin but with grinning skull-like faces: often *Danse Macabre* images showed the living body both youthful and ageing, alongside the decomposing corpse and the unfleshed skeleton. Indeed when Hamlet and Laertes in the First Quarto text are wrestling in Ophelia's grave, their live bodies entangled with a newly dead corpse and with long-dead remains, the stage exhibits a classic *Danse Macabre* iconography.[19] Hamlet himself of course alludes to this tradition when he describes how 'a king may go a Progresse through the guts of a Begger' (2693), and in the graveyard scene talks of the 'fine Reuolution' (3280) which brings all flesh to one final resting place. Similar juxtapositions of the living, the corpse in deathbed or shroud, and the denuded skull, all linked into a continuous and unbroken cycle, appear in images such as *The Judd Marriage*, which shows the living couple touching hands on a skull, while below them lies a shrouded but uncovered corpse; or in John Souch's painting of *Sir Thomas Aston at the Deathbed of his Wife*, which shows the widower with hand on skull and his wife pictured twice, once living and once dead.[20]

---

[16] Douglas Bruster, 'The Dramatic Life of Objects', in Gil Harris and Natasha Korda, *Staged Properties in Early Modern English Drama* (Cambridge, 2002), p. 17.

[17] See Thomas Fisher, *A Series of Antient Allegorical, Historical, and Legendary Paintings Which Were Discovered in the Summer of 1804 on the Walls of the Chapel of the Trinity at Stratford upon Avon in Warwickshire*. Most of the plates are annotated as 'Drawn 1804 and published 20 April 1807'. Plates reproduced in Clifford Davidson, *The Guild Chapel Wall Paintings at Stratford-upon-Avon* (New York, 1988), pp. 10–11. Fisher did not see the dance of Death, which was exposed in 1955 and drawn by Wilfrid Puddephat: 'The Mural Paintings of the Dance of Death in the Guild Chapel of Stratford-upon-Avon', *Birmingham Archaeological Society Transactions*, 76 (1960). Drawing reproduced by Davidson, Plate 19.

[18] 'From sodaine death / Good Lorde deliuer us', 'The Letany', quoted from *A Booke of Christian Prayers, collected out of the auncient writers, etc.* (London, 1578, 1581), p. 127. In this popular manual known as *Queen Elizabeth's Prayer-Book* the Dance of Death riots in the margins of the text, so 'sodaine death' is amply illustrated by images of skeletons seizing the living, skulls, piles of bones and corpses.

[19] Carol Rutter describes the stage of Hamlet as filled with 'bodies presented in all stages of post-mortem recuperation, from ghost-walking Hamlet to fresh-bleeding Polonius to mouldering Yorick to Priam of deathless memory'. See Carol Chillington Rutter, *Enter the Body: Women and Representation on Shakespeare's Stage* (London, 2001), p. 28.

[20] Anonymous, *The Judd Marriage* (1560), Dulwich Picture Gallery; John Souch, *Sir Thomas Aston at the Deathbed of his Wife*, (1635), Manchester City Art Gallery.

But the point about Yorick's skull is that it is not a mere anonymized object readily available as a visual aid to generic satire, lamentation or *memento mori* (like the skull that lies on the floor, almost kicked aside, in the powerful 1544 portrait of Sir Thomas Gresham in the art collection of the Mercers' Company),[21] but an individualized skull, the recognizable remains of someone known and loved. As Andrew Sofer puts it, 'naming the skull transforms the scene. It is a moment of unmetaphoring in which the conventionalized figure of speech has suddenly become humanized.'[22] As such the skull occupies a liminal position (as in Hamlet's evocation of the living Yorick), between life and death, since it can still (unlike the anonymous bones of the skeleton) resemble, or be held to resemble, the living person whose life it formerly contained. Although the skull is composed of more than twenty-two separate bones they are in Gray's words 'almost immovably connected'.[23] Even in advanced decomposition the skull retains its unique rounded completeness and its capacity to retain facial features – such as cheekbones and teeth – that are identifying characteristics of the living face. The teeth are often a focus of attention in this context, not just because they provide the skull with a parodic human expression, but because they are in life an integral part of the expressive language of the face: the only part of the skeleton, in fact, not covered by soft tissue and therefore visible, and so contributory to the notorious similarity of the skull to a living head.

At the same time, with its hollow orbits, empty vomer and enigmatic grin a skull is disturbingly unlike any living face, except one very close to death. In short the human skull is a textbook representation of what Freud called the 'uncanny', which primarily consists in 'doubts whether an apparently animate being is really alive; or conversely whether a lifeless object might not in fact be animate'.[24] Examples given in Freud's essay are waxwork figures, dolls and automata.[25] Any representation involving such liminal ambiguity between life and death fits into the category of 'uncanny', such as the superb illustrations to Vesalius's *De Humani Corporis Fabrica* (1543), which show

a skeleton adopting various human postures: leaning on a shovel, possibly weeping with head in hands, even contemplating another skull. Ruth Richardson has described these as akin to 'X-rays', seeing in cross-section through the active living body to view its internal frame.[26] At the same time the figures recall irresistibly the sardonic skeletal jesters of the Dance of Death. The Hamlet-like skeleton with his hand on a skull which appears on sig. Kv1 is haunted by his living counterpart, as from the verso page the image of a man holding a skull clearly shows through (Vesalius, sig. Kv1).[27]

III

Skulls on stage are even more 'uncanny' because of what Sofer calls 'their disturbing ability to oscillate between subject and object' (Sofer, p. 90). In the *memento mori* tradition the skull is passive, a visual aid or object-lesson. In the *Danse Macabre*

---

21 Anonymous, *Sir Thomas Gresham* (1544), Mercers' Company. This was also a wedding portrait, since it bears an inscription 'AG [Anne Gresham] love, serve and obei TG'.

22 Andrew Sofer, *The Stage Life of Props* (Ann Arbor, 2003), p. 98.

23 Henry Gray, *Anatomy Descriptive and Surgical* (Bath, 2001), p. 19.

24 Sigmund Freud, *The Uncanny* (1919), trans. David McLintock (London, 2003), 135. The definitions are sometimes attributed to Freud, but he was quoting from a paper 'On the Psychology of the Uncanny' (1908) by Otto Jentsch.

25 'Uncanny' is obviously also a fitting description for artefacts constructed from human remains: Byron's drinking cup fashioned from a skull; the 'auto-icon' of Jeremy Bentham at University College, with its mummified head; or the 'plasticized' remains turned into sculptures in Gunter von Hagens's exhibition 'Body Worlds' ('The Anatomical Exhibition of Real Human Bodies').

26 'Did they seem to contemporaries as extraordinary as Roentgen's X-rays did in the 1890s?' 'The Skull Beneath the Skin', illustrated lecture in series *Facing Death*, National Portrait Gallery (January 2005). I am grateful to Dr Richardson for supplying me with her notes.

27 Vesalius saw himself as a kind of Resurrection Man *vis-à-vis* the science of anatomy, which in his view needed to be 'recalled from the dead'. See his preface '*To the Divine Charles V, the Mightiest and Most Unvanquished Emperor: Andreas Vesalius' PREFACE to his books On the Fabric of the Human Body*', Andreas Vesalius, *De Humani Corporis Fabrica* (Basel, 1543).

the death's head is alive and active among the living. When Hamlet spoke to Yorick's skull on the London stage around 1600, the dead object was given a role in the *dramatis personae*, transubstantiated into a living character, placed 'centre stage in the act of performance' (Sofer, p. 94). 'Once we focus on it, the skull decenters our own "objective" grasp of its stage symbolism and our presumption of autonomous gazing from outside the emblem's "frame"' (Sofer, p. 92). As in the disturbing fantasy of the ventriloquist's dummy that comes to life, once the actor begins to speak on the skull's behalf, he also begins to invest the skull with autonomous vitality. 'The object cannot speak' writes Scott Dudley, 'it has no agency of its own. If it is to signify at all, it can do so only as a subject makes it speak.'[28] This semiotic transference was wickedly parodied in the famous Morecombe and Wise *Hamlet* sketch, where the skull was routinely asked 'What do you think of it so far?' and replied (the comedian working its jaw and supplying the voice), 'Rubbish!'.[29]

In this respect the skull operates as a particularly compelling exemplar of 'the power of stage objects to take on a life of their own in performance' (Sofer, p. 2). On stage the distinctions between animate and inanimate objects, the live body of the actor and the physical property he manipulates, are quite different from those that pertain outside the theatre. Petr Bogatyrev of the Prague School of semioticians argues that as everything on stage signifies, then everything participates in a universal semioticity that occludes the difference between live and dead objects. All stage objects become 'signs of a sign of a material object',[30] at a double remove from the real.

Thus the 'function of the stage property duplicates that of the theatre itself: to bring dead images back to life' (Sofer, p. 3). Props in general are 'haunted mediums' that 'ventriloquize an offstage, absent subject' (Sofer, p. 27). But this capability of resurrection is dependent on the specific function of the prop in action. The stage skulls of *Hamlet* illustrate what Jiri Veltrusky called a 'fluid continuum between subjects and objects':[31] objects can be on stage and lie relatively inert, as the skulls

first lie when excavated by the gravedigger. They can be used as objects, in the way Hamlet uses them as *exempla* in his sardonic and macabre satire. But when props acquire an independent signifying force, as when Hamlet engages in conversation with Yorick's skull, then 'we perceive them as spontaneous subjects, equivalent to the figure of the actor' (Veltrusky, p. 84).

This parallels what de Grazia, Quilligan and Stallybrass find in seventeenth-century *Vanitas* paintings, where 'objects have evicted the subject'.[32] In one example the skull is described as sharing the inert passivity of all 'still life': 'The omnipresent skull serves as a reminder of the common materiality of subject and objects' (p. 1). But for all its stillness the skull retains traces of a former subjectivity, bears ineradicable reminders of its occupation by an immaterial human life, and thus stands out from other objects in the painting. Though the painting is empty of subjects, 'a memory of one remains – the *memento mori* or skull, now an object among objects' (de Grazia *et al.*, p. 1). Objectified it may have become, but still it had a tongue in it once and could sing. 'A skull', Michael Neill explains, 'is at once the most eloquent and empty of human signs. Simultaneously recalling and travestying the head which is the source of all meanings, the seat of all interpretation, the skull acts as a peculiar and sinisterly attractive mirror for the gazer, drawing endless narratives into itself only to cancel them' (Neill, pp. 234–5).

---

[28] Scott Dudley, 'Conferring with the Dead: Necrophilia and Nostalgia in the Seventeenth Century', *ELH*, 66 (1999), 285.

[29] For this and other parodies see Derek Longhurst, '"You base football player!": Shakespeare in contemporary popular culture', in *The Shakespeare Myth*, ed. Graham Holderness (Manchester, 1988), pp. 65–7.

[30] Petr Bogatyrev, 'Semiotics in the Folk Theatre', in *Semiotics of Art: Prague School Contributions*, ed. Ladislav Matejka and Irwin R. Titunick (Cambridge, MA, 1976), p. 34.

[31] Jiri Veltrusky, 'Man and Objects in the Theatre', in *Prague School Reader on Aesthetics, Literary Structure and Style*, ed. and trans. Paul L. Garvin (Washington, DC, 1964), p. 84.

[32] 'Introduction' to *Subject and Object in Renaissance Culture*, ed. M. de Grazia, Maureen Quilligan and Peter Stallybrass (Cambridge, 1996), p. 1.

Thus the skull already possesses an overcharged, dangerous capability even outside the semiotically saturated environment of the theatre. Hence its use on stage is multiply powerful. Nowhere is this more apparent than in the use for purposes of representation or performance of a real human skull. When Peter Hall was rehearsing *Hamlet* in 1975 he records the use of a real skull in rehearsal:[33]

We rehearsed the graveyard scene this morning with a real skull. The actuality of the scene was immediately apparent; actors, stage management, everybody aware of a dead man's skull among us.

When Polish pianist and composer Andre Tchaikovsky died in 1982, he 'bequeathed his skull to the Royal Shakespeare Company for use in *Hamlet*': 'Wrapped in a brown paper-parcel', Stanley Wells recounts, 'it arrived on the general manager's desk one morning along with the rest of the post.'[34] Pascale Aebischer records that in 1989 when Mark Rylance was rehearsing the role, he asked the props department 'whether it would be possible to use the real skull that was donated to the RSC as Yorick's skull'.[35] Rehearsal notes confirm that the company did use it, with a similar impact to that recorded by Peter Hall, but then stopped short of using it in performance, as noted by Mark Rylance's wife Claire von Kampen (quoted Aebischer, p. 86):

As a company we all felt most privileged to be able to work the Gravedigger scene with a real skull . . . However collectively as a group we agreed that as the real power of theatre lies in the complicity of illusion between actor and audience, it would be inappropriate to use a real skull during the performances . . .

There is also a suggestion that some 'primitive taboo' may have operated to inhibit the use of an identifiable actual skull as signifier of an identifiable fictional skull in a live theatrical performance. 'Because the property disturbingly kept its extrafictional and extratheatrical identity as the property of Andre Tchaikovsky the pianist, it resisted the company's attempts to appropriate it as an accessory' (Aebischer, p. 89). Tchaikovsky's skull was discarded, but a cast of it constructed for the produc-

tion. This conflict between Tchaikovsky's aspiration after posthumous celebrity ('Remember *me*!') and the company's determination to contain the unruly sign echoes the debates about ownership acted out in *Hamlet*. Who owns a dead body or an exhumed skull? Who owns a grave? Its previous occupants who are being turfed out to make room for more? The corpse for whom the grave has been re-dug? The gravedigger who has made it and claims artisanal property in it? The mourners who dispute its status or Hamlet and Laertes who leap in and compete for ownership of the grave and devotion to its intended occupant? In 1982 Tchaikovsky's family contested the terms of his will in the courts but lost their case. The judgement endorsed Tchaikovsky's right to will his remains and the RSC's right to appropriate them as a 'property'.[36]

But such attempts to appropriate the stage 'property' (that which 'belongs to', is appurtenant or appropriate to, the drama) in the case of the skull come up against what Martin Esslin calls 'involuntary semiosis': 'material objects on the stage or screen may contain signifiers that the originators of the performance (the designer, the director) did not intend to be perceived'.[37] Frances Teague quotes a definition of the theatrical prop as an

---

[33] *Peter Hall's Diaries: The Story of a Dramatic Battle*, ed. John Goodwin (London, 1983), p. 195.

[34] Stanley Wells, *Shakespeare For All Time* (London, 2000), p. 398.

[35] Pascale Aebischer, *Shakespeare's Violated Bodies: Stage and Screen Performance* (Cambridge, 2004), p. 86.

[36] Another fascinating case of disputed ownership of the skull occurred when Major Robert Lawrence received a serious head wound in the Falklands War in 1982. Medical staff took photographs of his brain through the wound and later used them in a presentation to demonstrate their surgical skills. Lawrence saw them for the first time when he attended a lecture on the achievements of battlefield surgery. He subsequently acquired and used them to a different purpose in his autobiographical account of the Falklands War, John Lawrence and Robert Lawrence, *When the Fighting is Over* (London, 1988).

[37] Martin Esslin, *The Field of Drama: How the Signs of Drama Create Meaning on Stage and Screen* (London, 1987), p. 46.

'unanchored physical object',[38] meaning that it
is literally free to be moved around the stage,
but suggesting also its semiotic indeterminacy and
instability: 'A property can carry multiple meanings, which may sometimes conflict' (pp. 16–17).
As Douglas Bruster puts it in language appropriate to Yorick's skull, such mobile material objects
lend themselves to a wide range of dramatic actions:
'they can be variously possessed, traded, lost, found,
concealed and evaluated' (Bruster, p. 17). The Victoria and Albert Museum has an early photogravure
of a skull prepared for teaching, probably in the
Royal College of Surgeons (some of the bones have
been removed). The skull must in reality have been
mounted, anchored, on a wooden plinth, but the
support has been removed from the print, so the
skull floats eerily, 'unanchored' in nebulous space.[39]
The image is profoundly 'uncanny', signifying in
ways never intended by the physicians who originally constructed and used the skull as a pedagogic
visual aid.

At least one other hopeful has followed
Tchaikovsky's lead and left the RSC a skull. This
was aspiring actor Jonathan Hartmann whose application to join the company had been routinely
rejected, and who obviously felt this was the only
way he would ever get onto the stage. He stipulated that when used, the skull should be credited
in the programme: 'the skull of Yorick is played
by the skull of Jonathan Hartmann'.[40] The outcome of this bequest remains to be seen. When
American comedy actor Del Close died in 1999
he bequeathed his skull to Chicago's Goodman
Theatre, which he had helped to found, so that
it 'may be used to play Yorick, or for any other
purposes the Goodman deems appropriate'. In this
case the theatre has embraced the gift, exhibiting
the skull in a glass case in the Artistic Director's
office, and using it as a static prop in at least one
production.[41] These bids for thespian immortality
are obviously testimony to the strength of actorly
ambition, as strong as death. But is it more than the
vanity of players? Even as an inert decorative object
the skull inevitably draws attention to itself. Placed
among other objects into a *Vanitas* painting or foregrounded on stage, its semiotic power is multiplied.

To the actor the opportunity of playing Yorick is
clearly irresistible, since the role brings the skull
into that liminal half-light between life and death
that the theatre so eloquently adumbrates. The skull
is neither object nor subject, neither person nor
actor, neither character nor role. It is speechless yet
expressive, blank but eloquent, empty yet replete
with signifying potency. What actor would not
wish to play, and be, such a skull? To survive into
theatrical immortality, to cheat death, to exist as a
dead subject among the living?

IV

These stories problematize the relationship
between the living and the dead; but there has
never been a time when that relationship was
unproblematic. Early modern social attitudes
towards death have been well charted in recent
years. Philippe Ariès[42] has traced the transition
from the ancient world, where the dead were
treated as impure and placed outside the city
(giving rise to the differentiation between 'polis'
and 'necropolis', cities of living and dead), to
the medieval Christian world where 'the dead
ceased to frighten the living, and the two groups
co-existed in the same places and behind the same
walls' (Ariès, p. 30). Via Christian faith in the
resurrection of the body and the practice of wor-
shipping ancient martyrs and their tombs (Ariès,
pp. 30–1), the taboo separation of living and dead
was eroded: tombs were built round cemeteries,
churches became 'surrounded and invaded by the

---

[38] Frances Teague, *Shakespeare's Speaking Properties* (Lewisburg,
1991), p. 15.
[39] See Mark Haworth-Booth, ed., *Things: A Spectrum of Photography 1850–2001* (London, 2005), pp. 34–5.
[40] See David Lister, 'Yorick, I'll play his skull!', *The Independent*,
1 March 1995.
[41] *Chicago Tribune*, 27 July 2004; *New Improv Page*, 14 January 2005. Available at www.fuzzyco.com/improv/archives/
000215.html [Accessed 25 October 2005]. By contrast the
replica skull used in Kenneth Branagh's film was presented
afterwards to Ken Dodd as a memento.
[42] Philippe Ariès, *The Hour of Our Death*, trans. Helen Weaver
(Paris, 1977).

dead' (Ariès, p. 34). Christians were 'gathered together within the sacred enclosure, completing the bond of association between the dead and the living' (Cressy, p. 465). In the Middle Ages the place of the dead is sanctified, not polluted, so consecration becomes a proper preparation of the ground to be blessed by their presence. Grave lots were dug over and over again, the bones extracted and placed in ossuaries. Hence as Ariès shows, the emergence of a distinction between 'cemetery', burial-plot and 'charnel', the ossuary where bones dug up to make room for new bodies were placed (pp. 54–5). After the fourteenth century charnel houses became places of exhibition (Ariès, p. 61). Charlemont in *The Atheist's Tragedy* describes the charnel house as a 'convocation-house for dead men's skulls'.[43]

Thus in the Middle Ages living and dead co-existed far more closely than in the ancient or the modern worlds. As Clare Gittings puts it, 'throughout the Middle Ages there was a far greater perception of continuity between the states of being alive and being dead than we feel today'.[44] Death was a transitional state: the dead waited for resurrection, and remained amenable to the touch of prayer. Purgatory was a liminal domain within which the dead remained communally bound to the living; or in Gittings's terms, 'The doctrine of purgatory ensured that the living and the dead were closely bound by ritual ties' (Gittings, p. 22).

The Reformation in England altered all this. The chantries fell silent, and the dead disappeared into a void. As Anthony Low puts it, the bereaved were abandoned to a silence when confronting the dead.[45] Theologically there was a sudden and disruptive shift from corporate to individual expectation of judgement and resurrection. Michael Neill writes, 'The protestant denial of Purgatory . . . suddenly placed the dead beyond the reach of their survivors . . . then death became a more absolute annihilation than ever' (Neill, p. 38). Eamon Duffy describes the reformed funeral service as 'an act of oblivion, a casting out of the dead from the community of the living into a collective anonymity'.[46] The loss of Purgatory 'affected . . . the social relationship between the living and the dead' (Cressy,

p. 386), enforcing a new degree of separation, with the consequence of severe psychological trauma.[47]

These changes in official doctrine affected popular emotions about the status of human remains. Ariès draws a distinction between two strands of historical belief: the view derived from Paracelsus and Jewish medicine, and to be found in some late seventeenth-century medical treatises, that the cadaver retained traces of life; and the view derived from Seneca and the ancient world, that soul and body were utterly separate. The latter was espoused by the orthodox Christian elite and became the view of modern science. At the beginning of the seventeenth century these questions were still clearly alive. Does life belong to the whole body or to its elements? Do human remains retain traces of vitality? In popular belief it was felt that bodies could still feel, hear, bleed at a murderer's touch. Could the skull of a dead person in some way bear the residue of that person's life? Can these bones live?

This takes us exactly to the point where Hamlet's communing with Yorick's skull serves as a textbook demonstration of these residual and emergent ideologies. Just as the skull itself is a liminal object, lying uncannily between life and death, so Hamlet's relationship with it lies between past and future, between Rome and Canterbury, between medieval and early modern views of death. From the new reformed perspective the skull is not only an empty shell, a discarded remnant of a vanished life, 'a

43 *The Atheists Tragedy, or the Honest Man's Revenge*, 4.3.73, in *The Plays of Cyril Tourneur* (Cambridge, 1978).

44 Clare Gittings, *Death, Burial and the Individual in Early Modern Britain* (London, 1984), p. 20.

45 Anthony Low, '*Hamlet* and the Ghost of Purgatory: Intimations of Killing the Father', *ELR*, 29 (1999), p. 463.

46 Eamon Duffy, *The Stripping of the Altars: Traditional Religion in England 1400–1580* (New Haven, 1992), p. 494.

47 The 'Protestant soul', Natalie Davies writes, was 'left with memories, unimpeded and untransformed by any ritual communication with the dead'. Natalie Davies, 'Ghosts, Kin and Progeny: Some Features of Family Life in Early Modern France', *Daedalus* (1977), 95. 'The denying of Purgatory thus caused grievous psychological damage: from that point forward the living were, in effect, distanced from the dead' (Llewellyn, p. 27).

thing – Of nothing' (2658–60), it is also unwhole-some, toxic, 'a pollutant that threatens hygiene' (Llewellyn, p. 16). If soul and body part absolutely and irrevocably at the moment of death, then the corporeal remains have no meaning or value, are merely garbage, to be concealed or destroyed as soon as possible. Autolysis, putrefaction, the return to dust: these are simply God's methods for dispos-ing of unwanted waste matter. Protestant polemicist John Polyander in *A Disputation Against the Adora-tion of Reliques* described human remains as 'the bones and garments of rotten bodies returned into ashes', 'rotten reliques of dead bodies', 'dust and putrefaction'.[48] In this sensibility the skull, evicted from its resting-place in grave or charnel, stink-ing of decay ('And smelt so? Puh', 3388) brings the alarming spectacle of what Ariès called 'wild death' into the hygienic domain of the living.

In conferring humanity on Yorick's skull how-ever Hamlet speaks from, perhaps even for, an older theology. In this context Yorick's skull is a relic, sanctified by the vanished presence of the life it contained, eloquent in its very deadness and hol-lowness of the absence that life has left behind. The skull is a memento, even a 'monument' to the memory of the dead. John Florio's English–Italian dictionary *A World of Words* (1598) identi-fied 'the rest that remains, the ashes of bones of the dead' with both 'Reliquia: a relic' and 'mon-ument'.[49] Through such relics, as Scott Dudley puts it, 'the past continues to live in the present' (Dudley, p. 282). 'We cannot really speak with the dead', affirms Jurgen Pieters, but 'through the texts and other relics they have left us', the possibility of some kind of 'communication or transaction' arises.[50] The mortal body remains in some myster-ious way blessed by the vanished presence of the life departed; and if Purgatory exists (as the Ghost of Old Hamlet affirms it does), then the skull is a link with the suffering spirit that still needs, and can still benefit from, our prayers. 'The continuing life of the soul, to which the relic refers, endows the relic itself with an ongoing life and potency' (Dudley, p. 282).

Karen Coddon is correct then to state in her essay on *The Revenger's Tragedy* and 'necrophilia'

that here 'the body of death is at least symbolically conflated with the body of desire'.[51] But to define this desire for the dead as 'necrophilia' is potentially misleading. Erich Fromm offers a typically modern psychoanalytic view of necrophilia in *The Anatomy of Human Destructiveness*:

[For the necrophile] . . . only the past is experienced as quite real, not the present or the future. What has been, i.e., what is dead, rules his life . . . the past is sacred, nothing new is valuable, drastic change is a crime against the 'natural' order.[52]

Fromm explains necrophilia as a symptomatic response to the loss of certainty and to destabil-ising change. But in his love for the dead, exempli-fied in his loyalty to the ghost and his affectionate recollections of Yorick, Hamlet is responding to a deeper rapprochement of loss and desire: desire for the dead that have gone before, the dead we have always with us; the loss we cannot repair for the dead we are obligated in perpetuity to mourn. And in attempting if only briefly to hold 'confer-ence with the dead',[53] Hamlet is also attesting to the enduring belief in their continuing existence.

Certainly this desire can participate in the dam-aging perversion of necrophilia, as graphically rep-resented in *The Revenger's Tragedy*, where tongu-ing the poisoned skull with the rough enthusiasm of a 'slobbering Dutchman', the Duke licks the toxin that will kill him, 'kiss his lips to death'. But Middleton is only exaggerating what Shake-speare made implicit in *Hamlet* a few years earlier:

---

[48] John Polyander, *A Disputation Against the Adoration of the Reliques of Saints departed* (Dordrecht, 1611), I. 54, 65.

[49] John Florio, *A Worlde of Wordes, or Most copious, and exact Dic-tionarie in Italian and English* (London, 1598).

[50] Jurgen Pieters, *Speaking with the Dead: Explorations in Literature and History* (Edinburgh, 2005), p. 130.

[51] Karen Coddon, '"For show or useless property": Necrophilia and *The Revengers Tragedy*', *ELH*, 61 (1994), 71.

[52] Eric Fromm, *The Anatomy of Human Destructiveness* (London, 1974), p. 339. Fromm echoes the commonsense views of both Claudius and Gertrude, who accuse Hamlet of exactly such disabling 'necrophilia': 'Do not for euer with thy veyled lids / Seeke for thy Noble Father in the dust' (250–1).

[53] John Webster, *The Duchess of Malfi*, 4.2.22, ed. Elizabeth Brennan (London, 1964).

that the relationship between the living and the dead is grounded in desire, a Lacanian desire generated by loss, absence, lack of the loved presence. In 1919 Freud stated flatly that 'the goal of all life is death'.[54] 'Life has only one meaning', said Lacan, 'that in which desire is borne by death' ('*le desir est porté par la mort*').[55] Foucault spoke of 'the Death that is at work in suffering, the Desire that has lost its object'.[56] All these formulations concur in the paradox coined by Jonathan Dollimore: 'Death itself is the impossible dynamic of desire'.[57] In this context the uncanny skull, with its unmistakable deadness and its disturbing similarity to the living being, performs a central and pivotal function and role.

V

As Ariès shows, while the ancients feared not being buried properly, Christians feared what might happen to the dead body to impede its resurrection in the flesh (Ariès, p. 31). Anxiety over proper ritual burial was replaced by anxiety over the future fortunes of the corpse. A typical early medieval prohibition was recorded in the thirteenth century by William Durandus:

May this sepulchre never at any time be violated, so that I may return to life *sine impedimentum* when He comes who is to judge the living and the dead.[58]

The famous inscription on Shakespeare's own grave in Holy Trinity Church Stratford echoes this old imprecation:

GOOD FREND FOR IESVS SAKE FORBEARE,
TO DIGG THE DVST ENCLOASED HEARE:
BLESTE BE YE MAN YT SPARES THES STONES,
AND CVRST BE HE YT MOVES MY BONES.

Here we find an old fear of the grave's violation indicating a somewhat Catholic concern for the fate of Shakespeare's remains. The concern, whoever conceived it, over possible violation of the grave proved not without foundation, as the remains have of course been the object of intense curiosity, even to the extent of regular concerted campaigns proposing their exhumation. The tomb has inevitably become a site of dispute over Shakespeare's identity: whether it contains a body at all, whose body it might be.

The motivation of those willing to transgress the tomb's exhortation and open the grave was to some extent articulated in the language of science. Their objective was either to confirm details of Shakespeare's appearance, so elusively recorded by the various extant portraits; or to prove that the grave's occupant (if it has one) is someone other than Shakespeare. These contradictory motives have enthused Stratfordians and anti-Stratfordians respectively: if the bones in the grave match the Droeshout engraving, then a link between man and work is established; if the grave were empty or otherwise occupied, this would fuel the mystery around theories of alternative authorship. Fantasies about finding manuscripts buried in the tomb are held in common: they might confirm once and for all Shakespeare's authorship, or they might be in someone else's handwriting. James Rigney finds in this tomb-raiding curiosity 'an archaeological concern to locate the authentic remains of the author and flesh them out in the lineaments of the artefact'.[59]

At the close of the nineteenth century there was a vigorous public debate about whether Shakespeare's tomb should or should not be opened. Supporters advocated exhumation as a means of testing the portraits, and even photographing the remains before their inevitable dissolution. 'Think of a photograph of Shakespeare', mused J. Parker

[54] Sigmund Freud, *Beyond the Pleasure Principle and Other Writings*, trans. John Reddick (London, 2003), p. 78.

[55] Jacques Lacan, 'La Direction de la cure', in *Ecrits* (Paris, 1966), p. 642.

[56] Michel Foucault, *The Order of Things: An Archaeology of the Human Sciences* (London, 1966), pp. 376, 387.

[57] Jonathan Dollimore, 'Desire is Death', in de Grazia, Quilligan and Stallybrass, *Subject and Object*, p. 373.

[58] Guilelmus Durandus, *Rationale Divinum Officiorum* (1286), 5: xiv; translated and cited Ariès, p. 32.

[59] James Rigney '"Worse than Malone or Sacrilege": The Exhumation of Shakespeare's Remains', *Critical Survey*, 9 (1997), 78.

Norris: '"in habit as he lived". Would not such a relic be of inestimable value to the world?'[60] Very old exhumed corpses have been found to retain their form and the garments they were buried in intact, though these corrupt quickly once exposed to air. But Norris echoes a description of the Ghost in *Hamlet* ('in his habite, as he liued', 2518). Shakespeare himself of course is reputed to have played the Ghost on stage, so it would be in keeping for his 'Canoniz'd bones Hearsed in death' to 'burst their cerments' (632–3) as he returns to resolve our questions. 'If we had but Shakespeare's skull before us', wrote Clement Ingleby, a Trustee of the Shakespeare Birthplace Trust, 'most of these questions would be set at rest for ever'.[61] Even the anticipated photograph of the remains would, in Norris's phrase, be a 'relic of inestimable value'.

Ingleby argued for disinterment, 'a respectful examination of the grave', on grounds of a legitimate 'desire, by exhumation, to set at rest a reasonable or important issue respecting the person of the deceased while he was yet a living man':[62]

Beyond question, the skull of Shakespeare, might we but discern in it anything like its condition at the time of interment, would be of still greater interest and value.

(29)

Ingleby's proposals were vilified as vandalism and sacrilege. Local Stratford dignitaries were clearly concerned about the Stratford monopoly on Shakespeare's remains: 'Photographs of Shakespeare's skull', complained Stratford councillor Alderman Gibbs, 'would, doubtless, have a large sale all over the world'.[63] J. O. Halliwell-Phillips argued that if the skull were found and compared to the Holy Trinity bust, any discrepancy would suggest that the skull could not be Shakespeare's. This would in turn confirm the earlier rumour that Shakespeare's skull had in reality been stolen from the grave, acquired by a 'Resurrection Man' and taken to America by phrenologist Johann Kaspar Spurzheim. A phrenological drawing, dated 1807 and attributed to Georges Cuvier, and which can be held to match the Chandos and Droeshout portraits, purports to have been taken from Shakespeare's skull. And who would pay 6d to view a tomb that had been proven not to contain the authentic skull of Shakespeare?

In any case, Gibbs asserted, the portraits of Shakespeare were obviously accurate, as they showed a man with a huge skull capable of containing the Shakespearean brain:

It is quite clear to all physiologists and phrenologists that the brain of Shakespeare must be enclosed in the skull of a fully developed man, the structure of whose head must be similar to that shown by the bust in the chancel.

(quoted Rigney, p. 86)

As Mary Thomas Crane has recently observed, 'Portraits of Shakespeare emphasize the large dome of his forehead, accentuated by a receding hairline; he must have had a brain'.[64] Gibbs may also have been aware of the story that John Milton's skull proved on exhumation to be disappointingly flat and low-browed, lacking the distinctive 'supraorbital development' marking the skulls of both Shakespeare and Sherlock Holmes as repositories of unusual brains. Recently Petrarch's grave has been opened and found to be occupied by the skull of a woman. Ironically this is exactly what happens in Belgrave Titmarsh's Victorian burlesque play *Shakspere's Skull and Falstaff's Nose*. The hero Dryasdustus, a Shakespeare scholar bent on proving Shakespeare's plays were written by his ancestor Dryasdust, hires grave-robbers to open Shakespeare's tomb. They find and produce the skull – 'His fame was crumbled into dust, / Except

---

[60] J. Parker Norris, 'Shall we open Shakespeare's Grave?', *Manhattan Illustrated Monthly Magazine*, 19 (July 1884), 73. Ingleby quotes Norris from the *American Bibliopolist* (April 1876): 'If we could get even a photograph of Shakespeare's skull it would be a great thing' (Ingleby, *Shakespeare's Bones*, p. 41).

[61] C. M. Ingleby, *Shakespeare's Bones: The Proposal to Disinter them Considered in Relation to their Possible Bearing on his Portraiture* (London, 1883), p. 34.

[62] Ingleby, *Shakespeare's Bones*, pp. 30, 2.

[63] Reported in the *Stratford upon Avon Herald*, 5 October 1883.

[64] Mary Thomas Crane, *Shakespeare's Brain: Reading with Cognitive Theory* (Princeton, 2000), p. 14. See also Sir Arthur Keith. 'Shakespeare's Skull and Brain', in *Tenements of Clay: An Anthology of Biographical Medical Essays*, ed. Arnold Sorsby (New York, 1975).

the skull' (Titmarsh, p. 23) – but it proves in reality to be 'feminine'. This displacement of the overdeveloped, high-browed skull of the cultural hero by an inferior specimen – that of a low-brow, or even a woman – represents the kind of risk to cultural stereotypes entailed in exhumation. Charles Dickens during an earlier exhumation campaign was grateful that the Stratford grave remained inviolate, that Shakespeare's tomb 'remained a fine mystery', and no bardic skull had been produced and exposed in 'the phrenological shop windows'.[65]

VI

These stories continually enact and re-enact a dialectic of desire and disappointment. Although by this stage articulated in modern scientific terms of phrenological mapping and photographic commemoration, this appetite for discovery remains recognisable as that familiar old hunger for the restoration of a lost presence, the necrophiliac desire for 'conference with the dead'. These Victorian scholars and enthusiasts coveted Shakespeare's skull with the reverence usually afforded to the relics of saints. Their aspiration to re-fit the authentic skull back into the portraits was not just to test the accuracy of portraiture, but to reassemble Shakespeare's fragmented parts into something resembling the living man. The prospect of finding in the grave not the true remains but a substitute, such as the skull of a woman, provoked in them profound anxieties of potential disappointment and disenchantment. Most chilling of all was the possibility of finding nothing: proof that no-one had ever been buried there or simply evidence of the inexorable universality of decay. As Clement Ingleby recorded, the latter was a distinct possibility:

I am informed, on the authority of a Free and Accepted Mason, that a Brother-Mason of his had explored the grave which purports to be Shakespeare's, and had found nothing in it but dust.

(31–2)

Dust to dust, as the common phrase reminds us. But the phrase comes from the Christian burial service, and there it precedes an affirmation of faith in some kind of return: 'in sure and certain hope of the Resurrection to eternal life'. Like Stephen Greenblatt we began with a desire to speak with the dead and equally we shall end with it. But not just to speak, since our desire for the dead encompasses also a desire for that fragile body with which the soul in its earthly life irrevocably and ineradicably interacted. Hence the 'almost imperceptible shift' noted by Ariès in early modern England and France from 'familiarity with the dead' to 'macabre eroticism' (Ariès, p. 376). If human remains, more strongly than any other personal memento or monument, could form a link between living and dead, then love for the departed must inevitably have gravitated towards those remains, and the remains themselves have become invested with an aura of divinity. The Eros in 'macabre eroticism' was not so much a perversion as a god. In Hamlet's attachment to Yorick's skull and in the Victorian scholars' coveting of Shakespeare's, we find a residual nostalgia for a historical culture in which the body was central. In Francis Barker's words,

The glorious cruelties of the Jacobean theatre articulate a mode of corporeality which is structural to its world . . . it represents a generalised condition under which the body, living or dead, is not that effaced residue which it is to become, beneath or behind the proper realm of discourse, but a materiality that is fully and unashamedly involved in the processes of domination and resistance which are the inner substance of social life.[66]

Modern science has by no means effaced this nostalgia. In surgical anatomy or in forensic science, human remains, though of course devoid of vitality, are nonetheless a source of knowledge: they speak to us. In popular TV dramas about criminal forensics, scientists are often shown talking to corpses or bones. This approach is not continuous with the

---

[65] *The Letters of Charles Dickens*, ed. Georgiana Hogarth and Mamie Dickens (London, 1893), p. 111.
[66] Francis Barker, *The Tremulous Private Body: Essays in Subjection* (London, 1984), p. 23.

ancient pagan or early modern Protestant horror of the dead as toxic pollutants, but instead converges with the medieval and early modern Catholic view of the dead as alive, speaking, still accessible to inquiry, prayer and love. 'Necrophilia', as Karen Coddon puts it, 'yokes together science and seduction' (Coddon, p. 71).

VII

The skull in the portrait of John Evelyn with which we began looks towards both past and future. It glances back through the *memento mori* tradition to the Roman banquets where a grinning skull exhorted revellers to *carpe diem*, enjoy the fugitive moment. But as an anatomical specimen it also looks forward to an era of scientific discovery and understanding. It acts as a salutary reminder of mortality and a prompt towards righteous living, but, in the context of Evelyn's marriage, it celebrates a strange union of love and death. The hollow skull echoes the vacancy that awaits all flesh; but also adumbrates in Jonathan Dollimore's words, 'the hollowing of life from within into desire as loss' (Dollimore, p. 381).

In much the same way Hamlet's commentary on Yorick's skull is both scientific and religious, both sceptical and reverential, both Protestant and Catholic.[67] Warned by Horatio against considering things 'to[o] curiously', Hamlet's 'Imagination' nonetheless follows the logic of decomposition to imagine Alexander the Great's dust 'stopping a bung-hole'. At the same time his rehabilitation of the skull into the garment of flesh testifies to a reverence for human remains as sanctified relics of the departed. Desire is born of death ('*Le desir est porté par la mort*', Lacan, *Ecrits*, p. 642); death is 'the impossible dynamic of desire' (Dollimore, 'Desire', p. 373). I covet your skull.

---

[67] See Mark S. Sweetnam, '*Hamlet* and the Reformation of the Eucharist', *Literature and Theology*, 21 (2007), 11–28.

MARTIN DROESHOUT *REDIVIVUS*: REASSESSING THE FOLIO ENGRAVING OF SHAKESPEARE

JUNE SCHLUETER

I

Among the most familiar portraits of Shakespeare is the engraving that graces the title-page of the 1623 First Folio of Shakespeare's plays (see illustration 40). Unlike other portraits purporting to be the playwright, the engraving should present no question of authenticity, for the publication date establishes its *terminus ab quo* and Ben Jonson's attendant verses lament the 'Sweet Swan of Avon' and note the figure 'was for gentle Shakespeare cut'. Nor is the engraver's name in question, for below the portrait is his signature: 'Martin Droeshout Sculpsit London'.

But there are two Martin Droeshouts in the records of early modern London, and the question of which of them engraved the famous title-page has not been settled. Was it the elder Martin, who was born in Brussels but spent much of his life in London? Or was it his nephew, who was born in London in 1601?[1] The London records mention the elder several times, identifying him as the son of John Droeshout, a painter, and brother of Michael, an engraver; he himself is called a painter. The younger is mentioned only once, upon his baptism; but there are several references to his father, Michael, and his older brother, John, who were both engravers.[2]

In 1991, following years of uncertainty and assumption, two articles provided new evidence on the Droeshouts. But the evidence was of two kinds, and the authors came to opposite conclusions: Mary Edmond contended that the elder Martin

was the likely engraver of Shakespeare;[3] Christiaan Schuckman believed it was the younger.[4]

Astonished that some thought a case could be made for the younger Martin, Edmond pointed out that 'there is absolutely no positive evidence that the younger Droeshout ever practiced as an engraver'; indeed, apart from the record of his baptism in London in April 1601, there was 'no positive documentary evidence about him at all'.[5] But there *are* London documents on the elder Martin and several speak to his profession. A 1608 grant of denization identifies the elder Martin as a painter of Brabant.[6] The 1617 Registers of the

---

Individual notes acknowledge the help I received with particular aspects of this essay. More generally, I am grateful to my husband, Paul Schlueter, and to the Skillman Library staff at Lafayette College for their research assistance.

[1] The elder Martin also had a son named Martin; born in 1607, he would have been 16 when the First Folio was published. No one has suggested him as a candidate.

[2] Examples of the work of Michael and John may be found in Arthur M. Hind, *Engraving in England in the Sixteenth and Seventeenth Centuries: A Descriptive Catalogue with Introductions, Part II: The Reign of James I* (Cambridge, 1955), Plates 108–10, 249, 113 and 213.

[3] Mary Edmond, '"It was for gentle Shakespeare cut"', *Shakespeare Quarterly*, 42 (1991), pp. 339–44.

[4] Christiaan Schuckman, 'The Engraver of the First *Folio* Portrait of William Shakespeare', *Print Quarterly*, 8 (1991), pp. 40–3.

[5] Edmond, '"It was for gentle Shakespeare cut"', p. 339.

[6] *Calendar of State Papers, Domestic Series, of the Reign of James I, 1603–1610, Preserved in the State Paper Department of Her Majesty's*

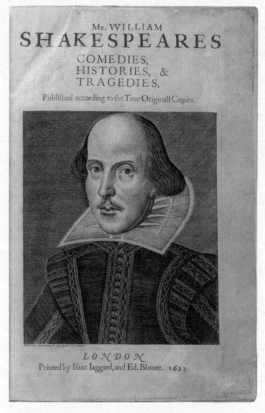

Mᵣ. WILLIAM
SHAKESPEARES
COMEDIES,
HISTORIES, &
TRAGEDIES.
Published according to the True Originall Copies.

LONDON
Printed by Isaac Iaggard, and Ed. Blount. 1623.

40. Droeshout engraving of Shakespeare on the title-page of
the 1623 First Folio, signed in London.

search of the London records, however, and her
sure identification of the elder Martin as a painter,
her comment about the younger Martin also holds
for the elder: 'there is absolutely no positive evidence that the [elder] Droeshout ever practiced as
an engraver'.

Schuckman's essay is as provocative as Edmond's,
for it announces his discovery of ten Martin
Droeshout engravings in the Biblioteca Nacional,
Madrid. All are signed, and nine are dated 1635–40
or appear in books published in Madrid during
those years; on four, the Droeshout signature
indicates, in the same hand, the place where
the engraving was done: 'en Madrid'. Schuckman particularly notes an (undated) engraving of
Francisco de la Peña, done in Madrid, that bears

Austin Friars Dutch Church in London place the
elder Martin, his wife Janneken, and six children in
Crossed (or Crutched) Friars and identify him as a
painter.[7] The elder Martin is in the 1617 inventory of 'handycraftmen' members of the Dutch
Church living within the City; he is said to have
dwelled there for 33 years and is listed as a denizen,
a poor householder and a painter.[8] A 1635 reference identifies him as a 'limner', born in Brussels
and living here (in the Parish of St Olave, Aldgate
Ward) 30 years.[9] Moreover, just before publishing
her essay on the Droeshout engraving, Edmond
uncovered a record that identifies the elder Martin
as a freeman of the Painter-Stainers' Company.[10]
And she provides archival evidence that a member
of the Painter-Stainers' Company could well have
practiced engraving.[11] Despite Edmond's assiduous

Public Record Office, ed. Mary Anne Everett Green (Nendeln,
Liechtenstein, 1967), p. 397.

7 *Returns of Aliens Dwelling in the City and Suburbs of London*,
The Publications of The Huguenot Society of London 10, Part 3,
ed. R. E. G. Kirk and Ernest F. Kirk (Aberdeen, 1907), p. 179,
citing Dutch Church Registers, vol. 10, no. 47.

8 *Returns of Aliens Dwelling in the City and Suburbs of London*,
The Publications of The Huguenot Society of London 10, Part 3,
ed. Kirk and Kirk, p. 146, citing Dutch Church Registers,
vol. 10, no. 12, and vol. 1, no. 40.

9 Irene Scouloudi, *Returns of Strangers in the Metropolis 1593,
1627, 1635, 1639: A Study of an Active Minority*, Quarto Series
of the Huguenot Society of London 57 (1985), p. 278, citing
State Papers Domestic, MS 16/305/II.ii. Edmond corrects
Scouloudi's assumption that the '30 years' refers to the elder
Martin's time in England rather than in Aldgate Ward (p. 341,
note 13).

10 Edmond, '"It was for gentle Shakespeare cut"', pp. 340 and
340, note 3, citing Guildhall MS 5667/1: 'at a meeting on 19
September 1634, "Mr Marcus Garrett", "Mr Drossett", and
another man, acting as "Assistants in the Search", reported on
some very bad workmanship they had inspected'.

11 Edmond, '"It was for gentle Shakespeare cut"', p. 340.
Records of Antwerp's St Luke's Guild confirm such variety of membership in the painters' company there, as well as
the preparation of many of the company's members in several
trades. Crispyn vande(n) Broeck, for example, a student of
Frans Floris, named in 1555–6, was a painter, designer and
engraver. And Carel Liefrinck, identified as a painter in the
1556–7 membership list, was both a painter and a copper
engraver. See Jan van der Stock, *Printing Images in Antwerp:
The Introduction of Printmaking in a City, Fifteenth Century to
1585*, trans. Beverley Jackson (Rotterdam, 1998), Appendix 1.

41. Droeshout engraving of Francisco de la Peña, signed in Madrid (undated).

signatures on the 25 extant London works make a convincing case for a single engraver, whose (dated extant) work began in London with the 1623 Folio and concluded in Madrid in 1639 or 1640.[14] Throughout his analysis, Schuckman assumes that both the London and the Madrid engravings were the work of the younger Martin. Inexplicably, he never admits the possibility that the single engraver could have been the elder.

Key to the resolution of which Martin did the portraits, title-pages and book illustrations that bear the engraver's signature is the question of which Martin emigrated to Spain – or accepted

a strong stylistic resemblance to the Shakespeare portrait (see illustration 41).[12] He also examines the signatures, noting their variety. Five use a full or nearly full version of the name (three of these use a monogram that entwines the 'DR' of the surname and/or the 'MAR' of the first name), and five use an abbreviated form (all with a monogram that entwines the 'DR' of the surname and/or the 'MAR' of the first name, with the 'DR' monogram standing as the surname). Moreover, those that employ the fuller version reveal an intriguing change of name: from 'Droeshout' to 'Droeswood' or 'Droeswoode', 'wood' being the English equivalent of the Dutch 'hout'.[13] For Schuckman, the 1623 Folio signature, the only one using the full name 'Martin Droeshout', offers one more example of such variety. His comments on artistic style and his observation that variety also typifies the

---

12 Schuckman, 'The Engraver of the First *Folio* Portrait of William Shakespeare', pp. 40–1 (fig. 25).

13 The cryptic signature has resulted in cataloging difficulties. Elena Páez Rios, in *Iconografia Hispana, Catálogo de los Retratos de Personajes Españoles de la Biblioteca Nacional*, vols. 2–5 (Madrid, 1966–70), uses 'Woode, Marten R. D.' in the index and variously transcribes the signature on the four engraved portraits as 'MRtin de Roswood', 'M AR. D. B. R. (Marten de Rooswod or Woode)', 'Martin RD.', and 'Marten RD Woode'. In *Repertorio de Grabados Españoles en la Biblioteca Nacional*, vols. 1 and 3 (Madrid, 1981–3), she uses 'Woode, Marten R.', with 'Droeswoode, Martin' and 'Roswood, Martin' as crosslistings. Here and in *Iconografia Hispana*, she corrects a misattribution of the portrait of Juan Perez de Montalbán, signed 'Marteen R D' (actually 'Martin' followed by the 'DR' monogram), to Martin Rodriguez. (In identifying the ten Madrid engravings, Schuckman relies on the Páez Rios catalogues.) Although one can only guess at why the younger Martin anglicized his name, his reason could have been political. Jonathan I. Israel, in 'The Politics of International Trade Rivalry during the Thirty Years War: Gabriel de Roy and Olivares' Mercantilist Projects, 1621–1645', *The International History Review*, 8 (November 1986), pp. 517–49, offers this description of Spanish–Dutch relations prior to (and continuing through) the years Droeshout was in Spain: 'By the later years of the Twelve Years Truce (1609–21), the Dutch were seen in Madrid not just as rebels and heretics but as subverters of the world economic order and colonial system' (p. 517).

14 Schuckman is cautious about extending the date to 1640, but the engraved title-page for *Conjuracion del Conde Juan Luis Fiesco Escrita*[,] *en lengua Toscana por Agustin Mascardi*[,] *Traducida en Castellano por Don Antonio Velazquez*[,] *Dedicada Al muy noble y muy ilustre Señor Don Joseph Strata Cavallero de la Orden de Sant-Iago Commendador de las Casas de Toledo y Señor de la Villa de Robledo de Chavela y Sus aldeas* does bear that date, with title, 'Año 1640', and Droeshout's signature in the same hand.

a commission there. Schuckman assumes it was the nephew, proposing that the younger Martin emigrated between 1632 (the date of the last known London engraving) and 1635 (the date of the first known Madrid engraving). But Schuckman only glances at the London records and he does not acknowledge Edmond's observations about the elder Martin. For although she was unaware of the Madrid engravings at the time of her argument, Edmond points out that London's printed Calendar of State Papers for 1635 omits the elder Martin from a list of artists living there.[15] And she observes that the only post-1635 London record that may be positively identified with the elder Martin dates from 1641, when his name appears in the Dutch Church Registers in connection with his youngest child's admission to that congregation: '1641, Dec. 26. Daniel Droessaert with testimony of his father, Maerten Drossaert'.[16] Hence the elder Martin could have been away from London from 1635 to 1639 or 1640.

But the case for the elder Martin's absence from London during these years is problematic, for despite the omission of his name from the printed Calendar, it does appear in the 1635 return of aliens. The census entry, under 'Aldgate, 12 Nov 1635, St. Olaves, Hartstreet', reads: 'Martin Drussett Lymner borne in Bruzills and Jane his wife borne in Antwerpe have lyved heere 30 yeares have six children all borne heere'.[17] The elder Martin's residence in London as late as November 1635 makes it unlikely that he was the engraver of the coat of arms of Gaspar de Guzmán Olivares in Tractatus Absolutissimus de Triplis . . . , by Antonio Cabreros Avendaño,[18] and the portrait of Juan de Avila in Vida de . . . Juan de Avila, by Luis Muñoz,[19] both published in Madrid in 1635. Moreover, another document, which Edmond does not notice, indicates that the elder Martin was in London in 1638. On Friday, 6 July [=16, N.S.] 1638, in London, Martin Droeshoudt, along with Timotheus van Vleteren (minister of the Dutch Church from 1628–32 – 'dienaer der Nederduytsche gemeente') and Henric Pauwels (a painter, also of Dutch origin), signed a declaration concerning a legacy of Wessel Boots to his children.[20] If we can infer

from the body of work that Droeshout's presence in Spain was sustained rather than occasional, then the elder Martin could not have been the Madrid engraver.

The case for the elder Martin weakens further when one considers the subject matter of the Madrid engravings. As Schuckman observes, the engraver's earliest (extant) commission in Spain was the coat of arms of Gaspar de Guzmán, Count-Duke of Olivares, 'a staunch supporter of the Spanish Counter-Reformation'.[21] Other Droeshout engravings depict Catholic saints and Counter-Reformation iconography; among the most explicit is the illustration that follows the title-page of Novissimus Librorum Prohibitorum et Expurganatorum Index showing the Church as Warrior stamping out Heresy, Error and Temerity.[22] Schuckman concludes that the engraver advocated

15 Edmond, '"It was for gentle Shakespeare cut"', p. 341, citing Calendar of State Papers, Domestic Series, of the Reign of Charles I, 1635, 591–4.
16 Edmond, '"It was for gentle Shakespeare cut"', p. 342, citing Lionel Cust, 'Foreign Artists of the Reformed Religion Working in London from about 1560 to 1660', Proceedings of the Huguenot Society of London, 1901–4, p. 62.
17 SP 16/305/II.ii/C.
18 The full title is Tractatus Absolutissimus de Triplis, Seu Eorum Poena, ad Elucidationem l. 18. tit. 5. lib. 9. Recop. Tum novitate præclarissimus, cùm singularitate maxima præditus, & tá praxi difficilis discussionis, quàm juris enucleatione creperus, sed utilitate maximus, & omnibus adprimé necessarius. Ex utriusque litteraturae fulcris compactus, by Don Antonio Cabreros Avendaño Madridensi I.C. Exc^mo Olivarum Comiti Dicatus.
19 The full title is Vida y virtudes del venerable varón el P. Maestro Juan de Avila, predicator apostólico, con algunos elogios de las virtudes y vidas de algunos de sus más principales discípulos, by Luis Muñoz.
20 The entry is transcribed in Epistulae et Tractatus: Cum Reformations Tum Ecclesiae Londino-Batava, ed. Joannes Henricus Hessels (Cambridge, 1897), p. 1769. Edmond notices a 28 February 1640/1 record – 'Mr Drosset made A motion about his Sonn' – a reference too vague to be helpful (Edmond, '"It was for gentle Shakespeare cut"', p. 342, citing Guildhall MS 5667/1, 155).
21 Schuckman, 'The Engraver of the First Folio Portrait of William Shakespeare', p. 42. Guzmán was also a patron of artists, including Velázquez, who painted Guzmán on horseback, c. 1635, and a portrait of Guzmán, 1638.
22 The full title is Novissimus Librorum Prohibitorum et Expurgandorum Index. Pro Catholicis Hispaniarum Regnis, Philippi IIII.

Catholicism and 'clearly became a Catholic',[23] a suggestion consistent with the absence of any mention of the younger Martin, beyond the baptism, in the records of London's Dutch Church. By contrast, the elder Martin's name appears repeatedly in those records, from 1592 through 1641, tracing his own admission to the congregation, his two marriages, the baptisms of his seven children and the admission of three of his children. There are miscellaneous references as well, and the 1638 declaration that the elder Martin signed was also signed by the Dutch Church minister. Although it is risky to make assumptions about the religious and political sympathies of an artist based on a work of art, so sustained a record of the elder Martin's commitment to the Protestant faith renders problematic any proposal that it was he who did the decidedly Catholic, Counter-Reformation engravings in Madrid.

But might *both* Martins have been responsible for the body of engravings that bear the Droeshout signature? Might the elder have done the London engravings, including that of Shakespeare, and the younger those in Spain? Despite the absence of evidence (beyond the engravings themselves) that *either* Martin was an engraver, isn't it possible that *both* were? While the proposal has its attractions, the chronology of the work argues against it. For although the elder Martin had lived in London for decades before the First Folio was published, there are no known Droeshout engravings before 1623.[24] Moreover, although there are some two dozen London engravings, with dates ranging from 1623 to 1632, there are no known London engravings after 1632; the next known engravings appeared in Madrid in 1635.[25] The chronology points to a single engraver.

Droeshout's penchant for the monogram is also suggestive, for the London engravings, like those from Madrid, entwine the 'MA' or the 'MAR' of Martin, the 'DR' of Droeshout, or the initials 'MD'. As with the Madrid engravings, the London work also reflects variation in the spelling of 'Martin'/'Marten' and three different lettering styles for the initial 'M': roman, italic, and swash. Most compelling is the strong similarity between two signa-

tures, one from London – indeed, the Shakespeare engraving – and one from Madrid. A comparison of the full name signatures on the title-page of the 1623 Folio (London, 1623) and the title-page of *Politica Militar en Avisos de Generales* (Madrid, 1638) (see illustration 42) leaves little doubt that the signatures are in the same hand.

The scenario, then, that chronology, style, signatures and the subject matter of the Madrid engravings urge – and that is supported by the London records – is the one that Schuckman assumes: the younger Martin, born in London in 1601, began his

---

Reg. Cath. Ann. 1640. See Schuckman, 'The Engraver of the First *Folio* Portrait of William Shakespeare', p. 43 (fig. 28).

23 Schuckman, 'The Engraver of the First *Folio* Portrait of William Shakespeare', pp. 42, 40. (Schuckman discusses a 1624 record of a Martin Droeshout's having been admitted to the Dutch Church in London. Uncertain whether the reference is to the elder or the younger Martin, he speculates about Catholic sympathies. The reference, however, is almost certainly to the third Martin, son of the elder Martin.)

24 Two comments are appropriate here. First, Malcolm Jones, 'English Broadsides – I', *Print Quarterly*, 18 (2001), pp. 149–63, suggests the possibility that Droeshout's portrait of William Fairfax and his *Saints* might be from 1621 or 1622 (p. 152). In addition, Jones publishes, for the first time, a later state of a 1623 Droeshout engraving entitled *The Spiritual Warfare* (pp. 153 (fig. 142), 154, 157–8), available in the Bruce Peal Special Collections of the Library of the University of Alberta, Edmonton, Canada, Wing S5002A. Jones's research suggests that the 22-year-old may already have been an established engraver when he did the Folio Shakespeare. Second, the unsigned title-page engraving in the 1615 edition of Helkiah Crooke's *Makrokosmographica* includes two flanking figures that are similar to those in the 1631 title-page engraving that bears Droeshout's monogram, but there is no reason to conclude that Droeshout did the earlier engraving. For as the sub-titles of both editions indicate, the illustrations were collected by Crooke from the 'best authors of anatomy', especially Gasper Bauhinus and Andreas Laurentius. A review of anatomy books reveals that similar illustrations, including those on the 1615 title-page, appeared earlier in Juan Valverde de Amusco, *Historia de la composicion del cuerpo humano* (Rome, 1556). I am grateful to William Schupbach, Iconographic Collections Curator at the Wellcome Library, London, for his help in identifying sources.

25 Jones, 'English Broadsides – I', offers a solid argument for affixing a 1635 date to Droeshout's *Four Seasons*, which would make this his last London commission before his departure for Spain (pp. 152, 154).

42. (top) Signature on the engraved title-page of the First Folio (London, 1623) and (bottom) Signature on the engraved title-page of *Politica Militar en Avisos de Generales* (Madrid, 1638) ('Sculpsit' is squeezed to avoid the edge of the plinth).

career as an engraver at age twenty-two (possibly a year earlier – see note 24). He did at least twenty-four engravings in London, with dates ranging from 1623 to 1632. Sometime between 1632 and 1635 (probably 1635 – see note 25), he went to Madrid, where he did work dated, or published, 1635–40. My research has uncovered additional engravings from Madrid, including one that puta-tively, though problematically, extends the younger Martin's presence there to 1644.[26] But except for that one engraving, which is a cut-out version of one published in 1638, we lose track of the younger Martin after 1640 and, a year later, of the elder Martin as well.

When I began my research on the two Martin Droeshouts, I was hoping that I would be able to confirm Edmond's argument for the elder Martin, for in addressing the question of which Martin did the 1623 Folio engraving, Edmond has been assiduous in finding and assessing archival records. Indeed, even when she wrote the entry on Martin Droeshout for the Grove *Dictionary of Art* in 1996 and the *Oxford Dictionary of National Biography* in 2004,[27] she did not yield to Schuckman's assumption that it was the younger Martin who was in Madrid. Nor should she have, for it is only with the range of documents now before us that the case for the younger Martin finds compelling support.

Archival research is an incremental process, and it is possible that the future will yield additional documents – in Madrid, London, Belgium, New Spain, or elsewhere. But given the constraints on the case for the elder Martin, it is likely that any further new evidence will only strengthen the con-clusion that the signature on the 1623 engraving of Shakespeare belongs to the twenty-two-year-old Martin Droeshout.

II

Before closing this discussion of the Folio engraver, I would like to present additional new evidence

---

[26] The document is an 80-stanza poem by the Portuguese-born writer Manuel de Faria i Sousa, Cavallero d' la Orden de Christo, entitled *Nenia En el fallecimiento del Excelentissimo Señor Dõ Joseph Lopez Pacheco i Acuña Côde de S. Estevã de Gormaz i Marques de Moya, Hijo Unico del Gran Marques de Villena, Duque de Escalona el Excelentissimo Señor Don Diego Lopez Pacheco i Acuña. Dedicada a S. Excelécia.* It is a nenia, or funeral song, for Diego Lopez Pacheco's only son, who died in 1643. (The father, Gran Marques de Villena and Duque de Escalona, served as Viceroy of New Spain, in Mexico, from 1640–2.) Of particular interest is the title-page, which presents an engraved architectural monument with square piers on either side, the central compartment containing the title, the two faces of the plinths, the authorial attribution, followed by 'Madrid 1644'. The engraved signature – 'Martin Droeswoode sculp-sit' – appears at the foot in the niche between the plinths. Unfortunately, although the (red ink) inscriptions in the cen-tral compartment and the top and side cartouches are partic-ular to the 1644 document, the design and the Droeswoode signature are not; they also appear in *Politica Militar en Avi-sos de Generales*, by Francisco Manuel de Melo, dated Madrid 1638. The manuscript is in the Biblioteca Nacional, Buenos Aires. For their help with this document, I thank Erin Blake, Curator of Art and Special Collections, Folger Shakespeare Library; Eric Luhrs, Digital Initiatives Librarian, Lafayette College; and Francisco A. Marcos-Marin, Professor of Span-ish, The University of Texas at San Antonio, who kindly examined the document for me when he was in Buenos Aires. Other Droeshout engravings, which Schuckman does not notice, are an elaborate title-page for *Segunda parte de las exce-lencias de Dios, su Madre, y sus Santos. Por Fr Pedro de Tevar Aldana Padre de la Provincia de Castilla de la regular Obseru-ancia. De los Frayles Menores Predicador del Rey N. Sʳ. Califi-cador del Consejo de la general Inquisicion natural de la ciudad de los Reyes*, published in Madrid in 1639, and an illustration in *Primera parte de la vida del V. y Rmo. P. M.Fr. Simon de Roxas . . . del Orden de la Santissima Trinidad de Redemptores*, by Francisco de Arcos, signed in Madrid and published there in 1670. Both books are in the Biblioteca Nacional, Madrid, but Páez Rios

concerning the Droeshouts. Until now, it was thought that John and Mary Droeshout emigrated from Brussels to England *c.* 1569 and that their two sons, Michael and Martin, were born in the 1560s, before their parents' departure.[28] The assumption may be attributed not only to several references in the London records indicating that Michael and Martin were born in Brussels but also to a troublesome transcript of an entry in the 1593 return of aliens stating that John and Mary Droeshout had been in England twenty-four years. It is not hard to see how Edmond and others, relying on these records, assigned the Droeshout emigration to *c.* 1569.

Nor is it difficult to see how Edmond deduced that 'John and Mary had six children, Michael and Martin born in Brussels in the late 1560s and two sons and two daughters born in London between circa 1574 and 1589'.[29] The relevant portion of Irene Scouloudi's 1985 transcript of the 1593 return reads: 'DRUSSAIT, JOHN and Mary, his wife, householders, 2; born in Brussels (Brisle); painter; two sons of 19 and 15, two daughters of 12 and 4 years, all English-born . . .'[30] If the four children referenced in the 1593 return were all born in England and Michael and Martin were born in Brussels, then John and Mary must have had six children.

But Belgian documents tell a different story. The Brussels archive has yielded a marriage record for the senior Droeshouts and a baptismal record for their son Martin. John and Mary were married in Brussels in 1572/3; the elder Martin was baptized in Brussels in 1573/4. Both events took place in the Onze-Lieve-Vrouw van de Kapel (the Church of Our Lady). The record for the senior Droeshouts reads: 'Jan Droeshout, Maijken De Looze gudilana 13 jan. 1572 stijlo brab'[31] (see illustration 43). The baptismal record for the elder Martin reads: 'die septima baptizatus est Martinus filius Jões [Joannes] Droessaert; susceptor Martinus De Loose et Gertrudis Clemens' (the seventh [of January] Martin Droeshout, son of John Droeshout, is baptized; godparents Martin De Looze and Gertrude Clemens) (see illustration 44).[32] Moreover, the 1593 London return does

not state that the four Droeshout children were 'all English-born', as Scouloudi reports. That column of the return actually reads:

2 sonnes one 19 another
15 & 2 daughters one 12
4 borne in England[33]

The four-year old was, indeed, born in England, but the others were not.

includes neither in her listing of Woode engravings in *Repertoria de Grabados Españoles*.

27 *The Dictionary of Art*, ed. Jane Turner, vol. 9 (New York, 1996), p. 299; *Oxford Dictionary of National Biography*, ed. H. C. G. Matthew and Brian Harrison, vol. 16 (Oxford, 2004), p. 935.

28 See, for example, Edmond, '"It was for gentle Shakespeare cut"', p. 341, and Hind, *Engraving in England in the Sixteenth and Seventeenth Centuries: A Descriptive Catalogue with Introductions, Part II: The Reign of James I*, p. 341. (Edmond points to several errors in Hind's account of the Droeshout family. Indeed, there are several more. Although Hind's work on engraving in England is magisterial, his narrative on the Droeshout family needs to be read with caution.)

29 Edmond, '"It was for gentle Shakespeare cut"', p. 341.

30 Scouloudi, *Returns of Strangers in the Metropolis 1593, 1627, 1635, 1639: A Study of an Active Minority*, *Quarto Series of the Huguenot Society of London* 57, p. 173.

31 The item appears in 'Transcriptum Registrum Matrimonialis Ecclesiae Parochialis B. Mariae V. de Capella', which lists marriage licenses issued from Christmas 1572 ('Sponsalia contracta a Festo Nativitatis 1572 stijlo Brab'). By local custom, the couple would have married soon after – in late January or February 1572/3 ('gudilana' may refer to Maijken De Looze's place of origin or, possibly, to her membership in the Church of St Gudule).

32 Paul de Clerck, amateur genealogist and a volunteer at the Rijksarchief Leuven, has been immensely helpful in my research on the Droeshouts in Belgium. It was he who uncovered the marriage record and referred my further query to Henri De Greef, who located the baptismal record. The Rijksarchief Leuven is the repository for Brussels church records; it also holds LDS-microfilms of the parish and civil records of the old province of Brabant: Brussels, Flemish Brabant, and Walloon Brabant. I am also grateful to de Clerck for reviewing my transcripts of Flemish hand.

33 I am grateful to D. J. Pohl of The Huguenot Library, London, for photocopies taken from the microfilm of the manuscript on file there. The 1593 return of aliens is part of the Dugdale MS at Merevale Hall; it is bound in vols. 3 and 4 of the manuscript of *The History of Warwickshire*, by Sir William Dugdale.

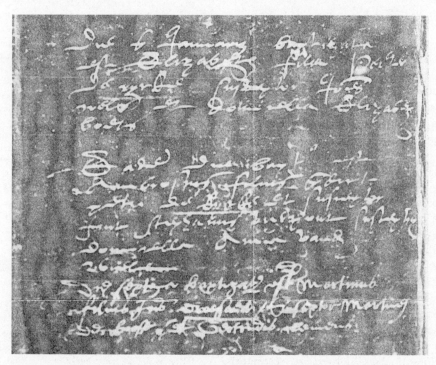

43. Marriage record for John and Mary Droeshout.

44. Baptism record for the elder Martin Droeshout.

Clearly, the assumption that John and Mary emigrated to London in or about 1569 needs amending, as does the consequent assumption that there were six Droeshout children. There were, in fact, other Droeshouts from Brussels who arrived in London in the late 1560s – Hans (John) and Hendrick, both joiners[34] – and it may be that English commissioners mistakenly incorporated material from the 1569 record for John and Margaret Droeshout into the 1593 entry for John and Mary Droeshout. In any event, there is no known record of John Droeshout in London prior to 1583, when he is listed, as a Dutchman and a painter, in an inventory of strangers in Broad Street Ward.[35] John's name first appears with Mary's in 1585, when the two were admitted to the Dutch Church congregation.[36] The first reference to the family in London is a 4 November 1587 Lay Subsidy indicating that John and Mary, their two sons, and a daughter were living in Broad Street Ward.[37] Hence it is safe to assign a 1583–4 arrival to the Droeshout family.

A 1583–4 arrival date is consistent with the 1617 Dutch Church Registers, which state that the elder Martin had 'dwelled heere' for thirty-three years and Michael for twenty-nine. The four-year disparity may be explained by an entry in the 1593 return, which reads: 'Mychaell Drowshot . . . born in Brussell in Brabant, but dyd remayne sumtyme in Andwarpe, sometyme in Fryzeland, and sometyme in Zeland, and from thence came hyther. A graver in Copper, which he learned in Brussell.'[38] One could read the entry to mean that Michael came to London with his family. But it is more likely that he came to London a few years after his family in c. 1583–4 and, sometime after 1587, returned to the continent to learn copper engraving. Another 1593 entry, described as a 'duplicate return', states that Michael has been '3 years in the realm'.[39] If both the 1617 record ('twenty-nine years') and the 1593 record ('three years') are accurate, then it would appear that between 1587 and 1593, Michael was on the continent for three or four years.

It should be noted that the Brussels baptismal record for the elder Martin is consistent with the age of the elder son in the 1593 London return:

born in 1574, Martin would have been nineteen when the census was taken. Moreover, a London

34 See Edmond, '"It was for gentle Shakespeare cut"', p. 341. In fact, the 1568 records include only the two joiners: 'Henry de Drossart, denison, joyner, his wif, and ij children; John de Drossart, his brother; they go to the Dutche churche' (1568 return of aliens and Lansdowne MS, vol. 203); also, 'Hendrick de Drossaert' and 'Hans de Drossaert' (Lansdowne MS 10, ff. 123, 124, no. 30) (*Returns of Aliens Dwelling in the City and Suburbs of London, The Publications of The Huguenot Society of London* 10, ed. Kirk and Kirk, Part 3, p. 367, and Part 1, p. 385). The 1571 return of aliens also includes entries for 'John Drussett, joyner, borne in Brussett, in England and in the said warde [Saynt Fosters Paryshe] v yeares'; 'Margarett Drussett, his wife, borne in Cleveland, in England iiij[or] yeares, and in the said ward a quarter of a yeare' (*Returns of Aliens Dwelling in the City and Suburbs of London, The Publications of The Huguenot Society of London* 10, ed. Kirk and Kirk, Part 1, p. 412); and 'Henricke de Drossart, of Bruxells, joyner, came about iiij[or] yeres past for religion, Jacounbia his wif, Peter, Henry, and Maudlyn, his children, and Mary his servant' (*Returns of Aliens Dwelling in the City and Suburbs of London, The Publications of The Huguenot Society of London* 10, ed. Kirk and Kirk, Part 2, p. 132). Judging from records of their widows's remarriages, John died before 1577 and Henry before 1585.

35 *Returns of Aliens Dwelling in the City and Suburbs of London, The Publications of The Huguenot Society of London* 10, ed. Kirk and Kirk, Part 2, p. 318, citing Cecil Manuscripts 210/14.

36 November 1585 (*Returns of Aliens Dwelling in the City and Suburbs of London, The Publications of The Huguenot Society of London* 10, ed. Kirk and Kirk, Part 2, p. 387). Cust transcribes the particular record: '1585, Aug. 28. Jan Droeshout et uxor Malcken [sic – Maicken] with attestation fr. Brussels' (p. 62).

37 Edmond, '"It was for gentle Shakespeare cut"', p. 341, citing *Returns of Aliens Dwelling in the City and Suburbs of London, The Publications of The Huguenot Society of London* 10, ed. Kirk and Kirk, Part 2, p. 405, citing Lay Subsidies, London, 145/253. The record erroneously lists the middle child as Phillipp rather than Michael: 'John Drowsar, and his wiffe, Martyn, Phillipp, and Jane Drowsar, his three children' (*Returns of Aliens Dwelling in the City and Suburbs of London, The Publications of The Huguenot Society of London* 10, ed. Kirk and Kirk, part 2, p. 405).

38 *The Life, Diary, and Correspondence of Sir William Dugdale*, ed. William Hamper (London, 1828), p. 511; *Returns of Aliens Dwelling in the City and Suburbs of London, The Publications of The Huguenot Society of London* 10, ed. Kirk and Kirk, part 3 Additions, p. 444.

39 *Returns of Aliens Dwelling in the City and Suburbs of London, The Publications of The Huguenot Society of London* 10, ed. Kirk and Kirk, part 3, p. 146, citing Dutch Church Registers, vol. 10, no. 12; and *Returns of Aliens Dwelling in the City and Suburbs of London, The Publications of The Huguenot Society of London*

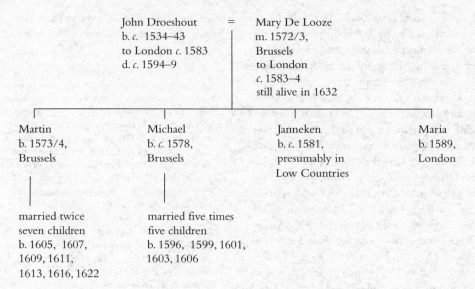

John Droeshout b. *c.* 1534–43 to London *c.* 1583 d. *c.* 1594–9	=	Mary De Looze m. 1572/3, Brussels to London *c.* 1583–4 still alive in 1632	

Martin b. 1573/4, Brussels	Michael b. *c.* 1578, Brussels	Janneken b. *c.* 1581, presumably in Low Countries	Maria b. 1589, London
married twice seven children b. 1605, 1607, 1609, 1611, 1613, 1616, 1622	married five times five children b. 1596, 1599, 1601, 1603, 1606		

baptismal record for Maria, Martin's younger sister, places her birth at 1589, making her the four-year-old. The other two children, then, would be Michael, until now thought the eldest, born *c.* 1578 (age fifteen), and a sister, Janneken, born *c.* 1581 (age twelve).[40] In listing the ages of the children, the 1593 entry provides information that is indispensable in establishing the composition and chronology of the Droeshout family.

To summarize: the convergent records in Brussels and London yield this amended configuration of John and Mary Droeshout's family: married in Brussels in 1572/3, John and Mary emigrated to London *c.* 1583–4; the couple had four children: Martin, born 1573/4 in Brussels; Michael, born *c.* 1578 in Brussels; Janneken, born *c.* 1581 on the continent (almost certainly in the Low Countries); and Maria, born 1589 in London.

I also have additional information on John, the elder Martin's father. Although John and Mary married in Brussels in 1572/3, the senior Droeshout had roots in Antwerp. Indeed, it was in Antwerp that he learned his craft: records of the Antwerp St. Luke's Guild for 1554 include the young Hans (John) Droeshout as an apprentice to the painter Michael Coecke (born *c.* 1527),[41] son of Pieter Coecke van Aelst (1502–50), dean (in 1537) of the Guild and court painter to Charles V.

I have information on the younger Martin's two brothers as well. John (1599–1651/2), an engraver, was made a free Brother of the newly formed Clockmakers' Company in 1632; in 1637, he took an apprentice, Daniel Jolly; he paid his membership fee ('quarterage') until 1647[42] and (as Edmond notes) died in 1651/2. His younger brother, William (b. 1603), may have been associated with the tapestry works at Mortlake (southwest of London), a manufactory staffed by

---

10, ed. Kirk and Kirk, part 3, p. 160, citing Dutch Church Registers, book 10, no. 40.

40 Maria's baptism is recorded in the Dutch Church Registers in London, but her older sister's is not, leaving the birthplace of the Droeshouts's third child uncertain.

41 See *De Liggeren en Andere Historische Archieven der Antwerpsche Sint Lucasgilde/Les Liggeren et Autres Archives Historiques de la Guild Anversoise de Saint Luc*, transcribed and annotated by Ph. Rombouts and Th. Van Lerius (Antwerpen/Anvers, 1872), p. 188.

42 Brian Loomes, *The Early Clockmakers of Great Britain* (London, 1981), p. 199. Loomes explains that the Company's earliest members, of necessity, were 'Brothers' rather than 'Freemen', the latter a title reserved for those who did their apprenticeships with the Company. As a Brother (who assumed the title 'free Brother', as did others), John was not able to take an apprentice on his own; when he apprenticed Jolly in 1637, he did so through Oswald Durant, who attained Freeman status in 1636/7.

Flemish weavers, royally chartered in 1619 and active until 1703. A 'Wilhelm De Drossate' appears on a 5 April 1640 list of members of the Dutch Church of London residing at Mortlake, but with a note indicating that he had left: 'Wilhelm De Drossate vertrocken'. And William stood godfather at a baptism at Mortlake in 1629.[43] A later Mortlake record, dated 1678, mentions a 'Martinus Driesvolt'. That year, a petition signed by Francis Poyntz at Mortlake asked the King and Council 'to consider the position of some Roman Catholic tapicers under the anti-Catholic law. These had been brought over by royal encouragement in setting up the tapestry manufacture

there is no known record of this marriage, as there is for the other four, the Lay Subsidies of 1598 and 1600 for Aldgate Ward, Duke's Place, list Dominick as Michael's wife. The records indicate the following sequence of events: in 1595, Michael married Susanneken; in 1596, a son, John, was born; by 1598, Michael had married Dominick; in 1599, a son, John, was born. The recording of Dominick's name as Michael's wife and the naming of Michael's two sons 'John' suggest that the first John died; indeed, Michael, who was only seventeen when he married Susanneken, may have faced the death of both his firstborn and (in childbirth?) his wife.

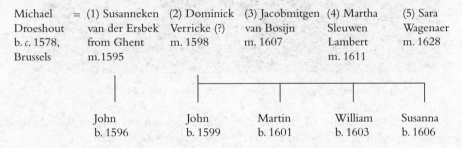

| Michael Droeshout b. *c.* 1578, Brussels | = | (1) Susanneken van der Ersbek from Ghent m.1595 | (2) Dominick Verricke (?) m. 1598 | (3) Jacobmitgen van Bosijn m. 1607 | (4) Martha Sleuwen Lambert m. 1611 | (5) Sara Wagenaer m. 1628 |

| John b. 1596 | John b. 1599 | Martin b. 1601 | William b. 1603 | Susanna b. 1606 |

here, and would be obliged by the proclamation, unless relief were granted, to leave the country'.[44] The reference is most likely to a next generation Droeshout, the nephew (William's son or Martin's) named in John's 1651/2 will. (Interestingly, Edmond reads the fact that a nephew was the only named blood relative as an indication that the younger Martin had either died or left the country.)[45]

Finally, I should say a word about the younger Martin's mother, for until now it has been assumed that she was Michael's first wife. In describing the younger Martin, S. Schoenbaum states that he was the 'son of Michael Droeshout and his wife Susannah van der Ersbek'.[46] Similarly, Edmond states that Michael married four times and that 'by the first wife, Susanneken van der Ersbek from Ghent, . . . he had four children'.[47] But it is almost certain that the mother of Michael's four surviving children was Dominick Verricke (the spelling is uncertain, given the illegibility of the handwriting). For although

The appended Chronology abstracts the records of the Droeshout family from 1572/3 to Michael's death in 1638 and provides several items from

---

43 The Mortlake lists for 1640, 1655 and 1663 are published in W. G. Thomson, *Tapestry Weaving in England from the Earliest Times to the End of the Eighteenth Century* (London and New York, 1914), pp. 96, 98. In an e-mail communication, Wendy Hefford of the Victoria and Albert Museum advised that in Thomson the list headed '1655' begins with the membership list of 1640, which was derived from records of the 1620s and 1630s. I am grateful to Hefford for the record of the baptism: on 1 March 1629, William stood godfather to Elizabeth, daughter of Hendrick de Bock (Guildhall MS 7382).

44 Thomson, *Tapestry Weaving in England from the Earliest Times to the End of the Eighteenth Century*, p. 105. Thomson cites a 1672 date, which Hefford corrects in 'Flemish Tapestry Weavers in England: 1550–1775', in *Flemish Tapestry Weavers Abroad: Emigration and the Founding of Manufactories in Europe*, ed. Guy Delmarcel (Leuven, 2002), p. 59.

45 Edmond, '"It was for gentle Shakespeare cut"', p. 342.

46 S. Schoenbaum, *Shakespeare's Lives* (Oxford and New York, 1970), p. 10.

47 Edmond, '"It was for gentle Shakespeare cut"', p. 342.

45. Watercolour signed by Martin Droeshout, from album of Michael van Meer, 1614–15.

the 1640s and later. While many of the dates reference records already published by Cust, Kirk and Kirk, Scouloudi, Edmond and others,[48] the new evidence presented in this essay both extends and revises that base of information.

III

As Edmond's research shows, the London records clearly establish the elder Martin's profession as a painter. Until now, however, there have been no examples of his work. Recently, I examined an *album amicorum* belonging to Michael van Meer, a northern European who had origins in Antwerp, lived most of his life in Hamburg, and spent a year-and-a-half in London in 1614–15, where he obtained signatures of English royalty, noblemen, and others.[49] The album contains numerous coats of arms and watercolor illustrations, including a painting of Ceres, Bacchus, and Venus (with Cupid) on a monumental pedestal engraved with the message 'SINE CERERE ET BACCHO FRIGET VENUS' (Without food and wine, love grows cold,

fo. 475v), a familiar trope in early modern European art[50] (see illustration 45). On the base of the pedestal is the contributor's signature: '1615 MARTIN DROESHOVDT'.

But which Martin Droeshout contributed the painting of the classical gods to the van Meer album? Here, there is little doubt that it was the

---

[48] Those not cited in the notes to this essay are: *The Marriage, Baptismal, and Burial Registers, 1571 to 1874, and Monumental Inscriptions, of the Dutch Reformed Church, Austin Friars, London,* ed. William John Charles Moens (Lymington, 1884); *Lists of Foreign Protestants, and Aliens, Resident in England 1618–1688,* ed. Wm. Durrant Cooper (London, 1862); *A Calendar of the Marriage Allegations in the Registry of the Bishop of London: 1597–1648,* vol. I, ed. R. M. Glencross (London, 1937); and *The Inhabitants of London in 1638. Edited from* MS 272 *in the Lambeth Palace Library,* vol. I, ed. T. C. Dale (London, 1931).

[49] See June Schlueter, 'Michael van Meer's *Album Amicorum,* with Illustrations of London, 1614–15', *Huntington Library Quarterly,* 69 (2006), pp. 301–13. The van Meer album is at Edinburgh University, La.III.283.

[50] See Konrad Renger, 'Sine Cerere et Baccho friget Venus', *Gentse Bijdragen tot de Kunstgeschiedenis en Oudheidkunde,* 24 (1976–8), pp. 190–203. The motto appears elsewhere in the van Meer album as well (fo. 501).

elder. For below the carefully executed painting is the signatory's dedication to the album owner, which reads: 'Dits ter gedachtenisse van den erewerdigen ende Eedelen ende goeden vrint Michell van Mere' (This is in remembrance of my venerable and noble and good friend Michael van Meer).[51] The mature, fluent (though less than exemplary) hand and the styling of van Meer as a 'good friend' make it likely that van Meer offered the uncle, not the fourteen-year-old nephew, a page in his album. Moreover, though inscribed in London, the dedication is in Flemish, which also points to the elder Martin, for this was the language of his and van Meer's birthplace; preferring it over English would have been an earnest of friendship, evoking, as it did, their common origin in Brabant.

The watercolour further secures the elder Martin's membership in the community of artists in London; and it offers the first pictorial evidence of his identity as a painter in colour. (In 1991, Edmond observed that 'Martin Droeshout is entered as "limner" in the aliens' return of 1635, although, so far as we know, he did not paint miniatures'.)[52] Though the elder Martin is no longer a candidate for the engraving of Shakespeare, this painting, along with the references to him as a painter, renews, and encourages research into, E. A. J. Honigmann's proposal that the elder Martin did the painting that formed the basis for the Shakespeare engraving.[53]

APPENDIX: A DROESHOUT FAMILY CHRONOLOGY

- Brackets indicate that the date is inferred from, but not specified in, archival records.
- Unless otherwise specified, 'Martin' refers to the elder Martin.

1570s

1572/3   Jan (John) and Maÿken (Mary) Droeshout marry in Brussels (13 January)
1573/4   Martin baptized in Brussels (7 January)
[1578]   Michael born in Brussels

1580s

[1581]   Janneken, Martin's sister, born [on continent]
[1583]   John arrives in England
[1583–4]   John's family arrives in England
1585   John and Mary admitted to Dutch Church
1587   John and Mary listed in Lay Subsidies, Broad Street Ward, St Peter le Poor and All Hallows, London Wall Parishes, three children
1588   John listed in Dutch Church Registers as householder
1589   Maria, Martin's sister, born in London
[c. 1589–90]   Michael returns to continent, learns copper engraving in Brussels

1590s

1592   Martin (age 18) admitted to Dutch Church
[1593]   Michael returns to London
1593   John and Mary listed in return of aliens, March through May, householders, two sons and two daughters

---

51 I am grateful to Paul Franssen and Lia van Gemert of the University of Utrecht for reviewing my transcript of the Flemish dedication.

52 Edmond, '"It was for gentle Shakespeare cut"', p. 340. It is conceivable that the elder Martin was the painter(/friend) van Meer commissioned to do other London paintings in his album.

53 E. A. J. Honigmann, 'Shakespeare and London's Immigrant Community Circa 1600', in *Elizabethan and Modern Studies Presented to Professor Willem Schrickx on the Occasion of His Retirement*, ed. J. P. Vander Motten (Gent, 1985), p. 147. Also see Edmond, '"It was for gentle Shakespeare cut"', p. 344. Edmond points to London records linking the elder Martin, Marcus Gheeraerts II, John Taylor and John Droeshout (the elder Martin's nephew), all members of the Painter-Stainers' Company, and proposes that Gheeraerts may have done the lost painting. I would add that the 1593 return of aliens lists, on the same page as the senior John Droeshout, Cornelius Johnson, probably the father of the Cornelius Johnson (1593–1661) once thought to be the painter of the 'Janssen' portrait of Shakespeare.

1593 Michael listed in return of aliens, March through May, chamber keeper, Broad Street Ward

1594 John, Mary, and Martin (age 20) listed among Dutch Church Members, Aldgate Ward, Duke's Place

[1594–9] John dies

1595 Michael (age 17) admitted to Dutch Church

1595 Michael (age 17) marries first wife, Susanneken van der Ersbek of Ghent

1596 John, Michael's first child, baptized (the child must have died young – see 1599 below)

1598 Michael and second wife, Dominick Verricke (?), listed in Lay Subsidies, Aldgate Ward, Duke's Place

1598–9 Mary, John's widow, and son listed in Lay Subsidies, Aldgate Ward, Duke's Place

1599 John, Michael's second child, baptized

1599 Michael and wife listed in Lay Subsidies, Aldgate Ward, Duke's Place

1600s

1600 Mary, John's widow, and son listed in Lay Subsidies, Aldgate Ward, Duke's Place

1600 Michael and second wife, Dominick, listed in Lay Subsidies, Aldgate Ward, Duke's Place

1601 Martin, Michael's third child, baptized ('the younger Martin')

1602 Martin (age 28) marries first wife, Anna Winterbeke of Brussels (widow of Hans Sele of Rouen)

1603 William, Michael's fourth child, baptized

1603 Janneken, Martin's sister (age 22), marries Guillame Beijart

1604 Martin (age 30) marries second wife, Jannekens Molijns of Antwerp

[1605] Martin and wife living in Aldgate Ward, Parish of St Olave, Crossed (Crutched) Friars

1605 Johaneken, Martin's first child, baptized

1606 Susanna, Michael's fifth child, baptized

1607 Martin, Martin's second child, baptized

1607 Michael (age 29) marries third wife, Jacobmijntgen van Bosijn, widow of Daniel Blommaert

1608 Martin granted denization

1609 Maria, Martin's third child, baptized

1610s

1611 Michael (age 33) marries fourth wife, Martha Sleuwen Lambert, widow of Jan Lambert

1611 David, Martin's fourth child, baptized

1613 Hester, Martin's fifth child, baptized

1616 Anna, Martin's sixth child, baptized

1616 Maria, Martin's sister (age 27), marries Dierick Wessels of Swol

1617 Martin listed in Dutch Church Registers (English and Dutch versions) among painters within the city; from Brussels, denizen, six children, has lived here 33 years

1617 Michael listed in Dutch Church Registers (English and Dutch versions) among goldsmiths, silversmiths, jewellers, and diamond cutters; from Brussels, three children, has lived here 29 years

1617 or 18 Martin listed in Dutch Church Registers among handycraftmen within the walls of the city, Crossed (Crutched) Friars, painter, wife Janneken, six children born here

1617 or 18 Michael listed in Dutch Church Registers among handycraftmen in the suburbs of London, St Martin, silversmith, wife Martha, three children born here, has lived here 30 years

1617 Michael (age 39) made free of the Goldsmiths' Company

1618 Martin listed in certificate of strangers, Aldgate Ward

1618	Michael listed in certificate of strangers, Aldersgate Ward

1620s

1621	Martin and wife listed in Lay Subsidies, Aldgate Ward, St Olave's, Hart Street
1622	Daniel, Martin's seventh child, baptized (Martin age 48)
1623	Engraving of Shakespeare published in First Folio
1624	Martin, Martin's son (age 17), admitted to Dutch Church
1624	Maria, Martin's daughter (age 15), admitted to Dutch Church
1627	John, Michael's son (age 28), secures license to marry Anne Ward
1628	Michael (age 50), widower, marries fifth wife, Sara Wagenaer, widow of Jacob Sele (Jaques Selam) of Antwerp
1629	William, Michael's son (age 26), stands godfather for Elizabeth, daughter of Hendrick de Bock, at Mortlake
1629–32	Additional signed, dated London engravings

1630s

1632	Mary, John's widow, mentioned in letter from Simon Ruijtinck, former Dutch Church minister, whose books were packed up in her house
1632	John, Michael's son, made a free Brother of the Clockmakers' Company
[1632–5]	The younger Martin goes to Madrid
1634	Martin's name, along with that of Marcus Gheeraerts II, appears in first Court Minute Book of Painter-Stainers' Company
1635	Martin and wife Jane listed in return of aliens, Aldgate Ward, St Olave's, Hart Street, six children born here; described as limner

1635–44	Signed, dated Madrid engravings
1637	John, Michael's son, takes an apprentice, Daniel Jolly, in the Clockmakers's Company
1638	Martin, with Timotheus van Vleteren (former minister of Dutch Church) and Henric Pauwels, signs declaration concerning a legacy of Wessel Boots to his children
1638	Michael listed as householder, Aldersgate Ward, St Leonard's, Foster Lane
1638	Michael dies

1640s

1640	Anne, wife of John, Michael's son, dies
1640	William, Michael's son (age 37), listed among members of the Dutch Congregation of London at Mortlake, but having left
1640/1	'Mr Drosset made A motion about his Sonn' (which 'Mr Drosset' is unclear)
1640	Last known Madrid engraving
1641	Daniel, Martin's son (age 19), admitted to Dutch Church
1647	John, Michael's son, pays final quarter-age to Clockmakers's Company

1650s

1651/2	John, Michael's son (age 52), 'Of St Bride's, Fleet St., London, Ingraver', dies; wife Elizabeth proves will 18 March; neither brother (Martin or William) is mentioned in will; only blood relative named is a nephew Martin

1670s

1678	a Martinus Driesvolt is mentioned in petition from Mortlake regarding Roman Catholic tapicers (possibly the nephew named in John's 1651/2 will)

CANONIZING SHAKESPEARE: *THE PASSIONATE PILGRIM, ENGLAND'S HELICON* AND THE QUESTION OF AUTHENTICITY

JAMES P. BEDNARZ

. . . and finding you . . . so carefull and industrious . . . to doe the author all the rights of the presse, I could not choose but gratulate your honest indeavours with this short remembrance.

Thomas Heywood to Nicholas Okes[1]

The concept of a Shakespeare Apocrypha assumes an absolute distinction between authentic and fake versions of his plays and poems, since its very existence is predicated on the idea of a Shakespeare Canon against which it is defined. But Shakespeare scholars have come to realize in line with a New Textualism that the dream of an absolutely fixed canon, the guiding principle of the New Bibliography, is illusory. We will never have Shakespeare verbatim. Although the texts of *Venus and Adonis* and *Lucrece* are clearly authoritative, even a cursory glance at the three versions of *Hamlet* reveals the impossibility of constructing an authentic edition. Compounding this difficulty, inferior early editions of Shakespearian texts – the 'bad' quartos – can occasionally include wording that appears to be more genuine than that found in comparably better copy. A current heightened awareness of the historical conditions under which Shakespeare's work was written and disseminated through manuscript, print and performance has prompted a re-examination of how these modes of production have shaped and continue to shape what 'Shakespeare' means.

One of the results of this investigation has been a critical re-estimation of William Jaggard's motives in publishing *The Passionate Pilgrim* that challenges Swinburne's memorable characterization of him in 1894 as 'an infamous pirate, liar, and thief' whose collection was a 'worthless little volume of stolen and mutilated poetry'.[2] One of the strangest twists in Elizabethan literary history is the fact that Jaggard, one of the principal publishers of the Shakespeare First Folio (1623), should also earlier have produced a collection of twenty poems called *The Passionate Pilgrim* (in two editions between September of 1598 and 1599; expanded in 1612), with a title-page attribution to 'W. Shakespeare', even though probably only five of these lyrics (1, 2, 3, 5 and 16) are his.[3] Since definitive attributions cannot be established for 4, 6, 9 and 12, and even viable counter-attributions have never been offered for 7, 10, 13, 14, 15 and 18, *The Passionate Pilgrim* has come to occupy a strange position in the Shakespeare canon as a mixture of the authentic and fake. No credible scholar believes that Shakespeare wrote all twenty poems in the volume,

---

[1] Thomas Heywood, 'Epistle' to the printer Nicholas Okes, *An Apology for Actors* (London, 1612), G4r.

[2] Quoted from Algernon Charles Swinburne, *Studies in Prose and Poetry* (London, 1894), p. 90.

[3] Joseph Quincy Adams, in the introduction to his facsimile version of *The Passionate Pilgrim* (New York, 1939), conclusively proved that the Folger Library fragments, sigs. A3–A7, without a title-page, were part of an earlier edition than that preserved in the Trinity College and Huntington Libraries. Since the collection's printer T. Hudson set up his shop in September of 1598, it is possible, then, that the Folger fragments might have been printed in the final months of that year, if not in 1599.

but questions remain as to how much of it is his and to what extent Jaggard was aware that some of his poems were not authentic.

I

Late twentieth-century editions of Shakespeare's collected works illustrate the current ambiguous status of Jaggard's collection. No major editor includes the expanded version of 1612, but G. Blakemore Evans prints all twenty poems as a set from the 1599 octavo, Stanley Wells and Gary Taylor present only a selection, out of context, as occasional poems (if they do not duplicate lyrics already in their collection and cannot be proven to have been written by someone else), and David Bevington excludes them entirely.[4] Having been integrated into John Benson's collection of the *Poems* in 1640, these lyrics were in the past routinely printed as Shakespeare's until the nineteenth century, even though, by 1656, Abraham Cowley had already complained of those stationers who, 'like *Vintners* with sophisticate mixtures, spoil the whole vessel of wine, to make it yield more *profit*'. 'This has been the case with *Shakespear, Fletcher, Jonson* and many others', he observes, 'part of whose Poems I should take the boldness to prune and lop away, if the care of replanting them in print did belong to me.'[5] Cowley might have been particularly disturbed by Benson's decision not only to print *The Passionate Pilgrim* but to use as his copy text the third edition of 1612, which included nine long translations from Ovid by Thomas Heywood. 'To modern historians', Adrian Johns observes, 'it often appears that the introduction of printing led to an augmentation of certainty', although to 'contemporaries, the link between print and knowledge seemed far less secure.'[6]

Even though some current critics, such as David Kastan, have forgivingly contextualized Jaggard's behaviour in printing *The Passionate Pilgrim* under Shakespeare's name as 'the kind of irregular, opportunistic practice that most stationers had on occasion engaged in', others have attempted, wrongly I believe, to vindicate Jaggard completely from Swinburne's charge that he had deliberately perpetuated an act of literary fraud when he published a mix of authentic and inauthentic poems under Shakespeare's name.[7] Joseph Loewenstein's study of *The Passionate Pilgrim*, for instance, exemplifies an exaggerated emphasis on Jaggard's innocence. 'It might be argued in Jaggard's defense', Loewenstein writes, 'that a Jacobean stationer's "Shakespeare" might be very nearly generic'.[8] There are, however, serious problems with this re-conceptualization based on the generic meaning of 'W. Shakespeare', and one is the absence of either this name or the epithet 'Shakespearian' to characterize other writers in either the Elizabethan or Jacobean periods. When Nathaniel Butter blazoned the playwright's name across the title-page of *M. William Shakspeare: His Chronicle Historie of the life and death of King Lear* in 1608, he did so to distinguish Shakespeare's version from all others, especially from the anonymous *True Chronicle History of King Leir* published in 1605. And when Thomas Thorpe published *Shakespeare's Sonnets* in 1609, he similarly employed the author's name to specify its composer. Nevertheless, Loewenstein concludes that

---

4 See *The Riverside Shakespeare*, ed. G. Blakemore Evans (New York, 1997), 2nd edn; *The Oxford Shakespeare: The Complete Works*, ed. Stanley Wells and Gary Taylor (Oxford, 1986), and *The Complete Works of Shakespeare*, ed. David Bevington (Longman, 1997), 4th edn. The Oxford text omits 1, 2, 3, 5, 8, 11, 16, 19 and 20.

5 Cited by Arthur Marotti in *Manuscript, Print and the English Lyric*, (Ithaca, 1995), 263–4. Later, Richard Farmer, having read Heywood's complaint, criticized the false attributions of the revised *Passionate Pilgrim* in his influential *Essay on the Learning of Shakespeare* in 1767, and Edmond Malone cut three of Jaggard's poems that had been rejected by Ling – 8, 19 and 20 – from his 1807 edition of *The Plays and Poems of William Shakespeare*.

6 Adrian Johns, *The Nature of the Book: Print and Knowledge in the Making* (Chicago, 1998), p. 171.

7 David Scott Kastan, *Shakespeare and the Book* (Cambridge, 2001), p. 57.

8 Joseph Loewenstein, *Ben Jonson and Possessive Authorship* (Cambridge, 2002), p. 60.

for Jaggard the name 'Shakespeare' signified a type of literature, regardless of who produced it, rather than the work of a particular person, since the name suggested the whole category of quality love poetry. 'Shakespeare', he writes, 'was a marker of "family resemblance" among poems and a source thereby of borrowed meanings and borrowed value – it should perhaps not go without saying that the borrowing of meanings and of value is one of the functions of the generic within the literary system; even the merely competent acquired gilt by association'.[9] But the convention of generic categorization which had already been fixed by such titles for poetic anthologies as *The Paradise of Dainty Devices* (1576) or *The Gorgeous Gallery of Gallant Inventions* (1578) did not use proper names. 'The poems of *The Passionate Pilgrim* are thus "Shakespearian" or "Shakespearistic", if they are not Shakespeare's', Loewenstein concludes, minimizing Jaggard's possible duplicity in creating a volume inflated with fakes. Loewenstein, however, concedes that Shakespeare's name on the title-page of *The Passionate Pilgrim* 'may be the effect of a stationer's confusion, of his unconcern, or of his shrewdness', but from this phrasing it is not quite clear if he is implying that Jaggard's 'shrewdness' involved deliberate deception.[10] For the most part, however, Loewenstein represents Jaggard's use of Shakespeare's name as a cryptic professional deployment common in early modern print culture that only seems devious to us because of our misunderstanding of the stationer's historically contingent but fully justified conception of literary property and poetic discourse.

Loewenstein's main problem in assessing Jaggard's collection stems from the Foucauldian paradigm he employs, which makes it impossible to distinguish between real and fake examples of a writer's work. In 'What is an Author?' Foucault maintains that the erasure of the concept of authorial agency is a fundamental imperative of contemporary criticism, since the 'author-function' is solely a result of textual circulation, even though he simultaneously celebrates Marx and Freud as 'founders of discursivity', who are 'not just the authors of their own works', but

writers who have 'produced' the 'possibilities and rules for the formation of other texts'.[11] So that even though he characterizes Shakespeare, Marx and Freud as being unable to control the historical reinterpretation of their thought, Foucault implicitly assumes the very idea of authorship he supposedly revokes. Indeed, this and a wide range of self-contradictions that have arisen in the recent application of Foucault's theory of authorship to the study of early modern English literature have been cogently articulated by Brian Vickers in *Shakespeare, Co-Author*.[12] Perhaps the most damaging effect of Foucault's theory for a study of *The Passionate Pilgrim* is its refusal to acknowledge a difference between the work of 'Shakespeare' and the 'Shakespearistic'. Severed from any notion of even the most historically contingent authorial agency, philosophically bound to assume the ontological parity of *all* 'Shakespeare' texts, Foucault's approach is incapable of either coming to terms with Jaggard's strange mixture of relatively authoritative and delinquent texts in *The Passionate Pilgrim* or accounting for his deliberate adulterations.

The problematic nature of Loewenstein's analysis is shared by Margreta de Grazia's account of the pre-Malonean editing of Shakespeare's verse from Jaggard's *Passionate Pilgrim* to John Benson's *Poems* of 1640. Benson epitomizes early modern printing practice for de Grazia in that he 'appears not to have distinguished between what Shakespeare had written and what had been ascribed to him or associated with him in print; nor was he interested in

---

9 Loewenstein, p. 60.
10 Loewenstein, pp. 64 and 60.
11 Michel Foucault, 'What is an Author?' *Textual Strategies: Perspectives in Post-Structuralist Criticism*, ed. Josue V. Harari (Ithaca, 1979), pp. 141 and 154.
12 Brian Vickers, *Shakespeare, Co-Author, A Historical Study of Five Collaborative Plays* (Oxford, 2002), especially 'Appendix II: Abolishing the Author? Theory *versus* History', pp. 506–41. For an equally compelling examination of the problems that beset editorial theories that propose to reject author-based approaches to bibliography, see G. Thomas Tanselle, 'Textual Criticism at the Millennium', *Studies in Bibliography* 54 (2001), 1–80.

singling out Shakespeare's experience from commonplace occasions and conventional Ovidian encounters'.[13] Benson and Jaggard operated, according to de Grazia, in an early modern manuscript culture in which 'ascription worked synecdochally to refer to a poem's production and reproduction, the stages of its materialization being less than entirely distinct when the making of a poem was often a remaking of or a response to a prior composition'. The printed anthologies, she concludes, 'must have adopted' this 'synecdochic mode'.[14] But what are we to make of William Jaggard, who seems to have been shrewder than Benson insofar as he knew, with certainty, as I will soon indicate, the source of some of his misattributed poems? To begin, even tentatively, to address this question, we need to examine a different side of early modern editing. For Jaggard's 'shrewdness' in publishing *The Passionate Pilgrim* involved what some of his contemporaries saw as a violation of professional ethics (albeit in a milieu in which these violations were quite common), leading two interested readers – Nicholas Ling in 1600 and Thomas Heywood in 1612 – to challenge his representation of 'Shakespeare'. The advertisement of Shakespeare's name on the title-page of *The Passionate Pilgrim* owes more to market forces than to the mentality of the scriptorium.

II

Of the five poems in *The Passionate Pilgrim* that we know Shakespeare wrote, the first two, derived from manuscript circulation, provide the earliest datable versions of 'When my love swears that she is made of truth' (1) and 'Two loves I have, of comfort and despair' (2), and they differ (the first substantially) from Sonnets 138 and 144 in Thorpe's 1609 edition of *Shakespeare's Sonnets*.[15] The last three, reprinted with some changes, were probably based on either of the two early quartos of *Love's Labour's Lost* (published in 1597 (in a lost edition) and 1598): Longaville's 'Did not the heavenly Rhetoric of thine eye' (3), Berowne's 'If Love make me forsworn, how shall I swear to love?' (5), and

Dumaine's 'On a day (alack the day)' (16).[16] Of the remaining poems, several can be identified with

---

13 Margreta de Grazia, *Shakespeare Verbatim, The Reproduction of Authenticity and the 1790 Apparatus* (Oxford, 1991), p. 169.

14 de Grazia, pp. 169 and 170. See also Margreta de Grazia and Peter Stallybrass, 'The Materiality of Shakespeare's Text', *Shakespeare Quarterly* 44 (1993), 255–83.

15 Opinion concerning the authenticity of these two sonnets is divided. Colin Burrow in his introduction to *William Shakespeare: The Complete Sonnets and Poems* (Oxford, 2002) suggests that Jaggard's collection 'may derive from a version by a transcriber' (107), but he also admits that its rendition of 138 'may well represent an early state of the sonnet' (76). Arthur Marotti, supporting the first of these propositions, concludes that Jaggard's versions of 138 and 144 are memorial reconstructions in 'Shakespeare's Sonnets as Literary Property', *Soliciting Interpretation: Literary Theory and Seventeenth-Century English Poetry*, ed. Elizabeth D. Harvey and Katharine Eisaman Maus (Chicago, 1990), pp. 143–77; 151–2. But Edward A. Snow, in 'Loves of Comfort and Despair: A Reading of Shakespeare's Sonnet 138', *ELH* (1980), 462–83, assumes that Jaggard's 138 prints an authentic early draft, which Shakespeare later revised to produce Thorpe's version. Snow's analysis, however, is based on literary assumptions rather than bibliographic facts, and I agree with Marotti that Jaggard's transcription of 138 had been corrupted through circulation. Consider, for instance, its odd ninth line, which asks why the poet's mistress is lying about her age: 'But wherefore says my love that she is young?' In the *Sonnets* only the poet is ever described as being old, never the lady, who has no need to conceal her age. In Thorpe's version the mistress pretends to be honest and the poet pretends to be young in an arrangement that conforms to their characterization in the rest of the sequence. But in Jaggard's version of 138, however, we encounter an anomaly – an older woman – in a textual change that ruins Shakespeare's witty differentiation of lies involving *her* unfaithfulness and *his* vanity. The tainted provenance of *The Passionate Pilgrim* should, in any case, caution us against accepting the poem's legitimacy. Can the same volume that offers such a corrupt conflation of Marlowe's and (probably) Ralegh's famous poems be counted on to furnish an entirely accurate early version of Sonnet 138? Jaggard's unreliable copy cannot plausibly be used to chart Shakespeare's revision of his work between 1599 and 1609.

16 Jaggard's poems 3, 5 and 16 appear in slightly altered form in *Love's Labour's Lost* 4.3.57–70, 4.2.106–19 and 4.3.99–118 (without lines 112–13). Quoted from *The Riverside Shakespeare*, ed. G. Blakemore Evans (New York, 1997). Only the 1598 quarto of *Love's Labour's Lost* is extant, but the contention that the comedy had first been published a year earlier has recently been supported by Arthur Freeman and Paul Grinke, 'Four New Shakespeare Quartos?', *The Times Literary Supplement*, 5 April 2002, 17–18, who cite Philip Tandy's mid-1630s

contemporary authors, including Bartholomew Griffin (11), perhaps Thomas Deloney (12), Christopher Marlowe, and probably Sir Walter Ralegh (19).[17] The inclusion of Richard Barnfield's poetry in *The Passionate Pilgrim* provides proof that Jaggard knowingly stuffed his collection with verses by other writers in order to pad out his core poems, and that he placed four of these genuine poems (1, 2, 3 and 5) at the opening of the volume in order to create an initial sense of legitimacy in an anthology dominated by falsely attributed verse. In his recent introduction to the Oxford *Complete Sonnets and Poems*, Colin Burrow writes that in the final analysis the origin of the texts included in Jaggard's anthology are 'a mystery', since there is 'insufficient evidence to reach a certain conclusion about how these poems came into Jaggard's hands, or about the kind of copy from which the printer of the volume was working'.[18] But that is not the case, as he nevertheless recognizes, in regard to Barnfield's two poems.

We can be absolutely certain that Barnfield wrote 'If Musique and sweete Poetrie agree' (8) and 'As it fell upon a Day' (20), because they had previously appeared as 'To His Friend Maister R. L. In Praise of Musique and Poetrie' and 'An Ode' in a short collection called 'Poems in Divers Humors' that comprises the final section of *The Encomion of Lady Pecunia: or the Praise of Money*.[19] And the title-page of this book records not only that it was written '*By Richard Barnfeild [sic], Graduate in Oxford*', but also that it was printed in 1598 by John Jaggard, William's brother. Thus, while Jaggard's transcription of Bartholomew Griffin's sonnet from *Fidessa, More Chaste than Kind* (1596) as poem 11 shows differences in lines 9–12 from the previously published text, making it attractive to hypothesize an intermediate manuscript between the printed poem and Jaggard's copy, Barnfield's lyrics, on the contrary, faithfully duplicate their published source. John Roe, citing Edwin E. Willoughby and Joseph Quincy Adams, accepts as most plausible the theory that Jaggard used a commonplace book for some of the poems. But he also acknowledges the element of trickery in the collection. 'All his editors agree', Roe concludes, 'that Jaggard was practicing

a deception on the reader.'[20] The almost identical transcriptions of Barnfield's two poems in the Jaggard brothers' two collections consequently provide conclusive evidence that William Jaggard knew that poems 8 and 20 were really Barnfield's when he published them as Shakespeare's. If the print market escalated the trend toward literary attribution, the opportunity it afforded stationers to increase profit by fraudulently using a famous author's name also increased the incidence of misattribution. Jaggard might perhaps have been confused or mistaken about the exact authenticity of some of his poems – although this is not

---

catalogue of the books of Edward, second Viscount Conway (1594–1655), which lists a copy of 'Loves Labours Lost by W: Sha: 1597'. The play's 1598 title-page describes this quarto as having been 'Newly corrected and augmented / By W. Shakespere', although H. R. Woudhuysen in Appendix 1 of his Arden3 edition of *Love's Labour's Lost* (London, 1998) notes that early modern publishers' claims to have improved copy are not trustworthy (302–3).

[17] John Roe, *William Shakespeare, The Poems* (Cambridge, 1992), p. 246, and Colin Burrow, *Complete Sonnets and Poems* (Oxford, 2002), pp. 79–81, conclude that Bartholomew Griffin who wrote 11 probably penned all four of the sonnets on the subject of Venus and Adonis (poems 4, 6, 9 and 11). But C. H. Hobday, 'Shakespeare's Venus and Adonis Sonnets', *Shakespeare Survey 26* (Cambridge 1973), pp. 103–9, speculates, against the grain, that they are Shakespeare's. While I agree with Roe and Burrow that these four sonnets are not by Shakespeare, the stylistic variations in them pointed out by Hobday might still indicate composition by more than one non-Shakespearian author.

[18] See Burrow, *Complete Sonnets and Poems*, p. 76.

[19] Verses from 'Poems in Divers Humors' are quoted from *Richard Barnfield, The Complete Poems*, ed. George Klawitter (London, 1990), pp. 81–6.

[20] Roe, *The Poems*, 54. In his introduction to *The Passionate Pilgrim*, Joseph Quincy Adams had previously written that although Jaggard might have used a manuscript collection for some of the poems, he was still 'guilty of deliberate and purposeful misrepresentation' (xii) in reproducing the two Barnfield poems from 'printed texts' (xiv). Katherine Duncan-Jones's statement in *Ungentle Shakespeare: Scenes from His Life* (London, 2001), p. 136, that William Jaggard 'got hold of a manuscript that contained the twenty poems in his collection, reflecting the taste and/or personal associations of its compiler which accommodated both Shakespeare and Barnfield', thus does not account for Jaggard's familiarity with and dependence on the printed source of Barnfield's two poems.

provable – but he certainly understood the family provenance of 8 and 20.

In assessing Jaggard's collection, it is important not to overlook its irregularity of ascription. Since the two Barnfield poems are so thoroughly and cleverly integrated into *The Passionate Pilgrim*, Burrow's suggestion that Jaggard 'did for a brief time imagine that he had got his hands on the genuine article' seems unlikely. This becomes clear if we consider the most popular hypotheses about the genesis of the collection as a whole. In his sophisticated bibliographical analysis of *The Passionate Pilgrim*, Burrow lists four possible theories about the origin of Jaggard's copy: (1) that it came from Shakespeare's own manuscript, which included a few poems by others; (2) that it was based on a manuscript circulated by a group of poets; (3) that it was formed as a manuscript miscellany removed from its original authors; and (4) that it consisted of a collection fabricated by Jaggard who combined the two manuscript sonnets with three lyrics from the published *Love's Labour's Lost*, the Venus and Adonis sonnets, and 'pieces of unknown authorship'.[21] And although he tries to remain as open-minded as possible, Burrow nevertheless observes that most editors 'incline' to the fourth option, and appears to lean toward this opinion himself. But Burrow's schematization oddly neglects sufficiently to include an account of the origin of the two Barnfield poems (8 and 20), which require a different explanation for their appearance in *The Passionate Pilgrim*, since the choice to include them cannot be explained as the result of either generic or synecdochic processes of manuscript compilation. Since these non-Shakespeare poems were not of 'anonymous origin', they can only adequately be explained by assuming a fifth case: that Jaggard knowingly combined whatever manuscript material he had (including inferior versions of two of Shakespeare's sonnets) with excerpts from at least one printed text by an explicitly identified contemporary poet whose work he fraudulently attributed to Shakespeare.

Jaggard apparently copied 8 and 20 from his brother's edition of Barnfield's poetry, primarily because Barnfield admired and imitated Shakespeare and his poems could be passed off as Shakespeare's, even in so far as they echo the two metrical forms used by the collection's five genuine poems. Poem 8 employs the sonnet form (with three quatrains and a couplet) that Shakespeare uses in 1, 2, 3 and 5; and 20 matches 16, an Anacreontic verse in trochaic tetrameter that Shakespeare had originally composed for Dumaine's recited lyric 'On a day' in *Love's Labour's Lost*. In the 1598 quarto of the play, 'On a day' is described by Dumaine as being an 'Ode', and the original stage direction indicates that he '*reades his Sonnet*' (F3ᵛ). Berowne jests that it will show that 'Love can varrie Wit', but after it is read, its style and rhetoric are not criticized. In performance the poem might have been slightly moving, if read as a whimsical confession imbued with a tone of endearing self-mockery. The verbal and formal resemblances between Shakespeare's 16 and Barnfield's 20 are apparent in their opening lines:

On a day (alacke the day)	As it fell upon a Day,
Love whose month was ever May,	In the merry Month of May,
Spied a blossom passing fair,	Sitting in a pleasant shade,
Playing in the wanton ayre, . . .	Which a grove of Myrtles made, . . .

Jaggard needed more Shakespeare poems than the few he had if he wanted to publish a collection, so he added Barnfield's 'An Ode', the title of which signals its indebtedness to Shakespeare's poem. Jaggard might have hoped that readers would accept Barnfield's melancholy handling of the same genre as a complement to Shakespeare's lighter, playful lyricism, illustrating the poet's variations on a theme. What made the poems particularly similar was their mutual responses to the eighth song of Sir Philip Sidney's *Astrophil and Stella*, which begins:

In a grove most rich of shade,
Where birds wanton music made,
May, then young, his pied weeds showing,
New-perfumed with flowers fresh growing.[22]

---

[21] Burrow, *Complete Sonnets and Poems*, p. 58.

[22] Quoted from *Sir Philip Sidney: Selected Prose and Poetry*, ed. Robert Kimbrough (Madison, 1983), 'Eighth Song,' lines 1–4.

In Sidney's poem, Astrophil coaxes Stella to be affectionate by observing, 'This small wind, which so sweet is, / See how it the leaves doth kiss', and then asking, 'if dumb things be so witty, / Shall a heavenly grace want pity?' (lines 57–8; 63–4). Shakespeare plays on this passage, when he has Dumaine speak of how the 'wanton air' of the 'wind' finds a satisfaction he does not: 'Air, quoth he, thy cheeks may blow, / Air, would I might triumph so!' (4.3.107–8). Yet where Shakespeare's response to Sidney is brief and whimsical, Barnfield's imitation, although closer to the latter's melancholy mood, lacks his corresponding lightness of touch. Instead, Barnfield extrapolates a series of turgid aphorisms that rival Polonius's advice to Laertes: 'Faithfull friends are hard to find: / Every man will be thy friend, / Whilst thou hast wherewith to spend / But if store of Crowns be scant, / No man will supply thy want' (lines 32–6). In attributing Barnfield's poem to Shakespeare, Jaggard expected readers to accept these platitudes as genuine, judging that the similarities these poems shared (with allowance for variation) overweighed their differences.

III

In Captain William Jaggard's *Shakespeare Bibliography*, written in 1911, the author defends his ancestor and namesake by imagining the most innocent scene possible: that 'the manuscript brought to the printer may have been written entirely in Sh–'s hand'. 'It is quite feasible', he adds, 'that Sh– copied the others' poems and added them to his own for some ulterior purpose, as an anthology'.[23] But the Elizabethan Jaggard's willful replacement of 'Barnfield' with 'Shakespeare' was, on the contrary, part of a shrewd marketing ploy that capitalized on Shakespeare's name to induce readers to buy *The Passionate Pilgrim*, through the sale of which Jaggard alone, as a stationer, benefited financially. It was contrived to satisfy the growing desire to read more of Shakespeare's poetry by substituting the work of a lesser known writer whose verses might not be so easily recognized. Such a move is based on a perception of the difference between canonical and apocryphal works that is consciously violated.

Jaggard's flaunting of Shakespeare's name occurred at the very time when Shakespeare's writing began to be increasingly celebrated by his contemporaries, such as Francis Meres, whose *Palladis Tamia, or Wit's Treasury*, published in 1598, praises Shakespeare with Sidney, Edmund Spenser, Samuel Daniel, Michael Drayton, Thomas Warner, Marlowe and George Chapman for having enriched the English tongue, which they have 'gorgeouslie invested in rare ornaments'. These writers are, he asserts, the equivalent of Homer, Hesiod, Euripides, Aeschylus, Sophocles and Aristophanes among the ancient Greeks, and Virgil, Ovid and Horace among the Romans. Meres, of course, in a well-known passage mentions Shakespeare's affinity with Ovid, whose 'sweete wittie soule' seems to live 'in mellifluous & hony-tongued' Shakespeare's *Venus and Adonis, Lucrece* and 'his sugred Sonnets' that were being circulated in manuscript 'among his private friends'. Like Ovid and Horace, who claimed that their own work would last forever, Meres continues, 'so say I severally' of the writing of Sidney, Spenser, Daniel, Drayton, Shakespeare and Warner. Not only does Meres add Shakespeare's name, along with Spenser, Daniel, Drayton and Nicholas Bretton, to his list of the best lyric poets, but he includes it as well among the finest 'Tragicke Poets', the 'best Poets for Comedy', and, with Spenser and Ralegh, among the 'most passionate' composers of 'Elegie'.[24]

This appreciation of Shakespeare as one of England's greatest poets was paralleled by the first appearance of his name on the title-pages of his plays. In 1598, Cuthbert Burby's edition of *Love's Labours Lost* proclaimed that it was 'Newly corrected and augmented By W. Shakespere', and Andrew Wise attributed the second quarto of *Richard III* as well as the second and third

---

[23] Quoted from Hyder Edward Rollins's introduction to *The Passionate Pilgrim by William Shakespeare* (New York, 1940), p. xxxiii.

[24] Francis Meres, *Palladis Tamia, Wit's Treasury, Being the Second Part of Wit's Commonwealth* (London, 1598), pp. 281–2.

quartos of *Richard II* to 'William Shake-speare'. Then, in 1599, Wise added Shakespeare's name to the title-page of the second quarto of *1 Henry IV*.[25] Jaggard might have seen the title-page of *Love's Labour's Lost* when he was assembling *The Passionate Pilgrim*, and he consequently brought to Shakespeare's poetry a typographic convention that had previously only been used to advertise his drama. Shakespeare apparently decided against adding his name to the title-pages of *Venus and Adonis* (1593) and *Lucrece* (1594), a citation he might easily have secured from Richard Field and John Harrison, their publishers. Symbolically turning his back on the general readers who inspected his title-pages, he revealed his identity instead within the covers of these volumes, in signed dedicatory letters to his patron, Henry Wriothesley, the earl of Southampton, that impart the formal illusion of coterie intimacy to the public medium of print. When Thomas Thorpe published *Shakespeare's Sonnets* a decade later, he consequently followed Jaggard's, not Shakespeare's, precedent in featuring the poet's name on the title-page of his non-dramatic verse.[26]

But, unlike Thorpe who had abundant material for his 1609 edition of the sonnets, Jaggard faced a situation in which demand outstripped supply, and he sought out specimens of the plausibly 'Shakespearistic', a task that was made easier by contemporary imitations of Shakespeare's verse by weaker poets such as Barnfield. Jaggard's disguise of 'Barnfield' as 'Shakespeare' was conveniently facilitated by the former's admiration of the latter, an attitude that Barnfield shared with Meres and similarly expressed in print in 1598. When Jaggard took 'In Praise of Musique and Poetrie' and 'An Ode' from Barnfield's collection (which was published in the same year as *Palladis Tamia*) to attribute them to Shakespeare, he must have seen the two short poems that were printed between them, which, read together, offer coordinated diachronic and synchronic assessments of English literature from Chaucer to Shakespeare. Barnfield's first poem, 'Against the Dispraisers of Poetrie', traces a literary history of English verse from Chaucer, through Gower, and the earl of Surrey, to Sidney and George Gascoigne, and exults in the fact that

James VI, the 'King of Scots (now living) is a Poet'. This poem is then followed by 'A Remembrance of some English Poets', which numbers Shakespeare, along with Spenser, Daniel and Drayton, among the four greatest living writers:

> . . . *Shakespeare* thou, whose hony-flowing Vaine,
> (Pleasing the World) thy Praises doth obtaine.
> Whose *Venus*, and whose *Lucrece* (sweete, and chaste)
> Thy Name in fames immortall Booke have plac't.
> Live ever you, at least Fame live ever:
> Well may the Bodye dye, but Fame dies never.[27]

Shakespeare's 'Name', according to Barnfield, had been entered in fame's 'immortal Book' for his having written *Venus and Adonis* and *Lucrece*. Shakespeare had already achieved the most exalted status that a contemporary writer could enjoy in the eyes of Meres and Barnfield, indicating the potential marketability of his name for stationers such as Jaggard. What would Barnfield have thought when he saw the next poem in his collection, 'An Ode', attributed to Shakespeare by his publisher's brother, someone who should have known better? He might have been either indignant, secretly pleased, or both. He might have been

---

[25] The recent discovery of Philip Tandy's early seventeenth-century catalogue reference to 'Loves Labours Lost by W: Sha: 1597' (see note 16 above), however, broaches the possibility that Shakespeare's name appeared on this title-page a year earlier than is currently assumed by, among others, Lukas Erne in *Shakespeare as Literary Dramatist* (Cambridge, 2003), pp. 57–8.

[26] Lois Potter in 'Shakespeare's life and career' in *Shakespeare: An Oxford Guide*, ed. Stanley Wells and Lena Cowen Orlin (Oxford, 2003), 11, incorrectly describes *Venus and Adonis* as 'the first publication that had his name on the title-page'. And Peter Hyland, *An Introduction to Shakespeare's Poems* (Houndmills, 2003), p. 197, mistakenly asserts that Shakespeare's name 'was for the first time on the title-pages of the fifth and sixth Quartos of *Venus and Adonis*' in 1599, while 'prior to that it had appeared only in the dedication'. Conforming to the typographic convention employed in the first edition, Shakespeare's name never appeared on the title-pages of *Venus and Adonis* during his lifetime. And it was only in the year of his death, 1616, that *Lucrece*, now fully described as *The Rape of Lucrece*, was first attributed on its title-page to 'Mr. *William Shake-speare*'.

[27] Richard Barnfield, *The Complete Poems*, p. 182.

angered to find his work used to counterfeit 'Shakespeare', and he might have been flattered that some readers thought that his writing was good enough to be substituted for that of a poet he emulated.

IV

In tracing the early modern construction of authorship, one must be especially observant of the fact that not all London stationers employed the same standards of attribution. This became an issue when, soon after *The Passionate Pilgrim* was published, Nicholas Ling, whom we assume to be the primary editor of *England's Helicon*, a rival miscellany released in 1600, reprinted four of Jaggard's poems and implicitly denied that Shakespeare had written three of them by either re-attributing them or stripping them of ascription.[28] Jaggard's collection ends with a series of six poems (15–20) sectioned off by an internal title-page that calls them 'SONNETS to sundry notes of Musicke'. From these six poems, Ling selected four for either reprinting or textual substitution with various changes (16, 17, 19 and 20). Most importantly, he correctly attributes only 16, Dumaine's 'On a day', to 'W. Shakespeare', while challenging the attributions of 17 ('My Flocks feed not'), 19 ('Live with me and be my love') and 20 ('As it fell upon a day'). Ling consequently saw through Jaggard's reckless attribution of 20, 'As it fell upon a Day', to Shakespeare, and he pairs it with 17 ('My Flocks feed not, my Ewes breed not') as non-Shakespearian.[29] Indeed, to emphasize his point that these two poems are not by Shakespeare, Ling prints 17 and 20 together, following the validated 16, with a rejection of their forged pedigree; they are now called '*The unknown Shepherd's complaint*' and '*Another of the same Shepherd*', and they appear with 'Ignoto' instead of 'W. Shakespeare' printed at their conclusions. Although 17 has not been conclusively proven to be Barnfield's, Ling's identification of 17 and 20 as being by the 'same' poet provides support for the thesis that Barnfield wrote it, since we know that he composed 20.[30]

The current theory that Shakespeare's name acted generically or as a kind of synecdoche in the case of *The Passionate Pilgrim* appears, in view of this more complex situation, anachronistically postmodern. It is also unhelpful as a theoretical tool to the extent that it obscures our sense of how *The Passionate Pilgrim* was constructed in reference to its genuine intertexts: Shakespeare's unpublished Sonnets, *Love's Labour's Lost, Venus and Adonis* and *Romeo and Juliet*. Jaggard selected Barnfield's work because it matched part of this canonical template. He also correctly assumed that Barnfield's poems would be hard to identify by most readers. Indeed, his 'Ode,' between 1598 and 1600, travelled the entire circuit of possibilities in the Elizabethan literary system, from being printed as the work of the relatively unknown Barnfield in *Lady Pecunia*, through re-attribution to the 'immortal' Shakespeare as poem 20 in *The Passionate Pilgrim*, to being reduced to anonymity in *England's Helicon*. In the process, Ling even chopped off its plodding didactic conclusion – lines 27 to 56 – making it an even better although less authentic poem.

But Ling's greatest service to literature was to find a superior replacement for 19, 'Live with me and be my Love'. The editor of *England's Helicon* knew that Marlowe, not Shakespeare, had written 'Come live with me and be my Love' (by 1593, the year of his death) in six brilliant, not four botched, stanzas of iambic tetrameter, and that Jaggard's one-stanza response called 'Love's Answer' was actually part of a six-stanza rejoinder, probably by Sir Walter Ralegh. In *England's Helicon*, what most scholars still believe to be Ralegh's response to Marlowe is printed above his name, although this ascription was later covered by pasted cancel slips

---

[28] *England's Helicon* was printed 'by I. R. [John Roberts] for John Flasket', under the patronage of John Bodenham. For background, see Hyder E. Rollins, ed., *England's Helicon 1600, 1614*, 2 vols. (Cambridge, MA, 1935), I, pp. 1–6.

[29] All quotations from this collection are from the facsimile reprint of the 1600 edition, *England's Helicon*, ed. D. E. L. Crane (London, 1973).

[30] 'My Flocks feed not' (17) had previously been printed as an anonymous song lyric in Thomas Weelkes's *Madrigals to 3, 4, 5, and 6 voices* (London, 1597).

that read 'Ignoto'.[31] In place of Jaggard's horrendous copy, Ling provides excellent versions of both 'The passionate Shepherd to his love' and 'The Nymph's reply to the Shepherd', which he fully prints for the first time, hence becoming as important a figure for an understanding of the inception of Marlowe studies as he is for an understanding of Shakespeare bibliography. Observe, for instance, how Jaggard and Ling print the first stanza of what had already become a favourite pastoral poem and song:

Live with mee and be my Love,	Come live with mee, and be my love,
And we will all the pleasures prove	And we will all the pleasures prove,
That hilles and vallies, dales and fields,	That Vallies, groves, hills and fieldes,
And all the craggy mountains yield.	Woods, or steepie mountaine yeeldes.

Ling's superior version fixes Jaggard's first line, by supplying an accurate rendition of its well-known opening. Marlowe himself implies that the poem contains the extra syllable of the first iamb in his self-parody of the lyric in The Jew of Malta. When Ithamore promises Bellamira that she 'Shalt live with me and be my love', his phrasing parallels the cadences of the perfect iambic tetrameter of the first and last lines of the version printed in England's Helicon: 'Come live with mee, and be my love', which is slightly varied at the poem's conclusion to 'Then live with mee, and be my love' [italics mine].[32] In the second couplet, Ling's text also shows a more sophisticated sense of rhythm and language that avoids the clichés of 'hills and vallies' and 'craggy mountains', even as it preserves the appropriate rhyme word 'yeeldes' that Jaggard's version mars. Consequently, rather than conjecturing that Jaggard had obtained an earlier, less adept, shorter version of Marlowe's poem, one that preserved his original phrasing, closer to its source in Catullus's Carmina V ('Vivamus . . . atque amemus'), it is more reasonable to assume that Ling's six-stanza poem replaced Jaggard's truncated inferior copy with a better, more authentic text. A similar kind of replacement would have occurred in 1609 when Thorpe printed a superior version of 'When

my love swears that she is made of truth' in Shakespeare's Sonnets. It is not only that Jaggard's version of Marlowe's poem has been obviously cut from six stanzas to four (with a one-stanza response in the so-called 'Nymph's Reply'), but that 'Live with mee, and bee my Love' does not as a whole match the quality of Ling's copy and what we expect from the best of Marlowe's verse.

In his address 'To the Reader, if indifferent', at the opening of England's Helicon, Ling (who disguises his own identity under the reversed initials 'L. N.') affirms his vigilance in attempting to make correct ascriptions, in opposition to stationers such as Jaggard who do not strive for accuracy, when he states that

If any man hath beene defrauded of any thing by him composed, by another mans title put to the same, hee hath this benefit by this collection, freely to challenge his owne in publique, where else he might be robed of his proper due. No one thing being here placed by the Collector of the same under any mans name, eyther at large, or in letters, but as it was delivered by some especiall coppy coming to his handes. (A4ʳ)

His concern for the difficulty of ensuring accurate nomination, Ling explains, stems from his conviction that 'the names of Poets (all feare and dutie ascribed to her great and sacred Name) have beene placed with the names of the greatest Princes of the world, by the most authentique and worthiest judgements' (A4ᵛ). The visual impact of Ling's determination to give each poet and poem due credit is apparent in the typographic conventions of the layout of England's Helicon, in which each work is separated from the others by a line above and below it. In its own unique space, each poem is then exhibited between its title and either the author's name, pseudonym, initials or 'Ignoto', followed by the word 'FINIS'. The volume's typographical

---

[31] See Marcy L. North, The Anonymous Renaissance: Cultures of Discretion (Chicago, 2003), p. 76. North also notes the multiple possible sources for the editorial tasks that I have assigned to 'Ling' in this paper.

[32] The Jew of Malta 4.2.116 is quoted from Christopher Marlowe: The Complete Plays, ed. J. B. Steane (London, 1969).

code leads readers to focus on the relation between poetic artifacts and their creators.

V

But despite his concern for giving Shakespeare proper credit for what he had written, Ling's transcription of 'On a day' (16) was heavily indebted to Jaggard's volume, and he might not have known of the poem's earlier appearance in *Love's Labour's Lost*. Jaggard had treated Shakespeare's 'On a day' as one of a set of lyrics that either had been or should have been set to music when he included it in a special section of his collection devoted to song, and Ling subsequently published the poem as a free-standing lyric for which he invented the title *'The passionate Sheepheards Song'* as an improvisation on *The Passionate Pilgrim*. Ling's text accordingly reprints Jaggard's verbal error in line 2 ('Love whose month *was* [in place of *'is'*] ever May') and omits the same couplet that Jaggard had cut: Dumaine's protest, 'Do not call it sinne in mee, / That I am forsworne for thee' (E3ʳ). But Ling was alert enough to Shakespeare's prosody to correct Jaggard's error – copied from *Love's Labour's Lost* – of ending line 16 with the word 'throne'. *England's Helicon* prints this line correctly for the first time by substituting the word 'thorne' to complete the rhyme with 'sworne' in the sixth couplet. Nevertheless, Ling's own appropriation of Shakespeare's work also has to be factored into our approach. For even though he was adamant about assigning proper credit to writers, the editor of *England's Helicon* aggressively shaped the collection's poems to articulate his overarching pastoral theme. Thus, Jaggard's 'lover' of line 7 becomes Ling's 'Sheepheard'. For Ling, as for so many other stationers of the period, the transmission of early modern texts involved the dialectical impulses of conservation and adaptation. So that if, on the one hand, he was at the beginning of a long tradition of editors who have attempted to sort out what Shakespeare had actually written from what he had not, he also, on the other, felt free to adapt what he printed to make it explicitly fit the design of his pastoral collection.[33] And although he tried to be accurate about attribution, Ling thought

of title-creation as being legitimately within his purview as an editor intent on marketing an independent product. His creativity also extended to his having probably invented the name of Marlowe's most famous poem, *'The passionate Shepherd to his love'*, which similarly reflects Jaggard's influence. Ling might or might not have known that Shakespeare had already called Marlowe a 'Shepherd' (3.5.88) in *As You Like It*, especially in reaction to this poem. *England's Helicon* created in its pages a shepherd nation of poets whose collected works offered its anxious turn-of-the-century readers an imaginary space of pastoral *otium* in which the best recent writers, both dead and living (such as Sidney, Spenser, Marlowe and Shakespeare), mingled their voices. Shakespeare might even have felt privileged to have his 'ode' included in what is now widely viewed as the best Elizabethan verse anthology. He might also have been pleased to have been cleared of having written some of Jaggard's falsely attributed poems. One editorial strategy behind *England's Helicon* was to rectify as far as possible problems of attribution in order to document the growth of a literary culture that was metaphorically imagined as the rejuvenated sacred well of the Muses discovered on native soil. Ling consequently wanted to be for different reasons both accurate and novel.

In his title *The Passionate Pilgrim*, Jaggard evokes the sonnet improvised by Romeo and Juliet (1.5.92–105) in which she describes him as her 'Good pilgrim' to define 'Shakespeare' through his most passionate style at a time when the play was tremendously popular. Ling might have similarly gotten the idea of including a token poem by Shakespeare in his collection (numbering him among Sidney, Spenser, Marlowe and the earl of

---

33 Ling, however, ends the poem with a unique variant that might either be deliberate or accidental: Jove is described as 'Turning mortall for *my* [instead of *"thy"*] Love'. Still, Ling's editorial practice as a whole was inconsistent. Hyder Rollins, in his introduction to *The Phoenix Nest, 1593* (Cambridge, MA, 1969), p. xli, for example, notes the verbal corruptions that *England's Helicon* introduces into the nine poems Ling reproduces from that collection (one printed twice).

Oxford, those other 'shepherds' in *England's Helicon*) because of the recent stage success of *As You Like It*. *England's Helicon* was registered in the Stationers' Record on 4 August 1600, the same day on which *As You Like It* was entered 'to be staied'. Although the play was never printed until Edward Blount and Isaac Jaggard (William's son working in association with his then blind father) subsequently registered it on 8 November 1623 for the First Folio, it is possible that the success of Shakespeare's pastoral comedy at the Globe encouraged the editor of *England's Helicon* to reprint one of the dramatist's available pastoral poems.[34] Taken together, the play and poem indicate the extent to which Shakespeare's audience and readers would have strongly identified him with the pastoral genre at the beginning of the seventeenth century, when he became, on the model of Spenser and Sidney, a shepherd-poet.

VI

In a recent bid to exonerate Jaggard's use of Shakespeare's name on the title-page of *The Passionate Pilgrim*, Max W. Thomas seeks to reverse what he sees as a long tradition of Jaggard-bashing by insisting that the publisher was entirely justified in what he had done. Jaggard 'owned the rights to all of the texts that he included', Thomas argues, explaining that the poems 'in the 1599 edition belonged to him by virtue of his having assembled the previously unpublished (and unclaimed) materials for the collection'. They belonged to Jaggard, he concludes, through 'the unwritten code of uncontested publication'.[35] But this is not entirely true: of the five Shakespeare poems, for instance, three had previously been published. This code might be evoked to justify Jaggard's publication of Sonnets 138 and 144, but it does not apply to his reprinting of the three lyrics from *Love's Labour's Lost*. Jaggard had no right to print these three poems, even if we admit that he might not have known their origin. 'On a day', was printed by three different stationers between 1598 and 1600, without a transfer of rights, in *Love's Labour's Lost*, *The Passionate Pilgrim* and *England's Helicon*. The creation of miscellanies of previously published material was a matter of dispute among stationers, concerning the conditions under which they could print excerpts from each other's works without infringing on each other's privilege. Both Jaggard and Ling were dealing in a grey area of trade ethics (verging on piracy) and, although *England's Helicon* was successfully registered, Ling's defiance of any stationer who might accuse him of theft (for reprinting previously published poems) shows the extent to which he was willing to manipulate his interpretation of copyright:

> Noew, if any Stationer shall finde faulte, that his Coppies are robed by any thing in this Collection, let me aske him this question. Why more in this, then in any Divine or humaine Authour: From whence a man (writing of that argument) shal gather any saying, sentence, similie, or example, his name put to it who is the Authour of the same. This is the simplest of many reasons that I could urdge, though perhaps the nearest his capacitie, but that I would be loth to trouble my selfe, to satisfy him.
>
> (A4ʳ)

Ling tendentiously argues that he, as an editor, should have the same liberty to print poetry found in other texts as a divine or humanist is given in quoting citations from scripture or the classics (with proper ascriptions). His point is that in the case of his one Shakespeare poem, for example, neither Burby nor Jaggard had the right to accuse him of stealing their property because he was only exercising the same fair use of quotation commonly employed in scholarly exegesis. Since

---

[34] For the argument that *As You Like It* was produced at the Globe in 1600 (just before *England's Helicon* was published), see James P. Bednarz, *Shakespeare and the Poets' War* (New York, 2001), pp. 117–30, 267–8.

[35] Max W. Thomas, 'Eschewing Credit: Heywood, Shakespeare, and Plagiarism before Copyright', *New Literary History*, 31 (2000), 281. Thomas's argument is especially undermined by his eccentric reading of Heywood's metaphoric admission that his lines were 'not worthy his patronage' under whom Jaggard had published them as a reference to Heywood's actual patron, the earl of Worcester, rather than to Shakespeare (284–5).

England's Helicon evidently has none of the features of an ordinary critical treatise, however, Ling's claim looks more like a cover for recycling available material. Jaggard and Ling's differences, then, had less to do with the ownership of Shakespeare's poetry than with a rivalry to represent him on their own terms. Jaggard makes up only two titles for his collection, *The Passionate Pilgrim* and 'SONNETS to sundry notes of Musicke', but the editor of *England's Helicon* invents many. *England's Helicon* thus initiates a process of canon formation in its effort to ensure the authenticity of Shakespeare's texts by exercising editorial scrutiny in challenging the growing apocrypha that had begun to accumulate around his name. But this impulse to preserve correct ascription is nevertheless linked to a concomitant transformation of Shakespeare's work from Dumaine's ode into the passionate shepherd's song.

There is no clear indication that Shakespeare was upset by the first two octavos of *The Passionate Pilgrim* which had appeared in bookstalls by 1599. But it is rare to have any evidence of this kind. He might well have been displeased and felt he had no remedy. Heywood, however, in a now famous passage, cited below, tells us in 1612 that Shakespeare was indeed disturbed by Jaggard's misrepresentation of his name in the third edition. Heywood's contempt for both Jaggard's technical incompetence and dishonest business practices surfaced in that year, as a result of the publication of the third enlarged octavo edition of the book that he now called:

THE PASSIONATE PILGRIM, OR *Certain Amorous Sonnets, between Venus and Adonis, newly corrected and augmented, By W. Shakespeare*. Whereunto is newly added two Love-Epistles, the first From *Paris* to *Helen*, and *Helen's* answer back again to *Paris*.

Although one might argue that Shakespeare is not cited as the author of the 'Love-Epistles' mentioned above, the new title certainly leaves the deliberately misleading impression that Shakespeare had personally revised and augmented the volume. It implies that he had not only fixed whatever errors existed in the second octavo, but that he had also written the epistles between Paris and Helen as variations on the sonnets supposedly passed between Venus and Adonis (which Jaggard seems here to conceive as the first 20 poems of the prior editions). But Thomas Heywood, not Shakespeare, had written the two new epistles between Paris and Helen, just as he had composed the other seven that are not mentioned on Jaggard's title-page but which are included in the volume. All nine of these new and longer poems were actually translations by Thomas Heywood, mainly from Ovid's *Heroides*, *Art of Love* and *Remedies of Love*. And, as in the case of Richard Barnfield, Jaggard was fully aware that all of the new poems that he published were Heywood's, not Shakespeare's, because he had published them under Heywood's name in *Troia Britannica* (1609) three years earlier.

In a letter 'To my approved good Friend, Mr. Nicholas Okes', the printer of *An Apology for Actors* in 1612, Heywood lists Jaggard's series of 'dishonesties' in printing his poems. Jaggard had ruined *Troia Britannica* and refused to append a list of *errata*, Heywood complains, and, what was worse, he had added several of its poems under Shakespeare's name to the third edition of *The Passionate Pilgrim*. Concentrating on Jaggard's title-page which implies that Shakespeare was responsible for these Paris–Helen epistles, Heywood publicized his private grievance:

Here, likewise, I must necessarily insert a manifest injury done me in that worke, by taking the two epistles of Paris and Helen, and Helen to Paris, and printing them in a lesse volume under the name of another, which may put the world in opinion I might steale them from him, and hee, to doe himself right, hath since published them in his own name: but, as I must acknowledge my lines not worthy his patronage under whom he hath publisht them, so the author, I know, much offended with M. Jaggard (that altogether unknowne to him), presumed to make so bold with his name.[36]

---

[36] Thomas Heywood, *An Apology for Actors* (London, 1612), G4^{r-v}.

Heywood is upset that Jaggard had blatantly published his poems as Shakespeare's, because he fears that readers will think that he had stolen them from Shakespeare in *Troia Britannica*, and that Shakespeare, to prove they were his, had added them to the third octavo of *The Passionate Pilgrim*. Furthermore, like Barnfield, who was similarly victimized, Heywood admires Shakespeare as an extraordinary poet possessing skills beyond his own. But, most importantly, he tells us that Shakespeare was 'offended' at the manner in which Jaggard had 'made so bold with his name'. Shakespeare, like Ling before him, had found Jaggard's misattributions disrespectful. If Barnfield had the opportunity to confront Jaggard about the unauthorized use of two of his poems under Shakespeare's name (in all three editions of the same collection), he probably would have said something similar to what Heywood modestly protested. Heywood bases his criticism of Jaggard on the assumption that stationers owe their authors certain 'rights of the presse' (G4^r). These rights are not codified in law but exist as a simple principle of commercial ethics in the book trade: publishers should try to deal as fairly as possible, according to the conventions of the time, with questions of attribution and copy, since they were directly correlated with their authors' 'reputation' or 'credit'. This was, however, what might best be called a matter of civility not law. But even in this environment, in which 'authors had few legal rights to intellectual property, and notions of authorial copyright were almost nonexistent', Marcy L. North observes, there still were 'small ways for less entitled participants to balance the power' that stationers exercised.[37] Heywood took advantage of one of those small strategies when he criticized Jaggard's lax professional standards and argued that there were basic unwritten 'rights' that have nothing to do with the physical possession and ownership of books but with the ancient custom of allowing certain writers to derive symbolic capital from the texts they had been instrumental in producing. Some publishers recognized these rights for contemporary vernacular writers and others did not, especially when it

was to their advantage to upgrade attribution. Was there even a single case of someone else being given credit for Shakespeare's genuine plays or poems by early modern stationers? Shakespeare's predominance in late Elizabethan theatrical/literary culture was arguably equalled but not surpassed by fellow poet-playwrights. Considerations about adding or deleting a writer's name were more complex than a purely legal context suggests, and differences concerning this issue do not entirely follow a professional divide between stationers and authors, as is evident in Jaggard's and Ling's contrasting practices.

The contention that authors did occasionally have some say in matters of attribution is indicated by the fact that Jaggard was intimidated enough to print a second title-page for the third octavo from which he removed Shakespeare's name.[38] Because Heywood retaliated and shamed Jaggard in print, his complaint endures, although there seems to have been more social pressure to remove Shakespeare's name than to add Heywood's. Rather than clarifying these issues of provenance for his readers, Jaggard's solution was to make the enlarged *Passionate Pilgrim* anonymous. But even then, the collection must have still held the allure for some readers of being authentically Shakespeare's, based on its long-standing appearance as his work.

VII

In the early modern book trade, we might conclude, there were few pirates but abundant piracy, since even mainstream stationers, as Adrian Johns points out, operated in a world of improvised ethics and strategic morality regarding the fine points

---

[37] North, *The Anonymous Renaissance*, p. 56. See also Vickers, *Shakespeare, Co-Author*, pp. 517–27, for contemporary protests against plagiarism.

[38] In response to criticism, Jaggard cancelled the title-pages of unsold copies and replaced them with others without Shakespeare's name. The Bodleian copy, formerly owned by Malone, as Burrow, *Complete Sonnets and Poems*, p. 79, points out, preserves both the original and its replacement.

of attribution and copy ownership.[39] The most remarkable aspect of Jaggard's story however is that his persistence in printing unreliable versions of Shakespeare's work inevitably led to his role as one of the principal publishers of the Shakespeare First Folio in 1623. For even after Jaggard had been persuaded to remove Shakespeare's name from the title-page of *The Passionate Pilgrim*, he was again involved in the publication of apocryphal Shakespeare works in 1619 when he printed the poet's name on the title-pages of *A Yorkshire Tragedy* and *1 Sir John Oldcastle* as part of the ten so-called 'Pavier quartos', the first attempt to issue a selected collection of Shakespeare's drama. Yet Jaggard's involvement with the Pavier quartos seems directly to have led to his being recruited by John Heminges and Henry Condell of the King's Men to become, along with his son Isaac and Edward Blount, one of the main publishers of the First Folio. In May of 1619, after the first three Pavier plays had been printed, in what was probably an attempt to halt production of the quarto collection, William Herbert, the Lord Chamberlain, wrote his well-known letter to the Court of Stationers banning the publication of any of the King's Men's plays without their authorization.[40] But because the players needed a stationer who would be interested in their own grand project of producing the First Folio, and because Jaggard was willing to do the job, the players invited him to join their syndicate a few years later.[41] Indeed, he might also have been perceived as having established a kind of *de facto* copyright through his involvement with the 1619 Pavier quartos. Collaboration between the printer and players was apparently considered to be mutually beneficial. Under the guidance of Heminges and Condell, he and his son Isaac then produced a volume of Shakespeare's plays that preserves, with all its manifest imperfections, some of the greatest and most respected works in world literature. After continuously producing suspect versions of Shakespeare's poems and plays, he had finally reached an accommodation with the King's Men that transformed him into the playwright's canonical printer, the first in a long line of editors who have inevitably tried, following his lead, but always in slightly different ways, to produce an authentic text.

Jaggard has consequently left a curiously divided legacy. He can be celebrated as the publisher and printer of the First Folio, which, with all its flaws, remains one of the greatest achievements of world culture, and he can also be reviled for being one of the tainted sources for John Benson's degraded anthology of Shakespeare's *Poems* in 1640.[42] Through Benson's volume, which includes the entire expanded 1612 edition of *The Passionate Pilgrim*, Jaggard's deception, despite Ling's and Heywood's best efforts, corrupted the subsequent printing of Shakespeare's collected poetry. As a result, after more than four hundred years, *The Passionate Pilgrim* still assumes a paradoxical place

---

[39] Johns, *The Nature of the Book*, pp. 166–7.

[40] Herbert's letter appears in *Records of the Court of the Stationers' Company, 1602–1640*, ed. W. A. Jackson (London, 1957), p. 110. Pavier and Jaggard's reaction to the ban was to backdate plays, leaving the erroneous impression that their edition of *Sir John Oldcastle* had been printed in 1600 (as was the play's original quarto). This ruse was first detected by W. W. Greg, 'On Certain False Dates in Shakespeare Quartos', *The Library* 9 (1908), 113–31, and corroborated by William Neidig, 'False Dates on Shakespeare Quartos', *Century Magazine* (October 1910), 912–19. See also W. W. Greg, *The Shakespeare First Folio: Its Bibliographic and Textual History* (Oxford, 1955), pp. 9–17, and Leo Kirschbaum, *Shakespeare and the Stationers* (Columbus, 1955), pp. 227–42.

[41] The aggressive business strategy Jaggard employed in publishing Shakespeare's work parallels his activity in printing playbills. In 1593, with the death of John Charlewood, Jaggard petitioned to obtain this monopoly, which went to James Roberts (who married Charlewood's widow Alice). Roberts however discovered in 1602 that Jaggard was illegally furnishing the Earl of Worcester's Men with playbills and mounted a complaint against him that ended with an arrangement to allow Jaggard to rent the privilege of supplying that one company. Then, sometime between 1606 and 1615, Jaggard acquired Roberts's business and legitimately secured the monopoly. See Greg, *The Shakespeare First Folio*, pp. 22–3.

[42] Nevertheless, not all of Jaggard's influence on the printing of Shakespeare's plays was salutary. Despite his key role in publishing the First Folio, he posthumously exerted a damaging effect on the Third Folio, whose second issue, published in 1664, included *1 Sir John Oldcastle* and *A Yorkshire Tragedy*.

in the Shakespeare canon, where it is, by turns, included, altered and excluded from the collected works. Of late the collection has begun to receive a little more attention, and one of the things this attention reveals is that the pruning and replanting of Shakespeare's poetry that Cowley envisioned in 1656 – the job of remedying the adulteration of the canon with apocrypha that Jaggard initiated – had already begun in 1600, tentatively and in a small way, with *England's Helicon*.

REREADING SHAKESPEARE: THE EXAMPLE OF RICHARD BRATHWAIT

RICHARD ABRAMS

Reade him, therefore; and againe, and againe: And if then you doe not like him, surely you are in some manifest danger, not to understand him. And so we leaue you to other of his Friends, whom if you need, can bee your guides: if you neede them not, you can leade your selues, and others. And such Readers we wish him.

In the Preface to the 1623 Shakespeare First Folio, John Heminge and Henry Condell urge repeated, even guided reading of an often obscure playwright. Their salute to Shakespeare as 'so worthy a Friend' in the epistle to the Herbert brothers re-echoes midway in the ensuing address 'To the great Variety of Readers': 'we pray you do not envie his Friends, the office of their care, and paine'. Then the circle of friends expands mysteriously. In the passage cited above, Shakespeare's former colleagues conclude the preliminaries by referring readers to 'other of his Friends' who can supply guidance, unless 'you neede them not [and] can leade your selues, and others'. Who are these other friends into whose tutelage Heminge and Condell discharge the less capable reader? Recent attention to the matter has produced only halting commentary.

Supporting a tentative proposal by Heidi Bray-man Hackel (which she then backs away from), this article proceeds from the inference that Shake-speare's first editors imagined a community of read-ers helping each other to understand – the same community envisioned in the Address's first sen-tence, stretching 'from the most able, to him that can but spell'.[1] The editors' fantasy of a read-ing group centred on the Folio has its basis in a familiar early modern practice. Though Heminge and Condell (or the syndicate to which they lend their names)[2] stop short of presenting Shakespeare's oeuvre as a sacred text, they insinuate an analogy between the interpretive enterprise swirling around their friend's big book and the scene taking place in myriad Protestant households where families, gath-ered round the Bible, help each other to drink the milk of the pure word. On this model (supported by the admonition to 'Reade him . . . againe, and againe', echoing pastoral advice to make a habit of Bible-reading),[3] Shakespeare within years of his

---

I am grateful to Benjamin Bertram and Edward Pechter for their astute suggestions.

[1] Heidi Brayman Hackel, 'The "Great Variety" of Readers and Early Modern Reading Practices', in *A Companion to Shake-speare*, ed. David Scott Kastan (Oxford, 1999), pp. 139–57, writes that Heminge and Condell may regard the Folio's ablest readers as helpful to others in reading the playwright (p. 142) but concludes that their main intent is to clear the stage for writers of other preliminaries, who were once friends to the living Shakespeare. It's unclear how such writers could be con-sidered 'guides' to deficient readers. Rather, it's hoped that the expert reader, sufficient to lead himself, will also 'leade . . . others'. See Hackel, *Reading Material in Early Modern England* (Cambridge, 2005), pp. 72–4, 98.

[2] For discussion of 'the syndicate fronted by Heminge and Con-dell', Leah Scragg, 'Edward Blount and the prefatory material to the first folio of Shakespeare', *Bulletin of the John Rylands Library*, 79 (1997), 117–26.

[3] Hackel, 'Great Variety', p. 149: 'In urging readers to turn again and again to the folio, Heminge and Condell distance the volume from ephemeral trifles, situating it instead as a volume, like Scripture or a scholarly text, that demands and rewards rereading'. David Bergeron, *Reading and Writing in Shakespeare* (Newark, Del., 1996), p. 14, remarks that in the

death is already regarded as something more than a provider of literary entertainments. He has become an exacting sage from whom 'the wiser sort', in Gabriel Harvey's phrase, may derive wisdom to disseminate among the less learned. To hear the Folio's 'Presenters' tell of the matter, seminars are busily forming, friends shepherding friends along twisting paths. By receiving instruction from 'other of [Shakespeare's] Friends', inexpert readers may avoid pitfalls of simplification which leave the mere pleasure-seeker in 'manifest danger' – like an unlettered soul in spiritual peril – 'not to understand him'.

To turn from Heminge and Condell's high hopes for their friend ('such Readers we wish him') to the documentary record of early Shakespeare conversation is to experience a steep drop. Of the afterlives of Shakespeare's plays in the minds of early playgoers and readers, we know next to nothing. Lively conversations must have taken place, sensibilities may have been reshaped, but the ferment of early Shakespeare culture is lost to us. Readers' traces survive in the form of marginalia and commonplace-book transcriptions but yield 'less than we need to do much with them'; lacking 'personal or creative intensity', the early annotators skirt the excitements that induced them to buy and read Shakespeare in the first place.[4] Nor are we on much happier ground when we arrive among critics with faces. A gulf separates Simon Forman's recoil in the theatrical presence of Autolycus ('Beware of trusting feigned beggars or fawning fellows') from the young Milton's bookish homage two decades later to 'those Delphick lines' that 'make us Marble with too much conceaving'. But what are the implications of such remarks for trends in Shakespeare's early reception-history? Did the 'identified' spectator engage the sedulous reader in dialogue? When in the early years of Shakespeare publication did Shakespeare *study* gel? What sort of guidance did the Folio editors imagine expert readers imparting to the less adept?

Though the precise divulgences of Shakespeare's best early readers lie beyond recovery, I attempt in this essay a small-scale salvage operation. Drawing on extensive unreported primary materials,

I undertake to read over the shoulder of a single early reader of Shakespeare – or more pertinently, in Heminge and Condell's sense, a *re*reader of Shakespeare, one who did 'Reade him . . . againe, and againe', discussed him with friends and interpreted him to the less able. In a literary career spanning six decades and encompassing more than fifty separate volumes, Richard Brathwait lived through enormous changes in 'Shakespeare', from the still-active playwright to the institution patronized by Thomas Rymer, Margaret Cavendish and John Dryden. His corpus yields a staggering number of allusions to the stage and its most celebrated writer, allusions constituting an unexploited resource for the study of drama before the closing of the theatres. If Milton speaks from the mountaintop, Brathwait dwells in the foothills. Struggling for comprehension, he questions Shakespeare's artistic decisions, extracts ethical lessons from drama, depicts friends meeting to discuss tragedies, and in time of personal grief steers his course with reference to a Shakespearian model. In the sheer variety of his negotiations, Brathwait may be the most multifaceted early witness to Shakespeare who has yet come to light. Though his writings antedate the dawn of formal interpretive criticism in English, his complex appropriations verge at times on critical readings, answering to Heminge and Condell's hope for interpreters to the unlearned. Indeed, Brathwait himself may have served as a partial inspiration for that fantasy.

In praising Shakespeare as a writer worth rereading, Heminge and Condell transparently pursue commercial ends. But cogent arguments have lately been advanced to suggest that the Folio plays were construed early on, and possibly intended, as reading texts. The hypothesis of the plays' conscious literariness, urged by Richard Dutton, Lukas Erne and others, receives a modicum of

---

Epistle to the Herbert brothers the Folio assumes the 'quasi-religious status' of 'a consecrated text'.

[4] William H. Sherman, 'What Did Renaissance Readers Write in Their Books?' in *Books and Readers in Early Modern England: Material Studies*, ed. Jennifer Anderson and Elizabeth Sauer (Philadelphia, 2002), pp. 119–37: 133, 137 n.41.

confirmation from the kinds of attention paid by Brathwait. Attending the London stage in the twilight of Shakespeare's career, Brathwait saw some marvellous plays and was fully responsive to their theatrical power. Richard III and Antony and Cleopatra (as Shakespearian characters), Boult, Trinculo, Malvolio, Oberon and the great Jack all live by name within his pages. But Brathwait's mind runs not only to character and plot but also to Shakespeare's perceived ideas. Consistent with Heminge and Condell's portrayal of a thinker whose subtleties have just begun to be explicated by his living friends, Brathwait views *Romeo and Juliet* and *Hamlet* as plays reaching a philosophical hand to suffering – a hand he himself is eager to assist. Whether in viewing the tragedies as founts of compassionate wisdom Brathwait also holds interlocking views of authorial agency, of the plays' wisdom as Shakespearian *teachings*, is less clear. He never names Shakespeare as he does 'Rabbi Ben-Johnson', but this may be because Jonson set himself up as a critic, drawing fire (four years after Jonson's death: 'Fetch me Ben. Johnsons Scull, and fill't with Sacke').[5] Jonson excepted, Brathwait's handling of Shakespeare is in line with his handling of other playwrights, and his associative leaps among Shakespeare's works give the impression of at least an inchoate sense of a Shakespeare canon such as we find in Francis Meres.

Richard Brathwait (1588–1673), a country magistrate for many of his eighty-five years, was educated at Oxford and Cambridge but took degrees at neither. The second son of a Kendal barrister, he was next sent to London to study law but became absorbed in the public theatre, for which he aspired to write. On his father's death in 1610 he returned home to Cumbria; however, problems in the settlement of his father's will and an undoubted taste for London living landed him back in the capital where, evidently on more than one occasion, he was jailed for debt. On his elder brother's death in 1618, he became head of his family, taking up the duties of a country gentleman and eventually siding with the royalists in the civil war. Brathwait's avocation as a writer was lifelong, though two main periods of productivity stand out: from 1611 to 1622,

and again from 1630 to 1641. Conversant with half a dozen languages, he wrote across a wide variety of genres including love lyrics and histories, eclogues and satires, courtesy books and local colour, moral treatises and racy fiction, political allegory, spiritual autobiography, 'characters' and – his most popular work – a picaresque travel diary. Only toward the end of his career do we find stageplays (and those in Latin). This is curious because Brathwait later insisted on his youthful success at playwriting. However, if plays from his early years fail to survive or never existed, his abiding interest in the genre is manifest in his early and continual citation of theatrical works.[6]

Before turning to Brathwait's Shakespeare, we should acknowledge that the field of allusion-study is mined with subjectivity. ''Tis with our judgements as our watches, none / Go just alike, yet each believes his own'. The bad news – that it was ever thus – is attested by the frequency with which *The Shakspere Allusion-Book* (re-edited 1932) flags its entries as uncertain. The good news is that controls newly introduced into the field with the emergence of electronic text archives permit cross-checking of suspected allusions for rarity. In *The Devills White Boyes*, Brathwait recalls the corruption of Charles I's judges: 'honest men went to wrack, and every Iack might be made a Sir Iohn, for an hundred pounds'.[7] A Shakespearian

---

5 Brathwait, *The History of Moderation* (London, 1669), sig. F4ᵛ; *A Preparative to Studie, or, The Vertue of Sack* (1641), sig. A2ʳ (the STC attribution to Francis Beaumont is impossible. Alternative attributions have included Brathwait's friend Thomas Heywood and his putative collaborator, John Taylor the Water Poet).

6 The latest biography is by now an antique: Matthew Wilson Black, *Richard Brathwait, An Account of His Life and Works* (Philadelphia, 1928). For Brathwait's preferred spelling of his name, without terminal -e, see Black, p. 13 n.10. Brathwait's unsupported claim of early contribution to the stage appears in *A Spiritval Spicerie: Containing Sundrie Sweet Tractates of Devotion and Piety* (London, 1638), sig. S11ʳ. Gerald Eades Bentley doubts his veracity, *The Jacobean and Caroline Stage*, vol. 3 (Oxford, 1956), p. 40.

7 Brathwait, *The Devills White Boyes: or, A Mixture of Malicious Malignants* (London, 1644), sig. A3ᵛ. *White Boyes* may be a collaboration with John Taylor the Water Poet. This and

parallel suggests itself. But do I dare trust the chord struck in my memory or must I discount my association, realizing that I know more Shakespeare than I know other early modern writers? To judge whether Brathwait's phrasing is derivative, I turn to the largest archive of searchable texts, Chadwyck-Healey's *Literature Online* (*LION*), and proceed as follows.

I wish to examine all passages in which 'Jack' and 'Sir John' occur in reasonable proximity to each other and in the same sequence as in Brathwait. The passage's rhythms are important; Jack → Sir John implies aggrandizement; Sir John → Jack implies abatement. *Literature Online* uses the Boolean search commands OR, AND and NOT, and the proximity operator NEAR. The latter might serve; using NEAR, I could then manually cull instances of the desired sequence from my pool of results. But more efficient is the command FBY (followed by), recognized by *LION*, though not universally by other databases. On a *LION* text-search page I click Advanced Search Options, select under Literary Period the field of Renaissance (1500–1660), then enter in the Keywords window the search string <iack* FBY.20 sir ioh*>. This string will call up all passages in which 'sir ioh*' succeeds 'iack*' within twenty words (an arbitrary large number). The truncating asterisks allow for variants such as 'iacke', 'iohn', 'iohnn', and 'iohan'; and I shall further tick the Typographical Variants checkbox to allow /j/ as a variant for /i/.[8] I am ready to search.

Among all texts archived in the *LION* database, these search procedures turn up only two further instances of the sequence, Jack → Sir John, both in *2 Henry IV*. They include the reminiscence that launched my suspicion of Brathwait's indebtedness: 'Jack Falstaff with my familiars . . . Sir John with all Europe' (2.2.123–5). Despite the precaution of searching widely, however, I recognize that the case for Brathwait's phrase as a Shakespearian echo is far from airtight. *LION* has many shortcomings: it indexes prose non-fiction only thinly, often omits the preliminaries of indexed publications, and ignores variant readings. Nor would the case be airtight if the archive were comprehensive; there always remains the possibility of coincidence. Still,

though *LION* is at present a crude instrument, it serves to delimit a field. Fifteen years ago we could only have guessed whether the Jack → Sir John sequence is distinctive. With *LION* and other databases rapidly becoming available, we can refine that guess.[9]

Other factors taken in conjunction with rarity may strengthen the case for an allusion. In Brathwait's comment on corruption under Charles I, the judges' preferment parallels Falstaff's crooked rise to prominence. Or take Brathwait's half-title for a collection of satires, 'The honest ghost'. A *LION* search for the string <honest* NEAR.3 ghost*> yields only *Hamlet*, Brathwait and a discardable phrase in Suckling ('some honest Lovers ghost', in which 'honest' modifies 'Lover' rather than 'ghost'). As in the case of Jack/Sir John, the echo is enhanced contextually; Brathwait's honest satires expose what's rotten in the state of England. Furthermore, a phrase in a title is expected to bear full weight of interpretation. A Shakespearian source seems assured. Or take Brathwait's phrase, 'bring forth Male-children'.[10] *Macbeth* has 'men-children', but early allusions are seldom scrupulous, and Brathwait's slip may register pressure from Shakespeare's pun on 'male' ('Bring forth men-children only, / For thy undaunted mettle should compose / Nothing but males' (1.7.72–4)). Finally, clusters of suspicionable echoes, such as we shall later assemble from a memorial poem of Brathwait's steeped in *Hamlet*, enhance credibility through

---

other proposed Shakespeare echoes are previously unreported, except as noted.

8 For a still more comprehensive search, one may click the spelling-variants option to the right of the Keywords window and accept relevant prompts. *LION* transcriptions sometimes confuse long /s/ with /f/ and neglect the tilde marking an elided /m/ or /n/, producing such errors as 'copare' for 'cōpare' ('compare') and 'cofirm' for 'cōfirm' ('confirm'). When critical to the search, both the correct spelling and likely misspellings should be searched separately.

9 The Chadwyck-Healey database *Early English Books Online* (*EEBO*), based on the Short-Title Catalogue, promises, when complete, to dwarf *LION*. As far as possible, I have cross-checked *LION* against *EEBO*, recording relevant additions.

10 Brathwait, *Ar't Asleepe Husband: A Boulster Lecture* (London, 1640), sig. D4ʳ.

mutual reinforcement. The same principle applies to Brathwait's conflation of passages from discrete Shakespearian texts. The world is 'a Tragick Theatre' populated by actors:

but their Play-bill bears no better style then A Comedy of Errors. To see a Man turne himselfe into all shapes like a Camelion, or as Proteus, transforming himselfe into every prodigious forme.[11]

Other writers besides Shakespeare (in *3 Henry VI*) share the chameleon–Proteus nexus, but Brathwait's additional reference to *Comedy of Errors* tends to confirm a Shakespearian source for 'Camelion . . . Proteus'.[12] Such conflations are not infrequent in Brathwait. The one I wish to explore involves the intricate pairing of a Shakespearian comedy and tragedy over the length of a narrative poem.

DREAMING *ROMEO AND JULIET*

Though modern critics rightly applaud Shakespeare's witty alignment of *Romeo and Juliet* with the burlesque love-tragedy of Pyramus and Thisbe (not to mention the averted love-tragedy of Lysander and Hermia) in *A Midsummer Night's Dream*, scholarly study reveals that the bare-bones analogy descended to Shakespeare ready-made. To five established, pre-Shakespearian texts in English linking Pyramus and Thisbe with Romeo and Juliet, we may add three precursor-texts and two *novelle* published soon after the plays' first performances.[13] These ten texts collectively evidence a tradition independent of Shakespeare. But Shakespearian influence is unmistakable in Brathwait's 'LOVES / *LABYRINTH: / OR / The true-Louers knot*', an unreported epyllion of almost 2200 lines printed in his collection, *A / STRAPPADO / for the Diuell. / EPIGRAMS AND / Satyres alluding to the time* (London, 1615). Though *Loves Labyrinth* is not the first text to draw on both *Romeo and Juliet* and *A Midsummer Night's Dream*, it's the first deliberately to link the two plays – a venture more remarkable for its being undertaken during Shakespeare's lifetime.[14] On *Loves Labyrinth's* title-page Brathwait declares his intent to redeem 'A Subiect heereto-

fore handled, but now with much more proprietie of passion, and varietie of invention, continued'. That the improprieties marked for correction are Shakespeare's is indicated by Brathwait's further stipulation of his subject as 'The disastrous fals of two star-crost / Louers Pyramvs & Thysbe'.

Loves Labyrinth's extensive prefatory verses include a brief envoi, 'The Author vpon his infant Poeme', explaining that the poem was composed in 'youth's minority', the author's 'infancy / Of Age, Art, Iudgement, Knowledge, and of Wit'. The containing volume, *A Strappado for the Diuell*, is mainly a collection of satires, so it's unclear why Brathwait also includes an anti-satire (the unpublished manuscript may simply have weighed heavily on him). Nor can the poem's date of composition

---

[11] Brathwait, *The Two Lancashire Lovers: or, The Excellent History of Philocles and Doriclea* (London, 1640), sig. O3[v].

[12] Fond of playing with Shakespeare's titles, Brathwait again cites the title of *Comedy of Errors* in *Lancs. Lovers*, sig. K2[v], and in a passage reported in *Shakspere Allusion-Book*, re-ed. John Munro, 2 vols. (London, 1932), 1.468. *Spiritvall Spicerie* (London, 1638), sigs. Q5[v]–Q6[r], has 'A / long *winter night* seemed but a *Midsummer nights dreame*'. *Times Curtaine Dravvne, or The Anatomie of Vanitie* (London, 1621), sig. F8[r], has 'Thus did I loue, thus was my labour lost'. 'Labour of love' and 'lost labour' are proverbial but, in *LION*, only Shakespeare, Brathwait and Robert Tofte, alluding to a performance of Shakespeare's play, link the phrases. The last stanza of Part 2 of Brathwait's *Barnabæ Itinerarium, or Barnabees Iournall* (1638; sig. M1[r]) has 'A Shop . . . / Where Young vends his old Tobacco, / As You Like It' (his italics). Surprisingly rare in pre-1650 usage, the phrase appears in *LION* only in Shakespeare. *EEBO* adds Nicholas Breton and Sir Edward Dering.

[13] René Pruvost, *Matteo Bandello and Elizabethan Fiction* (Paris, 1937), pp. 70, 76, 84, 93, 94, notes collocations in Rich, Pettie, Grange, Whetstone, Robinson; cf. Arden2 *Dream*, ed., Harold F. Brooks (1979), p. xlv. Unreported collocations include a second passage in George Pettie, *A Petite Palace. Of Pettie his Pleasure* (London, 1576), sig. D2[v]; Thomas Peend, *The Pleasant Fable of Hermaphroditus and Salmacis* (London, 1565), sig. B4[v]; 'student in Ca[m]bridge', *A Poore Knight his Pallace of Priuate Pleasures* (London, 1579), sig. B3[r–v]; Richard Stanyhurst, *Thee First Foure Bookes of Virgil his Æneis* (Leiden, 1582), sig.Q1[v]. The *novelle* are Emanuel Ford, *The Most Pleasant Historie of Ornatus and Artesia* (London, 1599?), sig. E1[r], and John Hind, *The Most Excellent Historie of Lysimachus and Varrona* (London, 1604), sig. N2[r–v], plagiarizing Pettie.

[14] *Wily Beguilde* (London, 1606) alludes casually to both plays and to *The Merchant of Venice*.

be fixed with exactitude. But if, taking Brathwait at his word, we add twenty-one years to his birthdate of 1588, we obtain the terminus ad quem of 1609. *Loves Labyrinth* may have been composed earlier; *Blurt, Master Constable* (*c.* 1607) adapts some of the same material Brathwait uses. Yet the outside date of 1609 remains attractive, for in that year Brathwait arrived in London and succumbed to the allure of the public theatre.

By the 1630s the phrase, 'star-crossed lovers', was in common use; however, prior to *Loves Labyrinth* the only attested usage is Shakespeare's.[15] Brathwait's advisedness in taking up Romeo and Juliet's epithet as a half-title (as he later takes up 'honest ghost') to describe a pair of lovers traditionally cognate with them is evident in the dedication, which invites readers to come 'see these star-crost louers', and in the 'Argument of Pyramus and Thysbe', which opens with an echo of *Romeo and Juliet*'s first-act Chorus: 'Childrens loue and Parents hate, / Pure affection cros'd by fate'. These dinning allusions suggest the poet's basic strategy. In restoring Pyramus and Thisbe's dignity, Brathwait not only writes against the Shakespeare of *A Midsummer Night's Dream* but recruits the Shakespeare of *Romeo and Juliet* as a collaborator.[16]

Though Brathwait calls his lovers star-crossed, he departs from Shakespeare in failing to work through the ironies of fate operative in their catastrophe. Instead, coarsening hints in *Romeo and Juliet*, he heaps blame for the children's deaths on their parents, especially Thisbe's. Her father insists on marrying his daughter to wealth. Her mother is vindictive: her 'eies [Thisbe] feared more then anie other'.[17] The mother's officiousness appears early on; as the lovers pledge eternal love, 'in comes her mother, / which made them take their leaue one of another'.[18] Absent in Golding, the detail seems to derive from the Nurse's interruption of Romeo and Juliet's vows in the balcony scene. A page later Brathwait writes, 'Hearbs yeeld a soueraigne cure to euery wound, / but for loues cure, in hearbs no vertue's found'. The gratuitous herbal imagery recalls the Friar's entry in 2.2, while the Friar's *festina lente* on his exit in the same scene, 'They stumble that run fast' (95), re-echoes in Brathwait's

chastisement of parents who 'Made hast . . . yet hasted not; / Till they saw their children lie, / Arme in arme full louingly'.

In another set of displacements Brathwait conflates Pyramus and Thisbe's rendezvous and deaths in sight of Ninus's tomb with *Romeo and Juliet*'s final scene. Arriving at the lovers' appointed meeting-place after the lion drives Thisbe into hiding, Pyramus lets his imagination run wild along Shakespearian lines. His apostrophe to the stony tomb, 'Didst thou her bewty in thy shrine inter? / Didst thou immure her in thy marble toombe?'[19] places us with Romeo at the door of Juliet's tomb, though a subsequent break-in would be pointless: Thisbe is not within. When Thisbe returns to find her lover dying, however, she herself takes up the fantasy of entry and double interment. Imagining a site of multiple burials ('compile[d] bones'), she implores the tomb, 'Open thy marble bosome and receiue, / two friends at once in one renowmed graue'. And when Pyramus dies, he does so in literary company. Romeo imagines 'death's pale flag' advanced in Juliet's face, overwhelming 'Beauty's ensign . . . / . . . in [her] cheeks' (5.3.94–6). Brathwait shifts the conceit from heroine to hero. Pyramus 'might whilst he suruiu'd and bore the sway, / his purple flags in euery coast display', but when he dies, 'death, pale death now swaies'.[20]

A final set of similarities appears in scenes of lovers' meetings. Following Ovid, Brathwait jumps into his tale after Pyramus and Thisbe are already acquainted, meeting daily at the wall. No opportunity exists for parallelism with Romeo's meeting Juliet at the ball or his espial of her on her balcony. But Brathwait devises a limited

---

[15] Expanding the string to <star* cros* FBY.4 lou*> adds Robert Tofte in his Shakespeare-influenced *Alba. The Months Minde of a Melancholy Louer* (London, 1598).

[16] At first glance it may appear that Brathwait writes against not Shakespeare's but the mechanicals' mistreatment of Pyramus and Thisbe, but 'handled' (in 'A Subiect heeretofore handled'), and 'varietie of invention' point to an author.

[17] Brathwait, *Labyrinth*, sig. s8ᵛ.

[18] Brathwait, *Labyrinth*, sig. R7ᵛ.

[19] Brathwait, *Labyrinth*, sig. T6ʳ.

[20] Brathwait, *Labyrinth*, sig. V4ᵛ–V5ᵛ.

correspondence. Thisbe arrives at her woodland rendezvous heralded by her own 'piercing eyes':

> which shon so bright,
> that they gaue day vnto a gloomy night:
> So that each Wood-nimph, Faune and Satyre there,
> rose from their caues perceiuing light appeare.[21]

The chief woodland denizen deceived by this false dawn is Sylvanus, 'god of woods and desert groues', who, roused by Thisbe's radiance, shakes off sleep 'long before his time', hastens to meet the new arrival and falls in love. Though no Petrarchan cliché is more familiar than the beloved's shining eyes, Shakespeare refreshes the figure in the smitten Romeo who, suddenly aware of Juliet at the ball, senses a diffuse radiance that later becomes focused in her eyes. With giddy hyperbole Romeo declares that Juliet's eyes, set in the heavens, would make birds 'sing and think it were not night' (2.1.64). The conceptual parallels with Sylvanus are strong and the tone similar. In both texts, a deceptive unknown radiance invades the natural realm, turning night to day. Though the comparison is more precarious than earlier ones, Brathwait's conception probably owes something of its whimsical particularity to Romeo's first encounters with Juliet.

If Brathwait 'dreams' Romeo and Juliet in the guise of a redeemed Pyramus and Thisbe, he also picks up detail from *A Midsummer Night's Dream*'s frame-story. Besides the doomed lovers, the poem's chief character is the shag-headed Sylvanus. The genius loci of an enchanted wood at whose fringe the lovers dwell, watched over by a 'watrie Moone',[22] Sylvanus bears a recognizable descent. Like Oberon conjuring wild beasts ('ounce, or cat, or bear, / Pard, or boar with bristled hair' (2.2.36–7)) to teach Titania a lesson, Sylvanus determines on Thisbe's rejection of him 'to command some sauage beast' – the lion – 'vpon her, whom he lou'd'.[23] And Oberon's henchman is also slyly present, at least in borrowed phrasing. Puck concludes his epilogue, 'Give me your hands, if we be *friends*, / And Robin shall restore *amends*'; Brathwait concludes his envoi by commending his narrative 'Freely to th' World, that she may *friendly mend* it' (sig. R6[r]; my italics in both).[24]

In the main, though, *A Midsummer Night's Dream* serves as a grab bag of effects, while *Romeo and Juliet* drives Brathwait's narrative. And what it drives the narrative *toward* is a moral, imagined by Brathwait as the play's own. That moral, though trite in itself, is the product of a broad understanding of the social use of tragedy that seems also to derive from Shakespeare.

---

21 Brathwait, *Labyrinth*, sig. T1[v].

22 Brathwait, *Labyrinth*, sig. S4[r]. The phrase, 'watery moon', searched with the string <watr* FBY.9 moon*>, appears only in Turberville, Robert Greene and *Dream*; the alternative spelling <water*> adds only *Richard III*.

23 Brathwait, *Labyrinth*, sig.T3[v]. Further evidence of Oberon's presence behind Sylvanus appears in a text of Brathwait's composed no more than two years after *Loves Labyrinth*'s publication but withheld from the press for decades. In *A Solemne Ioviall Disputation: The Smoaking Age, or, The Man in the Mist* (London, 1617), sig.O3[v], Brathwait notes with regard to Chaucer that his '*Comments*' (i.e. *A Comment upon the Two Tales of our Ancient, Renovvned, and Ever-Living Poet Sr Jeffray Chaucer, Knight*, London, 1655) are 'shortly to bee published' (Black, *Brathwait*, p. 146, finds material from *Strappado* in *Comment*). *Comment* twice invokes Oberon. Linking 'King Oberon [and] Queen Mab' (sig. L4[r]), Brathwait offers a distinctive gloss, 'the Fayries Midwife' (sig. M2[v]); *LION* records only this instance of the phrase and Mercutio's. More substantially, Brathwait renders the 'night-spell' intoned by the Miller's Tale's carpenter: 'Fawns and Fairies keep away, / While we in these Coverts stay; / Goblins, Elves, of Oberon's Train, / Never in these Plains remain, / Till I and my Nymph awake' (sig. C8[r]). Metrically recalling Oberon's final verses ('Now, until the break of day / Through this house each fairy stray'), the chant simultaneously modifies the fairies' protective incantation, replacing natural threats (spotted snakes, hedgehogs, newts) with the 'Goblin . . . of Oberon's Train' (Puck) who materializes in Titania's bower. The same chant loosely translates or forms the basis of a macaronic passage in Thomas Randolph's *Cornelianum Dolium* (1638), putatively worked on by Brathwait after Randolph's death (Black, *Brathwait*, pp. 82–6). *Cornelianum*, 3.5, refers to '*Igne fatuo, Robin goodfellow*' and '*Satyrie, Faunis vulgo* Fairies', but omits Oberon. Pyramus and Thisbe's reminiscences of their sylvan trysts also echo Oberon: 'O many times haue we two sported there', and 'manie time and oft haue we two plaide' (sig. X2[r]); cf. 'I with the morning's love have oft made sport' (*Dream*, 3.3.390).

24 Puck's 'amends' reechoes in the final couplet of the epilogue-like conclusion to the *Comment* on the Miller's Tale, sig. E6[r].

MORALIZING TRAGEDY

Besides contributing to Brathwait's reworking of the Pyramus and Thisbe story, *Romeo and Juliet* lies at the heart of the poet's thinking about tragedy. On the eve of the publication of *Loves Labyrinth*, Brathwait reflects:

what can be more pleasant, or more profitable, then in the Theatre of mans life; so, to be made wary and wise by other mens harmes (and that without harme) as to sit in safety, and yet to be instructed in all parts [theatrical roles] without ieopardy: chusing out examples of all kind, which thou maist apply vnto thy owne peculiar vse.[25]

When Brathwait revives these musings a few years later, he has *Romeo and Juliet* in mind. The 'best of humane blessings', he avers in *The Shepheards Tales* (1621), is 'To sit secure and in a safe repose, / To view the crosse occurrences of those / Who are on the Sea'. Though the ensuing tales bear scant resemblance to anything in Shakespeare, Brathwait unveils his touchstone when he invites his dedicatee, Richard Hutton, 'To reade how Starre-crost louers lost their loue', thereby experiencing, 'what you nere felt, nor ere did prove; / Poore Swainlins crost where they affected most'.[26] The figure of vicariously acquiring experience through reading gains in authority, moreover, when in the first tale it is taken over by a rustic wordsmith, Technis, based on Brathwait himself.[27]

In a memoir dating from 1638 Brathwait recalls how, defying his father's wishes that he become a lawyer, he exchanged 'Suits' for 'Scenes'.[28] The character Technis similarly abandons legal studies on his father's early death (paralleling Brathwait's father's), preferring the liberal arts. Sharing memories with fellow shepherds of his happy days in Athens (recalling Brathwait's days in London), Technis asks rhetorically, 'Is it delightfull Shepheards to repose, / And all-alone to reade of others woes?' Pastoral repose is pleasant, he concedes, yet such rural delights pale beside the lordly pleasures afforded by places of learning:

Why there [in Athens] in Tragick Stories might we spend
Whole houres in choice discourses to a friend.

And reason of Occurrents to and fro,
And why this thing or that did happen so.
Might it content man, to allay the loade
Of a distemperd minde to walke abroad,
That he might moderate the thought of care
By choice acquaintance, or by change of ayre?
What noble consorts might you quickly finde
To share in sorrow with *a troubled minde*?

(my italics)[29]

Several points may be made. The recurrent figure of repose certifies that the passages under discussion lend themselves to joint elucidation. Auditors 'sit in safety' in a theatre; Hutton 'in a safe repose' devours tales of star-crossed lovers; Technis's shepherds in 'repose' 'reade of others woes', their pleasures falling short of the Athenian students who spend 'Whole houres in choice discourses' of 'Tragick Stories' (later 'tragick Scenes').[30] Of these passages, the most relevant is the third, with its conjuration of an interpretive community. Like the skilled readers called on by Heminge and Condell to explain Shakespeare to the less adept, Technis

---

[25] *The Schollers Medley, or, an Intermixt Discovrse vpon Historicall and Poeticall Relations* (London, 1614), sig. P1ʳ.

[26] Brathwait, *The Shepheards Tales* (London, 1621), sig. A1ʳ⁻ᵛ. Citations follow a separately bound version of the work (*STC* #3584). A second 1621 version of the text, beginning at sig. M8ʳ of *Natvres Embassie: or, The Wilde-Mans Measvres* (London, 1621; *SR* 1619), omits passages relevant to my discussion. *Natvres Embassie* returns to Pyramus and Thisbe in a short narrative poem, 'Love to the Last', which shows no influence from *Dream* or *Romeo* but ties the lovers to Hero and Leander, prominent in *Loves Labyrinth*. J. W. Ebsworth, in the introduction to his edition of *A Strappado for the Diuell* (Boston, 1878), pp. xviii–xix, argues that *Natvres Embassie* was planned as a sequel to *Strappado*.

[27] Black, *Brathwait*, pp. 23–32, observes Brathwait's autobiographical habit in his fictions, and, p. 120, notes Technis's similarities to Brathwait.

[28] Brathwait, *Spiritval Spicerie*, sig. T1ᵛ.

[29] Brathwait, *Shepheards Tales* sig. A4ᵛ–A5ʳ.

[30] Brathwait, *Shepheards Tales*, sig. B7ᵛ. '[C]hoice acquaintance' reechoes suggestively in 'Even so should I in my choise of acquaintance, desire more to enjoy his company; who hath beene usefully vers'd on the Theatre of History', *A Survey of History: or, A Nursery for Gentry* (London, 1638; an expansion of *Schollers Medley*), sig. Ddd3ᵛ.

and his companions spend hours in conversation, shaping the afterlives of tragic tales.

Note the phrases in italics: 'Of a distemperd minde to walke abroad' and 'a troubled minde'. They echo *Romeo and Juliet*'s first scene in which Benvolio tells of Romeo's melancholy ('A troubled mind drive me to walk abroad' [117]). Similarly pertinent is the love-duet in *A Midsummer Night's Dream*'s first scene, in which Lysander and Hermia anticipate Technis's companions' reasoning to and fro of tragic tales. Setting their course by 'aught that I could ever read, / Could ever hear by tale or history' (132–3), the beleaguered comic lovers speak as though, sitting securely in a theatre, they learn from Romeo and Juliet's play, running in repertory with their own, how to escape their counterparts' tragic fates. The analogy may be a bit of a stretch. No verbal parallelisms such as those linking the Technis passage to the Benvolio passage link it also to the comic lovers' dialogue. But because Brathwait thought hard about *Romeo and Juliet*'s relation to *A Midsummer Night's Dream*, we may speculate that he read in Hermia and Lysander's ruminations a witty allusion to Romeo and Juliet's travails. Not impossibly, their dialogue may even have encouraged his meditation on the profit to be extracted from tragic theatre.

What benefit does Brathwait imagine his readers deriving from reasoning to and fro about the plight of a Romeo and Juliet-conformed Pyramus and Thisbe? The answer lies in *Loves Labyrinth*'s dedication to 'vnhappy lovers':

Repose thee then vnhappy louer heere;
And see loues fal in tragick measures fram'd;
That when thou seest a louer loose his deere,
Thou of like chance may neuer be asham'd
Since thou art but as other louers were.
　For shame its none, to loose whats scarce begun,
　But shame is't not to doe what should be done.[31]

Rather than counselling flight on the heels of Hermia and Lysander contemplating their star-crossed lot, Brathwait advises readers to 'repose' themselves (that word again) in his tale, resisting shame. True lovers must 'neuer be asham'd' of love's trials, Brathwait insists in his dedication's close, signing himself love's 'passion-pittier' ('passion' in the sense of suffering). The phrase recalls his title-page promise of a subject, previously handled, 'but now with much more proprietie of *passion . . .* continued' (his italics). 'Passion' is also a keyword in the poem itself, in which Brathwait sympathizes with the 'distractions passionate' that Shakespeare mocked. For example, when he commends a pathetic Thisbe, 'nibbl[ing] out a stone or two' from the wall, or an equally pathetic Pyramus, 'hugg[ing] his pillow . . . Supposing it was Thysbe', his aim is to shield his readers, 'vnhappy lovers', from shame by teaching them that even the greatest lovers at times appear ridiculous.[32]

Romeo and Juliet's moral, as Brathwait reads the play, emerges most vividly from a passage near the end of the poem, displaying the bathos to which true love must sometimes descend. Depicting Thisbe's suicide, Brathwait seizes on a hilarious piece of Shakespearian stage-business preserved by Edward Sharpham's *The Fleire*, in which a character exclaims, 'Faith like *Thisbe* in the play, a has almost kil'd / himselfe with the scabberd'.[33] Brathwait echoes this routine, draining it of satire. In fifty lines of perfect deadpan, he depicts his heroine, taking Pyramus's weapon in hand, yet hesitating, not because she fears death but because she is incompetent to determine the business end of a sword:

Poore wench she knew not how to vse the blade,
　for other armour Nature had her made . . .
At last by reason, reason did acquaint,
　which was the pummell, which the fatall point[34]

Eventually casting off maidenly modesty ('other armour'), Thisbe throws both shame and squeamishness to the winds, plunging the sword into her breast. Similarly, Brathwait's readers, 'vnhappy lovers', must stay love's course even at the risk of appearing foolish. By scorning shame they bear witness to the fires of their passion.

---

[31] Brathwait, *Labyrinth*, sig. R4ᵛ.
[32] Brathwait, *Labyrinth*, sigs. S6ᵛ, S2ʳ, R8ʳ.
[33] Sharpham, *The Fleire* (1607), sig. E1ᵛ.
[34] Brathwait, *Labyrinth*, sig. X6ʳ.

In specifying Pyramus and Thisbe's sexual bravery as steadfastness against shame, Brathwait looks again to *Romeo and Juliet*. Though we are unaccustomed to viewing Juliet as a breakthrough in sexual frankness, Mary Bly demonstrates from early theatrical imitations of the play that Juliet's 'erotic fluency' had a liberating effect on early audiences. Masked in night, Juliet excuses herself from the 'maiden blush' that would else 'bepaint [her] cheek', and in diction verging on carnality ('Come night, come Romeo; come') imagines night freeing her to 'Think true love acted simple modesty' (2.1.128; 3.2.16–17). When the Nurse mutters, 'Shame come to Romeo!' Juliet retorts, 'He was not born to shame. / Upon his brow shame is ashamed to sit' (90–2). Brathwait echoes the phrasing, advising his readers not to let shame deprive them of love. The last lines of the dedication to unhappy lovers, with its two 'shames' and one 'ashamed' ('neuer be *asham'd* . . . / (for *shame* its none . . . / But *shame* is't)' (my italics)) exactly matches Juliet's pattern of triple repetition.[35]

And not only is *Loves Labyrinth*'s moral an extrapolation from *Romeo and Juliet*, but so too are the poem's inscribed readers. *Unhappy* lovers: the primary sense of luckless, ill-starred, rather than just sad, is underscored by the dedication's synonymous use of 'haplesse louer' and by Brathwait's concern that 'like chance' which befell Pyramus and Thisbe may befall his readers. By way of solace, the dedicatory poem, which opens by summoning 'louers, crost by louers fate', to 'Come . . . see these star-crost louers', promises the same readers, 'beames of comfort in the night, / Of your discomforts'. The beams, of course, will be emitted by love's risen martyrs, Pyramus and Thisbe, who in death become metaphorical stars raining down benign influence on their spiritual progeny. By the same token, in adopting his lover-readers as Pyramus and Thisbe's protégés, Brathwait implicitly places them under the protection of Shakespeare's star-crossed lovers, whose epithet he borrows in the dedication's opening.

Which brings us back to the Folio 'Presenters'. When Heminge and Condell in 1623 glance at 'other of [Shakespeare's] Friends, whom if you need, can bee your guides', their view of reading Shakespeare as a communal endeavour may represent only a slight advance beyond circumstances already in place. Not only does the conjured image of a reading group correlate with arrangements described in 1621's *Shepheards Tales* of friends gathering to reason of tragic occurrents, but 1615's *Loves Labyrinth* had already guided readers in the moral interpretation of the love-tragedy in which it is steeped. True, Brathwait fails to mention Shakespeare and not all readers would recognize his narrative as a mediation. Even Brathwait's disclaimer that his text corrects the improprieties of an earlier version of Pyramus and Thisbe's story might have been insufficient to prompt 'him that can but spell' to look beyond the present rendering to a Shakespearian original. But just as surely, 'the most able' would recognize that it was Shakespeare's business Brathwait went about. If Heminge and Condell knew *Loves Labyrinth*, whose containing volume, *A Strappado for the Diuell*, is remembered in 1640 as having won its author fame (in an appendix I take up the matter of the Folio editors' and Brathwait's overlapping circles of acquaintance), they may well have read the poem as a gloss on *Romeo and Juliet*, numbering its author among Shakespeare's 'friends' competent to 'leade [himself] and others'.[36] And even if they knew nothing of *Loves Labyrinth*, the virtual synchronicity of Brathwait's 1621 evocation of listeners discussing tragic tales with the Folio editors' call for guided reading is suggestive. Quite simply, Shakespeare conversation is in the air. As Heminge and Condell embark on

---

35 Mary Bly, 'Bawdy Puns and Lustful Virgins: The Legacy of Juliet's Desire in Comedies of the Early 1600s', *Shakespeare Survey 49* (Cambridge, 1996), pp. 97–109. 'Shame' is also a keyword in Hippolytus's admonition to Phaedra, appended to *Loves Labyrinth*'s Pyramus and Thisbe tale, but in the admonition, the shame is meant to stick. The Phaedra myth has ties to *Dream* (Arden2 edn, pp. lxiii, lxxx). Refracted through Theseus and Ariadne, it may also have inspired Brathwait's title figure of a labyrinth.

36 A pseudonymous poet signing himself 'Joan. Patridophilus' writes in a commendatory poem to Hum[phrey] Mill, *A Nights Search* (London, 1640), 'laud on Brathwait waiting did abound, / When a Strappado for the deuill he found'.

their publishing venture, it's noteworthy that the London book market casts up an analogue to the editors' model of expert readers steering lesser lights to a more profound reading experience. In helping weak readers to a moral (however platitudinous) to take away from *Romeo and Juliet*, Brathwait exemplifies the kind of 'friend' whose assistance Shakespeare's former colleagues rely upon to bring their own deceased 'Friend' before a wide reading public. Though contemporaneous discussion of Shakespeare is hard to come by, the perspective that emerges from study of Brathwait's early career is that the Folio's publication was a timelier event than we have appreciated.

BRATHWAIT AND *HAMLET*

After a relatively lean decade, Brathwait in the 1630s returned to abundance, coming under Shakespearian influence in intimate writings that revisit the theory of *The Shepheards Tales* and the practice of *Loves Labyrinth*. In 1617 he married Frances Lawson who bore nine children and died in 1633. Vowing to write annual poems of commemoration, Brathwait got only as far as 1639, when he remarried, bidding Frances a final farewell. In four extant memorial poems (the 1637 and 1638 poems are lost or were never written), Brathwait styles Frances 'Panarete', all-virtue, himself taking the name of 'Philaretus', virtue's lover.[37] The first of the *Anniversaries upon his Panarete* builds on Technis's view that tragic tales help readers to endure real loss, and it displays links with *Loves Labyrinth* so elaborate as to suggest that Brathwait had *Loves Labyrinth* open before him as he cast about for directions in funeral elegy.[38] But in mourning Panarete the firmest directions he takes are from *Hamlet*.

A favourite text of Brathwait's, *Hamlet* lends words and phrases that stick in the poet's vocabulary for decades.[39] Weeping Niobe is a conventional emblem of grief, so pervasive as to be nearly untraceable in its transmission. But Brathwait's usage unquestionably derives from Hamlet's mother following her husband's hearse, 'like Niobe, all tears' (1.2.149). Among almost three hundred palpable hits for <niob*/nyob*> in the

Renaissance section of *LION*, only Brathwait and Shakespeare juxtapose 'Niobe' with 'all', Brathwait doing so six times in passages displaying additional debts to *Hamlet*. For example, the 1639 memorial echoes Hamlet's disdain for 'seems', for ostentation in mourning. New widows flaunt the 'seeming weed of Sorrow: these belye / Their sable habits with a teare-forc'd eye', and press:

> Towards their Husbands graves: where they appeare
> All Niobees; clasping the fatall Beare
> With an affected zeale; and to ingrave
> More Sceanes of sorrow leape into his Grave[40]

---

[37] The *Natvres Embassie* version of *Shepheards Tales*, sig. O7[v], introduces a virtuous lady, Panaretus [*sic*]. The name appears conspicuously in Josuah Sylvester's elegy for Prince Henry, *Lachrimæ Lachrimarum, or The Distillation of Teares Shede for the Vntymely Death of the Incomparable Prince Panaretus* (London, 1612). The expanded edn of Brathwait's *Essaies vpon the Fiue Senses* (London, 1635) includes devotional pieces attributed to the 'personated' Panarete and 'Philaretvs, his Instructions to his Sonne'. See Appendix.

[38] The most prominent links appear in an alternate dedication of *Loves Labyrinth* to Brathwait's recently deceased patron, Sir Richard Musgrave ('Upon the Dedicatorie'). Granting the dedication's incongruity, Brathwait remarks: 'A sadder straine would better fitting be / Drain'd from the streames of graue Melpomene, / Where euery sentence might that passion breede'. 'Melpomene' and 'passion' recur in an epigraph to the tragic muse in *Anniversaries upon his Panarete* (London, 1634, sig. A2[v]; hereafter *Panarete I*), and 'sadder straine' in line 3 (and only there in the searchable Brathwait canon) of the Anniversary itself. Similarly, *Panarete I*'s second epigraph, to Niobe, telling of Brathwait's nine children standing in for the muses, echoes *Loves Labyrinth*'s ending in which the nine muses, enumerated (again, only here in the digitized canon), mourn Pyramus and Thisbe's deaths.

[39] The earliest compelling reference to *Hamlet* I find in Brathwait is *A New Spring Shadovved in Sundry Pithie Poems* (London, 1619), sig. B2[v]: 'neuer rac't / Out of the Table of our Memory' (unindexed in *LION*). The string <table of FBY.9 memor*> is paralleled only by Shakespeare and Massinger, but Massinger says nothing about razing/wiping out.

[40] Brathwait, *Astraea's Teares: Panaretees Trivmph: or, Hymens Heavenly Hymne* (London, 1641), sigs. E8[v]–F1[r]. Brathwait's other juxtapositions of 'all' and 'Niobe' occur in the last lines of *Raglands Niobe: or, Elizas Elegie* (London, 1635), sig. B6[v]; *Survey*, sig. Fff3[v]; *Lancs. Lovers*, sig. M8[r]; and *The Arcadian Princesse; or The Trivmph of Ivstice* (1635), sigs. A6[v], Kk7[r] (unindexed in *LION* but in *EEBO*, which adds near-misses by James Shirley and Thomas Rogers).

Catching up a skein of recent allusions in Brathwait's writing, including an epigraph to the First Anniversary (1634) and the title of a spinoff elegy, *Raglands Niobe* (1635), the 1639 allusion to Niobe betrays its Shakespearian basis by glancing at Gertrude's hypocrisy and Laertes's leap into Ophelia's grave.

Brathwait's most striking allusion to *Hamlet* occurs in line 2 of the first of two literary epitaphs for Panarete appended to the First Anniversary:

> For rites of holy Church which Christians have,
> Quires of blest Angels sing her to her grave[41]

The allusion of course is to Horatio's adieu, 'Good night, sweet prince, / And flights of angels sing thee to thy rest' (5.2.312–13); and it says much about Brathwait's esteem for Shakespeare that in commemorating his wife he reaches for a secular text, putting it to a use normally reserved for sacred verse. The epitaph, moreover, balances a reminiscence of another famous funerary passage in *Hamlet*. Seven lines into the Anniversary, Brathwait echoes Hamlet's first extended utterance, his refusal to be denoted by his customary suit of inky black:

> Nor will I cast my Sorrowes on my backe,
> Nor cloath them, as our Painters vse, in blacke;
> Such clothing's meere dissembling: many weare
> A sable habit, and distill a teare[42]

The coordination of echoes appears to be deliberate; in opening and closing the Anniversary, Brathwait draws on passages occupying equivalent positions in Shakespeare's tragedy, adroitly interweaving memorial allusions to Old and Young Hamlet.

Elsewhere in the same Anniversary, Brathwait justifies his memorial poem's incongruous turn to theatre, staging an internal debate between the faculties of Reason and Passion. Resuming the role of 'passion-pittier' performed in *Loves Labyrinth*, Brathwait takes up his own Passion's (sorrow's) complaint against Panarete's early death. '[Y]ou'l say shee dyed young', he challenges his sorrow in the voice of Reason, 'And might by course of Nature have liv'd long':

> Goe to th'Embrodred Theatre of ours
> Deckt with variety of choicest flowers,
> Where you shall find some meldew'd in their prime,
> Some blasted, others pruned 'fore their time;
> Not one 'mongst tenne but culled in their youth,
> And those are left, doe perish in their grouth.[43]

Commending the tragic theatre where virtue as a rule dies young, Brathwait as Reason argues that by witnessing deaths on the stage Passion ought to have acquired a tolerance for the injustice of Panarete's early passing. The argument recalls *The Shepheards Tales*' defense of fictions to the effect that stage-characters' misfortunes inure spectators to life's hardships. Brathwait, in other words, reminds himself of his own instruction. In the person of Reason schooling Passion, he practices what, as Technis, he preached.

Brathwait's specification of the *embroidered* stage alludes to the floral embossment of theatrical costumes (and hangings?). The figure is evidently important, calling up a matching image of the virtuous dead as 'choicest flowers' blasted in their prime, but Brathwait's intent is far from clear. Is there a nod to literature's power, like embroidery, to preserve and commemorate? Stitched in the memories of playgoers, tragic heroes live on, ornamenting the place of their death, the stage. Or is the point that theatrical 'flowers' are *mere* embroidery, *mere* artificial persons, from whose suffering spectators soon detach themselves, in the process of detachment rehearsing recovery from real-life loss? Whatever the main consideration, Brathwait's

---

41 Brathwait, *Panarete I*, sig. C7ᵛ. An epitaph for the Brathwaits' deceased child similarly concludes, 'While Angels sing my Lullabee', sig. C8ʳ; cf. Robert Southwell, *Saint Peters Complaint* (London, 1602), sig. M1ʳ: 'Let Angels sing his lullabie'. The idea of a substitution for orthodox burial ritual, carried forward in Panarete's epitaph with its repeated 'for' phrases ('for rites'; 'for hallow'd candles', etc.), may correct upward Ophelia's maimed rites ('For charitable prayers, / Shards, flints, and pebbles', *Hamlet*, 5.1.224–5).

42 Brathwait, *Panarete I*, sig.A3ʳ.

43 Brathwait, *Panarete I*, sig. B8ᵛ–C1ʳ. To my ear, the diction calls up Hamlet's father cut off in the blossoms of his sin, with additions from the mildewed Claudius (but I may be listening too intently).

importation of the theatre into a memorial poem is audacious. Though the Anniversary doesn't quite say, 'Cheer yourself up, attend plays as an antidote to grief', it comes close to saying that.[44] 'Go to the theatre' means 'take the theatre (metonymic for the stories enacted there) as an example (of virtue dying young)'. But to put a finer point on the matter: to feel the force of the example, you need to *go to* – to betake yourself physically to – the theatre, or to read playbooks.

Small touches heighten the incongruity of commending the stage in a memorial poem. The omission of the word 'tragic' (context determining the meaning, 'go to the *tragic* theatre') allows notions of levity to infiltrate. The salute to floral embroidery reverses the poem's censure of artificiality, indeed, of 'flowers of Rhetoricke'.[45] Brathwait's tolerance for theatre jars with his censure of 'Mimick Mourners' playacting grief, and jars, too, with his disdain to travesty his woes 'with description upon ev'ry part / To make my griefe a curious Scene of Art'.[46] Yet for all these misgivings, the bereaved poet turns nostalgically to his old flame, the theatre, for what it can teach him of tragic necessity. In a way Brathwait's ambivalence resembles Hamlet's, whose impatience with theatricalized mourning scarcely diminishes his delight in the players' arrival, his endorsement of 'the play' as 'the thing', and his amused contemplation of a theatrical career upon procuring for himself a pair of embroidered shoes.

A year later in the Second Anniversary, Brathwait bemoans the First Anniversary's failure to reverberate with the reading public. Underlying his lament is Hamlet's 'rogue and peasant slave' soliloquy in which, having shirked his authentic cue for passion, Hamlet feels shamed by the First Player's lustily bewailing a fictional Hecuba. Unlike Hamlet, though, Brathwait declines to take blame, shifting the fault onto unfeeling readers. How is it possible, he asks, that authentic 'Scenes of griefe, should not afford a teare' while

> ev'ry trifling toy
> Sprung from the ashes of consumed Troy
> Can force distreaming passion, though this woe,
> This feined woe, were many yeares agoe.[47]

Hamlet's First Player, 'forc[ing] his soul so to his whole conceit' as to produce 'Tears in his eyes' for burning Troy (2.2.555–7), is notionally intact in Brathwait's actor working the same terrain, able to 'force distreaming passion', while Brathwait's own 'unequall'd Subject' leaves readers dry-eyed. The antitheatricalism gibes with the First Anniversary's refusal 'To make my griefe a curious Scene of Art'. And as Hamlet embraces the players while disdaining theatricalized mourning, so Brathwait is ambivalent. Even as he complains about fiction's unrivalled power to stir grief, he illustrates his case with a theatrical fiction, drawing on *Hamlet* as an authoritative source of antitheatrical critique.[48]

In tracking these echoes, we should not be unduly surprised to encounter the stage's greatest melancholic in mourning poems commending 'th'Embrodred Theatre', but Shakespeare's tragedy serves Brathwait as more than just a source of allusion. We underestimate the extent of Brathwait's indebtedness if we think of him opportunistically borrowing from *Hamlet* to illustrate independently formed attitudes of grief. Mourners in 1633 were under no compulsion, after all, to position themselves on the tiredness of the fashion of funeral sable, nor to ponder the efficacy of real versus feigned tears in prompting sympathy. If these issues find their way into the Anniversaries, it's not because Brathwait alludes, exactly, looking to

---

44 Stephen Gosson writes in *The School of Abuse*: 'When you are greeved, passe the time with your neighboures in sober conference, or if you can read, let Bookes bee your comforte . . . looke for no salve at Playes or theatres, lest that . . . to leave Phisick, you flee to inchaunting', *Markets of Bawdrie: The Dramatic Criticism of Stephen Gosson*, ed. Arthur Kinney (Lewiston, N.Y., 2003), p. 117. To be sure, 'greeved' doesn't necessarily imply death. Still, Gosson's stress on vigilance against the theatre in time of dejection points up the boldness of Brathwait's advice.

45 In *Panarete I*, sig. B2[v], Brathwait opposes artificial flowers to Panarete's natural beauty; cf. his misgivings about 'imbroder'd Spring' in *Panaretees Triumph*, sig. E6[v].

46 Brathwait, *Panarete I*, sigs. B2[r], B1[v].

47 Brathwait, *Panarete II*, sig. A3[v].

48 The ambivalence runs deep; in *Panarete II*, sig. A7[r], Brathwait derides the theatre so vigorously that he feels compelled to correct a possible misimpression: 'I'm no Stage-Stinger'.

Hamlet for exemplification of already held beliefs, but because at a deeper level the play sets the agenda for his mourning. Interpellated by Shakespeare's great tragedy of bereavement, Brathwait derives from *Hamlet* a set of concerns deemed proper to grief precisely because of their Shakespearian provenance. The poet's profound ethical regard for Shakespeare, which disposes him to draw emulously on *Hamlet* in the intimate act of mourning his wife, is witnessed by the Anniversaries' borrowings from other Shakespearian plays and by indications elsewhere of Brathwait's career-long obsession with the Bard.[49] For instance, five years after the publication of Shakespeare's Sonnets, Brathwait lifts the final couplet from Sonnet 13 ('deare you know, / You had a father, let your sonne say so', in Brathwait's version).[50] Though this near-verbatim borrowing is long-established, its implications have registered only faintly with scholars. Until Benson's 1640 edition, the Sonnets were virtually unknown, or at any rate unquoted; Brathwait anticipates by two decades the next writer (Suckling) to display intimate knowledge of them. His early borrowing argues an exceptional responsiveness on Brathwait's part to whatever issued from Shakespeare's pen. Though the term is anachronous, we can do worse than to think of Brathwait as Shakespeare's fan. Understood in this way, Brathwait's echo of Horatio's farewell to Hamlet in his proposed epitaph for Panarete not only adds Shakespearian dignity to his wife's obsequies but is *self*-dignifying. Precipitating in his own grief a Shakespearian thematics, casting his sorrows in a respected idiom, the widower validates himself as a mourner.

Brathwait's supra-literary investment in Shakespeare presumably exceeds Heminge and Condell's fondest hopes for their friend's book, but there may be a sense in which Shakespeare's first editors, rhetorically overreaching, map the ground that Brathwait will soon occupy. Their wry warning of a 'manifest danger' besetting inexpert readers makes two points. If you're not a fan of Shakespeare's, you probably don't get him: relinquish your place among the literati, dropping back to the ranks of 'him that can but spell' (but first you may want to reread him or consult experts). And

second, your soul may be in a parlous state – the comic exaggeration (as suggested earlier) echoing Protestant traditions of Bible study in which a failure to understand entailed the risk of damnation. To be sure, Heminge and Condell's playful mystification of Shakespeare's theatrical 'scriptures' is far from full-blown bardolatry. In the 1620s and 1630s Shakespeare was not yet a universal taste, much less a god. Yet many who liked Shakespeare already loved him 'this side idolatry'. Among these was Brathwait, whose echo of Horatio's goodnight to the sweet Prince signals more than just a moment's infatuation with a pretty line.

---

49 Like *Hamlet*, *Richard II* is a frequent source of elegiac sentiment for Brathwait; e.g. an extended passage on his wife's last words, beginning, 'No Syllable is lost' (*Panarete I*, sig. C3ᵛ), derives from John of Gaunt's dying soliloquy, 'the tongues of dying men / Enforce attention, like deep harmony' (*Richard II*, 2.1.5–6). The sentiment is commonplace and direct comparison of end-terms may be unconvincing, but confirmation is abundant. In *Panthalia: or The Royal Romance* (London, 1659) Brathwait writes: (1) 'The words of dying men should enforce the deepest impression' (sig. C2ʳ; <dying man*/men* NEAR.9 enforc*/inforc*> yields only Gaunt's speech and Brathwait; 'deep' is a further link); and (2) 'Dying mens words ever reteine the deepest impression: especially when we consider how that very mouth . . . shall be injoyned to a perpetuall silence, and never impart the least . . . syllable of a word . . . to the world any more' (sig. O8ʳ). 'Impressions', 'syllable', 'perpetuall [cf. "eternall"] silence' and 'attention', all echo *Panarete I*. Elsewhere, Brathwait twice echoes *Richard II*'s 'nothing can we call our own but death' (3.2.148): 'nor can we say / Ought proper ours saue Sin', *New Spring*, sig. B2ᵛ; 'Man hath nothing . . . which he may properly call his owne, save Time', *Five Senses* (1635), sig. F5ᵛ.

50 Leo Daugherty, 'A 1614 Borrowing from Shakespeare's Sonnet 13', *Notes and Queries*, 29 (1982), 126–7, citing *The Poets VVillow: or, The Passionate Shepheard* (London, 1614), sig. F8ᵛ. *VVillow* contains many more probable echoes; e.g., the next stanza ends: 'Oh let this after age thine Image find / By some record which thou shalt leave behind' (cf. Sonnet 9.6). Two stanzas later: 'Those freeborne blossomes of thy tender prime' (cf. Sonnet 3.10). Another stanza concludes, 'for where he thought to finde conte[n]tment most, / In that same place he was the greatliest crost' (sig. C3ʳ; cf. Sonnet 29.8). Brathwait, *Smoaking Age: Chaucers Incensed Ghost* (1617) has: 'To force him leave what he had us'd so long' (sig.O3ᵛ; cf. Sonnet 73.14). *VVillow* treats further of a phoenix and a turtle and Venus and Adonis.

What is Brathwait's aim in incorporating an allusion to Shakespeare in his wife's epitaph? Is his intent to move pity by creating equivalence with the beloved Hamlet, who also 'dyed young[,] prun'd 'fore [his] time'? Is there a dream of sanctification, of calling down Shakespeare's blessings on the deceased? What if *Frances*, a composer of meditations in her own right, were primarily the one who admired the 'flights of angels' passage, prompting its inclusion? Though none of these conjectures can be compelling without evidence, each perhaps captures something of the force of a theatrical allusion's incongruous encroachment on the sacred space of epitaph. And whatever resonance the allusion possessed for Panarete's eulogist, it may be argued that by extracting the line from the stream of events in *Hamlet* and inscribing it in modified form as an epitaph on page or headstone, Brathwait claims for this one passage in Shakespeare the supreme readerly attention Heminge and Condell deem the rightful lot of their friend's greatness.

A year before Frances Brathwait's death, a second Shakespeare folio came into print with three new prefatory poems. The finest of these, the young Milton's 'Epitaph on the admirable Dramaticke Poet, W. Shakespeare', displays views similar to Brathwait's in the Anniversaries. Admiration in Milton's 'Epitaph' turns out to possess unsettling overtones of habitation, of being taken thrall by Shakespeare's genius. Three times Milton uses the prefix *in*: Shakespeare has built a monument '*in* our wonder and astonishment'; he prints readers' hearts 'with deep *Im*pression'; he lies '[s]epulcher'd *in*' our imaginations and spirits. Only twenty years earlier such hyperbole might have seemed outlandish, but in the interval Shakespeare's writings have attained a degree of cultural penetration; indeed, Milton's conceit of the admirer's 'fancy of it self bereaving' finds an echo in a fellow Second Folio praise-giver's depiction of playgoers 'Stolne from [them]selves' by Shakespearian wonders.[51] A difference between the two passages, though, and one that swings the Miltonic text in Brathwait's direction, is that Milton addresses the reading experience, as opposed to the broad theatrical experience, of Shakespeare. His topic is the afterlife of Shakespeare's words,

how they effect their displacement of the reader's subjectivity. Milton's account belongs to the same cultural moment as the Panarete anniversaries in which allusiveness goes beyond a mere ransacking of *Hamlet* for tropes and trophies. Instead, Brathwait thinks Shakespearian thoughts, gives over his voice to Shakespearian approximations of his emotions. The condition of being ventriloquized, to Milton tantamount to being struck dumb, sits easily with Brathwait, who displays influence without anxiety. And of course it's Brathwait's example, remarkable in the 1630s, that will move towards the centre as 'literature, philosophy, and thought', in Emerson's neologism, are 'Shakespearized'. Brathwait's self-authorization via self-effacement will become a posture increasingly familiar as writers in English, rereading and absorbing Shakespeare, come to regard him not just as a fellow writer to allude *to*, but as a tonality resident in and constitutive of their native language.

APPENDIX: BRATHWAIT'S CIRCLE OF ACQUAINTANCE

How far-ranging were Brathwait's theatrical connections? Can he have known Shakespeare or have been known to Heminge and Condell? The evidence, though inconclusive, is suggestive at least of the latter. Presumably having taken up part of his Cumbrian inheritance by the year of *Loves Labyrinth*'s publication (1615), Brathwait remained in touch with literary London, possibly dividing his time between the country and the capital. His closest theatrical friend was Thomas Heywood, whose 1612 *An Apology for Actors* (sig. G3[r]; written *c.* 1608) mentions Kendal, two miles from Brathwait's principal estate, as one of England's busiest theatrical hubs outside London. That same year, Heywood reports Shakespeare's offence at misattributed poems in *The Passionate Pilgrim*. Two

---

[51] Milton and 'IMS' quoted from Second Folio facsimile in *EEBO*. Paul Stevens compares the tribute to Shakespeare's 'hart robbing lines' in the last Parnassus play, 'Subversion and Wonder in Milton's Epitaph "On Shakespeare"', *English Literary Renaissance* 19 (1989), 375–88: p. 385.

years later, in 1614, Brathwait borrows from the Sonnets and, in *The Schollers Medley*, dedicated to Shakespeare's early patron Southampton, calls Heywood, 'My Iudicious friend' (sig. E4^r). He and Heywood remain friends until Heywood's death in 1641. Brathwait also continues on good terms with Southampton till the Earl's death in 1625, writing a funeral elegy, now lost, to which he alludes in 1638 (*Survey of History*, sig. A4^r).

On 10 July 1614 Shakespeare's Stratford friend John Combe dies. It is Brathwait who in *Remains after Death* (1618) reports the notorious epitaph ('Ten in the hundred') attached to Combe's monument, which will later be attributed apocryphally to Shakespeare.[52] The basis of Brathwait's association with Stratford around the time of Shakespeare's final residence there is unknown. A possible link is Thomas Posthumus Digges of Reigate, Surrey, co-dedicatee (with Thomas Gainsford) of *Strappado for the Diuell*, whom Brathwait hails as his Maecenas. T. P. Digges was a second cousin to Dudley and Leonard Digges, the stepsons of Shakespeare's testamentary overseer Thomas Russell, and he eventually sold the estate on which the Digges brothers were raised. The London house of Russell's second wife, Anne (St Leger Digges) Russell, neighboured those of Heminge and Condell, and her country house neighboured Heminge's birthplace. Heminge attended Dudley's wedding, signing as a witness. Leonard was Shakespeare's eulogist.[53]

Though by Brathwait's account the proper appreciation of 'Tragick Stories' is a communal endeavour, most of the poet's literary friends can only be guessed at. In 1614 William Browne of Tavistock published *The Shepheards Pipe*, with additions by George Wither, called Roget, and Christopher Brooke, called Cuddy. Within the year 'Roget' published a sequel, *The Shepherds Hunting*, with poems by 'Willy' and 'Cuddy'. Michelle O'Callaghan argues that the circle shared an agenda; their work is 'a product . . . of an Inns of Court culture characterized by a high level of political consciousness and collective literary activity'.[54] Brathwait, an Inns of Court-man, was Wither's exact contemporary and admirer; his writings show influence from both Wither and Browne.[55] That influence extends even to intimate texts: Wither's *nom de plume* in *Faire-Virtve, The Mistresse of Phil'arete* (1622) may underlie Brathwait's Philaretus. Or influence may travel in the other direction: Brathwait's *The Shepheards Tales* (1621) introduces a virtuous lady Panaretus (*sic*). Indeed, Wither and Brathwait may both be indebted to Browne's 1614 elegy for his friend Philarete (Thomas Manwood). Wither's corpus like Brathwait's is vast, and Browne's considerable. All three bear investigation with an eye to parallel strands of Shakespeare allusion. Similarly, Thomas Heywood and John Taylor the Water Poet may yield interesting correlations.

---

[52] Brathwait, *Remains*, sig. L2^v; printed with Patrick Hannay, *A Happy Husband* (London, 1619).

[53] For an account of the Digges family (excluding T. P. Digges), Leslie Hotson, *I, William Shakespeare, do appoint Thomas Russell, esquire* (London, 1937). I wish to thank Deborah Digges Barasch for correspondence concerning her family history.

[54] Michelle O'Callaghan, 'Literary Commonwealths: A 1614 Print Community, *The Shepheards Pipe* and *The Shepherds Hunting*', *The Seventeenth Century* 13 (1998), 103–23: 104; '"Now thou may'st speak freely": Entering the Public Sphere in 1614', in *The Crisis of 1614 and The Addled Parliament: Literary and Historical Perspectives*, ed. Stephen Clucas and Rosalind Davies (Aldershot, 2003), pp. 63–79: 72–4.

[55] In *Strappado* Brathwait hails 'louely Wither . . . bonny Browne, / . . . and their Cuddy too'. *The Shepheards Tales* is modelled on Browne's *The Shepheards Pipe*, and Wither's *The Shepherds Hunting*; *Strappado*, on Wither's *Abuses Stript and Whipt*.

SHAKESPEARE PERFORMANCES
IN ENGLAND, 2006

MICHAEL DOBSON

JANUARY 2006

Well before its inauguration, the RSC's Complete Works Festival – a drive to stage or host productions of every play in the canon in Stratford between April 2006 and April 2007 – is already making 2006 an unusual year for the classical repertory in England. For one thing, it results in there being no Shakespeare at all on offer in Stratford for the first three months of the year, with the RSC playing adaptations of Chaucer and Dickens (reserve national poets?) while they gather their resources for what the publicity department is calling The Essential Year. The company administrators with whom I have corresponded sound slightly perplexed and, looking at the intricacy of the Complete Works Festival performance schedule available on the company's website I can see why. Every Stratford venue possible has been mobilized: productions are to be mounted in the Royal Shakespeare Theatre (prior to its closure for internal remodelling); in the Swan; in the temporary 900-seat Courtyard Theatre (a large corrugated steel shell occupying the Other Place car-park, due on completion to open with a revival of Michael Boyd's production of the first tetralogy of histories, described in *Survey 55*); and, as if just to demonstrate which organization is the real spiritual and temporal power in Stratford-upon-Avon nowadays, the RSC has even gone beyond their own premises to borrow an extra performance space from the Church of England, conscripting Holy Trinity Church for a very brief run of *Henry VIII* in the late summer. One other local body has

mucked in too: what is perhaps the least popular play in the canon, *Timon of Athens*, is to have a short autumn run in the Birthplace Trust's little lecture hall at the Shakespeare Centre on Henley Street. (I am at first surprised by the absence of The Other Place from all this, but apparently the RSC's last remaining studio theatre is due to become the lobby of the temporary Courtyard for the duration of that structure's life.) The exhausted RSC staff sound relieved, however, by an unexpectedly high level of box-office demand. A scheme to sell 'golden tickets' admitting their holders to as many performances as they liked of every production in the Festival at £1,000 a time had to be abandoned, since, although the company anticipated applications for such tickets only from a handful of millionaires, enough of their hardcore fans noticed that this price would actually represent quite a good deal – about £27 a ticket, even if you only saw each show once, and substantially less if you rented the ticket out to your friends in between – for the bookings department to have been snowed under with requests.

SPRING

2 MARCH 2006

Meanwhile, the National has at last revived the Complicite *Measure for Measure*, first seen for only a few performances in 2004 (see *Survey 58*), though in a different space – the proscenium-arch Lyttelton rather than the much larger Olivier – and with a slightly altered cast. Having the Duke played by the production's director makes an obvious A-level sort of sense, but Simon McBurney has less gravitas and far less menace than had David Troughton, and the still, momentary face-off between Vincentio and the released Barnardine in the last scene, for example, is far less arresting than it was. As if fulfilling the Duke's promise to the Provost, 'We shall employ thee in a worthier place' (5.1.530), McBurney has promoted Angus Wright to the role of Angelo, where he is convincingly and at times almost touchingly gauche but far less neurotically antiseptic than was Paul Rhys. As if to overcompensate for his comparatively sympathetic manner, however, he is more visibly cruel to Naomi Frederick's Isabella: as she faces the audience, stiff and appalled, towards the close of their interview in 2.4, he unbuttons her blouse and then, standing behind her, cuts through the front of her bra at 'Fit thy consent to my sharp appetite' (2.4.161) using the razorblade with which he earlier cut his arm at 'Blood, thou art blood' (2.4.15), thereby exposing her breasts to the audience. The supportive way of reading this directorial decision would be to say that it deliberately creates an uneasy complicity between the audience's voyeurism and Angelo's lust, to be recognized and immediately disowned, but it still feels exploitative, over and above what it does within the terms of the production.

28 MARCH 2006

On tour at the Grand Theatre in Wolverhampton, Bill Bryden's modern-dress-with-rapiers Birmingham Rep production of *Romeo and Juliet* is distinguished principally by a fine Mercutio, Gus Gallagher, who, as well as putting over the sexual jokes as energetically as any school party could wish, takes the trouble to mind about getting killed. Instead of throwing away 'No, 'tis not so deep as a well' (3.1.96ff) as a bitter but essentially stoical triumph of wit in the face of mortality, Gallagher eschews the customary stiff upper lip in favour of the riskier but much more plausible option of exhibiting maximum pain, shock, anger and an absolute terror of dying: the floundering, crying, shouting, choking spectacle is appalling, and it renders Romeo's subsequent loss of control far more convincing and less arbitrary than it can often seem. What is less convincing about this production (quite apart from principals Jamie Doyle and Anjali Jay, who are never wholly comfortable with the verse or even the vocabulary) is Bryden's decision to have the Prince of Verona represented only by a tape-recording of Sir Donald Sinden: instead of appearing in person to part the opening fray, banish Romeo and editorialize over the last act's corpses, this Prince merely booms fruitily from the public address system, while those hapless flesh-and-blood members of the cast currently on the stage are obliged to stop what they are doing and gaze abjectly upwards towards the balcony. I learn later that this curious device, fatally reminiscent of the disembodied voice of authority which periodically tells the Teletubbies that it is time for bed, has been used before, but why so undramatic and ludicrous a directorial choice should ever have been repeated baffles me.

22 APRIL 2006

It is the weekend of the Birthday celebrations in Stratford, with all their touchingly absurd pomp, and the Complete Works Festival is at last under way. In the marquee where the official lunch for those who have processed from Birthplace to Grave takes place (a meal which on this occasion comes complete with speeches by Janet Suzman, Carol Rutter and a grandly undisembodied Sir Donald Sinden), it soon becomes clear that as a desperate gambit for energizing Stratford by inducing a sort of exhilarated panic throughout the ranks of the RSC, the Complete Works Festival is already a roaring success. Among the guests at the lunch are members of the Baxter Theatre Company, one of the first of the Festival's visiting companies, who have brought Janet Suzman's production of *Hamlet* from Cape Town, and even their palpable collective shock at the murder of their original Guildenstern, Brett Goldin, just before their departure from South Africa less than a week before seems like a bracing and unaccustomed breath of wind from a less predictable theatrical world elsewhere. It is a terrible shame, then, that the sample of work by the RSC that is on offer in the evening as this year's official Birthday Performance and the first show in the Festival, Nancy Meckler's production of *Romeo and Juliet* in the main house, should be as weak as it is. The set represents a piece of sandy ground with a pit on one side of it and an artistic-looking dead tree at the back, and as the audience settle into their seats it resembles nothing so much as a Debenhams window display awaiting the arrival of some fashionably dressed dummies. Sadly, that is pretty much what the cast of this production become, comprehensively paralysed by a directorial concept which the merest GCSE drama student could have recognized as a non-starter before the first rehearsal. Elegantly kitted out as Mediterranean peasants in their best clothes, and puzzlingly accompanied by several small children, including a little girl in rabbit pyjamas, the cast arrive in two groups and ceremonially throw a collection of weapons – knives, handguns, agricultural implements – into the pit and then cover it with a tarpaulin before the play gets under way. Having thus disarmed themselves, those members of the cast who now start to perform *Romeo and Juliet* while the rest look on are strangely ill-equipped for the opening brawl scene, and in this and every other piece of combat (in a play punctuated throughout by violence which needs to impress the audience as completely lethal) the actors do not actually attack each other but instead exhibit competitive displays of macho tap-dancing under low neon light, enhanced by the rhythmic thumping of the ends of what look like vertically held billiard cues against the stage beside their feet. Those whom the script nonetheless insists get fatally injured during such encounters have to collapse spontaneously at pre-agreed moments, as if suddenly afflicted by terminal bunions. This manner of staging the fight scenes is probably less helpful in terms of narrative and emotional impact than cutting them entirely would have been, and the non-fight scenes aren't much less alienating, played with an odd not-quite-naturalistic clumsiness that I finally decide, in a fit of charity, may be deliberate. During the duel between Romeo and Tybalt the two actors get sufficiently cross about each other's tap steps to throw down their billiard cues and try to resort to the real weapons that were earlier thrown into the pit, but they are prevented from so doing by lookers-on; however, the little girl in the rabbit pyjamas gets upset anyway, and is taken off to bed. I find myself wishing at this point that the real Sir Donald Sinden in the audience would stand up and announce that it is time everybody else went to bed too, but alas he does not. It is only when I inspect the oversized programme at the end of this long evening that I learn from a note that what the audience were supposed to infer was that we were watching two rival Sicilian peasant families who once had a fatal feud but who now remind themselves not to kill each other by ritually staging a tap-dancing open-air amateur performance of Shakespeare's *Romeo and Juliet* every year. Obvious, really: I'm sure it happens all the time. The little girl, I gather, was being kept up late to watch this farrago because when she gets older she will have to play Juliet every year herself. I cannot blame her for being unhappy about the prospect.

27 APRIL 2006

The house-lights dim, and at the centre of the stage of the Royal Shakespeare Theatre a black grand piano, which is soon having uncomfortable ominous chords hammered out of it by the black T-shirted musician who sits hunched on its stool, stands on top of an upturned white one. Shafts of cold white light shine across the dim stage from the wings. At the back of the stage stand three or four impassive and unappealing middle-aged white men in charcoal business suits. Another, more overweight and even less appealing, is downstage in front of the piano. Very slowly, he begins to undress, folding his clothes at his feet. As far as the show that is just beginning is concerned, clearly, there is no beauty and no colour and no melody in the world, and the audience who find themselves attending this joyless monochrome cabaret are emphatically not to be indulged – unless, that is, what they most want to have indulged is a revolted misanthropy. These first five wordless minutes of the Münchner

Kammerspiele's *Othello*, directed by Luk Perceval, would make the perfect comic undergraduate parody of every cliché an English audience might have expected on coming to see a specimen of modern German theatre. But then the dialogue starts, and the surtitles, and two things become clear: firstly that the bulging actor now down to his underwear is representing Brabantio, and secondly that it is all going to be even more dispiriting than this opening has already suggested. Feridun Zaimoglu's adaptation, edited down to two hours by the company's dramaturg Marion Tiedke without even the escapist comfort of an interval (though some audience members decide to make their escape well before the end without one), transforms every character in *Othello* into one more foul-mouthed Iago, so that even if your German does not extend much beyond the words 'scheisse' and 'hure' you will understand a depressingly high percentage of this script without any recourse to the simultaneous translation. The contents of the stage, however, miscegenating pianos and all, are sufficiently monotonous and unattractive to send one's eyes to the surtitles for much of the time regardless, where one finds oneself reading *Othello* as reductively paraphrased by a highly aggressive sociopath with a penchant for picturesque obscenity. (I will spare you any direct quotations, but you can take my word for it that by comparison *The Skinhead Hamlet* is a rich, ebullient, Chaucerian celebration of human possibility.) Numbed if they are lucky, most of the Stratford audience sit trying to tame this ugly cocktail of racism, misogyny and homophobia (in which Othello, though referred to throughout even by Desdemona as 'Choco', is played by an undisguisedly white actor, Thomas Thieme, and Sheri Hagen's black Emilia seems to be left loitering at the edge of the stage for much of the show purely to launder some of the script's extreme representational violence against women and minorities) by making wild surmises about the cultural context from which this show has incongruously travelled to the familiar safe red plush of the RST. The adaptor is of Turkish extraction, so are the grotesques which he is putting through a vastly simplified version of the plot of *Othello* intended as an angry outsider's satire on the attitudes of white Germany? How offensive did this show seem in Munich, and was its offensiveness purposely designed to shock a complacent bourgeoisie out of their prejudices, or does Zaimoglu just genuinely suffer from a virulent dramaturgical equivalent of Tourette's syndrome? From the evidence of the show itself, seen away from its home constituency like this, it would be just as possible to hypothesize that the Münchner Kammerspiele's regular audience must consist of baying neo-Nazis as to picture an auditorium full of anxious and masochistic liberals. Iago for once completes and even gets away with the murder of Cassio, savagely tearing up his business suit afterwards for good measure; Othello apparently gets away with the murder of Desdemona, whose death on this occasion, like Thisbe's passion, ends the play; and Luk Perceval seems to have got away with a show substantially indistinguishable from the equally scatological, life-hating and inanely keyboard-dominated Shakespeare adaptations that over the last few years have been directed in Spain by Calixto Bieto. I suppose it is refreshing to go to the RST and see an *Othello* that is there not as a routine piece of pre-approved British state culture but purely because the Complete Works Festival needed a visiting *Othello* for a week or so and this one happened to be available, but it was a great deal more refreshing to get out into the open air after it had finished.

29 APRIL 2006

From one that surprisingly got into the Festival to one that surprisingly didn't, Northern Broadsides' three-part *The Wars of the Roses*, which the company selected for their 2006 programme before they had heard that Michael Boyd would be reviving his own 2000–1 production of the first tetralogy as the Complete Works Festival's own chosen rendering of the life of Henry VI and the rise and fall of Richard III. Hence this robust, flat-vowelled cycle boasts an impressive tour schedule but one that doesn't include Stratford. During its stay in Liverpool, the whole enterprise can be seen at the Playhouse in a single Saturday, with *Henry VI* (essentially, parts one-and-a-half) at 11am, *Edward IV* (the rest of part 2 and an athletically trimmed part 3) at 4pm, and then *Richard III* at 7.30pm. This makes for a fairly exhausting but undeniably grand day out, and few of the sizeable majority of the near-capacity audience who have been in the theatre for most of the preceding twelve hours by the time the battle of Bosworth has been lost and won are not enthusiastically on their feet during the ensuing curtain call. Among much else, Barrie Rutter's production demonstrates the superior effectiveness of drumming over tap dancing as a substitute for naturalistic stage fighting: in the successive military conflicts that punctuate the sequence, culminating in a Bosworth Field that could have held its own at a music festival in Burundi, individual combats are supplemented by confrontations between rival teams of percussionists. Mark Stratton's Talbot, indeed, goes into battle pushing a wheeled contraption that is in part medieval tank and in part a one-man-band's attack drum kit, from the midst of which he issues forth with a battle-axe for his duels with Joan la Pucelle. Throughout, the changing fortunes of the contending armies are as audible as they are visible, as their rival rhythms and heraldic fanfares batter and shriek to dominate the auditorium, easily making up in energy and excitement what the stage armies lack in numbers. More than half of a twenty-one-strong company double as the show's accomplished band as well as doubling, tripling and sometimes quadrupling their speaking roles: Jacqueline Redgewell, for instance, is a fine alto saxophonist as well as Duchess Eleanor of Gloucester, Lady Bona and the widowed Duchess of York, while even Maeve Larkin, playing the more structurally important female roles of Joan la Pucelle and Lady Anne, spends far less time resting between their scenes than she does playing the violin.

Despite these conspicuous and conspicuously strong female performances, the company is so dominated by barrel-chested middle-aged northern men that the first two parts of the trilogy sometimes resemble the contention between York and Lancaster as re-enacted by those two cities' respective aldermen, and it almost comes as a relief when towards the middle of *Edward IV* York's variously vicious sons begin to achieve some dramatic pre-eminence over the stolid ageing warlords and senior clerics who have held the plays together to date. Given the size and demographics of the company, Conrad Nelson's vigorous, weaselly Richard of Gloucester inevitably finds himself employing some surprisingly mature and well-nourished-looking citizens in some surprisingly menial positions during *Richard III*, but fortunately most of Rutter's troupe are just as capable of producing a well-characterized underling as they are of marshalling military or ecclesiastical dignity. Rutter himself manages what is perhaps the most thorough transformation of the day. He has cast himself, in the best traditions of the actor-manager, as a commanding Richard of York for *Henry VI* and *Edward IV*, a role in which he is undeniably strong but during which he displays an unfortunate habit of fixing the audience's eyes with a manic glint towards the end of each major soliloquy, spreading his arms as if threatening to embrace them, and then stalking slowly and unblinkingly backwards into the wings after the final couplet. (I find myself wondering whether he picked this particular mannerism up from Macready.) But after a tremendous death-scene in *Edward IV*, during which his voice seems to discover a whole new bass register and his performance a sudden shocked and belated capacity for pity, he returns in *Richard III* as the conscience-stricken second murderer of Clarence in 1.4, a man who here gives a persuasive impression of having been just morally confused enough by a whole disappointing lifetime of under-rewarded and degrading service to have rashly agreed to try out a first assignment as a hit-man even after retirement age. Overall, with its simple, heavy wooden scaffold set and deliberately coarsened make-do period costumes, Rutter's is a version of the first tetralogy which perhaps has little to say about these plays which wasn't said in Hall and Barton's famous rendition forty years earlier, but it is no less gripping for that and as potent an introduction to the pleasures of Shakespeare's histories in performance as provincial audiences are likely to get.

46. *Richard III*, Northern Broadsides, dir. Barrie Rutter, 2006. Conrad Nelson as Richard at the head of his army, 5.5.

4 MAY 2006

On the stage of the Swan, fitted with a circular rake from which rises a commanding central flat rectangle, a sentry in hooded camouflage fatigues is already standing with a rifle beneath a cyclorama of gathering clouds as the audience take their places. Presently the house lights fade and only the foggy blue of a night which the soldier's anxious vigilance has already imbued with palpable tension remains. Suddenly raising his rifle to challenge the fellow-soldier who, entering from the rear of the stalls, has come to relieve him – '*Who's there?*' – the sentry seems on the very point of firing, and for a tiny moment the whole audience sit involuntarily up, ready for the shock of a gunshot. We were expecting the line, but we weren't expecting it to be delivered in such complete deadly earnest. Something of this utter seriousness and conviction character-izes the whole of Janet Suzman's Baxter Theatre Centre production of *Hamlet*: we were expecting the rest of the play too, but weren't expecting that to be delivered in such complete earnest either.

The Denmark this nervous African sentry is defending is very much a modern state, though precisely how it is to be understood in relation to the racial politics of post-apartheid South Africa remains a puzzle for an audience unfamiliar with its home context. Adam Neill's initially cheery, corduroy-clad Horatio, trying to twinkle Tauriq Jenkins' grim Marcellus out of his belief in ghosts until he too sees the greatcoated, peaked-capped Old Hamlet (and hears the eerie, sonorous snore-come-groan which is all that the ghost can utter before the cock crows), is a Jewish university academic, perhaps a junior lecturer in philosophy; his student-age friend Hamlet, as played by Vaneshran Arumugam, is a lithe South African Asian who will consider whether to be or not to be while carrying out Tai Chi exercises. Roshina Ratnam's Ophelia would once have been classified as 'coloured' too, while as Rosencrantz and Guildenstern Marcel Meyer and Nicholas Pauling are a pair of spoiled white students who have trouble with the unaccustomed Tweedledum and Tweedledee-like ties they don when summoned to the court. Claudius, however, as impersonated by John Kani, looks like an ANC veteran who on acceding to the crown has ruthlessly taken over the security apparatus of the *ancien regime*: giving an impressive presidential wave at the start of 1.2, and then standing on the central rectangle behind a seated Gertrude as he delivers his lecture against unmanly grief, he grips the queen's shoulder hard to enforce her compliance with his stated party line as, clearly overruling her own real views, he tells Hamlet that the prince's intent in going back to school in Wittenberg is 'most retrograde to *our* desire' (1.2.114), where the first person plural is clearly marital rather than royal. At this line, on Claudius's slight but definite nod, armed guards promptly appear to block all the exits.

Arumugam's Hamlet, however, though angered by this, is not subdued: he refuses to accept the public handshake then riskily offered by Claudius at 'Our chiefest courtier, cousin, and our son' (1.2.117), and his reply to his cowed mother's repetition of her husband's injunction ('I pray thee stay with us, go not to Wittenberg', 1.2.119) pointedly rebukes her for expressing Claudius's desires rather than her own – 'I shall in all my best obey *you*, madam' (1.2.120). His subsequent rendition of 'O that this too, too solid flesh would melt' (1.2.129) is disappointing after this carefully observed little confrontation – this is a Hamlet better at scoring points off other characters than at simply inhabiting his own, more lucid in action than in reflection – but Suzman's 1.2 beautifully sets up both the cat-and-mouse game with the king and what will emerge as an especially searching portrait of the Claudius–Gertrude marriage. If anything, the performances are slightly too big for the Swan, or at least their points are underlined with more emphasis than one has come to expect from the RSC house-style that this theatre usually hosts, but this is all part of the prevailing impression this show gives of being definitely and unforcedly serious: it has something of the rawness and energy that can characterize the best student productions, but with far more technical accomplishment and a far greater sense that the play matters more than do the individuals playing it.

With all the gains provided by the company's freshness and unfamiliarity, however, come some losses: excited and moved by the show as this Stratford audience is, I for one, as I have already suggested, find myself wishing I knew more about the specific resonances that these casting decisions and these costuming choices must have carried for the Baxter's own crowd back in Cape Town. What does it mean when a South African Asian Hamlet adopts an antic disposition by donning what look like prison-camp clothes, wearing khaki shorts and carrying a blanket and an enamel cup and plate? Clearly he is reiterating in another register his sense that Denmark is a prison, and that he is being detained in Elsinore against his will, but what other connotations does this particular kit bring with it in South Africa? Which African language is it in which Claudius attempts briefly to pray aloud at the end of 'O, my offence is rank . . .' (3.3.36ff), and what should it tell us about his origins and social identity? And why does Dorothy Ann Gould's troubled Gertrude, once her worst suspicions about Claudius are confirmed during the closet scene, start to wear clothes that make her look exactly like Winnie Mandela? (She is particularly good in her encounter with the mad Ophelia, incidentally, who finds the Queen in 4.5 smoking a nervous cigarette outdoors and has to be covered with the horrified Gertrude's fur wrap when she starts trying to remove her blouse as she sings.) Presumably the righteous Old Hamlet, doubled with Claudius by John Kani (whose work in Athol Fugard's *The Island* has already made him an honorary detainee of the apartheid era), is implicitly being identified with Nelson Mandela (and in the closet scene he appears up on the balcony behind the other actors looking as if imprisoned), but Suzman's programme note instead appears to link Mandela with Hamlet junior: 'the world is very well aware of a remarkable

47. *Hamlet*, Baxter Theatre Centre, Cape Town, dir. Janet Suzman, 2006. John Kani and
Dorothy Ann Gould as Claudius and Gertrude.

individual, an aristocrat among souls, incarcerated against his will, who took himself on a prolonged spiritual and intellectual journey while awaiting his rightful place to be restored to him'. For the time being one just has to put these nagging pieces of frustrated curiosity about the implicit politics of this production aside and immerse oneself in the narrative, which when it is played this urgently is easy enough to do. It seems characteristic of Arumugam's extroverted forcefulness in the title role that at the end of this *Hamlet* he not only stabs and poisons Claudius but strangles him as well – appropriate, too, to the strength and authority with which Kani has endowed the usurper. If ever there was a Claudius who was going to need a lot of killing, this was him.

10 MAY 2006

It is a terrible anticlimax to go within a week of this striking *Hamlet* to see the first play mounted under Dominic Dromgoole's regime at Shakespeare's Globe, his own production of *Coriolanus*. Dromgoole has rashly taken on two shows to direct himself in his first season as Artistic Direc-

tor, and this one, perhaps as a result, looks as though it has had too little rehearsal and much too little thought. The default settings established under Mark Rylance are clearly all still in place: the whole season has a moderately tenuous theme ('The Edges of Rome', which for this purpose extend beyond the world metropolis dramatized in *Coriolanus*, *Titus Andronicus* and *Antony and Cleopatra* to encompass the Hellenic location of *The Comedy of Errors*); the unfortunate actors in this opening production have to wear reconstructions of what somebody thinks Elizabethans would have worn when playing Romans; and the audience in the yard are continually having their space half-jokily invaded by bits of the action – the show culminates, for example, with a bathetic echo of Olivier's famous death-fall, when Jonathan Cake's beefy Coriolanus is stabbed at the very front of the stage and falls slowly forwards, to be caught by the extras who have been elbowing the central standees out of the way in order to do so for the preceding two minutes. (The whole incident looks about as spontaneous as a singer's rehearsed leap into a hireling-crammed mosh-pit during a pop video.) There is no genuine dramatic conflict in

48. *Hamlet*, Baxter Theatre Centre, Cape Town, dir. Janet Suzman, 2006. Vaneshran Arumugam as Hamlet.

the show at all, which is entirely dedicated to making Coriolanus look admirable, if at times comically eccentric, and which never seems to have considered the option of allowing anyone to recognize the validity of what the tribunes have to say against him; instead Sicinius and Brutus are played so as to resemble trades union leaders as caricatured in the *Daily Mail* during the 1970s. Despite one intelligent reading of one line – 1.7.76, 'O' me alone, make you a sword of me', played as an intent prayer to Mars – this is exactly the facile, half-embarrassed *Coriolanus* the Globe might have staged at any time over the last ten years, and a poor omen for the new management.

19 MAY 2006

At the Bristol Old Vic, Anne Tipton has directed *The Taming of the Shrew* in a satisfyingly detailed, inventive, modern-dress production which is nonetheless as striking for what it shares with Greg Doran's RSC rendition of 2003 as it is for what it has come up with independently. Unlike Doran, it is true, Tipton leaves the Induction uncut (faint shades of Michael Bogdanov here, as Geoffrey Beever's Sly irrupts ad-libbing from the stalls, to be found drunkenly asleep on the stage by a bowler-hatted Hooray Henry of a Lord) and, unlike Doran, Tipton has Katharina at first played entirely as a victim. Even within the world of the play, it is very surprising to hear Flora Montgomery's pretty, crestfallen elder sister described as a shrew, and Petruccio's rough wooing fails to provoke her into much beyond depressive sulking. Richard Dillane's Petruccio, though, like Jasper Britton's in 2003, is a reckless, charismatic heavy drinker visibly upset about his father's death and very serious about falconry, who is surprised by his own response to Katharina at their first meeting, has some reservations about the here thoroughly gratuitous taming to which he subjects her after their wedding, and finally cracks and starts trying to comfort her (which is clearly all she needed all along) immediately after he has seen off the tailor in 4.3. He does so, moreover, by giving her his favourite old green cardigan to wear over the tattered petticoat and wellingtons in which she arrived at his house, so that she arrives back in Padua wearing a costume strikingly similar to the curious outfit in which Alexandra Gilbreath's Katharina finally accepted herself as a wife in 2003. Like Britton and Gilbreath too, Dillane and Montgomery finish the evening in a happy alliance against their more conventionally respectable peers: after her gleefully over-the-top submission speech, he empties the attaché-case full of banknotes which is the prize of the men's wager all over the dining table at which his shocked in-laws are seated and on which the two have been standing during her lecture, and the happy couple walk out together then and there, leaving Hortensio's final congratulations as an awkward, face-saving bid to break the shocked silence which ensues. Despite Montgomery's surprising sparklessness in the earlier part of the play, Katharina and Petruccio's scenes are often funny – a green hoover in the line-up of Petruccio's servants that greets them at his house, for example, occasions some intricate touches – but for once they are given a run for their money in this respect by the subplot which here, for example, boasts an excellent Tranio by Samuel Roukin who has all sorts of fun aping Lucentio's educated accent, demanding in 2.1, for example, that he should be allowed 'free eccess' to 'Bienka'. There are some impressive pieces of design, too: the way in which Hannah Clark has devised a set in which a Paduan plaza can become the interior of Minola's house merely by a lighting change and the turning of two replicas of the Venus de Milo (another pair of simultaneously idealized and damaged women to add to the play's existing collection) is especially slick.

21 MAY 2006

The Complete Works Festival today throws up a real curiosity in the Swan: a 3pm Sunday matinee, directed by William Oldroyd, consisting of the RSC's currently touring version of *The Knight's Tale*, part of Mike Poulton's two-part adaptation of selected Canterbury Tales (the whole company of which have been brought to Stratford for the day, without costumes or props), and then, after an interval, the same cast giving a rehearsed reading, on the same bare stage, of *The Two Noble Kinsmen*. Two main points stand out: one, that most of *The Two Noble Kinsmen* follows exactly the dramatic structure that any adaptor of this poem would use (since the second item on this double bill show is in most respects very like the first), except for the brilliant elaboration and counterpoint provided by the Jailer's Daughter's scenes; and two, that the Jailer's Daughter (here played by Lisa Ellis, a mere Third Queen before the interval, given that this role has no counterpart in the Chaucer) isn't nearly such a good part if you are still stuck behind a script and aren't finding the syntax very easy.

25 MAY 2006

I return to the Swan four days later for an altogether less minimalist piece of work, Gregory Doran's *Antony and Cleopatra*, which boasts in one of its leads an Honorary Associate Artist whose public profile has been transformed since he last worked for the RSC nearly twenty-five years ago, Patrick Stewart, and in the other the RSC's current reigning tragedienne, another Associate Artist, Harriet Walter. The theatre is crammed and expectation is high, and, as I take my seat and start admiring the understatedly Romano-Egyptian cracked terracotta finish of the stage's back wall, I notice that Doran has cannily placed into the opening of his show a reflection of our own impatience for the arrival of the star performers we have paid to see. Pacing up and down the right-hand side of the stage, well before the house-lights go down, are three men in Roman military uniforms. Two of them look as though they have had a long journey and all three are visibly irritated at being kept hanging about like this – if this were a modern-dress production rather than a characteristic specimen of what Doran and his usual designer Stephen Brimson-Lewis do with plays set in Roman times (which is normally something voluptuously West

49. *Antony and Cleopatra*, RSC, Swan Theatre, dir. Gregory Doran, 2006. The court at Alexandria in 1.1: Patrick Stewart as Antony, Harriet Walter as Cleopatra, with waiting messengers.

End and tending towards *Ben Hur*), they would be looking at their watches each time they sigh, but being well-trained RSC play-as-casts they do not even glance towards their classically naked wrists. Even after the lights dim on the dot of 7.30pm they are still kept waiting, looking with occasional anxiety and annoyance towards the entrances, as do we, and it is only when our shared impatience is finally reaching the point of definite affront – who does Stewart think he is to treat a live audience in this cavalier fashion? Just because he made all that money in *Star Trek* and *X-Men*! – that a smirking bare-chested figure in white harem trousers holding an ornate leather whip comes dashing stealthily up through the front stalls and onto the right-hand corner of the stage, sees the soldiers, holds up the whip to show it to them with a silly snigger, presses his finger to his lips with a loud 'Ssshh!', and then runs onwards, to disappear off backstage right. The

audience just have time to wonder whether that really was Patrick Stewart, and the soldiers to look at each other in disbelieving fury, when he comes running hilariously back in the opposite direction, this time pursued by a magnificent woman with jet-black shoulder-length hair, in cream silk and a turquoise and gold necklace, who now has the whip herself and is shrieking with laughter. That was Patrick Stewart and Harriet Walter as Antony and Cleopatra. The door at the side of the right-hand stalls closes behind them and they are gone, and this little powerless brush with self-indulgent celebrity is over, and the largest of the three waiting soldiers can at last burst out with the indignant comment that has been building up in him since before we even arrived at the theatre: 'Nay, but this dotage of our General's / O'erflows the measure'. It is a tremendously clever opening gambit, not just cue-ing Philo's speech but giving the audience a share in the emotion and the experience which informs it, and from here onwards the show's level of energy never flags: as the Alexandrian court sweeps onto the stage in a flurry of laughter and fans and colour and the spreading of a blue silk cloth ('Look where they come!'), and Antony and Cleopatra settle to another bout of performing their infatuation to one another and to the world, it is already clear that this is to be an *Antony and Cleopatra* that will have been well worth waiting for.

Stewart's performance throughout the evening is a shining advertisement for what a little global or even intergalactic celebrity can do for an actor: I saw him several times in Stratford in the days when he was still being cast as Enobarbus (a role he played for Trevor Nunn in 1972 and then again for Peter Brook in 1978 before finally graduating to his triumvirship all these years later), and remembered him as a rather cold, stiff, self-regarding performer, perhaps most notably as a remote, slightly affected Leontes (in 1982) who never seemed genuinely involved in anything that happened to him. Tonight, however, he is barely recognizable, and not only thanks to a curly, cropped grey wig. There is a warmth and impulsiveness to his Antony, that I wouldn't have thought him capable of in his pre-Hollywood days, and a literal flexibility. When one of the still-irate messengers dares to interrupt the kiss into which he and Cleopatra, profiles to the audience, dissolve on 'Then must thou needs find out new heaven, new earth' (1.1.17) – 'News, my good lord' [*the kiss continues regardless. Only just controlling his anger.*] 'From *Rome*' – Antony breaks off from Cleopatra, still holding her waist in his hands, and leans backwards towards the messenger, his face a perfectly horizontal mask of irritation and amused weary tolerance and his entire spine momentarily and exuberantly curved into a letter C. An easy spontaneity based in hubris is the keynote of his performance throughout the first half of the play: serenely confident of his ascendancy over Octavius, he suavely makes his concessions at the triumvirs' summit in 2.2 to show that he can afford to do so rather than because he feels he must, and when the civil war is finally under way he decides his overall battle-plan at Actium

with no better rationale, not just on the spur of the moment but in mid-sentence: 'Canidius, we / Will fight with him by . . . [*slightly extending this monosyllable while he looks upward as if mentally tossing a coin*] . . . sea' (3.7.27–8). Once Cleopatra, whose preceding rebuke this display of overconfidence is designed to answer, has loyally endorsed this choice in front of the officers, Antony cannot reverse the decision without losing face, though it is clear from his ensuing conversation with the soldier who points out the advantages of fighting by land that he soon wishes he could, albeit briefly. In Antony's parting 'Well, well; away!' (3.7.66), the first two words express a world of misgivings but the last, as he averts his eyes from the soldier and abruptly turns back to the business of maintaining his gallantly smiling performance with Cleopatra, betrays a habitual lazy strategy of averting his mind from unpleasant thoughts rather than confronting them. This Antony loses the world almost because of a little social accident – had Cleopatra, Canidius and the soldier only encountered him in a slightly different order or not in earshot of each other at all, he would obviously have fought by land – and Doran succeeds once again in convincing his audience that it didn't have to happen this way, that the tragedy could always have happened differently or not at all.

The larger surprise in Stewart's performance, however, is how compelling he continues to make Antony after the defeat at Actium: instead of lapsing into a leaden, underplayed drunken sulk for the encounter with Thidias in 3.13, for example, as many actors do, he is filled with all the neurotic energy of complete despair, displaying a ranting, twitching state of alternating reckless bravado and unbearable self-loathing in which the savage and here convincingly gory whipping to which he subjects the over-familiar messenger looks as much like a sudden externalization of his fury with himself as of his antagonism towards Octavius. Sending his angry challenge to single combat, he is on the edge of complete incoherence, scarcely able to hold the shape of a whole sentence in his mind, such is the pressure of his humiliation at finding himself at the mercy of his younger colleague:

50. *Antony and Cleopatra*, RSC, Swan Theatre, dir. Gregory Doran, 2006. On Pompey's barge, Antony (Patrick Stewart) passes the wine-bowl to an apprehensive Octavius (John Hopkins), 2.7.92.

'Tell him he wears the rose / Of youth upon him, from which the world should note [*sudden bathetic lapse of concentration*] / Something particular' (3.13.19–21). This debilitating combination of fear and self-reproach seems to render Antony only intermittently capable even of seeing the people around him (so that Cleopatra's 'Not know me yet?', 3.13.160, has to be accompanied by a risky grasping of his arms and an attempt to meet his eyes to force him actually to look at her), and his recovery from it, first into the affecting if slightly out-of-control sentimentality with which he bids his sad captains farewell in 4.2 and then into the short-lived courage and military success of the first day's fighting outside Alexandria (4.4–4.9), comes as a profound relief. Both the audience and Antony himself are able to take a measure of comfort from the lucidity with which he finds himself able to face his own death: the generosity of

spirit with which he responds to the defection of Enobarbus stays with him throughout his dialogue with Eros (whose sudden suicide, since this subordinate would be unable to remove his breast-plate without arousing Antony's suspicions, is carried out, shockingly, by the slashing of his carotid artery). To surprisingly moving effect, Antony has regained his sense of humour and even the pain of his mortal but ineffectual self-wounding cannot rob him of it. When Diomedes arrives on the scene and tells him that he was sent to the now supine Antony by Cleopatra, Stewart leaves a little pause before asking '*When* did she send thee?' (4.15.117), and in response to Diomedes' 'Now, now, my lord' he rests his face against the stage, closes his eyes and allows himself a rueful, appalled laugh before asking 'Where is she?', with an ironic, weary, Northern stress on the first word. Hoisted precariously into the monument (the Swan's upper gallery along the back of the stage), he touchingly maintains this intimate amusement at Cleopatra's penchant for histrionics almost to the last: after his request 'Give me some wine, and let me speak a little' is answered not by attention but by the beginnings of a tirade of Cleopatra's own – 'No, let me speak, and let me rail so high / That the false hussy Fortune break her wheel, / Provoked by my offence' (4.16.44–7) – Antony makes a conscious affectionately satirical joke at finding himself having to interrupt her for the thousandth time in their relationship even so as to be allowed to speak his dying words – '*One* word, sweet queen.' (4.16.47). It is one of the distinctions of this production that Antony's passing is, unusually, as moving as Cleopatra's in its own right rather than simply being an event moving her towards her own suicide, which is often the only death in the play which the audience are given either time or cause to regret.

This unusual parity between Antony and Cleopatra is a feature of Doran's production from the first: more visibly witty and mercurial than Antony though Walter's serpent of old Nile may be, the comedy of her taunts and teasingly simulated changes of mood in the first act is played for his amused comprehension as well as for that of the audience, and the success-rate of their respective strategies for dealing with one another's moods is about equal over the course of the play. After the atrocious rebukes provoked by her apparent flirtation with Thidias, for example, she holds off from accepting Antony's restored faith in her ('I am satisfied', 3.13.170) for a long pause as they stand square-on to one another, before finally she allows him to lean his head forward against her breast, both of them exhausted by the row that has now passed and both equally conscious of this pose as the self-conscious tableau of two people resigned to being stuck with one another for better or worse, tantrums and all. Walter's Cleopatra, though her vulnerability and her ability to lose herself completely in extreme emotion are both perfectly genuine (her anger with the messenger who tells of Antony's marriage to Octavia, if funny, is only laughable in an appalling way rather than because it is played with a knowing sparkle for the

audience's benefit), is sustained by a poised self-knowledge: sometimes she has to assert her dignity, sometimes disown it (most clearly at the start of 1.5 when, weary of dancing with her attendants at the opening of the scene, she sits down, removes what turns out to have been a wig and contemplates her crop-haired face in a mirror), but she is never ludicrous and never stupid. There is nothing vainly operatic about her suicide, either: she has decided that death is her only option the moment she hears that Antony is dying, and instead of slowing the play down while she indulges in grand poetic recitations she plays the whole of the fifth act with concentrated, speedy purpose. Her great elegy for her lover, 'I dreamt there was an Emperor Antony' (5.2.75–99), rather than functioning as a free-floating set piece, is carefully designed to win over Dolabella into betraying Caesar's real intentions, and later in the scene it is a note of fear in Iras's voice as she utters the word 'dark' in 'and we are for the dark' (5.2.189) which motivates Cleopatra's subsequent word-painting of an imaginary Roman stage travesty of her court, a strategy designed solely to convince Iras as rapidly as possible that death would be preferable to adorning Caesar's triumph. The final tableau of Cleopatra's death – wig restored under metal Egyptian headdress, on a centre-stage throne flanked by two flaming tripods – is no less affecting for being this time recognizably a suicide carried resolutely out under extreme pressure rather than the stately exercise in ritual self-glorification which it can become.

Completely entrancing as Walter's Cleopatra always is (and, watching it, one is only surprised that at fifty-five she hasn't been cast in the role before, so perfectly does its combination of the poignant, the graceful and the temperamentally impossible suit her gifts), her performance offers less novelty than does one given in a less obviously showy role, that of Octavius. John Hopkins here plays the youngest of the triumvirs not as a cold, Machiavellian master of spin who simply waits for Antony to fail, but as a seething mass of mingled hero-worship and resentment, who when we first meet him feels genuinely afraid of Pompey and deeply betrayed by Antony's failure to send military assistance earlier, and who finds the older man's urbanity, military record and easy authority absolutely intolerable in person. The little social contest at the opening of the triumvirs' meeting in 2.2, as he and Antony briefly pause over the tricky protocol of which of them should sit down first at the other's request, is here not effortlessly won by Octavius, as is customary, at all. Instead of smugly relaxing into his chair in response to Antony's 'Sit, sir' (2.2.31), Hopkins's unbearably tense Caesar is so provoked by the potential sarcasm of the 'sir' that on his 'Nay, then' he attempts to flounce angrily out of the meeting altogether and he has to be pacified and almost dragged back into the conference by Maecenas and Agrippa. The relation between Octavius and his attendants in this production is indeed well-nigh the opposite of how it is usually played: instead of being mere yes-men who obediently parrot the strategies he has dictated to them in advance, these older political attachés almost function as his tutors and diplomatic nursemaids, obliged to reiterate and paraphrase in a more measured and gubernatorial tone the speeches which Octavius blurts out in the heat of the moment. He is predictably uneasy among the more experienced warriors on Pompey's barge, only just holding his own in the full-scale macho song-and-dance number that is 'Come, thou monarch of the vine', and he takes what opportunities he can to try to disconcert Antony whenever he has him on anything that could be regarded as his own territory: parting from Octavia in 3.2 after she and Antony are married, for example, Octavius gives her a lingering kiss on the mouth in a vain attempt to provoke Antony into a response other than the weary tolerance and curt farewell which he receives. (When Octavia subsequently arrives back in Rome in 3.6, by contrast, her brother is only angry with her, refusing any physical contact and leaving her alone at the end of the scene in one of the three chairs that had earlier appeared at the summit, so that for a moment she becomes a failed implicit replacement for Lepidus as peace-making third triumvir.) The keynote of Hopkins's entire performance is struck by the line by which he responds to Antony's challenge to single combat at the opening of 4.1:

instead of relating Antony's inappropriate and desperate taunts with amused detachment, he comes rushing onto the stage red-faced, with his assistants in anxious pursuit, clutching the document in his hand and shouting 'He calls me boy!' in as unstatesmanlike a manner as could be imagined. Only gradually does this Octavius start to learn to become Augustus: he has at last grasped the importance of public relations by 4.6, when we find him dictating 'The time of universal peace is near . . .' (4.6.4–6) to a scribe, but the news of Antony's death catches him completely off-balance – at first he is merely frightened and angered by Decretas's arrival with the bloodied sword, as if fearing assassination, and Maecenas and Agrippa once more have to rationalize and excuse the sobbing outburst which is his immediate response on gathering what the sword implies. When he finally meets Cleopatra in 5.2 he shades and averts his eyes, as if he has never met a mature femme fatale before and is afraid of being seduced, but he just manages to retain his temper on finding how her suicide has cheated him. There is now nobody for him to have to look up to, and that is both a triumph and something entirely desolating.

In a less crowded year, this production might deservedly occupy almost all of this article: whole essays might be written about the skill with which its scenes flowed onto and off the Swan's stage, about how Chris Jarman's soothsayer emerged from under the blue stagecloth after Antony and Cleopatra's departure in 1.1 having served invisibly as their cushion throughout the scene to date, or about how Ken Bones's Enobarbus had to insist on making Maecenas and Agrippa, determined to leave promptly and without him after the triumvirs' meeting, listen to the Cydnus speech at all – a speech which completely won over Agrippa, though Edmund Kingsley's priggish Maecenas indignantly defended virtue and Octavia as best he could (which, comically, wasn't very well – describing Octavia, after a spluttering half-pause, as 'a blessed lottery' at 2.2.249 seemed like damningly faint praise). The one reservation I might record about this colourful, vivid, engaging and always theatrically intelligent production would be a familiar anxiety about how or even if it was intended to connect with the world(s) of its audience: there was, for instance, only one moment at which it appeared to signal an awareness of more recent instances of Middle Eastern empire-building and empire-losing, and that was the death of Pacorus at the start of the often-cut 3.1. This was a wonderfully arresting moment: from the end of the thoroughly jovial party scene on Pompey's barge, with Enobarbus and Menas, their brief relationship clearly on the verge of going beyond the homosocial, departing towards the latter's cabin, the lights abruptly changed to the dazzling faintly tawny sunlight of a desert and, screaming, a man with his hands tied behind his back and a canvas bag over his head came running blindly onto the stage. Two Roman soldiers appeared behind him and one fired a crossbow: there came a sound effect of its flying shaft and the thump of its arrowhead entering the bound man's back and he fell forward, the arrow protruding. 'Now, darting Parthia, art thou struck' began the more senior of the Romans in a satisfied tone, as though the execution of this hostage marked an ordinary but particularly bracing start to a day's work. It was a shocking moment, but not least because it offered a glimpse of potential topicality absent from the remainder of this rich but otherwise self-enclosed show.

SUMMER

7 JUNE 2006

The Russian franchise, if that is the word, of Cheek by Jowl brought Declan Donnellan's all-male production of *Twelfth Night*, first seen in Moscow in 2003, to the Oxford Playhouse before it appeared in London as part of the Barbican International Theatre Event and in Stratford as part of the Complete Works Festival. The show has all Donnellan's characteristic simplicity and lucidity – the whole company arrive together on stage in dark evening dress at its opening, and only when they have all uttered the word 'Father' (to quote the surtitle rather than the line) does one young actor separate from the rest and, supplied with a hat, metamorphose into an anxious Viola, before the remainder become Orsino's court for 1.1. At 'O, when mine eyes did see Olivia first' (1.1.18) another actor is ritually supplied with accessories to become Olivia, and at the end of the scene both this new-made Olivia and the staff of Orsino's court remain motionlessly present on the stage while Viola, now clad in a pale yellow dress, enters from the auditorium for her dialogue with the sea-captain. Orsino's court and Olivia's are both rather gloomy places (until the second half, when the overall dress code will change from dark evening wear to cream linen, as if Viola's dress has proved contagious), and both aristocrats are obliged to spend a certain amount of time signing things at the same large desk. (As ever with this company, the small amount of furniture is put to clear and significant use: Olivia, for example, fatally cedes her authority to Cesario by gesturing that he should sit in her official chair in order to deliver his message from Orsino.) Olivia's steward (played by Dmitry Shcherbina), though, looks unusually young and handsome, even though it is easily possible to see that his mistress is rather uncomfortable with him by the way in which she will only smoke behind his back. (Social distinctions throughout this household are often marked by who is prepared openly to smoke in front of whom.)

Once again, I feel shut out of some of the production's finer points by the experience of being reliant on surtitles, which here provide a lamentably ill-typed abridgement of Shakespeare's text which provides no clues as to where the Russian translation the actors are speaking may vary from it. In a superbly Slavic rendition of the catch scene, 2.3, for example, which features four whole bottles of vodka smuggled into the house in a plastic bag, the main song which Evgeny Pisarev's wizened, dapper little Feste performs (in part sitting on Sir Toby's knee, so that with his white face make-up and rouged cheeks he resembles a ventriloquist's dummy) clearly isn't a mere translation of 'O mistress mine', as the delighted laughter of recognition which issues from the many expatriate Russians in the audience confirms, and to judge by further Russian laughs elsewhere there are lots of other

51. *Twelfth Night*, Cheek by Jowl, dir. Declan Donnellan, 2006. The catch scene, 2.3: Alexander Feklistov
as Sir Toby Belch and Dmitry Diuzhev as Sir Andrew Aguecheek.

incidental gags in the translation which the surtitles are keeping quiet about. What needs no translation, however, is this scene's unaccustomed violence: this Sir Toby, played as a gone-to-seed bully by Alexander Feklistov, strikes Maria in the face at 'Am I not consanguineous?' (2.3.74) before lapsing into lachrymose penitence under the table. Their marriage (which on this occasion they arrive onstage to reveal themselves during the last scene) is not going to count as much of a happy ending, and at the very end of the evening everyone else seems to be at risk of violence too. The reunion of the twins is simply and beautifully staged as per the untranslated Shakespeare – after a superbly blocked sequence in which the mutually recriminating Orsino, Olivia and Cesario chase one another in accelerating circles around Antonio and his guard – but in one piece of rewriting which the surtitles do not conceal, Malvolio's letter is not produced and his exit line is postponed. After arriving in the disordered clothing of 4.2, apparently having escaped from the darkened room by himself, to learn how he has been gulled, he leaves in cowed silence, and then silently returns a few lines later in immaculate tails, the perfect obedient servant again, to hand

out glasses of champagne from a tray to the happy couples and their well-wishers. It is only when Orsino has finished his last speech and everyone has a glass that Malvolio, checking that he is unobserved, stalks down to the front of the stage, looks straight into the audience and, in an unaccustomed, savage tone, announces that he will be revenged on the whole pack of them. It is perfectly imaginable that he has put strychnine in the champagne, and that only the concluding blackout which immediately follows his line preserves us from seeing its effects on the rest of the cast.

15 JUNE 2006

Back in Stratford, meanwhile, the Complete Works Festival continues with Tim Supple's altogether more colourful and physical production of *A Midsummer Night's Dream*, produced by Dash Arts with the financial support of the British Council. There are no surtitles at all for this show, despite the fact that its actors between them use seven of the different languages found across India and Sri Lanka, but fortunately for Anglophone audiences, one of these (for interesting historical reasons) is English.

52. *A Midsummer Night's Dream*, Dash Arts, Swan Theatre, dir. Tim Supple, 2006. 4.1:
Joy Fernandes as Bottom, Faezeh Jahali as Peaseblossom, Archana Ramaswamy as Titania.

Equally ignorant of each of the six other languages at work tonight, I am unable to detect any meaningful pattern in when they are and aren't used; it appears as though the performers are simply allowed to play a similar proportion of their respective roles in their respective first languages, with enough English used at regular enough intervals to keep monoglot Anglophones abreast of the action.

Spoken language, in any case, is hardly the sole point of this show, which transforms the Swan into something between a temple, a playground and a circus ring: the stage has been covered in a layer of red soil (covered by great sheets of silk for the scenes in Theseus's palace), which by the end of a very athletic show has begun to invade the clothes of anyone seated in the front two rows. An uncharitable account of this production, putting the least generous construction on its explanatory programme notes, would say that Tim Supple had been given a budget to travel around the Indian subcontinent cherry-picking the best talents in a range of local types of performance and had then simply gone through the script of *A Midsummer Night's Dream*

deciding where they could each show off their respective acts to best effect, thereby assembling a show masquerading as a Shakespeare revival but really offering a composite, exoticized vision of India for audiences of *de facto* tourists. (The most glaring instance of this would be the Indian boy who provides the text's main excuse for the whole exercise, brought onto the stage in the person of Ram Pawar to perform athletic feats as close to the Indian rope trick as makes no matter, feats so excitingly risky that the show was nearly forbidden by health and safety officers before it even opened.) It is difficult to sustain this critique, however, in the face of Supple's *Dream* itself which, while undeniably offering the pleasures of exotic effects in spades – the glass harmonica, ritually unveiled from under sea-green silk at the front of the stage by the performer who will become Puck to call the play into being! the martial-arts percussion-punctuated quarterstaff combat between Oberon's and Titania's respective spirits, fought out in a wood near Athens that is definitely a jungle! the strip of dangling red silk that becomes Titania's bower-cum-sari as she winds herself up into it, pulling the end up after her as she disappears into what has become a suspended cocoon! – does ground itself in an intelligent, original and cogent reading of the play. (It is also so consistently enjoyable – not least, frankly, because its cast are all unnaturally good-looking and wear few clothes, and those beautiful – that criticism is largely in abeyance for its duration.)

This is, for example, a *Dream* which threatens to turn into *Così fan Tutte*, in that one of the things the lovers are forced to learn in the wood is the limited strength of their own mutually unaided fidelity. It isn't just that some of them are acting under the influence of what is here a wonderfully physicalized magic – to administer the love-charm, Puck and Oberon practically wrestle with each respective sleeper and throw red dust into their faces as if delivering a blow – but that all of them, faced with real opportunity, are liable to find their adherence to monogamy faltering. Protest against Lysander's charm-inspired advances though she does in 3.2, for example, Shanaya Raffat's responsive, visibly tempted Helena is on the point of yielding to them until Demetrius awakens and interrupts, and were it not for Oberon's dispatching of Puck to separate would-be lovers and would-be combatants at the end of the scene – which he does, spectacularly, by entangling them in an enormous elasticated spider's web, woven between eight poles fitted into sockets around the edges of the stage – individual willpower alone would be insufficient to maintain the loyalty even of those characters not under the influence of the spell. The reunion and reintegration of not just the couples but all the disparate elements of this production – including a superbly charismatic Bottom (Joy Fernandes) whose outfit after his translation into an ass includes not just ears affixed to an elasticated denim headband but a gourd worn below the waist which is adorned with a red condom – within the wedding celebrations of Act 5 is both a relief and a miracle, complete with acres of red silk, semi-modern wedding clothes, and thousands of falling petals. When did I last see an audience standing to applaud at the end of a show in the Swan? At the end of Suzman's *Hamlet*, come to think of it, and I don't think that this just rep-

resents a hospitable impulse to be indiscriminately nice to all this season's foreign visitors. This Festival really is bringing some unaccustomed stimulation and excitement to what can be one of the tamest towns in the Midlands.

22 JUNE 2006

Business as usual in the Swan a week later, though, when I catch up with a matinee of Marianne Elliott's well-reviewed RSC production of *Much Ado About Nothing*. This is one of those shows that has simply chosen a particular design-friendly setting and then shoe-horned the allotted Shakespeare play into it willy-nilly; the programme is full of information about Cuba on the eve of Castro's revolution, the stage is decorated with coloured light bulbs and neon signs which give every impression that Leonato's family live at a nightclub in downtown Havana, and the main attraction of this production is already being supplied while the audience arrive in the form of some very expert pastiche Latin American dance music composed by Olly Fox. Tamsin Greig's performance as Beatrice consists almost entirely, in between the slickly choreographed dance sequences which punctuate the action, of striking tango-friendly poses in tight skirts and high heels while looking mulishly stubborn, and she largely overpowers Joseph Millson's amiable softie of a Benedick; Bette Bourne plays Dogberry, irrelevantly and to precious little comic effect, as a heavily made-up recreational cross-dresser. Every joke is underlined as if for the benefit of the comically illiterate (Benedick's antics concealed behind a potted shrub in 2.3 are predictable to the extent that their very lameness almost becomes funny despite itself), and the unhelpful conceit of setting this play in 1950s Cuba is finally pushed well over the edge of absurdity when a fugitive Don John, in an interpolated between-scenes moment after the rest of the cast have finally detected his treachery, is seen donning a beret somewhere out in the maquis and raising a rifle in revolutionary salute. If I were a living relative of Ché Guevara I would be tempted to sue this production, but the glamour of its loud music and

53. *Titus Andronicus*, The Ninagawa Company, Royal Shakespeare Theatre, dir. Yukio Ninagawa, 2006.
Hitomi Manaka as Lavinia.

the popularity of Tamsin Greig from her work in television comedy and in *The Archers* will doubtless guarantee it a sold-out London run regardless. This is the perfect rendition of a Shakespearean comedy for people who would otherwise go to their salsa class that night instead.

The evening show in the Royal Shakespeare Theatre is something altogether more estimable, however, namely Yukio Ninagawa's *Titus Andronicus*, for which dangerous-looking Japanese warriors, clad in white costumes that hybridize Roman motifs with the shapes and weapons associated with the samurai period, are already warming up in the foyer well before the advertised starting time. In the auditorium itself, the immense white set is still being assembled, with actors and stagehands gathered informally about the stage among mobile rails of costumes and, disconcertingly, racks of prop severed heads, well after the audience have taken their seats. Huge white flats with blank Romanesque windows and doors still have what appear to be fragments of their blueprints projected onto them, behind wide lateral steps which lead down into the stalls. Announcements in Japanese come over the tannoy system from invisible stage managers but,

rather spoiling the spontaneous Brechtian demystification effect this is presumably intended to produce, these informal instructions have all been translated in advance and can be read on the surtitle boards at either side of the stage. The most striking is rendered as 'Please bring the wolf downstage, and clear the costume rails.' Sure enough, into this emptying forum comes a twelve-foot high statue of the infant Romulus and Remus and their adoptive mother, and this immense wolf is present for much of the show as an unmissable symbol of the predatory savagery that always has been somewhere at the centre of Rome's identity since long before Titus declares the city to be a wilderness of tigers. Presently the house-lights dim and, after a white-clad Saturninus and Bassianus have initiated their rhetorical conflict from rival windows in the flats, an appalling procession comes down the left-hand aisle through the stalls and onto the stage. Led by Kotaro Yoshida's Titus, a white-bearded Samurai general whose uniform includes outsize epaulettes, ranks of warriors are bearing perspex coffins containing the white plastic corpses of his slain sons, and dragging in chains a spectacularly beautiful, feral Tamora and her three living children. After the eldest of these, Alarbus, is subsequently dragged off stage to be sacrificed, Titus's own sons bring mutilated fragments of a plastic dummy back on with them, each ort decorated with the red streamers which Ninagawa, following Brook, adopts as code for blood throughout this production. These sons each resemble a smaller version of Titus; when he turns against Bassianus and Mutius later in the scene, the others tremble and waver inward and outward around him with a sort of collective animal indecision, their simultaneous desire to assail and to flee from their father making them behave exactly like a litter of beaten hunting dogs.

I suspect that any account of this *Titus* would dwell on its design and such visual moments as this, even were it written by someone fluent in Japanese: this is a relentless, powerful spectacle of a production, using what to judge by the surtitles and their correspondence to the staged action is a close, literal and very full translation of Shakespeare's text (prepared for the occasion by Kazuko Matsuoka). My own impression is that it neither seeks nor achieves anything much like intimacy (the great speeches seem comparatively undifferentiated and their content is very much demonstrated to the audience rather than confided in them), relying for its impact not on soliciting or even much permitting a close emotional engagement with the experiences of any of the characters but on exhibiting the content of their various living nightmares in the most unforgettably grand and ruthless stage images that Ninagawa and his team of designers (Tsukasa Nakagoshi, Tamotsu Harada, Lily Komine, Chimaki Takeda) can devise. Most of these involve very red streamers seen against very white backgrounds; even the rape of Lavinia takes place in a white wood, full of man-size white single-leaved plants like giant pennywort, and the appalling spectacle of Lavinia's re-entry afterwards, streamers trailing from mouth and wrists, is prepared for by the if anything worse spectacle of a gleeful Chiron and Demetrius preceding her, naked save for the smaller streamers which cover their genital areas as the unconcealed traces of the sexual violence they have perpetrated. After Titus is later kissed by Lavinia at 3.1.248, streamers dangle from his mouth too, and his embrace of

the madness that has taken over his world is soon signalled by another astonishing stage-picture as, clutching a red-streamer-bedecked plastic amputated hand, with further streamers trailing from his maimed wrist, he lolls backward against the statue of the wolf, uttering a terrible mirthless rasping laughter.

It is a laughter which nonetheless sounds quite like the speech audible everywhere in this production: without a better knowledge of Japanese I couldn't say whether that language always sounds like the soundtrack to the really nasty bits in a martial arts film, but I can say that the main vocal variation in this production is provided by Rei Asami's terrifying, Cruella-deVil-to-the-power-of-ten performance as Tamora. Posing as Revenge, she takes her voice an octave up and well-nigh sings to Titus in a wheedling manner reminiscent of Peking opera; finally made aware (after Titus has broken Lavinia's neck with a shocking crack and then cradled her corpse, Cordelia-like, in his arms) that she has eaten her sons (their faces, grotesquely, suddenly revealed within the pie-dish), her voice rises even further into an impersonal short-lived shriek like escaping steam. After the noisy, bassoon-accompanied massacre which ensues, the production's last sound is provided by Young Lucius: left holding Aaron's baby son, so far from disappearing with him into the rosy sunset pictured by Julie Taymor's film he stands paralysed in the centre of the stage, uttering, at painful, long intervals, a hopeless inarticulate scream. It is perhaps the summary which best suits this fierce, unflinching but oddly remote and inhuman production.

JULY 2006

For some reason, the following month's theatregoing is predominantly disappointing. On the 4th I see Sean Holmes's RSC production of *Julius Caesar* in the main house, a noisy, incoherent, shouting piece of work during which John Light's hoarse Brutus delivers his stoical prose oration at Caesar's funeral as if it were an outburst of hysteria, and Ariyon Bakare's Mark Antony is then greatly

hampered by the fact that the corpse of Julius Caesar got up and walked away during 'O pardon
me, thou bleeding piece of earth' (at 'And Caesar's
spirit, ranging for revenge', 3.1.273), so that instead
of being able to show the crowd Caesar's bloodstained mantle and then Caesar's mangled corpse
he has to make do, rather bathetically, with showing them Caesar's bloodstained mantle and then
showing them some more of Caesar's bloodstained
mantle. (It seems painfully unjust that with so
many good productions passing rapidly through the
repertory, the shows being seen most often in the
largest RSC venue throughout the summer should
be this one and Nancy Meckler's *Romeo and Juliet*.)
On the 6th I am allowed into the new Courtyard
to watch the technical rehearsal of Michael Boyd's
Henry VI Part 1, from which it is clear that the show
will be much as it was in 2000, which is fine, and
that the new theatre bears a worrying resemblance
to an oversized Swan, with poorer acoustics, which
is less so, especially given that this temporary auditorium is supposed to represent a rough sketch for
the projected permanent remodelling of the RST.
(To Boyd's evident delight, however, the Courtyard has much higher flies than the Swan from
which to lower actors rapidly and perilously on
ropes.) The run of really interesting visiting shows
in the Swan itself is broken on 13 July, when I
watch Barbara Gaines's Chicago Shakespeare Theatre productions of both parts of *Henry IV*. Grateful as I always was to this company when I lived in
that city, this is not the best example of their work
I've seen, an affair of stuck-on beards and mous-
taches, would-be medieval leather jerkins, coarse
acting and bizarre padding (Falstaff looks like a cross
between Santa Claus and Humpty Dumpty) that
adds up to a show of a kind which in England one
might expect to see performed in a village hall or a
vicarage garden but which would normally be kept
safely away from the subsidized professional theatre.
The main feature distinguishing Gaines's *Henry IV*
from any such indigenous production is its odd collection of pronunciations, with some of the cast
unable to bring themselves to speak the lines in anything other than a constrained, embarrassed would-
be English accent, and some of them, especially

around Eastcheap, feeling that broad comedy (and
to this day I've never seen an American production of Shakespeare that recognized any other kind)
demands something more rootin' and tootin'. And
then on the 25th I go to what sadly remains one of
the last places on earth one should go in the hope of
avoiding amateurishly coarse Shakespearean comedy, the replica Globe, where Christopher Luscombe has directed *The Comedy of Errors*. This, as
its programme unashamedly proclaims, is *The Comedy of Errors* in the manner of *Carry on Cleo* and *Up
Pompeii*: a campy nonsense of skimpy tunics and
curled fringes in which nothing serious is ever at
stake for any of the characters, so that even when
Antipholus and Dromio of Syracuse are being pursued through the streets in the fourth act in peril of
their lives they only employ standard British music-
hall comedy run variant number 4, the one where
most of the runner's energy is diverted into silly
locomotive-like arm movements and an exaggerated rising onto the balls of the feet. It is impossible
to care whether they get caught or not, and, crimi-
nally, this show even squanders the talents of one of
the country's best percussionists, Phil Hopkins, on
providing cymbal-smashes and cowbell-bonks and
facetious thumps on the bass drum to accompany
such vacuous slapstick routines throughout. Clever
as Luscombe may be as a comic actor himself, his
production gives the lamentable impression that it
has been designed solely to appeal to Ned Sherrin.

14 AND 15 AUGUST 2006

I should record (or perhaps 'confess' is the right
word) that due to absences from within a reasonable range of Stratford during parts of the summer
I manage to miss both the Complete Works Festival's visiting American *Love's Labour's Lost* and its
home-produced *Henry VIII*, but I am pleased not
to miss this summer's Shakespearean offerings in
Regent's Park. Rachel Kavanaugh's *The Taming of
the Shrew* is certainly the best piece of her work I
have seen yet, though like Anne Tipton's in Bristol
it has much in common with Greg Doran's production of the same play three seasons ago. With
an attractive design by Kit Surrey that places the

action around a little Italian square in the late 1940s (Hortensio, usefully, runs a café in one corner, from whose tables one can get a nice view into Bianca's bedroom window when she accidentally-on-purpose fails to draw the curtains), this production too is dominated by a well-nigh alcoholic Petruccio, though John Hodgkinson is far more saturnine than his Bristol counterpart. A tall, gloomy man whose pepper-and-salt jacket bears a black armband in sincere grief for his dead father, this Petruccio gives the impression that he has rarely before left the family estate in the country, 'young' only in the sense that it is only now, on the verge of middle age, that he has been forced to take on an independent life outside the family business, and it is clear as he makes his unsmiling promise to marry Katharina for the benefit of her sister's suitors that he is prepared to do so because essentially he does not care what happens to him at all. When not miserably consuming grappa at Hortensio's café, twirling an aluminium ashtray idly and neurotically with one finger as he does so, he resorts constantly to a hip-flask kept in his breast pocket, every bit as visibly unhappy in the first act as is Sirine Saba's Katharina. Saba makes a much more distinctive and high-octane shrew than did Flora Montgomery in Bristol, wearing frumpish pyjamas in 2.1 as she ties up her negligee-clad blonde minx of a sister with a dressing-gown cord and then dismembers her soft toys, but nothing short of the violence with which she resists Petruccio's wooing in the dialogue which follows – before which Baptista, outrageously partial to Bianca, refuses to allow Katharina to go and dress – could ever have roused Hodgkinson's depression-numbed suitor into any kind of response. When she accuses him, not unreasonably, of being withered and he replies ''Tis with cares' (2.1.234) without irony, as if surprised at her perceptiveness, he is still his dismal old self, but as he studies her more closely during his ensuing speech of praise ('I find you passing gentle . . .', 2.1.237–51) he almost begins to smile, genuinely acknowledging the presence of another person for the first time in the play. As Katharina, waiting impatiently for her bridegroom in 3.2, sits at the café table and begins absent-mindedly to spin an ashtray with one finger it is clear to the audience that these two misfits – who in this reading share an inability to take life as lightly or insincerely as those around them – are made for one another, something which they delightedly recognize themselves when they finally notice this shared tic during the concluding feast at Baptista's house. In between, the taming scenes are laundered as often before by being presented as Petruccio's essentially benign attempt to force his new bride to confront the physical harshness of his own long past out on a rural estate, but in kicks, retorts and an eventually amused sarcasm Saba gives about as good as she gets, and by the end of the evening it is hard to grudge the couple either their happiness or their triumph over Dominic Marsh's particularly smug Lucentio. Saba and Hodgkinson are temporarily and successfully paired again as Titania and Bottom in Kavanaugh's *A Midsummer Night's Dream*, in which Hodgkinson, interestingly, is genuinely a Bottom who would be happier playing a tyrant than a lover (his Pyramus sounds like a parody of Irving's Richard III), but overall this is a much less fresh production, its miked-up, muddy fairies in Victorian underwear and bovver boots faintly reminiscent of John Caird's back in the early 1990s.

AUTUMN

6 SEPTEMBER 2006

This *Dream*, however, is a good deal more enjoyable than Dominic Dromgoole's *Antony and Cleopatra* at the Globe, another under-rehearsed production mounted in this venue's usual recreated-clothing-of-the-period, in which Cleopatra's indefinably tatty court resembles the ill-disciplined tail end of the eleventh day of Christmas as celebrated at Theobalds or Hampton Court in the olden days. Frances Barber puts on a brave show as Cleopatra, but the show is sabotaged not only by some dreadful blocking (the whole onstage cast keep getting lined up laterally along the stage between the pillars like a school photograph, so as to become all-but-invisible from two sides of the stage) but by its casting. Dromgoole had to find his Antony just as Patrick

54. *Titus Andronicus*, Shakespeare's Globe, dir. Lucy Bailey, 2006. The surviving Andronici fire their message-bearing arrows in 4.3.

Stewart was receiving his rave first-night notices in Stratford, and apparently nobody was prepared to risk the comparison except Nicholas Jones. Jones made a fine Polonius in Trevor Nunn's *Hamlet* two seasons ago, but this seems to be about the limit of his range in Shakespeare and this de facto *Polonius and Cleopatra* makes a thoroughly unexciting and sexless spectacle. The riskiest piece of casting, however, turns out to be that of the asp: returning to the yard for the second half, I notice a warning sign reading 'Please note that this performance features a live snake.' 'Oh yes', a volunteer usher tells me, 'they do use a live snake at the end, unless it's being too frisky that day.' So do they have to audition the beast before every single performance to check that it isn't in too scene-stealing a mood? The idea of a reptile given to over-acting intrigues me but I am disappointed, when the last scene eventually comes around, to see Barber using what is clearly a rubber substitute. Well, it was only a matinee, and I suppose show-business convention demands that every now and then a big chance should be given to the understudy.

The evening show, however, Lucy Bailey's *Titus Andronicus*, is a different matter altogether. When I return to the Globe a couple of hours later I find it transformed, its pillars and the frons scenae wrapped in black fabric and a sort of semi-translucent black circular awning with a hole in the middle covering the entire building like a lid. By fitting this last structure in particular – based partly on the velarium that shaded the crowds in Nero's Colosseum, partly on the sun-pierced ceiling of the Pantheon – Bailey and her designer William Dudley have managed at last to make this space feel at once focused (not least because the temporary roof vastly improves the acoustics) and potentially dangerous. Well before the action begins, being in the yard already feels a little like being in the arena before the lions arrive, and it turns out to be almost as perilous. I have always resisted the Globe's mannerism of using expanded entries and exits through the crowd in the yard, and even staging parts of whole scenes there, but Bailey takes it to such lengths in this *Titus* that it ceases to seem like a desperate bid for attention or a vote of no confidence in the stage proper and instead genuinely redefines the space, abandoning any pretence to Elizabethanism, as a venue for a split-level promenade performance overlooked from the balconies. Saturninus and Bassianus mount rival scaffolding towers on castors in opposite corners of the yard to make their campaign speeches (parked here when not in use, where the stage meets the back wall), which their supporters rush alarmingly through the audience to bring them into firing range of each other's insults, but the gladiatorial keynote of this production isn't fully established until Titus makes his processional entry through the yard and up onto the stage proper. Anticipating his line about Rome being a wilderness, his Gothic prisoners wear cat-like warpaint on their faces that makes them resemble only recently caged tigers, while his sons and their fellow warriors wear modern skateboard knee and elbow pads artfully cut and styled to suggest Roman armour and baseball boots with the toecaps cut off to suggest sandals. This version of Rome clearly isn't the world we live in, but it isn't definitely remote from it either, physically threatening a large proportion of the audience at regular intervals (I get one foot painfully stood on, for example, when actors are moving back the crowd at the front of the yard in order to stretch a piece of camouflage netting outwards from the stage to produce the pit into which Bassianus, Martius and Quintus fall in 2.3.) Nor does Bailey spare them anything of the play's own internal violence, eschewing the stylization favoured by Ninagawa. Lavinia's mutilation, and all its sequels, are rendered completely naturalistically, with all the stage blood which that implies, and however many people may assure us that violence in the theatre is no more shocking than it is in the cinema, I see more people faint this evening (four or five just

immediately around me in the yard) than I have ever seen pass out during *Pulp Fiction* or *Dog Day Afternoon*. By the time Marcus presents her to her father, Lavinia has been wrapped from head to foot in a bandage-like costume, blood seeping through from her wrists, as if already part-mummified, but if anything her performance becomes even more painful later on: hitherto completely numbed with shock (so that her failure to identify her assailants earlier is completely understandable), she cannot write the names of Chiron and Demetrius in the sand in 4.1 without experiencing a terrible involuntary complete recall of their crime, crying inarticulately aloud as she struggles to wield the stick between her stumps in pain that is as much mental as physical.

At the centre of this show, Douglas Hodge's Titus looks too young to have lost quite so many sons as the script records, but he nevertheless gives a forceful impression in the first half of the play of being gradually roused from a deep inner torpor of grief (and submission to an unrealistically idealized loyalty to the Roman state) and into a terrible vulnerability. Where he really excels, however, is in the second half, when on that awful laugh after learning how Aaron has tricked him out of his right hand he awakens into a permanent state of nightmare in which there is nothing serious left to lose. Though Bailey's *Titus* lacks the spectacular grandeur and eerie cruel beauty of Ninagawa's, it has a much more developed sense of the black humour that is never far away from Elizabethan and Jacobean revenge tragedy, and Hodge puts on a fine and terrible turn as a Titus who has clearly seen all those Jack Nicholson films and in a perverse way is determined to find what mad enjoyment there may be in destroying what is left of the world. Eyes flashing and teeth bared, for example, he almost laughs at himself for involuntarily trying to draw back the string of his bow with his missing hand in 4.3, a gag he repeats in the last scene when he tries to lick the same absent fingers in his guise as chef. The extent to which Titus is reduced to the savage malicious glee that has always characterized Aaron – here splendidly and full-bloodedly played by Shaun Parkes – is admirably clear in this rendition of the

55. *King John*, RSC, Swan Theatre, dir. Josie Rourke, 2006. Tamsin Greig as Constance, 3.4.104.

play, though, unlike Aaron, Hodge's Titus never wholly loses his capacity for compassion: in the last scene (after entrapping Geraldine James's fine Tamora, whose earlier performance as Revenge comes complete with a classical theatrical mask) he kills Lavinia with a dreadful tenderness, suffocating her, Othello-like, rather than violating her ruined body any further. Rough around the edges as some of its verse-speaking remains, this is easily the most consistent and cogent piece of work I have seen in this space, and I hope future directors here will find it a liberating precedent.

7 SEPTEMBER 2006

In Stratford, the Complete Works Festival continues with a matinee of Josie Rourke's little gem of a *King John* in the Swan. This is an intricate, beautifully cast production throughout, which opens with an interpolated pageant of John's (first) coronation, an experience ruined for the insecure king by the imagined figure of the rightful heir, young Arthur. The boy, clearly invisible to the presiding bishop, skips mockingly around John and sits defiantly in his throne like Banquo's ghost at the feast, and even after this projection of his fear and guilt

has departed the newly crowned monarch hardly dares mount the throne, sitting only uncomfortably and with a hunted look once he does. Though he shows profound relief when his mother joins him on the stage he can still muster only with difficulty the resolve to hear out and defy the French ambassador. Richard McCabe, the perfect tragicomic actor, makes a superb John, his short neck and potentially toad-like bearing ideally suited to this portrait of a man tormented or at least persistently undermined by his own self-conscious unkingliness. He seems forever to be trying out a different attitude, none of them comfortably his own, as in a virtuoso rendering of the dialogue by which he finally commissions Arthur's murder. Even after his immensely long, evasive preamble (3.3.19–55), McCabe's King John still manages to achieve three false starts in a single line, 3.3.59: '[*primly*] Good Hubert. [*looks at Hubert, feels he has not caught the right tone, tries again. Putting a blokeish arm around Hubert, in a man-to-man, smiling tone*] Hubert. [*feels this is too flippant and uncomfortably intimate: stands apart and tries for royal gravity instead*] Hubert, [*then much more wheedlingly, and as if he has only just noticed Arthur upstage*] throw thine eye / On yon young boy'. Despairing of ever fully convincing anyone, he increasingly lapses after his mother's death into a state of near-infantile solipsism, telling his last special friend the Bastard about his renewed truce with Pandulph (at 5.1.62–5) in a sort of baby talk, and sucking his thumb after he has been poisoned. Just as illegitimate in his own way but altogether more decisive, Joseph Millson's Bastard makes the perfect foil and antitype to this touchingly eccentric usurper, more powerful and also considerably funnier in this role than as Benedick, and Tamsin Greig's penchant for conspicuous, non-negotiable obstinacy is put to much better use in a nervy, vitriolic performance as Constance than in her merely awkward Beatrice. Despite its handsome medieval trappings (including some lovely simulated little candles all over the house for the start of the second half), Rourke's production is alive to the political as well as the personal resonances of this play for its present-day audience: the Bastard, as if having a premonition of Kenneth Branagh's *Henry V*, sings 'Deo gracias Angliae' after the victory in 3.2, and the last word is taken up like a football chant of 'Inger-lund' by the English soldiers whom we have already seen abusing a dead Frenchman during the battle sequence. Illegal wars and war crimes as tools of national self-definition clearly aren't new.

The evening's performance in the main house, though by a much more famous director, is altogether less diverting. This is Peter Stein's *Troilus and Cressida*, which, visiting the Complete Works Festival after opening at the Edinburgh Festival the previous month, is this director's first Shakespeare to be performed in English rather than in German translation. A strong cast of English actors (among them Henry Pettigrew and Annabel Scholey as the lovers, Paul Jesson as Pandarus, Ian Hogg as Agamemnon, Adam Levy as Paris) look lost on a large, empty metallic-surfaced stage that eventually tilts slowly and portentously up to an angle of about 45 degrees, so that the final battle can appear to be taking place on a roof. A sentence in the programme by Stein himself dedicates the show to John Barton, 'whose 1968 production influenced my vision of the play and my desire to do it', but while Stein has clearly imitated some aspects of

Barton's production very closely – most obviously its costuming, with the warriors clad in little more than leather jock-straps and Homeric helmets – it is hard to believe that Barton's version was anything like this humourless, unengaging or poorly paced. This three-and-a-half hour show feels as long as the Ring cycle, and slightly less witty.

28 SEPTEMBER 2006

Thank goodness, then, that the RSC have invited a perfect antidote to visit the Swan later this same month in the form of Kneehigh Theatre, an eight-actor and four-musician-strong troupe from Cornwall who have brought their half-cabaret, half-children's-theatre-for-adults adaptation of *Cymbeline* to represent the play in the Complete Works Festival. Devised and written by Emma Rice and Carl Grose (who play the Queen and Posthumus respectively), this is a splendidly perky and inventive piece of work, deploying simple resources to maximum effect: the four-piece band are placed on a structure of metal scaffolding on the stage which also provides an upper acting area and, at stage level, a simple gate – between the bars of which Craig Johnston's disgusting Cloten will get his head memorably stuck after trying to serenade Imogen, to be released only when his nurse-come-dominatrix of a mother arrives and turns out to be equipped with a tube of KY jelly. This is an extremely funny show throughout, often much more thoroughly at the expense of the characters than is Shakespeare's version (Posthumus and Imogen, for example, are here a very unglamorous pair of losers who achieve a happy ending despite themselves; this Posthumus can only just bring himself to part with the watch he gives his bride at their enforced parting in place of the original's bracelet), but I worry at times during the evening as to whether it would be nearly as amusing to an audience less familiar with their Shakespeare than are the usual crowd at the Swan. Interspersed with cabaret-like songs commenting on the action, which has usually been transposed (as in the case of the watch) to a bathetic modernity (the disguised Imogen, for example, becomes not Fidele but

56. *Cymbeline*, Kneehigh Theatre, adapted by Emma Rice and Carl Grose, dir. Emma Rice, Swan Theatre, 2006. To the strains of 'A song about leaving your love', Posthumus (Carl Grose) voyages reluctantly away from Britain. His T-shirt bears the slogan 'Every breath a death'.

'Ian'), the Kneehigh *Cymbeline* in many respects resembles a Victorian burlesque, but like the best Victorian burlesques it has some canny things to say about the play on which it draws. It is very keen to focus on the lost childhood of the missing princes, for instance, and on Cymbeline's emotional state since their disappearance. The show begins with the cast gradually turning the gate into a little shrine to the absent children, one by one affixing bunches of flowers, photographs and abandoned toys to the door of this now empty nursery and, between them, one letter at a time, these nameless homage-paying mourners graffiti the word 'REMEMBER' on a piece of cardboard with a spray can. After this, however, Kneehigh are just as unashamed as is Shakespeare about using a flagrantly stagey device to expound the details of the back-story. Replacing the informative lord and

his inexplicably ill-informed interlocutor from the opening of 1.1, Mike Shepherd, who elsewhere plays both Cymbeline and Belarius, now appears in drag as one 'Joan Puttock', a panto dame of a local woman just returning to the court after being absent for some years on the Costa Brava, who insists on telling the audience her memories of the princes' disappearance before prompting Pisanio (in this version Imogen's waiting-woman, played by Kirsty Woodward) to fill her in on the king's remarriage, the forbidden match between Imogen and Posthumus, and so on.

Once this task is complete, more elaborate story-telling methods can come into play, some of them picturesquely and delightfully unnecessary. As Posthumus sets reluctantly off for Italy, for example, a bottomless cardboard rowing boat is suspended from his shoulders, and he mimes rowing himself very slowly off the stage while the band sing a song about parting, little toy fish wobbling at the end of wires fixed to the sides of the boat and little toy seagulls wobbling at the end of wires fixed to his parodically British bowler hat. (This boat is used again when he and Iachimo return to Britain in Act 4, now wearing military tin hats which also, ludicrously, have little toy seagulls fixed to them on similar wires.) At other points, mime replaces passages of speech: Iachimo's removal of the unwitting Imogen's bracelet, with its electrifying long aside, for example, becomes a wordless and very funny sequence in which Róbert Luckay's sleazy Italian playboy winds up wrestling elaborately with Imogen's sleeping body, in a manner that seems to parody the final pas-de-deux between hero and unconscious heroine in the Macmillan ballet of *Romeo and Juliet*. (Just when he has got the watch off one wrist she has somehow managed unconsciously to slip it onto the other while he is disentangling himself from her arm, and so on.) Elsewhere, dialogue is retained despite the elimination of characters: for the embassy from Rome, the role of Caius Lucius is cut, and instead two silent ambassadors wheel a tape recorder and a large cardboard cut-out of a smiling Marcello Magni to Cymbeline's court. One of them switches on the tape recorder and goes round behind the picture, puts his arms out through two holes at its shoulders and, to irresistibly comic effect, makes appropriate arm-gestures to accompany Magni-as-Caesar's pre-recorded request for tribute. (When Cymbeline refuses to pay, the ambassadors turn the cut-out around to reveal a portrait of a furious Magni on its obverse instead, then change the tape and make suitably angry Italian gestures through the holes to accompany a pre-recorded declaration of war.) Throughout, only a few lines survive unaltered from Shakespeare's script – much of 'Fear no more the heat o'th' sun,' for instance, the marvellous 'Do't, and to bed, then!' after Imogen learns that Pisanio has only decoyed her to Wales to kill her (3.4.100), and 'O for a horse with wings!' (3.2.48) – more surprisingly, given how little this Imogen looks like the horsey type. Often, though, such lines are kept only so as to be burlesqued

by what follows. The princess's next remark, for instance, also survives intact, but only for the sake of a laugh produced by a new sequel: '[*very loud and joyous*] He is at Milford Haven! [*pause, then just as loud and emphatic*] Where's Milford Haven?! [*runs up stairs inside scaffolding to consult a globe: then surprised and slightly baffled*] It's in Wales!' But the unusual pleasure of watching any kind of Shakespeare production without always knowing precisely what the characters are going to say next is not to be understated, though I still cannot help regretting the losses that the small size of this cast inevitably dictates in the reunion scene, which here does not provide anything like the gloriously baroque conclusion that it does in the original. What instead provides a fine and oddly haunting ending, though, is a creepy epilogue-like sequence that finally restores all the missing contents of that empty nursery: to the strains of a lullaby, Cymbeline looks on from the background as Posthumus and Imogen slowly climb into one single bed and Guiderius and Arviragus into another. After all their adventures, they are all good little children again, and in this guise, settling themselves contentedly to sleep, we leave them.

10 OCTOBER 2007

At the Barbican Theatre, more rewriting, though of a less thoroughgoing kind, is on offer in Lev Dodin's Maly Theatre production of *King Lear*, visiting from St Petersburg. The first scene of this production – played on bare floorboards in front of large timber St Andrew's crosses and vertical beams – is pleasingly unfussy, though it follows Kosintsev's example in adding the Fool to this scene's dramatis personae. He here enters in companionable half-drunken merriment with Lear through the front stalls and then takes up position at a piano downstage right where he will spend much of the rest of the evening accompanying the action with a wistful little ragtime tune. The trouble with this show is that having established its own clear, spacious, non-naturalistic style in this opening scene it can't seem to find anywhere else to go: the ragtime tune gets tedious surprisingly

57. *King Lear*, Maly Theatre of St Petersburg, dir. Lev Dodin, 2006. A dream sequence in the fourth act: Elizabeta Boryaskaya as Goneril, Elena Kalinina as Regan, Daria Rumantseva as Cordelia.

quickly, Peter Semak's Lear seems to get into a rut of cracked-voice self-pity almost as soon as he arrives at Goneril's palace, and visually the uniformly monochrome costumes become so boring that even Kent and Gloucester decide to take theirs right off in the storm along with Lear and Edgar. More frustratingly, the surtitles, which with few exceptions offer only a thin ration of untranslated Shakespeare, clearly offer only a very partial idea of the script the actors are actually using, which I gather is a highly colloquial, modern adaptation of the play. In the second half especially much of Shakespeare's plot is replaced by what looks like a series of dream sequences: similar sexual encounters between Edmund and Goneril and Edmund and Regan, during which both women cry out the word 'Father!' as the lights fade; a reunion scene between Lear and Cordelia in which they are the only characters present on the immense empty stage; and most strikingly a sort of ballet performed by a vision of all three sisters in white Elizabethan dresses, gavotting in turn with a half-dressed Lear. The best I can say is that this might well have been a very interesting production for Russian speakers. Dodin himself, who has the reputation of being a theatrical guru of the stature of Peter Brook, joined the cast to take a curtain call at the close of this London press night (is this customary in Russia?), but the applause seemed polite rather than eager.

27 OCTOBER 2006

I somehow manage to miss Peter Hall's visiting *Measure for Measure* in the Courtyard – by report, a methodically spoken, Jacobean-dress, unremarkable specimen of his latterday manner – but do get to what ought to be a more stimulating and engaged show, the Cardboard Citizens' production of *Timon of Athens* at the Shakespeare Centre in Stratford. The idea of having this professed 'homeless people's theatre company' stage a version of a script that is, after all, about becoming homeless after falling massively into debt must have looked like a good one when the show was commissioned, but Adrian Jackson's show is in the event much less coherent than anyone can reasonably have expected. The evening begins as a quite funny parody of one of those business seminars that seek to use Shakespeare as a tool for demonstrating how to make contacts and influence people ('Look at his message in *Hamlet*', urges a microphone-bearing young man in a Burton's suit, 'always prioritize your to-do list!'), but why such a seminar leader should be intermittently compering such a virulently anti-business play as *Timon* is never adequately explained. Once this conceit has been substantially dropped after the interval, the play is periodically interrupted instead by video footage of interviews with a squatter and with a man seeking the legal right to live in a hut in some woods, and any concentration on the play's own special moral hysteria is further dissipated by the sharing of the role of Timon between three different actors. Each of them, furthermore, makes extensive use of a large hand-held microphone, which in such a small venue is physically as well as aesthetically irritating, while just to prove that somebody on the production team has read one of those essays about this play's use of dog imagery, every time the text mentions anything remotely canine somebody offstage with another microphone makes a painfully loud barking noise over the loudspeakers. The most interesting aspect of the evening is probably watching the audience arriving at the start of the evening and being told by Cardboard Citizens' assistants to fill out a lapel badge specifying their first name and profession and to indicate by a colour-coded sticker into what income band they fall. On 27 October the overwhelming majority are impecunious retired academics and they are not much amused.

10 NOVEMBER 2006

The University of Michigan at Ann Arbor have laid on a conference about Shakespearean performance to coincide with a one-month residency of the RSC's current productions of *Julius Caesar*, *Antony and Cleopatra* and *The Tempest*, and while attending this event I not only revisit the first two but finally catch up with the latter, which ran at the main house in Stratford from late July through early October and will transfer to the Novello in London in spring 2007. Rupert Goold's production is likely to be remembered more for the sheer audacious novelty of its setting than for anything else, but if and when one can take one's eyes and one's mind off this *Tempest*'s extravagant, lavishly counter-intuitive mise-en-scène it offers much else to enjoy. Giles Cadle's visual effects are foregrounded from the very start, when the arriving audience find themselves looking at an immense drop bearing an image of a 1930s radio set which looks as though it has been massively enlarged from a Tintin comic, and the self-conscious daring of the production is then flaunted when, as the house-lights fade, the audience hear not the opening lines of Shakespeare's dialogue but a recording of the BBC shipping forecast, stolidly promising extreme bad weather in the North Atlantic. As this bulletin fades in its turn, the round dial of the radio first lights up to become the cathode ray tube of a radar set, its cursor scanning in circles to the pinging of sonar, and then turns translucent, and we find ourselves watching the first scene of *The Tempest* as if through a porthole, the crew and passengers glimpsed below the decks of a modern ship, with the text's naval commands occasionally brought from the bridge by sailors descending an iron ladder but more often relayed over a tannoy.

Nothing so far has suggested we are in the Mediterranean somewhere between Tunis and Naples – in fact geographically it all looks more like the world of *The Cruel Sea* than that of *The Aeneid* – but this production's magnificently silly central idea is only fully revealed after the ship appears to sink before our eyes in a clamour of 'Mayday's and the discharge of a red Very light: suddenly the drop,

58. *The Tempest*, RSC, Royal Shakespeare Theatre, dir. Rupert Goold, 2006. The betrothal scene, 4.1, in a wooden hut in the Arctic: still in the pyjamas in which he was shipwrecked, Ferdinand (Nick Court) is warned against taking advantage of Miranda (Mariah Gale) by Prospero (Patrick Stewart). Note the magic garment made of North Polar animal furs on the back of the door.

briefly showing a projection of the sea as it might appear to the drowning, becomes a screen on which is projected falling snow, before lifting on a set that reveals the interior of a strange wooden hut that is quite clearly somewhere in the Arctic, with snow stretching whitely away beyond its roofless rear wall towards a backdrop horizon. With his back to us stands a man wearing a magic garment that is on this occasion made from the skin of a polar bear, and beside him, rather appalled, stands a young woman in a short red coat. These people are Patrick Stewart as Prospero and Mariah Gale as Miranda, for whom this hut appears to serve primarily as a schoolroom: I have never seen Miranda played more exquisitely as an earnest home-schooled only child, and I find myself warming to her the moment she primly and eagerly raises her hand in response to Pros-pero's 'Canst thou remember / A time before we

came unto this cell?' (1.2.38–9). This memorable Miranda is counterpointed by an equally distinctive Ariel, played by Julian Bleach as a gloomy white-faced frost-demon, low half-human voice forever half-echoing with added reverb; he still seems to be at some important level imprisoned in the cloven pine where he howled all those winters out before Prospero's arrival.

If you can only stop trying to work out how any storm could get a ship from Tunis to what appears to be somewhere beyond Spitsbergen, or how come Prospero seems to have been inducted as some sort of shaman (who instead of staging the customary classical masque in act 4 has three vaguely Native American spirits take Ferdinand and Miranda through most of a cod Inuit betrothal rit-ual), or how come some of the castaways are sur-viving in only pyjamas and lifejackets while others are only just fending off terminal exposure in thick blankets, or why the stage floor often looks like cracked ice floes but nobody ever seems to worry about falling through into the sea, or whether the hungry castaways would really tuck that eagerly into a magic banquet that consists here of a dead raw walrus dragged in on a sledge, and whether the skull on Prospero's desk is really that of Sycorax (as a nod towards it seems to suggest when he mentions her at 1.2.258–60), and if so what he did with her, then these three performances can between them keep this *Tempest* just about cogent, at an emotional level at least. (John Light's conventionally crawling Caliban, unusually, somehow never seems to matter anything like as much.) Bleach's Ariel is sufficiently jealous of Miranda to use her sleeping body as a sofa while he recounts his doings in the opening storm in 1.2 but still yearns with slow frozen resentment for his freedom; Miranda, irresistible to Ferdinand through the sheer quivering intensity of her attention, needs to leave school and her only partly understood though revered father as soon as possible; and this preoccupied, practical, unmelodramatic Prospero – for whom Stewart, in this extremely northern latitude, revives as much of his native Yorkshire pronunciation as he can – finally achieves a breakthrough into something like resolution not when he decides to renounce revenge in favour of virtue but when in the final scene he suddenly and spontaneously embraces Miranda, just when neither of them was expecting it (at 5.1.202). The whole show ends as it begins, with a fancy effect: dismissed at last, on a set that now represents the snowy ground outside the hut rather than its interior, Ariel goes into the abandoned dwelling and soon appears to have set light to it: as it begins to burn there is a sudden firework-like whoosh and suddenly the sky beyond bursts out into the aurora borealis. (So this chill spirit – who in this production does not sing about how merrily he will live now under the blossom that hangs on the bough, since he has probably never seen any – appears to have been joyously released to become the Northern Lights, or was that celestial illumination a mere coincidence or metaphor and has he really only committed a fiery suicide?) Prospero's epilogue seems an off-centred, almost irrelevant pendant after this, since this is a production which has never sought a language in which it might speak to the audience independently of the special effects which he is now obliged to renounce. This is a peculiar, wantonly perverse, expensive sort of *Tempest*, but I suspect that it will be remembered with pleasure as well as with an amused near-disbelief.

17 NOVEMBER 2006

Back in Stratford, I find myself a week later beginning to wonder whether one incidental purpose of the Complete Works Festival may be to undermine the reputation of the German theatre. (And where are the French in all this, anyway?) After years of dreaming of getting to see the Berliner Ensemble, I am in the Courtyard watching Claus Peymann's visiting production of *Richard II* and it looks like an anthology of some of the dullest theatrical clichés that have already bedevilled Peter Stein's *Troilus* and the Münchner Kammerspieler *Othello*: monochromatic set and costumes (a plain white stage and white flats, black suits on Bolingbroke's faction, white on Richard's), lots of empty space and a drearily non-committal style of acting that seems deliberately not to engage with either the emotional or the intellectual content of the piece. Peymann's actors, just in case we were to take the events of the play too seriously, have been provided with half-clownish white face make-up, but a pervasive note of incipient mirthless burlesque only really blossoms into the famous German sense of humour around Richard's hapless queen. Played on this occasion by the equally hapless Hanna Jürgens she is obliged to faint at least once during every scene in which she appears, and this little running gag, though not dropped thereafter, achieves its maximum effect in the gardeners' scene. I had anticipated something distracting in the way of watering in this scene when I first noticed a tap set in the stage-right flat before the play began, but I admit that I hadn't anticipated that a hosepipe would be used by one gardener to turn a wheelbarrow-load of topsoil dumped onto the stage by the other into a small swamp of mud, so that when the queen faints this time her white dress can get all muddy. Laugh? I nearly went home. Everyone gets pretty muddy by the end – handfuls of mud and some tin cans are even thrown against the flats from offstage after the deposition scene – and this production is likely to be remembered more vividly by the RSC's cleaning staff than by its audiences. Thomas Brasch's translation has Richard murdered by his uncle York rather than by Sir Piers Exton, but this production gives so few clues about why you should care who did it or even whether they did it that the fact hardly seems worth recording.

WINTER

12 DECEMBER 2006

At least the last Festival show I shall see before 2007 is a cheerful one. A theatregoing year that began with revisiting Greg Doran's *Dream* on its London transfer and included two welcome attendances at his *Antony and Cleopatra*, both of them among the best work he has done, ends with what is liable to be remembered as his biggest if perhaps most endearing folly to date. I am in the stalls of the Royal Shakespeare Theatre for the press night of *Merry Wives, The Musical* ('based on the play by William Shakespeare, adapted by Gregory Doran, music by Paul Englishby, lyrics by Ranjit Bolt'), contemplating an enormous drop bearing a 1930s-style postcard-like printed image of Windsor Castle, and reminding myself strenuously that some earlier musical adaptations of this play (by Verdi and Nicolai and Vaughan Williams) have actually been quite good. To judge from the overture, this one is not going to be as memorable musically (the score hovers between pastiching the classic musicals of the 1930s and 1940s and sending them up, with occasional lurches into Lloyd-Webber around Anne Page and Fenton), but as the picture of Windsor Castle is hoisted away upwards the set at least promises some visual wit. A street of half-timbered houses recedes into the centre-stage distance, peopled by bustling heavily miked-up actors representing Windsor townspeople whose costumes nicely hybridize the 1590s with the 1930s – this is mock-Tudor deluxe, and when Simon Callow's Falstaff arrives to take up residence at the Garter Inn he does so on a motorbike, with a kilted Bardolph, a semi-punk Pistol and a spivvish Nym crowded into a sidecar. (With his goggles and cap Callow looks at first glance rather like Mr Toad and indeed that is much the performance which Callow gives for the rest of the evening.) This conceit produces some nice intricate sight gags – Alistair McGowan's Ford, for instance, carries a furled umbrella and a vaguely Elizabethan satchel as he sets off in doublet and waistcoat towards what is evidently his job in the City – and it enables Stephen Brimson Lewis to have all sorts of fun devising nice semi-Ginger Rogers outfits for the wives and a half-Elizabethan, half-Disney-*Snow-White* look for Anne Page; but it does produce one immediate problem, which is that nothing in this show's version of Windsor looks like anyone's idea of normality, even when one has allowed for the fact that everybody on the stage keeps bursting into song under sudden follow-spots the whole time. It is very hard for the comedy in *The Merry Wives of Windsor*, however the script is adapted, to achieve much leverage without some shrewd common sense of what ordinary everyday life would be like, and this show's delightfully whimsical design turns out to blur the play's central issues still further later on when the dubious, disreputable, male interior of the Garter Inn is represented by almost the same configuration of the set as the domestic, respectable, female interior of Mistress Ford's house.

This show has not primarily been devised with the intention of clarifying *The Merry Wives*, however, but with that of turning it into a vehicle for someone who has otherwise grown out of Shakespeare's unrewritten roles for women, namely Dame Judi Dench, who arrives in the fourth scene (to the credit of this audience, without receiving an entrance-round) wearing a tawny wig that makes her look remarkably like Imelda Staunton. She is playing, of all people, Mistress Quickly, who from incidental go-between has been promoted in Doran's adaptation almost into leading

59. *Merry Wives, The Musical*, RSC, Royal Shakespeare Theatre, dir. Gregory Doran, 2006. 1590s meet 1950s in an all-singing 3.3: Alexandra Gilbreath as Mistress Ford and Haydn Gwynne as Mistress Page put Simon Callow's Falstaff into the buck basket.

lady. Whereas Shakespeare suppressed the fact that he was recycling this character from an Eastcheap which, inexplicably, neither she nor her erstwhile parasite Falstaff ever seems to remember, Doran imports whole substantial passages from both parts of *Henry IV* and even the knowledge of her future marriage from *Henry V*, so that Quickly can reproach Falstaff for his breach of promise to marry her, accuse him of bankrupting her tavern so that she has had to accept work as Dr Caius's housekeeper, waver over a renewed proposition which Falstaff somehow manages to fit in between attempts on Mistresses Page and Ford, and finally get herself together and get her show on the road in the company of Ancient Pistol. Structurally, this overbalances the play entirely – the exquisite symmetry of its plotting, by which everything comes together and is settled at Herne's Oak, is quite lost, the other subplot gets fatally squeezed so that Dr

Caius and Parson Evans have a whole duet about how they are going to plot revenge on the host of the Garter but never put any such plan into effect, and the wives themselves are further hindered from establishing their stories and their values at the heart of the show. It isn't much of a help musically either, since Dench, whatever her other virtues, is not the world's greatest singer, and committing her to a duet with Simon Callow, who is not the world's greatest singer either, only by a much larger margin, is positively irresponsible. But the whole enterprise, if rather arch and constantly on the edge of the saccharine, is at least good-natured, and nobody is going to grudge this cast the enjoyment which they seem genuinely to be deriving from the whole absurd business. The level of sheer expertise that has gone into the choreography, the mise-en-scène and the score is humbling, and many performers familiar from the RSC's non-musical work turn out to be more than competent at both song and dance: Alex Gilbreath as Mistress Ford, Haydn Gwynne as Mistress Page and Paul Chahidi as Dr Caius among them. Dench, furthermore, gets two sight-gags which are almost worth tolerating Anne Page's songs for, one when she enters from centre back stage down the set's receding high street and stands for a while in baffled amazement in front of a house which for the purposes of perspective has been constructed so as to be only just as tall as she is, and once when, at the climax of the wives' vigorous semi-hoedown number in the second half, a body-double in a copy of her wig and costume cartwheels vigorously across the stage from one set of the wings to the other before Dench re-enters, simulating a slight attack of dizziness. It's as close as this December is going to get to a designated official RSC panto.

All this and interesting promenade productions of *Pericles* and *The Winter's Tale* still to be seen in the Swan, and many further star turns still to look forward to during the remaining third of the Complete Works Festival: McKellen as Lear, Janet Suzman as Volumnia and Eve Best as Rosalind among them. Come the end of April 2007, we will perhaps find the time to work out what this whole exercise will have added up to, once the RST and the Swan are both closed for the internal rebuilding and the frantic international party has come to an end, and which aspects of The Essential Year will continue to be part of RSC practice hereafter. But, for the moment, the strains of *Merry Wives, The Musical* fade away.

PROFESSIONAL SHAKESPEARE PRODUCTIONS IN THE BRITISH ISLES JANUARY–DECEMBER 2005

JAMES SHAW

Most of the productions listed are by professional companies, but some amateur productions are included. The information is taken from *Touchstone* (www.touchstone.bham.ac.uk), a Shakespeare website maintained by the Shakespeare Institute Library. *Touchstone* includes a monthly list of current and forthcoming UK Shakespeare productions from listings information. The websites provided for theatre companies were accurate at the time of going to press.

ANTONY AND CLEOPATRA

Royal Exchange Theatre Company. Royal Exchange, Manchester, 23 February–9 April.
www.royalexchange.co.uk
Director: Braham Murray
Antony: Tom Mannion
Cleopatra: Josette Bushell-Mingo

AS YOU LIKE IT

Young Vic Theatre Company. Wyndham's Theatre, London, 3 June–3 September.
www.youngvic.org
Director: David Lan
Rosalind: Helen McCrory
Celia: Sienna Miller
Set in 1940s France.

Creation Theatre Company. Headington Hill Park, Oxford, 3 June–9 August.
www.creationtheatre.co.uk
Director: Charlotte Conquest

Royal Shakespeare Company. Royal Shakespeare Theatre, Stratford-upon-Avon, 5 August–13 October.
www.rsc.org.uk
Director: Dominic Cooke
Rosalind: Lia Williams

Nottingham Playhouse and Belgrade Theatre, Coventry. Royal Lyceum, Edinburgh, 17 September–15 October.
www.lyceum.org.uk
Director: Mark Thomson
Rosalind: Emma Cunniffe

THE COMEDY OF ERRORS

Creation Theatre Company. The Spiegeltent, BMW Group Plant, Oxford, 28 January–19 March.
www.creationtheatre.co.uk
Director: Charlotte Conquest

Northern Broadsides Theatre Company. West Yorkshire Playhouse, Leeds, 21–6 March and tour until June.
www.northern-broadsides.co.uk
Director: Barrie Rutter
Touring with *Sweet William* (see Miscellaneous).

Queen's Theatre, Hornchurch, 15 April–7 May.
www.queens-theatre.co.uk
Director: Bob Carlton

Set in Times Square, accompanied by musical numbers.

Sheffield Theatre Company. The Crucible Theatre, Sheffield, 19 May–11 June.
www.sheffieldtheatres.co.uk
Director: Jonathan Munby
Duke and Dr Pinch: Hilton McRae

Illyria Theatre Company. Tamworth Castle, Tamworth, 27–28 May and tour until August.
www.illyria.uk.com

Northcott Theatre Company. Northcott Theatre, Exeter, 13 July–13 August.
www.northcott-theatre.co.uk
Director: Ben Crocker

Royal Shakespeare Company. Royal Shakespeare Theatre, Stratford-upon-Avon, 15 July–29 October.
www.rsc.org.uk
Director: Nancy Meckler

CYMBELINE

New Shakespeare Company. Open Air Theatre, Regent's Park, London, 1 June–3 September.
www.openairtheatre.org
Director: Rachel Kavanaugh
The first Cymbeline in Regent's Park for over 50 years.

HAMLET

Royal and Derngate Theatres. Derngate Theatre, Northampton, 17 March–3 April.
Director: Rupert Goold
Gertrude: Jane Birkin
The stage designed to resemble the auditorium of the Derngate Theatre. The political elements were reduced and Fortinbras was cut.

Heartbreak Productions. Tour June–August.
www.heartbreakproductions.co.uk

Haymarket Theatre Company. Haymarket Theatre, Basingstoke, 16 September–8 October.
www.haymarket.org.uk
Director: John Adams

English Touring Theatre. The Playhouse, Oxford, 23 September–1 October and UK tour until November.
www.ett.org.uk
Director: Stephen Unwin
Hamlet: Edward Stoppard
Gertrude: Anita Dobson

Wales Theatre Company. Grand Theatre, Swansea, 19–29 October and Welsh tour.
www.walestheatrecompany.com
Directors: Michael Bogdanov and Kirsty Jones
Translator: Gareth Miles
Production alternated nightly between Welsh and English language.

ADAPTATION

Rosencrantz and Guildenstern are Dead
English Touring Theatre. Oxford Playhouse, 20–28 May, and UK until July.
Director: Stephen Unwin
Playwright: Tom Stoppard

The Secret Love Life of Ophelia
The Ramshorn Theatre, Glasgow, 30 May–4 June.
Director: Bruce Downie
Playwright: Steven Berkoff
A series of imagined letters between Hamlet and Ophelia.

BALLET

Hamlet
Welsh Ballet Company, UK tour May–December.
www.welshballet.co.uk
Choreographer: Darius James

HENRY IV PART 1

National Theatre Company. Olivier Theatre, London, 16 April 2005–22 July.
www.nationaltheatre.org.uk
Director: Nicholas Hytner
Falstaff: Michael Gambon
King Henry IV: David Bradley
Hal: Matthew Macfadyen

HENRY IV PART 2

National Theatre Company. Olivier Theatre, London, 26 April–2 July.
www.nationaltheatre.org.uk
Director: Nicholas Hytner
Falstaff: Michael Gambon
King Henry IV: David Bradley
Hal: Matthew Macfadyen
Shallow: John Wood

HENRY V

ADAPTATION

After Agincourt
Doges of War Company. Etcetera Theatre, London, 8–13 February.
Playwright: Peter Mottley
Director: Gareth David-Lloyd
Set in The Boar's Head seven years after the battle of Agincourt, with Pistol recounting events at the battle.

HENRY VI PART 1

The Wars of the Roses: Part 1: House of Lancaster
Generator Company. Playbox Theatre, Warwick, 18, 20–1, 26, 27–8 May.
www.playboxtheatre.com
Director: Stewart McGill
Adaptor: Richard Pearson

HENRY VI PART 2

The Wars of the Roses: Part 2: House of York
Generator Company. Playbox Theatre, Warwick, 19, 21, 26, 27–8 May.
www.playboxtheatre.com
Director: Stewart McGill.
Adaptor: Richard Pearson

JULIUS CAESAR

Royal Shakespeare Company. Swan Theatre, Stratford-upon-Avon, 18 November 2004–26 February 2005 and UK tour.
www.rsc.org.uk
Director: David Farr
Touring with *The Two Gentlemen of Verona*.

Theatre National du Chaillot. Teatro Espanol, Grand Theatre de la Ville. Barbican Theatre, London 14 April–14 May.
Director: Deborah Warner
Brutus: Anton Lesser
Cassius: Simon Russell Beale
Antony: Ralph Fiennes
Portia: Fiona Shaw
Employed over a hundred extras for crowd scenes.

KING LEAR

Royal Shakespeare Company. Albery Theatre, London, 13 January–5 February. Transfer from Stratford.
www.rsc.org.uk
Director: Bill Alexander
Lear: Corin Redgrave

Chichester Festival Theatre. Minerva Theatre, Chichester, 7 May–10 September.
www.cft.org.uk
Director: Steven Pimlott
Lear: David Warner

ADAPTATION

Lear

Sheffield Theatre Company. Crucible Theatre, Sheffield, 9 March–2 April.
www.sheffieldtheatres.co.uk
Playwright: Edward Bond
Director: Jonathan Kent
Lear: Ian McDiarmid

Our Lear

Theatro Technis, London, 26 January–6 February.
Director and Adaptor: George Eugeniou

LOVE'S LABOUR'S LOST

Theatre Set-Up. Tour June–August.
www.ts-u.co.uk

ADAPTATION

The Big Life

Theatre Royal, Stratford East, 23 February–4 March; Apollo Theatre, London, May–December.
Composer: Paul Sirret
Director: Clint Dyer
Musical version involving four men arriving in fifties Britain from the Caribbean.

MACBETH

Out of Joint Theatre Company. Wilton's Music Hall, 6 January–5 February.
www.outofjoint.co.uk
Director: Max Stafford Clark
Macbeth: Danny Sapani
Lady Macbeth: Monica Dolan

Almeida Theatre Company. Almeida Theatre, London, 13 January–5 March.
www.almeida.co.uk
Director: John Caird
Macbeth: Simon Russell Beale

Royal Shakespeare Company. Albery Theatre, London, 10 February–5 March. Stratford transfer.
www.rsc.org.uk
Director: Dominic Cooke
Macbeth: Greg Hicks
Lady Macbeth: Sian Thomas

York Theatre Royal Company. Theatre, Royal, York, 28 February–19 March.
www.yorktheatreroyal.co.uk
Director: Damian Cruden

Chapterhouse Theatre Company. UK tour June–September.
www.chapterhouse.org

The Lord Chamberlain's Men. Osborne House, Isle of Wight, 3–5 June and UK tour until August.
www.lordchamberlainsmen.co.uk
Director: Lucy Pitman-Wallace

Stamford Shakespeare Festival. Rutland Open Air Theatre, Tolethorpe Hall, Tolethorpe, June–July.
www.stamfordshakespeare.co.uk

Oxford Shakespeare Company. Wadham College Gardens, 27 July–19 August.
www.oxfordshakespearecompany.co.uk
Director: Chris Pickles
All-male production.

Derby Playhouse Theatre Company, Derby, 24 September–22 October.
www.derbyplayhouse.co.uk
Director: Karen Louise Hebden
Macbeth: Brian Protheroe

Leicester Haymarket Theatre Company. Haymarket Theatre, Leicester, 6–28 October.
www.lhtheatre.co.uk
Director: Paul Kerryson

ADAPTATION

Macbeth
Centre for New Theatre at CalArts (California). Almeida Theatre, London, 26 October–5 November.
www.almeida.co.uk
Director: Travis Preston
Stephen Dillane's solo interpretation on a bare stage with a single prop (chair), with a relatively uncut text.

Shakespeare's Sisters – As Good As It Gets
Works Well Productions. Everyman Theatre, Cheltenham, 23 September–1 October and small UK tour.
www.everymantheatre.org.uk
Playwright: Jonathan Shelly

Wyrd Sisters
Threadbare Theatre Company. Upstairs at the Gatehouse, London, 11–29 October.
Adaptor: Stephen Briggs
Adapted from the novel by Terry Pratchett, and includes parodies of *Macbeth* and *Hamlet*.

OPERA

Macbeth
Opera Holland Park. London, June.
Composer: Verdi
Director: Olivia Fuchs

MEASURE FOR MEASURE

Shakespeare's Globe Theatre, London, 6–16 October and USA tour.
www.shakespeares-globe.org
Director: John Dove

Tara Arts, UK tour September–December.
www.tara-arts.com
Director: Jatinda Verma

MERRY WIVES OF WINDSOR

Rain or Shine Theatre Company, UK tour June–August.
www.rainorshine.co.uk

Peter Hall Company. Theatre Royal, Bath, 29 June–4 August.
www.theatreroyal.org.uk
Director: Peter Hall

Stamford Shakespeare Festival. Rutland Open Air Theatre, Tolethorpe Hall, Tolethorpe, July–September.
www.stamfordshakespeare.co.uk

Wild Thyme Productions. Upstairs at the Gatehouse, London, 7–17 July.
Director: Stephen Jameson
Treated as a farce and set in post-war Windsor.

OPERA

Falstaff
English Touring Opera. UK tour October–December.
Composer: Verdi
www.englishtouringopera.org.uk

Falstaff
Music Theatre London, UK tour April–June.
Composer: Verdi
Set in a golf club near Windsor with Alice Ford behind the bar at the nineteenth hole.

A MIDSUMMER NIGHT'S DREAM

Royal Shakespeare Company, Royal Shakespeare Theatre, Stratford-upon-Avon, 31 March–September.
www.rsc.org.uk
Director: Gregory Doran
Bottom: Malcolm Storry

British Touring Shakespeare Company. Queen Square, Bristol, 5–17 July.

www.bristolshakespeare.org.uk
Part of the Bristol Shakespeare Festival.

Creation Theatre Company. Headington Hill
Park, Oxford, 7 July–10 September
www.creationtheatre.co.uk
Director: Zoe Seaton
Cast of eight with all characters doubled except
Puck.

Chapterhouse Theatre Company. UK tour
June–September.
www.chapterhouse.org

The Festival Players. UK tour June–August
www.thefestivalplayers.co.uk
Director: Michael Dyer

Peter Hall Company. Theatre Royal, Bath, 29
June–6 August.
Director: Peter Hall
Benedick: Aden Gillett
Beatrice: Janie Dee

Sheffield Crucible Theatre Company. Crucible
Theatre, Sheffield, 21 September–5 Novem-
ber.
www.sheffieldtheatres.co.uk
Director: Josie Rourke
Benedick: Sam West

Centurion Theatre Company. The Courtyard
Theatre, London, 2–27 November.
www.thecourtyard.org.uk
Director: Michael Sergeant

BALLET

A Midsummer Night's Dream
Welsh Ballet Company. UK tour April–June.
www.welshballet.co.uk
Choreographer: Darius James
Music by Mendelssohn.

The Dream
Royal Ballet. Royal Opera House, London, 7–8,
11 June.
Choreographer: Frederick Ashton

OPERA

A Midsummer Night's Dream
The Royal Opera House, London, 25
November–3 December
www.royaloperahouse.org
Composer: Benjamin Britten
Director: Olivia Fuchs

MUCH ADO ABOUT NOTHING

Heartbreak Productions, UK tour June–August
www.heartbreakproductions.co.uk

OTHELLO

ADAPTATION

Desdemona: A Play About a Handkerchief
Strathclyde Theatre Group. The Ramshorn
Theatre, Glasgow, 30 May–4 June.
Playwright: Paula Vogel
Director: Sara Harrison

OPERA

Otello
Royal Opera House. The Royal Opera House,
London, 28 June–16 July.
Composer: Verdi
Director: Elijah Moshinsky

Otello
Glyndebourne Opera Company. Glynde-
bourne, Lewes, 24 July–28 August.
www.glyndebourne.com
Composer: Verdi
Director: Peter Hall

PERICLES

Shakespeare at the Tobacco Factory Theatre
Company. The Tobacco Factory, Bristol, 10
February–19 March.
www.sattf.org.uk
Director: Andrew Hilton
Pericles: Nathan Rimmell
Favourably reviewed.

Shakespeare's Globe Theatre Company. Shakespeare's Globe Theatre, London, 6 May–2
October.
http://shakespeares-globe.org
Director: Kathryn Hunter
The title part separated into Pericles the elder
and younger, played by different actors.

RICHARD II

Ludlow Shakespeare Festival. Ludlow Castle,
Ludlow, 25 June–9 July.
www.ludlowfestival.co.uk
Director: Steven Berkoff
Loosely set in Victorian England with Richard
II resembling Oscar Wilde.

Old Vic. The Old Vic Theatre, London, 4
October–26 November.
www.oldvictheatre.com
Director: Trevor Nunn
Richard: Kevin Spacey
Bolingbroke: Ben Miles
Modern dress production drawing upon media
manipulation of twenty-first-century politics.

Playbox Theatre Company. The Dream Factory,
Warwick, 15–19 November.
www.playboxtheatre.com
Director: Stewart McGill

RICHARD III

Kaos Richard III. Kaos Theatre Company. UK
tour February

www.kaostheatre.com
Director: Xavier Leret

ROMEO AND JULIET

Young Vic Company and Vesturport Company.
Playhouse Theatre, London, 13 November
2004–2 January 2005.
Director: Gisli Orn Gardarson

Royal Shakespeare Company. Albery Theatre,
London, 16 December 2004–8 January 2005.
Stratford transfer.
www.rsc.org.uk
Director: Peter Gill

Derby Playhouse, Derby, 28 May–2 July.
www.derbyplayhouse.co.uk
Director: Stephen Edwards

Chapterhouse Theatre Company. UK tour
June–August.
www.chapterhouse.org

Manchester Royal Exchange. Royal Exchange
Theatre, Manchester, Manchester, 7
September–22 October.
www.royalexchange.com
Director: Jacob Murray

Birmingham Repertory Theatre Company. Birmingham Repertory Theatre, 30
September–22 October.
www.birmingham-rep.co.uk
Director: Bill Bryden

ADAPTATION

Mercutio Rising
Primrose Hill Players. Etcetera Theatre, London,
8–20 November.
www.etceteratheatre.com
Playwright: Dominic Carroll
A monologue for Mercutio.

PROFESSIONAL PRODUCTIONS IN THE BRITISH ISLES

BALLET

English National Ballet.
Coliseum, London, 11–15 January.
Composer: Prokofiev
Choreography: Rudolf Noreen

Birmingham Royal Ballet. UK tour January.
www.brb.org.uk
Choreographer: Kenneth MacMillan

The Kirov Ballet. Royal Opera House, London,
22–23, 25 July.
Composer: Prokofiev
Choreography: Leonid Lavrovsky

SIR THOMAS MORE

Royal Shakespeare Company. Swan Theatre,
Stratford-upon-Avon, 9 March–3 November.
www.rsc.org.uk
Director: Robert Delamere

THE TAMING OF THE SHREW

Chapterhouse Theatre Company. UK tour
June–September.
www.chapterhouse.org

ADAPTATION

Kiss Me Kate
Tristan Baker Productions and CCO Theatrical
Ltd. UK tour February–July.

The Tamer Tamed
Minack Theatre, Penzance, 1–5 August.
www.minack.com
Playwright: John Fletcher

THE TEMPEST

Shakespeare's Globe Theatre Company. Shakespeare' Globe Theatre, London, 6 May–2
October.
http://shakespeares-globe.org

Director: Tim Carroll
Prospero: Mark Rylance
Psychological production where the only visible characters were Prospero, Caliban and
Ariel. The cast of three were accompanied
by dancers and classical chorus.

British Touring Shakespeare (with Facsimile
Theatre Company). UK tour July–August.
www.britishtouringshakespeare.co.uk

Liverpool Playhouse, 4–22 October.
Director: Philip Franks
Prospero: Christopher Ravenscroft
Set in a dilapidated theatre in an English seaside
town.

ADAPTATION

The Tempest
Southwark Playhouse, London, 25 January–12
February.
www.southwarkplayhouse.co.uk
Director: Tom Wright
Prospero: Hilton McRae
Ninety-minute version intended for schools,
with a cast of eight.

The Tempest
Ant Theatre Company. Brockley Jack Pub, London, 13 September–9 October.
www.anttheatre.com
Director: Simon Beyer
A gender-reversed interpretation featuring Prospera and her scheming sister Antonia.

Tossed!
Pants on Fire Theatre Company. People Show
Studios, London. 26 April–7 May.
www.pantsonfiretheatre.com
Director: Peter Bramley
Featuring six Ariels.

TROILUS AND CRESSIDA

Clwyd Theatr Cymru. Anthony Hopkins Theatre, Clwyd Theatr Cymru, Mold, 10 February–5 March.
www.clwyd-theatr-cymru.co.uk
Director: Terry Hands

Shakespeare's Globe Theatre Company. Shakespeare's Globe Theatre, London, 6 May–2 October.
http://shakespeares-globe.org
Director: Giles Block

TWELFTH NIGHT

Fervent Theatre Company. The Broadway Theatre, Catford Bridge, London 8 February–5 March.
Director: Mike Bernadin

Mercury Theatre. Mercury Theatre, Colchester, 3–26 March.
www.mercurytheatre.co.uk
Director: Dee Evans

Royal Shakespeare Company. Royal Shakespeare Theatre, Stratford-upon-Avon, 22 April–10 October.
www.rsc.org.uk
Director: Michael Boyd
Feste: Forbes Masson
Malvolio: Richard Cordery
Viola: Kananu Kirimi

New Shakespeare Company. Regent's Park Open Air Theatre, London, 30 May–1 September.
www.openairtheatre.org
Director: Timothy Sheader
Toby Belch: Desmond Barrit
Loosely set on a nineteenth-century Spanish colonial island.

West Yorkshire Playhouse, Leeds, 17 September–22 October.
www.wyp.org.uk
Director: Ian Brown
Pre-World War II setting.

Theatre Royal Plymouth and Thelma Holt. Theatre Royal, Plymouth, 26 September–8 October and UK tour.
Director: Patrick Mason
Malvolio: Matthew Kelly
Feste: Hilton McRae
Viola: Honeysuckle Weeks

ADAPTATION

Twelfth Night – The Musical – Five Go to Illyria
Qdos Entertainment. Yvonne Arnaud Theatre, Guildford, 20–3 July; Assembly Rooms, Edinburgh, 5–29 August.
Adaptor: Gyles Brandreth
Director: Carole Todd
A comic adaptation including a selection of popular songs and Shakespeare in person at the piano.

Twelfth Night – The 1960s San Francisco Psychedelic Musical
Company Aurora / Western Connecticut State University, Gilded Balloon. Edinburgh Fringe, 6–28 August.
Adaptor and Director: Sal Trapani

THE TWO GENTLEMEN OF VERONA

Royal Shakespeare Company. Swan Theatre, Stratford-upon-Avon, tour September 2004–May 2005.
www.rsc.org.uk
Director: Fiona Buffini

THE WINTER'S TALE

The Watermill Company. The Watermill Theatre, Newbury, 20 January–12 March and UK tour.
www.watermill.org.uk

Director: Edward Hall
All-male cast.

Shakespeare's Globe Theatre Company. Shakespeare's Globe Theatre, London, 6 May–2 October.
http://shakespeares-globe.org
Director: John Dove
Leontes: Paul Jesson

MISCELLANEOUS

The Dresser
Duke of York's, London. 28 February–15 May.
Director: Peter Hall
Sir: Julian Glover
Norman: Nicholas Lyndhurst

The Hollow Crown
Royal Shakespeare Company. The Royal Shakespeare Theatre, Stratford-upon-Avon, 3–19 March.
www.rsc.org.uk

Director and devisor: John Barton
Cast included Harriet Walter, Alan Howard and Donald Sinden.

Theatre of Blood
Improbable Theatre and National Theatre Companies. Lyttelton Theatre, London 9 May–27 August.
www.nationaltheatre.org.uk
Adaptors: Lee Simpson & Phelim McDermott.
Director: Phelim McDermott
Edward Lionheart: Jim Broadbent
Adaptation of the horror film starring Vincent Price.

Sweet William
Northern Broadsides. UK tour April–June.
www.northern-broadsides.co.uk
Playwright: Alan Plater
A view of Shakespeare from the viewpoint of contemporary Elizabethan friends, including Shakespeare as a character (touring with *The Comedy of Errors*).

THE YEAR'S CONTRIBUTIONS TO
SHAKESPEARE STUDIES

1. CRITICAL STUDIES
reviewed by MICHAEL TAYLOR

LOCAL SHAKESPEARES

All Shakespeare criticism is irrepressibly local. As recent literary theory has insisted, we can't help but read or play him in ways that inevitably expose our own positions – ideological, historical, geographical – whether we like it or not. Some criticism likes it a great deal and, responding to the metacritical impulse of our times, self-consciously, not to say cathartically, examines the myriad ways Shakespeare's texts take on the camouflage of the cultures in which they find themselves. An omnibus case in point is Celia R. Daileader's street-smart, provocative, sometimes infuriating book, *Racism, Misogyny, and the Othello Myth: Inter-racial Couples from Shakespeare to Spike Lee*, which traces the career of the Othello story in a series of local reworkings of it, from a vulgar recension by Thomas Dekker in the seventeenth century, *Lust's Dominion; or, The Lascivious Queen*, to Spike Lee's movies in the twentieth which, comfortably in the Dekker tradition, celebrate the machinations of 'snaky white women'. He and before him other writers such as Aphra Behn in her tragedy *Abdelazar* (1676) and her novella *Oroonoko; or, the Royal Slave* (1688), Coleridge in *The Rime of the Ancient Mariner* (1798), Edgar Allen Poe, Mary Shelley in *Frankenstein*, James Fennimore Cooper in *The Last of the Mohicans* (1826), Emily Brontë in *Wuthering Heights*, Bram Stoker in *Dracula*, Margaret Mitchell in *Gone with the Wind* – all are mesmerized by what Daileader

calls the 'siren-song of Othellophilia', doomed, like Coleridge's mariner, to retell a version of the same story of inter-racial or inter-cultural tragic love.

By and large Daileader looks on these compulsive appropriations with a jaundiced eye. Especially (so she believes) their inherent misogyny and racism. She notes, for instance, how three marquee novels of the twentieth century – Faulkner's *Light in August*, Ralph Ellison's *Invisible Man* and Richard Wright's *Native Son* – 'valorize black manhood at the expense of women, and above all women of colour'. She is particularly disheartened by the treatment of women in these largely male-authored texts (Aphra Behn's is no exception here): they flaunt the 'masculinist-racist obsession with the sexuality of white women', with their black sisters as 'marginalised subjects of the suppressed counter-narrative'. It is nearly always a question of white women and black men: 'in Anglo-American culture from the Renaissance onward, the most widely read, canonical narratives of inter-racial sex have involved black men and white women, and not black women and white men'. In the unsuppressed thrust of these transmutations' main narrative the white woman is nearly always the pathetic, deluded victim who has to die 'because she loves the monster. This is the pornographic secret of horror'. To make matters worse the women often collude with their tragic fate. Bram Stoker's Lucy, for example, 'must be rendered just sluttish enough to serve as the novel's central sacrifice'. She is just one in a line of 'hyper-sexualised . . . inter-racialist heroines'.

This, then, is Othellophilia at its ugly work. But one might argue that Daileader's own brand of Othellophilia mythicizes *Othello* itself, the *fons et origo* of Othellophilia. This is particularly the case in her disdainful understanding of the character of Desdemona whom she manages to turn into a collusive Lucy, a snaky white woman, a hyper-sexualized inter-racialist heroine. In Daileader's 'self-consciously eccentric' interpretation Desdemona is cast as a more pallid Tamora from *Titus Andronicus*, 'not so much the antithesis of the monstrous Tamora, but a more psychologically sophisticated version of her', who conspires in her own 'degradation and murder', who, when asked who has killed her, replies 'bafflingly' 'I myself' (5.2.133), who wants to go to Cyprus with Othello because 'The rites for why I love him are bereft me' (1.3.257), revealing thereby an insatiable female sexual appetite which 'severely problematizes' her as a virtuous woman (it is somehow not virtuous to want to make love to your new husband), who parades her 'infuriating naivety – not to say flat absurdity' when she asks Iago if she is truly the whore Othello calls her, 'Am I that name?' (4.2.121). The line in full reads: 'Am I that name, Iago?': the – perhaps unintended – omission of Iago's name here is an indication of Daileader's lack of interest in his agency generally in her eagerness to blame Desdemona. (More nuanced reservations about Desdemona's character can be found in some of the essays in *Approaches to Teaching Shakespeare's "Othello"*, to be reviewed later.) This uncharitable reading of Desdemona suggests to me that the siren song of Othellophilia has seduced Daileader into its opposite, a form of Othellophobia, that is not just self-consciously eccentric but in its own way as misogynist as the constructions of the male writers she castigates.

Another book of local readings – South African by and large – Martin Orkin's *Local Shakespeares: Proximations and Power*, focuses on some of Shakespeare's male characters, those in four of the last plays, *Pericles, Cymbeline, The Winter's Tale*, and *The Tempest*. But first Orkin finds it necessary to write a lengthy, largely theoretical preamble on the nature of different kinds of reception – or (as he puts it) how Shakespeare might be read in Timbuktu. Very differently, as we might imagine, from anywhere in Europe (or South Africa, for that matter). And the difference is magnified for his chosen vantage point in that the plays themselves proffer a problematic masculinity, an 'equivocal masculinity' (and not just in the romances), which Orkin oddly describes as a 'recurring muscle of thought'. The particular muscle that Orkin wants to flex is the refuting one: that is, he wants to see if he can find in Shakespeare's treatment of masculinity the possibility of a number of readings antagonistic to the patriarchal closure that the plays seem to endorse. Hence the question he asks about that 'iconic text within Western culture', *The Tempest*: 'In what ways might [it] be the bearer of a related simultaneity of (multiple) contradictory content?'

The wording of this question throws up another more important one that dogs the reader throughout the book. Are the book's insights worth the effort it takes to clamber over Orkin's castellated prose to get at them? He is, to begin with, the most periphrastic of writers. 'Even these senses entail potential for semantic problematisation', he solemnly tells us, and, having achieved that potential in the phrasing itself, continues to do so, as in the following representative mind-bender: 'but it also shows male cognitive dysfunction as approximating what patriarchy constructs for female intellection'. His book is full of indigestible mouthfuls: 'when collocated with this dimension', 'proposing the factor of proximity', 'processually problematized'. Sometimes the confusion is increased by his combining the long-winded with a needlessly disruptive syntactical displacement as in the following remarkable sentence about Leontes's language: 'His rhetoric, as it were, like mental pathogens emanating from an inner fear, interpolates in turn, via the air through which his speaking language travels, the objects of his gaze, elides their sexual fidelity, so to speak (re-)animates particularly Hermione in a contaminating way.'

None of this would matter all that much (though it would always matter some) if the rough ways led to clearings of intellectual insight. But although it's always interesting to read about the manner in which Shakespeare is appropriated, contested and assimilated by other cultures, the large claims Orkin makes for the significance of South African renderings of Shakespeare's plays for a better understanding of the plays themselves seems to me to be a nonstarter (at least it is from the examples he gives in this book). I was interested to learn, in other words, how it was important for an African reading of *Othello* to interpret the handkerchief in terms of African magic, '*muti*'. Or how, let us say, Yael Farber's *SeZaR* (a version of *Julius Caesar*) emphasizes an inquiring woman's gaze, so important in a country that has such a high incidence of rape. I was just as interested in the way an African reading can appropriate what's already in Shakespeare in the way Othello appropriates things Venetian 'to achieve agency'. But the simultaneity of contradictory intent in the plays, to use Orkin's words, doesn't have much light thrown on it from the African perspective. For me, the strange chapter on *The Winter's Tale* seen in the light of Pedro Almodóvar's *All About My Mother* (and vice versa) sums up the weakness of this approach. The play and the film are discrete entities in this chapter forced into an arbitrary, uneasy conjunction where not much of value is said about either, whether considered together or separately.

We stay in the same locality with Natasha Distiller's *South Africa, Shakespeare, and Post-Colonial Culture*. Like Martin Orkin, Distiller is out to 'theorise and illustrate the working of culture in a situation of socio-political inequality'. Like him too she makes much of Homi Bhabha's theory of hybridity in an attempt to move into an area outside of rigid cultural categorisation. Where her emphasis differs from Orkin's is on the ways in which South African responses to Shakespeare's works, taken (approximately) on their own terms, seize on their viability for a dissident application. How to achieve agency, in other words, with things Shakespearean. For Distiller, the Shakespearian thing operating most powerfully in the black South African

dissident appropriation of him is his humanism, his 'liberal humanist values', the very thing (as she apologetically confesses) viewed with such suspicion by the radical Shakespeare scholarship she so clearly admires. So the hybridity she isolates is a 'specifically inflected humanism', a 'new, or redefined humanism', one which 'enabled and shaped political and personal resistance to colonial abuses', or one in which human beings 'in the lived reality of their humanity, find ways to survive brutality and create beauty'. In a word, '[t]he liberal humanist subject in South Africa can also be the resisting, anti-apartheid cultural activist'. Humanism has at least the 'discursive potential to be used in the service of the political left'.

To the remaining liberal humanists among us her 'contentious' thesis doesn't have the jaw-dropping effect she thinks it has. Many of us have always found in Shakespeare's humanism much discursive potential for the political left (especially of the democratic variety). She regards her uncontentious analysis, however, as so iconoclastic as to necessitate, like Orkin, a heavily theoretical introduction extending over the first two chapters. Like his they are also heavily repetitive and exhibit peculiarities of punctuation and syntax and such oddities as the compulsive use of quotation marks not only around 'Shakespeare' but also around 'him', 'his' and 'he'. There are no running titles anywhere in the book but (again like Orkin) there are neologisms (e.g. the strange looking and sounding 'conscientations'). Most of all like Orkin, her book is at its liveliest in describing how Shakespeare is transformed into a black South African Shakespeare – by Solomon Plaatje, for example, the translator of Shakespeare into Setswana, and by the *Drum* writers in Sophiatown (a South African Elizabethan England in miniature). This African Shakespeare is written by and largely about men and is the Shakespeare of an educated elite, 'bourgeois, creative, and embattled'.

In its own way, Christopher Warley's *Sonnet Sequences and Social Distinction in Renaissance England* – a difficult, subtle book – is also concerned with the working of culture in a situation of socio-political inequality. Here, though, the local is on

our doorstep, and the victims of social disturbance are not South African Blacks but those icons
of Metropolitan literary culture, Sidney, Spenser,
Shakespeare and Milton. Or, rather, not so much
them as their elusive and untrustworthy projec-
tions, the speakers of their sonnet sequences,
especially in the manifestation of their 'internally
contradictory desires . . . their paradoxical urges to
distinguish themselves'.

Warley begins the book with two necessary
introductory chapters outlining its theoretical
premises: a heavy reliance on the work of Pierre
Bourdieu, Fredric Jameson's 'ideology of form', an
elastic redefinition of standard terms such as 'class'
(for Warley 'a unique process of social differentiation' or 'the question of the socially incommen-
surable') and, most importantly, 'social distinction'
which for him means, on the one hand, 'the continual situating of individuals, independently of
their will, within a social structure' and on the
other hand – a very different other hand – 'the
participation of individuals in the transformation
of "the categories of perception"'. Somewhere
behind these internally contradictory desires for
the same linguistic unit lie the prevarications in
the definitions of such maid-of-all-work terms as
ideology.

We have come a long way clearly from what
Dante Gabriel Rossetti had in mind when he
coined the term 'sonnet sequence' in 1880. For him
the emphasis was on the sensibility of the individual subject and his discussions of the poems were
oblivious to the sonnets' social and political dimensions, as has mostly been the case with discussions
of them ever since. And yet, as Warley argues,
these writers' sonnets demonstrate a wide range
of cultural events: English Calvinism (Anne Lok),
colonial activity in Ireland (Spenser), mercantilism
and a new language of economics (Shakespeare),
the book trade and absolutism (Milton) and the
reinvention of a masculine, aristocratic imaginary
(Sidney). A social revolution was in the offing and
these sonnet sequences unknowingly participate in
social struggle: they 'tend to articulate a series of
social and linguistic contradictions'. On the one
hand, they imagine an idealized social order: Anne

Lok's Calvinist God, Sidney's nobility, Spenser's
Irish landlord, Shakespeare's young man. On the
other, their language and what Warley calls their
conceptual apparatus undermine such idealization.
The sonnets are in fact supremely distinguished by
'undecidability and unrequitedness'. In them two
different languages of social distinction are at odds:
'an allegorical, lyric authority, and a representational, narrative authority'.

Shakespeare's 'gendered objects of desire' are
pursued, in a chapter called '"Till my bad Angel fire
my good one out": engendering economic expertise in Shakespeare's sonnets', in terms of the financial metaphor; hence the importance in Sonnet 144
of 'angel' as a monetary unit, and so the line 'Till
my bad angel fire my good one out' has reference
to 'bad money driving out good money'. Warley
has the grace to warn us that his pursuit of the
financial metaphor in this chapter (and other similar
'social' metaphors elsewhere in the book) doesn't
necessarily provide 'access to a more fundamental
substructure', but does provide somehow or other
a 'tacit metadiscourse able to tie together all these
possibilities into a coherent meaning'. Announcing
this large and slippery claim provokes and presumably justifies a lengthy discussion of financial matters in the sixteenth century, culminating in the
observation that the poem's angels conceal 'a complex of economic, social, and political forces entangled in the problems of inflation and the value of
currency'. Can this poem – or any of the others
by Shakespeare that Warley investigates – bear the
weight of this kind of analysis? In an extensive consideration of this line, the recent Oxford edition of
the sonnets says nothing about the workings of a
financial metaphor here though it does mention the
exceedingly remote possibility of a glancing allusion to the practice of smoking foxes from their
holes. The New Penguin Shakespeare does talk
about the line as 'touching' on the financial apoph-
thegm, 'bad money drives out good' (known as
Gresham's Law), but Warley himself tells us that this
formulation was not actually coined by Gresham at
all but was an invention of a British economist in
the nineteenth century. A similar evidential trajectory occurs in Warley's discussion of Shakespeare's

opening sonnet, 'From fairest creatures we desire increase', where for Warley's purposes increase has to mean financial interest or profit. The Oxford edition only goes so far as to note that 'A faint play on the sense "profit" (OED 4) reminds us that this is a poem to a potential patron'. Nothing can gainsay the subtlety and enthusiasm of Warley's pursuit of his thesis in this and the book's other chapters. In many respects it's a fascinating read. But all the time I was reading it I was troubled by my sense that in too many cases of Warley's interpretative choices bad angels were firing the good ones out.

In Lisa Hopkins's *Shakespeare on the Edge: Border-crossing in the Tragedies and the "Henriad"* the local takes the form of liminal, threshold spaces on the edges of geographical locations and countries of the mind. Indeed, the book is particularly insistent to present the geographical in Shakespeare as a stepping-stone to the spiritual; the border really in question turns out to be the eschatological one: the 'geographical proves to intersect with the eschatological in a more complex way than ever before' as she writes climactically of *King Lear*. Sometimes the stepping-stones are dangerously wobbly as, for example, in her attempt to make her discussion of islands, Ireland in particular, germane to her treatment of *Othello*: 'The play's characters, in short, are like islands, uneasily afloat, dangerously permeable, and subject to attack on all sides from fluids which threaten to engulf entirely their already imperilled individuality'. The impressionistic strain, in more than one sense, engulfing this judgement is a persistent feature of her book.

The local here is decked out in New Historicist anecdote and allusion, as the book traverses the borders between the plays' texts and their circumambient cultural geography, and is sometimes, as we have already seen, at the mercy of the runaway imagination we associate on occasion with New Historicist writing. We are told, for instance, that Henry IV's lines – 'Shall now, in mutual well-beseeming ranks, / March all one way' (*I Henry IV* 1.1.14–15) – undo his speech 'because the March is also the title of the English border with Wales'. When Hopkins makes the familiar argument that

Hal steers a course between Falstaff and Hotspur, choosing neither definitively but internalizing bits of both, she then adds (with an unconvincing 'of course' and an even more unconvincing 'closely') that '[t]his, of course, is closely analogous to the mechanisms by which the embryonic British Empire was attempting to establish itself'. Fanciful extrapolations such as these are to be found frequently in her book: the word 'cable' in *Othello* 'irresistibly suggests anchors' (the suggestion is only too resistible in fact); in *Hamlet* Gertrude's description of Ophelia as a 'mermaid' 'might even be reminiscent of the lewd caricatures' depicting Mary, Queen of Scots in the shape of a mermaid, and in the same play in the word 'escotted' we 'may well be meant to hear a pun on the Scots'. It comes as no surprise that her larger judgements should be equally tenuous and equally confidently expressed as in this one on *Macbeth*: 'Indeed I want to argue that *Macbeth* can be read as a sustained lament for the lack of a water border between England and Scotland, in the absence of which each leaches uncannily into the other.' What I find more uncanny is the unexpected concluding sentence of her Conclusion in which all the plays she has considered manage to leach into each other: 'Ultimately, I think that these plays register a sustained protest at a Scottish king's rule of England and at the foreclosing of religious possibilities which it is seen to represent.' What a lot of ground that 'ultimately' has to cover.

A fair amount of ground from a geographical and historical point of view is covered by *Shakespeare in the Worlds of Communism and Socialism*, but the book is narrowly local ideologically speaking. (Even more narrow than its title suggests as 'the world of socialism' only has a supernumerary existence in the title of Zoltán Márkus's piece, 'War, Lechery, and Goulash Communism: *Troilus and Cressida* in Socialist Hungary'.) It explores Shakespeare's 'complex, uneasy, and unpredictable alliance . . . with communist ideology' and it does so, as does Edward Burns's study of *Richard III*, largely in terms of the productions of the plays – I can't recall the poetry even being mentioned – 'since performance more sharply delineates issues of malleability and unpredictability than published accounts'. Apart from the book's last essay, an unexpected if fascinating history of Marxist criticism in North America by Sharon O'Dair, all the book's nineteen essays record examples of the fraught and coy dalliance of communist directors and actors with what Robert Weimann calls 'the greatest cultural text of modern Western civilisation' (5,000,000 Chinese students in middle school currently study Shakespeare). It is his essay which especially focuses on the way in which all bets are off when you bring together such a volatile group as professional actors and a director: a lengthy period of rehearsals often sabotages in a flurry of creative interplay – or in Weimann's terms an exposure to 'multivocal mediation and response' – the 'ideology of any preconceived notion of the play's given or desirable meaning'.

Multivocal mediation and response, as these essays tell us, run the gamut from enthusiastic, idealistic co-operation with the aims and ambitions of the communist state through a retreat into aestheticism ('areas of aesthetic refuge') to an outright (though often camouflaged) attack on communist censorship and restrictions, as is the case, for example, with the 1973 production of *Troilus and Cressida* in Hungary in which the play was 'a Trojan horse of sorts to smuggle critiques of present politics and society into a theatrical representation of Shakespeare's account of the Trojan War'. Many of the essays concern themselves with showing us how, in Irena Makaryk's words, 'censorship breeds sophisticated interpreters' whereby, as Martin Hilský writes in his essay on the Czech experience, 'Shakespeare's politically harmless verses acquired special resonance'. Sometimes it is the case that 'sweet indeed are the uses of adversity'. Indeed, Krystyna Skuszanka, the Polish female director, goes so far as to bemoan the fact that since liberation Poland, in her view, hasn't produced any valuable theatrical productions of Shakespeare.

We are all more or less familiar with the notion of a subversive-working Shakespeare production in an oppressive state. Less, perhaps, with the communist love-affair in the thirties with Shakespeare's comedies, despite Stalin's proclamation in 1935,

'Comrades, life has become better, life has become more joyful', and despite Marx's notion that 'humanity broke with its past in a merry mood'. These observations are quoted in Laurence Senelick's essay on *The Taming of the Shrew* where, rather sophisticatedly, a Soviet production of the play in the thirties stressed the complicity between Katherina and Petruccio as anticipating the socialist ideal. In 1936 *Much Ado About Nothing* was performed 600 times to packed houses in Moscow in a spirit of historical optimism with Shakespeare 'as the poet of the rising class'. Concomitantly, as Senelick tells us in his essay on the Okhlopkov *Hamlet*, in the thirties neither *Hamlet* nor *Macbeth* was in favour as they weren't examples, unlike *Othello*, of 'optimistic tragedy'! While *Hamlet* may not have been in favour in the thirties it was (and is) the play that dominated theatre production in all communist and non-communist states – 'Germany is Hamlet' – including Cuba and China. How it would have been interpreted differed from jurisdiction to jurisdiction and the book asks us – and shows us why it asks us – not to flatten distinctions on the Tolstoyan principle that 'All unhappy colonies are unhappy each in its own distinct way'.

Kate Emery Pogue's *Shakespeare's Friends* attempts to give flesh and blood to the local. Not an easy task as Shakespeare was 'resolutely private'. A typical case in point is Pogue's reconstruction of the putative friendship between Drayton and Shakespeare: 'The establishment of a friendship between William Shakespeare and Michael Drayton rests on a tangential fact, an unsubstantiated anecdote that refuses to die, and the logic of likelihood.' What we find throughout the book is the predominance of the logic of likelihood in the face of so few facts, tangential or otherwise, and not all that many immortal anecdotes either. And so Pogue has to rely upon problematic deductions from the workings of a frustrated-sounding commonsense: 'they would have taken that natural interest in each other of people who come from the same small corner of the world'. But all the 'would haves', 'must haves' and 'surelys' on which so many sentences are hinged are no replacement for facts or even anecdotes; they herald instead an over-indulgence in unsubstantiated and unsubstantiatable imaginary encounters such as the following amiable suggestion: 'Shakespeare lived within a short walk of the Hemingeses and the Condells and visiting their lively, busy homes, filled with babies, growing children, and apprentices, must have given Shakespeare a break from the loneliness of his rented lodgings.' 'Must have given' despite the overwhelming impression we get from Shakespeare, as Pogue herself insists, of an 'introverted personality, chary of his privacy'.

We should be grateful, however, to have Shakespeare's friends and possible friends convivially gathered together in one place, despite the note of cosy familiarity in the treatment of them which runs throughout the book (and despite the desperate inclusion of 'friends' such as Queen Elizabeth and King James). The book is sensibly divided into different clumps of friends: those in Stratford, those in the theatre and those in London. Pogue makes a nice distinction between Londoners and Stratfordians: Shakespeare's mature Stratford friends 'mirrored the traits he cultivated in himself; they were intelligent, practical, wealthy, successful, upper-middle-class gentry'; his London friends were 'conservative, family-oriented, actor-managers from his company'.

One of Shakespeare's dearest posthumous 'friends' is the subject of a book of essays edited by Katherine Romack and James Fitzmaurice. Margaret Cavendish, the Duchess of Newcastle (1623–1673), was born the year Shakespeare's First Folio was published and her extraordinarily prolific career as a writer (25 plays, fiction, essays, biography, autobiography) was deeply marked by Shakespeare's works, especially her plays. She took from Shakespeare ideas for characters, plots and dialogue, all reverentially reworked for her own purposes. What these purposes were is explored by this book of essays which, as its editors argue, 'represents the first sustained attempt to place an early modern woman writer in dialogue with a male contemporary'. And what a male contemporary.

From our perspective the most interesting essays are the ones that deal with Cavendish's appropriations of particular Shakespeare plays: Alexandra G. Bennett's 'Testifying in the Court of Public Opinion: Margaret Cavendish Reworks *The Winter's Tale*' and Katherine Romack's '"I wonder she should be so Infamous for a Whore?": Cleopatra Restored'. Romack's essay, strategically placed at the end of the book, touches on many of the themes and attitudes explored in the essays that come before it. Cavendish anticipates Dryden's re-rendering of *Antony and Cleopatra, All for Love* (1677), in transforming Cleopatra from 'an exotic representative of the danger of female deception and desire, to a character firmly anchored to the domestic virtues of love, honesty, and even chastity'. Where she differs from Dryden (and from every other seventeenth-century interpreter of Shakespeare's play) is to make Cleopatra's virtue gamesome, prickly and self-assertive. Cleopatra plays the whore in her play (as she does in Shakespeare's) making 'companionate marriage' a sexy business: unlike Dryden's Cleopatra Cavendish's 'sweeps in, breasts bared, to bring a playful sexuality into marriage and render it fun'.

Local Shakespeare couldn't get more local than in the 'trawling expeditions' of Penny McCarthy's 'plodding detective story' *Pseudonymous Shakespeare: Rioting Language in the Sydney Circle* which attempts no less than to overthrow the world of Shakespeare scholarship by catching in its net a number of minor pieces of writing never before associated with Shakespeare but now confidently ascribed to his authorship. The implications of such discoveries, the true harvest of the catch, are spelled out in an Introduction that runs full tilt against received opinion about Shakespeare's early days in a startlingly assured, not to say pugnacious, manner. Plodding they certainly aren't. McCarthy wants us to know in no uncertain terms just how revolutionary her revisionary readings are. These include: a reinterpretation of texts both by Shakespeare and by some of his contemporaries; the ante-dating of contemporary allusions to the 'historical Shakespeare'; earlier dates for most of Shakespeare's works; the identification of Shakespeare's 'lost' early occasional lyrics, elegies, sonnet sequences, accounts of progresses, a romance, dedicatory poems, a pamphlet, a prose translation, a 'pseudo-historical treatise'.

It's those troublesome 'lost years' again. Where was Shakespeare and what was he up to in the years between leaving Stratford-upon-Avon in the mid-1580s and his appearance in London in the early 1590s? Was he up north teaching? Was he travelling on the continent? Or was he, as McCarthy contends, happily ensconced in a minor serving capacity in the aristocratic, rebelliously Protestant household of the Earl of Leicester and 'spoiled by all because of his talents . . . bossing the other boys, startling everyone with his proficiency in languages . . . sniggering and splashing in the fountains'? And also writing of course. But writing under a series of pseudonyms, mainly pseudonymous initials, of which the most important is 'the cheeky' RL, conventionally thought up to now to have been a number of people (for example Robert Langham and Richard Lichfield) but really in fact William Shakespeare.

I don't think, to begin with, that McCarthy ever satisfactorily explains why Shakespeare had to go to such desperate lengths to avoid writing under his own name and in so many permutations. The examples she gives of the poetry of the combined RLs sound to my ear more like the 'Shakespeare' of the largely discredited poem 'Shall I die?' than, say, *Titus Andronicus* or *Venus and Adonis*. But the first question that springs to mind is why no one before Penny McCarthy ever twigged that RL and all the others were really WS in disguise. The answer lies in the extraordinary lengths that Shakespeare and his mentors took to protect Shakespeare's identity (for whatever reasons), and the corresponding lengths that McCarthy has had to go to to unearth RL's 'real' identity. The book is full of phrases that reveal the arduous nature of her struggle to breach such perversely encoded material: 'perilous sub-texts', 'extraordinary after-lights', 'false personas', 'involuntary little betrayals' and so on. It's no wonder then that the pursuit of the pun and word-play generally is the life-blood of this book. And here is a not entirely untypical example. In order for a Jacobean audience to realize that the eponymous hero of Chapman's *M. d'Olive* (1607)

is really M. Shakespeare they would have had to work out in the blink of an eye (or its aural equivalent) that his 'Frenchified name' concealed 'a line from "William" to "olive" via Greek "Elaiso/n" means "made of olive"; "of olives" – genitive plural – is "elaiôn". Elizabethan "w" was quite soft. So "[w]elaion could well have stood for "[W]illiam"'. We can see from this why RL was such a tough nut to crack.

A lot of work has gone into this book but its procedures and conclusions are unconvincing. I can't prove her findings wrong of course but the whole convoluted enterprise lacks plausibility not helped by such eccentric claims as the one that argues that *Macbeth* must have been composed by Shakespeare before 1592 because of its heavily 'Senecan' language. The 'young' Shakespeare had yet to find his 'own vernacular voice'.

WIDER HORIZONS

Robert N. Watson's *Back to Nature: The Green and the Real in the Late Renaissance* is a work of great distinction and it is impossible to do justice to its scope, density and eloquence in a short review. Its two chapters on Shakespeare's works, one on *As You Like It*, the other on *The Merchant of Venice*, occur in a book that spreads its net widely: a lengthy Introduction – two chapters – that wrestles with theoretical issues (with a section on Shakespeare specifically, 'Shakespearean Drama and Cartesian Doubt'), Marvell's Mower poems, Metaphysical and Cavalier poets, Dutch painting of the seventeenth century, Thomas Traherne. The chapter on *As You Like It* is linked with the one on Marvell in the second Part of the book entitled 'Paradoxes: Alienation from Nature in English Literature'; that on *The Merchant of Venice* to Thomas Traherne in the last Part, 'Solutions: the Consolations of Mediation'. The book's bold reach, as one may see from this short description, is policed and disciplined by an exacting and precise frame of reference.

Watson calls his chosen period – the sixteenth and seventeenth centuries – late Renaissance rather than early Modern because in its despairing search for philosophical and epistemological certainties in a world where doubt was king, there was a drive back to nature to try to find an unfissionable reality in the natural world. Back in time, that is, in the mistaken belief that there was a time back sometime when human beings lived in a state of oneness with nature, when there was some 'posited certainty'. With great élan and cleverness, Watson 'explores artistic responses to this nostalgia for unmediated contact with the world of nature' and his explorations take in not only the pot-pourri of the works quoted above but issues of theology (especially Protestant theology), epistemology, politics, ecology, gender and science.

Regretfully, I have to restrict myself to Watson's chapters on Shakespeare, but it should be emphasized that only a full reading of the book can do justice to what he has to say about Shakespeare. The chapter on *The Merchant of Venice* in particular gets wonderful resonance from following on from Watson's discussion of Dutch painting in the seventeenth century and leading into his discussion of the 'otherworldly worldliness' of Thomas Traherne. Everywhere you turn in this book there are phrases to relish and complexities to unpick; it's a little like reading Northrop Frye at his most persuasive; you're never quite sure, as with Frye, what the next sentence has in store for you, though you know from previous experience it will land on some fruitfully teasing proposition or some unexpectedly enlightening congruity. If at times you feel, as is occasionally the case with Frye, that the reach has exceeded the grasp, Watson would be the first to agree. Looking back on what he has written on *As You Like It*, for instance, he can see only 'a self-interested, appropriative simulation of the play, instead of the play itself' (rather in keeping with his general thesis about the vapourish nature of reality). He's worried that 'evidently no one else has seen the same play I claim to see, the same original intent, the same organic form'. Elsewhere he talks of 'awkward twists and wrong-footed landings', of 'barking up the wrong recursive tree', of being 'a reckless driver through their field' (art history), of making 'a silly comparison', and so on.

In *As You Like It*, the return to nature, as Watson sees it, is fundamentally a frustrating business for its characters (and for us): despite its good humour and happy ending the play is basically dubious 'about the prospects for any authentic involvement with the natural world'. What Watson sees that no one else has seen is the significance of the way in which the play is permeated with the idea of likeness – 'we can know things only as we liken them, never in or as themselves' – a play packed with similes and 'if' clauses that by their very profusion 'stand between us and any pure encounter with absolute reality'. They push us away from reality more than they draw us into it, as his opening analysis of the play's title intimates: 'In the four syllables of its title, *As You Like It* contains both the words used to signal simile, and places "like" as a barrier between "you" and "it".' It is not for nothing that *Hamlet* is the next play to be written: 'arguably the most epistemologically skeptical play of all'.

I must confess to being less convinced by Watson's discussion of *As You Like It* – though I don't think he's barking up the wrong recursive tree – than I am by his discussion of *The Merchant of Venice* where it seems pretty clear that he's barking up the right one. While Watson's account gives due weight to the play's well-known explorations of dubious moral conduct, despiritualized capitalism, racist contempt, casuistic argument and, although he's well aware that the play's invitation to a figurative reading makes it a labyrinth 'strewn with expired theories and mutilated conclusions of countless scholars', he nonetheless insists on the necessity to listen for and respond to the play's 'deep allegorical melody'. It's difficult perhaps to hear it through the surface noise of equivocation and counter-equivocation although that noise itself is in fact melody's descant. For *The Merchant of Venice* is a play that praises mediation, reconciles us to approximation, to intuition, to imperfect readings, to 'a diversified portfolio of uncertainties', to the 'transitional and transactional', to a world of 'likelihoods, representations, and imperfect approximations', to 'some amalgam of intuition and tradition'. It exemplifies '"negative capability" in overdrive'. It teaches its audiences how to 'decipher familiar moral lessons in the intricate language of the modern market-place'. If *As You*

Like It warns us that partial resemblances are untruths, *The Merchant of Venice* reminds us that these are all we have; we're stumbling ahead 'to a soft landing in the new Christian dispensation' with Launcelot and Jessica; if, with Portia, we are able 'to dance to her domestic music with enough lowercase grace . . . the uppercase Grace may take care of itself'. Although I think that what Watson says is true anyway about *The Merchant of Venice*, it would be difficult to take issue with what he says when he says it in writing as fine as this.

It's a bold critic, one might think, who can, so late in the day, write a book, as R. W. Maslen has done, entitled *Shakespeare and Comedy*. (Can *Shakespeare and Tragedy* be far behind?) In fact the 'and' here doesn't really justify the means as the book, with the exception of a chapter on *Measure for Measure*, restricts itself not only to Shakespeare's Elizabethan comedies – on the rather hapless premise that 'a book has to end somewhere' – but to one aspect only of their comedy, its aggressive, subversive, not to say demonic conjuration of a 'raucous and abrasive' laughter in the service of a democratic, levelling intelligence. If this view of Shakespeare's early comedies sounds perhaps more Rabelaisian than it should, it gets a kind of negative justification from Maslen's notion that comedy in Shakespeare's time was 'fundamentally indefinable', that the 'comic moment' had a 'precariously contingent status' and, more positively, that the history of comedy in the theatre 'was inseparable from that of class conflict' (these early comedies were a counter-check to tyranny), that Shakespeare's comedy – comedy generally – gives 'a voice to the otherwise voiceless'.

What's conspicuously missing here in this discussion of Shakespeare's early comedies is the countervailing notion that they continue to give a voice to those who have always had one. To justify that *and* in Maslen's title, in other words, consideration would have to have been given to aspects of Shakespeare's comedy other than just its anti-authoritarianism. Surely these early plays in particular also display a much more conformist, playfully irresponsible kind of comedy: one that indulges,

for instance, a Sidneyan aristocratic delight in trifles light as air or a pointless paronomastic playfulness. The rather old-fashioned character of this book is reflected in its confident promotion of how characters speak their words or how their characters are to be interpreted in speaking them; hence there are a number of intensely subjective, casually unverifiable judgements: 'the facile music' of the courtiers' speeches in *Love's Labour's Lost*, for instance, the 'conspicuous wisdom' of Antonio in *The Merchant of Venice*, the 'fragile heartiness' of Don Pedro in *Much Ado About Nothing*, 'the voyeuristic glee' of Rosalind in *As You Like It*, the idea that Bottom in *A Midsummer Night's Dream* is a 'fitting role model for all classes in the play', the 'spontaneous mismatch' of Isabella and Vincentio in *Measure for Measure*. Considered in the light of these examples there's a certain irony in Maslen's later judgement that 'any sign may be misread, and the tone of any witty comment may be mistaken'. Perhaps not surprisingly, given his take on comedy, Maslen's chapter on the comic underpinning of the tragedy *Romeo and Juliet* is one of the strongest in the book. As he says, the wit comes breaking through the tragic events as if the tragedy had been 'infected with comedy as if by a virus'. But he should have stuck to Shakespeare's Elizabethan comedies: his discussion of *Measure for Measure* is by and large a rather pedestrian re-telling of the plot.

Andrew Hadfield's *Shakespeare and Republicanism* has no trouble justifying its conjunctive title but steps back from boldly dispensing with the connective altogether, unlike Robin Headlam Wells's gauntlet-dropping *Shakespeare's Humanism* (to be reviewed later). There are two main reasons why Hadfield can't call his book *Shakespeare's Republicanism*: one is that republicanism in Shakespeare's time was so contradictory and difficult to pin down; the other that Shakespeare as a systematic thinker was just as contradictory and just as difficult to pin down. Nonetheless, so Hadfield claims, Shakespeare was much less conservative than we think – 'a highly politicised and radical thinker, interested in republicanism', in fact, working 'within a culture of political argument' for a theatre which had a tendency to wriggle free of ideological formations. And he wasn't the only one. Marlowe, Jonson, Spenser, Sidney and Chapman (to name but a few and not all of them dramatists) display a marked interest in republican government, though none as intensely as Shakespeare who 'narrates more of the republican story than any other dramatist working in Elizabethan and Jacobean England, as well as applying the lessons of a history of the republic to the English crown'. Thus Marlowe's work doesn't have Shakespeare's articulate (if evasive) political theory, but nonetheless it is 'relentlessly hostile not just to Kings, but to the conception of hereditary kingship, and political power preserved in the hands of the very few'.

Hadfield buttresses his discussion of Shakespeare in the second part of his book with a Part I that concentrates on the republican nature of the culture in the 1590s on the welcome principle that 'radical thinking would be better served by more historical analysis and less theory'. He shows us that republicanism as a topic was ubiquitous at this time, a constant ghostly presence, and so was criticism of it. People read and discussed the works of George Buchanan (1506–82), the Scottish thinker, who was a great admirer of the Venetian Republic (as were many other intellectuals), Tacitus, Sallust and Suetonius (who wrote histories of Rome), Lucan whose *Pharsalia* was 'a key text in the grammar school curriculum, and certainly a work against tyrants and arguably a republican classic', Cicero, especially his *De Officis* (*Of Duties*) and *De Amicitia* (important for an understanding of *Julius Caesar*), the Greek author Herodian (AD *c.* 165–250), Polybius and other writers advocating forms of republicanism. Hadfield notes that England was constantly implicitly and explicitly compared to the Roman republic especially with its institution of Parliament and that there was a close link between religious political thought and republican texts, so that 'republican examples and republican arguments could be used alongside similar religious arguments for the deposition of unjust and tyrannical princes'. On the other hand, Hadfield warns, we have to acknowledge republicanism's 'inchoate nature as well as its existence as a series of related, overlapping and sometimes contradictory points';

we have to remember that 'the history of republicanism was discontinuous, fractious and confused, not a smooth development towards a clearly perceived goal when a full form of the idea was finally produced'.

These caveats need to be borne in mind in any reading of Shakespeare. Not so much for the Roman plays themselves (obviously), nor for the first history tetralogy (less obviously), but for works such as *Venus and Adonis* and *Hamlet*. In the case of the tetralogy, Hadfield argues that it represents Shakespeare's *Pharsalia*; he's 'Lucanizing English history', and he chooses to begin his career as a writer of history plays with the minatory reign of Henry VI because it had 'a bearing on current political issues and . . . also represented one nightmarish vision of the future'. The malignant ghost haunting these plays, Hadfield acutely observes, is Julius Caesar, 'constantly reminding the audience that civil war is likely to produce a dictator'. Less persuasively, Hadfield draws on contemporary politics in his treatment of *Venus and Adonis* and *The Rape of Lucrece*: it's a stretch to see Lucrece's suicide 'as a displaced assassination of the king' and even more of one to read Venus as Elizabeth I on some occasions and not on others – not, that is, on occasions such as the following where Venus 'With blindfold fury . . . begins to forage; / Her face doth reek and smoke, her blood doth boil, / And careless lust stirs up a desperate courage'. As for *Hamlet*, 'this messiest of plays', it seems that 'uncovering a political archaeology is especially problematic', as Hadfield goes on to demonstrate with his contention that we're dealing here with a play that 'confronts its audience with the dilemma of how they would act when faced with an unjust and unpalatable succession'. I doubt that any audience, then or now, would take Hamlet's political dilemma so personally.

Nonetheless, Hadfield is right to argue that Shakespeare remained interested in republican issues throughout his writing career. He's also right to argue that with the death of Elizabeth interest in republican issues waned: in *Measure for Measure*, for instance, 'numerous plot motifs' show us that 'republicanism is no longer a viable, current political philosophy'. And the same can be said for the plot motifs of *Othello* and *Antony and Cleopatra*. So it is by no means clear, as Hadfield himself concludes, that Shakespeare was a completely convinced republican. But as with so many claims for Shakespeare's convictions there's enough there to write a book about it.

Early modern English puritans have been called many things and have had to assume many historical burdens. For that matter, many of the period's fictional characters who are self-evidently not puritans in any precise sense have been called puritans or quasi-puritans or puritans in all but name, with Shylock as a notably striking example (e.g. in Wells's *Shakespeare's Humanism*, p. 18). In Kristen Poole's *Radical Religion from Shakespeare to Milton: Figures of Nonconformity in Early Modern England*, the overlooked figure of puritan nonconformity she thrusts into the spotlight couldn't be less like Shylock: we're talking here counter-intuitively about the puritan as transgressive hedonist, the 'puritan bellygod', 'the drunken, gluttonous, and lascivious puritan'. The puritan bellygod who immediately springs to mind is, of course, Jonson's Zeal-of-the-Land Busy in *Bartholomew Fair* who is a self-advertising puritan, as his adopted name hilariously signifies. The Shakespearian transgressive hedonist who also immediately springs to mind is, of course, Falstaff, whose name does not, however, unmistakably suggest a puritan sensibility, though it does offer a number of possibilities for jocose deconstruction as does his maker's. (Poole notes this and compares it with names such as More Fruit, Faint Not and the like.)

It doesn't seem to me the case that Falstaff, either in name or in characterization, exposes a puritan sensibility, although it is true that his frequent recourse to a puritan vocabulary and his mugging of puritan attitudes are aspects of his sly and satiric humour. So I don't think it's convincing that Falstaff 'established a model for the grotesque, carnivalesque puritan which would predominate for decades to come', nor do I think it true that 'Falstaff – in all of his sack-swilling glory – both catalyzed and epitomized the early modern representation of the stage puritan'. Poole, herself, doesn't

give any examples of these early modern representations of the stage puritan, apart that is from Falstaff himself, but deflects the argument instead into the controversy surrounding the case of Martin Marprelate and Sir John Oldcastle, Lord Cobham, reputed leader of a Lollard insurrection in 1414, the model for Falstaff and the provider of his original name. At this point in the book it seems to me that Poole has wandered away from her subject, to return to it only in her later discussions of Jonson, the Family of Love, Thomas Edwards's *Grangraena*, Milton and Samuel Butler, all of which are embedded in a consideration of some 250 pamphlets, tracts and sermons. The book ends with a discussion of Samuel Butler's *Hudibras* which 'continues the tradition of the grotesque puritan dramatized by Falstaff' but unlike Falstaff is a bellygod 'expulsed by the carnival crowd' whereas both Falstaff and his carnival followers, as we know only too well, were expulsed by the turncoat Hal, busy in his Zeal-of-the-land role as Henry V. Who is the 'real' puritan here?

Unrealities of another kind are canvassed by many of the essays in *Shakespeare, Marlowe, Jonson: New Directions in Biography* edited by Takashi Kozuka and J. R. Mulryne. There's a rueful tone to a number of them in this collection especially the ones on Shakespeare who gets the lion's share (eight for him, four each for Marlowe and Jonson). J. R. Mulryne opens the proceedings and sets this tone with a directional introduction, 'Where We Are Now: New Directions and Biographical Methods', where where we are now turns out to be somewhere like where we were once before. As is so often the case in Shakespeare criticism, in other words, something new turns out to be a revised estimation of an original revisionism, a 'newer new historicism (or post-new historicism)', replacing in this case an exhausted 'theory-led approaches' approach. (This confident assertion may well raise some hackles.) Before it moves on to summarize and assess the essays that follow, the Introduction continues in admonitory vein to warn potential biographers to avoid the danger of becoming biographical fantasists or narcissists indulging a kind of 'biographical self-fashioning'.

And yet, at the same time, it also goes on to say, it's salutary to be aware of a necessary element of pleasurable self-discovery or self-disclosure in what you're doing. There's often a vibrant liberty taken by some critics in interpreting Shakespeare's life (witness Katherine Duncan-Jones's *Ungentle Shakespeare*).

Mulryne's carefully worded advocacy of a radicalized *via media* is given a much more trenchant expression in Blair Worden's essay, 'Shakespeare in Life and Art: Biography and *Richard II*', the first essay after the Introduction (not much of the media about this via). Shakespeare, Worden flatly tells us, 'is unknowable'; his writings 'prove of no help' for understanding him as a man (*pace* Honan, Greenblatt and a host of others). In fact, says Worden, warming to his task, 'the gap between artistic achievement and biographical explanation of it seems unbridgeable, sometimes embarrassingly so'. And yet 'so vast and bright a mirror as his plays will reflect any preconception, however dim or distant, that is placed before them'. (We might compare this wise observation with Alison Shell's remark in a later essay, 'in recent years, many people seem to have *wanted* Shakespeare to be a Catholic, and wanting is a dangerous thing to do'.) Before we despair of being able to know anything positive about Shakespeare, Worden admits that we do get biographical information of an important kind from an examination of local conditions and the pressures of theatrical authorship. He illustrates this with a masterly rebuttal of the widely indulged argument that it was Shakespeare's *Richard II* that was played before Essex's followers on the eve of his doomed attempt to rid Elizabeth's court of its inner circle of misguided flatterers (or so he believed).

Biographical scepticism widens urbanely in John Carey's essay 'Is the Author Dead? Or, the Mermaids and the Robot' to take in the judgements of literary criticism themselves. He wants us to know up front exactly where he stands: 'I should make it clear from the outset that I have never understood how statements about what is valid or invalid in literary criticism can support themselves.' Most critics now subscribe, he believes, to a productive indecisiveness, but we get so often 'the paradoxical situation that biographical criticism is ruled out because of its inevitable uncertainty, yet inevitable uncertainty is acknowledged to be the condition of all critical enquiry'. It isn't true, he then says, in a series of ringing negative judgements, that a poem is a 'single definable entity' (despite what Wimsatt and Beardsley say), and – above all – it isn't true that the author is or ever was dead. One might suspect that these opening essays (I almost called them opening salvoes) were deliberately arranged in order of wrist-slapping intensity to climax in Alan H. Nelson's brief, somewhat cranky piece 'Calling All (Shakespeare) Biographers! Or, a Plea for Documentary Discipline'. In keeping with this collection's emphasis on history, it is, above all, he tells us, important to make some kind of new discovery about Shakespeare to justify yet another biographical venture. (Many would take issue with this stringent requirement.)

After these initial flurries, things calm down a little. Richard Dutton's 'Shakespearian Origins' asks us not to be so London-centred in exploring Shakespeare's life. Peter Holland in his 'Shakespeare and the DNB' pursues the book's concerns in an interesting area: 'to find New Directions in Old Biographies, directions that remain crucial to the current practice of biography'. Alison Shell is measured and sensible in answering her question 'Why Didn't Shakespeare Write Religious Verse?' She notes Shakespeare's 'high level of silence and evasion where religion is concerned' (a gentle rebuke for the stridency of recent claims where Shakespeare's religion is concerned) and, in another nice phrase, characterizes the history of allusion-spotting as 'full of small unprovable optimisms'. Her essay juxtaposes Shakespeare and the Catholic poet, Robert Southwell, concluding that these 'two writers represent two different ways to live one's imaginative life – and, in the end, two utterly different modes of moral accountability'. John W. Velz traces Shakespeare's move from using the Bishops' to the Geneva bible in 'Shakespeare and the Geneva Bible: The Circumstances' but doesn't draw any firm biographical conclusions from this. However, some firm, not to say large, optimisms are drawn from Helen Cooper's essay 'Guy of Warwick, Upstart Crows and Mounting Sparrows' where a possible allusion to Shakespeare as Sparrow, 'a high mounting lofty minded sparrow', in the anonymous *The Tragical History, Admirable Atchievements and various events of Guy earl of Warwick* gives us, if true, information about his association with the theatre company used in the service of Anglican polemics, his relationship with his fellow actors and playwrights, possible evidence for the dating for *King John* and an alternative route of influence to Marlowe.

The sections dealing with Marlowe and Jonson are well worth reading, especially the essays by Charles Nicholl and Patrick Cheney on Marlowe, and the ones by Lloyd Davis and Julie Sanders on Jonson. I should, though, make special mention of Ian Donaldson's sprightly written piece, 'Looking Sideways: Jonson, Shakespeare and the Myths of Envy', in which the standard view of Jonson 'as the natural loser, the spiteful pedant, the man with bloodshot eyes, squinting balefully at his successful rival' is undoubtedly a later malicious fiction. And Donaldson answers in a strongly worded affirmative his musical question, 'Did the two men ever learn, like Crosby and Sinatra, to sing in harmony?'

Jason Lawrence's study *'Who the devil taught thee so much Italian?': Italian Language Learning and Literary Imitation in Early Modern England* culminates in a chapter on Shakespeare in which Lawrence's essential conclusion, fully prepared for by the introductory chapter on language learning in Elizabethan England and the following one on Samuel Daniel, is that in all likelihood Shakespeare learnt his Italian from manuals of instruction such as John Florio's *Florio his First Frutes* (1578) and his *Second Frutes* (1591), both parallel-text dialogue manuals for learning Italian. These manuals emphasized the importance of translation in the learning of the language especially from writers such as Petrarch and Boccaccio. This doesn't mean to say that Shakespeare did not know Florio personally or did not receive private instruction from him or some other language teacher. Nor does it mean that Shakespeare could necessarily speak the Italian language more or less fluently or if at all. But it does mean that he could read Italian probably with ease and

that in all likelihood read the Italian sources for his plays in both the original Italian and in various English translations.

Lawrence's book is yet another nail in the coffin of those small-French-and-less-Italian schools of thought about Shakespeare's understanding of modern European languages. It is carefully argued, straightforwardly expressed, responsibly researched. But for the life of me I can't understand why Lawrence chose (I almost said chooses) to write his book in the historical present. Is it because he believes that his rather dry account (clearly the product of a doctoral dissertation) will somehow become more immediate, more lively, if what happened in the past seems to be happening in the here and now? For me, this singular choice tended, in its awkward self-advertisement, only to make a plain account awkwardly plain.

Neither plain nor awkward, Maureen Quilligan's *Incest and Agency in Elizabeth's England* begins and ends with an unusual interpretation of *King Lear*'s Cordelia. But although Cordelia seems in structural terms to be the target of the book this is not really the case. As Quilligan puts it late in the last chapter: 'The need to understand another Shakespearian character in a slightly different way is far less pressing than the need to understand the unread women authors of the Renaissance, and if attempting to reperceive Cordelia, however alien it makes her, helps us towards this understanding, it's worth taking the risk.' These aren't exactly fighting words. Quilligan's apparent discomfort in making Cordelia alien to us, even though the interpretation is only 'slightly different', must stem (I assume) from her sense of our heavy investment in the notion that Cordelia's rejection of her father in the play's first scene is 'a radical defiance of patriarchal authority', that in this first scene she displays female agency at its most startling and uncomfortable (especially for her father and perhaps also for us). Not so, argues Quilligan. On the contrary, her silence in response to her father's childish and 'incestuous' attempt to establish her as the all-loving daughter is in fact in obedience to a greater cultural and patriarchal authority: to be 'chaste, obedient, and most of all *silent*'. She is in essence teaching Lear (did he but know it) his patriarchal duty. We misread her (and Desdemona in similar circumstances) if we fail to see that she is here announcing the 'most conservative obedience to the traffic in women'.

The unread women Quilligan most wants us to become acquainted with and understand are the ones who come between these discussions of Cordelia: Elizabeth I, Margaret of Navarre, Penelope Devereux Rich, Mary Sidney Herbert, Countess of Pembroke, Mary Wroth and the not exactly unread Britomart (from Spenser's *Faerie Queene*). It is around these women that the anthropological argument swirls. It is they who by not behaving like Cordelia break the social bonds, assume a real or symbolic incestuous authority, and assert their agency in the act of writing. It's the argument, however, about Cordelia that interests us as Shakespearians (though the chapters on Elizabeth I and Mary Wroth in particular are well worth reading). In Cordelia's case it seems to me that Quilligan is unnecessarily diffident. Most readers and playgoers feel that Cordelia's function at the beginning of the play is to remind Lear of larger social/feudal/natural obligations. She's wincingly right in what she says and Quilligan's anthropological take on her position is well within the parameters of this larger interpretative structure. Where Quilligan is more controversial is to argue that the Cordelia who lands an army on Britain's shores in the last scenes of the play is different from the Cordelia of the first scene: she now subscribes to Lear's incestuous dream of intimacy, she exhibits a transgressive female autonomy and her death would have been regarded by Shakespeare's audiences as an appropriate (if regrettable) punishment. Maybe so, but I suspect that their response might well have been closer to ours (and Dr Johnson's) – more visceral than judgmental.

Robin Headlam Wells's *Shakespeare's Humanism* is both visceral and judgmental. It takes up arms against what Wells clearly perceives as a sea of postmodernism to claim that Shakespeare is much less our contemporary than postmodernism thinks he is. And Wells perhaps speaks from bitter experience when he argues that '[a]cademics find that it's not easy to get papers hostile to postmodern orthodoxy published in *PMLA* or the top Shakespeare journals'. Postmodern orthodoxy, Wells claims, denies the proposition that Shakespeare was a humanist; to the contrary, since the 1980s it has argued that Shakespeare and his contemporaries were, like the postmodernists themselves, anti-essentialist, who constructed their characters in a postmodern spirit as artifacts of cultural contingency. In this respect, so Wells believes, the postmodernists are yet another example of a cult of enthusiastic devotees of a particular intellectual position who claim Shakespeare as one of their own. The history of Shakespeare criticism is littered with such (mis-)appropriations.

Yet, as Wells also cheerfully maintains, there's nothing particularly wrong with reading any Shakespeare text creatively against the grain; you can bend it to your own *weltanschauung* if you wish but you should not confuse your exercise in deconstruction 'with an attempt at authentic reconstruction of a past intellectual world' – you should not, that is, confuse a so-called presentist approach and an historicist one. Why not instead, Wells asks, admit that Shakespeare's plays are shot through with humanist themes and ideas and then deconstruct them (if that is what interests you) 'rather than claim that he was a post-modernist *avant la lettre*'. (I suspect that many postmodernists admit and do exactly that.) Postmodern readers may not be interested in these humanist ideas as such – which is fine – but for others, for historians, 'the appeal of the past is its otherness: they do things differently there'.

And so the book takes a number of Shakespeare's plays and attempts to defend them against postmodern readings by seeing how differently they do do things there. (And it is clear from Wells's examples that the differences matter and are different in the ways he says they are.) In the process, Wells floods his book with secondary references, historical mainly, but also readings from recent works in 'archaeoanthropology, evolutionary psychology and neurobiology that [have] transformed modern thinking on social behaviour, the mind, and the mystery of human creativity'. So Wells creatively combines the thinking of Shakespeare's day with that of the most recent meditations from the neo-Darwinists and the like, a challenging body of evidence, as the book's last two sentences convincingly proclaim, 'powerful enough and sufficiently well established to give us the confidence to challenge the orthodoxies that are seldom questioned in modern primers on Theory, and to re-endorse the human universals without which criticism cannot exist, and history becomes impossible. It may even help us to recognize Shakespeare's humanism for what it is.'

A clutch of books from the Accents on Shakespeare series might well stand as articulate (sometimes bewilderingly articulate) witnesses for the justice by and large of Headlam Wells's observation that there's nothing too much wrong with reading Shakespeare creatively against the grain. These three books offer a range of the Accents' formal structures: *Spiritual Shakespeares* (with its revealing plural) is a collection of essays from a diverse group of critics intent on exploring the range of Shakespeare's spirituality; Gabriel Egan's *Green Shakespeare: from Ecopolitics to Ecocriticism* is a straightforward monograph, an experiment in 'ecocriticism' with a number of Shakespeare's works as the specimens to be examined; Linda Charnes's *Hamlet's Heirs: Shakespeare and the Politics of a New Millennium* is a series of 'discrete' essays by her, 'independent meditations' as she calls them, on the after-life of *Hamlet* and *The Henriad* in the 21st century.

It might be useful to step back a bit and try to see the three books as a group, how they differ from unaccented books on Shakespeare, how they resemble (and also differ from) each other. Most noticeably, all of them come at you bristling with intention, offering in each case 'a Shakespeare inflected in terms of a specific urgency'. We need to be reading Shakespeare, that is, as though our lives depended on it, no more so than in *Green Shakespeare* whose Shakespeare, all unbeknownst to him of course, mapped out for future generations ways of making connections with the natural world (and the cosmological) that, if properly heeded, would help us in our own efforts to come to terms with and do something about a world on the brink of an ecological disaster. Or, in our spiritually benighted age, a pursuit of Shakespeare's spirituality, as *Spiritual Shakespeares* urges us, 'might reinvigorate and strengthen politically progressive materialist criticism'. Spirituality of some kind, and why should it not be the Shakespearian, 'may be a necessary supplement for radical materialism', or even 'a revolutionary alternative'. Or we may be able to grasp the 'truly radical democratic potential' in *Hamlet* and *The Henriad*, as Linda Charnes would have us do, from her readings of Shakespeare in *Hamlet's Heirs*. And by so doing we might, among other desirable outcomes, be better placed to understand and deal with the undemocratic ways of administrations like George Bush's.

The three books operate at a high level of cerebration. It's not for nothing perhaps that the (unacknowledged) portrait of Shakespeare on their covers – on all the Accents' covers – is a colour-tinted photograph of the 1740 life-size statue in white marble of Shakespeare to be found in Poets' Corner in Westminster Abbey. It's a representation of Shakespeare as thinker, pensively leaning on a pile of untitled books and pointing with his left hand to a scroll at the base of the statue on which there is a quotation from *The Tempest*. The scroll isn't in the photograph which cuts Shakespeare off at hip-level. (A pity really for *Spiritual Shakespeares*, as Shakespeare's pointing forefinger has picked out the word 'temples' from Prospero's quotation.) All three books then celebrate Shakespeare as a 'living thinker' (*Spiritual Shakespeares*) with the emphasis very much on the 'living'. In fact, although techniques for dealing with his works may vary, all the Accents books think of him as writing proleptically for and somehow about us. In keeping with his status of advanced thinker, the Accents books talk about him in the company of other advanced thinkers. And these aren't, by and large, the usual run of literary critics but philosophers, theologians, cultural critics and sociologists. In the Introduction to *Spiritual Shakespeares*, for instance, written by its editor, Ewan Fernie, *the* acknowledged thinker of the book, apart from Shakespeare, is Jacques Derrida (sharpened politically by Alain Badiou and Slavoj Žižek): most chapters are 'cued by or resonate with' him. In the case of *Hamlet's Heirs* its vocabulary is heavily Lacanian and Žižekian, and in *Green Shakespeare* it would be useful to have studied the works, say, of Henri Lefebvre, Herbert Spencer and Charles Darwin before taking up the book. *Hamlet's Heirs* and especially *Spiritual Shakespeares* sprinkle their chapters with technical German terms from philosophy and sociology (*gemütlichkeit*, *Verleugnen*, *nachträglich*, *Gelassenheit* etc.), while *Green Shakespeare* talks about such things as chlorofluorocarbons, positive feedback reactions and negative feedback loops. So these books are quite the workout, intellectually speaking.

As far as Headlam Wells is concerned, as we've seen, there's nothing pernicious in reading Shakespeare against the grain unless you distort or deny or colonise his intellectual position. Wells doesn't say anything, as far as I remember, about the distortions or denials or colonisations of Shakespeare's texts themselves. How do Shakespeare's texts fare then in being bent to the Accent critics' wills and agendas; do they emerge unscathed or, if they are scathed, does it matter? The fashionable position to take these days is to deny the relevance (or even existence) of the capacity to do harm to such a free-flowing text as Shakespeare's texts where they can mean only what we think or make them mean. That is, they have no intrinsic meaning in themselves; they are there for us to construct our meanings from them. (I'm reminded of Roger Beale's cartoon in the *Financial Times* depicting a crusty old don telling an undergraduate that 'Shakespeare is important, of course, but its true value lies in what I have to say about it'.) All the Accents books make liberal use of Shakespeare's texts, of course, quoting from them and referring to them constantly. They certainly are living presences in all the books under review.

Living but sometimes maimed. I think it fair to say that all three Accents books on occasion treat their chief witness for the prosecution somewhat cavalierly. It's the usual sort of thing. In Lowell Gallagher's 'Waiting for Gobbo' in *Spiritual Shakespeares*, for instance, a heady pursuit of the spiritual ramifications of gift-giving (mainly in the context of 'philosophical debates' between Jacques Derrida, Jean-Luc Marion, Emmanuel Levinas and Alain Badiou) pounces on Old Gobbo's gift of a dish of doves for his son's employer, Shylock. It's important for the essay as a whole that this gift be seen as having 'subliminal provocations' under Marcel Mauss's notion of the unquantifiable surplus of the gift. (We might note, in passing, that the Gobbos 'belong to the periphery of the play's social world', performing in the 'suburbs of the main action', and that the gift-giving itself is in the periphery of those suburbs.) The gift's subliminal provocations do not include an explicit reason, or any reason apparently, for having been given; the essay's argument demands that the offering of the gift is 'without explanation'. Bearing in mind the peripheral nature of this incident, its very fleetingness in the scene's economy, it's surely of importance to take into account the evidence we may have, however indirect, that some kind of explanation is in the air. What evidence there is suggests that Old Gobbo's gift to Shylock does not in fact acknowledge the 'face' of Shylock (in Emmanuel Levinas's terminology), is not an impossible gift (in Derrida's and Marion's sense of the term). When Old Gobbo says 'I have brought him [Shylock] a present' it comes between two questions, 'How dost thou and thy master agree?' and 'How 'gree you now?' These questions are ignored by Gallagher. But there is presumably a connection to be made between this reiterated concern for the relationship between employer and employee and the bringing of the gift. (This is borne out by the way in which Old Gobbo seamlessly switches to Bassanio as the gift's recipient when he learns that Launcelot has a new master who needs to be propitiated.) So it's not true to say that there is no explanation for Old Gobbo's gift even though the explanation is not spelled out (as of course it couldn't be in the circumstances). What Old Gobbo wants to do with his gift for Shylock is to sweeten his son's standing with his employer. It's very much a gift, that is, with an ulterior motive.

A similar disinclination to take Shakespeare into account occurs in Ewan Fernie's 'Introduction: Shakespeare, spirituality and contemporary criticism' with the claim he makes with regard to Talbot in *Henry VI Part 1*. According to Fernie (who, by the way, misattributes his opening quotation from *Richard III*: it's Prince Edward who is 'a shadow like an angel', not Clarence's father-in-law), when Talbot is apparently trapped by the Countess of Auvergne in her castle his scornful reaction, 'my substance is not here', is evidence of 'a colossally elevated spiritual subjectivity'. It isn't. A few lines later (unmentioned by Fernie), a triumphant Talbot winds his horn and produces onstage the British army (or its representatives) which turns out to be 'his substance, sinews, arms, and strength' (2.3.63). A chastened Countess begs his pardon for having mistaken 'The outward composition of his body' (2.3.75). Now it may just be possible to squeeze out a spiritual dimension from the 'substance' under question, but to talk of its being an indication of 'a colossally elevated spiritual subjectivity' seems to me to be a colossal exaggeration (at best). Sometimes the urge to make one's point, to push home the argument, involves a simple misreading, or perhaps a wishful-thinking reading. In her essay 'The Hamlet Formerly Known as Prince', for example, Linda Charnes is so determined to get us to see Hamlet's father's 'manifest narcissism' that she talks of his 'most emulate pride' in wagering with the king of Norway. But the reference is in fact to Fortinbras of Norway not Hamlet of Denmark.

Another familiar way of textual misrepresentation is to leave Shakespeare far behind by indulging in a kind of wanton interpretative freedom. Although all three books enjoy themselves along these lines, the most unrestrained in this regard is Gabriel Egan's *Green Shakespeare*. In his essay on *Henry V*, for instance, he draws our attention to Shakespeare's use of the word 'jutty' to mean 'jut over' as in 'as doth a gallèd rock / O'erhang and jutty his confounded base' (3.1.12–13). Shakespeare compares this natural phenomenon to the ferocious physiognomy of the British soldier whose brow he imagines to be the gallèd rock. Not content with this imaginative leap, Egan provides another (or series of others) by noticing that the word 'jutty' (as a noun) is used in the contract for the Fortune

theatre to describe overhanging spectator galleries; so perhaps, he suggests, 'the partially completed Globe inspired the images of overhanging sea-cliffs and of helmeted brows'. A more egregious example of a runaway imagination, however, occurs in his cadenza on Gonzalo's line, 'long heath, broom furze, anything' (1.1.62–3), a line that the Oxford editor glumly describes as having 'suffered much interpretation'. Egan seizes upon the folio reading of 'firrs' for 'furze' and asks us to hear 'the word meaning shaped boards "call'd Furrs" nailed to warped floor timbers to make them level' and hence to the playhouse fabric called furs: Gonzalo by this concatenation 'is standing on brown furs, but special ones that have the quality of evoking a ship at sea during a storm'.

These departures from Shakespeare's texts attest, on the other hand, to the ambition and sheer *chutzpah* of the Accent writers and it would be churlish not to acknowledge the challenge and strength of their stimulating forays into what is, for most literary critics, uncharted territory. Churlish too not to respond to the wit of Linda Charnes, the monitory originality of Egan's Tillyardian connections between our natural world and Shakespeare's, and the 'fabrication of perverse affinities' celebrated by the essayists of *Spiritual Shakespeares*.

SHAKESPEARE FROM THE TRENCHES

Teaching Shakespeare's 'Othello' is the most recent dispatch from the pedagogical front. It is the latest volume in the series *Approaches to Teaching World Literature* and joins its fellow Shakespeare representatives on the world teaching stage, *Hamlet, King Lear, Romeo and Juliet* and *The Tempest*. Each of these volumes gives practising university teachers a brief opportunity – most of the essays are under ten pages – to describe the teaching strategies they use to increase their students' understanding and appreciation of Shakespeare's plays. There are a couple of ironies here. First, it's arguable that these Shakespeare plays (especially *Othello*) are the ones least in need of kick-start mechanisms or relevance face-lifts. Second, and relatedly, *World Literature* really means literature that most frequently gets taught in universities throughout the world; so the academic wallflowers that really need help with their teaching (when, that is, they do get taught) – *Timon, Cymbeline, Love's Labour's Lost, Measure for Measure*, etc. – never get the expert dancing partners they deserve (at least not so far in this series).

That said, there is much to commend in this volume on *Othello*. The heart of it is *Approaches*, the longer second part of the book consisting of twenty-one essays by different teachers subdivided somewhat arbitrarily into groups such as *Genealogies of Gender and Sexuality* (3 essays), *Approaches to Performance* (4 essays) and *Comparative Contexts* (4 essays). Really, all of them fall under the rubric of the fourth subdivision *Classroom Strategies* (4 essays) and most of them stray at times into the territories of the others. The longest essay in the collection, Michael Neill's '*Othello* and Race', doesn't once mention the classroom but its investigation of the simple difficulty of knowing/deciding whether the play is racist has obvious pedagogic value. 'Is the play racist?' is a very different question from 'was the play racist?' and Neill's formulation exposes one of the animating concerns of this collection: how best to bring Shakespeare's play into the life and times of today's students (again, not too much of a problem with *Othello* I would have thought). Hence Francesca T. Royster's teaching method in 'Rememorializing Othello: Teaching *Othello* and the Cultural Memory of Racism' consists of looking at the play through the lens of today's racist attitudes, while Emily C. Bartels' 'Improvisation and *Othello*: The Play of Race and Gender' adds gender to race in a fascinating description of how she uses role-playing in the classroom to read the play 'against the grain of stereotypes' to bring out the characters' 'loaded and malleable postures'. Cynthia Lewis's '"'Tis But a Man Gone": Teaching *Othello* as an (Anti)Revenge Play' finds relevance for today's students in examining the play in terms of 'a sophisticated argument against capital punishment in our society'. And Kathy M. Howlett's essay 'Interpreting the Tragic Loading of the Bed in Cinematic Adaptations of *Othello*' links the play

with O. J. Simpson's trial while talking about it in terms of spousal abuse.

On the other hand, it's just as pedagogically useful, so other essays argue, to explore *Othello* as an historical curiosity. And so Nicholas F. Radel in '"Your Own for Ever": Revealing Masculine Desire in *Othello*' teaches the play as 'an excellent way to introduce students to historically accurate understandings of same-sex desire and its place in the early modern period'. A particularly fruitful essay along these historical lines is Jean E. Howard's '*Othello* as an Adventure Play' which compares the play to 'one of the adventure dramas in which an Englishman goes to North Africa'. The contrast reveals a great deal about what is unique in Shakespeare's recasting of the adventure paradigm; the major difference of course is that the protagonist is not a white European but an African Moor: 'Shakespeare's genius in this play is to imagine what it might be like to make a black man the hero of a tragic tale of cross-cultural encounter, to imagine, so to speak, what the process English men were undergoing might look like from the other side.' Or, more microscopically, Geraldo U. de Sousa's fascinating essay, 'Unhoused in *Othello*', zeroes in on this word's 'rare and curious usage' throwing a strange and lurid light on the play's presentations of a fractured domesticity. The historical approach commandeers the textual in Michael Warren's 'Teaching the Texts of *Othello*' which looks at the quarto and folio texts in order to introduce students to the 'intellectual problems concerning the derivation and presentation of the texts of plays in modern editions'. And Douglas Bruster's essay, 'Teaching *Othello* as Tragedy and Comedy', rightly observes that the play's generic confusion is as useful as the textual from a teaching point of view.

In many of the essays much is made of teaching Shakespeare through the various available media, now indispensable in the classroom. Martha Tuck Rozett's essay 'Teaching Teachers: *Othello* in a Graduate Seminar' is performance oriented as are Samuel Crowl's '"Ocular Proof": Teaching *Othello* in Performance' and Miranda Johnson-Haddad's 'Teaching *Othello* Through Performance Choices' which deploys films that for the leading role star a Caucasian actor in blackface, an African actor and an African-American actor. This is an essay that makes an interesting companion-piece to Virgina Mason Vaughan's 'Teaching Richard Burbage's Othello' through which students will recognize that Shakespeare's Othello 'was not the essential black hero but the product of a white imagination represented by English actors to a white audience'. Other essays come at *Othello* illuminatingly via other writers and other works: Elizabeth Cary, Aphra Behn, Verdi, Vogel, Cinthio, Isak Dinesen.

I was particularly struck not only by these teachers' enthusiasm for the art and techniques of teaching but by their high regard for their students' capacities to profit from them. Joyce Green MacDonald's judgement of her students in 'Finding *Othello's* African Roots through Djanet Sears's *Harlem Duet*' conveys her own generous-minded zeal as a teacher as well as reflecting the open-mindedness shown by the essayists as a group: 'My inexperienced students, many of whom register for the course because they believe that studying Shakespeare will add intellectual value to their college education, frequently prove to be among my most imaginative and responsive.'

Inexperienced students will no doubt benefit from *William Shakespeare's "Hamlet": A Sourcebook* edited by Sean McEvoy and its companion volume on *Macbeth* edited by Alexander Leggatt, though a better title for these books would be A Resource-book rather than A Sourcebook. A very elastic definition of sources is involved here. Each book begins with a contextual overview to give them some historical ballast. This is followed by a chronology and then a section of extracts from contemporary documents such as 'A Homily Against Disobedience and Wilful Rebellion' in the *Hamlet* volume and King James's *Basilicon Doron* in the *Macbeth*. There is a section on performance that stretches back to the seventeenth and eighteenth centuries and includes twentieth-century cinema.

Where the books differ somewhat is in their editors' choice of material for the books' longest section, Interpretations. McEvoy's emphasis falls heavily on modern criticism, especially recent modern criticism (postmodern in the main): of the fourteen extracts that make up the interpretations from Modern Criticism four come from the years between 1900 and 1935; ten from those between 1986 and 2002; there is nothing, that is, from the fifty years between John Dover Wilson's *What Happens in Hamlet* written in 1935 and Terence Hawkes's astutely entertaining essay 'Telmah' in *That Shakespeherian Rag: Essays on a Critical Process* published in 1986. Leggatt's choice is more evenly balanced with essays from nearly every decade of the twentieth century even though there are four fewer than in McEvoy's Modern Criticism section.

McEvoy clearly favours a criticism that he believes to be non-authoritarian, improvisatory, text-centred and playful, and yet it could be argued that by favouring any kind of criticism, or period of criticism, all books of this kind are unavoidably authoritarian, tendentious in what they choose to leave out and keep in, and of course how they praise or fail to praise their chosen extracts. McEvoy to do him justice is aware of this: in the final useful and entertaining section of the book, Key Passages, he notes that 'any selection of passages for discussion at the expense of others will seem idiosyncratic, as some aspect of the play will be stressed at the neglect of others'. In both books I liked the introductions to these passages and also their annotations which often describe how particular productions in the theatre or the cinema rendered them.

McEvoy's *Shakespeare: The Basics*, first published in 2000, now revised, updated and reissued, also acknowledges that it 'outlines only one way of studying Shakespeare'. Nonetheless, such a restricted viewpoint is all that is needed apparently to cover the basics for any study of Shakespeare, though one could imagine an entirely different set of 'basics' forming the basis for another introductory study (as is indeed the case with David Bevington's *How to Read a Shakespeare Play*). One man's basics may be another's persiflage. McEvoy's, as we might have guessed from his take on *Hamlet*, involves the wholesale rejection of a criticism based 'predominantly on character, theme and plot' no matter how basic character, theme and plot may be thought to be to any understanding of Shakespeare's plays, or any other play for that matter. McEvoy is determined to restrict our access to the plays, however, to the social and political (as though they magically didn't involve character, theme and plot). His obsession with the plays' political contexts (as he conceives them) leads him to make a number of restrictive judgements usually at the expense of character and theme. Henry V, for example, is not 'fundamentally different from a thief like Pistol' or in *A Midsummer Night's Dream* 'the fiction of the magic potion is a metaphorical expression of the power of society to make people love in a way approved by the state' (he fails to mention Puck's ludicrous mistake in his handling of the potion – so much for the power of the state). Because McEvoy is so determined in his treatment of the tragedies to see the human suffering in them as 'the result of society's contradictory forces' he can argue reductively that Othello, black and foreign, 'cannot be accepted in the hierarchy of the Venetian state', a state represented 'in its most pure form' by Iago (we might imagine what the Duke and the Senators would have thought of that opinion) or that *King Lear* 'is based firmly on an idea of female subordination'. Despite his claim in the book's final pages that he welcomes dissent from his student readers he doesn't seem to leave much room for it.

David Bevington's *How to Read a Shakespeare Play* offers an entirely different set of basics for the study of Shakespeare's plays based firmly on the ascendancy of character, theme and plot. We might well argue that Bevington's notion of what is basic to an understanding of a Shakespeare play is, well, more basic than McEvoy's. We can't, after all, get much more basic in our questions than to wonder why the characters say what they say to each other, where the scenes are taking place, what the characters are wearing, how what they are wearing tells us whether they are soldiers, heralds, mariners, different nationalities, Moors, innkeepers, courtesans, witches, peasants etc. These are the concerns of the lengthy introduction. In it as well Bevington asks us to give Shakespeare a fair shake: abandon preconceptions, he urges his readers, read him

'aggressively, interactively, questioningly'. He tells us that we're dealing with a writer with a mammoth vocabulary and a wide range of reference (though, interestingly, he notes that Shakespeare doesn't mention Moses, David, Isaac or John the Baptist) and that each of his plays is a series of overlapping plays.

Bevington then takes us through six of Shakespeare's plays – *A Midsummer Night's Dream, Romeo and Juliet, Henry IV Part 1, Hamlet, King Lear, The Tempest* – pleasantly summarizing the plot of each one and every now and then making the odd astute observation: in *A Midsummer Night's Dream* (which he oddly contracts to *A Midsummer* rather than *Dream*), for instance, he observes that Oberon makes himself a cuckold to punish his queen, that it is Falstaff in *Henry IV Part 1* who introduces the subject of banishment and that in the same play Hotspur dies as a consequence of having been lied to by his uncle, that *Hamlet's* Denmark is an elective monarchy in the sense that the choice of the monarch is made by a small and elite group of well-born 'electors', and so on. Bevington mentions virtually no other critic nor does he refer to anything or anyone outside the plays themselves. He doesn't practise practical criticism nor does he tell us anything about the plays' performances. He hardly seems to be following his own advice to read Shakespeare aggressively, interactively and questioningly. Who is this book intended for then? It's astonishing (perhaps reassuring) that a book of 'basics' as basic as those to be found in this one can still find a niche in the super-competitive market of Shakespeare criticism.

If there's one work by Shakespeare that most readers would agree needs a helping hand by critics it's *A Lover's Complaint*. The editors of this book on the poem, Shirley Sharon-Zisser and Stephen Whitworth, are very conscious that they are breaking new ground as is indicated by the justifiable length of their introduction 'Generating Dialogue on Shakespeare's *A Lover's Complaint*'. After all, we're dealing with 'a lacuna in Shakespeare criticism and in the study of Renaissance narrative poetry', and hence the poem needs to be situated 'in its historical, cultural, generic, rhetorical, and psychological contexts'. This the book of essays proceeds to do, although it doesn't have very much to say about the poem's formal structure unfortunately – with the extraordinary exception of the last essay in the book by Sharon-Zisser – despite the Introduction's welcome conviction that 'we cannot refuse the critical engagement this poem demands, whoever its author'. Nor do they grapple with the question of the poem's authorship, a topic on which Brian Vickers is about to publish a book, *Shakespeare, 'A Lover's Complaint', and John Davies of Hereford* (Cambridge, 2007), reassigning it to John Davies of Hereford. Instead, the editors stress the need to talk about the poem in its literary context: other narrative complaint poems, Shakespeare's plays (especially the late ones), Shakespeare's sonnets.

And the social context of course. But contexts, literary or social, are sometimes just as slippery as the works that come from them. How convincing, for instance, is Paul Stegner's argument in 'A Reconciled Maid: *A Lover's Complaint* and Confessional Practices in Early Modern England' that the poem 'is indeed Shakespeare's most sustained treatment of the trauma caused by the transformation of penance in Tudor England'? In this reading the 'reverend man' takes on an unsustainable weight of significance, especially when Stegner argues that he must necessarily be 'a reformed clergyman'. A more likely explanation is the suggestion by Ilona Bell in a later essay that the religious connotations simply elevate the role played by the reverend man. The larger literary and social context is explored by Patrick Cheney's '"Deep-brained Sonnets" and "Tragic Shows": Shakespeare's Late Ovidian Art in *A Lover's Complaint*' (a reprint of chapter 8 of his book *Shakespeare, National Poet-Playwright* which I reviewed last year) in which he argues that the poem is important in the Shakespeare canon 'because it maps out a sad, complex model of national literary production' involving Marlowe, Shakespeare, Spenser, Ovid and Virgil.

Exploring a literary context, John Roe's 'Unfinished Business: *A Lover's Complaint* and *Hamlet*, *Romeo and Juliet* and *The Rape of Lucrece*' asks

provocative and productive questions such as 'Is the fickle maid a continuation of Ophelia? Is the reverend man a Polonius figure? Is the young man Hamlet?' The answer in each case is a stimulating maybe. Heather Dubrow's equally stimulating essay, '"He had the dialect and different skill": Authorizers in *Henry V*, *A Lover's Complaint* and *Othello*', explores this group in terms of 'the workings of power'. Ilona Bell deftly draws on both the literary and social context in her convincingly argued 'Shakespeare's Exculpatory Complaint'. This 'brilliant and surprisingly daring' poem, especially in comparison with ones in the same genre by Sir Henry Lee and Anne Vavasour, turns out to be 'an unabashed and unexpected defense of female patience, female speech, and women's lawful liberty'. Unlike many readings of the poem, in Bell's view the 'fickle maid' is no serving-wench, not that kind of maid, but is upper-class, well-educated and, most importantly, 'an heiress, free to marry according to her own desires'.

The book's last four essays, by James Schiffer, Jon Harned, Stephen Whitworth and Shirley Sharon-Zisser, let loose a rampaging Lacanianism on a poem whose very opacity and maidenly reluctance to tell all invite, I suppose, this kind of hermeneutic battering. Suffering ecstasy indeed. Sharon-Zisser's climactic piece of polysyllabic obscurantism is particularly depressing. The best that can be said for the kind of helping hand proffered by an essay such as this one is that it drives you back into the arms of the poem itself for solace and relief.

Edward Burns in his contribution on *Richard III* to the Writers and Their Work series makes no apology (as he puts it) for heavily favouring particular productions of the play in the theatre and cinema for their interpretative insights at the expense of 'academic' criticism. And the particular productions he's most interested in turn out to be – unsurprisingly – ones like Olivier's, Sher's and McKellen's, readily available on film and video, modern, iconoclastic, often eccentric, giving the play a vitality 'that commentators have more often than not been unable to'. His own informal and intensely readable treatment imitates the bravura of the actors he admires in strutting its stuff under such headings as 'Humping Lady Anne', 'Richard's Mum', and '"I Like You, Lads"'. One may see from the titles themselves the extent to which Burns has bought into the fairly recent theatrical obsession with the play as a tragedy of family and Richard as 'a charismatic psychopath' who expresses the Bakhtinian 'chaotic physicality of human life' especially in its perverse and dangerous 'sexual carnival'. He also buys into, perhaps necessarily, the modern theatre's exploitation of the Richard in *Richard III* as the product and outcome of the Richard in *Henry VI, Part 2* and *Part 3*. This 'remarkably coherent' personality stretching over the three plays 'may be in scholarly terms a fiction', may be 'frankly anachronistic', but is intensely appealing theatrically as we see him mutate into a 'child-killer', signalled by a 'kind of denial of the facts of childhood and family . . . that allows him to define himself as entirely independent'. Richard in this view does not become an adult until his conscience awakes 'the night before he dies'.

What does Burns mean, though, by 'scholarly terms' and 'frankly anachronistic'? That the play goes against the facts of history? Or that 'academic' criticism has a different *Richard III* in its sights? Often Burns himself seems to suggest that there is such another play within the play he primarily talks about – when, for instance, he tells us that Shakespeare would not have seen the four plays one after the other as they are so often produced today; or when in his section called Deformations of History he talks of the 'secret play' within the play which is 'a play of the fabrication of history'; or when he seems to deplore the disappearance of Margaret and the Scrivener in modern productions, sacrificed to 'the study of a troubled charismatic individual'; or when he talks about productions of the play seeming to be 'less about history than . . . about theatrical history'. Perhaps it is to 'academic' criticism that we have to turn to get a handle on this not so secret play within the play; perhaps the deformations of history are the product of the deformations of theatrical production.

As we may see from the above variety of heartfelt responses to Shakespeare, this irresistibly charismatic writer continues to trouble the minds of his twenty-first-century readers, as he did those of his readers in every century since his death in 1616. Shakespeare, more than any other writer, for complex cultural reasons (as well as some obvious Shakespearian ones), has the same effect on his readers and directors that *As You Like It* had on Watson's dazzled imagination who, as we recall, looking back on what he had written, saw only 'a self-interested, appropriative simulation of the play, instead of the play itself'. Much of the time, as witnessed by this year's crop of studies on Shakespeare, these 'simulations' of his works, and his life, frequently dazzling in themselves, make the reading of Shakespeare a more uplifting, intriguing and pleasurable experience. Sometimes, however, as we have also seen, they make it dismayingly incidental to the enthusiasms of other voices in other rooms.

WORKS REVIEWED

Bevington, David, *How to Read a Shakespeare Play* (Oxford, 2006).

Burns, Edward, *Richard III*. Writers and their Work (Horndon, Devon, 2006).

Charnes, Linda, *Hamlet's Heirs: Shakespeare and the Politics of a New Millennium*. Accents on Shakespeare (New York and London, 2006).

Chatterjee, Visvanath, *Ten Essays on Shakespeare* (Calcutta, 2006).

Daileader, Celia R., *Racism, Misogyny, and the Othello Myth: Inter-Racial Couples from Shakespeare to Spike Lee* (Cambridge, 2005).

Distiller, Natasha, *South Africa, Shakespeare, and Post-Colonial Culture* (Lampeter, 2005).

Egan, Gabriel, *Green Shakespeare: from Ecopolitics to Ecocriticism*. Accents on Shakespeare (New York and London, 2006).

Erickson, Peter and Maurice Hunt, eds., *Approaches to Teaching Shakespeare's* Othello (New York, 2005).

Fernie, Ewan, ed., *Spiritual Shakespeares*. Accents on Shakespeare (Milton Park, Abingdon and New York, 2005).

Hadfield, Andrew, *Shakespeare and Republicanism* (Cambridge, 2005).

Hopkins, Lisa, *Shakespeare on the Edge: Border-Crossing in the Tragedies and the* Henriad (Aldershot, Hampshire, 2005).

Kozuka, Takashi and J. R. Mulryne, eds., *Shakespeare, Marlowe, Jonson: New Directions in Biography* (Aldershot, Hampshire, 2006).

Lawrence, Jason, *'Who the devil taught thee so much Italian?': Italian Language Learning and Literary Imitation in Early Modern England* (Manchester, 2005).

Leggatt, Alexander, ed., *William Shakespeare's Macbeth: A Sourcebook* (Abingdon, Oxon, 2006).

Makaryk, Irena R. and Joseph G. Price, eds., *Shakespeare in the Worlds of Communism and Socialism* (Toronto, 2006).

Maslen, R. W., *Shakespeare and Comedy* (2005).

McCarthy, Penny, *Pseudonymous Shakespeare: Rioting Language in the Sidney Circle* (Aldershot, 2006).

McEvoy, Sean, *Shakespeare: The Basics*. 2nd edn (New York, 2006).

McEvoy, Sean, ed., *William Shakespeare's Hamlet: A Sourcebook* (Abingdon and New York, 2006).

Orkin, Martin, *Local Shakespeares: Proximations and Power* (London and New York, 2005).

Pogue, Kate Emery, *Shakespeare's Friends* (Westport, Conn., 2006).

Poole, Kristen, *Radical Religion from Shakespeare to Milton: Figures of Nonconformity in Early Modern England* (Cambridge, 2000).

Quilligan, Maureen, *Incest and Agency in Elizabeth's England* (Philadelphia, 2005).

Romack, Katherine and James Fitzmaurice, eds., *Cavendish and Shakespeare, Interconnections* (Aldershot, 2006).

Sharon-Zisser, Shirley, ed., *Critical Essays on Shakespeare's A Lover's Complaint: Suffering Ecstasy* (Aldershot, 2006).

Warley, Christopher, *Sonnet Sequences and Social Distinction in Renaissance England* (Cambridge, 2005).

Watson, Robert N., *Back to Nature: the Green and the Real in the Late Renaissance* (Philadelphia, 2006).

Wells, Robin Headlam, *Shakespeare's Humanism* (Cambridge, 2005).

2. SHAKESPEARE IN PERFORMANCE
reviewed by EMMA SMITH

On first reading, the subtitle to Christoph Clausen's comparative study of Verdi's and Shakespeare's *Macbeth* seems a little unwieldy: 'negotiating historical and medial difference'. Amplified by Clausen's own metaphor of travelling between his two texts as 'two nations', however, it offers three axes for the development of the field of performance criticism evidenced in the books under consideration. Performances in different times and places are usefully triangulated by a notion of performance as the translation of Shakespeare's texts into different media: visual art, film and music as well as theatre.

Stuart Sillars's *Painting Shakespeare: The Artist as Critic, 1720–1820* argues that the visual artists he discusses derive their inspiration from reading, rather than seeing, Shakespeare. He begins with John Wootton's 1750 painting *Macbeth and Banquo meeting the Weird Sisters*. Wootton depicts the two captains in plumed helmets and Jacobite drapes in the bottom centre of a forbidding khaki woodland scene from which three piratical female figures in chimneypot hats emerge, barefoot and leaning on sticks. Two birds are silhouetted against the bright break in the clouds. The composition of the picture bears down heavily on the figures, overwhelming them with the dark tones of windswept vegetation. It is one of sixteen colour plates – not enough – and 101 black and white illustrations to this volume. Sillars expertly sketches the ways in which this illustration draws on naturalistic painting conventions and on Gaspard Dughet and Poussin, rather than on the theatrical *Macbeth* reintroduced by Garrick, arguing that its context is textual and art historical rather than dramatic. In turning away from Banquo and towards the witches, Macbeth finds himself in the 'Choice of Hercules' trope popularized by Shaftesbury's 1713 essay on narrative in painting. But Sillars also notes that the painting, while apparently depicting the meeting in the play's 1.3, proleptically incorporates subsequent details – a magpie and an owl in a tree, anticipating the unnatural events attendant on the murder of Duncan, those flying birds 'mak[ing] wing to th' rooky wood' (3.2), the witches' cave and a cat from 4.1. The bright red of Macbeth's part-Scots, part-classical cloak might further be seen to anticipate his bloodsoaked deeds, pre-empting by a century and a half A. C. Bradley's identification of the play's particular chromatic character. This synchronic distillation anticipates in visual form the close reading practices of the twentieth century: as Sillars points out, in its combination of narrative and emblematic depiction, Wootton's painting participates in, even constructs, a discourse on the play which we would now recognize as critical. And he does this before criticism has really developed its procedures for discussing Shakespeare's plays.

That Shakespeare paintings might be more than secondary illustrations of plays and rather the layered and revelatory medium of the plays' reception and transmission makes it clear that Sillars's methodology is closely related to developments in performance criticism. That is, his visual texts *are*, rather than *represent*, performance, in that by translating the plays into visual form they select, interpret and accommodate Shakespeare for different ideological and aesthetic agendas. While the illustrations of the plays he discusses are as far from contemporary stage practice as Simon Forman's troubling recollection of those horses in the first *Macbeth*, the ways in which visual representations pre-empt, develop and elucidate eighteenth-century responses to Shakespeare in editing, performance and criticism are revelatory. There are some wonderful moments of detail: reading Hogarth's charcoal sketch of *Falstaff Reviewing His Troops* Sillars makes suggestive parallels between the artist's bravura, provisional medium and Falstaff's own improvisatory bluster; he skilfully unpacks Hogarth's *A Scene from Shakespear's 'The Tempest'* as a mock-nativity in which Prospero's island reforms Catholic iconography into native Protestantism; comparing two Fuseli line-and-wash *Hamlet* illustrations to their Etruscan vase painting prototypes, Sillars uncovers a darkly scopophilic eroticism in the painterly understanding of the play's psycho-sexual dynamic. The creative engagement

of Blake, Romney, Reynolds with Shakespeare's plays is seen as prototypically critical, and Sillars's own carefully interdisciplinary exposition crucially establishes illustration as engagement rather than decoration. It's a fine achievement.

More recent visualisations of Shakespeare's plays tend to be associated with cinema. The idea that Shakespearian films might themselves be interventions at once critical and creative is relatively recent, and the canon of films so discussed remains small – only Olivier's and Branagh's *Henry V* were named as exemplary pedagogic cinematic texts in a recent survey of the teaching of Shakespeare in British higher education. Diana Henderson's *A Concise Companion to Shakespeare on Screen* is indeed concise, but admirably broad-ranging. A chronology of world and cultural events alongside Shakespearian films is suggestive in its juxtapositions, offering a way of resisting the seductive present tense encouraged by the circulation of canonical texts on video and DVD. Thus George Sidney's *Kiss Me Kate* (1953) is placed alongside the televising of the Queen's coronation (as narrated by Laurence Olivier), the first Hollywood Cinemascope film (*The Robe*) and the death of Stalin; Parker's *Othello* and Branagh's *In the Bleak Midwinter* (1995) abut the O. J. Simpson trial and the establishment of amazon.com. Henderson's introduction suggests that the popularity of tragedies for film adaptation attests to their role in making sense, or revealing the senselessness, of the modern world; it is thus appropriate – and inevitable – that Almereyda's alienated, urban, cinematically self-reflexive *Hamlet* (2000) is the most cited film text. Robert Shaughnessy uses Almereyda's substitution of 'a film by Hamlet' for 'The Mousetrap' to discuss the prevalence of anti-theatricality in narratives of Shakespearian cinema. Discussing a marginalized, because overtly theatrical, *Hamlet* with Tony Richardson and revisiting Jack Jorgens's influential schema of 'theatrical', 'realist' and 'filmic' modes, Shaughnessy's contribution reminds us, like that chronology, of the need to contextualize Shakespearian cinema in time and place. For Elsie Walker, on nostalgia in *Looking for Richard* and *Love's Labour's Lost*, Almereyda offers an example of bricolage by which the Shakespearian film is understandable only in dialogue with other cinematic referents; Ireland is a spectre in this version for Mark Thornton Burnett; and Peter Donaldson elaborates on the idea of Ethan Hawke's Hamlet as an independent film-maker, fascinatingly reconstructing the original screenplay's juxtaposition of 'To be or not to be' with a video installation by the contemporary (and Shakespearian, at least nominally) artist, Bill Viola. If Almereyda is the new Branagh, the old Branagh isn't entirely forgotten: his Irishness is key to Burnett's article, Pascale Aebischer discusses suppressed homosexuality in his *Henry V*, and Barbara Hodgdon mentions Michael Keaton's aurally weird Dogberry in *Much Ado* in her nuanced chapter on acting styles. Elsewhere, Anthony Dawson sticks up for highbrow Kurosawa in an often resolutely pop-culture field; Douglas Lanier offers a characteristically clever reading of camp in Shakespeare parodies including *Tromeo and Juliet* and *Last Action Hero*, placing them in dialogue with the kitsch aesthetic of *Romeo + Juliet* and *Titus*; television Shakespeare, largely absent from the volume because its texts remain difficult to obtain, is represented by Roberta Pearson and William Uricchio's engaged account of recent Shakespeare documentaries including Michael Wood's *In Search of Shakespeare*. Cinematic Shakespeare studies seem alive and well, although Kathleen McLuskie's 'Afterword' has a mordant quality, in which film threatens to usurp the creative territory criticism has tried to reserve as its own prerogative, while critics of Shakespeare on film cling to an idea of a super-subtle reader of these commodified cultural products – the critic him- or herself? – educationally and exegetically superior to the films' implied spectator.

If the aim of Henderson's collection is to pause 'and mak[e] sense of our subject', there's something more restless about another cinematic collection, *Screening Shakespeare in the Twenty-First Century*, edited by Mark Thornton Burnett and Ramona Wray. Only six, or is it five, years into the said century, there are already a number of texts ripe for consideration: Almereyda is here a chronological starting-point rather than postmodern exemplar for these contributors, as seventy-six Shakespearian movie titles are identified between 2000 and 2005. Discussing a six-minute fashion commercial adaptation of *Romeo and Juliet* (2005), the editors discuss its deracialized, commodified aesthetic in which a fantasy Shakespeare is 'a magnet for negotiations about style, value, and cultural identity'. As this initial focus on the H&M commercial suggests, the range of cinematic Shakespeares is broad, taking in traditional adaptations such as Michael Radford's *Merchant of Venice* alongside Don C. Selwyn's *The Maori Merchant*. Samuel Crowl concludes his endorsement of Radford's film noting that, while the director is unlikely to essay Shakespeare again, 'the genre has been enriched by his *Merchant* and Pacino's Shylock'; nowhere else does the notion of Shakespeare film as a 'genre' seem so steady. Richard Dutton's analysis of Wood's television series discusses Wood's own careful maintenance of his own authority and the depiction of religious antagonisms in the context of early twentieth-first-century geopolitics. That 9/11 defines the nascent twenty-first century is a given of the collection – sometimes helpfully, sometimes rather tendentiously. Burnett writes of surveillance in three versions of *Hamlet*, arguing that the films can envisage new ways of seeing which escape the Patriot Act's regulatory scopic economy; Sarah Hatcheul relates Peter Babakitis's *Henry V* (2004) to media representations of the Iraq war; Carolyn Jess-Cooke argues that contemporary filmic engagement with Shakespeare mobilizes the contradictory global/local connotations of 'McShakespeare'; Suzanne Greenhalgh and Robert Shaughnessy examine television productions with ethnically mixed casts and settings to discuss cultural hybridity and the delicate possibilities of multiculturalism; Ramona Wray's work on the BBC's 'Shakespeare Re-Told' series analyses these modernisations alongside cultural reference points including Bridget Jones, modern televisual genres and the problems of and for twenty-first-century post-feminism. This is a collection more than simply quick off the blocks – although it is that too – but a stimulus to broader engagement with the most recent filmic epiphenomena. Henderson and Burnett/Wray both respond to and anatomize the fragmentary, montage qualities of contemporary cinematic culture in the fragmentary, montage style of contemporary academic publication: the essay collection. Saskia Kossak's 'Frame My Face to All Occasions': Shakespeare's Richard III on Screen is a more grand-narrative sort of intervention, with half the volume taken up with a history of Shakespeare on film from Beerbohm Tree's King John onwards. The book is less dutiful and more engaging when it settles to Richard III, particularly as refracted in gangster films including de Palma's Scarface, and in Neil Simon's The Goodbye Girl. In all, thirty-two screen productions are referenced: as Kossak identifies, this play above others seems to require 'extreme adaptation', witnessed by her work on Cibberian texts used by Olivier and Pacino.

Shakespearian characters do not sing on their own behalf: they get professional musicians to do it for them, unless they are mad, drunk, in their dotage or otherwise marked as unconventional. This insight early in David Lindley's excellent Shakespeare and Music is revelatory in helping us consider the charge of, say, Pandarus's or Feste's or Ophelia's songs on the stage, and exemplifies Lindley's deft touch in bringing music from editorial appendices into interpretative prominence. A contextual chapter glosses Lorenzo's unlikely paean to music as he and Jessica await the return of the other couples to Belmont in Act 5, outlining music's relation to neo-Platonism, to analogical theories, to fears of effeminacy, to reformed church practices and to mathematics. Lindley is fascinating on volume – recognizing that, aside from the trumpet, no available instrument offered high decibel sound and thus promoting the 'flourishes' so prominent in stage directions to particular aural authority. Henslowe's records for 1598–9 reveal expenditure of more than £7 on musical instruments for the Admiral's Men but records no payments to musicians, perhaps suggesting that the actors themselves acquired the necessary expertise. On specific plays and the ways in which music creates its intrinsic – and ambiguous – effects, Lindley is continually stimulating. Even relatively modest

musical effects – the use of the flourish, for example – become meaningful, as in the stage directions to the sequence on the castle walls in 3.3 in Richard II, with 'parle without, and answere within': a sequence which registers the aural challenge to Richard's singular sovereignty at this fulcrum of the play's shifting power dynamic. Dances in Romeo and Juliet, in Much Ado About Nothing and in Henry VIII are examined with particular attention to implied musical rhythms within the patterns of the characters' speeches. A chapter on song discusses Desdemona's 'willow song' and suggests that a familiar tune for Cassio's drinking song would add to the audience's complicity with Iago's plotting. Closing with The Tempest, Lindley suggests that in abjuring his magic, Prospero also loses control of Ariel and the music of the island, adding to the meiotic tone of the play's Epilogue. This is a short book with real power to encourage us to hear the plays' music, and is highly recommended. Christopher R. Wilson and Michela Calore's Music in Shakespeare: A Dictionary would be a good reference accompaniment: entries cover words with musical connotations across a spectrum of familiarity, giving early modern definitions where possible and then locating their Shakespearian referents. The entry for 'charm', for example, moves from Thomas Cooper's 1565 equation of 'charm' with 'song' to the use of the word as noun and verb in The Tempest: here, theatrical music is quite literally spell-binding. Related to this interest in Shakespeare's music is Christoph Clausen's Macbeth Multiplied, which compares Verdi's opera and the play. While the contextualization of the Jacobean Macbeth is sometimes over-familiar, many Shakespearians will be enlightened by the less habitual material on Verdi. Clausen's unpicking of Verdi's rendering of 'Is this a dagger which I see before me?' (2.1) argues that music has the advantage over other sorts of realization in constructing a flexible and nuanced sonorous representation of a dagger which both is and is not there.

Music in The Tempest and, perhaps less evidently, in Macbeth, is clearly connected to those plays' generic affiliations with masque. Barbara

Ravelhofer's booklength study of *The Early Stuart Masque: Dance, Costume, and Music* develops these associations. Much exegetical criticism of the masque constructs a historically, politically and aesthetically acute ideal spectator who has the mental key for the text's cryptogram of mythological references, court intrigue and allusions to other texts. Instead, Ravelhofer interposes a bewildered spectator – empirically, in the form of a Savoy diplomat Giovanni Battista Gabaleoni, disorientedly viewing Thomas Campion's Boxing Day masque of 1613 and unable to make sense of its action or verse, and more generally, in an imaginative reconstruction of the ways in which visual and aural meanings might be generated from multimedia masque performance. Attentive to performance spaces, Ravelhofer discusses choreography and staging, where geometric patterning and musical accompaniment were complementary. Her analysis of costume goes beyond the oft-reproduced Inigo Jones illustrations in a dazzling riot of description, where colour, texture and the sound of fabrics are important aspects of audience experience. Case-studies detail the sonic and visual contrasts between antimasque and masque, and, in contrast to previous studies, Ravelhofer argues for Ben Jonson as 'multimedia artist and collaborator' rather than rivalrous scriptwriter.

The role of court ladies in masque culture offers a challenge to histories of the contemporary public stage from which women are apparently entirely absent. A collection called *Women Players in England 1500–1660* takes on the challenge with a focus on non-elite performers and locations: women performed in alehouses, manorhouses, court and market square, watched by female spectators and patrons and, in presenting an inclusive idea of performance as 'any act of embodied display or representation intended for an audience', the collection breaks institutional and metropolitan as well as gender hegemonies. Performances of martyrdom by Catholic women such as Margaret Clitheroe, for example, are analysed alongside Mary Frith's extraordinary self-presentation at the Fortune Theatre, memorialised in Middleton and Dekker's play *The Roaring Girl*, and which Natasha Korda argues

should be stripped of its exceptional charge to reinstate Mary as a female performer within the cultural entrepôt of the London theatre world. James Stokes's archival research finds women paid for performance in Corpus Christi and related religious processional entertainments, and the regional volumes of the *Records of Early English Drama* project are trawled by other contributors. Commedia dell'arte and other European traditions are frequently referenced, indicating how normative native histories of English drama via the printed works of the public stage can construct the narrative they purport to represent, by excluding foreign – national, cultural, sexual – elements. Bruce Smith's essay on 'Female impersonation in Early Modern Ballads' uncovers theatrically multiple subject positions amid such iterated texts as 'The Daemon Lover' and 'The Fair Maid of Northumberland'. Jean Howard uses Heywood's Elizabeth plays to explore the ways in which the absence of women from the public stage simultaneously evokes and excludes the codes of femininity which both are and are not associated with the body sexed female. Women act *on*, if not *in*, early modern drama in ways which the collection begins to unpick, and it is salutary for the history of Renaissance theatre how frequently these investigations veer away from the urban world of London commercial theatre into alternative geographical, spatial and cultural locales.

A cluster of monographs and collections consider the performance of drama in its early modern context. Of these the most significant is Peter Holland and Stephen Orgel's volume *From Performance to Print in Shakespeare's England*, in a series entitled, bravely, *Redefining British Theatre History*. A sequence of top-drawer contributors – the relation between these redefiners and the implied previous definers is moot – usefully press on this claim, revisiting ontological and evidential questions with considerable energy and verve. It is as if the old chestnut of 'page to stage', modishly reversed in recent scholarship, has become itself a form of performance criticism, as *mise-en-page* partakes of a version of spatial staging closer to *mise-en-scène* than the chiastic formula quite allows.

Asking 'what does the text of a play . . . represent?', Orgel works with annotated texts stressing readerly engagement with printed plays, across a dazzling range of examples in which the material text contains not so much the play as the proprietorial reconstruction of it by its readers and owners. Proprietary control is the subject of Gary Taylor's work on the marketing of the 1623 *Folio*. Here early modern bookshops are 'performance spaces, where individuals acted out socially scripted interactive rituals of self-fashioning', and where the major protagonist is the bookseller. Taylor's reading of the preliminary materials in the Folio traces the attempt of Edward Blount and his co-stationers to create a luxury niche market for this expensive book, much of which had already seen print in cheaper formats. Here the text of the play represents an investment, a commodity, cultural capital, and Gabriel Egan's contribution to the volume develops Taylor's interest in marketing. Egan notes how the designation 'play' drops out of title-pages during the 1580s and 1590s, and traces the changing semantics of 'play' and its cognates as verb rather than noun. For John Jowett the text of *Timon of Athens*, printed in that Folio book, gives us a lens from which to construct, analeptically, the masque scene on the stage. Other sorts of performance are animated out of the printed book: the scene of Latin instruction, in Lynn Enterline's encounter with the drama of the grammar school classroom, the persona of Armin, resurrected from print traces by Richard Preiss, Gordon McMullan's design for the performance of 'lateness' in the last plays. The interest in Shakespeare on stage has, paradoxically, revivified the interest in Shakespeare on the page: Holland and Orgel's collection turns the page–stage binary into a Mobius strip.

Three books consider affect and the performance of passionate physicality on the early modern stage. Thomas Anderson's *Performing Early Modern Trauma from Shakespeare to Milton* is concerned with the traumatic past as it bears on the genre of history play. Rather than ameliorating or compensating for the losses generated by recent historical ruptures, Anderson argues that the cultural products fossilize that loss, using the tropes of 'memory's prosthesis' and 'the past's revenge', derived from psychoanalytically inflected models of traumatic historiography, particularly Holocaust studies. Thus Lavinia is a memorial to the Reformation narrative of Foxe's martyred bodies, and Marcus's question 'Shall I speak for thee?' (2.3) stands for the interrogation and articulation of that past by the early modern present. The fragmented and distracted bodies of *Titus Andronicus* maintain a vigil for the past, for the literally racked bodies and for the broken sacraments of Catholicism; the occluded circumstances of the death of Gloucester at the beginning of *Richard II* dramatise a refusal of amnesia in relation to the past; Jacobean revenge plays, in their encounter with the previous generations, freight their protagonists with the burdens of memory as well as of violence. An extended account of *Hamlet* – generically caught between history play and revenge tragedy – would have been an interesting addition to this elegant and suggestive thesis. In *Staging Anatomies: Dissection and Spectacle in Early Stuart Tragedy*, Hilary Nunn argues audiences for actors and anatomists overlapped in early modern London and that – it's not clear whether causally or merely coincidentally – theatrical violations of the body became more common 'as the practice of dissection gradually gained acceptance within the English medical community'. Nunn is attentive to dead bodies on stage, although not always willing to acknowledge the double charge of their representative force, since they are not actually dead, just as she identifies the material significance of unresponsive female flesh in drama while never quite acknowledging that this flesh is not female. Both studies employ dramatic verbs – 'staging', 'performing': in both cases metaphorical subtleties are carefully explored but the literal is rather ignored. Nunn's discussion of the tableau of the apparently dead bodies of the husband and children in *The Duchess of Malfi* quotes the stage direction's description of 'the artificial figures of Antonio and his children, appearing as if they were dead', but doesn't elaborate on the visual, thematic and ontological double-take if these figures were indeed represented by the living actors playing these roles, rather than, as she prefers, waxworks. Farah Karim-Cooper's attentiveness to representational modes in *Cosmetics in Shakespearian and Renaissance Drama* is prompted by Bosola's denigration of cosmetics and painting in Webster's play – and her account of the white lead and vinegar facepaint designating stage ghosts might be relevant to the depiction of the 'dead' Antonio. Because the early modern discourse of cosmetics is by turns didactic, satirical, medical, religious and anti-theatrical, her study is rich in contextual material. Sometimes less historically cautious material irrupts: 'Did early modern woman have a conscious desire to transform herself into the poetic embodiment of beauty? I would say yes.' Some evidence is forthcoming, but the singular 'woman' and the form of the question betray a politics of presentism which I would have enjoyed seeing theorized. A more explicitly feminist account of 'the reactionary practice of beautification' seems to be trying to get out from among the alert readings of *The Second Maiden's Tragedy* and Gloriana's lipstick moue in *The Revenger's Tragedy*. Karim-Cooper ends by evoking Shakespeare playing, *pace* Rowe, the Ghost in *Hamlet*: himself adorned with the cosmetic artistry intrinsic to, and anathematized by, the stage.

The Royal Shakespeare Company's new Courtyard Theatre, its home during the refurbishment of the old Memorial Theatre, has subsumed an earlier theatre building, The Other Place. Always, as that name suggests, perceived at an angle to the establishment theatre space, TOP's ideological and aesthetic commitments during the 1970s and 1980s are discussed in a timely monograph by Alycia Smith-Howard, *Studio Shakespeare: The Royal Shakespeare Company at The Other Place*. As the brainchild of Buzz Goodbody, TOP had a clear set of interlinked objectives aimed at breaking down barriers – cultural, hierarchical, regional, spatial, financial – between audiences and classical theatre. The recognizability of these aims three decades later emphasizes that TOP was ahead of its time. Smith-

Howard's unqualified admiration for Goodbody's mission enlivens this study even as it gives it a predictable shape: exciting, risk-taking theatre during her directorship, predictable, safe plays after her death. It is sometimes uncritical, as in its eulogistic last lines in which the idea of a 'pure and uncorrupted' way of doing theatre is apparently unproblematic. But Smith-Howard's account of rehearsal practices and for theatre as process rather than product draws heavily and importantly on new interviews and archival material about reading material, rehearsal exercises, improvised and therapeutic forms of encounter, and offers the most detailed reconstruction of this experimental period in the RSC's history. This is a study of personality – of Goodbody's, primarily, but also of the collective personality generated by close, studio and ensemble involvement with Shakespeare's plays, their characters and their audiences.

Shakespeare's ability to be translated through performance into other cultural contexts is attested by Monica Matei-Chesnoiu's *Shakespeare in Nineteenth-Century Romania* and Norbert Schaffeld's *Shakespeare's Legacy: The Appropriation of the Plays in Post-Colonial Drama*. Matei-Chesnoiu's contributors are largely concerned with linguistic and cultural aspects of translation and less with performance on stage, although they repeatedly identify curious points of correspondence between Romanian cultural politics and Shakespeare's plays. Schaffeld's collection is more concerned with performances – in Africa, India, Australia, the Carribean, and in Southeast Asia. It is hard work for the contributors both to describe the production or text and to encapsulate salient features of its cultural context, but the effort is worthwhile. Martina Ghosh-Schellhorn makes some trenchant comments about Janet Suzman's Market Theatre, Johannesburg *Othello*, arguing provocatively that she 'whitened up' John Kani and that the production spoke to and for South African whites. Richard Hubert's 'larrikin' New Zealand performance-piece *Hamlet: He Was A Grave Digger* (1998) repositions Shakespeare's tragedy within a parodic version of Antipodean culture, as a

Chips Rafferty, an iconic outback pioneer actor, watches his younger self as Hamlet: 'O that this too, too solid flesh would melt, thaw, and resolve itself into a dew. Bloody hot, innit?' Enough said.

Well, not quite. The most substantial volume in the field this year has been held back until the conclusion. Barbara Hodgdon and W. B. Worthen's *A Companion to Shakespeare and Performance* is a slam-dunk book – sustained, detailed, wide-ranging. If performance is embodied action for an audience, the contents pages stage an immediate sort of academic theatre. We've got Richard Burt doing his punning routine – 'Sshockspeare: (Nazi) Shakespeare Goes Heil-lywood', some nifty soft shoe shuffle with Laurie E. Osborne's 'Shakespearian Screen/Play', music hall wisecracking from Simon Palfrey and Tiffany Stern – 'What Does the Cued Part Cue? Parts and Cues in *Romeo and Juliet*', alliteration *and* parentheses in 'Guying the Girls and Girling the Shrew: (Post) Feminist Fun at Shakespeare's Globe' by G. B. Shand, and shared knowingness in Peter Holland's 'Shakespeare's Two Bodies', alongside the impeccable elegance of Richard Schoch's 'Shakespeare the Victorian' and Susan Bennett's mysterious 'Shakespeare on Vacation'. This is the catalogue flourish to an academic Ringling Bros and Barnum and Bailey – and the collection delivers. These two vectors – 'Shakespeare' and 'Performance' – produce a range of readings and emphases that are, above all, fun. Readers will find their own favourites among the contributions. Peggy Phelan's lucid explorations of connections between psychoanalysis and architecture thinks structurally about play texts and play spaces, imagining theatre – particularly in *King Lear* – as a self-denying space which stages its own disappearance and erases its own characters, even as it performs them. What is so striking about Phelan's work is its negotiation of apparently distinct fields and its incorporation of a language of – a feeling for – affect into scholarly prose. Bruce Smith suggests that John Manningham's cancelled 'Mid' in the diary entry recording the Middle Temple's *Twelfth Night* is a reference to 'midnight' not to *A Midsummer Night's Dream*, and goes on to

develop a great reading of time, rhythm and carousing in the play and its performances, including Nunn's film. Peter S. Donaldson's account of historical and game spaces in Taymor's *Titus* is significant and nuanced; Douglas Lanier listens to audio Shakespeares with a keen ear for accent and soundscape; Paul Prescott's work on theatre reviews denaturalises a genre often treated as transparent record; Carol Chillington Rutter's accounts of 'Maverick Shakespeare' by Northern Broadsides, Cheek by Jowl and the English Shakespeare Company combine telling performance detail with political nous; James Loehlin brings his customary insight to a pedagogically aware chapter 'Teaching through Performance'. Barbara Hodgdon's assuredly undogmatic introduction invokes disciplinary history and methodological range, ending by quoting Peggy Phelan's injunction to resist performance criticism as memorialisation 'for what one otherwise preserves is an illustrated corpse'. 'Is that,' Hodgdon asks, 'perhaps, the challenge that waits in the wings?' It is a good and important question, but if the subject here is a dead body, this is one hell of a wake.

WORKS REVIEWED

Anderson, Thomas P., *Performing Early Modern Trauma from Shakespeare to Milton* (Aldershot, 2006).

Brown, Pamela Allen, and Peter Parolin, eds., *Women Players in England, 1500–1660: Beyond the All-Male Stage* (Aldershot, 2005).

Burnett, Mark Thornton, and Ramona Wray, eds., *Screening Shakespeare in the Twenty-First Century* (Edinburgh, 2006).

Clausen, Christoph, *Macbeth Multiplied: Negotiating Historical and Medial Difference between Shakespeare and Verdi* (Amsterdam and New York, 2005).

Henderson, Diana E., ed., *A Concise Companion to Shakespeare on Screen* (Oxford, 2006).

Hodgdon, Barbara, and W. B. Worthen, *A Companion to Shakespeare and Performance* (Oxford, 2005).

Holland, Peter, and Stephen Orgel, eds., *From Performance to Print in Shakespeare's England* (Basingstoke, 2006).

Karim-Cooper, Farah, *Cosmetics in Shakespearian and Renaissance Drama* (Edinburgh, 2006).

Kossak, Saskia, *'Frame My Face to All Occasions': Shakespeare's Richard III on Screen* (Vienna, 2005).

Lindley, David, *Shakespeare and Music* (London, 2006).

Matei-Chesnoiu, Monica, ed., *Shakespeare in Nineteenth-Century Romania* (Bucharest, 2006).

Nunn, Hilary M., *Staging Anatomies: Dissection and Spectacle in Early Stuart Tragedy* (Aldershot, 2005).

Ravelhofer, Barbara, *The Early Stuart Masque: Dance, Costume, and Music* (Oxford, 2006).

Schaffeld, Norbert, ed., *Shakespeare's Legacy: The Appropriation of the Plays in Post-Colonial Drama* (Trier, 2005).

Sillars, Stuart, *Painting Shakespeare: The Artist as Critic 1720–1820* (Cambridge, 2006).

Smith-Howard, Alycia, *Studio Shakespeare: The Royal Shakespeare Company at The Other Place* (Aldershot, 2006).

Wilson, Christopher R., and Michela Calore, eds., *Music in Shakespeare: A Dictionary* (London, 2005).

3. EDITIONS AND TEXTUAL STUDIES
reviewed by ERIC RASMUSSEN

This *annus mirabilis* in Shakespearian editing welcomed two monumental editions: the Arden3 *Hamlet* and the Oxford *Othello*. I don't imagine that there are many Shakespearians on the planet who did not know of Arden's long-announced plan to present a groundbreaking edition of all three textual versions of *Hamlet*. The fact that Ann Thompson and Neil Taylor have prepared critical editions of Q1, Q2 and F – the latter two being the longest texts in the Shakespeare canon – in about a decade is an extraordinary achievement (it took Harold Jenkins thirty-six years to finish his Arden2 edition). Just as the 1982 Arden2 *Hamlet* marked the culmination of the tradition of conflated editions, Arden3 is a milestone in the recent history of version-based editing.

Thompson and Taylor have produced unapologetically conservative editions of all three texts. Those of us who have criticized version-based editions that do not follow their control texts will find much to applaud here. This is version-based editing at its best. Their Second Quarto text makes remarkably few emendations (128 compared to Jenkins's 297) and their Folio text preserves many more F readings than any previous Folio-based edition. My personal favourite comes in the opening line to 1.4 where Folio editors such as Gary Taylor, Philip Edwards and G. R. Hibbard all emend F's 'is it very cold?' to Q2's 'it is very cold'. Thompson and Taylor are surely correct in retaining this small but essential difference: Hamlet in the Folio is so distracted that he does not know whether it is cold or not and has to ask.

The texts are here presented as separate but not equal. Q2 is granted pride of place in the 'core' volume (titled simply '*Hamlet*', with full introductory material and critical apparatus; available in paperback, priced at £9) while Q1 and F appear in the supplementary 'companion' volume (titled '*Hamlet: The Texts of 1603 and 1623*', with a minimal introduction and scaled-down critical apparatus; currently available only in hardback, priced at £55). The practical consequences of this arrangement are obvious: although edited versions of each text are now available in the Arden3 series, only a happy few specialists will purchase the Q1/F volume; the great variety of readers will only buy Q2. For those interested in understanding the reasoning behind the decision to privilege Q2, Thompson and Taylor offer a refreshingly non-dogmatic apologia. They acknowledge that they do not have any strongly held convictions about the nature of the texts, confessing that 'the temptation to deny that we have a theory for any one text, let alone all three, is almost overwhelming'. At one point they even suggest that the length of a text alone might justify granting it priority; since Q2 is 'the longest text', printing it separately 'allows the two volumes to be

With thanks to Trey Jansen and Arthur Evenchik for invaluable assistance.

not too dissimilar in size'. (This makes little sense to me: as things stand, the Q2 volume contains 613 pages whereas the Q1/F volume has 368; if, in fact, a shorter text were featured in the main volume, *then* the two volumes would be closer in size.) Their 'agnostic' disposition notwithstanding, Thompson and Taylor ultimately concede that 'if one were forced to choose just one of the three early texts of *Hamlet* as, on the balance of the evidence, the most likely to have authority, it would have to be Q2'.

In the editors' view, Q2's 'authority' rests squarely on its derivation 'from an authorial manuscript'. But they elsewhere express a more tentative view of authorship, agency and authority ('We are not assuming that William Shakespeare was necessarily the sole author of every word in these early seventeenth-century texts, nor that we know the degree to which any of them represents the author's or authors' intentions'), which itself seems at odds with their lightly qualified assertion that the compositors' copy behind these texts was 'a pretty accurate record of what the author wrote and intended to write'. And when Thompson and Taylor address the issue of theatrical authority (in a statement of *Editorial principles* repeated in both volumes), things get a bit muddled:

since Shakespeare was the resident dramatist in an acting company, and since all three texts contain publishers' references to that company as being the play's provenance, the issue of whether or not 'playhouse practice' or 'actors' interpolations' have contaminated the author's text is not, for us, a major consideration.

This statement is inaccurate: only Q1 mentions an acting company ('acted by his Highnesse seruants'). Q2 manifestly does not contain a publisher's reference to an acting company; nor, as David Scott Kastan – one of the general editors of this edition – has pointed out, does the First Folio.[1] (I'm told that this statement has now been corrected in the first reprinting.)

Among the many highlights of this edition, for me, are the clear tables of press variants and compositors, the extended examination of the problematic act division at 3.4/4.1, and the study of

possible doubling patterns which reveals, remarkably, that each of the three texts could be played by a cast of eleven actors. This edition is consciously tailored (no pun) to the expanding UK undergraduate readership. The editors note that when the previous Arden edition of the play was published in 1982, only 10 per cent of school-leavers went to university; today, the figure is 'nearly 50 per cent'. Still, there are moments when Thompson and Taylor may be overestimating their audience. How many undergraduates will have a clue what is meant by the captions to figure 5 (a 'pre-Millais Ophelia') and figure 6 (a 'post-Millais Ophelia')? The painting of Ophelia by John Everett Millais is neither discussed nor illustrated in the introduction. (The caption notwithstanding, the photo of Jean Simmons tranquilly recumbent in the water, taken on set during the making of Olivier's film, is sublime.)

Thompson and Taylor's introduction is punctuated throughout by moments of quiet humour. Discussing the often *mano-a-mano* competition among textual editors, each one claiming that the play he has edited is the best in the canon, they wryly note that 'there are exceptions to this, as when a woman edits *The Taming of the Shrew*'. With a glance at the reconflated *Lear* in the Norton Shakespeare, the editors quip, 'Mercifully, you may feel, the general editors of the Arden Shakespeare have decided not to break all records by including a conflated text of *Hamlet* and making this the first four-text edition'.

This is an engaging introduction, but it's somewhat rough around the edges,[2] and also rather

---

[1] See Kastan, *Shakespeare and the Book* (Cambridge, 2001), p. 71.

[2] After claiming that 'the only features that these three *Hamlets* have in common are the name and designation of the chief character, and the fact that they are plays', the editors undermine their generalization by observing that 'some stretches of dialogue are virtually identical'. Having rightly observed that 'since the length of a line of prose is not a constant, a more meaningful comparison is between numbers of words in the three texts', Thompson and Taylor unaccountably proceed to use line counts, and inconsistent ones at that ('F lacks about 230 of Q2's lines, while Q2 lacks about 70 of F's lines' (p. 82) . . .

thin. Indeed, the fact that the introduction to the Arden3 *As You Like It*, also under review here, is *longer* than that to the Arden3 *Hamlet* comes as a shock. There is certainly worthwhile material in Thompson and Taylor's introductory essay – such as a detailed account of Captain William Keeling's journal entry about shipboard performances of the play off the coast of Africa in 1607 – but devotees of the Arden Shakespeare may feel that the relative brevity of the 137-page introduction and the concision of the commentary notes are not what they expect from this series. Jenkins's Arden2 included an extensive appendix of 'longer notes' devoted to some of the play's more famous cruxes: his discussion of the various critical responses to the question of Hamlet's age, for instance, ran to nearly four pages; Thompson and Taylor handle this issue in a commentary note on the Gravedigger's 'thirty' (5.1.153):

In Q2 and F Hamlet's age is given clearly, by this and by the Gravedigger's insistence at 163–71 that Yorick (whom Hamlet remembers) has been dead for 23 years. The Gravedigger in Q1 omits the first statement altogether and says Yorick's skull has lain in the earth 'this dozen years', perhaps indicating that Hamlet is 18 rather than 30, an age which would seem more appropriate to his status as a student.

Although a critical edition need not rehearse all previous commentary on a given line – this is an Arden, after all, not a variorum – the continuing fascination with *Hamlet* surely derives, at least in part, from an awareness that its problematic passages have been argued over for centuries, 'the sheer depth and breadth of tradition' as Thompson and Taylor call it at the opening of their introduction. And whereas Arden2 provided readers with a sense of the historical discussion of the problem of Hamlet's age, readers of Arden3 might not even know that a problem exists. (One wonders if this fundamental difference between the two might be sufficient reason to keep Arden2 in print, rather than rotating it out, as is standard when a new Arden3 appears.)

The number of substantive errors in each of the three texts prevents one from praising this edition's accuracy, but the typos are not howlers: in the Q2 text, for 'has' read 'hath' (1.3.87), for 'dishes to' read 'dishes but to' (4.3.24), for 'the stage' read 'a stage' (5.2.362); in the Q1 text, for 'inconvenient' read 'unconvenient' (2.29), for '*and* Players' read '*and the* Players' (9.0), for '*Enter* KING' read '*Enter the* KING' (10.0), for 'Whose' read 'What' (16.127); in the F1 text, for 'clear' read 'clearly' (1.3.96), for 'Thus' read 'So' (3.2.265), for 'answer' read 'answers' (3.2.313, though this is probably a deliberate emendation from Q2 that was not noted); line 3.3.26 is given to Rosincrance alone whereas F assigns it to '*Both*' Rosincrance and Guildensterne (on the idiosyncratic spelling of names, see below). Non-copy-text stage directions are often printed without brackets,[3] and the errata list for the textual notes is rather lengthy.[4]

F contains about 88 lines with no counterpart in Q2, while Q2 contains about 222 lines with no counterpart in F (p. 93).

[3] The following stage directions should be bracketed: in Q2, 'GUILDENSTERN' (4.4.8), '*Exit*' (4.5.73), '*Leaps in the grave*' (5.1.239), '*In scuffling they change rapiers*' (5.2.285), '*Hurts the King*' (5.2.306); in Q1, 1.97 SD '*The cock crows*' (1.97), 'CORAMBIS, GILDERSTONE and ROSSENCRAFT' (8.0–1), '*Rossencraft and Gilderstone*' (11.117), 'ROSSENCRAFT, GILDERSTONE' (11.125.1); in F, '*Rosincrance, Guildensterne*' (3.1.28), '*Rosincrance and Guildensterne*' (3.3.26), '*Rosincrance and Guildensterne*' (3.4.227).

[4] In Q2 collations, the relineation of 1.1.128–9 is not recorded; 1.2.67 for 'th' Sun' read 'th'Sun'; 2.2.0 two copy-text '*and*'s are deleted from the stage direction ('*Enter King and Queene, Rosencraus and Guyldensterne*') without note; 2.2.289 for 'the clowne' read 'The clowne'; 3.2.85.2 for '*attendant with*' read '*attendant, with*' and there is a stray parenthesis at the end of the note; 3.2.154 for '171' read '176'; 3.2.163 for '*Lord*' read 'Lord'; 3.3.50 for '*vp . . . vp*,' read '*vp . . . vp*,'; 4.3.28 Q2's duplicated speech heading '*King.King.*' could have been recorded; 4.7.127 for 'Chamber' read 'chamber' in Q2 citation; 5.1.35 for 'thyself' read 'thy selfe' in both instances; 5.1.112–13 for 'Q' read 'Q2'; 5.1.264 add '*om. F*'; 5.2.121 collation is incorrect, since the 'Sir' appears in Q2 as well, back at line 91; 5.2.258 for 'Q' read 'Q1'; a number of Q2 spellings probably should have been collated: tennatlesse (1.1.114), bedred (1.2.29), hundreth (for 'hundred' 1.2.236), reueale (for 'revel' 1.4.17), cleefe (1.4.70), windlesse (for 'windlasses' 2.1.62), vnwrong (3.2.236), margent (5.2.137); in the Q1 collations, the lineation changes at 2.117–18, 2.153–4, 5.31–3, 5.34–5, 5.43–9, 5.96–7, 5.105–6 and 11.12–14 are not noted; the expansions of Q1's '*Both*' at 5.113 SP and 115 SP are not noted;

The abbreviation 'this edn', meaning 'a reading adopted for the first time in this edition', must be the most misused convention in editing today. Having complained in these pages for many years about editors who use 'this edn' as shorthand for 'I'm too busy to look it up', I was encouraged by the seriousness with which Thompson and Taylor claim to have approached the task of giving credit where it is due: 'If we emend a word, add a stage direction or even make a significant alteration to a piece of punctuation, we must check to see if any of our predecessors made the same change and be scrupulous about acknowledging that precedent.' They admit to 'an extreme nervousness about claiming anything at all as original to this edition'. Unfortunately, that nervousness turns out to be warranted: many of their claims to originality do not stand up to scrutiny. At Q2 1.2.67, the reading 'in the "son"' should be credited to Dover Wilson's Cambridge edition rather than to 'this edn'; the 'Attendants' claimed to be original in the added SD at Q2 4.3.15.1 and F 3.6.16.1 were first added by Kittredge; the SD 'aside to Horatio' claimed to be unique to 'this edn' at Q2 5.1.213 and F 5.1.221 is identical to that in the Oxford Complete Works; the 'aside' stage directions claimed to be unique to 'this edn' at Q2 5.2.68, 70, 71 (F 5.2.84, 86, 87) all appear in Furness's 1877 variorum, where their ancestry is traced back to Capell; the emendation of Q2's 'dazzie' to 'dazzle' (5.2.99) is brilliant, but should be credited to Dover Wilson (*Manuscript of Shakespeare's 'Hamlet'*, 1.132) rather than to 'this edn'.

A curious pattern emerges in which identical added stage directions are credited differently in the Q2 and the F texts. As Polonius reads Hamlet's letter to Ophelia, the Q2 edition cites the origin of the obvious stage direction 'Reads' (2.2.114) as Johnson, but it should properly be credited to Rowe, and the F edition unaccountably claims that it is original to 'this edn' (F 2.2.114). The Q2 volume correctly credits the added stage direction 'To Polonius' (2.2.460) to Oxford, but F again claims that it is unique to 'this edn' (F 2.2.518). Similarly, the added stage directions 'aside to King' and 'aside to Laertes', which are correctly credited to Oxford in

the F volume (5.2.248), are claimed to be original to 'this edn' in Q2 (5.2.278).

The editors 'fervently hope that readers will study both volumes'. But those who do are bound to notice editorial inconsistencies between Q2 and F, especially when it comes to added stage directions. These inconsistencies may be as minor as the inclusion of a definite article in one text but not the other – 'Enter [a Player as the] Prologue' (Q2 3.2.133.1) versus 'Enter [a Player as] Prologue' (F 3.2.144.1) – or slight differences in the placement of an exit:

HAMLET Yours. 'A does well to commend it himself.

[*Exit Osric*]

(Q2 5.2.163)

HAMLET Yours, yours.

[*Exit Osricke*]

He does well to commend it himself.

(F 5.2.145–6)

(Interestingly, the added SD in Q2 is claimed to be unique to 'this edn', whereas the added SD in F is credited to 'Q1 *subst.*') Sometimes, these accidental differences are substantive. In Q2, Hamlet directs his exclamation 'How absolute the knave is!' (5.1.129) 'to Horatio' but apparently within earshot of the Gravedigger; in F, the same line is marked 'aside to Horatio' (F 5.1.135). Similarly, Polonius's 'O ho, do you mark that!' is marked 'to King' at Q2 3.2.107 but 'aside to King' at F 3.2.108.

The one editorial decision that strikes me as an error in judgement is the handling of proper names. In the Q2 text, the editors adopt 'conventional/traditional' spellings of names (e.g.,

---

7.340 in the Q1 reading for 'Th'arganian' read 'th'arganian'; 'Enter Horatio' at 9.41.1 should be credited to either Q2 or F rather than to Frank Hubbard's 1923 *PMLA* article on 'The Readings of the First Quarto of *Hamlet*'; 9.82.4 needs a note indicating 'duchess' is an emendation of Q1's 'Queene'; in the F collations, the expansions of F's 'Both' at 1.5.121 SP, 1.5.144 SP, and 2.2.264 SP are not noted; 5.1.213 SD is printed after line 214 in F; 5.1.289 SD the direction 'Exit Horatio', oddly credited to Pope, comes from Q2. In the F commentary note at 1.2.65 for 'F compositor' read 'Q2 compositor'.

'Gertrude' rather than Q2's 'Gertrard', 'Osric' rather than Q2's 'Ostrick'). But in the other two texts, they retain spellings that they deem to be 'substantively different' from the conventional ones. I would maintain, however, that Q1's 'Ofelia' (retained in this edition) is a simple spelling variant of 'Ophelia', and I do not see how the silent '*e*' in F's 'Guildensterne' makes it *substantively different* from Q2's 'Guildenstern'. In some instances, Thompson and Taylor's editorial practice is not only eccentric, it is also misleading. F's 'Rosincrance' may be substantively different from their Q2 edition's 'Rosencrantz', but Q2 actually reads 'Rosencraus' throughout.

Fans of Michael Neill's *Anthony & Cleopatra* in the Oxford Shakespeare series will not be surprised to learn that he has maintained his impeccably high standards in the new Oxford *Othello*. The text of this edition is close to perfect, missing only two apostrophes: for 'the ear-piercing' read 'th'ear-piercing' (3.3.354) and for 'is it' read 'is't' (3.4.79); the line numbers at 5.2.95 and 5.2.100 are off by one; there's a repeated sentence (with an interpolated phrase 'taking F as a possible revision') at the opening of the discussion of the *Indian/Judean* crux on page 464; and there are three trivial errors in the textual notes.[5]

Weighing in at 491 pages, Neill's *Othello* is the largest edition to date in Oxford's single-play series – and every rift is loaded with ore. In his introduction, Neill begins by placing *Othello* in a line of Shakespearian tragedies reflecting the pre-occupations and fears of societies far removed from the Jacobeans:

If the existential 'prison' of *Hamlet* was the place in which generations of post-Romantic intellectuals, following the example of Goethe and Coleridge, found the angst-ridden image of their own alienation; if, in the wake of World War II, it was the wasteland of *King Lear* that provided a mirror for humanity living under the shadow of holocaust and nuclear devastation; then, towards the close of the twentieth century, it was *Othello* that began to displace them both, as critics and directors alike began to trace in the cultural, religious, and ethnic animosities of its Mediterranean setting, the genealogy of the racial conflicts that fractured their own societies.

Neill distinguishes the tracing of such genealogies from a search for 'transhistorical continuities': 'Current historicist work', he writes, 'influenced as it has been by the sceptical methodology of Foucault', regards such continuities with suspicion. Thus Neill casts doubt on Virginia Mason Vaughan's 'apparent belief that our own culture and Shakespeare's participate in a single "discourse of racial difference"', and he dismisses 'the grossly simplified readings that assume the identical nature of Othello's and O. J. Simpson's predicaments in a world where "nothing has changed"'.

Neill, a master of critical diplomacy, navigates his synthetic summary of approaches to and productions of the play with steady evenhandedness. The moments in which he displays his talent for incisively sharp criticism are few, but well worth the wait, as when he describes the film *O* as 'unrelievedly pedestrian' and M. R. Ridley's remark in the Arden2 edition ('That a man is black in colour is no reason why he should look, even to European eyes, subhuman') as a 'painfully revealing turn of phrase'.

Neill's discussion of the emotional impact of *Othello* and the blurring of reality and fiction long associated with performances of the play highlights Paul Robeson's 'adulterous affair with Uta Hagen, his second Desdemona and wife of his Iago, Jose Ferrer', and he later points to Robeson's extraordinary avowal that 'Othello has taken away from me all kinds of fears, all sense of limitation, and all racial prejudice . . . *Othello has made me free*', which Neill aptly characterizes as 'a remarkable testament from the son of an escaped slave'. The assertion that Willard White, who performed in Trevor Nunn's 1989 production, was 'the first black actor to play Othello in the history of the Royal Shakespeare Company' seems to overlook Robeson's performances in Stratford at the Royal Shakespeare Theatre in 1959 (although this did predate the founding of the RSC by a year or so). In any event, Neill notes that 'the bravura of Ian McKellen's riveting

---

[5] In the textual note at 3.3.262 for 'quantities' read 'Quantities'; 3.3.455 for 'keeps' read 'keepes'; 3.4.89–90 should read '90–1'.

Iago so overwhelmed the dignified restraint of White's Moor that the play became more a study of psychopathic villainy than of racial conflict'.

I appreciate Neill's 'longer notes' on the military designations in the play, and would have been even more grateful for some sense of the Jacobean pronunciation of 'lieutenant'. Was it 'left-tenant' (as in modern British, but not American) and, if so, could it possibly relate to Cassio's 'the lieutenant is to be saved before the ensign . . . this is my right hand, and this is my left' (2.3.101, 105)?

Neill's superb text generally follows the Folio but parts company with his control text at the *sighs/kisses* crux at 1.3.150 (Q: 'She gaue me for my paines a world of sighes'; F: 'She gaue me for my paines a world of kisses'). He asserts that 'since it seems improbable that Shakespeare would have described such an extravagant expression of emotion as "this hint", the most plausible explanation is that the scribe's manuscript had become illegible at this point, and that "kisses" represents his conjectural substitution.' Having recently edited Folio *Othello* myself, I'd like to propose a defence of the F reading by quoting from the rationale that Jonathan Bate provides in our *RSC Complete Works of Shakespeare*:

Nearly all editions follow Quarto, even when Folio is their base-text. The assumption seems to be that Desdemona would not be so forward as to kiss Othello when he is still a comparative stranger. But 'kisses' for 'sighes' is an unlikely scribal or printer's error. In the usage of the period kisses could mean 'gentle touches', but it is also the case that Venetian customs of courtesy in the play are by any standard forward — Cassio greets Iago's wife Emilia with a kiss on arrival in Cyprus and Iago's manipulation of Othello plays intensely on the Moor's lack of ease with Venetian body language. A Desdemona who kisses Othello in the imagined pre-action of the play is a stronger, more active and interesting character than one who merely sighs in admiration for his charisma.

Neill's discussion of the textual issues surrounding *Othello* — a 'protracted history of debate', in his words — may be a bit too protracted to maintain the interest of any but the most inveterate specialists. Neill engages Ernst Honigmann at great length, and surprisingly repeats without qualification Honigmann's claim that 'with the exception of the so-called "Pavier quartos" — all of them reprints — not one of Shakespeare's plays had found its way into print between 1609 and 1621'. This statement is true if one is talking only about first editions, but since reprints are apparently included as well, then Q3 *Titus* (1611), Q3 *Hamlet* (1611), Q3 *Pericles* (1611), Q5 *Richard III* (1612), Q6 *1 Henry 4* (1613) and Q5 *Richard II* (1615) combine to disprove Honigmann's claim. It is disappointing that Neill does not attend to the most provocative discussion of the *Othello* texts in recent years: Leah Marcus's 'The Two Texts of *Othello* and early modern constructions of race', in which she argues that the play's 'most racially charged language' appears only in the Folio text.[6]

Neill's scrupulous historicism is reflected in his observation that 'the text of *Othello* printed here (like any other — including Q and F themselves) is to some extent a synthetic creature, shaped by editorial judgements and aesthetic preferences that are inevitably the product of a particular place and time'. In saying this, he in no way denigrates either his own textual labours or those of his predecessors. The collations to his edition, he writes with characteristic elegance, 'should be regarded for what they are — not as a mere scholarly accessory, but as a reservoir of poetic and theatrical possibility'.

Juliet Dusinberre's Arden3 *As You Like It* is constructed around the hypothesis that the play was first staged on Shrove Tuesday, 20 February 1599, before the queen and court in the Great Hall of Richmond Palace. Dusinberre argues, moreover, that the verse lines entitled 'to ye Q. by ye players. 1598' — transcribed in Henry Staford's commonplace book and first brought to light by William Ringler and Steven May, who conjectured that they were by Shakespeare — were spoken on that occasion as the epilogue to the play. Dusinberre makes a good case for this theory, observing that Touchstone's 'dreadful joke' that 'the pancakes were

---

[6] In *Textual Performances: The Modern Reproduction of Shakespeare's Drama*, ed. Lukas Erne and Margaret Jane Kidnie (Cambridge, 2004), 21–36.

naught and the mustard was good' (1.6.66) 'is only funny on one day of the year: Shrove Tuesday, Pancake Day, when in the Great Hall at Richmond courtiers were probably feasting on pancakes while they watched the play'.

Dusinberre finds much virtue in an *if*: many paragraphs of her introduction begin with some version of 'If the play was performed at Richmond on Shrove Tuesday in 1599 . . .' This speculation continues in the commentary, where the note at 1.3.101, for instance, glosses 'heaven, now at our sorrows pale' as 'sky, now faded in response to our sorrows; the onset of twilight' but then adds that 'If the play was first performed at court in February 1599, it was played "at night"' [the 'at night' a quotation from the payment to the Chamberlain's Men]. If the play dates from 1599, then Touchstone would have been played by Kemp rather than Armin. Quite a few of Dusinberre's notes attempt to link the role to Kemp, and some of the connections seem rather tenuous: 'Touchstone's courting of Jane Smile is in keeping with a possible performance of the role by Kemp, who was ribbed for being "amorous"' (2.4.50). Glossing 'I care not for my spirits if my legs were not weary' (2.4.2–3), Dusinberre suggests that this was 'possibly a stock joke of Will Kemp's – a celebrated dancer'.

Essex was in attendance at Richmond in February 1599, and Dusinberre frequently attempts to identify topical references to him. Some of these arguments, such as the gloss on Celia's image of the sieve – 'as fast as you pour affection in, it runs out' (4.1.197–8) – seem strained: 'by 1599 both Ralegh and Essex had experienced the running-out of the queen's affection'; the gloss on Duke Senior's characterization of Jaques as 'compact of jars' (2.7.5) asserts that 'the image had currency at court, for John Chamberlain wrote to Dudley Carleton on 15 February 1599 of the discontents fomenting around the queen's delay in commissioning Essex for Ireland: "The jarres continue as they did, if not worse, by daily renewing and our music runs so much upon discords that I feare what harmonie they will make of it in the end."' Commentary notes such as these offer a running 'documentation' in support of the February 1599

thesis, occasionally at the expense of some necessary question of the play that deserves to be considered.

The text of this edition is exceptionally good. In two places Dusinberre adopts a Second Folio reading without noting it (at 1.3.123 'be' is the F2 reading, F1 reads 'by'; at 5.2.55 'are' is the F2 reading, F1 reads 'arc'), and she silently adopts F4's 'cheerly' for F1's 'cheerely' at 2.6.13 and 17. In two stage directions the brackets are imprecise ('*Lords*' should be in brackets at 1.2.86, and at 2.70.2 for '[*dressed*] *as*' read '[*dressed as*]'). There are a few very minor errors in the collations,[7] and a brief moment of confusion in the textual discussion where 'quarto' is substituted for 'manuscript': '*As You Like It* was not printed in quarto, although a quarto must have been available for print'.

In addition to calling renewed attention to the 'To the Queen from the Players' manuscript, Dusinberre highlights a manuscript catalogue dating from 1669 in which *As You Like It* is named among plays from the old Blackfriars Theatre assigned to Thomas Killigrew for the new Theatre Royal. 'It is surprising that more has not been made of this document', she notes, 'in view of the many characteristics which might relate to the tastes of the Court and private theatres rather than those of the public audience'. Dusinberre does not observe that the Shakespeare comedies in this document (with the exception of *Much Ado*, which is omitted) are listed in the order in which they appear in the First, Second and Third Folios – *TGV*, *MW*, *CE*, *LLL*, *MND*, *MV*, *AYL*, *TS*, *AW* – a fact that may suggest a literary rather than a theatrical provenance.

The introduction has the splendidly wry feminist slant that one would expect from Dusinberre, one of the pioneers of Shakespearian feminist criticism. Noting the Puritan objections to cross-dressing on stage as potentially exciting homoerotic feeling

---

7 In the textual note at 2.7.97 for 'gentleness' read 'gentlenesse'; a textual note is needed for the emendation at 3.5.106; 4.1.198 for 'in, in' read 'in,in'; 5.3.33 for '&c.' read '&c.'; 5.4.80 for 'to' read 'ro'.

both in the actors and in the audience, Dusinberre parenthetically observes that 'What the many women in the audience were expected to feel was not part of the argument.' Noting that Celia's line 'We must have your doublet and hose plucked over your head and show the world what the bird hath done to her own nest' (4.1.192) was still being cut in the theatre as late as 1952, Dusinberre presses the point: 'Don't they force an audience to imagine genitals? And which sex of genitals are we – or certainly an Elizabethan audience – imagining?'

Dusinberre herself sometimes imagines genitals in improbable places (she glosses Touchstone's response to Corin's 'our hands are hard' – 'Your lips will feel them the sooner' [3.2.57] – as 'possibly a bawdy double entendre on female "labia" (vulva)'). On the other hand, Jaques's 'Have you not been acquainted with goldsmiths' wives, and conned them out of rings?' (3.2.263–5) is explained simply as 'Jaques suggests that Orlando has learnt his elegant answers from such a source', with no mention of the potential sexual meanings of 'quaint', French *con*, and 'ring'.

Most of the recently updated editions in the New Cambridge Shakespeare series have been those that originally appeared in the 1980s. With the progress of time, the series is now refurbishing editions from the 1990s. Angela Stock provides a new introductory section to supplement Brian Gibbons's *Measure for Measure* (first published in 1991) in which she usefully observes that although the Oxford editors are convinced that Middleton had a hand in the play, other authorship studies such as Jonathan Hope's *The Authorship of Shakespeare's Plays* (1994) and Brian Vickers's *Shakespeare, Co-Author* (2002) don't even mention this as a possibility. Stock's essay provides an amusing counterbalance to Gibbons's more formal prose: she not only describes modish productions, she interrogates them. 'But once the video projector, the surveillance cameras and the computer screens have been installed, mobile phones, life-style drugs, hand-cuffs and condoms have been distributed, and the actors have rehearsed scenes of physical and/or sexual violence that one has come to expect in Edward Bond or Sarah Kane,

what – after all – has been elucidated about the play?'

Two recent books have focused on agents that have been curiously overlooked in studies of the transmission of early dramatic texts: the publishers. David M. Bergeron's *Textual Patronage in English Drama, 1570–1640* usefully explores publishers' epistles dedicatory and addresses to readers, even finding new things to say about these paratexts in the Shakespeare First Folio. He points out that the Epistle Dedicatory addressed to William and Philip Herbert is printed in a large italic font with generous spacing, runs to two pages, with Heminges and Condell's names in roman. The address 'To the great variety of Readers' is in several respects the typographic opposite: printed in a small roman font, tightly spaced, limited to a single page, with the names of Heminges and Condell in italic. Bergeron argues compellingly that the typography was intended to convey visually the differences in status between the patrons and ordinary readers.

The only major error I found in Bergeron's book comes in his narrative account of Humphrey Moseley's attempts to secure a complete collection of play manuscripts for the 1647 Beaumont and Fletcher Folio, which

lacks only one play, according to Moseley: *The Wild Goose Chase*. Despite Moseley's efforts, his own wild goose chase, he has not turned up this text, presumably borrowed from the actors and '(by the negligence of a Servant) it was never return'd'. 'This Volume', Moseley adds, 'being now so complete and finish'd, that the Reader must expect no future Alterations.' The stationer's imagined fixed text does not ultimately prevail, as we know. Even *The Wild Goose Chase* eventually showed up, but not for Moseley.

In fact, the play did show up for Moseley, who published it in 1652. Unlike most single-text play publications, Moseley's *The Wild Goose Chase* was printed in folio, apparently so that it could be sold as a supplementary volume to the 1647 folio.

When Bergeron notes that in the preface to Q1 *Troilus & Cressida* 'the publisher poses as literary critic', he is picking up on one of the many excellent points made by Zachary Lesser in *Renaissance Drama and the Politics of Publication: Readings in the English Book Trade*. Lesser observes that the publishers, Richard Bonian and Henry Walley, seem to have been familiar with the details of the text of *Troilus and Cressida* – the odd word *clapper-clawed* is used both in their preface and in the play itself by Thersites – and that 'the preface is also a reading of the play'. (As a side note, since the issue of agency is important to both Bergeron and Lesser, they should probably have attended to William Elton's suggestion that the preface was written by John Marston, a friend of Walley's.)[8]

Lesser's study addresses the question of 'why a play seemed particularly vendible at a given time' and examines particular publishers' specialties. He suggests provocatively that Walter Burre may have specialized in dramatic texts that had been 'a disaster in the theatre' (*Catiline*, *The Knight of the Burning Pestle*), whereas Thomas Archer seems to have specialized in plays about women (*Every Woman in Her Humour*, *The Two Maids of More-Clack*, *The Roaring Girl*, *The Insatiate Countess*, *The White Devil*) and Thomas Walkley in plays that reflect a 'connection between the desire for mixed government and the desire for war' (*A King and No King*, *Phylaster*, *Thierry and Theodoret*, and *Othello*).

Lesser identifies the compositional technique of 'continuous printing', in which a verse line shared by two speakers is set on a single line, as one of the strategies publishers such as Burre used to establish the 'literary status' of a play text. He locates sixty-two first-edition plays from the period that manifest this 'continuous printing' and finds that such texts 'are more than twice as likely as the average printed play to contain Latin on their title-pages', another indicator of a play's literary status. He goes

on to observe that 'as drama began to become more acceptably literary matter, the number of continuously printed plays increased, and no decade in the period saw more plays thus printed than the 1630s.'

Lesser's book is a model of careful scholarship, thoroughly frustrating for a reviewer with a reputation for finding fault. I thought his assertion that '*The Jew of Malta* is the only extant sixteenth-century English drama to be first printed in the 1630s' had to be wrong, but my attempts to find another instance that would challenge this claim to uniqueness failed utterly (though Chettle's *The Tragedy of Hoffman*, written in 1602 but not published until 1631, comes close).

WORKS REVIEWED

Bergeron, David M., *Textual Patronage in English Drama, 1570–1640* (Aldershot, 2006).

Lesser, Zachary, *Renaissance Drama and the Politics of Publication: Readings in the English Book Trade* (Cambridge, 2004).

Shakespeare, William, *As You Like It*, ed. Juliet Dusinberre, Arden3 (London, 2006).

—, *Hamlet*, ed. Ann Thompson and Neil Taylor, Arden3 (London, 2006).

—, *Hamlet: The Texts of 1603 and 1623*, ed. Ann Thompson and Neil Taylor, Arden3 (London, 2006).

—, *Measure for Measure*, ed. Brian Gibbons, updated edition, New Cambridge Shakespeare (Cambridge, 2006).

—, *Othello*, ed. Michael Neill, Oxford Shakespeare (Oxford, 2006).

---

[8] Elton, 'Textual Transmission and Genre of Shakespeare's *Troilus*', in *Literatur als Kritik des Lebens*, ed. Rudolf Haas, Heinz-Joachim Mullenbrock and Claus Uhlig (Heidelberg, 1975), 63–82.

INDEX

INDEX

Traub, Valerie, 114n54, 169n9.4
Tree, Herbert Beerbohm, 186–7
Troughton, David, 285
The True Chronicle History of King Leir, 253
Tsubouchi, Shôyô, 132n9
Tukur, Uli, 197Fig.36
Tunstall [Dunstan], James, 21
Turberville, George, 274n22

Uchino, Masaaki, 136, 138
Uhlig, Claus, 369n8
Unwin, Stephen, 321
Uricchio, William, 355

Vanderhoof, Mary B., 218n17, 221n23
Vander Motten, J. P., 249n53
Vanita, Ruth, 84–101
Vaughan, Virginia Mason, 161Fig.24, 168, 349, 365
Vaughan Williams, Ralph, 184, 185, 186, 187, 188–91, 191, 192, 192n24, 194, 195, 317
Vavasour, Anne, 351
Veltrusky, Jiri, 228
Velz, John W., 342
Verdi, Giuseppe, 184, 187, 189–90, 190, 192n24, 317, 349, 353, 356
Verma, Jatinda, 324
Veronesi, Alberto, 190n20
Vesalius, Andreas, 227
Vestris, Lucia Elizabeth, 190
Vickers, Brian, 254, 265n37, 351, 368
Villiers, Sir Edward, 55
Viola, Bill, 355
Vleteren, Timotheus van, 240, 251
Vogel, Paula, 325, 349
Voltaire (François Marie Arouet), 215, 216–17, 218, 222

Walker, Elsie, 354–5
Walker, Greg, 61n8
Walker, Robert, 224Fig.39, 223–4
Walkley, Thomas, 369
Wallace, Bill, 211
Wallace, David, 81n39
Walley, Henry, 369
Walsingham, Sir Francis, 7
Walter, Harriet, 293, 294Fig.49, 294, 297, 329
Wannamaker, Zoe, 205
Ward, P., 46n55
Warley, Christopher, 332–4, 353

Warner, A., 42n22
Warner, David, 322
Warner, Deborah, 171, 172–3, 322
Warner, George F., 47n59, 51n10, 51n11, 52n17, 52n18, 52n19, 52n20
Warrack, John, 191n23
Warren, Jason Scott, 122n7
Warren, Michael, 348
Warwick, Earl of (Ambrose Dudley), 4–6, 8, 13
Wasson, John, 2n4
Watson, Robert N., 107n24, 337–9, 352, 353
Watters, Jack, 179Fig.33
Wayne, Valerie, 96n33
Webber, J. P., 184
websites, selected
    Early English Books Online (EEBO), 271n9
    hamletworks, 218n17
    Literature Online (LION), 271, 278
    Touchstone, 320–9
Webster, John, 109n33, 358–9
Wedel, Lupold von, 44, 45
Weeks, Honeysuckle, 328
Weelkes, Thomas, 260n30
Weimann, Robert, 123, 335
Welles, Orson, 111–12n39, 167Fig.30, 194
Wells, Robin Headlam, 125, 344–5, 346, 353
Wells, Stanley, 1n2, 168, 188n15, 193n27, 229, 253, 259n26, 341
Welsford, Enid, 59n3, 60n7, 61n9, 62n10, 62n11, 62n12
Werner, Sarah, 167Fig.30, 169n9.2
West, Sam, 325
Westcott, Jim, 180Fig.34
Westermarck, Edward, 76n21
Westfall, Suzanne R., 7n11, 54n27
Weston, Sir Richard, 69–70
Whetstone, George, 272n13
White, Paul Whitfield, 7n11, 54n27
White, Willard, 365–6
Whitgift, John, 13
Whitworth, Stephen, 350–1
Wickham, Glynne, 45n41
Wildgruber, Ulrich, 166Fig.29, 169n8.9
Wiles, David, 114
Willems, Michèle, 214–22
Willett, John, 174n10
Williams, Gordon, 103n7
Williams, Jano, 131n3

Williams, Lia, 320
Williams, Raymond, 59n3, 60n7
Willoughby, Edwin E., 256
Wilson, Christopher R., 356, 361
Wilson, John Dover, 58, 111n39, 364
Wilson, Robert, 21–2, 54
Wiltshire, Earl of (Henry Stafford), 68
Wily Beguilde, 272n14
Wimsatt, W. K., 214n1
Wingfield, Sir Richard, 69–70
Wingfield, Sir Robert, 69–70
Winny, James, 108n30
Winter, William, 116n59, 116n60
Wise, Andrew, 258–9
Wise, Ernie (Ernest Wiseman), 228
Wiseman, Susan, 129n33
Wither, George, 283
Witt, Johan de, 45
Wood, John, 322
Wood, Michael, 355
Woodbridge, Linda, 81n40, 84n2, 114n49
Woodvine, John, 209Fig.37
Woodward, Joan (*later* Alleyn), 51
Woodward, Kirsty, 311
Woolf, Virginia, 186n11
Wootton, John, 353–4
Worcester, 3rd Earl of (William Somerset), 7
Worcester, 4th Earl of (Edward Somerset), 7
Worden, Blair, 342
Worthen, W. B., 148, 150, 151, 152, 156, 360
Woudhuysen, H. R., 256n16
Wray, Ramona, 355, 356, 360
Wright, Angus, 285
Wright, Richard, 330
Wright, Tom, 327
Wringer, Leo, 162Fig.25
Wroth, Mary, 344
Wynne-Davies, Marion, 100n40

A Yorkshire Tragedy, 266, 266n42
Yoshida, Kotaro, 303
Yoshihara, Yukari, 130–40, 140n34
Young, Christopher, 144n12

Zadek, Peter, 166Fig.29
Zaimoglu, Feridun, 287
Zander, Horst, 132n10
Žižek, Slavoj, 345–6
Zarrilli, Philip B., 147n19